The American Exploration and Travel Series

Paul Wilhelm, Duke of Württemberg
TRAVELS IN NORTH AMERICA, 1822–1824

Paul Wilhelm, Duke of Württemberg

TRAVELS
IN
NORTH AMERICA
1822-1824

Translated by W. Robert Nitske
Edited by Savoie Lottinville

University of Oklahoma Press : NORMAN

BY W. ROBERT NITSKE:

The Complete Mercedes Story (New York, 1955)
The Amazing Porsche and Volkswagen Story (New York, 1958)
Rudolf Diesel: Pioneer of the Age of Power (with Charles Morrow Wilson, Norman, 1965)
The Life of Wilhelm Conrad Röntgen, Discoverer of the X Ray (Tucson, 1971)

BY SAVOIE LOTTINVILLE:

Life of George Bent: Written from His Letters by George E. Hyde (editor, Norman, 1968)
Soldier in the West: Letters of Theodore Talbot During His Services in California, Mexico, and Oregon (editor, with Robert V. Hine, Norman, 1972)

TRANSLATED BY W. ROBERT NITSKE AND EDITED BY SAVOIE LOTTINVILLE:

Travels in North America, 1822–1824, by Paul Wilhelm, Duke of Württemberg (Norman, 1973)

Library of Congress Cataloging in Publication Data

Paul Wilhelm, Duke of Württemberg, 1797–1860.
  Travels in North America, 1822–1824.
  (The American exploration and travel series, v. 63)
  Translation of Erste Reise nach dem nördlichen
Amerika in den Jahren 1822 bis 1824.
  Bibliography: p.
  1. Paul Wilhelm, Duke of Württemberg, 1797–1860.
2. Mississippi Valley—Description and travel.
3. United States—Description and travel—1783–1848.
I. Title.   II. Series.
F353.P3213   917.7'04'2   72–3596

Travels in North America, 1822–1824 is Volume 63 in The American Exploration and Travel Series.

TO
George J. Goodman
AND
George M. Sutton

WHOSE FRIENDSHIP AND SCIENTIFIC DISCERNMENT
CONTRIBUTED GREATLY TOWARD LIGHTENING THE
LABORS OF THE EDITOR AND THE TRANSLATOR OF THIS WORK

Translator's Acknowledgments

I would like to thank the Henry E. Huntington Library, San Marino, for allowing me to inspect and study the original proof sheets of Duke Paul's book with the author's own corrections, as well as a copy of the subsequent edition; the Alderman Library of the University of Virginia, Charlottesville, for the loan of the microcards of the book; Robert McCoy of the University of California at Santa Barbara for the loan of the instrument to project these cards; the Stadt Bad Mergentheim and the Württembergische Landesbibliothek, Stuttgart, for copies of periodicals and documents; and the Verkehrsamt der Stadt Stuttgart and the Staatliche Museum für Naturkunde, Stuttgart, for information pertaining to the collections of Duke Paul.

Finally, I am deeply indebted to my wife, Betty, for restoring grammatical sanity where great confusion reigned, resulting from the translation of an opposite system.

Tucson, Arizona   W. Robert Nitske
March 15, 1973

Editor's Acknowledgments

Gᴿᴀᴛᴇꜰᴜʟ acknowledgment is made by the editor of this volume to the University of Michigan Library for its courtesy in permitting examination and use of its copy of Duke Paul Wilhelm of Württemberg's account of his American tour, entitled *Erste Reise nach dem nördlichen Amerika in den Jahren 1822 bis 1824* (Stuttgart und Tübingen, Verlag der J. G. Cotta'schen Buchhandlung, 1835).

And to George J. Goodman, Regents Professor of Botany and Microbiology and Curator of the Bebb Herbarium of the University of Oklahoma, and George Sutton, George Lynn Cross Research Professor Emeritus of Ornithology and Curator Emeritus of Birds, Stovall Museum, in the same university, my thanks are but a token of the recognition they deserve for the long hours they devoted to correlating Duke Paul Wilhelm's natural science observations with modern systems and scientific names.

Cluff E. Hopla, George Lynn Cross Research Professor of Zoology in the University of Oklahoma; R. G. Webb, of Texas Western University in herpetology; and Dr. Harry Hoogstraal, Medical Zoology Department, U.S. Naval Medical Research Unit No. 3, came quickly to the editor's rescue in tracing difficult species or aberrant specimens from the Duke's collections. The encouragement of E. Raymond Hall, of the University of Kansas and its Museum, and the availability of his and Keith R. Kelson's *The Mammals of North America* greatly strengthened the editor's assault upon the mammal species mentioned in the author's itinerary. To Dr. Horst Janus, Hauptkonservator, Staatliches Museum für Naturkunde in Stuttgart, I return sincere thanks for making available the eight subjects from Duke Paul's *icones ineditae* reproduced in color in the present volume.

The availability of some thousands of rare books and periodicals bearing on the Trans-Mississippi West in the Frank Phillips Collection in the

Bizzell Memorial Library of the University of Oklahoma, and the unfailing helpfulness of its curator, Mrs. Alice M. Timmons, together constituted resources indispensable to the editing of this volume. And in his helpful suggestions to the editor, James J. Hill, Director Emeritus of the University of Nevada Library, contributed significantly to the development of many historical threads contained in the narrative, as did those of Thomas D. Clark of Indiana University, historian and bibliographer of the Old and the New South. Finally, to have had access to the vast resources available in the E. L. DeGolyer Collection in the History of Science and Technology at the University of Oklahoma, together with the highly informed guidance of its curator, Mrs. Marcia Goodman, was distinctly comforting to an editor adrift on the great and sometimes stormy sea of the natural sciences.

Norman, Oklahoma   Savoie Lottinville
March 15, 1973

Editor's Introduction

THE year 1822 was an inviting one for a young man of twenty-five whose immediate ambition was to widen his horizons by travel in the New World. The Old World, reordering itself after the black years of the Napoleonic Wars, was relatively peaceful, whatever the long-term consequences of the Congress of Vienna, which one realist charitably described as an "imperfect concert made by less than perfect statesmen." But peace there was, and it was good to small royal houses like that of Württemberg, whose King Friedrich meant to leave no stone unturned in furthering his nephew's renewed search for an education already well developed.

To Duke Friedrich Paul Wilhelm, the son of the King's brother, Duke Eugen Friedrich Heinrich of Württemberg, and Duchess Louise (born Princess of Stolberg-Godern), the intelligences from America were all good. Seven years had already elapsed since the disruptions of the War of 1812. The United States had signed treaties of "peace and amity" with the Indians of the upper Mississippi and Ohio valleys following the Peace of Ghent, at the insistence of the British with whom many tribes had been allied in the late conflict. A small tide of white emigration from Illinois, Kentucky, and Virginia was beginning to make itself felt on the frontiers of Missouri, admitted to statehood as recently as 1821. And inland transportation by steamboats, now increasingly plying the rivers, made the initial stages of exploration, at least, a good deal more comfortable than would have been the case a decade before.

From other, even more persuasive points of view, it was the best of times for an individual tour of exploration and scientific inventory-making. To be sure, an excellent beginning had already been made by the Americans. The voyage of discovery by Meriwether Lewis and William Clark in 1804–1806 to the far limits of the Louisiana Purchase had been the fulfillment of President Thomas Jefferson's dream of nearly a quarter of a century. It was quickly followed by the explorations of Zebulon Montgomery Pike, the sometimes "lost pathfinder" who had ascended to the headwaters of the Arkansas in 1806 before being ignominiously taken into custody by the Spaniards in their territory south of the Arkansas in Colorado. But for American science, the most electrifying information was that contained in Edwin James's *Account of an Expedition from Pittsburgh to the Rocky Mountains* of 1819–1820 under command of Major Stephen Harriman Long.

Here was perhaps the most carefully organized, most satisfactorily oriented expedition from the point of view of science, that had yet been sent into the Trans-Mississippi West. Its complement included such scientists as Edwin James, its botanist and geologist (and almost accidentally the author of its report); Thomas Say, the entomologist and conchologist; and Titian Ramsay Peale, the assistant naturalist and painter on the expedition, whose paintings and drawings for his scientific colleagues were of great importance to the report and to their subsequent scientific papers.

The young Duke knew of the first of the two volumes in Edwin James's account of the Long explorations, and in subsequent years he was to know both volumes and its atlas thoroughly, in either its Philadelphia or its London edition (the latter issued as early as 1823). While the American public would find the report less than practical, condemning it for its emphasis on geology, others would be engrossed by its descriptions, geography, accounts of Indian tribes met by the expedition, and its glossaries and vocabularies. In the end it would prove a landmark in the literature of American exploration, for historians if not for Daniel Webster, the popular spokesman who found it wanting.

Less specific but more pervasive was the influence exerted upon a young mind by the explorations and writings of one of his own countrymen, Alexander Freiherr von Humboldt, whose own investigations in the New World (principally South America and Cuba) had begun in 1799, two years after Duke Paul's birth (July 25, 1797, at Carlsruhe, Silesia). By 1822 many of the volumes projected by von Humboldt and his collaborator (and sometime teacher) Aimé Bonpland had been published at Paris in French, the dominant scientific language of the time.

It seems clear from the Duke's educational experience as a boy and young man that exploration and natural science held the trump cards. His royal uncle had made his education a matter of personal concern almost from the outset, securing for him the best available teachers, later placing him in the Gymnasium at Stuttgart. At the latter school, the equivalent of an English public school of the time, the young man had found the science teaching of Professor Dr. Lebert most exciting, in spite of the attractions of languages, whose mastery would mean much to his subsequent career. The Professor, who was of the school of such experimental and systematic scientists as Cuvier, Jussieu, Haüy, and Gay-Lussac, grounded his pupil thoroughly in the natural sciences and instilled in him a fondness for their wide scope and precise methods.

Whatever his own commitment to sound education, in this era to a considerable extent scientific, King Friedrich did not exempt his nephew from an opportunity to follow a military career, appointing him in May, 1806, a *captain à la suite* in his own guard (the boy was scarcely nine years old at the time). The actual extent of the Duke's experience in military affairs is unknown, but on May 20, 1817, he resigned his military commission as a major general and devoted himself exclusively to the study of natural science. The decision, his now firm devotion to science, and the accelerating pace of scientific investigation in post-Napoleonic Europe would make of him a life-long explorer, his projected trip to the United States only the first of several, and his other explorations the self-chosen rewards of his competence gained in the Western Hemisphere.

Duke Paul Wilhelm's *Erste Reise*, or "First Journey," as he subsequently chose to entitle it, began the first week in October, 1822, and lasted until the middle of February, 1824, when he returned to Europe. He chose to travel incognito as Baron von Hohenberg on a passport given a visa by the American consul at Hamburg, but, like others of his time and more recently, was quickly discovered by fellow-travelers (and later, by American frontiersmen) to be the Duke of Württemberg. He took with him his *Leibjäger*, or body servant, J. G. Schlape, who would manfully bring up the rear in the wilderness of the Trans-Mississippi West as his master moved determinedly towards the upper Missouri villages of the hostile Arikaras. While New Orleans was his immediate objective, his plans had originally called for an early departure from Louisiana for explorations in the "northern provinces of the former imperial empire" in Mexico. The revolutionary unrest in Mexico City, however, caused him to change his mind and to go to Cuba instead.

It was an entirely satisfactory alternative, inasmuch as von Humboldt and Bonpland had made a profitable sojourn in Cuba before him, as he later pointed out in writing the account of his travels. (Von Humboldt's *Essai politique sur le royaume de la nouvelle Espagne* had appeared in 1811, but his *Essai politique sur l'île de Cuba* did not appear until 1826, two years after the Duke's return to Europe.) What he found on the island in January and February, 1823, was essentially what von Humboldt had found, refracted in his own original way: a tropical wonderland for the natural scientist, a peculiar political climate (Cuba had remained loyal to Spain during the upheavals in Latin America two years earlier), and a race new to his experience, the Negro, consisting mainly of plantation slaves. His natural science observations while on the island were extensive.

By March 4, 1823, Duke Paul was back in New Orleans, from whence he would ascend the Mississippi to the mouth of the Ohio, thence up that river to the Falls of the Ohio at a point then called Shippingport, now within Louisville, Kentucky, which he reached by buggy for a brief but observant visit. His trip up the Mississippi and the Ohio on the fast-running steamer *Maysville* of two hundred tons, even though it braved night snags and continued running after dark, found him gathering information as he progressed—on military forts and trading posts for the Indians along the rivers; the names, linguistic connections, and condition of Indian tribes; the relation of United States to Spanish-Mexican interests west of the Mississippi; and, above all, the animal, bird, fish, reptile, and plant species he was able to observe on the journey.

Almost from the start of his voyage from Hamburg, the Duke had begun to set down according to their scientific designations the species he saw. He would continue the process on the two large river systems he pursued to Shippingport, and later, after an informative sojourn in St. Louis, on the Missouri. It was not, therefore, to be a bluebird but *Sialia sialis*, and not a pawpaw but *Annona tribola*, in the latter case sending his readers scurrying to their synonymies to find *Asimina tribola*. That he has since escaped such a comment as Henry M. Brackenridge's about Thomas Nuttall, the young English scientist whom Brackenridge met in John Bradbury's ascent of the Missouri with Wilson Price Hunt a dozen years before, is owing to both the historical and the scientific neglect of the Duke's work. "*Ou est le fou?*" asked the French boatmen when Nuttall was holding up their further progress. "*Il est apres remassée des racines,*" came the reply. But Duke Paul was himself so assiduous a searcher after roots that he would provide information on one of them which would be startling to some scientists a century and a half later.

The young explorer had introductions to a number of interesting people in Louisiana who helped to give direction and scope to the further education of a member of a royal house. Not the least of these was Louis Tainturier, a first-rate botanist on the Louisiana frontier, for whom the umbelliferous species, *Chaerophyllum tainturieri*, was named. In New Orleans he was entertained by the ebullient Vincent Nolte of German origin, a successful and combative merchant who liked to have notables as his guests (the Marquis de Lafayette would be his guest also, during his American tour of 1824–1825).

And it was thus that he found a ready welcome in and around St. Louis in the homes of the Chouteau family, particularly that of the aging Auguste Chouteau, the first citizen of the city he had founded fifty-nine years earlier when he was barely fourteen years old, as the agent of his stepfather Pierre de Laclède Liguest. From Chouteau he received further introductions, to be used as he proceeded upriver on one of the fur boats, sail- and cordelle-driven, of the Berthold, Chouteau, and Pratte interests (usually referred to by the Duke as the "French Missouri Company," a designation generally accepted in that era). What followed is an odyssey in which the stamina of a prince was repeatedly tested on the raw fur frontier and his future career determined. The latter would henceforth be committed to travel and exploration, ending only with his death in 1860.

His account of his travels, which would not be published until 1835, reveals not only what was happening on the Missouri River from St. Louis to present Chamberlain, South Dakota, but (unconsciously) what was happening to a young man of the blood. By 1815, in his eighteenth year, he had acquired some of the graces and not a few of the intolerances of the military class into which he had been inducted by his uncle the King. By 1823 he had absorbed much of the learning of his time, and with it some of the impatience of an intellectual. For readers of today, it is interesting to observe the changes in the man and his attitudes as he moved upriver, sometimes by boat, sometimes by an overland route, often by a cutoff from the winding Missouri River course. His reaction to a supper of clabbered milk and cold cornbread in the Ferrill cabin relatively early in the game gives way to the relish with which he tackles roasted bear meat and little else a few days later. Equally, his first reactions of mingled curiosity and intolerance to the crude frontier settlements on the lower Missouri are replaced by the disarming shyness with which he enters into shooting competitions with villagers (he was apparently not only a crack shot but the owner of a finely crafted double-rifle from Germany). Gradually, as he progresses farther and farther upriver, the Duke himself becomes a tolerant frontiersman, never far from ducal prerogative but adjusted, nevertheless, to his guides, Louis Caillou and Baptiste de Rouain; to the French-speaking boatmen, hard drinkers and undisciplined; and to the Indians he encountered from the beginning of his journey to its end.

It was in St. Louis, in fact, that the Duke, with an introduction to General William Clark, the Superintendent of Indian Affairs, had a full opportunity to know the great explorer and to sit with him at an audience

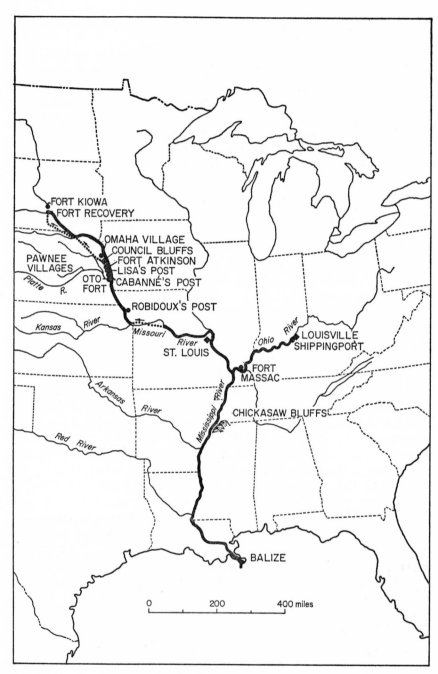

Route of Duke Paul's Travels in North America, 1823

for the Potawatomis. The dramatic picture he paints contains elements of tragedy he sensed but could not confirm—of a people quickly dispossessed of their vast holdings in the Ohio-Michigan-Illinois country after the War of 1812 by treaties negotiated in part by General Clark himself. The tableau he witnessses lacks on his part first-hand association with the Indians, to be sure. It clearly needs the elements of empathy and sympathy. But later, as the author moves among the Missourias, Iowas, Otos, Osages, and, most notably, the Poncas and Chauis, or Grand Pawnees, he becomes a frank champion of the Indian for his dignity, his frequent uncommon wisdom, and his often unsuspected charity. The royal carriage of the chiefs, particularly, found a ready response from the young traveler whose upbringing had given him long since the dimensions of *noblesse oblige.* His only trouble was that he could not abide boiled dog, which caused him to be reprimanded at an encampment of the Otos, a lesson he later reported manfully. (Lewis and Clark before him came to relish dog, horse meat, and roots in the absence of anything else, and the adventurous Captain B. L. E. Bonneville similarly developed a strong stomach during his explorations for his country in the 1830's.)

In the earlier scientific training of the young German, and in his reading from the journals and other accounts written by American explorers, he had developed a high regard for geography. Just so, he brought to the North American continent the necessary instruments for taking temperature, latitude and longitude, barometric, and humidity readings. He lacked only a good chronometer, a fact which would deprive him of accurate estimates of his locations when he was well up the Missouri. But the casualties to his other instruments, suffered when a buffalo stampede sent his horses in wild flight over broken ground in present South Dakota, would erase most remaining accuracy anyway.

As he ascended the rivers—the Mississippi, the Ohio, and, finally, the Missouri—he recorded known—and sometimes not well-known—landmarks, towns, villages, natural features, military establishments, and interesting geological formations. As one reads his account of the Missouri River from St. Louis to Fort Atkinson near present Omaha, it is possible to parallel his observations of places, Indian tribes, and natural features with those of Lewis and Clark, Henry M. Brackenridge, Edwin James, and Surgeon John Gale of the Missouri Expedition, as the annotations to the present translation of his work try to develop. The results may best be attributed to awareness and, when he had not been informed ahead of time, to sensitivity to information supplied by acquaintances along the route and by his French boatmen. Through it all runs, moreover, a considerably above average ear and eye for the human factor on the frontier.

The reader must not expect a gallery of frontier types, consciously drawn as Washington Irving, Charles Joseph Latrobe, or Count Albert-Alexandre de Pourtalès would do a decade later. The Duke was, after all, a natural scientist, and doubtless he would have been the first to disclaim being a literary portraitist. Nowhere in his account is this tendency more apparent than during his initial meeting with the eighteen-year-old Baptiste Charbonneau at the trading post run by Cyrus Curtis and Andrew Woods, upstream from the mouth of the Kansas River, in 1823. Like Meriwether Lewis and William Clark, he was apparently greatly taken with the youngster they named Pompey ("Pomp" for short), born to the Snake Indian woman, Sacagawea, and her French-speaking husband, Toussaint Charbonneau, from St. Louis, at the mouth of the Knife River in February, 1805, during the explorers' first winter in the wilderness. So much so that he offered to take him on his return downstream and overseas to Europe. There is no description of this historic young figure (whose age the Duke underestimated by two years), only the facts of his birth and parentage and the chronologically confusing statement that he "joined me on my return, followed me to Europe, and has since been with me."

But Duke Paul's people of the frontier are the people of fact, emerging strongly from the account, often in spite of less than strong delineation. They range from the now talkative Auguste Chouteau, full of memories going back to the beginnings of the Spanish regime in Louisiana; the old but menacing Baptiste de Rouain, hurling insults at a canoe-load of Indians descending the Missouri; the people of the Boone's Lick country, fresh emigrants from Kentucky viewing a European duke with wonderment; to the wounded survivors of the William Ashley battle with the Arikaras, half-drunk on the whisky they found floating down the Missouri from a boat which, like themselves, had met disaster upstream.

The Ashley fight and the abortive campaign by Colonel Henry Leavenworth and his troops against the Arikaras beginning August 9, 1823, would bring Duke Paul up short at the Missouri Fur Company post, Fort Recovery, on a small island just north of the mouth of the White River two weeks later. There he visited with, and was dissuaded from going farther by, the company partner, Joshua Pilcher. The Arikaras were not likely to be hospitable to whites of any persuasion, he was told. And thence he turned back upon the more than one thousand miles he had traversed from St. Louis, still collecting ethnology, specimens for his now large natural history collections, and geographical impressions.

To the main outline of Duke Paul's *Wanderjahr* must be added some estimate of its scientific merit, the biographical aftermath, and an estimate bibliographically, together with a projection of what may be added to the author's still-scant bibliography after a century and a half.

To an Elliott Coues, who gave scientific orientation to the Lewis and Clark journals, notably from the ornithological side, and to a Paul Russell Cutright, who only yesterday gave order to the long neglected Lewis and Clark herbarium in Philadelphia, this young German scientist on the frontier of the United States in the first quarter of the nineteenth century might be seen as something of a phenomenon. His original German text glosses species, treating them almost incidentally and often throwing them into footnotes, or running past them in the interest of the general reader's concerns, which were not scientific. But there are hundreds of species, named for the most part binomially, and also for the most part with the name of the taxonomist who brought them into the language of science. The effort on the author's part is clearly less directed to original discovery (in which he differed from his brilliant but eratic contemporary, Constantine Samuel Rafinesque) than to exact relation to species known and described previously.

In the post-Linnaean world in which Duke Paul was conducting his first non-European observations, a host of gifted naturalists was at work: Alexander Wilson, Benjamin Smith Barton, John Bradbury, George Ord, John Torrey, Benjamin Rush, William Maclure, Titian Ramsay Peale, Thomas Nuttall, Edwin James, and Frederick Pursh, to name only the obvious. As one examines his species, it is clear that the Duke was carrying with him, by boat and apparently even on mule or horse back, the manuals and other scientific works of such men, as well as those of some scientists of Europe. How else are we to assess an evident taxonomical precision?

To two well-known American scientists, George J. Goodman, the botanist, and George Sutton, the ornithologist and bird portraitist, who have been of inestimable aid to the editor and the translator of this volume, there are still a good many unsolved problems. The book is very little known to most scientists, apparently, and it seems to have escaped all but two of the modern works which tell us about recorded observations and the naming of the species, E. Raymond Hall and Keith R. Kelson, *The Mammals of North America* (2 vols.), and Robert Ridgway, *The Birds of North and Middle America: A Descriptive Catalogue* (10 vols.). In this, part of the trouble may lie with the fact that the book was a quiet one, quite unlike Prince Maximilian zu Wied's travels in both South and North America, which were widely translated and illustrated, in the case of his *Reise in das Innere Nord-Amerika in den Jahren 1832 bis 1834* (2 vols. and an atlas), with the paintings and drawings of Carl Bodmer. But the fact remains that the Duke's volume continues to call for the attention of synonymists of science.

A related but separate problem is that of priorities. What does science do with the Duke's *Mamillaria septentrionalis*, now known as *Coryphantha missouriensis*, which, when he observed it in eastern Nebraska, he likened to the pincushion cactus *Mammillaria simplex* Haworth he had seen in a Swiss greenhouse collection? A perhaps even more pointed example is the "*Aquilegia* . . . with very small light blue flowers, . . ." which Goodman tells me Nuttall sent in manuscript to Torrey and Gray as *Aquilegia canadensis β violacea* from a plant he had collected on "Big Blue River of the Platte" (the two rivers head within five miles of each other). Torrey and Gray listed it, but in synonymy, in the year 1838. There must be room for doubt that a frequent and rather decisive scientific dismissal by *nomen nudum* (a name without description or proper description) can actually apply in such instances.

Something has already been said about the Duke's regard for geographical location and the means of achieving it. In that context there may be more than a little room for a re-examination of the presently accepted limits to the range of the grizzly bear in the historic period. Equally, the Duke's travel account offers tantalizing fragments on the possible presence of the jaguar as far east as Louisiana. We know where in Missouri he saw and described two ticks, *Ixodes humanus* m. and *Ixodes cruciger* m., both of which (as indicated) he named. The former, according to Harry Hoogstraal, was applied to a specimen from Brazil by Koch in 1844, twenty-one years later; the latter fails entirely of notice. But the searcher after priorities doubtless will find in the account many other examples.

The standing of a scientist, very much like the standing of an explorer, depends in some considerable part upon his continuing and cumulative impact. The absence of this cumulative impact by Duke Paul was probably of his own doing. The further threads of his biography tend to make this fact clear, as my colleague, the translator of the Duke's volume, W. Robert Nitske, has found from his researches in Germany.

On April 17, 1827, Duke Paul married Princess Sophie Dorothea Caroline von Thurn und Taxis and was presented as his residence the former Deutschmeister Schloss at Bad Mergentheim, in the northeastern section of present Württemberg-Baden. The couple's first-born was a son, Maximilian, September 3, 1828, who followed a military career, dying in 1888.

Less than a year later, the Duke embarked upon his second trip to the United States, sailing from Bremen in April, 1829, for Santo Domingo. Eight months later, he arrived at St. Louis. His visit there and travel up the Missouri lasted from December 1, 1829, to February, 1830, when he reached Council Bluffs. Not to be deterred, as he was by the Arikaras in 1823, he departed from Fort Atkinson, of which he had given a classic description seven years before, stopped upriver with the Mandans, saw Fort Kipp and the Arikaras on the Missouri, and looked still farther for parts of the American wilderness to explore and record.

Ahead of him lay Fort Clark, which he visited, then touched the Rockies, moving on to Fort Tecumseh, living nearby with the Sioux and other tribes for three months. He had an opportunity to explore along the Yellowstone River and took it, along with glimpses of Blacksnake Creek. The Sauks and Foxes, ranging much farther west than was their custom, saw him at this time, their chiefs according him the treatment he seemed to merit as their equal. At the White River that winter (1829–1830), he was rescued by a Sioux upon whose father he had earlier bestowed a favor. Perhaps more dramatic was the fact that he met the Blackfeet, then and for another twenty-five years an almost constant threat to whites in or crossing their upper Montana country. He also met the Assiniboines.

To close his second journey, the Duke descended the Missouri in a small pirogue, the kind of enterprise, he stated, which could be successful in only ten out of one hundred attempts. By October, 1830, he was back in New Orleans, whence he departed December 21 for Tampico. Thereafter he crossed the Mexican mountains to Mexico City, going to Veracruz and thus on by ship to New Orleans. Back in the United States he had an opportunity to visit Cincinnati, Buffalo, Lake Erie, and Niagara Falls, before returning to Germany early in 1831.

At the meeting of German naturalists and physicians in Stuttgart in 1834, his paper with portions of his observations during his American travels, together with some of his drawings, was presented to the assembled scientists in his absence.

Beginning in September, 1839, the Duke was enabled to add to his already extensive collections, as well as his experience of other continents, by accepting an invitation to join a military expedition to the upper Nile organized by the *vali* (governor-general) of Egypt, Mohammed Ali I. The expedition covered upper Egypt, Nubia, and a part of Fazogl.

When the German traveler returned to Württemberg in August, 1840, he began to examine in detail the results of his travels and to bring order to his now vast collections (which would only become greater as his travels extended another twenty years). Looking ahead to publication (thus far, he had published only his first trip, the book appearing in 1835), he commissioned the historical painter Rosshirt to execute some ninety watercolors of plants and animals and a large painting of a Sioux encampment from descriptions provided by the Duke. The latter, completed in 1843, is now in Bad Mergentheim, and the watercolors are in private hands, only recently offered by sale to the Württembergische Landesbibliothek, Stuttgart.

Duke Paul had meantime made short trips to Algiers, England, France, and Austria. He was a not-infrequent attendant at the meetings of the *Kammer der Standesherren* (Chamber of Noblemen or Peers).

His subsequent travels, at least to the Americas, have given rise to some confusion. For example, when, in the year 1849, the Duke began a journey to North America which, with its continuations, would last until 1856, he was actually embarking upon his third trip to the United States, though it has often been referred to as his fourth. In the ensuing seven-year period, he would move from New Orleans to Texas, and, on his return, from New Orleans up the Mississippi to the Missouri-Illinois country, later to Texas again, Mexico, and from Mazatlán to San Francisco and other points in California (including a visit with John Sutter, whose domain was alive with gold activity in the summer of 1850). He went to Panama in the autumn of 1850, returned to New Orleans, traveled once more to St. Louis, which he reached in March, 1851, later visiting the Great Lakes, the upper Mississippi, and the Falls of St. Anthony. His trip in the autumn of 1851 to Fort Laramie was one which almost cost him his life, as indeed it threatened Balduin Möllhausen, his artist companion. In February, 1853, the Duke boarded a ship in New York which he hoped would take him to Australia but ended up in Brazil. From Bahía he went to Rio de Janeiro and Montevideo and enjoyed an extended visit in Uruguay.

An unexpected opportunity for further travel and adventure offered itself when the commander of the French post at La Plata offered Duke Paul transportation to the west coast of South America by way of the Straits of Magellan. He was thus enabled to visit Chile, Bolivia, Peru, and Ecuador, the great Andes chain to which he often refers in the present account. Thereafter he crossed the Isthmus of Panama and from New Orleans, which he reached late in October, 1853, he moved up and down the Mississippi Valley, visited the eastern, northern, and southern states, and finally returned to Europe late in July, 1856.

From this chronology and its accompanying itinerary, it is perhaps fair to conclude that the Duke made three trips to the Western Hemisphere— in 1822, 1829, and 1849, with one entry into the United States in 1823, two in 1829–1830, and three during the 1849–56 travels. There would be another, that of 1857, following the death of his brother and his decision to settle on the family estate in Silesia. There he determined to return once more to the Mississippi delta. Thus his sojourns in the United States were seven in all.

Still driven by ambition to see new lands and to collect for his continuously growing assemblage of natural history specimens, the German traveler sailed in 1858 for Australia. After a good crossing of ninety-four days, he arrived at Phillip Bay, New Holland, August 10 of that year. By mid-year of 1859 he had visited Adelaide, New Sydney, New Zealand, Tasmania, the Sundas, Ceylon, and China, returning by way of Egypt.

Once more the Duke returned to his long-delayed homework, this time to attempt to bring final order to long-neglected bundles of manuscripts and collections which, if they had periodically been brought to the attention of scientists and the general public, would have won for him the reputation which is the fruit of cumulative impact. But it was not to be. In November, 1860, he went down to his castle at Bad Mergentheim from his Carlsruhe residence. He had not been at Mergentheim long when he contracted a respiratory ailment, probably pneumonia, and on November 25 he died. He had still not succeeded in organizing the data and the narratives contained in more than one hundred journals, nor in placing with them in proper sequence and relation some one thousand drawings, charts, and sketches. The fruits of his collecting zeal, consisting of thousands of specimens, remained largely unreported to the scientific world. He was buried with court and military honors in a crypt of the Stiftskirche in Stuttgart.

There is reason to believe that Duke Paul Wilhelm's collections— geographical, ethnological, botanical, zoological, mineralogical, and antiquarian—were at his death the largest assembled by a private hand. Of the holdings in the museum established at Mergentheim, *Unsere Zeit*, the *Jahrbuch zu Brockhaus Conversationslexikon*, Volume V (1861), page 144, said, "In extent and content it is inferior only to a few of the large public collections and surpasses most of them." He was recognized by the University of Tübingen with a doctorate, *honoris causa*, and by many learned societies which conferred membership upon him: the Royal Leopold Academy, Vienna; the Société Imperial Zoologique d'Acclimation, Paris; the Society of Natural Sciences, Athens; and academies at London and St. Petersburg.

The power of a scientist or writer of *belles lettres* to survive his era depends to a considerable extent upon the corpus of his work, as well as its quality. When, as in Duke Paul's case, he pursues a course that can only be compared to that of a figure in a naturalistic novel, proceeding to his own demise from an original and persistent flaw, bibliography fails. But, as may soon be seen, a measure of balance may yet be restored by students of his career in another era, our own.

In the 1921 edition of his bibliography, *The Plains and the Rockies*,

Henry R. Wagner listed and described Duke Paul's account of his first American tour from the title page of the 1835 edition as his item No. 49. In the Grabhorn edition of 1937, Charles L. Camp, the editor of *The Plains and the Rockies*, makes it No. 58, other titles having been turned up for inclusion chronologically in this now classic listing of books significant to the history of the Trans-Mississippi West, 1800–1865. Camp's census of copies extant included those held by the Henry E. Huntington Library and Art Gallery, San Marino, California; the Library of Congress; and the private library of Mr. Thomas W. Streeter at Morristown, New Jersey.

The title page of the Duke's work reads *Erste Reise/ nach dem/ nördlichen Amerika/ in den Jahren 1822 bis 1824/ von/ Paul Wilhelm, Herzog von Württemberg./ Stuttgart und Tübingen,/ Verlag der J. G. Cotta'schen Buchhandlung./ 1835.*

The copy I have had the privilege of examining is that held by the University of Michigan Library, which very generously permitted it on interlibrary loan to the Bizzell Memorial Library at the University of Oklahoma. The cover, of paper over boards, measures 24 x 14.7 cm., the paper page being 23.4 x 13.6 cm. It came to the University of Michigan Library as a gift from L. L. Hubbard, a member of the University Board of Regents, on January 27, 1927. For his translation, my colleague W. Robert Nitske worked from the microcard copy held by the Alderman Library of the University of Virginia. He also had the opportunity to examine what must be considered the first German edition of this work (also noted by Henry R. Wagner and Charles L. Camp in 1937), in all likelihood produced at the Duke's own expense at Mergentheim by Johann Georg Thomm, 1828. "The original sheets of this work," says Nitske, who examined them at the Huntington Library, "on a slightly larger than book-size paper and with numerous corrections and additions made in ink, apparently by the author (the handwriting closely resembles a letter written in February, 1860, by Duke Paul to the Stadtschultheissamt now at Mergentheim) included eighteen pages of detailed journal entries of the sea voyage across the Atlantic. Listed are the date, exact longitude and latitude positions, and under 'physical observations' the precise barometer, thermometer, hygrometer, and wind readings are given. Above the original title,

Reise nach Nordamerika während den Jahren
1822, 1823, und 1824

was added *Erste*, suggesting that these corrections were made after the second trip had already been made (it began in 1829). The words *Verfasst von Friedrich Paul Wilhelm, Herzog von Württemberg* were not changed, but in the printed edition the *verfasst* (authored) was left off, as was his first name, Friedrich. The imprint, *Gedruckt von Johann Georg Thomm, Mergentheim, 1828,* was crossed out entirely and *Gedruckt* [printed] *1833* written in ink as a correction. The book as a formally published work, under book publishing auspices, appeared over the imprint of J. G. Cotta, Stuttgart and Tübingen, 1835."

A translation into English was carried out by William G. Bek of the Department of German of the University of North Dakota and published as *First Journey to North America in the Years 1822 to 1824, by Paul Wilhelm, Duke of Wuerttemberg* in *South Dakota Historical Collections,* Volume XIX (1938). This translation, which has been useful to those who do not command German or have no access to the 1835 edition, does not differentiate scientific names from the rest of the narrative and it contains no historical or scientific annotation by the translator. It does contain, as appendices, letters from Dr. Stenrel, the city archivist of Stuttgart; and Friedrich Bauser, archivist of a private address in Stuttgart, offering a manuscript of some nine hundred pages of materials drawn from Duke Paul's writings and other materials of a biographical character to the South Dakota Historical Society for "2200 to 2500 marks" as a basis for negotiation as of August 10, 1933 (I would receive a similar proposal from Germany some years later); and a "Statement of Biographic Facts Regarding Duke Paul of Wuerttemberg" by Friedrich Bauser.

During his travels in Europe, Charles L. Camp was able to secure a copy of a journal kept by Duke Paul during his third trip to the Americas, beginning in 1849. This copy is presently being translated and edited by David H. Miller, of the Department of Social Sciences, Cameron College, Lawton, Oklahoma. The much longer Friedrich Bauser narrative of the Duke's travels on this occasion, secured from the Württembergische Landesbibliothek in Stuttgart in 1966 by John Francis McDermott, of Southern Illinois University at Edwardsville, is in process of translation and editing by Professor Raymond Jürgen Spahn of that University and his wife, Betty.

But the Duke of Württemberg has hardly lacked attraction for others over the period of the last thirty-five years—roughly from the centennial of first extended publication of *Erste Reise* in 1935 to the present. Charles L. Camp had advanced a translation in typescript when the Bek translation made it abortive. In 1939 under the Department of History and the Graduate School of the University of Wyoming, Virginia Marie Speich's Master's thesis was completed. It was entitled "A Royal Voyager on the Ohio and Mississippi Rivers, 1822–1823; Introduction and Notes to Louis

C. Butscher's Translation of the First Seven Chapters of *Erste Reise nach dem nördlichen Amerika in den Jahren 1822 bis 1824* (Stuttgart und Tübingen, 1835) by Prince Paul of Württemberg."

Louis C. Butscher published "A Brief Biography of Prince Paul Wilhelm of Württemberg (1797–1860)" in *New Mexico Historical Review*, XVII, No. 3 (July, 1942), 181–225; and "Account of Adventures in the Great American Desert by His Royal Highness, Duke Paul Wilhelm of Württemberg," edited by Louis C. Butscher, in *New Mexico Historical Review*, XVII, No. 4 (October, 1942), 294–344. The former is important for its biographical synthesis, the latter for a blend of the Württemberg-Balduin Möllhausen account of their joint adventures in the American West in 1850–1851.

The year 1948 saw the completion of Sister Dolorita Marie Dougherty's Master's thesis, "First Journey to North America in the Years 1822 to 1824 by Paul Wilhelm, Duke of Württemberg: A Translation from the German," in the Department of History and the Graduate School of St. Louis University. Thus the weight of our familiarity with the German traveler's activities in the New World rests upon his extended, finished work of 1835 and fragments thus far of his journey of 1849–1856.

As Friedrich Bauser has indicated in his correspondence concerning the Duke's literary remains at Stuttgart, there is little or no trace of the notes the traveler may have kept, or formal writings that he may have done later, for the second trip to America beginning in 1829. This is a rich middle chapter in the story of the Missouri River fur trade, when some of its best characters were still alive and ready and willing to speak their lines to an old friend from the Württemberg line.

It appears that another record of a lifetime of travel, the natural science collections, scarcely even sorted, were either dispersed after the Duke's death or destroyed. Only those who work intimately with the skins of birds and animals and the dried specimens of the lower and higher plants can know the proportions of this loss to the natural history of a young America and an Old World.

The editorial notes contained in the present translation of Duke Paul's *Erste Reise* are in part his own, in larger part those of the editor. All of the Duke's notes are identified as such as they begin. All others are to be understood as editorial additions. Insertions in, or additions to, the Duke's notes are indicated by brackets. In a few instances I have bracketed genera, especially when the Duke left any room for doubt about his intent. But for the scientist as well as the general reader there can be little doubt about the author's wide-ranging command of North American natural science in the period of its infancy.

Norman, Oklahoma   SAVOIE LOTTINVILLE
March 15, 1973

Contents

Illustrations

Maps

Paul Wilhelm, Duke of Württemberg
TRAVELS IN NORTH AMERICA, 1822–1824

Author's Foreword

WHEN I undertook my first journey to North America, it was not my intention to present a complete historical travel report to the public. The purpose of the journey was rather to acquire knowledge of the country, its inhabitants and products, and, in case my total experiences would include sufficient material, to present that to the scientific world by publishing it in fragments or in separate papers.

With this intention I composed my diary. Only after repeated urging did I decide to present to the public these collected notes, arranged in logical order. Therefore I wish to ask indulgence if some defects are found or if often purely scientific and especially natural science subjects interrupt the thread of the narrative. These, as in most such travel descriptions, might tax the patience of the reader.

The acquisition of my collection was absolutely necessary. Since I intend to publish in separate treatises the geographic and natural-science observations of my two trans-Atlantic journeys, I have therefore gone into greater scientific detail.[1]

I ask the indulgence of scholars if individual mistakes or uncertainties have crept in, for I had to classify several objects immediately on my return in 1824, and they are perhaps now more accurately determined elsewhere. With others I needed larger reference works, especially such works which would have made possible accurate comparison through good detailed illustrations.

Furthermore, since larger works of this nature do not suit the general book trade, I have decided to publish separately several of my drawings of the regions which I traversed, and such items that may interest the public.[2]

---

[1] The reference here is to the author's journeys of 1822–1824 and 1829–1831 to the United States. Only his first journey received the extended publication he intended.

[2] The proposed separate publications containing "drawings of the regions" he traversed

3

Before closing this short foreword it is my duty to mention the friendly reception which I found everywhere in America, as well as the generous co-operation of the civil and military officials of the various American states, which greatly contributed to the success of my journey.

I have also every reason to express my warmest thanks to the several fur companies, now united as the American Fur Company, for the many friendly favors shown me during my two expeditions into the northwest of America.

---

had not been published at the time of the author's death in 1860. For the fate of the author's literary and scientific remains, see the Editor's Introduction, *ante*.

1

IMMEDIATELY on my arrival at Hamburg during the opening days of October, 1822, I was fortunate in finding a good opportunity to sail for New Orleans, and so did not have to remain there longer than was necessary to make the arrangements for my journey, to procure some badly needed additional scientific instruments, and to repair those that had become defective.

I expected to make the trip on the three-masted *Hyglander* of New York, which had the reputation of being a good sailing vessel, and whose most obliging and well informed Captain Walsh planned to leave in two weeks. As everyone knows, little reliance can be put in the announcement of a ship's probable date of departure. So many factors occur to postpone a sailing, but the main reason for the long delays so inconvenient to all passengers is that the ship's masters set the sailing date earlier to hasten as much as possible the loading of their vessel. This time, however, was a rare exception, for our vessel was ready to sail on the appointed day.

The entire cargo, linen (from Westphalia and Silesia), glass, and various other manufactured goods, was loaded, and I had all of my belongings put into my assigned cabin on the fifteenth, the day previous to the departure. But on the sixteenth, when I was already on board, the wind turned to the north, preventing our departure, and I returned to shore.

The captain had me called very early on the following day because the wind had changed to the southeast. However, it blew so faintly until eleven o'clock that it exerted hardly any noticeable influence on the sails. But the ship weighed anchor and by means of tow lines and with the aid of other craft was piloted into the current of the Elbe at noon and placed into position to continue its course slowly down the river with the help of the sails. Several other ships moved out with the *Hyglander*, among them a brig destined for Port-au-Prince on Santo Domingo. We advanced but slowly until evening and lost sight of Altona[1] very late.

Captain Walsh, who had remained in town for several hours on business, arrived on board just as the anchor was being lowered because of approaching nightfall and because of dense fog. Two pilots were aboard, one from Hamburg to pilot us through the Elbe into the open sea, and an Englishman from Dover who was to take us through the North Sea into the English Channel. Both would have command of the vessel at the moment the ship was set in motion. Though the Americans are excellent sailors, they rarely venture to sail the North Sea and the Channel without the help of an English pilot, especially after the equinox or during the short days of the winter when the sea is dangerous.

The trip from Hamburg to the mouth of the Elbe was not without difficulties, since one can sail only with a good south or southeast wind. Very light vessels can sail the Elbe with a slightly unfavorable wind, but with loaded ships this is utterly impossible. We took advantage of ebb tide and the southeast wind, but since the latter was only very faint on the first day, we moved very slowly down the river. At Stade[2] is a sandbank which larger ships can pass over only at flood tide or at the beginning of ebb tide and with a brisk wind. Our vessel had the rare luck to pass over this sandbank at fourteen feet of water, and since it draws thirteen feet I consider it a lucky chance that we were not delayed any longer. Under average conditions this sandbank is believed to be covered by eighteen feet of water, while at ebb tide it is covered with only eight feet. Sailing at night on the Elbe, as on most other river systems near the mouth, is not advised, and the cautious sailor drops anchor at the approach of night, yet this has also many inconveniences.

We were in the vicinity of Glückstadt at about noon of the eighteenth. The temperature was 50°, the weather foggy, and the wind blew briskly from the northeast by east. Thus we reeached Cuxhaven before sunset, but had to drop anchor on the roadstead because the wind was unfavorable to our entering the North Sea. During the night the wind changed to southwest by west and continued to blow from this direction uninterruptedly until noon of the twenty-third. I had ample opportunity to test my patience.

When on the morning of the twentieth countless gulls (*Larus marinus*, Gmel., *ridibundus*, Linn., *argentatus*, Lath., and others) congregated about our ship and even some dogfish stuck their heads out of the water, the

---

[1] A suburb of Hamburg, on cliffs of the right bank of the Elbe, five kilometers from the center of the city.

[2] A town west of Hamburg on the Schwinge River, five kilometers from its confluence with the Elbe.

sailors concluded that bad weather was coming. At about noon it arrived in the form of a violent southwest wind, accompanied by rain, increasing during the night to such fury that we feared the anchor cable would snap.

Toward morning of the twenty-first the storm subsided somewhat, ending in isolated wind gusts, and finally by evening actual calm prevailed. (The storm blew from the southwest by west during flood tide, but at the beginning of ebb tide turned to southwest by south and was then accompanied by rain. The temperature of the air rose from 52° to 56°, and that of the sea from 50° to 52°. The de Luc hygrometer rose [from the nineteenth to the twentieth] from 60° to 66°, and the barometer fell from 27″ 6.1′ "to 26″ 11.5′".)[3] This storm offered a foretaste of many dangerous storms to which I was subjected during the trip.

The stay at the roadstead of Cuxhaven could have tested even a sailor least inclined to be seasick, because the ship, riding at anchor and stripped of all sails, yielded to every movement of the sea with an irregular and rolling motion. Indeed, all of the passengers except myself lay miserably ill. I attributed my wellbeing to having previously made several sea voyages and to the fortunate faculty of not being affected by this malady.

On the morning of the twenty-second, with the beginning of the first moon quarter, the wind turned to the north, then to the northeast, and finally to the east and southeast. At the same time dense fog appeared and we could not think of setting sail. On the twenty-third, thick fog again prevailed, but with wind blowing briskly from the southeast the fog disappeared at about noon, and the anchor could be raised. Toward five o'clock in the evening we were opposite Helgoland and soon lost the lighthouse of the island from sight. That night we were in the deep waters of the North Sea itself. After midnight the violent southeast wind turned into a storm and continued the entire day of the twenty-fourth, driving the vessel swiftly towards the coast of England. At noon of the twenty-fifth we were at 53° 42′ north latitude and 2° 36′ east longitude from London. The wind turned to southwest by south and decreased very rapidly in velocity so that we were almost becalmed.

The sea was very rough during the entire night, while the wind again began to blow from the southwest by west. At about noon of the twenty-sixth it increased again in intensity, becoming a storm. When that day we

---

[3] Throughout, Duke Paul used the Reaumur temperature scale, but the translator has changed it to the Fahrenheit scale for simplification. The former, with a freezing point at zero and a boiling point at 80°, was widely used in Europe at the time. It was named for the French physicist René Antoine de Reaumur. The de Luc hygrometer, named for the Swiss physicist, J. A. de Luc, or Deluc, was based on the principle of the hair hygrometer but employed a strip of whalebone.

reached the heights of Northforeland[4] another calm set in, occasionally interrupted by single gusts of wind, creating a most uncomfortable situation for us near the English coast. Nevertheless, we luckily approached the mouth of the Channel, and at about five o'clock that evening were only one nautical mile from Dover, so that despite the approaching darkness, one could distinctly see the houses and the activity in the harbor. Our English pilot left us close to the town.

Despite the rough sea we were soon surrounded by a large number of boats offering all kinds of foodstuff for sale. These products were, however, so expensive on the English coast that one is wise to provide himself with all necessary items before departure. Because of the cool weather our captain had procured a considerable supply of fresh beef in Cuxhaven, and this was sufficient for three weeks for the cabin table.

Nothing of importance occurred during the night and our ship sailed on in the Channel, but in the morning the wind turned again to the northwest. We were fortunate to reach the Dungeness roadstead[5] where we anchored on good bottom. A few English naval officers came aboard and spent over half an hour in my cabin. They most kindly offered their services to attend to any business I might wish to transact on shore, and accepting this courteous offer, I wrote several letters, which they took care of.

In the vicinity of Dungeness the current of the Channel towards the northeast was already very noticeable. This has a decided influence on westbound sailings, making the journey very difficult during the stormy autumn and winter months. During the afternoon the wind changed to southeast by south, bringing good weather and awakening the hope in us of reaching the mouth of the strait and the Bay of Biscay without further hindrance.

During the clear days, which for short periods made our journey more agreeable and compensated us for the storms we had endured and the impenetrable fogs which so much offended our eyes, we could see the pleasant shores of England with their white chalk cliffs ornamented with patches of green grass, mirrored in the waves of the light blue sea. This formed a happy contrast to the dark and much higher coast of neighboring Normandy in the distance.

This scene, enlivened by many vessels sailing about in various directions, among them several armed vessels sailing proudly on their courses, under full sail, was a necessary inducement to raise our morale for the long sea

[4] On the east coast of England, north of Dover and at the eastern approach to the Thames estuary.

[5] On the south coast of Kent, eleven miles east of Rye.

voyage ahead. It must also fill everyone with respect for the art which has contributed so much to the advancement and civilization of the human race.

The two straits, the one separating France from England and the one Spain from Africa, may rightly be regarded as meeting places of vessels from all maritime nations. The life of these waters, with the great variety of ships traveling, has an uplifting effect on the observer and leaves him with indelible memories.

With a sharp wind blowing from southeast by south, we were at the tip of Cape Lezard Point (Lizard Head), the southwestern promontory of England, at noon of October 30. That same afternoon we lost sight of England having come from Dungeness along the coast past Beachyhead so close to Hastings and Thoreham that from the deck of the *Hyglander* we could actually count the windows in the houses. Because of changing wind to southwest by south during the night of the twenty-first, we made slow progress. At our entrance into the Aquatic Sea, or Bay of Biscay, the sea ran mighty high, many gulls and even storm birds (*Procellaria pelagica*, Linn.)[6] appeared near the ship, leaving no doubt of an impending storm.

The sky was only slightly clouded and the sun rose a bloody red. Towards evening the first fierce currents of air began and towards midnight the storm broke in its full fury from the southwest. Our most painstakingly prepared and excellent vessel withstood well the first violent attack of the storm, but even so lay on its side several times. We feared we would have to cut away the masts or see the ship take water. Luckily the *Hyglander* always righted herself again and with great dexterity cut through the most threatening waves, often entirely submerged when they broke over us. Many articles were washed off the decks, among them all of our poultry, a dire necessity on a sea voyage, and the sides of the vessel were greatly damaged. A wave damaged my cabin door at the very outset of the storm and the cabin was deluged, so that I had the greatest difficulty in keeping my books, papers, and instruments dry and undamaged from sea water.

All during the day of November 1 and the night following the storm continued unabated and when it subsided at noon of the 2nd, a calm, almost as dangerous as the storm, set in. During the storm two topgallant masts had broken and several sets of rigging were torn or badly tangled,

---

[6] *Procellaria pelagica* = *Hydrobates pelagica*, storm petrel, with other members of the family Hydrobatidae known traditionally to sailors as "Mother Carey's chickens," mythical harbingers of storms at sea.

but these minor mishaps could well be overlooked. We were fortunate to have escaped as luckily as we did.

After this storm, at noon of November 2 we were at 49° 39′ north latitude. The west longitude could not be accurately determined. The wind continued from the west, and with a high running sea the ship made very slow progress. I observed many marine birds drifting with the waves (among them *Puffinus anglorum*, Cuv., *Procellaria anglorum*, Gmel., *Carbo cormoranus*, Meyer, *Disporus alba*, Illiger (*Sula* M.) and *Sterna hirundo*, Linn., and others).[7]

Several schools of dolphins (*Dolphinus tursio*, Orca, Lacep., *Hyperoodon retusus*, Lacep., and others) floated near the surface of the water from the north to the southwest. When leaping, their entire bodies were at times visible above the water, and sometimes they disappeared for a distance of several hundred yards following the ship's course. They propelled themselves at times by leaping motions for a quarter of an hour uninterruptedly.[8]

During the night I could already observe the glowing of the sea, but not with the same splendor as later in the more southern regions. The mass of agitated water did not yet show that bright and almost fiery light peculiar to the tropical seas, but I saw several individual, brightly illuminated, star-shaped bodies glowing far down in the deep water, until they vanished from sight. These large luminous spots I even saw for a few seconds after water of breaking waves had been thrown on deck.

Unfortunately the regrettable scenes of November 1 and 2 were repeated on the morning of the seventh at 47° 25′ north latitude and 15° 34′ longitude west of Greenwich, when after calm and pleasant weather a new southwest by south gale broke with the same fury as the previous storm. After we had endured the hardships of this disturbance of nature, the wind fluctuated from east to northeast, northwest by north, then to northeast by east, and finally died away in a calm. The storm had driven us close to the Spanish coast and we were in the vicinity of Cape Finisterre at 43° 50′ north latitude and 15° 15′ west longitude.

From then on until the entrance to the trade-winds area we were still subjected to various changing strong winds from northeast, southeast, and southwest by west, but their violence decreased in proportion to our approach to the temperate climate. The air became clearer, the sky darker,

---

[7] The several marine species of birds here listed by the author all bear names of the older classifications with which he was familiar. They include shearwaters, petrels, cormorants, gannets, and terns.

[8] Cf. David Starr Jordan, *A Guide to the Study of Fishes*, I, 545; II, 213–14, 287.

the sun rose and set in a more beautiful yellow light, the beat of the waves became more regular, and that natural quiet prevailed which makes sailing on the vast and boundless great ocean far less dangerous than a journey on lakes bounded by cliffs.

San Miguel, one of the Azores islands, was clearly sighted on the fourteenth. By the structure of the rocky masses can be seen the volcanic origin peculiar to all the islands directly west of the African continent. On the morning of the sixteenth the wind turned to the northeast by north and on the next day to northeast by east. Thus we recognized with great joy the favorable trade wind, which indeed remained faithful to us until the twenty-ninth, luckily driving our vessel over the vast expanse of the Atlantic Ocean.

Nothing hindered us anymore and the peaceful mood peculiar during this season on the great ocean allowed a certain carefreeness so dear to the sailor on tranquil waters. Most of the sails could be set day and night, and our journey progressed rapidly. The air was almost always clear; showers were very rare; the mean temperature of the air during the day was 77° to 85°, at night 73° to 75°, and that of the water, from 30° north latitude on, between 77° and 81°. At the Tropic of Cancer we encountered thunderstorms, but not with such violence as in the vicinity of land. The glowing of the waters increased most from 30° to 25° north latitude, but diminished somewhat in the vicinity of the Tropic of Cancer. Near the 26° of latitude I already had begun to notice distinctly the pronounced shortness of dawn and twilight, and because of the dark color of the sky the individually brighter shining stars appeared on the firmament immediately after sunset. Jupiter was even visible when the sun touched the edge of the horizon, and hardly had the sun set when Sirius and Canopus appeared, ever increasing in brightness the more the splendid yellow light of the day star gave way to the dark tropical night.

After ten o'clock in the evening of November 25 many asteroids fell from a height of 40° to 45° in the direction from the south to the southwest, presenting a beautiful spectacle. I counted a considerable number and on various occasions saw several at one time. These meteors fell during a quarter of an hour's time. From that day on great masses of seaweed (*Laminaria pyrifera*, Lamoureux) appeared, which had been only rarely seen before on the surface of the water. These dense masses became more and more frequent as we approached the Gulf Stream, and as soon as we noticed this current on our course, the seaweed decreased again, perhaps caused by the motion of the sea. In the vicinity of the Tropic of Cancer, which we crossed for the first time on the twenty-fourth, the first flying fish and their pursuers, sharks and dolphins (*Exocetus volitans*, Linn., *Squalus carcharias*, Linn., *Coryphaena equisetis*, Bloch.) were noted, but in considerably smaller numbers than in the vicinity of the Antilles.

During a thunderstorm with violent electrical discharges on the twenty-eighth, the prevailing trade wind changed to a west wind. Thunder showers occured several times over a period of two hours. At half past ten the sky suddenly grew dark in the southwest and an extremely sudden violent storm rose, so that our sails had to be hurriedly taken in, but the point of the bowsprit to which the foremost sail was still attached was broken. This storm, resembling a tornado (frequent in the vicinity of the Antilles during the equinoxes), was so much more surprising because we were rather far from land. At about one o'clock the wind again rose furiously from the southwest, lasting until half past five, when the trade wind again set in.

My assumption that a violent west wind must be raging in the Antilles was confirmed. Such movements can be felt at sea several hundred miles from land. The southwest and northwest storms are especially frequent in the seas of tropical America, and they are more dangerous as one gets closer to the shore, giving too little warning to sailors to take in their sails. Because of the short duration they rarely set the sea in severe motion.

At noon on December 1st we were at 24° 32′ north latitude and 65° 36′ west longitude from Greenwich. The weather had again turned fine and clear, moonlit nights were so splendid that I could hardly bring myself to go to bed. On the afternoon of the second we observed a sailing ship steering from south to north. We came close enough to hail it and found that it was an American schooner sailing from Santo Domingo to Salem. From it we received the news that on November 28 a furious hurricane had raged in the Caribbean Sea.

The night of the third saw a full moon which passed the meridian almost in the zenith. The following night many asteroids again fell over a period of hours and in the same direction as on November 25. The current of the Gulf Stream now became so noticeable that it influenced the ship's course. The trade wind continued to blow, but decidedly weaker, favoring our journey.

At noon on December 6 Captain Walsh and I computed the longitude by the culminations of the moon and found no great difference between this calculation and the reading of my timepiece, which had a second hand. Although not an accurate instrument, and not to be compared with a real chronometer, it was to be preferred to the log for daily use on ship. Captain Walsh had a difference of only 2⅝ knots when compared with my watch, which had not been set back since October 20 and exceeded the astronomical longitude calculation by 1° 34′. The correct longitude at noon of the 6th was 75° 21′ west of Greenwich, the latitude 25° 48′ north. The heat was very oppressive that day, the sky was clear and violet blue. The thermometer rose to 86° and the barometer stood at 27″ 10.9′ ″.

Toward evening the wind turned from southeast by south to northeast. The night temperature was almost equal to that during the day (as can be seen in my meteorological journal). During the night several flying fish landed on the deck. I observed that this fish of the genus *Exocetus* appears with the coming of northeast or northwest winds, but this observation regarding the moves or wanderings of the flying fish should be experienced by travelers who traverse the equinoctial seas of northeastern America during the summer months. The natural history of these fish, particularly their economic life, is presently in great obscurity, and requires considerably more careful study.[9]

The next day was clear and the wind blew uniformly and rather strongly from the southeast. Although at noon some clouds formed, nevertheless we were able to determine the latitude and hoped to sight the first of the Lucayas Islands. According to my calculation, we should see Eleuthera with the unaided eye at about five o'clock with the same wind prevailing. That noon, on December 5, we were at 25° 45′ north latitude and 76° 40′ longitude.

I was not mistaken, and shortly after four o'clock the first helmsman from the height of the crow's nest on the foremast distinctly recognized the island.[10]

The island of Abaco, only forty minutes distant from Eleuthera, came into sight before sunset. We approached it within two miles and I could distinctly see its form and with a good Dollond telescope observed the main features of its vegetation.[11]

[9] *Author*: The flying fishes, according to observations made by Alexander von Humboldt, are characterized by the size of their swimming bladder, which is of advantage more for leaping through the air than for swimming. Though the fishes are able to keep themselves in flying motion out of the water for a while, they can do so only as long as their pectoral fins are moist. As soon as these become dry, the fishes need to moisten them again and must let themselves fall back into the water. Usually the flying fishes touch the water's surface three or four times before swimming again for a distance. The flying fishes of Japanese rivers are *Scorpinus dactyloptera*, *Porcus*, and *Scrofa*, which likewise have larger swimming bladders than other fishes. (Delaroche, *Annales du Museum*, Vol. XIV, p. 189).

[10] *Author*: As is known, Christopher Columbus at ten p.m. on Thursday, October 11, 1492, observed a light which seemed to be borne from place to place and communicated this fact to his page Pedro de Guttierez. The next morning at two o'clock the hope of the great sailor was fulfilled. It was the island Guanahani (San Salvador) located next to Eleuthera. [The dates above are old style. The actual site is probably modern Watling Island.]

[11] *Author*: The highest point of Abaco rises scarcely twenty-two yards above the level

The first sight of land brings elation to every seafarer. This impression is so much greater on that traveler whose imagination had busied himself in advance with a fantasy of a world entirely new to him. The recollection of the feelings of the discoverers of these shores, whose excited expectation was almost exceeded by reality, arouses wonderment at the great and magnificent scenes of nature in the soul of the receptive human being, and increases the desire for the perfection and the highest possible attainment of great and unselfish goals.

Abaco, as are most of the other islands of the Lucayan Archipelago,[12] is completely depopulated because of the lack of drinking water. The traces of a primitive population were erased by the cruelty of the conquerers at the beginning of the sixteenth century. The Spaniards sought to lure the inhabitants by cunning to Santo Domingo and Cuba, where even then the greater part of the primitive red race had died in the wars with the oppressors or in unbearable slavery.[13]

The Indians of these Lucayan Islands may have been related to the Indians in Florida with whom they seem to have had at least a close connection. They cultivated maize and cassava and lived in a manner similar to that of the inhabitants of the Greater Antilles. Since there is no record of their language, no comparison can be made with the dialect of the Appalachians.[14]

---

of the sea. The Lucayan Islands in many respects share the vegetation of equinoxial North America. The islands situated to the north have many of the genera peculiar to the southern tip of Florida, for example the royal palm (*palma real* of the French Creoles and undoubtedly identical with the *Oreodoxa regia* of von Humboldt) was distinctly discernible.

[12] The name given to the Bahamas by Columbus. English settlement began in the middle of the seventeenth century and royal control was exercised by the last quarter of the eighteenth century. Abaco consists of Great and Little Abaco islands, of which the latter is northernmost. Streams, then as now, were rare in the entire Bahamas group. But vegetation remains abundant on Great Abaco, where the Caribbean pine continues to offer forest products.

[13] *Author*: The population of Santo Domingo was probably exaggerated by the Spaniards at the time of discovery, when they estimated it at a million. Of this number, after fifteen years, only between fifty thousand and sixty thousand continued to exist. (Herrera, *Decad.* I, Lib. X, C. 12.) It is now assumed that the population of the island never exceeded three hundred thousand. How great therefore must have been the atrocities of the Spaniards in destroying 250,000 people.

The first deportation of the inhabitants of the Lucayan Islands occurred in 1508. (Herrera, *Decad.* I, Lib. VII, C. 3; Oviedo, Lib. III, C. 6; Gomera, *Hist.*, C. 41). Two ships were equipped for this purpose.

[14] The missing linguistic clue in Duke Paul's day has continued in ours to thwart comparisons between the Arawak, the principal Indian group of the Antilles in the sixteenth and seventeenth centuries, and the Calusas of Florida, who, however, numbered among their fifty villages an Arawak colony. The Calusas by 1600 were carrying on regular trading

On December 8 we reached the beginning of the Bahama Bank. The depth of the sea decreased suddenly and one can distinctly recognize the ocean bottom and objects on it. The bottom consisted of granular white calcareous earth and in many places was covered with seaweed. I noticed two genera (*Fucus natans* and *Laminaria pyrifera*, Lamour.), both of which grow on rocks in the sea and only accidentally drift to the Bahama Bank. Von Humboldt is of the opinion that these algae are proof of existing sea currents, and I share that opinion, especially where seaweeds occur in large amounts.

On my return from America to Europe I saw on the trip through the Gulf Stream the greatest amount of seaweed between northern latitudes of 26° to 33°. The various shades of the seaweed, graduating from a light, almost pale, to a dark color, may be due to their growth at a lesser or greater depth and to the influence of light. The Spaniards call the seaweed *zargossa*. Columbus found it first at 41° western longitude, and like all seafarers of his time, had to suffer by the superstitious belief of his crew regarding this innocent weed.

Countless sea crabs, mollusks, and rotatoria had made their home on these sea plants. Dolphins (*Coryphaena hippurus* and *equiselis*, Bloch) were busy hunting flying fish, which rose in great schools from the waves. Although I am not of the opinion that instinct of fear drives these creatures out of the water so that they escape their pursuers, it is nevertheless certain that these voracious enemies pursue them incessantly, following their course with the swiftness of an arrow.

A shark (*Squalus glaucus*, Bloch)[15] followed us the whole day, but would not take the hook baited with fresh pork which we cast for it. Ordinarily sharks swim close to the surface of the water and are surrounded by a wake of gleaming foam caused by the spinal fin which projects out of the water. The eagle-like frigate bird (*Tachypetes aquilus* with very long wings, commonly counted among pelicans and cormorants, has contrastingly short and small web feet) I saw for the first time on this bank.[16] It

expeditions to the Arawaks of Cuba. The Spaniards by 1508 had removed some forty thousand Arawaks from the Bahamas to Hispaniola, i.e., Haiti and the present Dominican Republic, to work in the mines there. Early records give us no clear view of the relations between the Timucuans of Florida and the Arawaks. Frederick Webb Hodge, *Handbook of Indians North of Mexico, Bulletin 30*, Smithsonian Institution, Bureau of American Ethnology, 2 vols., I, 195–96; II, 752–54.

[15] *Author*: Probably it was this variety which occurs frequently in the waters of the Atlantic coast, marked by a beautiful gleaming blue color. The specimen we saw was from ten to eleven feet long. [Possibly *Prionace glauca?*]

[16] Duke Paul's somewhat older fellow German, Prince Alexander Philip Maximilian zu Wied, a man equally dedicated to natural science, observed and named *Tachypetes aquilus*

competed with a long-tailed, brown bird of prey in the hunt of flying fish and mollusks floating on the surface.

Beautiful light blue jelly fish[17] swam in great numbers on the waves from southeast to north, seemingly torn loose from the cliffs of the southern islands. They caused a violent burning on the skin and lost their color immediately on coming in contact with alcohol.

That evening I saw an unknown storm bird (*Porcellaria*) which belonged to the smallest varieties, was dark brown, long-tailed, and had a white belly.[18]

We had to drop anchor in the evening since it would have been very venturesome to sail, even in the clearest night, such an uncertain sea, beset with shallows and cliffs, protruding or close under the surface of the water. The night was one of the most beautiful I had seen in the hot climate of the New World. It would be dull for the reader if I repeat the pictures which imprint themselves on the vivid imagination in these tropical nights. The sea was mirror smooth like waters of a great lake with moon and larger stars painted on it. The dark blue of the sky and silver coloring of sea produced a striking and impressive contrast. Even in daytime the different shades of the waters of the Bahama Bank, compared with those of the great ocean, furnished a characteristic picture of the torrid zone. The bottom of the sea was distinctly visible, and the water was colored a lightest aquamarine. The sky, on the other hand, appeared much darker and was reflected in the lighter surface of the water.

I made a few observations on the flow of the Gulf Stream pertaining to time and wind, which exert great influence on the strength of the current. Some 160 miles from the Bahama Islands one begins to feel the pressure of the waves to the east, not as great, however, as the pressure of the current to the northeast. At 73° 30′ west longitude from London, the thermometer hardly showed a difference of ¼ degree Fahrenheit at a depth of sixty fathoms. Later the current increased and rose to three English miles per hour, even with a strong southeast wind.

The salt content of the water showed only a slight difference from that of the great ocean, and the glowing of the foam was not as great any more. The reasons for this difference I shall leave to the physicists to explain.

Wied in his *Beitrage zur Naturgeschichte von Brasilien* (Weimar, 1825–1833), IV (2), 885. It is now *Fregata magnificens* Mathews, magnificent frigate-bird.

[17] *Author*: Belonging to the genus *Beroë*, whose rotary motion on the surface of the water is characteristic. Because of carelessness in transferring them into alcohol, the specimens so carefully collected by me were unfortunately spoiled.

[18] More likely one of the family of Hydrobatidae, storm petrels, though which of the eighteen species is difficult to determine.

The luminous particles, appearing like sparks in the surging water, vary in degree of luminosity in the different oceans and the various seasons of the year. Thus I was never able to see the illumination of the sea as striking as in the Gulf of Mexico during December, especially when the air was charged with electricity.

When, however, I traveled across the same waters in January 1824, the illumination was extremely faint, not in the form of illuminated foam, but only as single bright points glowing for several seconds like little stars in the turbulent sea.

I observed that the water of the Atlantic Ocean was always beautifully blue, and that of the Gulf showed a darker color with black shading. The extraordinary depth of the former and the coloring of the bottom of the latter may be the reasons for these phenomena. In the Gulf the sounding lead brought from a depth of sixty fathoms a dark slimy clay having a greasy feel and containing no sand particles.

The Bahama Bank is full of cliffs, and vessels drawing more than thirteen feet do not risk sailing along the Lucayan [Bahama] Islands. In addition, traveling here is very monotonous because of the current, which in certain areas amounts to five knots and during storms is dangerous. Hurricanes occur frequently here and blow with enormous, sudden velocity, giving the ship almost no opportunity to take in its sails. At certain seasons, especially during the autumnal and the vernal equinoxes, similar electric phenomena appear regularily at certain times of the day. Thus it is extremely difficult to protect oneself against such sudden hurricanes and at the same time continue the voyage with speed.

During such savage storms the sky suddenly grows dark, and the beat of the waves is short and violent. Ships which do not handle easily in a storm are in danger of being cast on the many cliffs and shallows. (During the frightful storms which raged in the West Indies towards the end of 1824 about two hundred vessels perished.)

Not only the elements but also pirates conspire against the seafarer, especially among the Lucayan Islands and along the coast of Cuba, and even more dangerous among the smaller islands in the Santaren Channel and the Tortugas Islands as far as Cape St. Antonio. The pirates possess rather large vessels, manned with crews of eighty to one hundred men, capable of running into most ocean inlets and there escaping pursuit by the cruising English and North American warships.

The pirates attack passing ships with the utmost boldness and are seldom satisfied with merely plundering the vessels, but kill or mistreat the crews, especially the captains and pilots, often in the most horrible manner.

On my arrival in New Orleans I saw the French ship *Alexandre de*

Bordeau which had been attacked and plundered on a trip from Vera Cruz to Havana on the coast of Cuba. The cargo of cochineal and money may have induced the pirates to action. Because of the Spanish officers aboard, the pirates were anxious to prevent its entering Havana or any other port of the island, and so took down all sails, cut the masts, and still unsatisfied with these horrible acts, poured nearly the entire supply of drinking water into the sea. Had it not been hailed by an American armed ship, the vessel would undoubtedly have been lost. Supplied with food and water, the unfortunate crew reached the mouth of the Mississippi. (In similar fashion some fifty ships met with misfortune in the course of a few months.)

Our ship's crew consisted of eighteen men. We carried only two inadequate cannon and in case of attack would have fared badly. Nevertheless, I had induced the captain to mount the best possible defense, because experience had taught how much a courageous counterattack can do in such cases. The timidity of a young agriculturist, who worked part time for his passage, amused me greatly. The ship's crew, sensing his fear, had greatly magnified the danger. This talk and the precautionary measures undertaken induced him to hide the small amount of money and few wretched articles of clothing he had in the most peculiar place.

We came close to the Sal Islands during the night and since the wind blew briskly, the vessel had to be turned to avoid running onto a sandbank at the approach to the islands. The morning of the 10th I could recognize the coast of Cuba, and at noon Matanzas lay ten English miles south of us. We crossed the Tropic of Cancer twice, at 11:28 o'clock at 80° 56′ west longitude and again at 5:42 o'clock at 82° 17′ west longitude, so that we approached Cuba at north latitude 23° 16′.

In the evening I distinctly saw the light tower of Fort Morro at Havana. The night was clear but towards midnight a thunderstorm with light wind arose. These thunderstorms occur at all seasons in the Gulf and the Antilles and often are of extraordinary violence. Electric discharges follow one another without interruption, so that ships not equipped with lightning rods are in danger of being struck. Waterspouts rarely destroy a vessel, but sometimes damage it. Thunderstorms in the torrid zone greatly exceed those of the northern latitudes in intensity and frequency of electric discharges. It is difficult to form a clear idea without witnessing them. Seen at night, the horizon appears dissolved in fire with great drops of rain pouring down in torrents illuminated brilliantly by the electric barrage. As is well known, much more rain falls on the east coast of America and the adjoining interior areas than in Europe or Africa at the same latitude. The electric detonations are by far more violent and frequent than in the above named continents. The thunderstorms of Africa, although extremely violent, are nevertheless much less frequent. The strokes are extraordinarily strong and the claps of thunder terrific, but of short duration as reported by travelers from the interior of Africa.

During the many thunderstorms which I observed at sea near the American coast as well as on the continent, I noticed that the electric discharges were usually associated with furious downpours of rain, following one another in rapid succession. During the spring months these storms, between the north latitudes of 35° and 45° on the Mississippi, Missouri, and Ohio rivers, continued for a long time. Often thunderstorms followed each other for several days, so that the interval between them hardly exceeded a few hours. During the storm the thunder rolled continuously, so that the observer could not differentiate one discharge from another. The reverberation resembled muffled bellowing, rarely could one hear a sharp clap, which characterized the thunderstorms of southern Europe. The electric discharges are likewise very frequent, but they were not violent, as I observed them during the winter months in the Gulf when they happened close to our vessel.

Lightning rods protect ships sufficiently, even though the conductors consist of only a single small-gauge wire. I observed only little if any change in the air temperature during a thunderstorm. Hot days were followed by sultry nights, the thermometer registering between 77° and 85°. The thunderstorms were rarely preceded by gusts of wind, but sometimes a brief and violent disturbance of air concluded this majestic spectacle. But I had no opportunity to observe this personally, because the thunderstorms which discharged in the Gulf while I was there were accompanied by oppressive heat and perfect calm. The storms occurring during March and September, the vernal and autumnal equinoxes, are very violent, but not nearly as dangerous as in the waters of the southern Antilles.

The coasts of Florida and Louisiana are very low and so can be seen only at a short distance, and not at all during the night. The danger is then increased, but it is still not as great as in the Gulf itself, which is dotted with small islands and madreporal reefs, as is the south and east coast of Cuba.

While for many years only few ships have been wrecked on the coasts of Florida, it is true that some had mishaps on the Tortugas Islands, on which one can easily become stranded during the night or under a dark sky.

The current of the Gulf Stream is on the average one and one-half English miles per hour from northwest to southeast. It is very difficult to determine longitudes correctly by means of the log, an imperfect method still unfortunately preferred to chronometers on most vessels, and thus leads to the greatest errors. (The usual price of a chronometer is 100 to 150 pounds sterling.)

During the night of December 11–12 an extremely furious storm rose. This magnificent spectacle was heightened by an extraordinary phosphorescence of the sea such as I had never before seen. Our ship seemed to be floating in a sea of light while the firmament was illuminated by incessant flashes of lightning. From aboard our vessel we could distinctly see the waterspouts accompanying these phenomena, and they terrified us with their terrible roars. To picture nature in that imposing display would be worth the effort of the greatest artists.

The following day was not so oppressively hot, the temperature rising at noon to 79°, but on the 10th the thermometer did not drop below 83°, even during the night. This cooling off, quite noticeable in tropical regions, seemed to have resulted from the recent violent storm, because our latitude of 26° 33′ could not yet exert a decided influence on the reduction of the heat of the air. Our longitude was 85° 10′ west from London.

Countless jellyfishes floated on the water about the ship. I noticed among them a small, very beautiful light blue colored variety, different from the previously mentioned genus *Beroë*. It is most arduous to capture these creatures. One of the ship's crew, however, decided to have a rope tied around him and be let down into the water to catch one, a trick not too difficult for a skilled swimmer in the windless air and calm sea. But this type of fishing might have ended disastrously through an unexpected incident. The young man had hardly been in the water a few minutes when I noticed a shark swimming speedily towards him. It would have devoured the daring sailor had he not been hoisted up in greatest haste.

This great shark[19] and another variety already mentioned (*Squalus carcharias* and *glaucus*) are very common in all waters on the east coast of America. These carnivorous fishes of enormous size belong to the most voracious inhabitants of the sea. Sailors of almost all nations labor under the delusion that a shark pursues especially those ships which have sick persons on board. Although the senses of the shark are probably not keen enough to ascertain this, it is undeniably true that they often follow ships for vast distances. If the sharks are overfed it becomes difficult to get rid of them. The olfactory sense of these fishes seems to be more perfectly developed than that of the other gill-breathing animals. In their voraciousness sharks grab the most indigestible objects, such as wood, and it is claimed by some that after opening their stomachs even iron and stones

[19] Possibly *Carcharodon carcharias*, the great white shark, the man-eater.

were found. They are rather easily caught on iron hooks baited with fresh meat fastened to a four- to six-foot-long chain.

At noon of the thirteenth the current ran at three knots and we were at 27° 53′ latitude and 86° 14′ western longitude. About five o'clock that evening, during fair weather and a 78° temperature, I heard a few muffled electric discharges without having been able to notice previous lightning. The sun set in a most beautiful golden glow, and during the night some sheet-lightning occurred in the eastern sky. At midnight several asteroids fell from an altitude of about fifty degrees from the south through southwest to west, leaving behind a trail which occupied seven to eight celestial degrees. The de Luc hygrometer recorded 63° at night, the thermometer 77°, and the barometer fell from 27″ 9.5′ ″ to 27″ 3.8′ ″. It was perfectly calm and nothing worth mentioning occurred the whole day.

Shortly before four o'clock in the evening we noticed in the northwest a small vessel which the captain recognized as a pilot boat from the mouth of the Mississippi, and in half an hour the pilot was aboard. It was weird not to have seen a human being other than our own company during almost two months and I was delighted to see a person who had left the land of my destination only a few hours before.

But this joy turned to grief at the news that in no previous years had the yellow fever raged to such an extent in lower Louisiana as in this one. For a traveler who was supplied with letters of recommendation, no news can be more disturbing than that the persons on whose courteous and obliging reception the success of the journey must in part depend might have fallen victim to such an epidemic. In 1823, on my return journey from the interior of North America, I was saddened by the news of the death of a highly valued friend. The yellow fever had indeed subsided, but there were still many dangerous cases of the disease, and there was no doubt that foreigners, especially Europeans, were not entirely safe.

The low coast, overgrown with tall reeds, on which the lighthouse at the main outlet of the Mississippi is located, was still fifteen knots away, according to the pilot, and we were forced to lay by at the approach of night. The sounding lead found bottom at sixty fathoms and brought up some hard clay.

The sun set beautifully, promising a better night ahead than the one we had passed. But about eleven o'clock a very strong wind rose from the northwest by north, cooling the air to 50°. Fortunately the wind did not last long and at nine o'clock in the morning it blew from the northeast, the thermometer rising to 55°. At ten o'clock I recognized several islands which surround the main outlet of the river.

I saw a highly peculiar phenomenon, the sudden discoloring of the water about half a mile from the outlet. The water of the Mississippi is yellow, due to the vast amount of clay it carries, and is in sharp contrast to the dark salt water of the Gulf. The clearing of the water occurs so suddenly that the fore part of the vessel seemed to float in yellow water while the aft part was in the darker water.

The temperature of the Gulf also changed over twenty degrees in a short time from 73° to 51°. On my return trip to Europe I investigated still more closely the increasing graduation of the warmth of the Gulf, but did not observe the mentioned clearing in the same striking degree.

As we began to sail up the Mississippi I saw for the first time those enormous tree trunks floating down the river, entwined one with another like rafts. They mark one of the main characteristics of all the great American rivers whose course lies through primitive forests.[20]

Annually the Missouri and the Mississippi and their tributaries tear away wide stretches of their banks which are overgrown with timber, especially during the receding of the waters. These uprooted trees, often massed together, must eventually reach the mouth of the Mississippi. They are torn loose by the tremendous force of the current, no matter how firmly their roots and branches may have become entangled with the bank over the years. During high water, these masses of trees, called correctly *embarras* by the Creoles, constitute almost insurmountable barriers for navigators and the traveler, who often must ride this terrible water system in a wretched *pirogue*. Only the most skilled swimmer can at times save himself from these dangers, and the novice trembles at the sight of these fearful scenes of nature.

During my year-long toilsome journey into the interior of North America, I had ample opportunity to become acquainted with these floating masses of wood which are stopped at the mouth of the river, held back by the force of the sea. Only few reach the high seas and are at once driven away by the current. The outlets of the Mississippi have, as a consequence of these accumulations of thousands of years of tree trunks, been forced into narrower areas. Since the water of the river in its regular inundations always washes over these natural wooden dams and each time leaves vast

[20] *Author*: Alexander von Humboldt compared the natural rafts of the Orinoco with the Chinampas of the Mexican inland lakes. The Indians on the Missouri and Mississippi make use of the same cunning of war which von Humboldt mentioned of the wild Caribs. In this manner the inhabitants of St. Louis on the Mississippi were once attacked by Indians clinging to drifting logs who had made themselves unrecognizable by body paint. They came very close to the small settlement. [The latter incident probably derives from Duke Paul's subsequent conversations with Auguste Chouteau. Cf. John Francis McDermott, ed., *The Early Histories of St. Louis*, 16.]

quantities of earthy deposits, these parts wrested from the sea became new and exceedingly fertile land. It does not seem improbable to me that the greater part of lower Louisiana, between Lake Pontchartrain and the Barataria Peninsula, which is now cut through by numerous channels of the Mississippi, may have at one time actually been part of the ocean. The graduation of vegetation confirms this still more, as will be made clear in the course of my description.[21]

The river banks of Louisiana were formed in the manner before described and are overgrown with the well-known giant grasses and a low variety of palm (*Sabal adansoni*).[22] Often huge sandbanks are encountered in these impassable tracts, which seemed to have been formed by the pressure of the sea.

Only the main outlet of the river with the Balize is navigable by larger ships, and a landing on the other banks by a hostile force would seem to me impossible. Attacks could only be made through Lake Pontchartrain or through Chandeleur Bay and Lake Borgne, as in fact the British did towards the end of 1814.

The Mississippi heaps great masses of clay soil at its outlets, often towering many feet above the surface of the water, resembling cliffs when seen from a distance. It is very difficult to pilot a vessel through these shallows, since these beds of clay, because of the force of the stream, change their position in a short time. Ships often remain stuck on them, but rarely suffer any damage, and after a few days are afloat again. We had a brisk wind and passed the most hazardous places in the mouth of the river rather quickly and without mishap. These shallows are between some islands, formed as mentioned above, and only sparsely overgrown with reeds.

At about noon we entered the actual river region, two miles from the Balize, the forlorn station of the pilots. Here the stream was over 600 *Toisen* [1,200 yards] wide and bordered by masses of decayed tree trunks,

---

[21] Two other European scientists and travelers who noted the Mississippi's land-forming proclivities below New Orleans were Joseph Nicolas Nicollet, *The Journals of Joseph N. Nicollet: A Scientist on the Mississippi Headwaters*, tr. by André Fertey and ed. by Martha Coleman Bray, 3–7; and Victor Tixier, *Tixier's Travels on the Osage Prairies*, tr. by Albert J. Salvan and ed. by John Francis McDermott, 27–34.

[22] *Author*: Sabal minor, Sabal adanosi. Pers. *T.I.* p. 399. *Cl. Hex. Trig.* Robin p. 337, Rafinesque, *Flora of Louisiana*, p. 16.

Rafinesque and Robin distinguish, moreover, a second variety of this palm, called by the Creoles *sabal adiantium* (Rafinesque, *Flora of Louisiana*, p. 17, Robin, p. 388). These palms are closely related to *Chamaerops humilis*, Linn., and *Palmetto*, M., which grows commonly on the rocky coast of Cuba among laurels and the *Cocolloba uvifera*. [*Sabal minor*, the dwarf palmetto.]

overgrown with reeds and palms. Nature seems to have destined this desolate region solely for the habitation of giant reptiles and countless mosquitoes.

Most of the waterfowl that spend the cold season in the south had already arrived. Millions of geese and many varieties of ducks covered the basin between the islands and the tip of land bordering the outlet of the Mississippi. Large numbers of dolphin darted to and fro in their short arched leaps. The great number of fish inhabiting the exits of the river attract these animals of the sea from the salt into the fresh water, but shocked by the cold of the river water, they soon return to the sea.

The alligators,[23] those giant and dangerous inhabitants of the waters of the warmer zones of America, seemed benumbed by the cold which was then already felt in Louisiana. They only protruded their shark-like noses above the surface of the stream, soon disappearing again, only to let themselves slide back into the mud beneath.

In the warmer seasons exceedingly large numbers of these animals inhabit the reed-covered banks of the river. It seems a mystery how these obviously voracious creatures are able to find prey enough to still their hunger, but nature provided them with a peculiar digestive apparatus. They require an extraordinary long period for their digestion, thus being able to live a long time without taking any food. When in March the sun's rays become warmer, the alligator awakens from its lethargic sleep, crawls out of its slimy bed and climbs onto the tree trunks projecting from the water. But overcome by drowsiness, this lazy saurian falls into a deep sleep despite the burning of the terrific heat. At that period alligators are entirely harmless, do not feed, and are often not even awakened by a shot fired at them.

As we approached the Balize a huge number of gulls swarmed about us and the entire region began to be more and more enlivened. The air became warmer, flocks of pelicans and swans flew about us in great circles, while in long processions, one lined up behind the other, white cranes and several kinds of heron flew from northeast to southwest.

At about three o'clock we were opposite the Balize, a little place subject to all the hardships of a most unhealthy, swampy, and entirely inhospitable region, and presenting a scene of greatest privation, where man

---

[23] *Author*: *Crocodilus lucius*. The real alligator. (Caiman à museau de Brochet, *An. du Mus.* I, 8 and 15, and II, 4. Tied. T. 4.) Wagler assigns the alligators to the genus *Champsa*. [There are two crocodilians in the U.S., *Alligator mississipiensis*, or American alligator, and *Crocodylus acutus*, a true crocodile inhabiting southern Florida and the Keys, the Greater Antilles, to the rivers of Colombia and Ecuador. *Mississipiensis* was the species the author encountered.]

subjects himself to hardship for the sake of gain. A stay during the hot season becomes unbearable because of the clouds of tormenting insects and the incessant croaking of frogs on the lower banks of the Mississippi. This lot also falls to many vessels if they are held up by contrary winds and can not sail upstream.

The few wooden houses are built on piles driven into water and mud, surrounded by tall reeds, and one goes from one house to another on wooden paths. The Balize is inhabited only by a few government officers and by pilots.

The customs officers immediately came aboard at our arrival and left after a few minutes. Our ship continued its journey, taking advantage of the favorable wind, and I was glad to forget the place where most of the inhabitants had become prey to yellow fever. The effects of this terrible disease were still noticeable on those who had recovered, a few of whom had come aboard ship. In the desire to set foot on land after a long voyage, no hindrance would have scared me from visiting even inhospitable Balize, but the captain and the pilot urged me to desist because seven or eight persons were still sick with the fever there.

The upstream banks were uniformly overgrown with tall reeds and dwarf palms, and only here and there a few willow bushes created a sad variation in the monotony of vegetation. The east bank formed a small promontory created by tree trunks drifted together. Climbing sufficiently high above deck to look over the giant grasses, one can see the sea, actually a part of the wide Chandeleur Bay, only a few hundred yards away from the isthmus which forms the two shores of the main outlet of the Mississippi.

Our ship cast anchor on the right bank of the river, and an extremely dense and cold fog during that night gave promise of fine weather on the following day. These fogs recurred regularly every evening and morning until my arrival in the city and during the entire time we had fine clear weather, the thermometer registering between 68° and 77° during the noon hours. These fogs may be the cause of the many catarrhal and rheumatic ailments that prevail in Louisiana during the winter months. The change from hot to cold is then very sudden. With the coming of fog after sundown the temperature falls usually from 65° or 59° to 41° or 39°. At midnight it usually rises by about four degrees, then falls again near sunrise to 36° or 39°, but rarely below freezing point.

Between nine and ten o'clock when the temperature rises, the fog becomes so dense that one can hardly distinguish objects at a distance of a few yards, but as soon as the temperature has reached a height of 45° to 50°, the fog falls in the form of an extremely fine drizzle.

In ascending wide, rapidly flowing rivers whose beds are uneven and filled with obstructions, the general rule is to keep to the side where the current is weakest. The counter-current (called *remoux* by the French) usually assists navigation, and the navigators who go up the Mississippi cleverly take advantage of this aid. The captain of our vessel knew the river intimately, and keeping as close as possible to the bank, he also frequently availed himself of cut-offs in the stream. This method of traveling was of great benefit to me, because I was able to observe the varying plant forms at closer range, but because of the great mass of logs which projected into the stream almost everywhere and sometimes as much as fifty paces, we were not able to get very close to the bank.

Various kinds of grasses alternated with *Miegia macrosperma,* most of them bearing ripe seeds but still resplendent in their freshest green.[24] Beautifully shaped fan palms mingled with willow bushes (*Callicarpa americana*) and a species of *Myrica cerifera* [bayberry]. All these increased the charm of this wild region, which already had excited me the previous day. On tree trunks some alligators sunned themselves. However, they rarely appear during the winter months.

Countless buzzards (*Cathartes aura,* Illig.) sat on tree stumps on the banks, without concern for the ship. This bird, inhabitant of all torrid and temperate regions of America, is one of the most useful creatures which nature in her wise economy has provided, stimulating in me the thought of nature and early history of people. The American buzzard shows no fear of man and is tolerated by most uncivilized people. As the region near the mouth of the Mississippi is much like that of lower Egypt, so also are the customs of the people inhabiting these lands similar, and their opinion and practices regarding these birds are the same.[25]

Two kinds of birds which the French call *troupials* were hopping about among the buzzards. Classed by older natural scientists among the ravens

[24] *Author:* The *Ludolphia* of Wildenow is related to the *Miegia* of Persoon. The American *Arunda* resembles in the main form the giant bamboo of Asia, as the genus *Gynerium* determined by von Humboldt in his *Plantes Equinoxiales,* and the bamboo which grows in Cuba are similar to the *Arundo bamboos* of East India. [*Miegia macrosperma* = *Arundinaria gigantea,* giant cane. For *Callicarpa americana* see p. 28 n.30.]

[25] *Author:* It is well known that the ancient Egyptians worshipped *Cathartes percnopterus.* Most of the primitive peoples of America regard the buzzard with superstitious awe; and in the Spanish colonies a fine of twenty piasters was imposed for killing a buzzard (Spanish *Aura tignosa, zamuro, gallinazo,* English turkey buzzard, French-Creole *carancro,* a corruption of carrion-crow, for the French Creoles of the West have no other name for *Aura*). The Spanish example has been emulated in some areas of the United States. [*Cathartes percnopterus* for the vulture (not buzzard) the Egyptians worshipped should read *Neophron percnopterus.* What he saw was the New World *Cathartes aura,* turkey vulture, or *Coragyps atratus,* black vulture.]

and magpies, they resemble our magpies in their habits, having long, wedge-shaped tails, which they keep in incessant motion.[26] The song of a gray bunting enlivened the reeds, their habits being similar to those of the black-headed reed bunting of Europe. The song of this bird (probably an *Emberiza*) and the cawing of a variety of crow (*Corvus ossifragus*, Wils.)[27] were the only sounds that broke the stillness of this region. These birds inhabit the banks of rivers in the warmer parts of North America and live off the remains of dead aquatic creatures. The noisy crows usually sat on tree trunks which were drifting down the stream, and occasionally I noticed a white headed eagle (*Haliaeetus leucocephalus*, Savig.) among them looking for prey.

At about three in the afternoon we reached Fort Plaquemine, which controls the wide river (about 1500 paces) and is located twenty-five miles from its mouth. This unhealthful place, consisting only of barracks and poorly fortified earthen breastworks, contained a garrison of a few hundred men, who die out almost annually. Established only a few years ago to protect New Orleans from any possible hostile attack from up-river, it is by no means recognized by the Americans as an important military position. The Mississippi, whose many outlets below the city so easily assist a landing of a hostile force and enemy movements, is being protected by new fortifications.

From Plaquemine on, the still swampy soil is firm enough in some places to support a more vigorous growth of plants. The willows begin to change from the form of a shrub to that of a tree. Scattered ash trees (*Fraxinus nigra*) and cottonwood, very similar to the Lombardy poplar, but not yet a fully determined type (*Populus deltoides*, Marsh. and *Diospyros virginica*, Linn.) constitute the first real groups of trees along the river bank. As in all the primitive forest in Louisiana up to a latitude of 35°, the trees are covered with a characteristic parasite (*Tillandsia usneoides*), usually called Spanish beard.[28]

---

[26] *Author*: *Icterus caudatus* and *Quiscala*. (*Quiscalus versicolor*.)

[The family Icteridae (Passeriformes, suborder Oscines) takes the substantive name American orioles, consisting of ninety-four species. This heterogeneous New World family includes such groups as oropendolas, caciques, grackles, American blackbirds, the American orioles or troupials, cowbirds, meadowlarks, and the bobolink. Old World orioles, the substantive name of most species of Oriolidae (Passeriformes, suborder Oscines) are a much more homogeneous group of twenty-eight species. The author probably saw *Cassidix mexicanus*, boattailed grackle, and the smaller common grackle, *Quiscalus quiscula*.]

[27] The fish crow of the Atlantic and Gulf coasts and some of the major river systems, a shore feeder.

[28] *Author*: The French *barbé espagnole* is different from the *Tillandsia* in Peru. "*Tillandsia usneoides, pedunculo monofloro brevi, caule ramoso filifiliformi-flexuoso*

Upstream, forests gain the upper hand more and more over grasses, and these, which still cover wide stretches, must make room for various kinds of trees. A few miles above Plaquemine[29] shrub-like plants appear, mixed with high and low tufted grasses and with some unbelliferous plants, forming a dense underbrush beneath the trees.

Several kinds of oak do not reach the characteristic form of trees, but appear in evergreen bush form. (*Ilex vomitoria, Myrica inodora, Callicarpa americana* are mingled among groups of Lauraceae.)[30] These seem to select indiscriminately dry as well as swampy places for their habitat. The many creeping plants, especially common to the New World, begin even here in their various forms. The varieties of creepers found in Louisiana are peculiar to North America and extend over a stretch of almost ten degrees of latitude. I shall find occasion later in this report to speak of their great variety and the luxuriance of their growth.

On the right bank opposite the military post was a plantation on which sugar cane and rice were grown. Started but recently, it was particularly interesting to me because it afforded me the first view of an American industry. The owner, a friend of the captain, came aboard for a moment. He made me a present of some oranges, which like most oranges produced in Louisiana, had thick peelings and very fibrous cell structure, caused probably by excess moisture in the soil. Orange trees grow very rapidly in Louisiana, and most have large broad leaves. Although this useful tree had been transplanted from the West Indies to Louisiana, it has retained neither the luxuriant form nor the pleasant flavor of its fruit.

The wind continued favorable, and although the river made several bends, the ship still was able to cover ten miles. A few miles above Plaquemine the river banks were again covered with low timber, and on the

---

pendulo, folis subulatofiliformibus. (*Flor. Peruv.* p. 43.) *Tillandsia usneoides, filiformis, ramosa intorta, scabra* (Linn. *Willd. I* c. p. 15.) *Cuscuta.* (Pluck, *Alm.* pt. 26, f. 5.)."

[*Fraxinus nigra* is too far south to be in range, but there are four other ash species in his area. *Populus deltoides,* cottonwood; *Diospyros virginica* is *D. virginiana,* the persimmon; *Tillandsia usneoides,* Spanish moss.]

[29] *Author*: Plaquemine derives its name from the many *Diospyros* growing in that region. In the regions of the New World occupied by the French and Spanish Creoles, plants abounding locally and physical peculiarities frequently give rise to place names. Anglo-Americans as well as immigrating Germans prefer the names of villages and towns of their old homeland, often applying the high-sounding names of great cities of the latter to their wretched cabins. The French Creoles apply the name of a village to even large cities, but the Anglo-Americans call two or three wooden shacks a town. [*Plaquemine* in French means persimmon.]

[30] These species are, respectively, yaupon, odorless wax-myrtle, and French mulberry, and the Lauraceae, or laurel family, in this area contain red bay, swamp red bay, spicebush, and sassafras.

left bank was a two-mile stretch with nothing but dwarf palms and ten-foot tall reeds. The sea is so close to this reed-covered area that it can be seen distinctly from the deck of the ship.

At our approach, great flocks of geese and swans rose from the reeds and settled on the waters of the Gulf. Occasionally one sees most miserable cabins along the right bank, surrounded by a few acres of cleared, poorly cultivated land. These settlements afford only a bare existence to their inhabitants, mostly of French Creole stock, who look sickly and haggard.

The vast numbers of wild animals which formerly inhabited these swampy parts now for the most part have disappeared or have withdrawn into the interior. Seldom does one see a deer or a racoon (*Procyon lotor*, Illiger). The most common game is the American rabbit (*Lepus nanus*, Schreber),[31] which despite persistent hunting can not be exterminated. The European domestic hog has here again reverted to the wild state, as it does wherever it has been deprived of human care. Of all the animals brought by the Europeans to the New World, the hog seems to prosper best.

The ever more frequently appearing trees have changed the banks of the river into a dense primitive forest. The cypress (*Cupressus disticha*), because of the swampy ground, attains the greatest height, its tops covered with long bundles of *Tillandsia usneoides*. Although the wooded region begins about thirty miles from the mouth of the river, it by no means resembles the regions further upstream, which consist of gigantic trees, impenetrable underbrush, thorn-bearing plants, and climbers (*Rhus, Similax, Begnonia, Vitis*, and others). These solidly grown woods give the banks of the upstream Mississippi their wild and primitive appearance, which must be considered characteristic of this mighty river.

The wood-covered swamps of Louisiana, where the cypress is the main wood type, are called *cypriaires* by the Creoles. The roots are rather peculiar. They grow from the ground to a height of three to four feet, forming a cone out of which grows the tree. During flood periods the cypress forests stand in a few feet of water, but after the continuous drought of the hot season the clay soil splits in wide cracks.

On the seventeenth I was able to go on shore for the first time near a small plantation and greatly enjoy the sight of living nature. This region was inhabited by many birds (such as *Turdus orpheus*, Edw., *Xanthornus spurious* [*Oriolus spurius*], *Picus pubescens*, Veill., *Ploceus oryzivorus*,

---

[31] Here probably *Procyon lotor megalodous*, but Hall and Kelson indicate *Lepus nanus* Schreber a composite of *Lepus americanus americanus* Erxleben and *Sylvilagus floridanus*, hare and rabbit, in Schreber 1790, *Die Saugthiere* . . . IV, 880–85, pl. 234B.

Cuv., *Xanthornus phoeniceus* [*Agelajus phoeniceus*, Veill.], *Loxia cardinalis, Silvia sialis*, and others).[32] I had an opportunity to shoot a number of them. It seemed peculiar to find so few insects in this region, although the day was warm enough to revive them, but perhaps an earlier frost was the responsible cause.

It had not rained since October, and I had to be constantly on guard to avoid making a misstep into the cracks of the torn ground. At a place covered with reeds and dwarf palms I attempted to step over tree trunks into my waiting boat, and here I saw close to me an alligator warming himself in the sun. It was the first time I had seen a live one at such close range. It held its jaws open and did not seem to notice me until I threw a piece of wood at it, then it glided slowly into the water.

Some fifty miles from the Balize the real sugar plantations started, and we reached the most appealing one about noon. Poorly clothed Negroes were occupied in cutting cane, the beautiful green of the leaves having already changed to yellow. During the night I saw a great number of fires started on the plantations to burn the unnecessary brush. They constituted in miniature that splendid spectacle which I later was to see on a large scale. Nothing surpasses the beauty of a hillside covered with fire, whose flames advance rapidly over a wide territory and resemble streams of lava. During the autumn months the banks of the Missouri are covered in this manner with fire and smoke, for the Indian tribes set the forests and prairies on fire on their hunting expeditions.

The mosquitoes and small stinging flies (*brulots* in French) tormented us, however not as severely as during the hot season. To the European, to whom this torture is not known in its full intensity, even these forerunners are unbearable.[33]

---

[32] *Turdus orpheus*, Edw., indistinct in the synonymies is probably one of the mocking birds; *Xanthornus spurius* (*Oriolus spurius*) = *Icterus spurius*, orchard oriole; *Picus pubescens* = *Dendrocopos pubescens*, downy woodpecker; *Ploceus oryzivorus* = *Dolichonyx oryzivorus*, bobolink; *Xanthornus phoeniceus* (*Agelajus phoeniceus*) = *Agelaius phoeniceus*, red-winged blackbird; *Loxia cardinalis* = *Richmondena cardinalis*, the cardinal; *Silvia sialis* = *Sialia sialis*, eastern bluebird.

[33] *Author*: Among the French and Spanish Creoles, the following differences between mosquitoes, *moustiques*, and *maringuins* are made:

Mosquitoes are small flies, of which the *brulots* are almost microscopic, of the genus *Simules* (*Simulum*), described by Latreille, *Histoire n. des crust, et ins.* Tome XIV, p. 294, and belonging to the order of *Tipulaires*. *Maringuins*, called *zancudos* by the Spaniards (*Lascanas largas*), belonging to our gnats and mosquitoes (*Cousins*). Although rich in species, of different size, and inflicting more or less painful stings, they are all included under the above names in the colonies. As creatures whose larvae live in water, their increase and decrease, and also their geographic distribution, depend upon the humidity of the climate.

At a great bend to northwest, which the river makes fifteen miles below New Orleans, is the quarantine station intended to protect the city from contagious diseases. However, the imperfect arrangement of the station does not seem to accomplish this. Ships carrying sick persons on board cannot be prevented from making contact with persons on the banks of the river before they reach the great bend, and since such persons can go unhindered to the city, the yellow fever, even if it did not originate in New Orleans itself, can thus be carried there indirectly.

We arrived about five o'clock in the afternoon at the point of the bend where the quarantine buildings are fenced in by palisades. Usually this place is called Detour des Anglais (English Turn). Adjoining these enclosures were a few wretched houses, either homes of the physicians or taverns. The inspecting physicians did not stay long on our ship, but with other ships lying there, we could not sail around the bend immediately. I utilized the evening by taking a walk through the forest and brought back several plants and animals that seemed peculiar to me.

Our captain suggested to his fellow sea captains that they assist one another, and by the combined force of all the crews of the vessels tow one ship after the other around the two-mile bend. This work detained us until noon, when we were able to hoist sail and continue our journey. Ships which cannot be towed from the banks must often wait for weeks for favorable wind.

During the day it was very humid and foggy. The de Luc hygrometer stood at 60°. Because of our delay that morning we were not able to cover more than seven miles, and at nightfall had to drop anchor opposite a plantation. From Detour des Anglais on, the region became more and more inhabited and planted with sugar cane and cotton. The forests which lie a mile to the rear serve as pasture for cattle.

Next day our journey was still slower than on the day preceding, because we were beset by either calm or fog. It was noon before the fog disappeared somewhat, but it returned again before sunset. The anchor was lowered and raised five or six times. At noon the heat rose to 70° and in the evening fell to 48°. At about six o'clock we were three miles from the city, having covered but nine miles all day.

Because the journey upstream, from the mouth of the river to the city, is usually a long one, a steamer makes a trip downstream every two or three days. Passengers who have to hasten their trip may take advantage of the return trip, and in 24 to 36 hours reach their destination. I preferred to stay aboard ship in order to have an opportunity to study the country better.

On the morning of December 21 the fog dispersed and we reached New Orleans at eleven o'clock. The ship tied up at the levee.

2

To describe the city of New Orleans
in detail in this report would be an unwarranted excursion into a wide
field. When this chapter was sent to the press, the public was already informed by several exhaustive works about this most important trade center
of the southwestern part of the United States. I may reserve it for a future
time to collect some pertinent facts. But I wish to state now that a city with
commerce so great, with political and commercial position dependent upon
general American policies, with extent and population so much on the
increase, must be subject to many changes. Thus, even the most truthful
and reliable account requires only a few decades to appear quite incorrect
and unrecognizable.

The old part of the city is quite different from the new, with its modern
structures. Only on the great square where the government buildings and
the cathedral stand and on the oldest streets, such as Chartres, Bourbon,
the Levée, etc., can one see now and then massive houses of French origin
built in former times. In the absence of building stone, the city drew upon
the forests for the material for wooden houses, whose French colonial
style and arrangement is calculated to meet the needs of a hot climate. In
contrast to these are the great solid brick buildings of the Anglo-Americans,
which remind one of the great seaports on the eastern coast of North
America, but the Creoles do not easily accustom themselves to them.[1]

New Orleans, gathering place of many nations, has a cosmopolitan

[1] Early New Orleans, dating from 1718, was built largely of split cyprus, but after the
disastrous fires of 1788 and 1794 the houses destroyed were replaced by structures of brick,
in the main. Wherever the rude structures of the early period gave way to new construction
of wood in the late eighteenth and early nineteenth centuries, the results were notable, as
may be seen today. Cf. Nathaniel Cortlandt Curtis, *New Orleans: Its Old Houses, Shops,
and Public Buildings.*

population similar to that of the large transatlantic seaports. A second Calcutta, it contains a mixture of peoples and customs, different in color and language, and bound together only by the vast and universal interest of world commerce. The greatest antithesis exists between the Creoles and the Anglo-Americans in language and customs, yet they amalgamate. Widely divergent in their opinions and religious views, they are united in politics and trade. Material gain finally wins over prejudice. The slave-trader and the Quaker meet amicably, and yet their concepts are diametrically opposed to one another.

Merchants of most of the commercial nations of Europe are established here, and the ear of the stranger hears every conceivable language of the educated and uneducated world. A foreigner meets a fellow countryman at any moment. In addition to the trade with Europe is the important inland and coastal trade, the connections with Mexico, Cuba, and part of the Antilles. Many of the political refugees from these parts choose New Orleans as their new home, and thus a Spanish population is formed, sharply separated from the French and the Anglo-American.[2]

But the real non-European population is that of the Negroes, in various nuances of color, and the few Indians roaming about the city. The Negroes, Mulattoes, and such, classified as either free or slave, constitute the major population of the city and the flat country. The high price of Negroes in Louisiana directs the traffic in human beings more and more to New Orleans.

Of the aborigines one sees only sad remnants in single families of Choctaws and Creeks wandering around town half-naked and ragged, selling trophies of the hunt and woven mats and baskets. Reeking of filth, full of vermin and usually drunk, these repulsive survivors of once mighty tribes now exhibit scarcely any signs of their nationality except the color of their skin. So degraded have they become that the most careful and keenest observer strains in vain to discover anything of a national characteristic which might remind him of their powerful forefathers.

Few harbors of the New World can boast of such lively ocean trade as the chief city of Louisiana. The enormous Mississippi, with its many navigable tributaries, brings here the greater part of the products of the United States, either for consumption or for further transportation. No

[2] Part at least of the Spanish population in New Orleans derived from France's cession of Louisiana to Spain by the secret treaty of Fontainbleau in 1762 as the French and Indian War drew to a close. Although Cuba was the Spanish administrative center for North America, New Orleans drew many Spanish colonial administrators and business interests to 1800, when France regained Louisiana by the secret treaty of San Ildefonso. Many Spaniards and Spanish-speaking colonials continued to live in New Orleans after the Louisiana Purchase of 1803 by the U.S.

33

trade center known to me accommodates as many steamboats, and no river system of the world furthers transportation by steamboats as does this.[3]

Under these conditions both trade and population would increase enormously if the climate and unhealthful situation did not disturb both. All strangers shun New Orleans from June to November to escape the deadly yellow fever. I arrived just at the end of such a terrible, all-ravaging epidemic. Owing to the slowness of our sea voyage I did not arrive at its peak. Many German countrymen who had not left the place had fallen victims to its plague. With the danger now over, strangers poured in again, and it was difficult for me to secure a room. Assisted by some merchants, to whom I was introduced with letters of recommendation, I was housed rather comfortably in a hotel on the great square near the Levée.

I cannot adequately describe the kind manner in which I was received, and the names of Mr. Teetzmann and Mr. Vincent Nolte will remain unforgettable to me.[4] Not only the Europeans residing here but also the Creoles of Louisiana are noted for their hospitality and kindness to strangers who are in need of their advice. The character of the Creoles shows a native good-heartedness coupled with French politeness. For the stranger and every guest, house, kitchen, and cellar are open. Easily susceptible to friendship, they feel themselves flattered by confidence and reciprocal approach. The Creoles are also great devotées of amusement, but it must be decorous. In all of their public entertainments good form is never lacking.

[3] In 1816, four years after Fulton and Livingston's steamer *New Orleans* became the first steam-propelled vessel to dock at the Port of New Orleans, half a dozen other vessels similarly propelled called at the port. For the interior trade, mostly entering New Orleans from upstream on the Mississippi or from other river systems, there were 1,881 flatboats. In 1821, the year before Duke Paul arrived, 287 steamships visited the port, together with 1,225 flatboats. The figure for steamers had risen to 608 in 1826, the flatboats continuing their decline. From as far away as Ohio and Pennsylvania, goods destined for New Orleans came by flatboat and *radeau*, intended partly for export and valued in 1830 at $22,065,518. The mélange was mighty—molasses, whisky, tallow, hay, lumber, lard, hams, bacon, barreled pork, hides, beef, lead, potatoes, cider, sugar, rum, salt, rice, indigo, and, above all, cotton and tobacco. Harry A. Mitchell, "The Development of New Orleans as a Wholesale Trading Center," *Louisiana Historical Quarterly*, XXVII, No. 4 (October, 1944), 933–63; Harold Sinclair, *The Port of New Orleans*, *passim*.

[4] Vincent Nolte, a member of the considerable foreign community settled in and around New Orleans, was a banker, merchant, and general businessman, well known to his contemporaries and to posterity for a flamboyance in his personal and autobiographical endeavors (Nolte, *Fifty Years in Both Hemispheres; or, Reminiscences of the Life of a Former Merchant*: New York, Redfield, 1854). He entertained Lafayette during the latter's American visit of 1824–1825.

The French Theater is a beautiful, modern building. The actors and the dancers of the ballet, who are brought from France at great expense, are well compensated. Although the Anglo-Americans, striving to equal the attainments of the Creoles, have also built a beautiful theater, there is still much left to be desired since they have to contend with many religious prejudices in public entertainment.[5]

During my stay in New Orleans several elegant balls took place at which the fair sex shone especially to advantage. The colored population also desires to have its amusements, but since they may not mingle with the whites, they have their separate meeting places, masquerades, and balls. The latter are occasionally attended by white gentlemen, but white women may under no circumstances appear there, and the native Creoles also avoid these gatherings, at least publicly, so as not to get into a quarrel with the ladies of New Orleans, who are most intolerant in these matters. This division of colors acts most unfavorably on the morals of the colored people, who must gradually diminish.

The European visitor to New Orleans for the first time must be peculiarly impressed that prices of many articles of trade, especially clothing, are so high when in the northern states they are almost as cheap as in Europe. The keen competition in trade must necessarily react on prices, and when this extends to these parts, prices here will also fall and adjust themselves to those existing at other seaports.

Food items are universally cheap, and prices in hotels and private boarding houses are not excessive. Cheapest are places on steamboats, by which most journeys are made. There good service and considerable cleanliness is maintained, with prices which can be explained only if one remembers that so many people in America travel, and that the steamboat is the principal means of transportation.

Resuming my story now, I will return to the chief city of Louisiana later. From earliest youth, the ancient as well as the modern history of Mexico, the splendid climate, the giant chain of the Andes Mountains[6]

[5] The author evidently refers to Théâtre Orléans, the third of that name, erected 1819. It was the most famous of the French theaters of New Orleans, but there were two others, St. Phillipe (1807) and St. Pierre (1808). The latter, from 1819 to 1823, was the American theater. Bernhard Duke of Saxe-Weimar recalled Théâtre Orléans as an early "theater in the round," with three rows of seats, offering during his visit of 1825–1826 French theatrical productions of a high order. Grace King, *New Orleans: The Place and Its People*, 265–66; Harold F. Bogner, "Sir Walter Scott in New Orleans," *Louisiana Historical Quarterly*, XXI, No. 2 (April, 1938), 423–42; Nelle Smither, "A History of the English Theater at New Orleans, 1806–1842," *Louisiana Historical Quarterly*, XXVIII, No. 1 (January, 1945), *passim*.

[6] Sierra Madre Occidental, inland from the west coast of Mexico, is essentially a con-

which traverse this region, and the wonders of nature and natural riches had spurred me on to study and to reflection, urging me to take a trip there.

When I left Europe I desired to carry out this plan and to investigate especially the northern provinces of the former imperial empire since they were less known. However, pressing circumstances compelled a change, and careful examination and consideration of the unfortunate conditions prevailing there caused me to make the sacrifice. The war-like unrest in that country, torn apart by party strife, and the seemingly finished Iturbide government made it difficult for a foreigner to make investigations which must always seem doubtful to a suspicious government.[7]

However, the time did not seem unfavorable to visit the Island of Cuba. The former policy of the Spanish government, barring its rich and important colonies to travelers, thus to hide these lands behind a veil of darkness, had been ended. Consequently interest became livelier to visit these formerly inaccessible regions. Alexander von Humboldt and Aimé Bonpland, specially favored by the Spanish government, had the rare fortune to visit almost all of equatorial America.[8] The extraordinary harvest to science which this journey brought consequentially urged other natural

---

tinuation of the Rocky Mountains of the U.S. and Canada; Sierra Madre Oriental, inland from the east coast of Mexico, is the other dominant chain. Neither is related to the Andes of South America.

[7] *Author*: Not until 1831 did I have the good fortune to travel in Mexico. Had I postponed my journey longer, the newer civil wars which tore the republic asunder would again have frustrated my plan.

[The Mexican Revolution, some ten years in the making, had been in progress the year before Duke Paul had begun his first trip to the Americas, and was successful by September, 1821, under the leadership of Augustín de Iturbe, who subsequently became emperor, abdicating in 1823, and was executed in 1824. The third president of the republic which followed was Anastasio Bustamente (1829–1832), overthrown by Santa Ana in 1832.]

[8] Von Humboldt (Friedrich Heinrich Alexander Freiherr) began his great South American, Cuban, and Mexican scientific explorations in 1799 in company with the French botanist and anatomist, Aimé Bonpland, a man four years his junior (b. 1773). The resulting thirty volumes entitled *Voyage de Humboldt et Bonpland*, often cited as *Voyage aux régions équinoxiales de nouveau continent*, which was Part I of the longer work, were begun in 1805, the year after their return to Europe, and were completed in 1834. Part III, *Essai politique sur le royaume de la nouvelle Espagne*, appeared in 1811, and *Essai politique sur l'île de Cuba* in 1826. Part VI of *Voyage*, consisting of seven volumes, was entitled *Nova Genera et species plantarum*, written by von Humboldt, Bonpland, and C. S. Kunth, appeared between 1815 and 1825. It is probable that Duke Paul had become familiar with von Humboldt's political views on Cuba before he published *Erste Reise*, since the latter did not appear until 1835. The internal evidence in his book makes clear that he knew rather thoroughly the main corpus of von Humboldt's and Bonpland's scientific findings. *Allgemeine Deutsche Biographie*, XIII, 358–83; *Nouvelle Biographie Générale*, VI, 651–55.

scientists and geographers to follow in the paths blazed by these men, who with the utmost exertion had surmounted apparently insurmountable obstacles.

Although the wars between the mother country and the colonies gave all of Spanish America a new political form, nevertheless by the observation of certain precautionary measures this time was not entirely unfavorable to travelers, except Spaniards. The political situation in Spain in 1822 also involved the Island of Cuba, one of the few colonies which had remained loyal, but where the idea of independence from the motherland was germinating.

Under former kings, much had been done for the enlightenment and scientific development of the island, and shortly after the adoption of the constitution in Spain, travelers were again permitted to enter the interior of Cuba, and the arbitrary behavior which the governors had formerly exercised towards foreigners was done away with. (This, ultimately, was the only benefit which Cuba derived from the constitution.) Yet I cannot help but believe that the general safety suffered during this period, because of the lack of governmental co-ordination, since nobody actually knew who was to command and who was to obey.

But disregarding this, many other conditions induced me to make the trip to Havana. Almost incessant rains during the winter had made Louisiana nearly impassable for the natural scientist, placing me in the unfortunate position of having to spend my time in idleness in New Orleans, and a succession of rheumatic illnesses followed the yellow fever and threatened to attack the foreign European and make him, most probably, unfit for distant journeys.

The vessels which lay at anchor ready to depart for Havana were wretched schooners, promising neither a speedy nor a safe journey, but fortunately for me the packet steamship *Robert Fulton* arrived at New Orleans from its regular trip from New York. Its fast journey to Charlestown and Havana would be made within a few days. Primarily designed for passengers only, it offered the traveler every imaginable convenience. I arranged for my passage and without any difficulty obtained a pass from the Spanish consul.[9]

Departure of the steamship was set for the sixth at daybreak, and to avoid all confusion on the part of passengers regarding their effects, we were obliged to board the preceding afternoon. The ship lay in the middle of the river, the day was stormy and it rained violently, a most unfavorable circumstance for the loading of my effects. I had decided to return to the

[9] Fulton had designed a ship of war for thirty guns, completed in October, 1814, as the *Demopolos*, which was later converted to commercial use and renamed the *Robert Fulton*.

city and spend the night there, but the nasty weather prevented me from doing that. There were many passengers on board the *Robert Fulton*. Most were destined for New York. Among the persons who wanted to stay in Havana were, besides myself, a few Spanish officers and a French family. Generally, they constituted good company and I had an agreeable journey.

During the night the sky suddenly cleared, the wind turned from west to northwest, and before daybreak the following morning the thermometer registered 26°. In countries where the sudden coming of cold weather is a rare occurrence, such changes have a most peculiar effect on everybody, even those accustomed to them. During my stay in Louisiana, as on the entire sea voyage, I had become quite adjusted to warm, or at least moderate, temperatures of the air, and therefore the freeze, which in northern Europe is one of the most common occurrences during spring and autumn, exerted as violent discomfort to my body as the most penetrating cold during our winter days.

Although frosts are not rare at the mouth of the Mississippi, the sinking of the thermometer below freezing at the 30th degree of northern latitude must be considered one of the interesting phenomena of the New World which has not been sufficiently investigated by the physicists.

Our departure was delayed from hour to hour, and arrangements did not get under way until eleven o'clock. The anchor fastened to a chain could not be raised, probably because it had caught on a log at the bottom. The great number of tree trunks in the river bed and the remains of sunken vessels create unsafe anchoring places near the city. Since the loss of the anchor, and especially the chain, is considerable for a vessel[10] the whole day was lost in futile efforts to raise them. Captain C. Chase, a pleasant and obliging man, preferred to stand the cost rather than further tax the patience of the passengers.

To cut the chain permission had to be obtained from the captain of the harbor. This was granted only on the condition that the captain would first work with all the power of his machinery during the night to loosen the anchor. Between ten and eleven o'clock the chain broke and the vessel became free. Because of the darkness, however, we could not get under way, and the captain decided to drop a second anchor. Peculiar misfortune willed that this anchor should also get caught and on the following morning had to be cut loose.

Toward morning hoarfrost formed and the thermometer showed 32°. We moved very rapidly downriver. The cold weather and the frost had

[10] *Author*: A large iron chain and the main anchor of a ship, weighing eighty tons, commonly cost between $250 and $300 in the ports of the eastern United States.

changed the appearance of the country. Most of the trees were completely robbed of their leaves, all the orange trees were frozen, and the tall grasses had changed their luxuriant green into melancholy yellow. The hoarfrost, which had covered most objects, disappeared with the first rays of the sun, and by ten o'clock the thermometer had risen to 50°.

I saw no alligators during that whole day nor did I hear the song of a single bird. Such is the effect of frost on the organism of living creatures in the warmer region of the earth, which, in the higher latitudes, would hardly attract the slightest attention.[11]

About one o'clock we passed Fort Plaquemine and reached the Balize at four o'clock. Here we stopped for almost an hour to buy a new anchor. The Fort always kept some on hand. After five o'clock the ship was piloted into the sea. With a brisk wind from the north we could travel under the combined power of steam and sail.

During the night the wind turned to the west and continued to blow in this direction during the remainder of the voyage. The sea was calm and the sky clear. At noon on the eighth we crossed 27° 41′ of north latitude and 87° 35′ west longitude, and at noon the next day we crossed 25° 44′ north latitude and 84° 24′ west longitude. At daybreak of the tenth we sighted the western coast of Cuba.

In the tropics dawn and twilight are of such short duration that only at sunrise could we recognize the coast lying before us. This was the heights which form the Pan de Mariel, bounded by a row of hills extending westerly to Cape St. Antonio to form the extreme promontory of the island in the west. East of the Pan de Mariel, at a distance of nine leagues and surrounded by a chain of hills which do not exceed a height of three hundred feet, lies the city of Havana (Spanish: La Habana. Actually the

---

[11] *Author*: A band of Choctaw Indians moving along the river not far from the Détour des Anglais confirms the experience that, of all living things, man, because of habit, is least irritated by the influence of weather, though his skin may be entirely bare. Most of the individuals in this band were entirely unclothed, despite the raw air. Woolen blankets, often worn by Indians, serve more as ornament than as dress. In New Orleans, and in general among the whites, they may be wrapped in blankets, summer or winter. In the wilderness of their secluded forests, however, they remain true to their custom of going bare at all seasons of the year.

[The Choctaws, one of the important divisions of the Muskhogean family, historically occupied middle and southern Mississippi but extended also into Georgia and Louisiana. De Soto met them in 1540. As various French *relations* show, they became friendly with the French, who increasingly entered their country on the lower Mississippi from the first quarter of the eighteenth century onwards. One of the best descriptions of them is that of Jean-Bernard Bossu, *Nouveau Voyages aux Indes occidentales* . . . (1768). translated in 1962 by Seymour Feiler as *Jean-Bernard Bossu's Travels in the Interior of North America, 1751–1762*.]

full name is: San Cristobal de la Nuestra Señora de la Habana; that is, St. Christopher of the Holy Virgin, etc.).

One of the most magnificent views opens at the approach of this harbor, undoubtedly holding first place among all the ports of the West Indies. The row of hills, forming the background and on the west and north touching on the coast, when seen from the distance, seem to be entirely bare of vegetation. Only giant palms cover the very summits of these hills. Even at a distance one recognizes by their growth, by their leaves shading into silver, and by the bulging tree trunks, that they are the splendid *palma real* (*Oreodoxa regia*, Hum.).[12] These palms grow thirty to forty paces apart in almost symmetrical order, and the long leaves of one seem to touch the other. Belonging to the most useful plants of the hot areas of America, at the same time they constitute, as do all palms, one of the greatest ornaments of their region.

The entrance to the harbor is protected against hostile attacks from the east by Morro Castle (Castillo de los Santos Reyes), and from the west by Fort La Punta (San Salvador de la Punta). The former stands on an eighty- or ninety-foot high cliff which drops abruptly into the sea. Its walls and towers resemble a castle of ancient times. On the cliffs are located the lighthouse and the signal poles. This important fortress commands with its cannon not only the sea but also the city and the harbor. On all sides along the coast, and also along the Bay of La Regla, a number of defensive works protect the city.

Seen from a distance at sea, the low-lying city is scarcely visible, but the hills, bordering the above-named bay in an amphitheater-like manner, present a picturesque view. The forts El Principe (San Carlos del Principe) and San Domingo de Atares situated a league southwest of the city, and Cabannas (San Carlos de la Cabanna) touching on the north on Morro, resemble fortified cities.

The higher suburbs (Spanish: *arrabales*), shaded on the south and west by cocoa palms and the large trunks of the dark leaved calabash trees (*Crescentia cujete* and *curcurbitina*) and orange trees, stand in sharp contrast to the surrounding dark foliage and present a magnificent picture. Adjoining the dwellings are the banana plantations, which when seen from a distance resemble light green squares on a sea-colored background. The surrounding hills around the city look like savannas.[13] In Cuba called

---

[12] *Oreodoxa regia*, Hum. = *Roystonea regia*, Cuban royal palm.

[13] *Author:* The words *savannas, llanos,* and *pampas* mean to the Spanish American in general large steppes devoid of trees. The grass-covered plains with scattered palms and other trees are ordinarily called *llanos* in Cuba, but the lands near habitations which are covered with grasses and herbaceous plants are called, because of the uses to which they are

potreros, they are covered with herbaceous plants and appear pale by contrast to the dark blue sky.

A special painting-like impression is made by the limestone quarries of the cloister of San Lazaro on the west coast, with its blinding white sharply contrasted against the hills covered with Indian fig. The nearer one comes to the land the more striking seems the vegetation which covers the coast composed of madreporic limestone. Originally formed from the shells of sea animals and hardened over thousands of years into rock, these areas are covered with those species of plants which require little soil for sustenance and whose ramifying roots and trailing stems draw their food from porous rocks. Thus, the geographic distribution of plant growth is in close relation to the geologic structure and the outward influence of the air.

In the dry parts of Africa, where the air is filled with particles of salt, the sandy surface supports nothing but countless varieties of stapelia, mesembrianthemums, and aloes.[14] In the moister air of warmer parts of America and on soil composed of decayed limestone and volcanic ash, especially the region along the seashore, manifold varieties of cactus are produced. The climate of the Cape of Good Hope is analogous to that of Australia and supports the different varieties of heather and Proteaceae, while the latter produces among its various plants the somewhat different, yet closely related *Mealleuca* and the *Casuarina*.[15] The great steppes of the colder parts of either North or South America, in the same latitude as the steppes of western Europe and northern Asia, likewise produce grasses that are analogous to form but marked by distinct differences.

Among the cactus-covered hills stretching along the eastern coast I noticed even from afar the *Coccoloba uvifera*,[16] one of the plants seemingly characteristic of the shores of tropical America.

Towards noon we were one English mile from Fort Morro and were signaled to stop. The Spanish pilot came aboard, and about half past twelve we sailed through the very narrow channel between La Punta and Fort Morro. For the first time we could now get a view of the city, the in-

---

put, *potreros*. Although the words *savannas*, *llanos*, and *pampas* have the same meaning, their application is not universal and they should be regarded as provincialisms employed in various Spanish areas of America. The word *savanna* is common in North America. The Spaniards of the Antilles and of the Tierra Firma use the expression *llanos* (from *llano*, meaning flat). The *pampas*, which name is customary in southern South America, are grass-covered plains, identical with those of the northwestern part of the New World.

[14] African plants with these generic names.

[15] Proteaceae, a southern hemisphere family, here African; *Melaleuca*, a genus of Australian and East Indian trees, the myrtles; *Casuarina*, a genus of Australian trees, the oaks, she-oaks, and beefwoods.

[16] *Cocoloba uvifera*, sea-grape.

describably beautiful bay, and of the little town of La Regla (Nuestra Señora de la Regla).

The sight of the city, one of the most important cities of tropical America and at one time the distribution center for the Spanish possessions of the New World, made an extraordinary impression on my senses, more like pictures in a dream than of actuality. The sight of Havana awakened rightly the remembrance of transitory political power. This proud city, justly calling itself a metropolis of the New World and accustomed to receiving in its harbor the products gathered from millions of square miles, saw its trade diverted into entirely different channels in scarcely twenty years. Formerly the principal maritime station of New Spain, Havana has now lost its dominating influence. A wise policy and favorable circumstances have again directed trade to it and not destroyed its wealth, but this would have happened even if the Spanish government had maintained its former policy.

Our ship dropped anchor in the middle of the harbor opposite the great warehouse called *Repeso* or *Almazen*. It is assumed that the harbor of Havana, where the ships anchor, is at 23° 9′ north latitude and 82° 23′ 37″ west longitude. (See von Humboldt, Part 6, Book 10, Chapter XXVIII, p. 74.)

Immediately after our arrival an officer with his guard came on board to collect the passports from the passengers. He treated me with special courtesy. Accidentally learning my real name, he relieved me of all customary formalities and left me free to go ashore at once, a favor which he granted only to the captain of the ship, to an American officer named Woole (an extremely amiable and educated man),[17] and to the Spanish officers.

I preferred to spend the night on board ship and to send my letters of recommendation ahead of me into the city to announce my arrival. It was a special desire of mine, on the first evening of my arrival, to enjoy undisturbed the pleasing impression which the splendid region had made on me.

Colonel Woole, who in the service of the United States had been charged with the inspection of the forts on the upper Missouri and Mississippi, and with whom I became well acquainted during my stay in New Orleans and on our trip, also preferred to spend the night on board ship. The acquaintance of this excellent gentleman later greatly benefited me,

[17] John Ellis Wool, subsequently a general officer (beginning 1826), was appointed inspector general of the army in 1816. His earlier career in the War of 1812, his tactics at Buena Vista in the Mexican War, and his Civil War service to 1862, when he was retired a brevet major general, gave him a long and distinguished record.

because in the course of my journey I touched on these regions. In the evening I received the visit of several persons from the city but declined to go ashore with them.

At daybreak on the eleventh Mr. Donnenberg, one of the most prominent German merchants then residing there, came to meet me with my effects and was so kind to provide quarters for me in his home. The whole day was spent in either making visits or receiving callers. Captain-General Don Sebastian Kindelan y Oregan, to whom I was introduced by the first English merchant, Mr. Drake, received me in a most courteous manner with his entire general staff, and returned my call at once. I also visited the General of Marines, Don Miguel Gaston, and the *intendado*, or President of Civil Affairs.

I occupied myself during the first days of my stay sightseeing in the city, of which I will say only a few words here because so important a place as Havana has been sufficiently described and is well known, and repetition would only tire the indulgence of my readers.

Surrounded by deep moats lined with masonry, the city is for the most part solidly built. Walls behind these moats are either non-existent or in a sad state of ruin, since Havana owes its fortified position solely to the forts and castles which guard it on all sides, except at the westerly landside, where it is less protected and open to attack. The streets are narrow, dirty, and unpaved. After every heavy rain and during the rainy season itself, the many holes in the streets are filled with water and mud, so that pedestrians cannot cross them without stepping ankle-deep into the muck. Most of the houses have only one, or at most, two stories, and the public squares are either irregular or very small.

The architecture of the churches is reminiscent of the sixteenth century. Built of squared limestone taken from the quarries near the city or brought from Vera Cruz, they are poorly suited to resist the destructive influence of the weather. Although the churches are large and spacious, they present a monotonous exterior and an interior arrangement devoid of good taste. The cathedral, one of the oldest in Havana and at the same time the church of the Bishop San Yago de Cuba, would remind one of the better places of worship in Europe if the interior had not been made unsightly by very poor oil paintings.

To the foreign traveler interested in the New World and its history, this church is nevertheless a monument of great value. Disregarding the fact that it is one of the oldest churches in this land, it is interesting because it contains the ashes of the mighty discoverer and the chains with which this great hero of the sea, as reward for his extraordinary deeds, was bound by the rudest ingratitude. The appropriate inscription on the mausoleum is brief and simple:

O Restos e ymagen del grande Colon
Mil siglos durad unidos en la Urna,
Al codigo santo de nuestra Nacion.
Z, fecit Habanae MDCCCXXII[18]

The private dwellings, most of which date back to the sixteenth and seventeenth centuries, are covered with bricks almost burned black; the rooms are spacious; the floors and ceilings are laid out with squared stones; the windows are high and wide without glass panes but supplied with old-fashioned wooden grates. In the interior little cleanliness prevails. The houses of the rich, especially those of foreigners, present in their entire arrangements the most refined European luxuries.

Among the larger squares, which might deserve that name, are the square before the government house and that before the theater. The government house is a newer building of squared stones in the Spanish style. In the lower story assembles the *cabildo*, or magistry, which supervises the administration of justice and enjoys many privileges. The prison for civil offenders is also part of this structure.

During my stay in Havana there were a great many prisoners in this prison. The worst criminals who await the death sentence were imprisoned in the same enclosure with persons who were held because of some small infraction of police regulations. (The same was true in 1831 in Mexico in the prison of Acordada, a remnant of old Spanish justice procedure.) By the adoption of the constitution and the presumable improvement of the judicial procedure the old laws had been completely neglected and all the accused had been held without trial, naturally impatiently awaiting to learn their fate. Before my arrival during the reign of Captain-General Cien Fuego a revolt broke out among the prisoners within these walls and was subdued only by the especially severe and decisive measures of the governor, without which the criminals would have escaped this poorly guarded prison.

The upper stories of the government house were arranged for the use of the commanding general and were fairly well furnished. The large square in front of the building adjoins the harbor. Here the water is

---

[18] "The remains and image of the great Columbus/ Will remain together in the urn/ The holy Creed of our nation / Done by Z in Havana, MDCCCXXII." Columbus died at Valladolid, Spain, May 20, 1506, fourteen years after his first voyage to the New World. In 1509 his remains were removed from Valladolid to Seville, and in 1541 they were again removed, this time to the Cathedral of Santo Domingo. Their present location is a matter of contested opinion. During his first voyage, having discovered Cuba, Columbus at first thought the island Cipango, i.e., Japan, rather than an island offshore from one of the American continents, of which he as yet had no knowledge.

sufficiently deep for ships to tie up for loading and unloading. On the north of the square are the barracks (Quartel de la Fuerza) surrounded by a wall, and adjoining the sea is a caiba tree (*Bombax caiba*)[19] into whose trunk an iron cross has been driven close to the roots. Legend says that at the time of the discovery of this place the first mass was read under this tree, and as a memorial this cross was inserted. The crown of this tree has died several times, but the caiba has renewed itself from its roots. It belongs to the oldest surviving monuments since it is claimed that this memorial dates back to 1494 from the time of Ovando, who circumnavigated Cuba and corrected the belief held by Columbus that Cuba was part of the American continent. It seems more rational to me that the cross was placed there in 1511 under the direction of Velasquez or by de Bara, the founder of Havana.[20]

The square at the theater is still less important than the one fronting the government building and is deserving of no mention. The theater is a large but poorly conceived building. The auditorium is very spacious, the arches are artistically built of cashew wood (*Cahoba anacardium occidentale*).[21] All decorations, however, were very bad and the actors belonged to the lowest class of artists.

Because the city is built on the right shore of the Gulf, it is longer than wide, and a line drawn along its boundary on the land side runs almost parallel with the harbor. The circumference would be considerable if the many suburbs, the *arrabales* or *carrios* of the Puerta de la Muralla (also called del Horcon, I believe), Jesus Maria, Señor de la Salud, and Guadaloupe, which extend in all directions, were included in the city. These suburbs, which I will mention later, have developed in recent times because the former government on the instigation of its engineers would not permit houses to be built within range of cannon in the city. A large number of persons from other parts of the island, drawn by various interests, have been attracted to Havana and have built there. The streets of the city were rather regular, but very narrow and the houses are erected without a definite building line, so that the whole has an irregular and angular appearance. At the same time, police ordinances are so poor and neglected that the greatest filthiness prevails in the city.

---

[19] *Bombax ceiba.*

[20] Diego Velasquez, who accompanied Columbus to Hispaniola in 1493 and in 1511 conquered the Arawak Indians, original inhabitants of Cuba, founded Havana in 1514–1515, which by 1519 had been removed to its present site. Nicolás de Ovando (1451–1511) was the first royal governor of the Indies, appointed 1501, arriving 1502.

[21] *Cahoba anacardium occidentale, nomen ambiguum: Anacardium occidentale* is the cashew.

In an atmosphere which is hot, and especially, during the rainy season, saturated with moisture, the strictest regulations are necessary for the conservation of health. The enormous filthiness of the streets and the bad drinking water undoubtedly contribute much to the indescribable epidemics of fever which visit Havana throughout the whole year but particularly during the hot months.

The drinking water, on which principally the poorer classes are dependent, is obtained from a creek, the Rio Armendoris (usually called Chorrera), which flows from a westerly region of the city. The water first flows through open country, entirely devoid of trees and shade, exposed to the intense heat of the sun. The bed from which the water system (*zanja*) takes the water is swampy, and the banks, on which only low bushes and a few swamp grasses grow, are a bottomless morass.

The bad condition of the water, already unwholesome because of its location, is increased by the unpardonable neglect on the part of the inhabitants of the suburbs, who deposit dead animals and the refuse of their homes on this swampy land. Such negligence should not be permitted in the hot zones of America, where fortunately countless buzzards (*Cathartes*) consume the fallen animals in a short time. I am convinced that the great mortality rate, especially among foreigners, is to be attributed to the consumption of this foul drinking water. Rich families have their drinking water brought by regularly scheduled ships from the region of Mantanzas and, although this water becomes very expensive, it undoubtedly contributes to the preservation of health.

Poor supervision by the police also manifests itself in the great confusion in the sale of different raw food stuffs. Thus, for example, the fish market is located at the wall near the great cathedral at the entrance to the harbor, a section exposed to the most intense rays of the sun. Since the fish peddlers and their goods are under no special control, their booths disseminate an unbearable stench from the vast number of putrid fish which are also offered for sale. In the meat booths, where fresh and dried meats (*tassajo*) are offered for sale, similar disorder and pestilential odors reign. The uneconomic handling of these items causes the high prices.

Personal insecurity in the city, but especially in the suburbs and the surrounding country, has recently reached its climax. During my stay in Havana not a night passed without several murders and thefts being committed. The government in an attempt to check crime in the city and its environs had charged a regimental captain of infantry named Arona and a number of soldiers with policing. Despite the resoluteness and severity of this man, and many murderers and robbers lost their lives while committing crimes, it was impossible to put a stop to this terror.

According to Spanish law, a person found near a corpse can be arrested as the possible murderer, therefore the misanthropic custom prevails in the city to hurry away from persons calling for help, and to bar one's doors and windows. The suburbs and the cities of La Regla and Guanabacoa are especially in ill repute. The road from one to the other, almost half a league long, leads through a desolate and hilly area which generally serves thieves as a hiding place. La Regla, as mentioned earlier, lies opposite Havana on the southeastern shore of the bay and is said to be the place for outfitting pirates who endanger the waters from Havana to Cape San Antonio.

The suburbs which have been built around the city and cover considerable space consist mainly of wooden shacks, among which only a few deserve the designation of houses. Only in recent years a few larger and more spacious buildings have begun to be erected outside the city. The suburbs will undoubtedly grow more beautiful, especially since it is reputed that yellow fever appears there less frequently and makes less progress than in the city itself.

The most important suburbs are Guadaloupe and Señor de la Salud, until now not built according to a definite plan, but with houses arranged along the most frequented streets and roads leading from the city to the country. The longest suburb extends parallel to the bay in the direction of Batabano and in this manner connects the city with a village a league away. The location of this suburb, Jesus Maria, is very beautiful. Houses are shaded by palms and other tropical trees and are surrounded by small gardens. Along the sea as far as the cloister San Lazaro extends a series of houses with a few attractive buildings and gardens.

The largest suburbs, however, are at the two extremes of the *paseo*. The *paseo*, running parallel to the west side of the city, may be regarded as the principal promenade outside of the city and consists of a broad avenue with wide pedestrian walks on both sides. The main avenue and the pedestrian walks are shaded by trees, some of considerable size and mostly taken from the interior of the island.

If this promenade were kept up it would compare favorably with the most beautiful promenades of Europe because of its wide variety of resplendent blossoming trees and also tropical evergreens. (Among others, *Bignonia stans*, very tall, *Sesbania* [*Agati*] *occidentalis*, *Hibiscus elatus*, *tiliaceus*, *Erythrina corallodendron*, *Poinciana* [*Caesalpinia*] *pulcherrima*, *Acacia Lebbeck*, *Melia sempervirens*, and others.)[22]

[22] *Bignonia stans* = *Tecoma stans*, trumpet flower; *Sesbania occidentalis* = *S. emerus*, Tamarindo de laguna; *Hibiscus elatus*, blue mahoe, Cuba bast; *H. tiliaceus*, mahoe, majagua; *Erythrina corallodendron*, one of the coral trees; *Poinciana* (*Caesalpinia pulcherrima*), "Barbados pride" or dwarf poincian; *Acacia Lebbek* = *Albizzia lebbek*, an Old

In the typical careless manner of the Spaniards, trees that die are not replaced with new ones, and thus this promenade goes to ruin. One enters the *paseo*, which is about six hundred paces long, by two gates. It begins not far from the sea near Fort La Punta. The southern end is bounded by a round place adorned with the marble statues of a few Spanish kings, for example, Charles III.

On Sundays and holidays almost the entire *beau monde* of Havana appears on this promenade, and since it is not customary for ladies of means to walk, one sees one *volanta* after another, each drawn by one horse (for only the governor and the bishop are allowed to ride in carriages drawn by two horses). On each slow walking horse sits a peculiarily dressed Negro slave, called a *calesero*.

In addition to the *paseo*, which, as stated before, is the best promenade for the people of Havana, there is also the Garden of the Bishop, the Quinta del Obispo. Established some time ago at considerable expense by the present Bishop de Espada, it is the most beautiful and interesting spot in the environs of the city. Reached by passing through a part of the suburb Señor de la Salud, which extends to the west along the Campo Marte, and frequented more by strangers who happen to be in Havana than by the inhabitants of the city, the garden is laid out on a portion of the bishop's country estate which was formerly used for pasture.

Since the whole country estate extends along a ridge of hills about half a mile long, one enjoys at various points in the garden a splendid view of the city, the harbor, and the surrounding country. Because all parts of the West Indies are adorned with the most luxurious vegetation, it does not require painstaking artistic skill to plan a large tract of land with glorious blooming nondeciduous plants. To complete the beauty of such a tract is only to lay out paths and avenues. This expedient was used by the Bishop in the establishment of the garden. However, the good taste of the Bishop prompted him to decorate the avenues and a square, which surrounds a small villa, with a number of wonderful tropical plants from all parts of the world. On several walks through this garden I gathered many plants distinguished not only by their beauty but also by their rarity.[23]

Formerly adjoining the *paeso* were many shacks for Negro slaves,

---

World species; *Melia sempervirens*, one of the Meliaceae, primarily of southern Asia and Australia.

[23] *Author*: Among the arboreal specimens were, in addition to a large quantity of fruit-bearing trees of the West Indies, notably the splendid trees of *Mangifera indica*, *Spondias mombin* and *myrobalanus*, the nucleiferous *Artocarpus incisa* of the South Sea islands, *Laurus persea*, *Marannon* or *Annona muricata*, *Annona squamosa*, and many others.

which the government permitted on the outskirts of the city. Now these have disappeared and in their place a botanical garden has been laid out, which, while occupying a large stretch of land, contains very few plants and deserves no further comment. In the hands of a skilled gardener, the extensive area of the botanical garden would make possible the cultivation of a vast number of plants from tropical regions and could be made an excellent halfway station for plants from the interior of tropical America and Europe. But the hostilities between the mother country and the colonies interfered with the consummation of such an enterprise.

The somewhat delicate plants of the North American continent, unable to endure a long journey by sea, could very easily be conveyed to Havana, where, with proper attention in the botanical garden, they could be propagated in perfect condition. From Havana, seeds and living plants can easily be shipped to European ports during the summer, as I have convinced myself by my own experiments. Almost all of the seeds which I took from Cuba to Europe retained their power of germination.

I found the botanical garden very much neglected, and the few plants contained in it were arranged without systematic order. There were found in it but few plants that do not already grow in the gardens of Havana or near the city. The Bishop's garden was in this respect much more interesting to the botanist, since it contained almost all of the flowering plants of the island, and in addition a great number of strange trees of which one could find but very few in the botanical garden. I found in the former the *Heliconia bihai* which had been brought from the interior of the island, but which I found nowhere else on my travels through Cuba. (So much more frequently did I find them later in Santo Domingo and on the eastern slopes of the Cordilleras.)

Beyond that, I saw a few beautifully flowering legumes, the seed of which I brought to Europe. So, for example, none of the palm varieties from the interior of the island, of which Alexander von Humboldt classified a few but of which several still seem to remain undetermined, have been transplanted into the Botanical Garden. Since I visited the island at a time when the palms bore neither fruit nor blossoms, it was impossible for me to classify them, and I deplore so much the more the carelessness of the garden superintendent. It would have been an easy matter for him to procure a few specimens from the interior of the country, or to raise young plants from seed and send them to Europe. The seeds of most palms do not endure the sea voyage. They spoil despite all the care with which they may be packed. Although almost all seeds brought with me to Europe germinated quickly and well, the carefully handled nuts of *Palma sombrero* (*Corypha tectorum*) and the *barrigon* palm (*Cocos crispa*, Humb.) and of *coroyo* (*Martinezia caryotaefolia?*) failed. On the other hand the seed of *palma real* (*Oreodoxa regia*) germinated easily.

In the Bishop's garden a few areas are planted with the giant bamboo peculiar to tropical America. It attains a height of thirty to forty feet, its stalks growing very close together. Although I had seen it in the interior of the island and also in the vicinity of Havana, especially on the *paseo*, I never saw it in such perfection as in the Bishop's garden. This variety of bamboo differs from the *Bambusa* of the East Indies.

The breadfruit tree (*Artocarpus incisa*),[24] peculiar to the islands of the Pacific Ocean, with which a few avenues in the garden are lined, had grown to considerable size in a short time. This useful tree of the nettle family produces the chief vegetable fruit of the South Sea Islands. The fortunate results with which the first attempts at cultivation have been crowned in Cuba encourage a further propagation of the same. Although the trees bore little fruit as yet, and during the month of January had not matured, they seemed to promise an abundant harvest. I did not find the *Artocarpus incisa* planted in the interior of the island, and found only a single tree on the coffee plantation of Mr. Andreas de Zayas. It bore ripe fruit. Even though every precaution was used, the completely developed seed spoiled during the voyage to Europe. The seeds of the breadfruit tree as well as those of the cacao (*Theobroma cacao*) usually lose their power of germination on a sea voyage. The cultivated breadfruit trees on the islands of the Pacific Ocean are, as a rule, sterile or their seeds do not completely mature. On the other hand the breadfruit tree introduced into the West Indies produces fully developed seeds. Although the pulpous pericarp of the *Artocarpus incisa* produces seeds in America, it contains, nevertheless, the nutritious, slimy and mealy parts in the same degree as those on the South Sea Islands. The climate of America seems to favor the growth of such plants whose roots or fruit yield a serviceable foodstuff.

In the temperate zone the cereals develop to the nearest state of perfection, and maize, which is peculiar to America, matures almost at any degree of latitude and has served New World peoples as food since time immemorial. The roots of the *Caladium esculentum*, of *Jatropha manihot*,

---

[24] *Author*: The streets of the entire island, as also the avenues of the gardens and plantations, are unfortunately not planted with useful trees, although the tropical heat ought to suggest such foresight for the convenience of the wanderer. Most of the fruit trees of the hot zone, such as *Mangifera indica* L., (*Mango*) *Psidium pyriferum* L. (*Guyaba*) *Achras sapota*, *Mammota* (*Mammai*), *Annona muricata* (*Guyabana, Marannon*), *Anacardium occidentale*, *Laurus persea*, *Eugenia yambos*, and many others combine with dense non-deciduous leaves an usually rapid growth. [In Cuba, *Eugenia* is a large genus of woody plants, Myrtaceae.]

of *Solanum tuberosum, Helianthus tuberosus, Oenothera, Psoralea,* etc.,[25] which are distributed most widely over the New World, contain a mealy nutritive substance in their roots. Almost peculiar to this area of the world they produce a somewhat narcotic substance, which, when eaten raw would classify them in part among the poisons.

The fruits of the American *Annona* varieties resemble in form and in nutritious content the *Annona muricata,* to which *Artocarpus incisa* is closely related. The pulpous fruits of almost all American plants are more papescent than juicy and, therefore, less palatable than nutritious.

If one considers the enormous amount of vegetable nutritive substance which the cultivated trees and nutrition-producing plants of America supply, and compares it with that of the nutritive plants of Europe and other continents, one is amazed to see how greatly nature has favored that continent.

When we compare the abundant harvest of maize, which matures to near perfection in almost all the climates of America, with the cereals of the Old World, it cannot be denied that maize furnishes a greater amount of nutritious substance on a smaller space and with less care than even rice, which in the warmer parts of the world is the most productive cereal.

The extraordinary benefit which the cultivation of the potato has brought to northern Europe during the last century seems to compensate the old continent in part for the harm which the discovery of the New World brought it.[26] The great amount of nutrient fruit which the banana tree yields affords the poorer classes, especially the slaves who inhabit the hot belt of America, a nourishing food. If we compare the space which the banana (*Plantanal*) plantation occupies with that required for our cereals there is no doubt that the banana on the same amount of space produces a greater yield of nutriment than the cereals.

In his statistical account of New Spain, Mr. von Humboldt, with his singular acumen, has sufficiently proved and explained everything that has

---

[25] *Caladium esculentum* = *Colocasia esculenta,* taro or dasheen; *Jatropha manihot* = *Manihot esculenta,* cassava, manioc, or tapioca plant; *Solanum tuberosum,* potato; *Helianthus tuberosus,* Jerusalem artichoke; *Oenothera,* evening primrose genus; *Psoralea* is of the Leguminosae, and one species is *P. esculenta,* Indian bread-fruit or Pomme de Prairie. Immediately following, *Annona muricata* is sour-sop.

[26] *Author:* I can by no means agree with the opinion of economists and students of public affairs that, with the introduction of the potato, land which was formerly used for the better cereals is now less advantageously cultivated. The great advantage which the cultivation of the potato brought to the sandy regions of northern Germany, especially where there is a dense population, is incalculable.

[A tropical crop, referred to *infra* as *Convolvulus batatas* (perhaps a *lapsus calami*), is the banana, genus *Musa. C. Batatas* is *Ipomoea batatas,* the sweet potato.]

been said heretofore. Although the banana is native to the hot zone of Asia and Africa, transplanted to America it prospers in no part of the world better than here. The same has been proved in regard to the coco palm and the sugar cane. Rice grows in Louisiana just as well as in Egypt and China at the same latitude.

In the northern parts of the New World our cereals, especially wheat, yield more abundant harvests in the United States than in Europe. On the other hand, the useful plants of the temperate part of the New World lose but little of their quality when transplanted to Europe. For this reason maize, and in the warmer regions, the banana (*Convolvulus batatas*) prosper very well.

A prolonged stay on the island of Cuba furnished the superior scholar Alexander von Humboldt the most reliable means to study the geographic and statistical data concerning Havana. He has compiled in his extremely valuable work, *Reise in die Aequinoctialgegenden der neuen Welt* (Part 6, Book X, Stuttgart und Tübingen, 1829) the most comprehensive and most important facts which have hitherto been published regarding this great city and its immediate surroundings. Collecting all tabulated records which had been compiled by the authorities up to the most recent times, Mr. von Humboldt with extraordinary diligence gave to the public in this manner a geographic review of Havana and of the island of Cuba which is remarkably complete. The description of Havana encompasses a period which extends to many later years than my observations regarding the population and commerce.[27]

The inhabitants of Havana, as of all of Cuba, consist of Creoles, or natives of white skin, Spaniards, foreigners of all nations here called *transuentes*, the free colored (*pardos*) by which are understood half-bloods of black and white ancestry, free blacks (*morenos* or Negroes), and slaves, who are either colored or black. Another race, the *zambos*, a mixture of

---

[27] The author's reference here originally appeared in his notes but like many other purely parenthetical notes has been transferred to the text by the editor. Von Humboldt's title, however, needs emendation to *Reise in die Aequinoctial-Gegenden des neuen Continents. In deutscher Bearbeitung von Hermann Hauff. Nach der Anordnung und unter Mitwirkung des Verfassers. Einzige von A. von Humboldt Anerkannte Ausgabe in deutscher Sprache.* What Duke Paul saw was an unauthorized German edition of six volumes, published 1815–1829, from the original Paris edition in French published in three volumes in 1814. In his *Vorwort* to the Hauff edition of 1859–1860, published by Cotta'sche Verlag, Stuttgart, von Humboldt, writing on March 26, 1859, spoke at last of the great pleasure that a German edition under his own supervision could give him. His publisher, in a separate statement in the same edition, referred to the scientist's unhappiness over the first German edition: "... *er mochte, wie er selbst schreibt, dies Buch niemals auch nur in die Hand nehmen* ..." Von Humboldt died six weeks later, on May 6, 1859.

Indian and Negro, is not seen any more, although there were some of them formerly in Guanabacoa.

Occasionally, but very seldom, Indians come over from Florida, and I saw a few families of them begging in the street. The majority of the population is colored. In 1810, the entire population of the city, without suburbs, was 43,175, of which number 18,361 were white, 10,294 free colored and blacks, and 14,520 slaves. Including the suburbs, in which La Regla may also be considered, there was a total of 96,304 souls, of which 41,227 were whites, 26,349 free *pardos* and blacks, and 28,728 slaves.

In 1825 Mr. von Humboldt maintained that the population, including about 6,000 soldiers, many foreigners, monks and friars, amounted to about 130,000 souls. This is probably correct since the population, because of the disturbances of 1823 and imperfect census, was estimated between 124,000 and 126,000 souls. Even though the population may have increased considerably between the years 1826 and 1832, there remains no doubt that it must have suffered great reductions due to the devastating cholera, mainly among the colored population.

Despite the frequently recurring epidemics of yellow fever, the white population, notably the foreign element, which is particularly affected by ailments due to the climate, has constantly increased, and the slaves lost by cholera have in large measure been replaced by purchases of slaves in the interior of the island. I dare to assume that a third of the loss occasioned by cholera has been replaced within a year.

Residence in Havana must be considered very unhealthful for the foreigner, and the frequent epidemics of yellow fever claim many victims. In recent times, through the aid of skilled foreign physicians, the evil has been greatly curbed. This is especially true in the military hospitals. Foreign sailors are also well taken care of and the mortality is certainly less here than in other American ports, such as New Orleans and Vera Cruz. It is now a question whether cholera will recur or not. At any event, it would be a great scourge in a country where there are so few means of preventing miasmatic ailments.

The Spanish soldiers brought from the home country and assembled here for military expeditions to the American continent were always subject to a kind of decimation. The extraordinary devotion and discipline of these Spanish troops dedicated to an almost certain death, their fine military bearing, their warlike spirit, and their bravery have instilled in me a high respect for the regular Spanish soldier. This spirit did not even deny itself during the critical period of my residence there, when their minds were unusually excited by the unrest prevailing in the mother country. A deep devotion to King Ferdinand manifested itself among the officers and also among the soldiers. Only a very few of the officers of the garrison constituted an exception. On the whole, the Spanish nation is a noble, vigorous people imbued with a love for fatherland and a sense of justice which can only be led astray by unfortunate circumstances. History teaches what power this people can develop.[28]

During the entire month of January the weather in Havana was extremely mild, although with the continual southeast wind the heat during the noon hours began to be oppressive. The thermometer stood between 63° and 68° during the night, rose to 77° shortly after sunrise, and during the warmest noon hours even reached 90°. (In January the highest thermometer reading was 88°, the lowest 68°. In the month of February, the highest reading was 90°, the lowest 59°.)

Despite the dry season, the narrow and low lying streets of the city were full of dirt, while in the higher regions the dust and the fine particles of limestone in the air were most annoying. Since Havana is much exposed to the northwest winds, rapid changes in temperature are not unusual, especially in the months of December and February. Then the thermometer falls appreciably, and it is said that in the highest areas around the city the mercury even reaches the freezing point.

With the advent of the first cold wind the yellow fever disappears, although isolated cases appear occasionally after such a time, to return again in the months of May and June. The dampness seemed peculiar to me, especially in the lower stories of the houses of Havana. This and a countless number of small ants made me anxious about my collections, particularily about my herbaria.

I had expected a much greater yield of specimens on my repeated daily walks in the vicinity of the city, but the region is not as rich in vegetable products as one might expect. The limestone of the coast bordering the sea is of Jurassic structure, and besides Crassulaceae[29] and thorn-bearing acacias, it produces but few herbs and grasses. On the madreporic formation washed by the sea there blossomed luxuriantly *Convolvulus maritimus* and also *Argemone mexicana*, a plant which I later found again on the volcanic highlands of the Andes.[30]

[28] As will be seen in subsequent passages, Duke Paul was capable of a degree of liberalism not unlike that of von Humboldt and a number of other German scientific and literary figures of the time. But his conservative prediction concerning Spain's position in Cuba would be tested frequently and adversely in the years to the end of the century, when the Spanish-American war closed the Spanish regime in the Island, three quarters of a century after the bulk of the Spanish empire in the New World had given way to republics.

[29] Crassulaceae, a family of succulent herbs of the order Rosales.

[30] Respectively, a morning glory and a prickly poppy.

The forts Cabanas and Morro are entirely surrounded by a closely inter-twined *tuna* (*Opuntia pseudo-tuna?*).[31] This *tunales* is rarely found mingling with other cactus varieties. Utilized in fortifications in southern America, it renders the surroundings of the fortress unapproachable. While, strangely enough, the long-barbed cacti surround the above named forts, the same service is afforded the fortifications to the west of the city by a great mass of *Cereus grandiflorous*.[32] Possibly the strong odor of its flowers and the subsequent decay of the same during the summer months may contribute much to the mortality of the city.

Another peculiar thing was to see not only *Crassulaceae* and acacias but also other shrubs and herbaceous plants live close beside one another. East of Fort Morro on the slope of Jurassic limestone I found large groups of a yellow flowering *Eupatorium* and, even at a height of several hundred feet, rather high bushes of the *Cocoloba*.[33] On excursions made west of the city and south of the bishop's country estate I found the vegetation much more luxuriant. Large grass-covered plots alternated with underbrush; on moist places the giant bamboo grew rank; and large stretches were covered with especially magnificent royal palms, their mighty trunks reaching heights such as I have seen no other palm in America attain.

Adjoining the suburbs are the villas of those people of Havana who begin to appreciate more and more the value of garden culture and the benefits of shade. Yet one will not find in Havana for a long time the luxuriance of the gardens surrounding the houses of Brazil and Santo Domingo. Much more inviting however is La Regla, which, because of its proximity to Havana, is counted among its suburbs. Exceedingly charming is the sight of the Gulf, which one can cross in a *lancha* at any hour. Negroes are always ready to effect the crossing for a few *pezzetas* (each about 20¢ U.S. money). Larger boats also make the trip regularly. At every hour of the day a cool sea breeze blows and a canopy protects one from the intense rays of the sun.

The city appears grandly picturesque with its many towers, forts, and castles, and the setting daystar glows splendidly through the palm-covered landscape, while the clear blue of the sea completes the brilliant tropic picture. And there are the black exotic forms of the Negroes, the brown faces of the Creoles, in contrast with the pale features of the foreign Europeans, the strange costumes of the country folk, and a harbor dotted with all types of ships and vessels. This region is still more enchanting at night, illumined by the exceedingly bright moonlight, when forms appear

---

[31] One of the cactus family.

[32] Another of the cacti.

[33] *Eupatorium*, a genus of the sun-flower family; *Cocoloba*, sea grape.

more fantastic and tropical nature more striking. Often during the cool of the evening I rocked in a boat on the waters of the Gulf admiring the magnitude of the natural scenes.

Connected with the larger water basin that forms the harbor of Havana along a bay is La Regla, a pretty, rather well built little town. It has a convenient anchoring place for smaller vessels. The inhabitants of La Regla therefore carry on a considerable trade, especially with coastal liners, which are however frequently misused for another, already mentioned very bad purpose. The population of La Regla, which in 1810 numbered 2,218 souls and since then may have increased by a third, consists of more whites than colored inhabitants.

The immediate surroundings consist of bare hills covered with grass and scattered palms. Among these I saw a group of *Cocos crispa*, a new kind determined by Mr. von Humboldt, which might be considered to belong to the *Monogynia*.[34] It is surprising that nature created among the many varieties of palms some individual forms that appear distributed in small groups in a very limited area. In my wanderings in Haiti and Mexico I found groups of palms, sometimes of very characteristic forms, which despite every effort I was not able to find again in other parts of these lands. In La Regla people seem to be more inclined than those in Havana to plant luxuriant trees, and the gloomy, often leafless *Erythrina* and acacias are replaced by bushes and trees that have perennial leather-like leaves.

Many of the fruit trees of the tropical zone, such as *Achras, Mammea, Persea,* mangoes and *anona*,[35] attain extraordinary heights with stately crowns and are a real blessing in the tropical zones and for this reason are common everywhere in the interior of the island. In Guanabacoa I also saw the first enormous trunks of *sapotier* (*Achras sapota*) richly laden with ripe fruit, which is pulpous but of cooling and agreeable taste.

The road to Guanabacoa is at first desolate and gives no idea of economic use of the land. The nearer one comes to this ancient Indian village the more the barren regions and shrubs disappear to give room to trees. Everything takes on a rural aspect, and the houses shaded by tall trees are surrounded by gardens, cornfields, and banana plantations. Oranges and lemons in all forms and varieties grow here in great abundance, the hot climate having helped these useful trees and fruits to multiply. The pineapples of Havana belong to the finest fruit of this sort. In the immediate

[34] *Cocos crispa*, one of the palms, perhaps of the *Monogynia* (*Monogenetica*).

[35] *Achras*, chicle or sapodillo; *Mammea americana*, mammee apple; *Persea* is the genus containing the avocado; mangoes are of *Mangifera indica*.

surroundings of the city they occur but rarely; in Guanabacoa, however, I saw many of extraordinary size.

In the neighborhood of this place there is a hill called Lomas de las Indios, marked by an enormous pile of rocks with a cross on the summit. The story is told that on this hill during the first years of Spanish occupation an encounter occurred between the Spaniards and the natives of the island, resulting in a huge massacre of the Indians not only by the sword but also by the blood hounds that were turned loose on them. I visited the hill, which, excepting the sad recollection of the gruesome sacrifice which the discovery of America had cost, shows few things worth mentioning. Botanically, I enriched my collection with a very low-growing, white-blooming *Malpighia* whose leaves resemble those of *Malpighia coccifera*, and a small-leaved *Echites* with rosy blossoms.[36]

Since I was most anxious to travel in the interior of the island and to the opposite coast, the invitation of an acquaintance, Mr. Henrique Desdier, came to me in good stead. He suggested that I should visit his estates in the interior which he held in common with his brother, Mr. Fernando Desdier. Though a native Spaniard, Mr. Desdier had by long residence in Hamburg mastered the German language so well that his speech could not be distinguished from that of a German. The accurate knowledge he had of the island of Cuba, his extensive acquaintance with the richest planters there, and his amiable character made him a most agreeable traveling companion for a stranger unacquainted with the language.

January 20 was set for our departure, and early in the morning of that day the *volante* stopped before my residence. First I visited the country home of Mr. Desdier in the suburb of Salud, a small, neat, and well-arranged building with a garden surrounded by a wall. In the latter were no fruit trees except a few orange trees and *guyavas* (*Psidium pyriferum*), a few very stunted pomegranates and figs. On the other hand I saw here for the first time the *Euphorbia tithymaloides*, the *Jenipha pinnatifida*,[37] a very beautiful unknown to me *Aristolochia*,[38] and a Cucurbitacée[39] with fully matured fruit. This latter cucumber-like climbing plant, with leaves and blossoms similar to those of *Momordica elatherium*, is characterized by the odd shape of its fruit, which is the size of a large, full-grown cucumber, multiseptate, with a hard leathery covering. The seeds are black, and when

[36] *Malpighia* (of the Malpighiaceae) is the genus which contains the Barbados cherry; *Echites* is a genus of the Apocynaceae, the dogbanes.

[37] *Psidium pyriferum* = *P. guajava*, the guava; *Euphorbia tithymaloides*, a spurge; *Jenipha pinnatifida*, perhaps of the genus *Janipha*, now *Manihot*.

[38] *Aristolochia*, Dutchman's pipe.

[39] Cucurbitaceae, a gourd.

ripe are in a loose, fibrous tissue through which they can easily fall. And so at every strong gust of wind these large but very light pods are set in motion and produce a rustling sound. A whole wall was overgrown with this plant and one fruit hung close to another. As is the case with all of the cucumber varieties, the seeds retain their power of germination for a long time. They developed well in Europe, bore perfect blossoms, and set fruit, which however could not be made to mature without effort.

I was most surprised at the sight of two splendid flamingoes (*Phoenicopterus americanus*) walking solemnly about in the garden, entirely red with black wing feathers.[40] These birds were quite tame and ate out of one's hand. I have never again seen any so tamed, although they are easily kept and can be raised with domestic fowls. Mr. Desdier was so kind as to make me a present of these beautiful birds, but unfortunately they did not stand the sea voyage.

At about ten o'clock in the morning we left the long suburb of Jesus Maria, and on the way to Batabano, past Fort Atares, we reached a rise, called Loma de San Juan. An excellent view of the city, the bay, and the sea opens up from here. The road is marked by scattered stems of *Yucca gloriosa* and the *Agave*,[41] and at first led through a sparsely settled and little cultivated land. The few dwellings are, moreover, very meager, since the land, covered with clumps of palms, is for the most part pasture land. A league from the town the road began to be extremely rough, and during the rainy season it is badly cut up by the many carts loaded with coffee and is left in bad repair.

Work on public roads is usually done by *maroons* (fugitive slaves) or other colored riff-raff, especially Negroes who can no longer be held in restraint by their masters and are turned over to the government as laborers. Such malefactors are used for the hardest public works, chiefly road building, bear iron neck bands with large prongs and heavy iron chains, and present generally a most repulsive appearance.

During the winter months, when the traffic is also the heaviest, the road is in the best condition because of the prevailing dryness. The road was quite crowded with people and carts, large troops of pack animals, two-wheeled carts drawn by huge oxen, single riders, and Negroes of both

---

[40] *Phoenicopterus ruber* Linn., the only species found in the West Indies. It was still occasionally being killed for food at the time of Thomas Barbour's writing in 1923 (Memoirs of the Nuttall Ornithological Club, No. 6, *The Birds of Cuba*, Cambridge, 1923, p. 34).

[41] *Yucca gloriosa*, a species of yucca, Spanish dagger; *Agave*, a genus of Amaryllidaceae, of which the century plant is one.

sexes with burdens on their heads passing by to haul the daily supply of provisions or the rich harvest of coffee and sugar to the capital.

Since the road was very narrow and full of holes and large stones, the loaded mules always tried to stay in the middle of the way, nor could the heavily loaded carts be turned out. Our progress at first was very slow. This was perfectly satisfactory to me, but not so to my companion, who desired to reach his hacienda at an early hour and complained bitterly about the heat. I was amused at the sight of the grotesque figures and every few minutes found something worth collecting, especially as the growth of vegetation became more luxuriant.

In the course of an hour we reached a large pasture called the *Potrero Bachoni*, where many head of cattle were grazing. Although I had already observed the size and beauty of the cattle in Cuba before, my expectation was surpassed by what I saw. Steers as well as cows are of remarkable beauty and size. Most of them are a rich dark color with huge, moon-shaped horns, like those of the Campagna Romana of the plains of Sicily. These herds of cattle were surrounded by flocks of birds that render them the same service as our starlings. Among them I noticed several varieties, *Cassicus niger*, and *Quiscalus (Icterus) versicolor*, which is also found in Louisiana.[42]

After we passed the *Potrero Bachoni*, the country changed suddenly in appearance and the soil took on a dark-red color. This very fertile soil, called *tierra colorado*, covered a large part of Cuba. Also called *tierra bermeja*, it is, according to Mr. von Humboldt's opinion, probably a mixture of oxidized iron, silica, and clay or red marl deposited over the limestone. This scholar called it Guinea limestone. The owners of plantations select this kind of ground, which covers a large part of the island, and also an almost pure deposit of coarsely granulated calcareous soil for the cultivation of coffee, whose roots prefer a hot and dry soil. Another kind of soil which is called black soil, or *tierra prieta*, is likewise fertile but contains more clay and favors best the cultivation of sugar cane. As soon as one reaches the red earth, the difference in productivity may be noticed, and large groves of tall trees and dense clusters of bushes entwined with climbing plants over the land.

Here I saw for the first time the small lemon, which is peculiar to the island, called *limonicilla* by the natives. In former times it must have covered large portions of the land. They use this small lemon not only to

---

[42] *Cassicus niger* = *Quiscalus niger* (Boddaert). Since no grackle-like icterid is common to Cuba and Louisiana, the author mistakes what he saw as *Quiscalus (Icterus) versicolor*. It probably was *Dives atroviolaceus*, the well-known Cuban blackbird.

press its exceedingly sour juice but Havana also carries on a considerable trade with the fruit preserved in sugar. I found this same variety again in Santo Domingo, where there are also two other varieties of citrus, one with round sour fruit and the other with sweet fruit similar to the orange. These trees grow tall in the wildest primitive forests and cannot be regarded as varieties of our pomegranate. Also, Mexico nourishes on the slopes of the cordilleras a few varieties of the citrus, and a more careful investigation will, no doubt, show that they existed there before the arrival of the Europeans.

A few tall acacias and erythrinas towered over the bushes of *Bignonia stans* and over low, pod-bearing bushes such as *Cytisus spinosus*, frequently intertwined with *Echites torulosa* and several species of the nice *Ipomoea*.[43]

Former travelers complained of the increasing destruction of the forests and bushes of Cuba. The more I approached the interior of the island the more excellent the timber became and I passed through large wooded sections in which giant tree trunks were still to be found. As far as I know, whatever may be destroyed by the *machete* (a long knife which is used for cutting bushes, the same as the *facao* in Brazil) of the planter, it is soon replaced by nature.[44]

Toward noon we reached the little place called San Yago. From here on nature became more prolific and more luxuriant, and the land was covered with greater forest areas. Coffee and sugar plantations, and with them the Negro population, became more numerous.

In the crowds of the city the blacks do not appear as striking as on the *ingenios*, where their genuine African character does not deny itself and both sexes are almost nude and exposed to the burning rays of the sun. Cuba, supplied with genuine Africans through the smuggling of Negroes from the Gold Coast, still preserves in its Negro blood the type which distinguishes this race. The genuine black is easily differentiated from the Creole Negro, who, the more he becomes acclimated, appears the more destitute and wretched.

Such a group of blacks, sparingly covered with brightly colored cloths, held its siesta, since it happened to be noontime, in the shade of an enormous *caiba*. Who would not have thought himself transported to

[43] *Bignonia stans* = *Tecoma stans*, trumpet flower; *Cytisus spinosus*, a leguminous shrub; *Echites torulosa* is of the Apocynaceae, *E. tomentosa* being the Savannah flower; *Ipomoea*, a morning glory.

[44] Barbour, *The Birds of Cuba*, reminds us that Cuba did not have in historic times the *foresta real* found in Central and South America, and that the accelerating pace of forest clearing for sugar-cane culture had made enormous inroads upon the sylvan areas of Cuba even half a century ago. But Oriente Province, among others, still shows some fine forest stands.

Africa at this sight? It seemed indeed as if the *caiba* reminded them of its kin, the baobab (*Adansonia digitata*) held holy by the superstitious belief of the Africans, and the sight of it carried them to the banks of the Niger.[45]

The forests through which we passed consisted of tall trees of *Cedrela odorata* and of *Bursera gummifera*. I also recognized *Brasiliastrum americanum* as well as the genuine *guaiac*.[46] Among these stems of balsams a few are of red bark similar in color to that of an Indian, and called *Indio desnudo*. Unfortunately I could not determine the tree because it was leafless. *Cecropia peltata* attaining an extraordinary height in Cuba, and I believe is called *jugrama*, with its large silver-colored leaves overtowers the highest tops of the thin-leaved gummiferous trees.[47] Fig trees with their dense, dark-green foliage and *Calophylum calaba* furnish a darker shading. To these are added a few climbing plants of the Aroideae with strangely shaped leaves, scattered palms breaking through the clusters of trees, and great masses of *Tillandsia* and *Bletia*, etc., which heaped one over the other, inhabit the forks of branches and live off the life of the trees.[48]

Great flocks of noisy parrots, hammering woodpeckers, melancholy cuckoos, called *arriero*, trogons with bright gaudy colors, brilliantly plumaged songbirds of all kinds, huge flocks of gregarious birds (*Cassicus*), also many gay butterflies with coloring peculiar to the hot zone, with it all a cloudless, dark-blue sky, a burning heat: and the true picture of the tropical zone is spread out to be viewed.

Before sunset I arrived at the *hacienda* of Mr. Desdier, called Ingenio del Rio Gange, because of its proximity to the small river Gange. I was received in the most friendly manner by the father and the brother of my companion. Hospitality is ebullient in all the Spanish colonies. The richest *quinta* and the poorest *milpa* are opened with equal cordiality to the stranger. One will never pass Creoles eating their meal without being most cordially invited.

[45] *Author*: As I was assured by trustworthy persons in Santo Domingo, the genuine African Negro who is transferred to this island really worships the enormous *caiba* or *mapau* (*Bombas caiba*) in the vicinity of Miragoane, apparently confusing it with the baobab. I myself measured this tree. The circumference was only slightly less than that of the largest baobab of Senegal, and the crown and branches nourished a countless number of parasitic plants.

[46] *Cedrela odorata*, Spanish cedar or cigar-box cedar; *Bursera gummifera*, Brazilian elemi; *Brasiliastrum americanum*, a hybrid of *Comocladia* (Anacardiaceae) and *Picrasma* (Simarubaceae); *guiac*, perhaps *Guaiacum*, lignum vitae.

[47] *Cecropia peltata*, one of the Moraceae.

[48] *Calophylum calaba* = *Calophyllum antillanum* of the Guttiferae; Aroideae, aroids or Araceae; *Tillandsia*, a genus of epiphytic plants; *Bletia*, a genus of orchids.

From gray antiquity this patriarchal custom has been transmitted to several nations of modern times, characterizing them by a simplicity of custom which brings them near a state of nature. Despite their predatory attributes, hospitality within the areas of their own huts is as sacred to the most bloodthirsty savages of North America as to the Bedouins of the desert and the warlike mountain people of the Caucasus. With the cessation of the bloody wars which laid Santo Domingo waste, hospitality even towards their former deadly enemies, the white Europeans, returned to the heart of the Africans on this island, and the destitute Negro in the primeval mountain forests shares his last cassava or banana with his former oppressors.

The region about the *hacienda* was very fertile. Nature is powerful and everything shows industry and diligence. The Negroes are, on the whole, well treated and their lot is endurable. At least they are better off than they were in their homeland. The most humane treatment is accorded them and mistreatment, so common in other slave countries, is extremely rare. The laws relating to the blacks, the *Code de los negros*, are among the most remarkable and most philanthropic statues recorded in the history of the colonies, and have made immortal the regent who gave them. By their benevolence toward the blacks, the Spaniards have atoned for the barbarity with which wild military zeal and the Conquistadore rapaciousness sinned against the red aborigines of America.

Whoever studies the history of the Spanish colonies and knows the character of the Spaniards must, on the whole, defend the action of the former Spanish government in the management of its domain. An early, powerful, and avaricious clergy in the mother country, influenced by the great monastic tradition, held to a detrimentally narrow trade policy. However, we must consider the appalling sacrifice which the discovery and conquest of the New World cost, as well as the age when these deeds were committed. Religious zeal coupled with persecution in Spain at that time (which even today remains peculiar to the Spanish clergy) crippled the over-extended monopoly of the machinery of state. In addition, we must consider the earliest population in the colonies as consisting in part of adventurers and indeed criminals, and finally, the often cruel, hostile, or at least unbending nature of the aborigines, even in the most civilized parts of this great continent.

The Spanish government and also the courts of audiencia and the Indian tribunal in Spain have for the most part enacted laws that were wholesome and intended to raise the well-being of the colonies. With truly wise paternalism they protected the poorer portions of the population and the dependent Indians against the presumptions of the too powerful clergy and the avaricious nobility.[49]

The cabinet of Madrid, seeking to protect its protégés against the excessive importation of luxury articles from Europe, hindered the trade of its European neighbors, but not the actual well-being of the colonies. Considering the child-like simplicity of the civilized Indians, their continued attachment to the Spanish crown, and the mildness with which they were treated, we must take back, in large measure the accusations which were voiced against the Spanish clergy.

I am far from defending all of the means employed by the clergy, nor yet from justifying them by the sanctity of religion. If, on the other hand, we weigh the barbarous idolatry of the Indians and their superstitious indolence, we cannot but agree that it required extraordinary means to convert them to Christianity and to hold them to it.

In times of peace the Spanish government would no doubt have assumed a different policy in regard to trade considerations and thereby would have removed the chief stumbling block. Studying carefully the conditions in Spanish America as they are submitted by the greatest of the present authorities in books of travel, Mr. von Humboldt, and considering the new republics as they are today, one cannot blame the Creoles when they yearn for a return to former times. Mr. von Humboldt has the absolute confidence and the universal respect of all natives of the educated class, and we see in his writings by no means attacks on the Spanish government of that time. The uncertain condition of Spain during the war with France and its own internal unrest made it difficult for the South American nations to accept one party or to accept the Junta of Seville as their master.

Restless ferment had to set in which finally resulted in separation. To this was added the free commerce with the rest of the world, and so these countries were irretrievably lost. The organization of new governments could not be effected with sufficient strength to face alone the dissension among the parties and the war with the troops of the mother country. Thus the administration of these countries followed the will of the most capable heads and the most successful generals. To this was added the influence and intrigue of foreign powers, which, by trade and other interests, are

[49] The courts of the audiencia in both provincial and colonial Spanish jurisdictions offered, in the beginning, relief to the citizen against the torts or excesses of administrative agencies. In this sense they were forerunners of those courts administering *droit administratif* in France, an order of the judicature slow to develop in Anglo-American countries. In the seventeenth and eighteenth centuries, courts of the audiencia became corrupted in Spanish colonial administrations.

bound to the republics. Moreover, a large body of idle soldiery to be employed and paid, the greatly increased demands created by the introduction of European luxury articles, and the very slight hope of final alleviation and settlement of all these difficulties were all troublesome factors opposing the well-being of the new republics.

Opposite the house of my host was a press for sugar cane, or *trapiche*. Since it was then harvest time it was in full operation. Consisting of three iron cylinders running parallel to one another, this contrivance lacked many of the improvements customarily used now in the pressing of the juice of the sugar cane in the sugar refineries of Louisiana, which have reached their greatest perfection. This press was driven by oxen ridden by small Negro boys. The pressed stalks were used as fodder for the cattle or for fuel, since whiskey distilleries had not been generally introduced.

On very large *haciendas*, however, I found even during my stay in Cuba that arrangements were fully advanced, and soon masses of machinery will limit the employment of many human workers. The Ingenio Gange kept some 300 adult slaves, of whom 180 were men and 120 women who had some 50 children. Such a plantation can produce 1,200 to 1,300 cases of sugar per year. The number of *arrobas* of coffee which can be produced by that number of slaves cannot accurately be determined because of progressively increasing production.

At the vesper hour all the blacks together with their *majorals*, their overseers, assembled on an open place near the *hacienda*. I was amazed at the number of genuine African Negroes whom I saw there and at the striking physiognomies characterizing the different tribes of the Negro race. It is therefore an easy matter for one who knows the Negroes to classify them as to their different nations and to guide oneself accordingly in the purchase of slaves, since certain tribes are preferred to others. Generally, all genuine Negroes are powerfully and muscularly built, the men often endowed with a truly gigantic strength and extraordinary endurance.

Although the various tribes show differences in the proportions of their bodies, the women are, on average, relatively small as compared with the men and, indeed, one could call them delicately built. Yet, here too, the different nations more or less deviate from one another, and in the mixture of their blood in America the various forms soon merge. Especially among the women there is then an inclination to obesity which gives rise to stout and awkward shapes.

While the women of several African tribes have coarse and repulsive facial features, others are characterized by striking beauty and most pleasing countenances. They do not have the flat, caved-in noses, protruding lips, and projecting skullbones which disfigure the Ethiopian race. It has

64

also been determined that not all the Negro women fade as quickly as is asserted by some travelers. Observing something of tribal peculiarities among the men and women of the genuine African race, with their strikingly ugly or beautiful forms, I usually found again, when I inquired concerning their origin, the facial characteristics of the various tribes. Although I have not seen the native tribes of Africa myself, I dare to assert that there prevails in Africa among the various tribes pronounced family similarities in which ugliness as well as beauty are inherited.[50]

During my stay on the island I examined various individuals of several tribes which were formerly imported into Cuba and which even now arrive there by way of contraband. The genuine Negroes are marked by incisions in their skin, tatooing, and disfigurements, as are other wild primitive people, whereby they indicate important events in their lives characteristic of their tribe or their rank. Therefore the imported Negroes of either sex, if they were imported after they had reached maturity, are easily distinguished from the Creole Negroes.[51]

[50] The application of "Ethiopian" as a generic for natives of Africa is of long standing (Shakespeare used it), however incorrect. Ethiopians then included Cushites, Hamites, and Semitic strains dating from the third milennium B.C. The Amhara and Tigrina ruling groups are Coptic Christians. Forty per cent of Ethiopians today are of Hamitic origin, Muslim in faith; there are also Somali, Danakil, Arabs, and Ethiopian Jews and Greeks.

[51] The author's analysis here and in subsequent numbered paragraphs obviously was derived from the more or less general knowledge of his time. It was then and is now difficult to establish type classifications for the peoples of Africa along purely physical lines because of prehistoric and modern migrations and mingling.

Broadly speaking, there are four main classifications: the Forest Negroids, the most numerous group, inhabiting most of Sub-Saharan Africa, characterized by brown to dark brown skin, kinky to woolly black hair, flat noses, everted lips. Second, the Nilotics, perhaps a variation of the Forest Negroid type, exhibiting taller, more slender physiques, narrower noses, less everted lips, inhabiting Rwanda, Burundi, Uganda, and the eastern Sudan. Third, the Bushmanoids or Bushman-Hottentots of Southwest Africa, characterized by yellow-brown skins, often in the females particularly by steatopygia. Fourth, Afro-Asiatic groups and Afro-Caucasoid peoples, such as the Fulani south of the Sahara in West Africa and many Somalis, characterized by both Negroid and Caucasoid features; most of them, but not all, are recent arrivals. Not to be left out are the Pygmies, who, however, are to be classified with the Forest Negroids.

The complexities of African language classification, little understood in Duke Paul's time, offer clues but no clear-cut correlations with physical types. The linguistic groups are (1) Congo-Kardofanian, spoken by most of Sub-Saharan Africa, embracing eleven subfamilies, one of the best known being Bantu (Benue-Congo), extending over a vast area and containing hundreds of languages; (2) Nilo-Saharan of eastern and north-central Africa, embracing half a dozen distinct divisions: Songhai, Saharan, Maban, Fur, Chari-Nile, and Koman; (3) Afro-Asiatic of northern and eastern Africa, consisting of Semitic, Berber, Cushitic, and Chad divisions; and (4) Khoisan of southern and south-central Africa. Cf. Melville J. Herskovits, *The Human Factor in Changing Africa* (Washington,

Here I list a few observations which I made on such individuals and, according to the statement of experts, having features and markings that are characteristic of their tribes:

(1) A girl of the tribe of Karavally, said to be fourteen years old, and quite fully developed. Head and frontal bone round, skull somewhat pressed in, back part of the head strong and arched towards the back. Chin not very prominent. Lips full, teeth large and brilliant white. Eyes brown. Hair very short and curly but not especially thick. Ears very small. Height of body, five feet, two inches. Proportions regular, only the hands too small in comparison to the feet. Hip bones very protruding, almost no calves. Color of skin brownish black. Imported into Cuba from Africa at the age of twelve and sold there. Spoke broken Spanish, was good natured and obedient, showed no mental capacity, and was of ugly appearance.

(2) Another girl, eleven years old, also a Karavally, almost mature and of somewhat darker skin. Back of the head also strongly arched, forehead round and high. Ears very small. Lips very thick and black. Eyes set far apart. Nose very flat, in the middle only slightly raised above the cheeks. Growth rather regular, but hips too far protruding. Feet turned in, large, with protruding ankles and flat heels. Good natured but stupid and ugly. Brought here a year and a half ago and ignorant of the language. Height, four feet, six inches.

(3) A man of about thirty years of age, a Karavally. Large strong Negro, five feet, ten inches tall. Round forehead, the middle of the head flat, but the back of the head strongly arched. Short, very curly hair. Small ears. Build very muscular, with flat and clumsy feet. Brownish black. Strong and sound, at the same time faithful and useful. Smuggled in since childhood, and able to speak the language.

(4) A girl, nine years old, Ganga. The back of the head not high. Eyes deep set. An abundance of curly hair. Very protruding red lips. Very regularly built. Shining black color. In Cuba only a few months.

(5) A handsome lad of fifteen, Ganga. Development of head as above. Three incisions on each cheek. Very white teeth and heavy pink lips. Well proportioned, five feet, six inches tall. Hands and feet not too large, calves poorly developed. Newcomer in Cuba and ignorant of the language.

(6) Man of twenty years, Lamba. Very dark black and well built. Round, somewhat pointed head, strongly arched behind. Deep eye sockets, but not particularily blunt nose and thick lips. Of strong physical build. Extremities not too large. Strikingly marked with two deep incisions on

1962); Joseph H. Greenberg, *The Languages of Africa* (Washington, 1963); Charles Gabriel Seligman, *Races of Africa* (New York, 1957).

each cheek, two small ones on the temples, and six on the forehead. On the abdomen a large tatooed cross with three broad lines radiating from it. Recently brought in.

(7) A man of twenty-five years, Congo Musinga. Small and very black with genuine Negro face, flat nose, thick lips, curly back part of head heavy hair, five feet, three inches tall. On his breast this black, who was a high ranking African, had a circle of deep incisions.

(8) A boy of eight years, Congo Bassura. Well built and very black, with straight legs, small feet and hands. Also circumcised.

(9) A large man of twenty-five years, Mandingo and Mohammedan, who could speak a few words of Arabic. Had from four to six lined rows of deep incisions on his breast. The Mandingoes are strong Negroes but more spoiled by their association with Moorish merchants than are the slaves from the interior of Africa.

(10) A handsome young woman of seventeen, Kaury, pitch black, with fine facial expression and extremely well built. Lips not very thick. Nose small but not blunt. Hair abundant and curly. Five feet, four inches tall. Very highly esteemed by her countrymen. Brought to Cuba only recently. Her owners treated her with the greatest consideration. An aristocratic person of her tribe, for her body was decorated throughout with parallel running incisions two inches long, which is said to be a great distinction in Africa and possibly, in the conception of the Ethiopians, adds great charm to beauty.

The Negroes generally are very superstitious and believe in the influence of evil spirits and sorcerers. Therefore, when first brought over from Africa they are afraid of every stranger. My diligent collecting of natural history objects and the few physical instruments which I carried with me brought me the reputation of being a wizard. The inherent curiosity of these people, especially the women and children, soon won out, and even though they were at first afraid and hid, they soon sought an opportunity to come near me.

Negroes imported into Cuba do not fall into that melancholy state of apathy which takes possession of their kind so easily on their arrival in other colonies, because they find here their own countrymen in a much happier condition than elsewhere, and the recollections of their native land may not always be the happiest. Slavery is certainly not the worst lot that can come to the Negro, but the revolting manner of transporting them to this country is against all human feeling. Danger threatens these unfortunates when, by a distorted sense of humaneness, the armed vessels of European nations pursue the slave ships. The horrible scenes which result in such hunts at sea alone outweigh the advantages gained by the proponents of the slave traffic.

Slavery will never be done away with in Africa, and all that the most humane theories have been able to do is to give the slave trade another direction and to make the lot of the blacks in Africa only sadder than formerly. The voice of humanity and genuinely noble desire inspired those societies which were formed in England and the United States to relieve the condition of the blacks by the abolition of the slave trade. But even so the evil is not extinguished with the decree forbidding their exportation into the slave countries.[52]

Through many centuries the employment of black slaves in the hot belt of the world has become an imperative necessity, so that a sudden emancipation of the Negroes would result in the most serious, I should say the most unfortunate, consequences to the owners of the slaves as well as to the slaves themselves. The ruin of one part of the population would make it also impossible for the other to exist, and the trade in the most important products of the tropical zone would be completely paralyzed.

However much I abhor the traffic in slaves and count it among the most degrading transactions that can sully mankind, I nevertheless fear that overly hasty measures regarding the emancipation of the blacks will have in their wake the most deplorable consequences for the latter themselves. The real means, however, of putting an end to the slavery of our black fellow beings lies in the beneficient laws which protect these unfortunates against despotic treatment and extremely severe punishment for such masters who abuse them. Furthermore the blacks should be given every possible means of acquiring their own freedom as soon as they feel themselves able to earn their own support.

I can never sanction the slave trade with the Gold Coast, since it is revolting to every sense of morality. Still, I believe that all coercive means devised against it will never attain their purpose, since in Africa the natives are oppressed in the most barbarous manner by their own rulers and are held in the most abject slavery. This shameful trade will not come to an end until all trade and communication with the west coast of Africa and Mozambique are given up. This cannot and never will be done.

In my excursions into the neighborhood of the *hacienda*, I could not

---

[52] Slavery, abolished in Cuba by Spain in 1886, actually did not cease until the close of the Spanish-American War (1898). It was not abolished in the British West Indian possessions until 1838, and in British India until 1843. Abolishment in French possessions was legislated in 1848, in Portuguese in 1858 (plus twenty years), in the U.S. by the emancipation proclamations of 1862 and 1863 and the Thirteenth Amendment of 1865; in Dutch possessions in 1863, and in Brazil in 1888.

help but admire the strikingly rapid changes of nature in the tropic zone. In some few trees these changes take place in a very short time. A few kinds shed their leaves suddenly and almost just as suddenly acquire new ones. Thus I saw a *caiba* which overnight was entirely bereft of its foliage, and another entirely without leaves but within the short period of two or three days was covered again with the most luxuriant green.

Thus I saw *Ipomoeas*[53] of which a few perennial varieties reached the very tips of the highest trees, while others, crawling along the ground in the early mornings unfolded their glorious leaves in various colors, but were deprived of all their ornament during the warm hours of the day. Affording a rich variation in the flora of Cuba, these *Ipomoeas* please the eye with their unrivaled charming appearance in delicate blue, red, yellow, white, and fringed blossoms.

Cuba, so rich in magnificent butterflies, affords even in the dry season a rich bounty for the collector. On the other hand, beetles are rare except during the rainy season. Even the hermit crabs, the land crabs, and the scorpions, called *alacran*, disappear, but it swarms with countless termites and obnoxious *cucarachas* of extraordinary size.

The proximity of the continent seems to have supplied the island of Cuba with a much greater wealth of bird life than neighboring Haiti and Jamaica. During my absence from Havana I myself collected more than fifty different species, among which several were unknown to me. The banana plantations were populated by greater numbers of *hudios* (*Crotophaga ani*),[54] and the beautiful white-headed parrot (*Psittacus leucocephalus*)[55] in great flocks enlivened the *ingenio*[56] trees which were resplendent with large amounts of ripe fruit. This variety of parrot is easily tamed and not at all shy, but is as yet rather rare in European collections.

Delicate turtle doves (*Columba jamaicensis* and *squamosa*),[57] smaller than those of the Carolinas, wander in pairs about the coffee plantations, and close under the windows of the houses the exceptionally dainty dwarf dove (*Columba passerina*)[58] seeks its food. Tropical America is very rich in these and supports several varieties. The denser forest on the other

[53] Morning glories.

[54] *Huidos*, Jews (here *Crotophaga ani* Linn., smooth-billed ani of the family Cuculidae, cuckoos and anis).

[55] *Psittacus leucocephalus* = *Amazona leucocephala*, the familiar Cuban parrot.

[56] *Ingenio*, plantation trees.

[57] *Columba jamaicensis* = *Leptotila jamaicensis*, the white-bellied dove; *Columba squamosa*, the scaly-naped or red-necked pigeon.

[58] *Columba passerina* = *Columbigallina passerina*, the common ground dove. The author probably saw the race *C. p. insularis*.

hand is inhabited by two larger doves (*Columba caribea* and *leucoce-phala*),[59] and in the bushes lives the cuckoo (*Saurothera*),[60] called *arriero*, different from the *vetula*, which I recognized as new and is distinguished by an unusually long tail. The *cambergo* (*Cassicus flavigaster*), a beautiful bird, shares more the habits of our oriole and lives in pairs.[61]

The most pitiful bird of this region is the trogon (closely related to *Trogon rosabella*) with strangely cut tail feathers and sharply hooked bill. The blood red underbelly is in sharp contrast to its splendid green back. This stupid bird sits with ruffled feathers on the lower branches of trees, and is so unwary that one can strike it dead with a stick.[62] So much more alive are, however, the *Muscicapa ruticilla*[63] and a dainty *Tanagra*[64] with white and yellow markings, and other vari-colored songbirds. I did not see any crows in Cuba,[65] though there are two varieties in Santo Domingo.[66]

Instead of the crow, Cuba has the *urubu* (*Aura tignosa*)[67] which has become very tame and is protected by law. The *zopilote*[68] of the Mexicans (*Cath. atratus ?* Wils.) does not appear in Cuba, and it is strange that these percnopters are not found at all in Santo Domingo while they inhabit the remainder of America.

The island sustains a great number of water and swamp birds and is in this respect much richer than its neighboring lands. It is peculiar that so many of these, especially varieties of ducks, seek the highest trees for the night. In the neighborhood of the *hacienda* on one evening I shot several

[59] *Columba caribea*, the ring-tailed pigeon; *Columba leucocephala*, the white-crowned pigeon.

[60] *Saurothera merlini*, the great lizard cuckoo, length 20 inches, tail, 11–13.

[61] *Cambergo* = *chambergo*, the Cuban or black-cowled oriole (*Icterus dominicensis*).

[62] The Cuban trogon (*Priotelus temnurus*), considered by James Bond(*Birds of the West Indies*) to be one of the most beautiful of the many splendid birds of the island.

[63] *Muscicapa ruticilla* = *Setophaga ruticilla*, American redstart.

[64] Possibly the stripe-headed tanager, *Spindalis zena*, but more likely the bananaquit, *Coereba flaveola*.

[65] Two crows, *Corvus nasicus* and *C. palmarum*, are known to inhabit Cuba, but neither is common there. In the opinion of Barbour (1923 *Memoirs of the Nuttall Ornithological Club*, No. 6, 106), the former is on its way to extinction, the latter "reduced to a few small bands... between Guane and the port of La Esperanza."

[66] *Author*: Both new, the *Corvus erythrophthalmus* m. lives in flocks on clusias and laurels, the size of the rook, noisy, steel-blue, with fire-red eyes, and the *Corvus palmarum* m. brownish black, scarcely as large as a jackdaw, lives solitarily on the trunks of palms, both in the vicinity of the Cibao Mountains in former Santo Domingo. [*Corvus palmarum* Württemberg remains but *C. erythrophthalmus* is now considered inseparable subspecifically from the species found in Puerto Rico, *C. leucognaphalus*, described in 1800 by Daudin (*Traité Orn.*, 2:231).]

[67] *Aura tignosa*, *Cathartes aura*, the turkey vulture.

musk ducks (*Anas moschata*) from the top of a *caiba*. This duck, as I later assured myself, always nests in high trees, is very common in Cuba and on the coast of Mexico, where with other tropical ducks and a great number of snipes and water fowl of all kinds, it inhabits the region of the mangrove trees (*Rhizophora mangle*).[69]

Cuba is most fortunate not to have a single poisonous reptile. Of snakes I saw only two species, one indeed very large and called *cobra maha*, and the other similar to the European *Coluber natrix*, both however quite harmless. Among the lizards I observed a few prettily colored *Anolis* (*Anolius bullaris, Lacerta bullaris*, L.), very dainty, lively creatures which live in trees and are curious because of the inflated pouches under their throats and their inordinately long breakable tails.[70] Formerly numerous in Cuba, the large leguans have now become rare, since the Negroes hunt them so much. So also the agouti (*Dasyprocta aguti*), one of the few mammals in Cuba, is becoming ever rarer and I had great difficulty in securing a pair of these splendid animals alive.

On the twenty-fourth, my host and I left the latter's home to visit one of the large plantations eight leagues to the west which was owned by one of his friends, Mr. Andreas de Zayas. It is supposed to be one of the largest on the island. Since we set out on our journey at daybreak, we arrived early at our half-way destination, the estate of a certain Mr. Hernandez, a polite and educated man who served us an excellent breakfast. Here I admired a very large palm with fan-shaped leaves. The entire stem and also its leaf stalks were covered with excessively hard and sharp barbs from three to four inches long. This fan palm is called *palma carojo* and seems to be very rare. The trunk before me must, because of its slow growth and extreme hardness of its wood, have been very old.[71]

In the neighborhood of the house a few very beautiful plants were in bloom, *Pancratium littorale, Bryophyllum calicinum, Poinciana pulcherrima, Passiflora quadrangularis, Besleria cristat*, and others. I also saw near the hedges *Duranta plumerii, Bauhinia prorecta, Mimosa sensitiva* (in

---

[68] *Zopilote*, black vulture. Bond, *op. cit.*, discounts the existence of this species, *Coragyps atratus*, in the West Indies.

[69] *Anas moschata* = *Cairina moschata*, the Muscovy duck, a large, heavy-bodied species called *Bisam-Ente* in German, and found from Mexico southward to coastal Peru and the La Plata estuary but *not* in the West Indies. The ducks shot by Duke Paul were almost certainly tree ducks of the genus *Dendrocygna*, one species of which, *D. arborea*, breeds widely in the West Indies.

[70] Of the family of Iguanidae, and mistakenly called New World chamelons, *Anolis* are here properly described.

[71] *Palma caraja*, sail palm.

tropical America there grow several *mimosas*, a sensitive plant, with leaves double and triple divided), and several *lantana*.[72]

Towards noon we reached a wooded region, called Monte de San Andreas, where I was fascinated by two beautiful climbing plants. The one is a cucumber-like plant, resplendent with many round, golden yellow fruits the size of an orange, bitter as the *colocynth*.[73] The other bore multi-locular pods and had leathery leaves. In the latter I recognized the *Feuillea cordifolia*, which in Santo Domingo is called *nandirobier*.[74] In this forest grew *Carica papaya*,[75] frequently wild among *Clusia, Cedrela, Switenia, Ficus*,[76] and others. Adjoining the forest were many *caffetalas*, or coffee plantations, the product of which grows best in this part of Cuba, and which produce also mocha beans, sold at the highest prices in Havana.

While the coffee grows tree-like even in the forests of Haiti, it is carefully pruned in Cuba, is never allowed to reach any height, and is systematically planted in equal rows. Very rarely will the careful planter allow the young trees to grow up under the protection of the banana. The soil of the area we passed over is composed of the most porous limestone, rather sparsely covered with the red calcareous earth of Guinea.

In the evening we reached the Caffetal de la Providencia of Mr. de Zayas. This gracious gentleman, a fine man of the world who commands the French language perfectly, had been advised of my coming and received me with great kindness and the entire *aisance* of a rich West Indian planter. From the interior arrangement of his house I could easily convince myself that I was in the middle of one of the islands in the Antilles. The rich people of Cuba, in the city as in the country, live as well as those in Europe, pay with heavy money good French and English cooks, have the most costly wines, and usually an open table to which persons recommended to them have a standing invitation. The oftener a stranger, if he is a distinguished and a respectable man, appears at such a house the more the host feels flattered and seeks to make the guest comfortable by favors and friendly acts.

Early on the following morning Mr. de Zayas conducted me about his

---

[72] *Pancratium littorale*, a member of the Amaryllidaceae; *Brophyllum calicinum*, *B. calycinum* = *Kalanchoe pinnata*, air plant; *Poinciana pulcherrima*, *Caesalpinia pulcherrima*, Barbados pride; *Passiflora quadrangularis*, grandilla; *Besleria cristat*, *B. cristata*, one of the Gesneriaceae; *Duranta plumerii*, *D. plumieri*, one of the Verbenaceae; *Bauhinia prorecta*, *B. porrecta*, one of the Leguminosae; *Mimosa sensitiva*, one of the sensitive plants.

[73] Colocynth, an Old-World vine allied to the watermelon, bitter apple, bitter gourd.

[74] *Feuillea cordifolia*, of the Cucurbitaceae.

[75] *Carica papaya*, papaya

[76] *Clusia* of the Guttiferae; *Cedrela*, Spanish cedar; *Switenia*, *Swietenia*, mahogany; *Ficus*, fig.

extensive estate. Between eight and nine hundred blacks were employed. I admired the sense of order and the good taste of my host, who had transformed his great *hacienda* into a Garden of Eden. Every coffee and sugarcane field was bounded by rows of splendid tropical fruit trees whose variety and beauty enchanted me. The delight that a carefully selected collection of fruit trees from all the continents having a tropical zone is to the friend of botany, I leave to the judgment of experts.

In giant height towered *Theobroma cacao*,[77] and *Laurus persea*,[78] which I later found again in Santo Domingo's primeval forests. Likewise I admired a large citrus variety with enormous fruit whose pulp was red and edible. The leaves of this lemon were characterized by very large folds, so that they appeared almost double. This citrus is a subdivision of *Citrus decumana*. Nowhere on the island did I see the cocoa palm more beautiful and more abundant, proof that this valuable plant also prospers away from the sea shore under the care of man. Great trunks of *Inga dulcis, Tamarinduc indicia, Spondias mombin, Mamea americana*, and *Mangifera indicia*,[79] although native of Cuba but rarely in great abundance, I saw on the plantation of Providencia as beautiful as on Haiti, an island whose fertility holds equal rank with that of Brazil.

After I had visited all the agricultural buildings and the fields of coffee and sugar cane, my delightful host invited me to inspect a wild wooded region and led me through some tall timber to the edge of a lake shaded by large trees, for the most part *Switenia mahogoni* and *Chamaefistula officinalis* inhabited by countless swamp birds. These birds, accustomed to enjoy undisturbed peace, were so tame that I could procure many for my collection. *Parra jacana*[80] ran along the edge of the water like domestic fowls. Even the discharging of guns could not make the herons desist from their warfare upon the fish in the lake and a black water hen (*Fulica leucopyga*)[81] swam quite unafraid at my very feet along the edge of the water. Of fresh water fish I noticed only one *Perca* between seven and nine inches long and one tiny *Pymelodus*.[82]

[77] *Theobroma cacao*, cocoa.

[78] *Laurus persea* = *Persea americana*, avocado.

[79] *Inga dulcis* = *Pithecellobium dulce* of the Leguminosae; *Tamarinduc indicia, Tamarindus indica*, tamarind; *Spondias mombin*, yellow mombin; *Mangifera indicia, M. indica*, mango.

[80] *Parra jacana* = *Jacana spinosa*, the American jacana, a water bird with extremely long claws.

[81] *Fulica leucopyga* = *Fulica americana*, the American coot, a water bird known to breed in the West Indies, but *F. caribaea*, the Caribbean coot, is, according to Bond (*op. cit.*), "rare in Cuba."

[82] *Pimelodus*, a genus of primarily South American cat fishes.

On the return I shot a beautiful thrush (*Turdus jamaicencis*)[83] and in the rotted trunk of a *Cecropia* I found a new *Passalus* which Mr. J. Sturm later classified under the name of *Passalus carbonarius*.[84] My attention was called to a small lazy falcon, called *San Antonio*.[85] This bird of prey will sit without moving for days on the top of the highest tree spying for game, and is probably different from *Falco sparverius* and rather resembles *Falco femoralis*. Later I shot one in Santo Domingo.

After a stay of three days I left the Hacienda de la Providencia and on the evening of the twenty-eighth I reached the *ingenio* on the Rio Gange. On the thirtieth I again departed at daybreak in order to visit the southern coast of the island about sixteen leagues distant which forms a part of the Bay of Xagua. I rode the whole day alternately through *haciendas*, pastures, and forest-covered stretches of land. At a distance of about seven leagues the exposed limestone and the red earth disappeared gradually and a black soil took its place. Now also appeared the *palma sombrero* (*Corypha tectorum?*) and scattered specimen of *palma filamentosa* (*Corypha miraguama*).[86] The more frequently the former appeared, so much the more *palma real* disappeared. I also found that the swampy places and small lakes, called *lagunas*, increased the further we advanced on the black soil. The *potreros*, or pastures, became more expansive and the trees of the higher altitudes disappeared, giving way to such trees and bushes as prefer a wet soil.

Before we reached the place selected by my companion for the night camp, the palms became lower, and it seemed to me that it was no longer that *palma sombrero* which I had observed a few leagues back. However, location has a decided influence on the development of the palms.

Mr. Desdier conducted me to the dwelling of a certain Mr. Juan Menendez in whose *desenganio* I likewise found a hospitable reception. Since night had not yet come, I used the rest of the day to hunt among the neighboring lagoons where there were many *parra* and white herons. Among the latter two varieties are to be distinguished, one as large as our common heron, entirely white, different from *Ardea egretta*, the other *Ardea candidissima*, only two-thirds as large as the first mentioned, milk white with the tips of the wings grayish black.[87] I also found two varieties of land turtles (*Emys*), of which one was of considerable size.

---

[83] Normal range, Jamaica.

[84] *Passalus carbonarius* Württemberg, one of the larger beetles.

[85] If *San Antonio* = *Cernicalo*, then it is *Falco sparverius*, the sparrow hawk.

[86] *Corypha miraguama* = *Coccothrinax miraguama*.

[87] The confusions which have arisen over herons in the white phase and in immaturity are discussed in Bond, *Birds of the West Indies*, 20–22.

The following morning we again started very early and passed through fertile cultivated sections, through pastures, also through swampy and unused areas. These parts left in the state of nature are called *cienegas* and are occupied by *Corypha maritima* and *Corypha miraguama*. *Corypha tectorum* disappears as does *Oreodoxa regia*. All these palms were discovered and determined by Mr. von Humboldt.[88]

At about noon we reached the dwelling of Mr. Freide, who lived very near the coast and owned large herds of cattle. His is the only part of all the *cienegas* and unfertile swamp land around there worth using for agricultural purposes. The very flat coast land comes close to his place and the muddy and salt-water-covered low shore extends in the form of several lagoons a few leagues inland.

Inhabited by many alligators, it is overgrown with mangrove trees or the hibiscus (*Hibiscus abutiloides*) abloom with beautiful red and yellow blossoms. I sought to penetrate this region with the aid of Negroes but in vain. The south coast of the island is so densely overgrown with mangrove trees, often many miles uninterruptedly, that one can not reach the land from the sea side nor the sea from the land side.

Mr. Freide had horses saddled for use and volunteered to guide us. Cleverly avoiding the swampy places, we traveled the distance of a league through tall grasses and *miraguama* palms to a place where the sea makes a small bay surrounded by mangrove trees. From here the open sea was visible. Six years later I sailed around these flat coasts, which are extremely dangerous because of their countless shallows and small groups of islands which serve pirates as hiding places. Since I had never seen the mangrove grow so large nor to such an extraordinary extent, it afforded me an unusual sight. From branches of the tree, root runners developed, reproducing the tree itself. This was most important to me and I remained two hours in that region enlivened by large colonies of swamp birds.

That evening, at my request, a hunt for alligators was organized, and one of these creatures was caught by the Negroes. It was only a small specimen of two feet and four inches in length, with pointed nose and thirty-eight teeth in the upper and thirty teeth in the lower jaw, quite identical with the *Crocodilus acutus* of Santo Domingo.

The Negroes insisted that the genuine alligator, though sometimes twelve feet in length, was not vicious here. Concerning the viciousness of the alligators, I must remark that local conditions must have an influence

[88] Von Humboldt, Bonpland, and Kunth, *Nova Genera et species plantarum*, had been published in its last and seventh volume by 1825, ten years before Duke Paul wrote the present account; it is likely that he had seen many of the earlier volumes in the set by 1822, the time of his departure for the New World.

requiring an explanation, for I have had the opportunity to observe three different kinds of alligators in America and can make the statement that the geographical distribution of these great saurians must also have an influence on their wildness.

The Louisiana alligator (*Champsa lucius*) is dangerous in some localities and quite harmless in others. On Santo Domingo the Negroes pay no heed to the *Crocodilus acutus* in the salt lakes of Mirebalais, but it is the terror of the inhabitants of Aquin and St. Louis. The same holds true in Mexico in regard to the *Crocodilus rhombifer*, which the Indians and the Creoles can distinguish readily from the *Crocodilus acutus*. They are accustomed to call the former *cayman* and the latter *alligator*. Insufficiency of food may have an effect on these carnivorous reptiles, as it has on other beasts of prey. Being crowded together in excessive numbers in certain localities may therefore increase their hunger. During their breeding time they are also more vicious than at any other period, but during the cold season in the northern part of America and during the dry season in the southern part they are entirely harmless and sunk in deep sleep.

On the second of February I returned to the *hacienda* on the Rio Gange, and on the fourth to Havana. During the entire journey I was accompanied by Mr. Desdier who honored me with obliging courtesy and supplied a large collection, especially of dry plants.[89]

[89] *Author*: Among the vertebrates of the first order I collected two mammals, the *Dasuprocta aguti*, and a small bat (*molossus?*). Of birds I collected: one vulture, *Cathartes aura*, three falcons, *Falco sparverius*, *Falco* (*Circus*) *uliginosus*, Edw., and San Antonio, which probably is not yet known; two owls, *Strix asio?* and a large black and white, dark-spotted one, perhaps not different from *Noctua nyctea*; one butcher bird, *Lanius carolinus*; nine fly catchers and tyrant birds, *Muscicapa ruticilla*, another similar one but marked with light yellow, probably not merely a variety (*M. flaveola mihi.*), moreover *M.* (*vireo*) *olivacea* and *M. cantatrix*, Wils., and yet two other doubtful genera. *Tyrannus ferox*, and a large dark gray tyrant bird with white and black markings, called *pitirri* in Cuba, *T. nigriceps*, Sw. ? ; one waxwing, *Bombicilla americana*; two tanagers *Tanagra multicolor* (*Fringilla zena*, Lin.), *Tanagra palmarum* (*Icteria*); two thrushes, *Turdus jamaicensis*, *Turdus polyglottus*; five warblers, *Sylvia*(*turdus*) *aurocapillus*, *Sylvia pusilla*, *Sylvia olivacea*, *trichas*, and one undetermined; one swallow, probably *Hirundo coronata* ? ; five buntings and finches; four Cassicans (*orioles*), *Icterus versicolor*, *Cassicus niger* (*Psarocolius*) *cajanus*, *flavigaster*; one starling, *Sturnus hypocrepis*, Wagler, different from *Alauda magna*, Gm.; two humming birds, *Trochilus gramineus* and *colubris* ? ; one kingfisher, *Alcedo alcyon*, called *Vulgo pitirri manglar*; two woodpeckers, *Picus radiolatus* and *ruficeps* ? ; two cuckoos, *Cuculus* (*Coccyzus*) *dominicus* ?, different from *Cuculus carolinensis*, and the *arriero*, a large bird, to be distinguished from the Cuculus (*Saurothera*) *vetula*; one *Couroucou*, *Trogon silens*, *mihi*, related to *Trogon rosalba*; two parrots, *Psittacus leucocephalus* and a very small parakeet with green back and dirty grayish-yellow speckled belly; two partridges, *Tetrao* (*Perdix*) *virginianus*, and a beautiful genus related to

Odontophorus rufus, Viellot; five doves, *Columba leucocephala, caribaea, jamaicensis, squam*ose ? and *passerina*.

I collected also: one plover, *Charadrius vociferus*; one crane, *Grus americana*, gray with pink, nude forehead, perhaps to be distinguished from the large white *Grus struthio*; eight herons, *Ardea alba, egretta, Candidissima herodias, ludoviciana, coerulea, virescens* and *cayennensis* (*Violacea*, Wis.) all well known; one wood ibis, *Tantalus loculator*; one flamingo, *Phoenicopterus americanus*; two ibises, *Ibis alba* and *rubra*; one spoon-bill, *Platalea ajaja*; one sea-lark, *Hemipalama* (*Tringa*) *semipalmata*; one stilt bird, *Himantopus nigricollis*; one *jacana, Parra jacana* but it is doubtful whether *Parra variabilis* can be called a separate genus; one mud hen, *Rallus virginianus*; one sultan, *Porphyrio martinicensis*; one water hen, *Fulica leucopyga*, Wagl.; one storm bird, *Procellaria Wilsonii*; two gulls, one not accurately determined, the other *Sterna fuliginosa*; four pelicans and *cormorants, Pelecanus thajus*; a large cormorant (*Haliaeus*), which occurs also in Mexico and in Louisiana, and comes close to *Haliaeus cristatus*, moreover, *Dysporus sula* and *tachypetes aquilus*; one plotus, *Plotus anhinga*; four ducks, *Anas moschata, Bahamensis, americana* and *caudacuta*.

Of saurians I collected a few: *Crocodilus acutus, Leguana cornuta*, a *polychrus* with nine stripes on his back, much smaller than *Polychrus VI vittatus*, the *mabouya* of St. Domingo; one *Anolius*, green with rose-colored throat pouch; two *Colubers* which are harmless; two *Chelonias* of the family of land turtles; and a few Batrachians, moreover about forty saltwater and four freshwater fish.

[The bird species which constitute the bulk of the collection described *supra*, now presumably lost as specimens to science, call for the following identifications. It is worth noting that the author's observation of *Trogon silens* precedes Temminck's *Priotelus temnurus* (1825) by two years.

[*Cathartes aura*, turkey vulture. *Falco sparverius*, American sparrow hawk. *Falco uliginosus*, Edw. = *Circus hudsonius*, marsh hawk. *Strix asio?* = *Otus asio*, screech owl, a species not found in the West Indies; the bird Duke Paul collected was probably *Glaucidium siju*, Cuban pygmy owl. "Large black and white, dark-spotted one," possibly *Asio stygius*, stygian owl, but certainly not *Noctua nyctea* = *Nyctea scandiaca*, snowy owl, an arctic species never reported from the West Indies. *Lanius carolinus* = *Lanius ludovicianus*, loggerhead shrike or butcher-bird. *Muscicapa ruticilla* = *Setophaga ruticilla*, American redstart. "Another similar one" probably a female or first-year-male American redstart, but possibly *Coereba flaveola*, bananaquit, a well-known West Indian bird. *M.* (*vireo*) *olivacea* = *Vireo olivaceus*, red-eyed vireo. *M. cantatrix*, Wils. = *Vireo griseus*, white-eyed vireo. *Tyrannus sulphuraceus* = *Tyrannus melancholicus*, tropical kingbird. *T. despotes*, Lich. = *Muscivora tyrannus*, fork-tailed flycatcher. *Tyrannus ferox* = *Myiarchus crinitus*, great crested flycatcher, a rare species in the West Indies (Bond); the bird Duke Paul collected might well have been *Myiarchus stolidus*, stolid flycatcher, a species found widely in the West Indies. "Tyrant bird" *pitirri*, *Tyrannus dominicensis*, gray kingbird or the larger *T. cubensis*, giant kingbird. *T. nigriceps*, Sw.? = *Myiarchus tuberculifer nigriceps*, a montane race of dusky-capped flycatcher found in Ecuador and Colombia; the West Indian race, *M. t. barbirostris*, found only in Jamaica, is considered by some taxonomists to be a full species. *Bombicilla* [*sic*] *americana* = *Bombycilla cedrorum*, cedar waxwing. *Tanagra multicolor* (*Fringilla zena*, Lin.) = *Spindalis zena*, stripe-headed tanager. *Tanagara* [*sic*] *palmarum* (*Icteria*) = *Phaenicophilus palmarum*, black-crowned palm tanager. *Turdus jamaicensis*, white-eyed thrush. *Turdus polyglottus* = *Mimus polyglottos*, northern mockingbird. *Sylvia* (*turdus*) *aurocapillus* = *Seiurus aurocapillus*, ovenbird. *Sylvia pusilla* = *Wilsonia pusilla*, Wilson's or black-capped warbler. *Sylvia olivacea* = *Peucedramus olivaceus*, olive warbler, a continental North American species not reported from the West Indies. The bird Duke Paul collected probably was olive in color, hence might well have been *Dendroica petechia*, yellow warbler, a wide-ranging species some plumages of which are decidedly olive in tone and without much yellow. [*Sylvia*] *trichas* = *Geothlypis trichas*, common yellowthroat. *Hirundo coronata*? = *Petrochelidon fulva*, cave swallow. *Icterus versicolor* = *Quiscalus quiscula*, common grackle, a species not found in the West Indies; the bird Duke Paul collected was probably the Cuban blackbird, *Dives atroviolaceus*. *Cassicus niger* (*Psarocolius*) = *Quiscalus niger*, greater Antillean grackle. [*Cassicus*] *cajanus*. The specific name *cajanus* does not appear in the synonymy of any species of the Icteridae; it does appear, however, in the synonymy of a cotingid, hence the bird Duke Paul obtained might have been *Platpsaris niger*, Jamaican becard, a not very handsome, somewhat blackbird-like species, glossy black above, sooty gray below. [*Cassicus*] *flavigaster* = *Icterus dominicensis*, black-cowled oriole, well known in the West Indies. *Sturnus hypocrepis*, Wagler = *Sturnella magna hypocrepis*, the Cuban race of the eastern meadowlark. *Alauda magna*, Gm. = *Sturnella magna*, eastern meadowlark. *Trochilus gramineus* = *Anthracothorax viridigula*, green-throated mango, not a West Indian species. The bird Duke Paul saw was probably the Cuban emerald, *Chlorostilbon ricordii*, a common species with brilliant green underparts. [*Trochilus*] *colubris*? Probably *Archilochus colubris*, ruby-throated hummingbird, a "not uncommon migrant" in Cuba (Barbour). *Alcedo alcyon* = *Megaceryle alcyon*, belted kingfisher. *Picus radiolatus* = *Centurus radiolatus*, Jamaican woodpecker. [*Picus*] *ruficeps*? = *Veniliornis ruficeps*, a rufous-headed woodpecker, a South American species. The bird Duke Paul collected might have been the Cuban Green Woodpecker, *Xiphidiopicus percussus*, one of the handsomest of West Indian birds. *Cuculus* (*Coccyzus*) *dominicus*? = *Coccyzus minor*, mangrove cuckoo, a rare species in Cuba. *Cuculus carolinensis* = *Coccyzus americanus*, yellow-billed cuckoo. *Arriero, Saurothera merlini*, great lizard cuckoo. *Cuculus* (*Saurothera*) *vetula* = *Saurothera vetula*, Jamaican lizard cuckoo *Couroucou*, probably an onomatopoeic local name for *Temnotrogon roseigaster*, Hispaniolan trogon, whose call is "a loud cock-craow" (Bond). *Trogon silens, mihi* = *Priotelus temnurus*, Cuban trogon, a beautiful species somewhat resembling *Trogon rosalba* = *T. collaris*, bar-tailed or collared trogon, of continental America. The call of the Cuban trogon is, according to Bond, softer than that of the Hispaniolan trogon—a possible explanation of Duke Paul's name *silens*. *Psittacus leucocephalus* = *Amazona leucocephala*, Cuban parrot. "Very small parakeet" probably *Aratinga nana*, olive- throated parakeet. *Tetrao* (*Perdix*) *virginianus* = *Colinus virginianus*, bobwhite quail. "A beautiful genus related to *Odontophorus rufus, Viellot* [*sic*]." Probably not a galliform bird at all, but one of the handsome quail-doves of the genus *Geotrygon*. *Columba leucocephala*, white-crowned pigeon. [*Columba*] *caribaea*, ring-tailed pigeon. [*Columba*] *jamaicensis* = *Leptotila jamaicensis*, white-bellied dove. [*Columba*] *squamose* [sic], red-necked pigeon. [*Columba*] *passerina* = *Columbigallina passerina*, ground dove. *Charadrius vociferus*, killdeer (plover). *Grus americana*, whooping crane. The crane Duke Paul collected was not that species, for his bird was "gray." What he took was a sandhill crane, *Grus canadensis*, a gray species that inhabits Cuba and the Isle of Pines. *Grus struthio* = *Grus americana*, whooping crane. *Ardea alba*, obviously a white heron of some sort, and probably the bird usually called the great white heron, the *Ardea occidentalis* of some authors (AOU *Checklist*, 1957), the white phase of *A. herodias occidentalis* by others (Hellmayr and Conover, 1948, Field Museum Natural History Zoological Series, 13, Pt. 1, No. 2, p. 170). [*Ardea*] *egretta* = *Casmerodius albus*, common egret. [*Ardea*] *Candidissima* = *Leucophoyx thula*, snowy egret. [*Ardea*]*herodias*,

Shortly before my arrival in the city, a thunderstorm overtook me and it began to rain in torrents. This was the first bad weather since my arrival in Cuba. During the month of February several such thunderstorms came which undoubtedly have much to do with the fertility of the island. The temperature of the air was not greatly reduced by these phenomena associated with great electric discharges. Of much more effect on the temperature were several north winds which came during the month. The thermometer sank to 55° and 59°, a point of cold which is felt painfully by the natives. At that time I saw the people of Havana, especially the women, wrapped up to their teeth in their mantillas. The cold air, particularly in the houses, caused a most uncomfortable sensation. Because of the almost continuous perspiring of the body, the skin is much more sensitive to cold.

Since, for my purpose, staying in Havana was not convenient, and since my collections suffered terribly from the moisture in my apartment, I accepted the invitation of a French physician, Mr. Le Dilly, to move to his residence in La Regla. For me this was so much more agreeable, for

---

great blue heron. [*Ardea*] *ludoviciana* = *Hydranassa tricolor*, tricolored or Louisiana heron. [*Ardea*] *coerulea* = *Florida coerulea*, little blue heron. [*Ardea*] *virescens* = *Butorides virescens*, green heron. [*Ardea*] *cayennensis* (*Violacea*, Wils.) = *Nyctanassa violacea*, yellow-crowned night heron. *Tantalus loculator* = *Mycteria americana*, wood ibis or wood stork. *Phoenicopterus americanus* = *Phoenicopterus ruber*, American flamingo. *Ibis alba* = *Eudocimus albus*, white ibis. [*Ibis*] *rubra* = *Eudocimus rubrus*, scarlet ibis. *Platalea ajaja* = *Ajaia ajaja*, roseate spoonbill. *Hemipalama* (*Tringa*) *semipalmata* = *Ereunetes pusillus*, semipalmated sandpiper. *Himantopus nigricollis* = *Himantopus mexicanus*, black-necked stilt. *Parra jacana* = *Jacana spinosa*, jacana. *Parra variabilis* = *Jacana spinosa*, jacana in first winter plumage. *Rallus virginianus* = *Rallus limicola*, Virginia rail, a species considered "accidental" in the West Indies. The bird Duke Paul collected was probably a king rail, *Rallus elegans*, a large bird found in Cuba and the Isle of Pines, or a clapper rail *R. longirostris*, another large species found widely in the West Indies. *Porphyrio martinicensis* = *Porphyrula martinica*, purple gallinule. *Fulica leucopyga*, Wagl. = *Fulica americana*, American coot. *Procellaria Wilsonii* = *Oceanites oceanicus*, Wilson's petrel. *Sterna fuliginosa* = *Sterna fuscata*, sooty tern. *Pelecanus thajus* = *Pelecanus occidentalis thajus*, a western race of the brown pelican; Duke Paul must have collected the eastern (nominate) race. *P. o. occidentalis*. *Haliaeus cristatus* = *Phalacrocorax atriceps*, imperial cormorant, a species that breeds on the coasts of southern South America, in Antarctica, and on certain subarctic islands; the "large cormorant" Duke Paul collected was almost certainly the double-crested cormorant, *Phalacrocorax auritus*. *Dysporus sula* = *Sula sula*, red-faced booby. *Tachypetes aquilus* = *Fregata magnificens*, magnificent frigatebird. *Plotus anhinga* = *Anhinga anhinga*, anhinga or water turkey. *Anas moschata* = *Cairina moschata*, Muscovy duck, a species found in the continental new world tropics; the bird Duke Paul collected was probably the West Indian tree-duck, *Dendrocygna arborea*. [*Anas*] *Bahamensis* = *Anas bahamensis*, white-*cheeked* or Bahaman pintail. [*Anas*] *americana*, American widgeon or baldpate. [*Anas*] *caudacuta* = *Anas acuta*, pintail.]

All of the foregoing data are from Professor George Miksch Sutton, who searched them out for the editor: "*Haud semper errat fama; aliquando et elegit.*"

the region of La Regla is in every respect more advantageous to the student of natural science than Havana.

Mr. Le Dilly occupied a spacious house which served at the same time for the reception of his patients. During my stay of several weeks, there were always a number of yellow fever patients there. Many of them recovered, because Mr. Le Dilly had an excellent method of treating this sickness. It differed greatly from the usual routine, which led the patients to certain death, used in most of the American cities.

The Creoles, especially the colored women, are most skillful in nursing patients of this kind, and their homely remedies, largely of the antiphlogistic healing method, have proven most effective. French physicians, who hitherto have combatted this disease of the West Indies most successfully, have convinced themselves of this method, as I myself have heard from the lips of skilled physicians in Santo Domingo, Havana, and New Orleans. The American physicians, however, who prescribe for almost every ill an excessive amount of mercury, are nothing less than lucky in their cures.

Of all the sea-faring nations, the English and the Spanish are least subject to yellow fever on board their warships, the former on account of the extremely rigid discipline and the excellent nourishment of their sailors and marines, the latter because of their moderation. The English marine hospitals are also a model of cleanliness and orderliness. They are also noted for the quality of drugs which they furnish the sick.

I was fortunate to have found reception at La Regla. In consequence of the exertions in the interior of the island, the cold bath which I had endured prior to my arrival in Havana, and the intensity of the sun's heat, which affects every European, I suffered a serious attack of climatic fever and was laid low in La Regla. Severe vomiting at first caused me to surmise that I must have eaten something harmful. Experts were divided on the diagnosis of my case and several were of the opinion that the consumption of a few oysters from the Manglares might be the cause of my illness. It is true that I had tasted a few of the small bivalves which were fastened to the coral banks and to the stems of the Rhizophora mangle but had found them so ill-tasting that they would not have enticed me.

Mr. Le Dilly soon recognized the true cause of my illness and treated me so skillfully that I was able to get up within a few days though still extremely weak. I only mention this incident in order to warn everyone who comes into a tropical region for the first time against great exertion during the hot noon-day hours, against sudden contraction of colds, and against the consumption of marine animals. Although fish, when fresh, are not usually harmful, caution is nevertheless advisable.

My collections were increased considerably in La Regla, and I had leisure to arrange and pack them. Since I had ascertained that in the neighborhood of La Regla there were several manchineel trees (*Hippomane mancinella*), I resolved to inspect these harmful, poisonous trees, particularly since there was in my house an African Negro who offered to accompany me there. He chose the noon hour, at which time the evaporations of this poisonous plant are not as dangerous as in the moist air of the morning or evening.

In order to reach them, I had to ride for some distance along the shores of the bay and then move along a mangrove-covered swamp connected with the bay. The manchineel trees (there were three average-sized trunks at the end of the stagnant body of salt water) do not attract one's attention by their outer appearance, since their shape and foliage resemble the mangrove very much. They were between fifty and sixty feet high and seemed to have no special influence on the surrounding vegetation.

Taking along sponges saturated with vinegar as a precaution, we approached under the protection of a strong sea breeze. The Negro cut several branches off the tree and a few unripe fruits, since the trees were no longer in bloom. I would have been ready to doubt the statements concerning the poisonous effect of these trees from which the natives flee with horror if, on my return, I had not felt nausea and headache like that of a person who for the first time smokes tobacco. The hands and face of the Negro who had come in direct contact with the tree swelled up and he had to vomit several times.

The external and internal use of sea water is regarded as the remedy for this narcotic intoxication. Certainly washing with vinegar and salt water and the consumption of a few drops of alkali in water is also effective. The smelling of narcotic herbs is sufficient to produce nausea and headache, therefore the deadly effect of the evaporation of an entire tree can be explained similarly, since its entire living organism pours out poisonous vapors.

Shortly before my departure from Cuba a fair was held at Guanabacoa which was attended by a great part of the people of Havana and the population of the neighboring country, thereby furnishing a characteristic picture of the manners, costumes, and customs of this island. In a row of booths and tents, as at every fair, there was a strange crossing of practices and amusements of a Spanish population with that of cultured Europeans and crude Negroes.

Spanish fandangos and boleros accompanied by bagpipes and castanets, French square dances and German waltzes to the music of wind instruments, African songs with a black orchestra that seemed to have been brought from the underworld, processions with burning tapers by day and night, drinking booths and gambling booths, land officers and naval officers, military uniforms of many nations, monks and friars, dandies, rich Creoles and elegant ladies, masks, harlequins and pantaloons, dirty rabble, thieves and beggars, prostitutes, nude Negroes, and colored people of all sorts intermingled here with one another.

But even in this confusion, Spanish politeness did not deny itself, a trait peculiar even to the lowest classes, distinguishing them from other nations. The irresistible inclination to gambling, which is common in the colonies, manifested itself here in its ugliest form. Large tables were occupied by monte and chussa players, the owners of these tables being privileged as are those of our gambling houses. At the tables of these sharpers all the expressions of distorted passion were depicted.

I was advised to overcome my repugnance and risk a chance at one of these gambling tables, since the owners of these institutions make common cause with one another and are in league with highwaymen and other low rabble. After I had deposited my gold piece I left and paid no more heed to its fate.

When I returned to La Regla dark night had descended. At the entrance of a narrow passage my *volanta* was suddenly halted, but they were not robbers, only armed men in the service of the police who, for the sake of my safety, conducted me through the passage.

Finally, I allow myself to add a few notes regarding the commerce of Havana. From January 1, 1822, to December 31 of the same year, there entered the harbor of Havana 72 Spanish warships, 69 of other nations, and 1,296 merchantmen, among them 386 Spanish, 669 American, 118 English, 62 French, 18 Dutch, 12 from Hamburg, 7 from Bremen, 6 Danish, 7 Portuguese, 4 Swedish, 2 piracy prizes, 2 Sicilian, 1 from Oldenburg, and 1 from Colombia.

Vessels going out were 64 Spanish and 69 foreign warships, 313 Spanish and 805 foreign merchantmen. From the harbor of Havana there were exported 261,795 cases of sugar, 501,529 *arrobas*[90] of coffee, 14,450 *arrobas* wax, 4,633 *pipas*[91] of sugar-cane brandy (*aguardiente de canna*), and 34,604 barrels of purified molasses. Accordingly, the exportation of sugar exceeded that of last year by 25,126 cases.

During the latter part of my stay the weather had become cold and stormy, and violent west and northwest winds made the departure of ships difficult. I had arranged passage to New Orleans on an American brig, the *Sarah Ann*, commanded by a Frenchman. For several days I had to wait

[90] The *arroba*, a Spanish measure, equals 3.32 U.S. gallons.
[91] One *pipa*, a Portuguese measure, equals 115.0 U.S. gallons.

for more favorable wind and better weather, for the sea ran very high and pounded with great force against the north coast of Cuba. Finally, on February 17, the storm subsided and the weather became fair. On the following morning at nine o'clock the brigantine weighed its anchors and made use of a faint wind from the southwest by south to leave the harbor.

A large number of foreign vessels, especially English, took advantage of the same wind for their departure to sail under the protection of the British fleet, which was just then cruising in sight of the city. The warships of the various flags had their hands full at that time to clear the sea of pirates, who made the waters of the West Indies unsafe. Never had this nuisance been as great as then. The sea ran extremely high and the ships battled severely against the waves. Indeed it was not until almost evening that we lost sight of Morro.

On the afternoon of the nineteenth at three o'clock, at 25° 3′ northern latitude and 83° 41′ western longitude, an armed vessel came near us. It identified itself as a privateer from Buenos Aires and had eighteen guns on board. It was great luck for me that I had not entrusted myself to a Spanish vessel, otherwise I might have started on a journey to La Plata instead of the Mississippi.

During the night the wind rose with increased intensity, first from the west and then from the northwest. On the twentieth great schools of dolphins appeared, traveling from the west to the northeast. The storm continued to rage during the night, but toward morning it turned to the southwest by south. On the twenty-second we passed 27° latitude and now the wind subsided. With the sea still running deep and very high our already leaky brig was tried to the utmost and our condition appeared intensely perilous.

On the evening of the twenty-third the wind rose with great fury, the storm coming from the northwest once more. These violent gusts of wind alternated with a heavy downpour of rain accompanied by loud claps of thunder, and this ended in a sudden calm which was more dangerous than the storm itself. The *Sarah Ann* became more and more leaky and drew so much water that a third of the crew had to work at the pumps.

Early on the twenty-fifth, before sunrise, the severe west wind had driven us so near Cape St. Blasio, about 29° 30′ north latitude and 85° 30′ west longitude, that there appeared little hope of saving the heavily damaged ship in the storm.

The great vessel, which was quite seaworthy, was now put in order for the utmost emergency, since the crew was scarcely sufficient for the pumps. The coast lying before us was a low sand dune, its background overgrown with reeds and coast palms, as are all the coastal regions of Florida and the

Mississippi. The higher land was a forest of pine trees (*Pinus palustris*).

At this critical moment the wind suddenly changed to the northeast. The weather cleared and on the morning of the twenty-seventh, at nine o'clock, a pilot from the mouth of the Mississippi came on board. With the excessive amount of water in the hull and with the faint wind, the brig could not make more than two or three knots. In the evening at seven o'clock we were at the main channel (*Grande Passe*) but could not enter because of the darkness and had to drop anchor at 29° north latitude and 89° 19′ west longitude.

With great difficulty the brig was piloted into the stream on the twenty-eighth but had to cast anchor two English miles from the Balize. After her leaks had been perfunctorily calked, the *Sarah Ann* reached the chief city of Louisiana on the fourth of March, ending an extremely difficult and slow journey.

3

During my final stay in New Orleans I found sufficient leisure to prepare myself for the somewhat difficult and tedious journey into the northwest interior of America. The season of the year and the high water level of the Mississippi were so favorable that a longer postponement would have become disadvantageous. There were also other factors which made the departure of the steamboat on which I engaged passage most desirable.

This year nature had adorned itself later than usual with her garment of spring, inspiring me with the hope that I might be able to observe the period of development of the revived plant world in upper Louisiana during the transition from the cold to the warm season. I was anxious to make this observation in a country located so close to the hot belt and yet so relatively close to the temperate climate that it consequently is strikingly different from the low-lying lands of the Old World at the same degree of latitude.

The cold winter of 1822 and 1823, with its extremely rapid changes of temperature from heat to frost, such as had not occurred at the mouth of the Mississippi in memory of man, reacted on all organic matter, but especially on the plant world, with that force which extremes always manifest, with their damaging effect, when they come intermittently after long intervals.

I contemplated making a stop of a few weeks at a point about fifty hours up the river and chose for this journey the steamboat *Feliciana*, which makes regular trips from New Orleans to Bayou Sara, a small settlement on the Mississippi not far from St. Francisville.

In the chief city I had been supplied with so many letters of recommendation by the best houses that I did not doubt for an instant that this well-meaning generosity would assure me the best reception. Mr. Louis Tainturier, a very well informed Creole and an enthusiastic student of nature whose friendship I had the good fortune of winning, wished to accompany me to Bayou Sara to pursue the same objective. He also made all necessary preparations for a short, but for him nevertheless interesting, excursion.[1]

Since strict regulations prevail on the steamboats in America and the hour set for departure ordinarily is observed to the minute, I was obliged to be on board of the *Feliciana* with my luggage on March 19, an hour before departure. Most of my friends in the city had accompanied me as far as the customs house, not far from which the steamboat lay at anchor, taking cordial leave of me and once more they reiterated every argument to make me waver in my resolve to travel up the Mississippi.

With sincere emotion I parted from these gentlemen, several of whom I was never to see again, and hastily betook myself on board the *Feliciana*. Mr. Tainturier almost came too late, because for him the leave-taking was more difficult than for me, for in the climate of the hot zone, so harmful to health, sensitive persons are greatly carried away by their emotions when they leave their friends and relatives, even though it may be for only a very short time. With his arrival on the boat the clock struck eleven, at the same moment the tow lines were loosened and the machinery started to move.

The steamboat *Feliciana* is one of the most complete vessels of its kind that ply the waters of North America. The pleasantness of its extra-ordinarily rapid speed, due to its excellent machinery, is increased still more by the comfort provided for the passengers. The two public rooms provided for gentlemen and ladies are simply and beautifully decorated and are kept very tidy. The fare was fifteen dollars per person from New Orleans to Bayou Sara and included, as is customary in America, three meals a day, namely at nine o'clock in the morning, two in the afternoon, and eight in the evening. However, still not satisfied with these luxurious meals, the Americans usually partake of light snacks at eleven and four o'clock.

The company which made the trip with me on the boat to Bayou Sara, or to other places along the river nearer the city, consisted of planters, French Creoles, as well as Anglo-Americans, several officers of the garrison at Baton Rouge, a family of traveling musical artists, and a few young ladies. In all, there were about thirty persons who tried to banish boredom in every conceivable manner, chiefly with games of cards.

When one has passed the last dwellings which might be called a suburb

[1] The author's traveling companion was the man for whom the umbelliferous species, *Chaerophyllum tainturieri,* was named.

of New Orleans, the left bank of the river spreads out in those desolate lowlands with swampy surface subject to the regular floodings of the Mississippi, where cypresses grow and occasionally a few leaf-bearing trees intersperse with some climbing plants. Nature seems to provide these regions in contrast to the bright, cheerful skies of latitude 30° with those gloomy evergreens whose depressing parasite, the tillandsia, heightens the melancholy impression still more.

If the mood which these forests produce were not dispelled by the reality of the burning heat of the sun and the sight of the alligators and the dwarf palms, the traveler would believe himself transported to the high latitudes of the far north. The opposite bank, on the other hand, is in cultivation, with a number of gardens and orange groves joining the houses of the planters, which supply the market of New Orleans at all seasons with vegetables and fruit.

At one o'clock in the afternoon our boat had already passed two bends in the river, the one extending from south to west, and the other at the sugar plantation of Forteus from south to northeast by north. The east bank of the river is everywhere more settled than the west bank, and here are many sugar plantations of whose arrangement I have spoken in the previous chapter.

In the vicinity of the dwelling places I frequently observed a willow with drooping branches, resembling our weeping willow, and also the *Yucca filamentosa*, which occurs in all of North America south of latitude 33°, developing its beautiful white cluster of blossoms in May, June, and July.[2] The not yet definitely determined cactus of Louisiana, different from *Cactus opuntia*, in contrast to most varieties of this generous genus prefers the moist rich banks of the river and will be more and more disposed of by the cultivation of the land. It is feared in Louisiana because of its barbs and is not used for enclosures of cultivated fields as is in Cuba its relative the *Cactus tuna*.[3]

Twelve miles from New Orleans, after the last of the above-named bends is passed, the journey extends northwestward along cultivated banks. The dwellings of the planters, who surround their houses with gardens and orange groves, appear most comfortable, and the large number of Negroes working in the sugar-cane and maize fields indicate the great prosperity which the inhabitants of lower Louisiana enjoy.

The abundant harvest of sugar cane and the huge demand for unrefined Louisiana sugar on the market make this branch of agriculture one of the

---

[2] *Yucca filamentosa*, yucca or Adam's needle.

[3] *Cactus opuntia*, a prickly pear; *Cactus tuna*, *Opuntia tuna*, a prickly pear.

most profitable, especially since sugar cane requires the least care of all the products of the colonies and is influenced less by weather conditions than any other useful plant of the hot zone.

Among all the nutritious plants in the family of grasses the Indian maize (*Zea mays*) yields the greatest harvest in the most varied climates of the New World, and the lower classes of people, especially the blacks, are used to this nutriment, preferring it over any other cereal. Moreover, maize requires almost no care in the warmer zones and yields multiple gain of its seed.

The river now runs for almost twelve English miles in a nearly straight line to the northwest. The dwellings of the richest planters of Louisiana are in this region. Their possessions, separated from one another only by their gardens and plantations, touch upon one another without interruption. In the manner of the French colonies they are divided into parishes (*paroisses*), a custom dating back to the earliest time of the colonization and settlement of Louisiana, or Nouvelle France, under the reign of Louis XV. The first church I reached among these parishes was the Red Church (*Église Rouge*), eighteen miles from the city.

The weather had remained beautiful during the entire day and the temperature of the air not too hot, although, to judge from appearances, the great heat in these parts threatened to come. The observation seems to be valid that after a cold winter in Louisiana heat with prevailing drought will set in earlier than ordinarily.

In the evening the foreign artists entertained the company with music, and that night but few passengers could sleep because some of our fellow passengers, all young people, had imbibed too much grog and spent the night until morning with noisy conversation and card games.

Since the moon shone and the night was fairly clear, the steamboat continued its journey uninterruptedly. This practice of traveling during the night is customary on the principal rivers in the United States, although, especially during low water, it is not without danger. For me this type of traveling was not desirable, for I was deprived of the sight of the land we were passing. And the noise of the machinery disturbed my sleep, which may perhaps happen to all passengers who for the first time travel on this kind of boat.

The steamboat made a distance of thirty-five miles up to the evening of the nineteenth, thus early in the morning of the twentieth of March we were near the outlet of the Bayou la Fourche, which empties toward the sea coast and near which the cohesive French Creole settlement bearing the same name forms a parish. Because of the darkness of the night I was not able to observe the location of the parishes, Bonne Chaire and Contrelles (Bona Cabra Church), situated on the right bank of the Mississippi.

Judging by the height of the deciduous trees, one can conclude with certainty that the ground is drier and more fertile than that of the areas nearer the city. The Mississippi makes several big bends before reaching the wide arms which flow out of the stream at Plaquemine, one in a southwesterly direction into the Gulf of New Spain, and one at Iberville from the north to the southeast emptying into Lake Maurepas.

The first of these bends extends from the south to the northeast and west, if the observer takes his direction coming upstream. Halfway around the bend, extending from south to north, is an island one and one-half English miles long and one-half a mile wide, ninety-two English miles from New Orleans. This island is situated in the middle of the river, dividing it into two almost equal parts. The edges of the island are heavily overgrown with a willow (*Salix nigra?*) which is common along the Mississippi, while the interior supports mainly poplars (*Populus deltoides*, Marsh, and *Diospyros virginica*, Linn.).[4]

The alligators, which I had not noticed at our departure from New Orleans, began to appear again, although not as numerous as at the mouth of the river below the city, or upriver in the region of Acheffalaya, the Red River (Rio Colorado de Nachitoches), and the Yazoo. Even though these creatures are not induced by the great population of the land to leave their habitat voluntarily, they must nevertheless, despite their vast increase, diminish by and by because they are destroyed in great numbers. Nature has limited the senses of these huge amphibia so much that they unconsciously approach impending danger. The poisonous snakes, however, find among the hogs and dogs such powerful enemies that they must retreat from the vicinity of inhabited places. Already vermin and noxious animals have greatly decreased in the inhabited parts of America.

The above-mentioned American lotus (*Diospyros virginica*, Linn.) which is closely related to its kin in Asia, where it lives under similar climatic conditions, is as much treasured as a food by the aborigines of the new continent as it was by the peoples of the Old World during the first period of Greek history.[5] This plant seems to have chosen as its main

---

[4] *Salix nigra*, the black willow, is probably correct; *Populus deltoides*, the eastern cottonwood; *Diospyros virginica* = *D. virginiana*, the persimmon.

[5] *Author*: The writers of Greece have applied the name lotus (λοτος) to several plants, even to some water plants, as the *Lotus aegyptia* of the Nile, a Nymphaea, the *nenuphar* of the Egyptians. Among the tree-like plants with edible fruits, the ancients understood the *Celtis australis* (French *micoulies*), the *coccamo* or *menicucco* of the Sicilians, moreover, two kinds of *Rhamnus*, the *zizyphus* and *jujuba* of the Africans, which Homer mentions in the Odyssey, likewise the *Diospyros lotus*, Linn. [The reference here is to *Diospyros virginiana*, the persimmon.]

habitat the banks of the Mississippi, where it is found growing singly and in groups much more frequently than in other places more distant from the river. The Europeans, while they also relish the fruit, which ripens in the late autumn, nevertheless cannot attribute to it that excellence which Homer does in his *Odyssey*, where he compares it to the food of the gods.

At about eleven o'clock we were opposite the church of Manchac, situated on the left bank of the river, where we let two passengers land. The houses of this parish are noticeably different in appearance, size, and excellence of arrangement from those further down the river. The decrease in the wealth of the planters living upstream is no doubt due to the branch of agriculture practiced here, for sugar cane, which does not prosper beyond Manchac, assures a much better income than cotton.

At noon the boat arrived at the outlet of Bayou Plaquemine, constituting one of the important outlets of the Mississippi from the north to the southwest, which makes possible the hydrographic connection in the western part of Louisiana. Those far-running branches make accessible not only the swampy deltas of the Mississippi and the Plaquemine, hardly accessible by road, but also the fertile strips of land of the Atacapas and the Opelousas.

The Bayou Plaquemine flows out of the Mississippi at 30° 13′ north latitude and 15° 17′ west longitude from Washington, and after a course of few hours in a westerly direction combines with the vast Bayou Acheffalaya, which also flows from the Mississippi in the region of Tunica at 30° 58′ north latitude and 15° 45′ longitude west of Washington. After flowing almost directly south, intertwined in a network system of greater or smaller water connections, it reaches the sea at 29° 15′ north latitude, forming Acheffalaya Bay. The little river La Fourche, running almost parallel to the Acheffalaya, which originates in the Mississippi at Donaldsonville, is separated from the Acheffalaya by swampy land through which several small rivers flow in a southerly direction to the sea.

The entire region between the Mississippi and the Acheffalaya to the mouths of these two rivers including the coast is dotted with a great number of lakes and channels connecting them. All of these are influenced by the inundations of the Mississippi, and the amount of water they contain is dependent on whether the river is high or low, but they are navigable only with small vessels and boats.

Perhaps no river in the world has so many outlets and water connections near its mouth as the Mississippi. Although it is not connected by means of channels with other rivers that empty into the sea, as for example the Orinoco with the Maranon via the Rio Negro, nevertheless the countless channels which the Mississippi forms with its own outlets or with the rivers that empty into it make it a unique example of this type among all the river systems of our planet known to us.

To discuss the entire supply system here would be an extensive piece of work which would furnish material enough for a separate treatise on geography. Because of my all too short stay in Louisiana I could not possibly obtain a complete view of the whole, and therefore I shall content myself to communicate only such conclusions as are absolutely necessary in connection with my journey and encompass general comparative geography.

The chart accompanying this chapter was drawn from the best source and on a reduced scale from the chart of Louisiana which is Number 31 of the *American Atlas*, published in 1823 by H. C. Carey and J. Lea in Philadelphia, and gives an accurate idea of the entire hydrographic system of the Mississippi from 33° down.[6]

The many lakes and morasses lying within the delta formed by the Mississippi and the Acheffalaya are almost all connected by channels. So, for example, Lac des Allemands, which is connected with the Mississippi by means of a channel, is also connected by tributaries with the lakes Quachi, Petit, and Bond, all of which pour their water through Lac des Îlets into the sea. Lac des Allemands has also its own outlet into the Bay of Barataria and is connected with the Mississippi. It has also a connection through the Bayou and Lake Chetimachas with La Fourche River, which, although pouring its waters into the sea, also has a connection with the Mississippi.

The lakes Verret and Poulourde are connected with the Acheffalaya not only through Berwiks Channel, but also by other connections. Above the Plaquemine, in the West Baton Rouge and the Pointe Coupée districts, the bayous Grosse Tête, Maringoin, and a few other channels likewise connect with the overgrown cypress region of both outlets of the Mississippi. The

---

[6] Duke Paul's reproduction of this map appeared following the advertisement pages of his publisher, J. G. Cotta'sche Verlagshandlung, Stuttgart and Tübingen, devoted to an early-day Exploration and Travel Series (*Reisen und Länderbeschreibungen der ältern und neusten Zeit* . . .). The present reproduction appears as close as possible to the author's reference to it in the text, i.e., on pages 92–93. His source was *American Atlas: A Complete Historical, Chronological, and Geographical American Atlas, Being a Guide to the History of North and South America, and the West Indies . . . to the Year 1822* (Philadelphia, Carey and Lea, 1823).

Even as the Duke was preparing his work for publication in 1834–1835, the Frenchman Joseph Nicolas Nicollet was fixing the geographical location of the mouth of the Mississippi in preparation for the explorations and the mapping of the upper Mississippi (Nicollet, *Report Intended to Illustrate a Map of the Hydrographical Basin of the Upper Mississippi River* . . . 26 Cong., 2d sess., *Senate Document 237*, 1843).

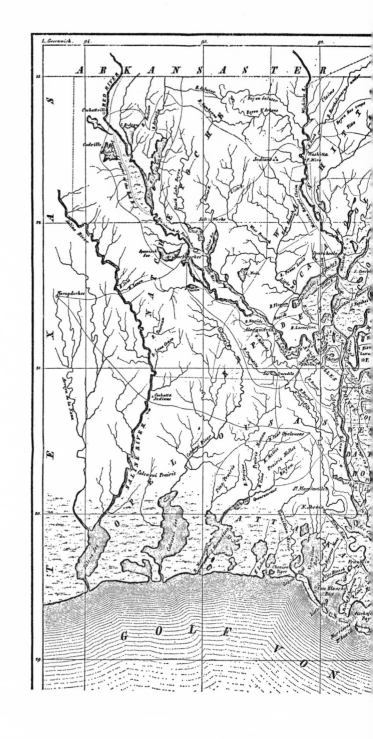

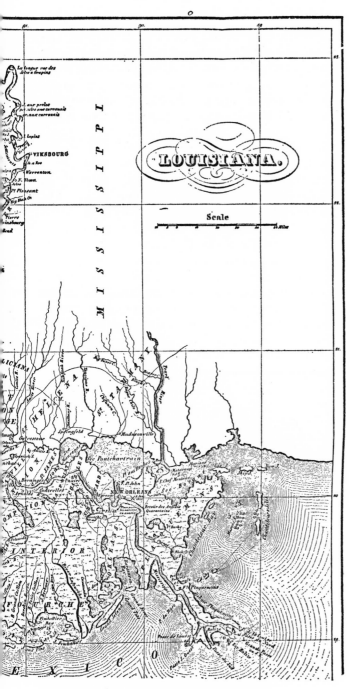

Louisiana (From Duke Paul's *Erste Reise*)

small rivers Boeuf and Crocodile which flow in the same direction as the Red River, north to southeast, after having originated in the region of the rapids of the latter river, unite in the Opelousas and after a short union separate again and flow in four divisions into the Acheffalaya. The larger of these arms attains importance only below Lac Chetimachas and under the name of Bayou Teche it waters the region of the Attacapus, whose main settlements, St. Martinville and New Iberia, are situated in a most fertile lowland country.

These lowlands, separated by low hills overgrown with tall grasses, herbaceous plants, and bushes scarcely as tall as a man, border the sea coast on the south, and because of its meager elevation above the level of the Gulf of Mexico this region is swampy and overgrown with tall reeds. The adjoining savannas, however, extend almost uninterruptedly to the north and west to the highlands of New Spain,[7] and with progressing settlement and cultivation of the land they will undoubtedly in later times constitute one of the most important sections of the new continent.

Since the Calcasue and Sabine rivers in Louisiana, which empty into the bays of like name, are navigable, the products of the Opelousas can be exported by the closest route, as can those of the Atacapas by way of Bayous Teche and Vermillion. The fairly well settled prairies Mellet and Mannou are connected with the sea by the Bayous Nepique, Canne, and Quencutortue, which empty into the Bay of Mermentas, but are, however, less suitable for navigation.

The tribes of aborigines, who in earlier times pursued the first settlers with hostility, have in part entirely died out or have withdrawn to a region between the Sabine and the Bravo Rivers. The few weak remnants of the red population of the Attacapas and Opelousas who still roam through the country are friendly and live by hunting and fishing. The Attacapas and Chetimachas, who live on the banks of the lake bearing this name and who were so greatly feared at the time of the discovery and settlement of western Louisiana, have, for but a few families, completely died out.[8] The already very much weakened Indians of Calcasue and Coshatta and

---

[7] New Spain was no longer valid as a geographical term in 1823, two years after Mexican independence, which removed Texas, New Mexico, and much of Colorado from direct Spanish control.

[8] The Attacapas, sole representatives of their linguistic branch, became known to the French explorers and religious as early as 1703, when Sieur de Bienville's men traveled among them in Louisiana. They once occupied much of the southwestern portion of that territory, hunting seasonally westward into Texas for buffalo. By 1885 there may have been no more than a dozen Attacapas surviving.

The Opelusas, according to John R. Swanton, were closely allied to the Attacapas and may have spoken a dialect of the latter language.

the friendly Tunicas and Choctaws,[9] who roam over all of Louisiana, constitute the last of the red population of this section.[10]

The savannas to 30° 15′ north latitude seem particularly well suited to the cultivation of sugar cane, while, on the other hand, those farther north seem to invite the cultivation of rice, cotton, and tobacco. Therefore stock raising should be profitable on the savanna and the large herds of cattle and horses ought to equal those that graze on the pampas of Paraguay and Buenos Aires.

The prairie situated between the Arkansas, Rio Colorado de Texas, and Rio Bravo del Norte already feed countless wild horses in addition to vast herds of bison (Spanish, *cibola*). The prairie Indians (*Indianos llaneros bravos*), Comanches and Pawnees and others who as mounted tribes resemble the Bedouins of the Arabian desert, catch these wild horses by means of long ropes with a noose made of bison hair and then break them.

The Spaniards make use of the same expedient with a skill that is peculiar to these people. This practice, which seems to have been trans-

The Chitimachas, also considered the sole representatives of their linguistic branch, were brought to terms by Bienville in 1706.

Hodge, *Handbook*, I, 114–15. 286; II, 139–40.

[9] For the Indians at Calcasue, see Athanase de Mézières, *Athanase de Mézières and the Louisiana-Texas Frontier, 1768–1780* . . . (2 vols.), edited by Herbert Eugene Bolton, II, 107n. Mézières indicated an Attacapa town. "Coshatta" appears in Jedediah Morse, *A Report to the Secretary of War of the United States, on Indian Affairs* . . . (New Haven, 1822). The tribe is the Koasati, an Upper Creek group speaking a language almost identical with that of the Alibamu, one of the Creek Confederacy in the eighteenth century and later, according to Hodge.

The Tunicas, largely sedentary, early became allied with the French (1699) and continued in friendly relations with the latter, thus escaping the fate of other Indian groups beset either by the French or by other Indians, or by both.

The Choctaws thrived in the forepart of the eighteenth century, in friendship with the French, later siding with the English, until they removed past mid-century across the Mississippi.

Indian cultures and ways in early Louisiana are depicted in Antoine Simon Le Page du Pratz, *Histoire de la Louisiane*, 3 vols. (Paris, 1758), II [203]–242; Hodge, *Handbook*, *passim*; Angie Debo, *The Rise and Fall of the Choctaw Republic*, 25–34.

[10] *Author*: In 1719 the Attacapas captured M. de Charleville and M. de Bellisle, who had lost their way while hunting. Since these natives lived far from the French settlements of that time on the Mississippi, they were not known to the settlers, and there existed neither a state of war nor of peace between them. Since M. de Charleville was very corpulent, he was killed at once with clubs and eaten. M. de Bellisle, however, was kept for a later feast but was freed by the timely intervention of his countrymen. In the treaty made between the French with the Attacapas, the latter had to agree as a principal condition to refrain from eating human flesh, but it is doubtful whether they fulfilled this condition. (*Mémoires de M. du Mont, sur la Louisiane; Histoire de la Louisiane par Le Page du Pratz.*) [The "M. du Mont" here is Georges-Marie Butel-Dumont, author of *Mémoires historiques sur la Louisiane* . . . 2 vols. (Paris, 1755).]

mitted by the Moors to the inhabitants of the Iberian Peninsula, has thus passed from the peoples of the Orient to those of the New World. The *lassos* which I brought with me and which I obtained from the Pawnees and the Arapahos are made of the hair of the bison and closely resemble those of the Kirghiz and the Kalmucks, only that the latter are made from the hair of the tail of horses.

The few houses which are at the mouth of the Plaquemine deserve no further mention, except to say that those travelers who wish to go to the western regions are allowed to land here and to find lodging. Provision is also made for the storing of goods and wares to await further transportation.

At Plaquemine the river makes a bend to the east to Bayou Manchac, usually called Rivière Iberville. Bayou Manchac forms a connection of the Mississippi with the sea from the north to the southeast through the lakes Maurepas, Pontchartrain, Borgne, and the Bay Chandeleur. During high water from the upper Mississippi, navigation to Florida is made possible through this natural channel so that ships do not have to follow the main stream via New Orleans.

At the little town of Galvestone the Iberville takes up the rather important Amitié River, which has its origin in the northern part of the state of Mississippi. Since the above named lakes are always supplied with sufficient water, and the Pontchartrain, which at Chef Manteur is connected by a deep channel with the continuation of Bay Chandeleur, navigation on the interior waters between the coast of Mobile and upper Louisiana will encourage the establishment of a number of settlements in the sparsely settled districts of Baton Rouge, St. Helena, and St. Tommany.[11]

A few miles above the outlet of Bayou Iberville, the first chain of hills rises from the low shoreland on the left bank of the Mississippi and connects with the interior solid land, thus protecting these areas against the periodic overflow of the river. These hills, attaining a height of scarcely one hundred feet, are a formation of secondary limestone, clay, and sand, and extend upward along the river through the regions of East Baton Rouge and a part of Feliciana between the little Bois Rouge River and the Mississippi, then extend northward into the state of Mississippi.

[11] *Author*: St. Helena in 1820 had a total population of 3,026 souls, of whom 2,164 were whites, 830 black slaves, and 32 free Negroes. St. Tommany had a total population of 1,723, of whom 1,053 were whites, 631 black slaves, and 39 free Negroes. East Baton Rouge had a total population of 5,220, of whom 3,012 were whites, 2,076 black slaves, and 312 free Negroes. The total number of inhabitants was 9,969 individuals of all colors and sexes. [All three of the above designations are of parishes, the equivalent of counties in other states, of which St. Tammany is the correct name for one, which has Covington for its capital; Baton Rouge, of East Baton Rouge; and Greensburg, of St. Helena.]

Along the river bed these hills have been eroded by the constant action of the river, so that in the center they have the form of bisected cones, and in their cuts these parallel-running layers, permeated by dark-colored veins, are distinctly visible. The abrupt walls are covered with some evergreen bushes, among them especially frequent are *Laurus sassafras*, Linn. and *Myrica caroliniensis*, Willd.[12] The trees on the hills are those leafy varieties common to the elevated parts of Louisiana and the southern part of the United States. The different varieties appear in separate clumps and I intend to speak of them in some detail in the course of my work.

We reached the small town of Baton Rouge about four o'clock in the afternoon and stopped there for about an hour. Built on terraces without order on the slope of a hill, the town is 138 English miles from New Orleans and numbers about 80 houses and 400 inhabitants. The population increases very slowly because of the fever prevailing here every summer. The houses are unpretentious one-story structures made of wood. In Baton Rouge a military force of between 400 and 500 regulars is stationed, quartered in a fort surrounded by palisades. The commandant of the garrison and several other officers were so kind as to pay me a visit on board the boat and expressed great interest in my undertaking. Several officers of higher rank were present at Baton Rouge, among whom I should mention General Atkinson who has become famous because of the military posts which he established on the Missouri and Mississippi.[13] There was also a colonel who had been commandant at Pensacola and who had received his education in the Karlsschule in Stuttgart.[14]

Not far from Baton Rouge in a valley formed by hills a German settlement, which does not have the appearance of great prosperity, is located. The extremely unhealthful climate and the many obstacles which all colonists have to face when first settling are sufficient reasons to dissuade all European immigrants from seeking their fortune in Louisiana.

That same evening we traveled eighteen miles farther upstream to the beginning of several islands which are called Îles du Prophèts. Because of

[12] *Laurus sassafras* = *Sassafras albidium*, sassafras; *Myrica caroliniensis*, bayberry.

[13] Baton Rouge Barracks, as a site, was first visited by Pierre Le Moyne, Sieur d'Iberville, in 1699 during an exploring expedition on the Lower Mississippi. The French made it a fort in 1719, but lost it in 1763 to the British, who garrisoned it. By 1803 it had passed to the U.S. with the Louisiana Purchase but remained in Spanish-French hands to 1810, when revolting American settlers occupied it September 23 of that year. It was more or less regularly garrisoned by the U.S. from 1810 and remained important militarily to 1882.

[14] Of General Henry Atkinson we will hear more in subsequent chapters. Which colonel commanded at Pensacola after the capture of Fort Don Carlos de Barancas from the Spaniards in 1818, during the Seminole campaign by generals Andrew Jackson and Edmund P. Gaines, is not clear.

approaching darkness, we cast anchor on the left bank of the river. Since the steamboat started early on the morning of the 21st, at dawn we were at the mouth of Thompson Creek, which flows into the Mississippi from the east. On its banks are a few cotton plantations notable for their rich yield. The soil is very fertile, especially for maize, which assures the most abundant harvest.

The river makes a turn to the northwest and then extends for almost sixteen English miles to the north along the coast of Pointe Coupée. The outlet of Fausse Rivière, which makes a horseshoe-shaped bend in direction to the west and north and surrounds Pointe Coupée like a bent lake, is to the northwest at a distance of two miles from Thompson Creek on the thinly wooded west bank of the river. Since I visited this region later I will reserve its description to another time and now pursue the thread of my story.

The left bank of the river, as far as Bayou Sara, is not settled at all and presents to the observer only a flat lowland, subject to the inundations of the Mississippi, a swampy forest consisting of cypresses and poplars permeated by many channels and morasses. In the somewhat drier places the ground is shaded by an impenetrable thicket of thorn bushes and clinging plants or the dense-growing giant reeds of the Mississippi (*Miegia macrosperma*, Pres.) which border the great stream as far as the mouth of the Ohio.[15] The low shore land on the east bank of the Mississippi is broken for some distance by a chain of hills connecting the heights of St. Francisville with those of Baton Rouge.

The first houses of the almost eighteen-mile-long parish Pointe Coupée extend to a place near the Fausse Rivière. The industry which is everywhere in evidence in this colony of French Creoles presents a pleasing contrast to the lack of development on the opposite bank, which is still left entirely in its primitive natural state.

[15] *Author:. Miegia macrosperma*, Pres., is closely related through its outward characteristics to *Arundo, Nastus*, and *Bambusa*. Walther calls it *Arundo gigantea* and he estimates its height correctly at twenty to twenty-six feet. He separates *Arundo gigantea* from *Arundo tecta*, with smaller leaves and occurring on the banks of rivers which flow into the sea and the morasses east of the Mississippi. Here belongs also *Ludolphia mississippiensis*, Willd., and other grasses, the study of which is generally neglected in this part of the world and is still in a state of great confusion.

The varieties of *Miegia* north of latitude 34° are much shorter than those of Louisiana. Since these blossom but rarely and since they resemble one another so much externally, errors are easily possible. I never saw the Mississippi reed bloom in its native habitat and only through the kindness of Mr. Desfontaines in Paris was I able to procure the blossom of this Arundinacee.

[*Ludolphia mississippiensis Willd.* is doubtful for Willdenow. *Ludolphia macrosperma* (Michx.) Willd. was based on *Arundaria macrosperma* Michx., a synonym of *Arundaria gigantea*.]

At half past nine the steamboat arrived at the settlement Bayou Sara, consisting of only a few houses and opposite the church of Pointe Coupée. Bayou Sara is really only a depot of St. Francisville, situated on an elevation one English mile from the Mississippi. The few wooden shacks, whose style would never permit them to be called houses, are inundated almost annually during the overflow of the Mississippi, and are really only stores or warehouses of the merchants of St. Francisville.

I had letters of recommendation at the latter place and found to my great pleasure one of my fellow countrymen. Mr. Holl from Ulm, in Bayou Sara who, although established in St. Francisville, also had a small warehouse on the banks of the river. I soon found myself surrounded by several Germans, who extended me a hearty reception and expressed the keenest pleasure in seeing a stranger who only a short while ago had left the beloved fatherland, and who now, visiting his brothers in a foreign land, could tell them everything that he knew regarding their true homeland. How joyously pass the hours in which the recollection of the plains arouses a common interest among people whom different conditions of life have held apart, and yet who, at great distances and under the most varied climates, feel a common bond.

After an hour I was obliged to interrupt this extremely pleasant conversation with my new friends, in order to accompany Mr. Nicholl, a wealthy planter from Pointe Coupée, to his home, a cotton plantation which he owns. I had received special recommendations to Mr. Nicholl in New Orleans and had become acquainted with this courteous and hospitable American aboard the *Feliciana*. As is the custom of the country, he did not fail to invite me to make his residence my home. Since I contemplated stopping some time at Pointe Coupée, I would have offended this obliging, cordial planter sorely if I had not accepted his invitation. Having given my German countrymen in Bayou Sara the definite assurance that I would visit them for a longer time a few weeks later, I parted from them with a melancholy feeling, deeply moved by their genial reception.

A few Negroes belonging to Mr. Nicholl had come across the river to Bayou Sara in a small boat to meet their master. I entered this boat with my new host while my friend Tainturier undertook to follow with the remaining passengers and the baggage in a barge. Since the Mississippi, which was at a high-water stage, flows very rapidly in some places, the crossing from one bank to the other usually takes a long time. The vessels must be rowed a great distance upstream near the bank, for the current is not as swift there as in the middle of the deepest part of the river. The boats must go far above the desired point on the opposite bank, then allow themselves to drift with the current in a slanting direction to the point of their destination.

With a strong and contrary wind, the passage in small boats is not only tedious but also somewhat dangerous, especially if one encounters great masses of driftwood and other obstructions.

Our small boat had difficulty in winding its way through the many willows (*Salix nigra ?*) which reached up from the water close to the bank. The sight of alligators with heads protruding from the water or resting on uprooted tree trunks, of which there are large numbers on the left bank of the river, entertained me during our passage, which lasted almost one and one-half hours. Not until two hours later did Mr. Tainturier, together with my servant, his little son, and the Negro slave, arrive at the residence of Mr. Nicholl.

The shaded dwelling of Mr. Nicholl, surrounded by catalpas and other native trees, the entire plantation, and the vast number of well-fed black slaves gave the impression of the best of order and affluence. This was so much the more to the credit of the owner, since he rarely resided in Louisiana and now had come merely on a visit to the Mississippi. Mr. Nicholl's entire family remained on his extensive estate in the vicinity of Richmond in the state of Virginia.

Barely after I had taken possession of the room that had been assigned to me and Mr. Tainturier, I made an exploratory trip into the wilderness bordering on the property of my host. All the dwellings of Pointe Coupée, extending for a distance of almost four and one-half German miles, are arranged in a row and separated from one another merely by the adjoining farm land. About fifty paces from the banks of the Mississippi, they are protected as much as possible against the overflow of the river by an earthen dam.

The cleared land of my host, amounting probably to eighty or one hundred acres, was in the form of a rectangle, with the narrower side bordering on the river. The soil was rich clay of extraordinary fertility, as was the cultivated land of Pointe Coupée, and exceptionally well suited for the production of cotton. The numerous rains had softened the plowed land so much that it was possible to wade through it only with the greatest exertion, in order to reach the adjoining cypress forest, actually a rather bottomless swamp. These swampy stretches of forest generally extend parallel to the river, are usually greater in length than in breath, are at times interrupted by pieces of dry land, and are frequently connected with one another and with the stream by small channels, owing their origin to the inundations of the river.

Such lands, overgrown with cypresses, oaks, and lotus, often contain clear water and a rather solid subsoil at not too great a depth. In hot years they would dry up entirely if their supply of fresh water were not replenished by springs and the overflow of the river. In places that are not too deep, a great number of water plants flourish of the families of the composite umbella and grass-like phanerogams, and also a multitude of mosses and lichens.

Swamps which deserve the name of morass or spongy bottomless brakes are more infrequent than those above described. They produce only a few arboreous plants and the well-known varieties of reeds of the lower Mississippi regions. These swamps have a slimy bottom of dissolved clay. Isolated and rarely connected with other regions, they are less subject to inundations. The poisonous gases arising from their surface during the hot season are undoubtedly the cause of the miasmatic ills of these parts which hurl so many people into the grave.[16]

The regions of stagnant waters support a wealth of chelonians, saurians, and batrachians which, in the steps of organic nature, reach from enormous size downwards. No other region of our earth produces them in such great numbers, variety, and curious shape. Although many varieties of families of these creatures are known to the natural scientist, nevertheless I am convinced that scarcely one-half of these swamp inhabitants of Louisiana and the adjacent country have been investigated and are classified under the existing systems.

Although I have diligently collected all reptiles which I could obtain and also received many contributions from persons who for years have busied themselves with collecting specimens, yet I possess, according to statements of trustworthy persons in Louisiana, scarcely one-third of the varieties which are known to those laymen. The attention of man in the observation of the animal and plant world is usually centered chiefly on those specimens which are interesting because of their usefulness or harmfulness, their striking size, or because superstition has attributed certain qualities to them.

The inhabitants of lower Louisiana, surrounded by primeval forests and unexplorable swamp regions, overlook the beauty of the gaudily plumaged birds and let their observation dwell on the horrible amphibians which, by their dangerous proximity and repulsive appearance, draw one's gaze to the ground. The history of the alligator and of the poisonous snakes, with all the peculiarities which characterize their lives, is quite amply known to every Creole, while he disregards other no less remarkable creatures simply because they cannot harm him. The Creole knows with certainty the name

[16] Malaria, transmitted by mosquitoes, and typhoid fever, among other diseases, were the culprits, rather than the gases generated by organic decay.

of every reptile that is shown him, yet he hardly suspects the name of the commonest bird or plant. Despite conviction, prejudice often turns people in all countries against entirely harmless animals.

While most of the inhabitants of our continent, for example, regard the completely harmless blindworm (*Anguis fragilis*, Linn.) as poisonous, the Creole on the Mississippi assures one with apodictic certainty that the bite of the toothless, quite innocent *Amphiuma* (Siren) is positively fatal after a few minutes without help. The variety of this creature which occurs commonly in Louisiana, especially in the Mississippi, was on several occasions delivered alive into my hands, and I had ample opportunity to convince myself by observation how little credence can be put in the stories concerning it, a species closely related to the Mexican *axolotl* (*Sirenodon oxolotl*).[17]

While examining the nearest swamp on the first day, I found many turtles warming themselves by the rays of the sun on the protruding roots of the cypress (*Cupressus disticha*) or on the rushes by the edge of the water. In addition to several small varieties I distinguished at once two turtles of the classification of *Trionyx* with a soft leathery shell. One was a *Trionyx ferox* (*tortue crocodile*), or a specimen related to the variety as determined by Pennant and Gmelin.[18] Belonging to the largest specimen of this order, this turtle has a pointed head provided with sharp, horn-like jaws which serve it as weapons. Its bite is extremely dangerous.

The inhabitants of Louisiana, especially the Negroes, who often have to wade through wet areas, dread the bite of this turtle more than that of the alligator. Usually only the tip of the head or the nostrils reach out of the water, the remaining part of the head and the long flexible neck are hidden under the leathery shell. At the approach of its prey or a vulnerable object, the turtle extends its neck and snaps about with extraordinary rapidity. Its flesh is not edible and disseminates an uncommonly strong, musky odor.

The other variety of *Trionyx* (*tortue à écaille molle*) was a small innocent creature with black-spotted, ash-gray, very soft shell. Later I found

---

[17] *Author*: *Gyrinus mexicanus*, *Naturalist's Miscellany*, No. 343; *Siren pisciformis*, *General Zoology*, Vol. III, Part 2, page 612 and pl. 140.

Gyrinus edulis or *Atolocatl*, Hernandez, *Hist. animant. et miner. Nov. Hisp. lib. unic.* Trat. V, cap IV, p. 77.

Anatomic investigations of Axolotl by G. Cuvier in *Recueil d'Observations de Zoologie et d'Anatomie Comparée*, collected by A. von Humboldt and A. Bonpland, VIII, page 160, pl. XII.

[18] *Author*: *Testudo ferox*, Pennent in *Philos. Trans.*, LXI, page 166, t. 10, f. 3. Gmelin, *S.N.L.I.*, page 1039. *Trionyn ferox*, B. Merrem, *Attempts to Form a System of Amphibians*, p. 20.

a similar specimen in the Ohio. But in the case of the latter the black spots were only separate dots and the head still more pointed. The remaining turtles, as I presume to judge after a fleeting glance, all belong to the *Emys* or river turtles. These creatures are somewhat timid, and at the approach of a person seek to conceal themselves by quickly submerging in the water.

Most of the plants, which had already developed blossoms, have not escaped the observation of botanists. The ground situated somewhat higher has a beautiful growth of trees on which the climbing plants, so common in Louisiana, have spread. The ground is covered partly with an impenetrable carpet of thorny plants of the genus *Rubus*,[19] whose twigs, thickly set with thorns, impose the greatest hindrance to every step and form a hiding place for countless poisonous snakes, extremely dangerous for one passing through.

A form of dam led over the swampy surroundings to a drier wooded region where the cattle are driven from the plantings to pasture. Though this dam is also intended for conveyances, it is nevertheless so muddy that I sank into the mire above my knees and could cross it only with the greatest effort. A black humus soil very different from the clay of the banks of the Mississippi, it must have originated from a great mass of decayed vegetable matter.

I was very glad to get into a region where I could find firm footing, for the uncertain going on boggy places where one is in danger of sinking at every step was extremely tiring. Moreover, it compels one to keep his eyes riveted on the ground, and this is most inconvenient to persons intending to make observations. I found very few herbs and bushes in bloom as heralds of the hot season in this wooded region so poor in plants of low growth. However, I made a rich find in ornithological specimens.

Found on all the river banks and in the swampy regions of all the warm parts of America, is the falcon *Milvus furcatus* (*Falco furcatus*, Catesby),[20] remarkable because of its forked tail and its gull-like appearance and flight. Flying in immense flocks at heights so great that they are scarcely visible to the eye, they suddenly dart down with unbelievable swiftness to secure their food, which consists of reptiles. This falcon is one of the most useful birds of this genus in the household of nature, for it captures and destroys countless poisonous snakes and other harmful crawling creatures.

[19] *Author*: *Rubus nitidus*, Raf., *angulatus*, Raf., *flagellaris*, Willd., *pubescens*, *fruticosus* (*villosus*) are the commonest varieties occurring in Louisiana. Among the climbing plants I noticed *Vitis riparia* and *Amelopsis bipinnata*, Mich. [*Rubus*, the brambles: blackberry, raspberry, etc.; *Vitis riparia*, wild grape; *Amelopsis bipinnata* = *A. arborea*, pepper vine.]

[20] *Falco furcatus* Catesby = *Elanoïdes forficatus* (Linn.), swallow-tailed kite.

Like the vultures (*Cathartes aura* and *atratus*, Wils.) it is so bold as to attack even a young alligator, and because of its great nimbleness its combat with these vicious saurians is never as protracted as that of the clumsy vultures. Of these also Mr. von Humboldt has furnished us some facts gathered on the occasion of his toilsome journey up the Orinoco (*Historische Reise*, Vol. III, Chapter XIX, page 439). On account of the speed of its flight, this remarkable bird not only flies over the interior portions of North America to rather high latitudes but also to the south, especially along the west coast through Mexico and Peru, where it was seen below 23° south latitude at Ilo and Arica in September (Père Louis Feuilée, *Journal des Obs.*, Vol. II, page 35).

On my return trip I saw on the fields large flocks of two different kinds of migratory birds (in French, *troupials*) which have the same habits as our starlings and do great harm, especially to the rice fields in America. They belong to *Icterus ferrugineus* (*Gracula ferruginea* and *Xanthornus phoeniceus*)[21] formerly classified among the orioles and distributed over a great part of South and North America. I found this beautiful bird, its black plumage marked by red spots on the wing joints under which spot runs a yellow band, very frequently during the summer months as far north on the Missouri as 43° north latitude, where it fed in the corn fields surrounding the settlements of the aborigines.

Satisfied with the collection I had made, I returned to the home of my host. A room had been prepared in the house in which my servant could prepare my collection, and we got to work at once, with Mr. Tainturier also lending a helpful hand.

Toward evening several persons of the neighborhood came to Mr. Nicholl's wishing to make my acquaintance. They overwhelmed me with expressions of kindness. There were among them some to whom I had been recommended, and naturally I had to promise that I would visit them at their homes. I was particularly pressed by a young German physician, Mr. Mueller, who had established himself on the Fausse Rivière, a two-

---

[21] *Author*: The genera *Ploceus*, Cuv. and Vieil., *Cassicus*, Cuv., and *Icterus*, which were formerly classified among the orioles and magpies, deserve special attention. I have classified *Gracula ferruginea* under *Icterus*, although because of its somewhat shorter and stronger beak it could be classified under *Cassicus*. *Gracula quiscala*, *bulbivora*, and *caudata* also belong to *Icterus*. *Cassicus* (*Xanthornus*) *phoeniceus* is Wilson's *Sturnus praedatornius* and Fernandez's *Acolchici. Nov. Hispan.*, page 14.

[The author's systematic concern for the Icteridae must strike latter-day ornithologists as prescient. *Gracula ferruginea* Wilson = *Euphagus carolinus*, the rusty blackbird; *Gracula quiscala* Linnaeus = *Quiscalus quiscula*, the common grackle; *G. bulbivora* = ?; *G. caudata* = ?; *Sturnus praedatornius* Wilson = *Agelaius phoeniceus*, the red-wing blackbird.]

hour's journey from here. He desired to have me visit him on the very next day.

Since the region and the location of the lake, which here has been given the name of False River surrounding Pointe Coupée like a horseshoe and connecting with the Mississippi, seemed particularly worthwhile to me, I accepted Mr. Mueller's invitation with pleasure.

4

On March 22 at about eleven o'clock
Mr. Mueller came for me. A few young men who had decided to participate in this pleasure ride joined us. The horses provided for this journey
were neither beautiful nor did their appearance indicate great endurance.
Nevertheless, they were praised by their owners as unsurpassable, and these
men spoke with as much conviction as does an Englishman when he
enumerates the fine qualities of his thoroughbred at a racing meet. The
horses of the Creoles in Louisiana are of only average quality and cannot
be good, since the Creole is accustomed to race over the worst roads at
full gallop.

The best-looking horse had been selected for me, a big sorrel, blind in
one eye. Brought from the northern states, in its time it may have been a
good horse. Lately many horses have been brought into Louisiana, whereby horse-breeding has gained greatly in importance.

The young men also wanted to persuade my friend Tainturier to participate in this pleasure ride. But Mr. Tainturier, in poor health and
almost sixty, seemed to me to be in no condition to undertake a ride of
several hours over roads in places partly covered with shallow water.
Moreover, I was convinced that he had not ridden a horse for a long time.
Nor did I like the horse belonging to one of the young people that had
been assigned him, and so I joined Mr. Nicholl and Mr. Mueller in their
pleas that the professor should devote his time to a short botanical excursion
on foot. Mr. Tainturier's small son, who desired to join the party, did not
agree with us at all, but finally and only with great pains our persuasion
prevailed.

I mounted my sorrel and was just in the act of riding away when a mishap detained us for a while. One of the horses began to buck, throwing his

rider very roughly to the ground. Most of the horses of the Creoles are wild and require a good rider.

The way led for a considerable distance past houses along the banks of the river. Some of the former are distinguished by good architecture, in so far as the houses of the Creoles can be said to be well built. The heat was extremely oppressive and the air as sultry as we have in Germany on the hottest summer days.

Turning away from the cultivated banks of the river, we reached the cypress forest, through which a recently laid out road led to the False River. The condition of all roads built through swampy, primitive forests varies with the seasons and the weather conditions. During a continued drought they are quite dry and comfortable for the traveler, but during uninterrupted rains or during high water on the river, the traveler is in danger of miring down in the spongy, water-soaked clay. At times a road may be intersected by bottomless pools, where the traveler must seek his salvation in swimming. Excepting the fact that I had to ride through a few wet places where the water came to the belly of a horse, and that I had to climb over some tree trunks which the wind had blown down, I encountered nothing unusual.

The extraordinary size and straight growth of the cypresses attracted my attention. They were resplendent with the freshest garment of spring, sharply contrasting with the gloomy gray of the Spanish moss (*Tillandsia usneoides*). The columnar, almost perfectly cylindrical trunks, in many instances from one to two yards in circumference, and the accompanying dark-leaved climbing plants (*Smilax* and *Tecoma*) present a most imposing contrast, making the regions of Louisiana unforgettable to the naturalist.

The dwellings situated on the Fausse Rivière resemble those of Pointe Coupée but do not have the size and conveniences of those belonging to the settlers on the banks of the Mississippi. The owners do not seem to possess as much wealth, even though they are not subjected to such frequent inundations as the settlers near the river. The only recently opened traffic and a certain lack of agricultural industry evidently prevent the inhabitants along the lake from utilizing all the advantages which they might derive from the location of their possessions.

The False River, as I have said, forms a horseshoe-shaped inland lake and is connected at its southern tip by a channel which may be regarded as an outlet of the Mississippi. At high water the floods of the Mississippi enter the channel and supply the lake with fresh water, and only in years when either an excessive amount of rain falls or the river attains great height does the lake overflow its banks, inundating the neighboring fields and adjoining forests. The lake has vast stretches overgrown with Mississippi reed (*Miegia macrosperma*). A varietyof *Paspalum* [grasses] also grows commonly in this region. The sharp leaves make wading through the swamps very hazardous. The Creoles of Louisiana are almost universally of the opinion that the False River was formerly the principal bed of the Mississippi. Although I know, as does every other traveler who endeavors to study the course of the great rivers in America which flow through flat regions, how these, and especially the Mississippi, change their courses and their banks, nevertheless, I see no satisfactory reasons for accepting the above assertion as true.

The greatest depth of the lake during the average stand of water is at most four or five feet. Generally all stagnant forest waters, which belong to the realm of the lower Mississippi and also many lakes at the mouth of this great stream, have characteristically shallow, spongy bottoms and are rarely deep. The shallow bed of the lake and also the peculiar fact that it obtains its water supply from the Mississippi through a channel at its southern end are, in my eyes, the main reasons against the opinions commonly held.

We stopped at Mr. Mueller's house. Our host did everything that his limited household could afford to receive his guests becomingly. The European who seeks his fortune and settles in the sparsely inhabited parts in the unhealthful climate of the New World must often subject himself to the direst and most oppressive privation to acquire even a small amount of wealth. Mr. Mueller seemed to find himself in this position, although by technical skill and generous conduct as a physician he must have acquired many friends in the entire region.

Various objects of nature were shown to me, among others a few remarkable aquatic animals from the lake, especially fish of which a few are still undetermined. The west bank of the lake, constituting a swampy wilderness and in many places supporting only Mississippi reeds, serves often as a hiding place for the Louisiana tiger (*Felis concolor*, Linn.).[1] This large beast of prey, despite its strength, exhibits but little courage and tears down domestic animals less frequently than the jaguar (*Felis onca*),[2] which surpasses it greatly in boldness and skill. The Louisiana tiger rarely, if ever, attacks human beings, except when it is seriously wounded and is unable to flee.

[1] *Felis concolor coryi* in this range of the mountain lion or puma.

[2] *Felis onca veraecrucis*, a subspecies of the jaguar, has a known historical range as far east as the western border of Louisiana. He will be mentioned again by implication in Chapter 5. Nothing in the Duke's remarks suggests that the species was on the Mississippi at that time.

The following morning Mr. Tainturier did not feel well, but neverthe-less accompanied me on a walk in the surrounding country, despite the sweltering heat and the mosquitoes, which had already begun to be un-bearable. Since I had shot a six-foot-long alligator, and despite my oppo-sition, he undertook the preparation of this animal. The unendurable smell which the Mississippi alligator disseminates, especially in the spring during the mating season, makes the skinning of these creatures an almost im-possible task. The entire house was so impregnated that I was scarcely able to stay in it. I am of the opinion that, if during the spring a live alligator were put into a cellar, any article of food would be spoiled by the diffusion of this strong musky odor.

I used the days of March 24 and 25 to visit several prominent planters at Pointe Coupée and also my German friends in St. Francisville. They again exacted from me the promise to spend the last days of my stay in Louisiana with them. On those visits I was not very successful with my observations, for the simple forms of life in this section present but few enticing pictures to the casual observer.

On the evening of the twenty-fifth, shortly after my return to the home of my host, a five-and-one-half-foot-long sturgeon (*Accipenser*) was brought to me. Taken from the river, this specimen was unknown to me, but the Creoles quite correctly call it *estourgeon*. It seemed to be very different from the spotted sturgeon (*Accipenser maculosus, An.d.Mus.*) of Canada. The meat resembled that of the Volga sturgeon but was not as tender.

On my arrival I found an invitation to a hunting party which was to take place near the settlement of Tunica, near the Isthmus of like name settled by French Creoles. Since the region about Tunica abounds in game and the hunt was to be made in my honor, the invitation by the Creoles was by no means unwelcome, and I accepted with pleasure.

The majesty of the forest had been greatly praised and it promised a rich find of specimens. The uniqueness of such a hunt for deer and bear in the swampy cypress forests, though very toilsome and dangerous because of the bayous, tested my patience, especially since I had entertained the hope of seeing, perchance, a few remaining members of the tribe of Tunica Indians, who are frequently seen in the Creole settlements. Even Mr. Tainturier could not suppress the desire to participate in this ride, which might mean his death. It was only with the utmost difficulty that I dis-suaded him from undertaking it.

At seven o'clock in the morning of March 26, in company with an acquaintance, my host, and my servant, we mounted our horses to start out for the home of Mr. Renon le Doux, who had invited me to the hunt. His place was twenty-three miles away, within the narrowest part of the peninsula of Tunica; called Racourcis by the Creoles, it is fairly well built up and populated. We hoped to reach it before night.

The banks of the Mississippi are at this place scarcely a mile apart, but the river flows a distance of thirty miles around the peninsula. Such bends are one of the characteristics of the Mississippi. It has this peculiarity in common with other American rivers, the Orinoco, the Madalena, the Marranon, and others that during high water overflow swampy plains. During high water, too, the Mississippi often breaks through the narrow loops of such bends, ordinarily without leaving its old river bed permanently for the newly formed channel.

The road runs along the bank of the river past the village. The parish of Pointe Coupée extends only five miles farther upstream from the residence of my host, and in the uniformly built houses of the planters no variation could be observed. A few beautiful Florida pines (*Pinus palustris*, Lambert, Rob, page 525, and *Pinus taeda*, Linn. [loblolly pine]) and gigantic catalpa trees attracted my attention. These are specimens of the few varieties of trees with which the inhabitants surround their houses.

At the last house in the village I found Mr. Meyer from Hanover, a farmer who had traveled in the same ship with me from Hamburg to New Orleans. He was staying with his brother, but in the course of the summer he died of climatic fever.

After passing Pointe Coupée, the next twelve miles of road led for the most part through the forest, and the last half of the way was particularly bad. At one place we had to wade through a shallow swampy bayou full of upset tree trunks where we could scarcely open our eyes for gnats and flies.

Extremely tired from the long ride in the sultry heat, we reached the home of Mr. le Doux at six in the evening and were received most hospitably. Soon a few Creoles arrived and the company became more lively. We ate our simple evening meal amid pleasant conversation, during which I, as a European, was asked many interesting questions about my fatherland, but especially about France. Since I was very tired, I soon excused myself from the company, threw myself on a straw mattress in the attic of the house, and would have wished nothing more than to go to sleep. But various circumstances prevented me from doing so.

One of these, a violent thunderstorm peculiar to these hot regions of America, was approaching, and the distant roar of thunder was uninterruptedly answered by the multi-voiced howling of Mr. le Doux' pack of hounds and the cacophonous croaking of countless frogs. In addition to this auditory treat one should imagine the unbearable heat and a billion small mosquitoes which are regarded as forerunners of intense thunderstorms.

Because of their almost microscopic smallness, these little pests pass through the finest mesh fly netting and thus make these protective measures entirely useless.

This torment did not last long, however, since a terrific storm set in and, coming from the forest region, it drew toward the river bottom, where it discharged itself with all the fury of the unfettered elements. It was impossible to distinguish the intervals between lightning and thunder. Through the cracks in the roof and between the logs which formed the walls of the house, my room was brightly illuminated. Stroke after stroke of lightning struck the cypresses on the bank of the river near the house.

After the storm had subsided somewhat, the rain fell in torrents, and since the roof, as I have indicated, was in poor condition, it was impossible for me to protect myself against the water pouring in from everywhere which soon covered the entire floor. The inhabitants of the house gathered, each one seeking to protect himself as best he could, and since the attic where I was, was the only endurable place in the house, everybody took refuge in it. The Negroes of my host, whose wretched huts were flooded, also joined us, crowding so densely that not even a mouse could have crawled between us. After two hours the rain finally ceased, the sky became clear, and the white and black assembly sought new sleeping places.

Hardly had the morning dawned when several men, accompanied by their hounds and horses, arrived at the house of my host. Their resolute manner, combined with a certain expressive courtesy, announced them at once as French Creoles. The Creoles of French origin, despite several intervening generations, have not lost the fine manners of their mother country, those manners which characterize the French nation so pleasantly. The natural and unrestrained manner of living has developed something frank in their behavior, which, coupled with the most sincere hospitality, is bound to win every stranger to them.

In the largest room in the house, which was still quite soaked with water, we hastily took a simple breakfast consisting of cornbread and ham, and at once prepared for the hunt. In the yard were six or eight horses and at least thirty dogs of crossed breeds which were to accompany the hunt. A few Indians of the tribe of Tunicas who dwell in this region had also come to accompany us. These people wore nothing but their blankets and seemed to rely more on their own legs than on the poor nags which were standing in the yard. They had black hair either hanging unbraided over their shoulders or tied together over their forehead, and all of them were supplied with long rifles which fired balls very well.

The French Creoles in Louisiana have become quite partial to the use of the double-barreled shotgun, which fires only shot. They are, therefore, inferior hunters to Americans of English or German origin and also to the Creoles of Canada and the upper Mississippi, who in their hunting make excellent use of the rifle and for the most part are excellent marksmen.

Our hunting party now set out. I mounted a fairly good horse and in a few minutes had reached the cypress forest. We soon found fresh tracks of game, and the whole pack was turned on them. A few of these dogs were good hunters, for soon we heard them picking up the scent. This was the wished-for signal. Creoles and Indians scattered in an instant in all directions in order to reach the various runways of the game. I must confess that the Creoles, contrary to my expectations, showed themselves as extremely bold horsemen in that horribly difficult terrain in the forest. No windbreak was too high, no thicket entwined with climbing vines too dense, and no lagoon too deep for them to ride through or to set out across. Their horses, although unsightly, did all that could be expected of them. And I at the side of a tall Creole, who stayed with me, owe it entirely to the excellence of his horse that I, outdistanced by all others, did not meet with an accident. No horse unaccustomed to these parts could have found its way among the swampy ground full of gnarled cypress roots and conical stumps.

My companion, a very jovial man, conducted me to a somewhat drier elevation where we made a halt. It did not take long until the hounds drove a deer past us which I shot and wounded. We followed the pack in great haste and soon got sight of the deer again. Presently a shot was heard and the deer fell. One of the Indians had headed it off and shot it. After this last shot all the hunters who were scattered in the forest came back and the hunt was ended. It was not possible to collect the dogs again.

The fallow buck, for there are not other varieties of deer left in the lower Mississippi region, had not yet shed its antlers, though it had exchanged its coat of winter hair for the red summer coat.[3] Even a month later this change had not taken place on the Ohio and Mississippi, six to eight degrees farther north, as I observed. The North American fallow buck (*Cervus virginianus*, Gmel.) is distributed throughout all of North America from the 25th degree to the 30th degree of latitude and is in some localities very numerous, although it is much pursued by the aborigines and also by the white settlers because of its excellent hide. In form as well as in its habits, it resembles the European fallow buck (*Cervus dama*, Linn.). Only the white spots on the ground color of red and the two black stripes on the haunches are lacking. The antlers are bent forward and are not palmated as are those of the European fallow buck, but are frequently

[3] The European fallow deer is unrepresented in the Western Hemisphere in the natural state. The subspecies here referred to is *Dama virginiana mcilhennyi*.

forked, the forks bending backward and also forward. In old deer several prongs may develop.

This variety of deer, despite the assertions of several naturalists, produces heavy antlers. I myself possess a pair of antlers with more than thirty prongs. The mating season is in October, when the deer fight viciously, and the young are born in May. Because of their forked antlers these deer become more easily entangled with one another than other varieties do. In the primeval forests of the Missouri I found many skulls of the fallow deer which were thus entangled and lay where the animals had perished. In their tracks I also found difference from those of our fallow deer, except that the hoof was somewhat narrower.

In order to avoid error I must observe that the French Creoles incorrectly call the fallow buck a roe deer (*chevreuil*). The roe deer is not found in all of North America, but several varieties of roe-like animals are found in South America. The colonists of English origin have been cognizant of a difference between the two varieties and call the American fallow buck correctly deer. On the other hand the great American red deer or stag, they call elk or élan, although this variety of deer (*Cervus major*, Say)[4] is entirely different from the élan, which the Canadians call *original* and which is found in much higher latitudes.

After I had returned to the house where I had spent the night, the Creole who had accompanied me on the hunt suggested that I should go along the banks of a forest creek that was connected with the Mississippi. He assured me we should find a large number of flowering plants which ordinarily grew on the banks. In this hope I was greatly disappointed, for except some clumps of yucca cactus just shooting up, a *Sesbania*, and a *Chelone*,[5] I found nothing but blackberry bushes and undeterminable grasses.

A few large alligators and turtles dived into their muddy abodes at our approach, and great swarms of mosquitoes announced the advent of the hot season. When we had almost completed our walk, my companion suddenly called me to be on my guard and showed me at a distance of three or four paces a coiled-up black snake which, by its upraised head and swollen neck, indicated its intention to strike us. I lost no time, and despite the outcries of my companion killed the snake with a large club. Upon closer examination it was found that this snake, which belongs to an order of real

[4] The wapiti or American elk, *Cervus canadensis*, which ranged over North America from northern Saskatchewan to central Louisiana. (*Cervus major* Ord, 1808, precedes Say.)

[5] *Author*: *Sesbania macrocarpa*, Muehl. I found this legume later rather plentiful in the vicinity of New Orleans and succeeded in making the plant bloom in Europe.
[*Sesbania macrocarpa*, the coffee bean. *Chelone obliqua*, the turtle head.]

vipers, was one of the most poisonous of its kind. The Creoles, who call this snake *serpent congo*, are uncommonly afraid of it because of the swift deadliness of its bite and because it ordinarily leaps with the swiftness of an arrow at the object which it intends to strike.[6]

On closer examination I found that this snake closely resembled a viper appearing on the mainland coast of South America which Mr. Alexander von Humboldt mentions. The inhabitants of Venezuela call it *cobra coral*, and as in the case of this latter, the bite is incurable after a few minutes. The Negroes, who usually go barefooted, fear it far more than the whites and Indians, who also do not like to step in its path.

The Creoles and Indians, as is well known, on their hunting trips and wanderings wear long stockings (*mitasses*) and soft shoes (moccasins) of strong and freshly tanned buckskin, which have been cured brown over a smoke of rotten and ill-smelling wood. This footwear is undoubtedly the best protection against the bite of poisonous creatures. The fangs of a poisonous snake which lie in a soft sheath rarely penetrate through this leather. Moreover, the snakes seem to have a special aversion to its strong odor. The rattlesnake, which is very numerous in some regions and, because of its size and its peculiar laziness does not like to go out of one's way, is very dangerous during wet weather. At this time when the sound of its rattles is scarcely audible, one can easily step on it and be bitten. The large fangs of the rattlesnake, however, do not penetrate soft leather, and I myself have seen an instance when these snakes would rather let themselves be stepped on than bite into the ill-smelling leather.

When I brought the dead snake into the home of my host, all those present showed the greatest terror. An unbelievable number of tales were told. Most of them bore the impress of exaggeration, although I do not doubt that some of them were true. For example, a short time before on a neighboring plantation, a young Negro had been bitten who, despite all the means that were applied, died in less than a quarter of an hour.

During my stay in Louisiana later, a horse was bitten in the fetlock of the right hind leg by a poisonous snake and died in a few minutes in violent convulsions. Since this occurrence was reported to me by very trustworthy

[6] In this passage and the one which follows it, there is room for confusion. What the author at first describes is the congo eel (*Amphiuma means*), an amphibian, not a pit viper (the true vipers do not occur in North America), and as such a nonvenomous species. The Creole name *serpent congo* may have been the cause of it all. On the other hand, the "coiled-up black snake" preceding seems to indicate a mature moccasin (*Agkistrodon piscivorus*), unquestionably a poisonous species and well known in the South. The ensuing comparison with von Humboldt's species and the name *cobra coral* suggest the eastern coral snake (*Micrurus fulvius*) or its kin, *M. euryxanthus*, normally with a habitat in the Southeast. The black description limits conjecture to the moccasin.

men an hour after it had occurred, I betook myself to the place. I found the horse extremely swollen and the skin of the abdomen raised in several places. In addition to the black color which had spread everywhere, I found large air bubbles, which were also found in the blood vessels, with the blood coagulated and black. The hind foot which had been bitten was very much swollen, although around the wound itself, apparently caused by a snake, the inflammation did not appear very large. In order to obtain more accurate results I should have examined more closely the intestines and main blood vessels, but despite all the money I offered, no Negro could be induced to undertake the opening.

I have in my collection several more specimen of vipers, common in Louisiana, which although they represent different varieties, nevertheless show great similarity. These vipers are much like the *Vipera prester* of Europe, the *Vipera cerastes* of Egypt without the small horns, and *Vipera nigra* (*Pelias nigra*, Merr.) in America, and others. They are all marked by a dark color shading from brown into black, and like all vipers, they have very wide, scale-covered, arrow-shaped heads with no pits before the eyes, and short, blunt tails terminating in a lighter color. For travelers I add this remark concerning the black poisonous snakes, that in Louisiana and also in a large part of the United States there are several kinds of entirely harm-less black adders which are characterized by striking length, with a uni-formly thin body and pointed head. They need not be feared in the least. In their mode of living and also in their shape, these adders completely resemble the ordinary blue European adder (*Coluber natrix*, Linn.), which frequently lives in running water, a habit the poisonous snakes do not have, since they prefer dry, rocky, and grassy regions.

That same day I rode back to Pointe Coupée. I encountered much trouble in wading through the above mentioned bayous. The thunder-storm which had raged that night had caused the swampy waters to be still more bottomless, and we had great trouble in getting our horses across. I arrived at home late very tired and thoroughly drenched and found my traveling companion, Mr. Tainturier, ill. The increasing heat together with the unaccustomed walks had caused a slight attack of fever, and despite this I had great difficulty in dissuading him on the following day from participating in an excursion to the southern region of the before mentioned False River. One of the Creoles of the neighborhood, Mr. Labattu, had invited me to accompany him, and I accepted this invitation because I expected the best results for my collection.

I used the entire day of the twenty-eighth for arranging dried plants and stuffing a few birds. Mr. Tainturier again filled the whole house with an unbelievable stench by preparing an alligator, which had been shot a few days before, and also several fish. The odor was so putrid that despite my zeal for natural science I could not make myself attend these preparations.

Probably the professor contracted on this day the germ of an illness from which I found him still suffering in January of the following year. I mentioned previously that nothing surpasses the dreadful odor of a decaying alligator. It is so exceedingly penetrating that an object, especially a cloth or woolen garment with which it comes in contact, remains permeated for months.

Early on the twenty-ninth at six o'clock Mr. Labattu came to the place where I was staying. In his company I rode a two-wheeled cart along the southern part of the parish of Pointe Coupée toward his home, about five English miles from that of Mr. Nicholl. There we took a boat and traveled down the river as far as the outlet of the fairly rapidly flowing channel which loses itself in the False River. The flat regions through which the Mississippi flows often cause this enormous river, through the power of the huge masses of water, to form new channels. These create then either new streams or lose themselves in swamps or lakes, or they effect wide spreading flooded flat land. The entrance of the channel was so covered with piled-up tree trunks that one could walk over the rapid stream with dry feet.

Our way led along the channel through a splendid dense forest of most beautiful native timber with an undergrowth of lianas and impenetrable reeds (*Ludolphia excelsa? Miegia macrosperma, Arundo gigantea* and *tecta*, Walt., and other giant reeds, which are more or less related to the bamboo).[7]

Numerous deer and bear tracks testified to the presence of these creatures and also that this region is sparsely settled. After we had walked for an hour we entered the dwelling of Mr. l'Abadie, a Frenchman born in Bayonne, and were received with the customary hospitality.

To captivate the naturalist the forest in the neighborhood teemed with rare birds, among them parrots, hummingbirds (*Trochyylus colubris*, Audub.), a few beautiful varieties of ducks (*Canard branchu, Anas sponsa*, Linn.), the splendid black woodpeckers with a white spot on its wings and large snow white bill (*Picus principalis*, Linn.), and the North American kingfishers (*Alecedo alcyon*, Linn.).

On the banks of the river I observed the cactus which is native in these parts. Its branches are as dark green as those of *Cactus tuna*, and the long spines fall off leaving a bristly beard.

Mr. Leandre, a Mulatto born in Santo Domingo and a rich and agreeable man, sent a cabriolet to take us to his dwelling, where we were to stay overnight. The way led for an hour through a dense forest. In Mr.

[7] All refer to *Arundinaria gigantea* and *A. tecta*.

Leandre's house, we found but few comforts, and despite all his efforts he was able to serve us no other beverage than whiskey, a spirit which the people drink with water. It takes the place of wine with many Americans. I could never become accustomed to this drink and so always had to drink the miserable water from the bayous, which always made me sick. The water of the Mississippi is mixed with clay, but it is cold and wholesome, while the stagnant waters, tepid and flat, take the odor of the many alligators which overcrowded them.

Finding these horrible creatures in such great numbers in the lake close to the house, I easily shot several of them with the rifle. They project their head and half of their neck from the water and remain in this position absolutely immovable, sometimes for hours. If one hits their brain directly over the eyes, they are dead at once, turn on their back and drift on the water for a few minutes, then sink and do not come to the surface again until decay has set in. During the warm season one sees these reptiles by the hundreds resting on the tree trunks, for they are not easily disturbed in their sleep. When the alligators wish to catch fish they congregate in large numbers, form a semi-circle, and beat the water until turbid with their tails. The fish, becoming confused, are driven into close quarters to be consumed by their enemies, who in such a drive often bite and wound one another.

If an alligator wishes to catch an animal, especially a hog which has gone into the swamp during the intense heat, it approaches very slowly under the water, seizes its prey quickly by the feet and draws it into the water to drown. When the animal is dead, the alligator drags it to the bank and consumes it. Similarly, it sometimes captures larger beasts of prey such as tiger[8] and bear.

Negro women who have to do their washing on the edge of the water have often had accidents in this manner. Wounded alligators will always seek the bank to die. The life force of these creatures is very great, the muscles of alligators will show movement two days after their head has been cut off. (The vital force of the muscles of amphibians is well known. The alligator, however, possesses without a doubt, the greatest galvanic energy of all saurians.)

On the lake, which I mentioned before, I saw many cormorants and a rare aquatic bird, the anhinga (*Plotus melanogaster*, Wils.). The ugly voice of the bullfrogs (*Rana ocellata*, Linn., *mugiens*, Merr., *clamitans*, Latr., and others) resounded from time to time making the already deso-

[8] *Felis onca veraecrucis* has ranged far up in eastern Texas and to and perhaps inside the western border of Louisiana. Hence "tiger" here (for jaguar) has some basis in fact. *Felis concolor coryi* Bangs, a subspecies of the puma, is another candidate for meaning at this point.

late region still more grim. A fierce storm was the forerunner of a heavy thunderstorm which came on the following day.

On the thirtieth the rain fell in torrents. Instead of cooling the air the heat rose to 88° and the de Luc hygrometer registered 70°. In the afternoon I left my kind hosts and returned to Mr. l'Abadie's where we had rested on the previous noon. (I must yet remark that at Mr. Leandre's house I saw the last surviving member of the now almost extinct but once mighty tribe of Chetimachas Indians. He was a youth of eighteen whose outward appearance showed nothing remarkable.)

In the state of Louisiana a great prejudice exists against the colored people of African descent. Negro slavery, which is tolerated in this state, is responsible for the separation of the whites and the colored people. The law forbids intermarriage of the two races, whereby naturally a separation must result between the free colored and pure whites. This must in the end have detrimental consequences, since marriage is the strongest moral bond which can befriend people of different races, who, through the force of circumstances, are obliged to inhabit the same land. Mutual enmity or contempt is the usual lot of those races which are prevented from intermarrying because of prejudice, religion, or politics. The history of all ages and nations furnishes proof of this, but the examples, results, and consequences of compulsory separation in America of the whites and the colored people are too new to require further mention.

The free blacks and those of different shades of color by no means have the rights of the whites. Since the Quadroons, the mixture of Negroes in the third and fourth rank, are as light colored as the white Creoles themselves, these separate naturally from the blacks and the Mulattoes and form a second class of this race which will have nothing in common with the Negroes. Mulatto and Quadroon women always aim at a so-called ennobling of their color and one rarely observes them marrying beneath their station. They live, especially in New Orleans, in illicit relations with white men, whereby morality is entirely undermined.

The mothers themselves bring about such unions and sell their daughters. In this transaction the beauty of the girl determines the price. The sum rarely exceeds a thousand dollars. These Quadroon maidens, often well behaved and well reared, then move to their privileged lovers, usually foreigners or unmarried young men. Normally they are only fed and clothed and when their paramour becomes tired of them they are left to their fate. This practice is common among the colored free even with the greatest mixture of white blood. They do not have the right to testify as witnesses in court, may not appear in the society of whites, even of the lowest class, and never eat with whites at the same table.

Despite the sincere respect which I have for the laws of the separate states of the great North American Union, I cannot but sense in these laws a threatening danger for the peace of the great republic. The most recent occurrences and indications of discord in the northern as well as in the southern states, the debates in the Congress at Washington, the lack of unanimity in the last presidential election, and other events have their origin in the different points of view regarding the treatment of the colored people and negro slavery.

Although slavery cannot yet be eliminated without the complete ruin of the planters in the southern states, nevertheless, it would be wiser for those states to approach the Negro and his descendants in a more sympathetic manner, for in no republican state can such separations remain, since they are unavoidably bound to bring with them a dividing spirit and inner discord in their wake. If the laws which have reference to this could not be annulled entirely, exceptions could be made in many instances. Although I do not like to inject political matters in a purely scientific account of a journey, I cannot refrain from saying that in a free state where the general welfare depends on equality of the classes and the avoidance of dangerous combinations, there cannot exist two castes among the inhabitants. The colored people might, in the states where they constitute a majority, become very dangerous in case their interests should induce them to demand by pressure or force those civil human rights which their fellow citizens would deny them.

I would ask any friend of humanity whether a respectable colored family may be justly excluded from cultured society simply because their ancestors came from Africa. That the Negroes can make use of reprisals and punish the whites with contempt, we have seen in Santo Domingo.

In the meantime the weather had become pleasant again and the clouds disappeared. After the rain the forests had a most beautiful luster and a fresh green, while during the winter the gray, beard-like pendant parasites had given the woods a peculiarly ancient appearance. Now they stood rejuvenated. The birds, too, had been aroused by the rays of the sun and were busy in the dense foliage, their songs forming a strange contrast to the cries of the parrots and the croaking of the great frogs.

We arrived at Mr. l'Abadie's at four o'clock in the afternoon and I found abundant opportunity for work, having received a large number of birds for stuffing which a few Indians had shot. I also killed two varieties of beautiful yellow headed parrots that same evening (*Psittacus caroliniensis*, Linn. and *Psittacus mississippiensis* ? Perhaps only a sub-variety).[9]

[9] The Carolina parakeet, once ranging from New York to the Dakotas, south to Texas and the east coast of Florida, has been extinct since about 1920.

Although they are very shy, one can approach them by hiding behind large trees and kill several with one shot since they sit so close together. The forest around Mr. l'Abadie's dwelling is in part overgrown with tall reeds. Such regions are almost impenetrable, and the bushes intergrown with climbing plants (*Tecoma, Bignonia, Philostemon, Ampelopsis,* and others) and raspberry shrubs make walking almost impossible.

The next morning, March 31, a hunt with many poor hounds was arranged, but since the hunters were badly posted they did not get a shot at the game. Then a plot of ground overgrown with vegetation was set afire, but it burned badly and drove out only a few rabbits and racoons (*Procyon loter* ? Ill.).[10] The practice of using fire in hunting is not bad and is common among the Indians. A large tract of wild undergrowth, reeds, or prairie is set on fire with the wind driving flames in the form of a crescent. Such a burning prairie presents a magnificent sight. The game, terrified by the approaching smoke, rushes into the range of the hunter. This method is especially good in the hunt for bears, for the bear is not brought to a stand as easily as the jaguar, and hounds are not anxious to attack him.

Leaving the home of our friend in the afternoon we rowed in our boat to the mouth of the channel. It was an unpleasant and slow journey up-river, particularly since we had to cross the river several times to escape the strong current. Finally, the Negro, entirely exhausted by the excessive exertion, brought us to the first house at Pointe Coupée. We collected our belongings and walked to the home of Mr. Labattu. I desired to return to my stopping place on that same evening because many birds had to be prepared. Mr. Labattu hitched his wagon, a conveyance consisting of a rickety cart with extremely refractory mules. Not wishing to run the risk of damaging my guns, I decided to walk. Exceedingly tired, I arrived at my place about ten o'clock and found everybody retired. After I had knocked for half an hour and quarreled with the Negroes, the house was finally opened up and I got some rest.

With regret I heard of the departure of my friend Tainturier. A serious illness had compelled him to return to New Orleans where the following winter I found him still ailing.[11]

---

[10] 1815. *Procyon lotor,* Illiger, *Abh. preuss. Akad. Wissenschaft, Berlin, 1804–1811,* pp. 70, 74. [Duke Paul's observations probably were for *P. lotor megalodous.*]

[11] *Author:* Since I did not observe a single tree or shrub which had not put forth new leaves, it may be appreciated by botanists if I mention the time when most of the deciduous trees and shrubs in Louisiana, between the 29th and 31st degrees of north latitude put forth new foliage. As my observations were made in the year 1823, and as in this winter the month of January was unusually cold, it may be assumed that on an average in warmer winters the vegetation develops ten days earlier.

March 1: *Fraxinus discolor*, Raf., *nigra lacera*, Raf., *Callicarpa americana*, Linn., *Bignonia capreolata*, Linn., *Tecoma radicans*, Juss., *Pagesia leucantha*, Raf., *Viburnum prunifolium*, Willd., *Aesculus flava*, Wild., *coccinea*, *Vitis integrifolia*, Raf., *Rotundifolia*, Mich., *Cordifolia*, Raf., *Aestivalis*, Mich., *Philadelphus inodorus*, Linn., *Frangula fragalis*, Raf., *Celastrus bullatus*, Linn.

March 5: *Fraxinus undulata*, Raf., *juglandifolia*, Mich., *tomentosa*, *aquatica*, Raf., *Acer saccharium*, Linn., *nigrum*, Linn., *Hypericum rostratur*, *fulgidum*, Raf., *Tilia stenapetala*, Raf.

March 10: *Rubus angulatus*, Raf., *Prunus virginiana*, *caroliniana*, Linn., *stenophylla*, Raf., *Acacia eburnea*. *Gleditschia triacanthos*. *Acacia glandulosa*, Willd. *Robinia pseudacacia*, Linn., *pulima*. *Cercis canadiensis*, Linn. *Acer dasycarpum*, Willd., *negundo*, Linn. *Castanea americana*, Raf. *Fagus americana*. *Diospyros virginiana*, Linn., *pubescens*, Pursh. *Annona tribola*, Linn. *Bignonia Catalpa*, Linn., *syringaefolia* (*Catalpa*), Pursh. *Philostemon radicans*, Raf. *Rhus typhinum*, Linn., *copallinum*. *Pseudopetalon glandulosum*. *Piela tomentosa*, Raf. *Juglans nigra*, *olivaeformis*, *Hykori*, Mich., *cathartica*, Darby, *laciniosa*, Darby, *porcina*, Darby, *myristicae-formis*, Darby, *tomentosa*, *scabra*, Darby. *Ulmus alba*, Raf., *pinguis*, Raf., *Salix denudata*, Raf., *ludovisiana*, Raf., *nigra*, Linn., *washitana*, Mag. Cat.

March 15: *Populus angulata*, Willd., *trepida*, Willd. *Betula lenta*, Darby. *Castanea pumila*, Darby. *Platanus occidentalis*, Linn. *Liriodendron tulipifera*, Linn. *Cupressus disticha*, Linn.

March 20: *Carpinus ostrya*, Darby, *americana*, Willd. *Quercus phellos*, Linn., *nigra*, Mich., *rubra*, Mich., *macrocarpa*, Mich., *falcata*, *lyrata*, *obtusifolia*, *aquatica*, *ferruginea*, and others.

[Of the above chronological inventories, Professor George J. Goodman, Curator of the Bebb Herbarium in the University of Oklahoma, refrained from observing, *Serit arbores, quae alteri saeclo prosient*, identifying them instead for the editor, as follows:

[March 1: *Fraxinus discolor* = *F. pennsylvanica*, green ash; *F. nigra lacera* Raf., presumably *F. lacera* Raf., as puzzling for Rafinesque's original identification as for Duke Paul's secondary observation in Louisiana; *Callicarpa americana*, French mulberry, beauty berry; *Bignonia capreolata*, trumpet honeysuckle; *Tecoma radicans* = *Campsis radicans*, trumpet vine; *Pagesia leucantha* = *P. acuminata*; *Viburnum prunifolium*, black haw, slightly out of range for Louisiana but the state contains four similar species; *Aesculus flava* and *coccinea*, probably varieties of *A. pavia*, red buckeye; *Vitis*, various wild grapes; *Philadelphus inodorus*, a mock orange; *Frangula fragilis* = *Rhamnus caroliniana*, Indian cherry, Carolina buckthorn; *Celastrus bullatus*, probably *C. scandens*, bittersweet.

[March 5: *Fraxinus undulata*, a Rafinesquian name not further identifiable; *F. juglandifolia*, likely *F. americana*, white ash; *F. tomentosa*, ?; *F. aquatica*, water ash; *Collinsonia verticillaris*, one of the mint family; *Cornus florida*, flowering dogwood; *C. polygamus*, likely *C. stricta*, blue-fruited dogwood; *Acer saccharium* = *A. saccharinum*, silver maple; *A. nigrum*: *A. nigrum* Mich., black maple not known so far south, possibly *A. leucoderme*, one of the sugar maples; *Hypericum rostratur* = *H. rostratum* = *H. densifolorum*, bushy St. John's wort; *H. fulgidum* = *H. fasciculatum*, bedstraw St. John's wort; *Tilia stenopetala* = *T. caroliniana*, Carolina bass wood.

[March 10: *Rubus angulatus*, one of the dewberry group; *Prunus virginiana*, choke cherry, if here accurately observed was out of its known range; *P. caroliniana*, Carolina laurel cherry; *P. stenophylla* = *P. angustifolia*, Chickasaw plum; *Acacia eburnea*, an Old-World species of *Acacia*; *Gleditschia triacanthos* = *Gleditsia triacanthos*, honey locust; *Acacia glandulosa* = *Desmanthus illinoensis*; *Robinia pseudoacacia*, black locust; R.

pulima, ? ; *Cercis canadiensis* = *C. canadensis*, red bud; *Acer dasycarpum* = *A. sacchari-num*, silver maple; *A. negundo*, box elder; *Castanea americana* = *C. dentata*, chestnut; *Fagus americana* = *F. dentata*, American beech; *Diospyros virginiana*, persimmon; *D. pubescens*, a possible variety of *D. virginiana*; *Annona tribola* = *Asimina tribola*, pawpaw; *Bignonia catalpa* = *Catalpa bignonioides*, southern catalpa; *Catalpa syringaefolia* = *C. bignonioides*; *Philostemon radicans* = *Rhus radicans*, poison ivy; *Rhus typhinum* = *R. typhina*, stag-horn sumac; *R. copallinum* = *R. copallina*, shining sumac; *Pseudopetalon glandulosum* = *Zanthoxylum clava-herculis*, Hercules club; *Piela tomentosa*, ? ; *Juglans cathartica* = *J. cinerea*, butternut; *J. laciniosa* = *Carya laciniosa*, shell-bark hickory; *J. nigra*, black walnut; *J. olivaeformis* = *Carya illinoensis*, pecan; *Juglans hykori*,? ; *Juglans porcina*, probably = *Carya glabra*, pig-nut hickory; *J. myristicae-formis* = *Carya myristi-caeformis*, nutmeg hickory; *J. tomentosa* = *Carya tomentosa*, mocker-nut hickory; *Juglans scabra*, ? ; *Ulmus alba* = *U. americana*, American elm; *U. pinguis*, a Rafinesquian name not identifiable; *Salix denudata*, the same; *S. ludoviciana*, the same; *S. nigra*, black willow; *S. washitana*, not identifiable;

[March 15: *Populus angulata* = *P. deltoides*, eastern cottonwood; *Populus trepida* = *P. tremuloides*, the quaking aspen, here out of range; *Betula lenta*, sweet birch, scarcely in range; *Castanea pumila*, Allegheny chinquapin; *Platanus occidentalis*, sycamore; *Lirio-dendron tulipufera*, tulip tree; *Carpinus ostrya* = *Ostrya virginica*, hophornbeam; *Carpinus americana* = *C. caroliniana*, ironwood; *Quercus phellos*, willow oak; *Q. nigra*, water oak; *Q. rubra*, northern red oak; *Q. macrocarpa*, bur oak; *Q. falcata*, southern red oak; *Q. lyrata*, overcup oak; *Q. obtusifolia* = *Q. undulata*, of southwestern U.S. range, perhaps a slip therefore for *Q. obtusiloba* = *Q. stellata*, post oak; *Q. aquatica* = *Q. nigra*, water oak; *Q. ferruginea* = *Q. nigra*.]

5

RETURN TO BAYOU SARA AND ST. FRANCISVILLE — DEPAR-
TURE ON THE STEAMBOAT *Maysville* — THE ACHEFFALAYA
— THE RED RIVER OF NACHITOCHEZ — FORT ADAMS —
NATCHEZ — THE STATE OF MISSISSIPPI — DEPARTURE
FROM NATCHEZ — THE YAZOO — POINTE ILLICHIO — THE
ARKANSAS.

O<small>N</small> the morning of April 1 we left
the home of Mr. Nicholl, who had departed during my absence in the
chemal (channel). After crossing the river to Bayou Sara on my arrival, I
was received by my German friends. In compliance with my wish, they
had written to New Orleans for information concerning the coming of a
steamboat destined for the state of Missouri. Their correspondent had informed them that the steamboat *Hekla* was scheduled to leave New Orleans at almost any hour loaded with freight for St. Louis, and it would be
ill-advised to await the departure of another steamboat, since four weeks
might pass before another vessel would put out for that city. I should
therefore keep myself in readiness to continue my journey and not leave
Bayou Sara.

This most unwelcome news compelled me to remain like a prisoner in
Mr. Holl's small house on the bank of the river awaiting the arrival of
the steamboat. The hope for an early departure seemed unrealistic. After
spending three days in Bayou Sara without a move and at night placing
watches on the bank of the river to hail every passing boat, I learned from a
passenger that, due to some unforeseen obstacles and lack of cargo, the
Hekla would not be able to depart for four or five days. At the same time
I was informed that the above-named boat was one of the worst on the
river and that it offered passengers few, if any, conveniences. It was therefore advisable to look for another chance, but I was reluctant to decide on
this since the success of my journey required my arrival in St. Louis the
latter part of April. Still, I was glad to have a few more days to make some
necessary preparations for my trip and to make a few explorations in this
region.

I did not permit myself to make any extensive excursions for fear of
missing a shipping opportunity. Nevertheless, not as closely confined as I

had been before, I could at least visit St. Francisville or roam on the other side of the river.

Thereby my collection grew visibly. I had ample leisure time to arrange and prepare the same. Since the region about St. Francisville assumes the form of a series of hills composed of clay and limestone, it presents a great variety of plant life and trees, making this region very rich by comparison to the opposite bank of the Mississippi.[1]

Here I found most of the trees and shrubs common in the southern part of the United States which love high and dry land. Among them were great stretches of magnolias, which in the summer season vastly increase the charm of these regions by their gorgeous blossoms.

The hilly landscape in such a warm climate is enlivened by a multitude of beautiful birds.[2] Many arrive in the spring months, migrating from the

[1] *Author*: Here I observed beautiful groups of *Laurus carolinensis*, Mich., *Ilex vomitoria*, *Olea americana*, Linn., *Magnolia glauca*, *grandiflora*, *Cephalanthus occidentalis*, Linn., several *Kalmia* in bloom, a beautiful *Prunus* and *Pavia*. Also I found in full bloom *Unisema sagittata*, Raf., *Lilium catesbaei*, Mich., *Pancratum liriosme*, Raf., a magnificent plant, *Iris rubescens*, Raf., *cuprea*, Pursh, with pale brown flowers, and many other plants belonging to this order.

[These species, *seriatim*, are: *Persea borbonia*, redbay; yaupon; *Osmanthus americanus*, devilwood; *Magnolia virginiana*, sweetbay; southern magnolia; buttonbush; *Kalmia latifolia*, mountain laurel; possibly *Aesculus pavia*, buckeye; *Pontederia lanceolata*, pickerelweed; leopard lily, pine lily; probably a *Hymenocallis*, the spider lilies; *Iris fulva*; *Iris cuprea* = *I. fulva*.]

[2] *Author*: Of the fine birds which I shot during my stay, I mention the *Cathartes stratus*, Wils., quite different from *Cathartes aura*, *Circus* (*Falco*) *ulginosus*, Edw., *Strix nebulosa*, Wils., *Tanagra ludoviciana*, Linn., *Muscipeta nunciola*, *Muscicapa viridis*, *Silvia protonotarius*, *agilis*, *flavicollis*, and several that are undetermined; *Turdus rufus*, *melodus*, *solitarius*, *orpheus*, *aquaticus*, *Hirundo americana*, *purpurea*, in the neighborhood of Bayou Sara, especially in trees. *Fringilla* (*Emberiza*) *Pecoris pratensis* (*Emberiza americana*), *Pyrgita savannah*, *albicolis*, *palustris*, *Fringilla ciris* (*vulgo le pape*, one of the most beautiful birds in southern Louisiana), *Cassicus ludovicianus*, *Psarocolius spurius*, *Corvus ossifragus*, *Picus pileatus*, *Erythrocephalus varius*, *auratus*, *Coccyzus* (Vieillot) *dominicus*, *Columba migratoria*, *caroliniensis*, Linn., *Ardea herodias*, *candidissima*, *Anas discors*.

[The foregoing species, identified *seriatim*, are:

[*Cathartes atratus*, Wils. = *Coragyps atratus*, black vulture. *Cathartes aura*, turkey vulture. *Circus* (*Falco*) *uliginosus*, Edw. = *Circus hudsonius*, marsh hawk. *Strix nebulosa*, Wils. = *Strix varia*, barred owl. *Tanagra ludoviciana*, Linn. = *Pheucticus ludovicianus*, rose-breasted grosbeak. Wilson described the western tanager, calling it *Tanagra ludoviciana* (type locality in Idaho). Linnaeus placed the rose-breasted grosbeak in the genus *Loxia* (1766). *Muscipeta nuncicola* = *Sayornis phoebe*, eastern phoebe. *Muscicapa viridis* = *Icteria virens*, yellow-breasted chat. *Silvia protonotarius* = *Protonotaria citrea*, prothonotary warbler. [*Silvia*] *agilis* = *Oporonis agilis*, Connecticut warbler. [*Silvia*] *flavicollis* = *Dendroica dominica*, yellow-throated warbler. *Turdus rufus* = *Toxostoma rufum*, brown thrasher. [*Turdus*] *melodus* = *Hylocichla mustelina*, wood thrush. [*Turdus*] *solitarius* = *Catharus guttatus*, hermit thrush. [*Turdus*] *orpheus* = *Mimus polyglottos*, equatorial regions, to make Louisiana a gathering place before redistributing themselves farther north. In the last days of March and the opening days of April countless flocks of wild pigeons begin their journey to more northern latitudes. The great numbers of these birds filling the air are unbelievable. In their abrupt descent it is not uncommon for them to injure one another because of the tremendous number coming together. It is not strange that by their burden they should crush the trees on which they roost in excessive numbers.[3]

Of mammals, I procured several specimens of the opossum[4] and the rabbit[5] which are common about Bayou Sara. The rabbit, usually called Virginia rabbit, in the United States takes the place of the European hare.

The little town of St. Francisville, with its warehouses at Bayou Sara on the river, is situated on the plateau of a hill about half an hour inland, as mentioned before. It is a very pretty little town, inhabited almost entirely by Anglo-Americans and Germans. The houses and the small Presbyterian church, which is situated nearly in the center of the place, are pleasing and neat. It also seems that this small town is more healthful than either Baton Rouge or Natchez.

mockingbird. [*Turdus*] *aquaticus* = *Seiurus noveboracensis*, northern waterthrush. *Hirundo americana* = *Hirundo rustica*, barn swallow. [*Hirundo*] *purpurea* = *Progne subis*, purple martin. *Fringilla* (*Emberiza*) *Pecoris* = *Molothrus ater*, brown-headed cowbird. [*Fringilla*] *pratensis* (*Emberiza americana*) = *Spiza americana*, dickcissel. *Pyrgita savannah* = *Passerculus sandwichensis*, savannah sparrow. [*Pyrgita*] *albicollis* = *Zonotrichia albicollis*, white-throated sparrow. [*Pyrgita*] *palustris* = *Melospiza georgiana*, swamp sparrow. *Fringilla circis* [sic] (*vulgo le pape*) = *Passerina ciris*, painted bunting. *Cassicus ludovicianus* = *Quiscalus quiscula*, common grackle. *Psarocolius spurius* = *Icterus spuricus*, orchard oriole. *Corvus ossifragus*, fish crow. *Picus pileatus* = *Dryocopus pileatus*, pileated woodpecker. [*Picus*] *Erythrocephalus* = *Melanerpes erythrocephalus*, red-headed woodpecker. [*Picus*] *varius* = *Sphyrapicus varius*, yellow-bellied sapsucker. [*Picus*] *auratus* = *Colaptes auratus*, yellow-shafted flicker. *Coccycus* (Vieillot) *dominicus* = *Coccyzus erythropthalmus*, black-billed cuckoo. *Columba migratoria* = *Ectopistes migratorius*, passenger pigeon. [*Columba*] *caroliniensis* [sic] = *Zenaidura macroura caroliensis*, the eastern race of the mourning dove. *Ardea herodias*, great blue heron. [*Ardea*] *candidissima* = *Leucophoyx thula*, snowy egret. *Anas discors*, blue-winged teal.]

[3] Here described is the passenger pigeon (*Ectopistes migratorius*), extinct since 1914, for which Alexander Wilson about 1810 estimated a passing flock at two billion birds. The most authoritative work on the species is that of A. W. Schorger, *The Passenger Pigeon: Its Natural History and Extinction.*

[4] *Author*: The North American marsupial, *Didelphis virginiana*, is about as large as a big cat or an average-sized fox. The ears are half black, the hair is silky, mixed with gray and black. I never found more than eight or ten young. [*Didelphis marsupialis pigra.*]

[5] *Sylvilagus*, restricted to the New World, contains eight species and more than sixty subspecies. The American hares, two subspecies of which (*Lepus californicus meriami* and *L. californicus melanotis*, both primarily west of the Mississippi) have ranges bordering Louisiana. The European hare is *Lepus europaeus.*

After I had spent eight days in fruitless waiting, a steamboat tied up at Bayou Sara and brought the news that the *Hekla,* for which I was waiting, could not yet, for various reasons, determine the day of its departure. It was also found that the boat was in very bad condition, and had acquired such a bad name because of various accidents it had been in, that scarcely any passengers would take passage on it. After careful consideration, I found myself compelled to change my travel plans. Instead of going up the Mississippi directly to the mouth of the Missouri, I decided to take passage on the first boat whose destination was the Ohio.

The months of March and April are very favorable for travel on the Mississippi, the Ohio, and their tributaries, because the melting snow and numerous rains raise the water level considerably, making travel less dangerous. It seemed reasonable to expect an early opportunity to go from Louisville, Cincinnati, or other places along the Ohio to St. Louis and to have the advantage of seeing the celebrated banks of the Ohio in the splendor of spring.

Soon thereafter, on the evening of April 8, a steamboat destined for the State of Tennessee came by. However I was unable to agree with the captain and was also scared off by the huge number of passengers crowding not only the inner space but also the upper deck. This missed chance was actually lucky for me for this boat perished on that journey.

On the tenth the steamboat *Maysville* bound for Louisville in Kentucky tied up at Bayou Sara for an hour to be supplied with wood. This boat, neither large nor new, also teemed with people, as had the earlier mentioned one. Nevertheless I secured passage on it, paying seventy-five Spanish dollars per person. The vessel was said to be a speedy traveler, and the captain was reputed to be an honest and courageous man. This latter fact should be carefully considered by every traveler, since one's comfort and good treatment while on board depend on the ship master's courtesy.

Almost all of the boats going up the Mississippi are overcrowded with passengers. From the upper regions of the river and from all its tributaries a countless number of flat-bottomed boats and small vessels drift down to New Orleans with produce of the land. There the owners sell the vessels as building material or as fuel and return as deck passengers on the steamboats. Often a large boat takes on two hundred such persons, who, by their noise and commotion, become a big annoyance to the cabin passengers.

About eleven o'clock the boat was set in motion and at the outset traveled along the uninhabited bank opposite Pointe Coupée. For two weeks the heat had reached such an intensity as is rarely felt in Germany during the hottest months. It rained but little and these rains made the atmosphere only more sultry. On the morning of my departure, at eight o'clock the

Indians of the Missouri and the Platte, by Charles Bird King
Young Omaha, War Eagle, Little Missouri, and Two Pawnees
(*Courtesy Smithsonian Institution, Washington*)

Chonocape (Big Kansas) of the Otos, by Charles Bird King
(*Courtesy Danish National Museum, Copenhagen*)

Sharitarish (Wicked Chief) of the Grand Pawnees, by Charles Bird King
(*Courtesy the White House, Washington*)

Ongpatonga (Big Elk) of the Omahas, by Charles Bird King

(Courtesy Thomas Gilcrease Institute of American History and Art, Tulsa)

Le Soldat du Chêne of the Osage tribe
(From Thomas L. McKenney and James Hall,
History of the Indian Tribes of North America)

Muskwaki of the Fox Indians, by Carl Bodmer
(*Courtesy Northern Natural Gas Company Collection, Joslyn Art Museum, Omaha*)

Big Soldier, by Carl Bodmer
(*Courtesy Northern Natural Gas Company Collection,
Joslyn Art Museum, Omaha, Nebraska*)

White Plume of the Kansa Indians, by Charles Bird King
(From Thomas L. McKenney and James Hall,
History of the Indian Tribes of North America)

thermometer registered 73°, the air was very clear, the de Luc hygrometer showed 52°, rising in the course of the day to 60°. Despite a strong wind from the west, which blew in about noon, we traveled up the stream at an unbelievable speed. The boat fully lived up to its reputation.

The fresh green of the poplars and willows combined with their wild surroundings made the rapid journey on the steamboat very pleasant. While the uninhabited left bank continuously presented primeval forests, the wooded region at the end of Pointe Coupée still contained scattered small plantations. The big bend which the river makes beyond Pointe Coupée, almost describing a complete circle from northeast to the west and south, forms a peninsula called Tunica after a now almost extinct Indian nation.

I have already mentioned seeing a few individuals of this nation, only a wretched remnant of a once powerful tribe, on the occasion of a hunting party in the neighborhood of Tunica. The little village of Tunica is situated on the left bank of the river not far from its bend to the northeast, and in its vicinity is also the island that bears the same name.

We left this island, overgrown with poplars, to our left and soon passed Bayou Tunica, located six English miles farther up the stream. Enormously tall poplars, oaks, ashes, and many other forest trees, entwined by giant climbing plants, adorned the banks of the river, which in turn were overgrown with impenetrable thickets of blackberry bushes. These trees, often one hundred and fifty feet high, of very great age, and of varied colors of foliage, fill the natural scientist with amazement. Farther up the stream the river banks become even wilder. Thorny smilax[6] and giant reeds make the forest almost impenetrable. The banks are very low, and the low land is swampy, harboring many alligators.

After the steamboat had passed the great bend, it took its course to the northeast past a group of islands called the Three Sisters. Here the left bank rises again to gentle hills covered with the finest leaf wood, great stretches of magnolia, catalpa, and walnut trees. On the right bank toward the mouth of the Acheffalaya [Atchafalaya] or Chefallo, whose remarkable water system must be considered one of the principal outlets of the Mississippi, I observed the continued flat and wild shore region where gigantic cypresses and poplars, clothed in dark green, a somber primeval forest, appeared in marked contrast to the attractive hills on the other side. These hills, so rich in picturesque forms and clothed with a variety of trees, are made tremendously more attractive by the varying light effects

[6] *Author*: *Smilax China*, *hasta*, Willd., and *Walteri*, Pursh, here take the place of the just as thorny *Smilax mauritanica* of southern Europe and northern Africa. [*Smilax China* could refer to *S. China sensu* Walter, which is *S. Walteri*. *Smilax hasta* = *S. bona-nox*.].

during the day. Against the intense blue of the sky, they present a great abundance of color, interspersed here and there by separate flats of meadows entirely devoid of trees.

The boat reached the mouth of the Acheffalaya about seven o'clock in the evening. Since the river bank is very flat and swampy, this arm of the Mississippi does not look nearly as wide as the amount of water which reaches the sea through this outlet might cause one to expect. The meager slope to the sea transforms the land between the Mississippi and the Acheffalaya into a delta which is permeated by countless channels flowing through swampland. During periods of flood stage, this region receives an immense amount of water from the Mississippi, which overflows its banks. Checked by numerous obstacles, the water gradually reaches the ocean, forming on its way great areas of bottomless swamps and lake-like bodies of water. The rapid current at the point where it leaves the Mississippi is gradually slowed until a flow of water is hardly detectable. In many places it resembles a dead channel. The mouth of the Acheffalaya lies at about 30° 56′ north latitude and 14° 46′ west longitude from Washington. The stream here makes another bend, twice intersecting the 31st degree of latitude.

After I had the Acheffalaya behind me, night had become complete. To take on wood and for some other reasons, the steamboat had to stop for several hours. About midnight the swifter current indicated the proximity of the confluence of the Red River.

The Red River which has its origin in the savannas of New Spain, and there is called the Rio Colorado de Nachitochez, is, after the Mississippi, the most important navigable river in the State of Louisiana. Its sources, owing their origin to a chain of mountains that separates the plains of New Mexico from the Rio Bravo del Norte, are only a few miles from the latter river, which runs from the north to the south almost parallel to the Mississippi.[7]

Travelers penetrating farther into the mountains experience many hindrances, severity of climate, and wildness of the inhabitants. These may account for the fact that so little scientific information is available concerning these regions. From the sea to the sources of the Arkansas, these mountains, except for a few mountain passes, are entirely unexplored by science. We would also be without adequate information about one of the sources of the Arkansas had it not been for the efforts of Major Long.[8]

---

[7] The Red has its sources in the plains of the Texas Panhandle, south of the Canadian River drainage. The Rio Bravo del Norte of the Spanish-Mexican provinces is the Rio Grande, rising in the San Juan Mountains of south-central Colorado.

[8] Major Stephen Harriman Long (1784–1864), who became a member of the Corps

The inhabitants of Mexico, who live in a continual war with the Indians, are poorly prepared to investigate this region, and travelers who go from Texas to Old Mexico hold to a southwesterly route towards Coahuila and commonly cross the Rio Bravo in the vicinity of San Fernando or farther downstream and from there turn to Monterrey or Natividad.

The Red River[9] receives several other rivers and bayous, of which only a few are navigable for important vessels. The most important river emptying into the Red River is the Washita. By this intricate water system the former has another connection with the Mississippi. The course of the Red River is interrupted by lakes, shallows, and rapids, but from Nachitochez and Alexandria it is navigable by steamboats and, as far as Coshatville, by other vessels. Since the region along the Red River is extremely fertile, especially suited for the cultivation of excellent tobacco, the land will increase more and more in population. In the future the region of the Red River will become one of the richest parts of the southern United States.

On account of the great darkness, which became particularly dense toward morning (for the journey was continued with all possible speed because of the high water), I could not observe the location of Fort Adams, which is close to the boundary line between the States of Mississippi and Louisiana at latitude 31°.

Also, on my return journey, the same hindrance prevented me from making observations, and I only add that Fort Adams formerly was a military post of importance. But since Louisiana and Florida have become

---

of Engineers of the U.S. Army in 1814, sought the source of the Arkansas, among other objectives, a dozen years after the less methodical Zebulon Montgomery Pike (1779–1813) had ascended the river in 1806. Cf. Edwin James, *An Account of an Expedition from Pittsburgh to the Rocky Mountains, Performed in the Years 1819 and '20, by order of the Hon. J. C. Calhoun, Sec'y of War: Under the Command of Major Stephen H. Long . . .* 2 vols. (Philadelphia, Carey and Lea, 1823); Zebulon Montgomery Pike, *Journals, with Letters and Related Documents,* edited by Donald Jackson, 2 vols. (Norman, University of Oklahoma Press, 1966).

[9] *Author:* The Red River flows through about seven degrees of latitude, from the 38th to the 31st degree of north latitude and 10° of longitude, from west to east. Of the lakes and rivers connected with it there are noteworthy, in addition to the forks that form it, the Bodeau, flowing from the northeast and forming a lake of like name at the point of confluence, also Lake Bistincan, formed by the Datche, Black Lake River (Lac Noir), Saline Lake, all coming from the north; further, Spanish Lake near Nachitochez in the southwest, all very unimportant.

The Washita, formed by the Black River and the Buffalo River, which have their origin at the 35th degree of north latitude, takes up several unimportant streams. By way of a bayou, the Catuff, which empties into the Washita at Lake Ocatahoola, it has a connection with the Mississippi.

possessions of the United States[10] and the population of Mississippi and Alabama has increased, the fort has been given up and is destined to become a complete ruin. Seven English miles east of Fort Adams is the little village of Pinkneyville.

On the morning of April 11 an impenetrable fog, unusual for this season, prevailed, preventing me completely from distinguishing any object on the adjoining shore, and only rarely the outlines of the rows of hills lining the left bank in many places could be made out. On the right bank occasional low ridges gently sloping and overgrown with Florida pines (*Pinus palustris*) soon disappeared and gave way to a low luxuriant forested bank.

Solid fog continued until noon, at which time we were in sight of several small islands situated above the mouths of the Little Buffalo and the Homochitto. Unimportant bayous meriting no description empty into the Mississippi on its left bank. About fifteen miles from Natchez the fog had almost disappeared. We were in the vicinity of St. Catharine's Creek, which flows between rather high hills and empties into the Mississippi. The above-named heights drop abruptly to the river, forming low mountains, and turn to the northeast, reaching the stream again at Natchez. They must be regarded as a continuation of a higher chain of mountains to the east which gently slope to the river, and on account of a white color, due to limestone, are called White Cliffs or Ellis Cliffs.

Six English miles from here is another island, three miles long, situated in the middle of the stream. At four in the afternoon we reached a row of houses on the bank. Located at the foot of a high hill, this forms the landing place, or if we should call it such, the harbor of Natchez. Sandbars and shallows make it difficult to land here during the low water and require the greatest care, with frequent soundings.

After landing the captain informed me, if I so desired, I should have ample time to view the appearance of the town until the approach of night. Of course I proceeded to take advantage of this opportunity at once, hastening through the muddy streets of the lower part of the town lined with shops and saloons, up the steep way leading to the top of the hill where the town of Natchez is located on its flat summit. Along the sharp slope, one hundred and fifty feet high, runs a street and one looks down

---

[10] Fort Adams, below Natchez at Loftus Heights (and therefore seen easily during daylight hours on the Mississippi), was established by General James Wilkinson on October 17, 1798, just six miles above the line defined by Pinckney's Treaty with Spain (Treaty of San Lorenzo), October 27, 1795. On the east bank of the Mississippi, it gave the U.S. powerful leverage on the lower river. It was closed in 1810. Francis Paul Prucha, *The Sword of the Republic: The United States Army on the Frontier, 1783–1846*, 54–55, 58.

as if into an abyss. The houses at the landing appear to lie perpendicularly below one's feet.

This poorly chosen location witnesses many accidents caused by great portions' of the mountain sliding down and covering up a considerable part of the town. As soon as the summit of the hill has been reached, one sees the little town of Natchez on the right. Rather well-built, substantial houses arranged according to a definite plan, with straight streets, etc., make a good impression. Natchez, located at 31° 33′ north latitude and 91° 15′ west longitude from London, contained some 300 to 400 houses. In 1822 it had 2,184 inhabitants, 1,448 were whites, and 736 were colored.

The population must have increased considerably since then, though the frequent epidemics of yellow fever do not allow this increase to be as rapid as in other places of the United States. Natchez is the chief market for all products of the interior part of the state of Mississippi and of several other adjoining eastern parts of the United States. The chief exports are cotton, tobacco, indigo, flax, hemp, maize, etc. The greater part of the cotton shipped via New Orleans to England is of exceptionally fine quality and its cultivation is becoming more and more extensive. The tobacco, on the other hand, which is of lower quality, finds fewer foreign markets.

The landing place can accommodate vessels of three to four hundred tons, and before the introduction of the steamboat merchantmen comfortably came from the mouth of the river as far as Natchez, though the distance of the town is three hundred English miles from New Orleans. Steamboats greatly furthered the trade of the state of Mississippi, as well as that of all states in North America which are located on navigable rivers. This includes the states on the Mississippi extending from 31° to 35° latitude, whose western border is the bank of the Mississippi River.

The most advantageous locations from the standpoint of commerce are the counties of Hancock and Jackson on the Gulf of Mexico. (The state is situated between 30° 10′ and 35° north latitude and between 11° 10′ and 14° 25′ west longitude from Washington.)[11]

For more than one hundred English miles the state of Mississippi constitutes a flat, in part, swampy country. But further on the land rises, especially toward the northeast, forming attractive elevated areas, mostly covered by dense virgin forests and abounding in springs. These have created several rivers of considerable size which empty either into the Mississippi or into the Gulf of Mexico. Among these are the Yazoo,

[11] *Author*: Although the circumstance should not be overlooked that the neighborhood of five or six border states could embroil it in political situations by which this state, through existing bad relations, may perhaps be most affected.

navigable for 150 English miles from northeast into the Mississippi, and Big Black and Homochitto, navigable for barely fifty or sixty miles and emptying into the Mississippi. In addition the Pearl River, navigable for 150 English miles, and the little Pascagoula, navigable for seventy miles, flow from the north and their mouths in Lake Borgne and the Gulf of Mexico are of greater importance.

The most fertile part of the state lies along the Mississippi River and extends forty or fifty miles inland. There are, however, many other fertile regions. The parts inhabited by the Choctaws are well suited for cultivation, and for this reason large sections of land have been bought from them and the Chickasaw Indians.

The Choctaws, as I have already said, are a peaceful nation. The numerous tribes roam over the neighboring states and rarely become undesirable because of theft or other acts incompatible with the social order in which they could become entangled. During my stay at Pointe Coupée and at Bayou Sara I frequently met up with these natives in the forest. On account of their roving habits and their dirtiness they might, perhaps, be compared with our gypsies, though, barring their drunkenness, they are better than the latter.

The same cannot be said of the Chickasaws. Their frequent wars with the whites, their many political entanglements because of the hostility of the English, French, and Americans, and finally their numerous feuds with neighboring Indian tribes have imparted to their character something of mistrust and hostility. These characteristics plus a certain avariciousness, cruelty, and drunkenness do not recommend this nation as neighbors.[12]

With all products of the United States prospering in Mississippi, European fruit varieties included, the great excess of food stuffs, and numerous rivers constituting a substitute for bad roads, making communication among the people easy, the state of Mississippi should increase rapidly in

[12] The Chickasaws merited the author's estimates of their warlike character, aggressiveness, and craft. They occupied territory in the early eighteenth century from northern Mississippi to the confluence of the Ohio with the Tennessee, eastward to Georgia and westward to the Mississippi River. They were frequently at war with their neighbors and all but annihilated on more than one occasion the tribes which sought to invade their homeland. They began their emigration west of the Mississippi in 1822, following land cessions to the U.S. in 1786, 1801, 1805, 1816, and 1818, by which the tribe relinquished holdings at Muscle Shoals, north of the Tennessee River, from the Tennessee to the west bank of the Tombigbee, and finally the lands which remained from the southern boundary of Tennessee northward. By treaties in 1832 and 1834, the Chickasaws remaining in the East were removed to Indian Territory (present Oklahoma). *American State Papers, Indian Affairs*, I, 648–49; II, 100–103, 164–65; Charles J. Kappler, *Indian Affairs: Laws and Treaties*, 3 vols. II, 10–12, 57–58, 93–94, 122–24, 259–66, 309–15.

population were it not for the great hindering factor, the destructive character of the climate for the European settler.[13]

The summers are, on the average, as uncomfortably hot as the winters, considering the latitude, are cold, wet, and foggy. In the late summer and the autumn, bilious fever and malaria rage, while in the winter and the spring rheumatism and bronchial troubles are common. To this must be added the occasional visitations of yellow fever, which rages in the settled communities, carrying away the inhabitants. The recurrent, terrible epidemics in Natchez furnish sad testimony on this point.

On a territory of 45,350 English square miles or 29,020,000 acres of land, the population amounted to no more than 75,488, about twenty inhabitants to a geographic square mile.[14] Most of these live in the country or in little settlements or small villages on the banks of the rivers. All of these, except Natchez and Monticello, the seat of the legislature and the state government, do not deserve the name of town.

In regard to the people, the same mixture of races is found as in Louisiana, with this difference, however, that the whites constitute the majority and that there are many free people. The Indians, who at the time of the first settlement were a source of danger, have either been exterminated or by surrender of their lands have been forced to emigrate.

[13] Much of Mississippi is semitropical with average mean temperatures sufficient to provide a long growing season. The average rainfall at Jackson is just over fifty inches. Settlers in the nineteenth century adapted easily to the climate.

[14] *Author*: The civil divisions of the state of Mississippi and the population in the year 1822 were as follows:

COUNTIES	WHITE	COLORED	TOTAL
Adams, including Natchez	4,005	8,171	12,176
Amité	4,004	2,847	6,851
Claiborne	2,840	3,125	5,965
Clowington	1,824	406	2,230
Franklin	2,277	1,544	3,821
Greene	1,063	382	1,682
Hancock	1,142	452	1,594
Jackson	1,300	382	1,682
Jefferson	3,154	3,668	6,822
Lawrence	3,919	997	4,916
Marion	1,884	1,232	3,116
Monroe	2,192	529	2,721
Perry	1,539	498	2,037
Pike	3,443	995	4,438
Warren	1,401	1,292	2,693
Wilkinson	3,937	5,781	9,718
Wayne	2,250	1,073	3,323
	42,176	33,372	75,548

Those still living in the state have to keep the peace. The great majority of the white population is of English origin, consisting for the most part of individuals who have exchanged the eastern states for the West. Since these migrations did not begin until the end of the past century, this great tract of land, as well as the entire western part of the United States, was formerly visited only occasionally by relatively few Spaniards and Frenchmen, brought by the hunt or by war with the Indians.

Impelled by greed for gold, Fernando de Soto was the first European to touch the Mississippi River. Landing early in 1539, this adventurer on his expedition from East Florida roamed with his companions through this region for several years and met his death on the Mississippi in May, 1542. The fairy-tale stories with which he tested the credulity of his age extended not only to the natives but also to the country itself and its products. His adventurous description seems to be substantiated by fact in only a few instances or not at all. It betrays the chief tendency of all Spanish adventurers of the sixteenth century, namely, by wonderful and alluring depiction to recruit new followers in their home country for their distant undertakings.

Like the conquerers of Peru and Mexico, de Soto describes the splendid establishment of several Indian towns whose princes were resplendent in costly garments and were surrounded by their retinues and courtiers. His fairy-tale description of the journey resembles in many respects that of [Francisco de] Orellana, whose great realms under the dominion of Amazon queens play a romantic role. But to both adventurers not all credit can be denied, for they were the first Europeans to discover and sail on the two greatest river systems in America.

Until 1682, when La Salle traveled down the Mississippi, little seems to have been known about the river. The name Louisiana, or Nouvelle France, dates back to the discoveries of this great explorer. The name Louisiana, now applying only to one state of the Union, formerly included the great tract of land bounded by the highlands of Mexico on the west, the Allegheny chain on the east, the Gulf of Mexico on the south, and the endless prairies of the Missouri and upper Mississippi on the north. Consequent to La Salle's discoveries, France claimed the overlordship of this region.

In 1716 the French established a settlement below Natchez for whose protection they built Fort Rosalie. Other settlers pushed ahead as far as the Yazoo, where they too built a fort which was destroyed by the Chickasaws in 1722.

Peaceful people, the Natchez at first sought to live in harmony and concord with the French. But repeated deeds of violence by the new settlers, also the presumptiousness of Chevalier Beauville, governor of Louisiana, and the cruelty of Monsieur de Chopart, commandant of Rosalie, incensed the Natchez to the extreme and they formed a union with the wild and warlike Chickasaw Indians in order to punish their oppressors. After the fortunes of war had been favorable to the Natchez on various occasions from 1723 to 1730, and they had inflicted great damage on their adversaries, treason and the imperfect execution of their plans delivered them finally into the hands of the French, who exterminated them completely.[15]

This horrible lot was in no way deserved by the unfortunate Natchez, since they belonged to the better and the more civilized Indians on the North American continent, and since the most unheard-of acts of cruelty had forced them into war against their oppressors. Through the inhumanity of immigrated Europeans, the Natchez therefore found an end similar to that of the equally innocent Guanches of the Canary Islands.

The few individuals of the once powerful nation of Natchez who escaped the murderous greed of their pursuers were lost among the Chickasaws and Creeks, who took them in and befriended them, and among whom remnants of their language are still found. After this blood bath, fear of the power of European arms held most of the Indiana tribes of the lower Mississippi in check. They stayed in their forests and swamps until the cession of the eastern bank of the Mississippi to England in 1763. The following year a regiment of soldiers marching upstream was ambushed by the Tunicas and badly beaten.

When I got back on board late that evening, I found that the captain was not inclined to continue the journey during the night. A dense fog had

---

[15] *Author*: On November 30, 1729, the Natchez Indians suddenly attacked Fort Rosalie and killed some six hundred Frenchmen. Chopart fell at the hand of a lowly warrior, since the chiefs regarded it beneath their dignity to lay hands on him.

[Fort Rosalie shows on the map in Le Page du Pratz, *Histoire de la Louisiana* (Paris, 1758) at a point on the east bank of the Mississippi below Pointe Coupée. Le Page, from personal observation, describes the adjacent Natchez town, the removal of which became a matter of fierce controversy between Sun of the Apple, Chief of the Natchez, and Sieur de Chopart, commandant of Fort Rosalie serving under M. Perier, governor of Louisiana. The resulting massacre of the garrison in 1729 cost the lives of Chopart and most of his seven hundred followers.

[The French between 1729 and 1731 defeated and dispersed the Natchez with the aid of the Choctaws, so that the former never regained tribal identity. They were of Muskhogean stock. The Beauville mentioned by the author is Sieur de Bienville, several times governor of Louisiana (first at the then capital, Biloxi, which he established 1701–1712; again beginning 1717, moving the capital to New Orleans, which he founded 1718; dismissed eight years later, he was reappointed in 1733, retiring to Paris in 1743). Le Page du Pratz, *op. cit.*, III, 231–262.]

settled on the river, and it was impossible to distinguish objects at any distance. Even when the fog lifted at about midnight, it was thought advisable not to start, because the irregular bottom a short distance upstream from Natchez makes navigation most hazardous in several places. The hazard takes the form of uprooted trees [sawyers] which have sunk to the bottom, and in shallow places their tops protrude to the surface of the water. Recent serious accidents had intimidated the pilots, inducing them rightly to pay more heed to the safety of the journey than to speed. Misguided ambition impels some steamboat captains to enter foolish races.

Since the water level was still high, no danger arose from leaving the deep stream channel. It was not necessary to follow all the bends of the river to take advantage of the weaker current. Since the vessel could take its course on the great expanse of water from one point of land to another, or from one bend to another, in a straight line, the loss of a few hours was of slight consequence. Night travel did not suit my purpose anyhow. There was still ample time for me to see the Ohio during the month of April. Even in May the Ohio remains high enough for steamboat navigation. Its many tributaries flowing between chains of high hills keep it sufficiently supplied with water.

During this night, and also during the succeeding nights that I had to spend on the boat, the greatest disturbance prevailed among the large number of passengers of all classes. The salon assigned fashionable travelers, those holding cabins, was so overcrowded that one could scarcely move. Many, not even having beds to sleep in, had to content themselves to lie on tables or in chairs. The company of travelers was of such a mixed character, I could not help but note the difference between my present fellow passengers and those aboard the *Feliciana*, also those on the steamboat *Robert Fulton*, on which I had made the trip to Havana. Excepting an old naval officer, I found no one with whom I, as a stranger, could associate.

I found neither inclination nor time for work because of the incessant commotion and the perpetual noise of so many people. The deck was so crowded with them that the captain requested me personally not to go up, in order to avoid being molested by rivermen from Kentucky and Tennessee who, being of a somewhat irritable nature and inclined to fighting, might easily cause trouble.

However, I must say for the honor of these people that, disregarding this fault, they are an industrious and upright class who have always distinguished themselves by courage, endurance, and honesty, and they certainly constitute one of the better elements of the immigrant population in North America. In addition to the mixed company and the limited space, a very unpleasant odor and an almost unbearable heat prevailed, and with it all a multitude of flies and mosquitoes and a great lack of cleanliness, of which I previously had but little cause to complain in America. All this caused me to find delight in the unusual speed with which the steamboat pursued its journey. But there was the disadvantage that I was prevented from making suitable observations and also deprived of the opportunity of recording more in detail the story of my trip to Louisville.

During the night another steamboat joined us. Both vessels started at daybreak, and now I had the opportunity to see the reputed speed of the *Maysville*. In less than two hours we had lost our companion boat from sight, despite the fact that the other applied all the power of its machinery. Our captain showed good judgment in keeping regular speed, in order not to risk damage to his boat.

The giant river carried countless trees, some quite dry and still covered with foliage which evidently had but recently been uprooted, while others had been in the river for a long time. Such trees often become entangled in great masses, to form mammoth piles on the banks and in shallow places, their branches and roots entwined. Here they decay in part or are again set adrift by the force of water at flood stage and start another journey. Thus one may see here trees of northern wood from the upper Missouri and Mississippi. After years of traveling, they reach the lower course of the river, then its mouth, where the principal crisis awaits them. Either they remain on the coastal shore and decay there or they drift out on the waves of the ocean to be caught by its currents, which finally cast them on shores of far distant continents.

The above-described savage character marked the Mississippi with monotonous regularity during our journey. Only seldom is the great solitude broken here and there by small settlements or wretched isolated huts, whose defective roofs shelter only woodcutters earning meager wages by supplying steamboats with necessary wood for fuel. Usually the boats stop once every twenty-four hours at such places. The business ordinarily does not take more than half an hour, and this was the only time that I had an opportunity to go on shore.

A few miles out of Natchez one sees the little river Fairchild, which, with several minor interconnecting lakes, constitutes the connection between the Mississippi and Washita. Several rather important islands, in part covered with huge trees, are located almost equidistant to the outlet of the rather broad Bayou Pierre, or Stony Creek, before which is the little settlement of Gipsonport, the capital of Clairborne County.

A few miles above Stony Creek there is a whirlpool which is more than half an English mile across, one of the largest in the entire run of the

Mississippi. Opposite the mouth of the Big Black River the stream forms a great bend, along which the western bank extends to a rocky point affording a beautiful sight. Here the enormous masses of river water break on the shore with extreme force, setting the floods of the great river in turmoil. Seeing this spectacle in the light of the setting sun in its entire magnificence, I could not help admiring the power with which our boat defied the resistance of the powerful current.

Not far from the western bank, near the whirlpool, is an inland lake nearly twelve miles long called Lac Joseph. It is said to abound in fish, and to my knowledge it has no outlet into the river.

In the course of the night of the thirteenth we passed several islands and also the unimportant settlements Pointe Plaisante, Palmira, and Warrington, and reached without mishap, still before sunrise, a beautiful row of hills, the Walnut Hills (Los Nogales), so named because of the large number of walnut trees that abound there. The wonderful effect which distinguished the splendid groups of deciduous trees in various shades of color, resplendent in the rays of the rising sun, signaled the abundance and variety adorning this primeval forest. I could distinctly make out the ashes, magnolias, and tulip trees.

The Yazoo, winding among a chain of rather high hills, empties into the Mississippi from the east a few miles above Walnut Hills. At its mouth grows a reed as yet undetermined. This together with *Equisetum praealtum*, Raf., and *Hyemale*, line the sandbars and the banks of many North American rivers from latitude 32° upward.[16] To the extent that the reeds replace the tall *Arundinaria*, they are mingled with the varieties of *Typha*, *Paspalum*, *Cyperus*,[17] and other aquatic plants which prefer a cooler climate, and they give the country a character similar to that of Europe and northern Asia.

Above the Yazoo we reached a large island which the Anglo-Americans call My Wife's Island, while the Creoles of French extraction call it Ile aux Assimines on account of the large number of *Annona tribola*, Linn.,[18] which grow there. Opposite this island on the west bank is the rather impressive settlement of Sparta.

On this day I frequently saw several migratory birds of the warmer zone. Several beautiful herons (*Ardea herodias*, Wils., *exilis*, Wils., *candidissima*, Jaeq.) frequented the lower banks or sat sadly on the branches or roots of lodged driftwood. The kingfisher (*Alcedo alcyon*)

[16] Two species of *Equisetum*, horsetail or scouring rush.

[17] *Arundinaria*, a bamboo-like grass; *Typha*, the genus of cat tails; *Paspalum*, a genus of grasses; *Cyperus*, a genus of sedges.

[18] *Annona tribola* = *Asimina tribola*, pawpaw.

flew piping, scared by every noise from the bushes along the bank. Huge flocks of ducks and diving birds, especially *Anas sponsa* and *Mergus cucullatus*, covered the bays and calm stretches of the river. Flocks of screaming parrots flew noisily across the Mississippi.

To hunt fish, the white-headed eagle (*Haliaeetus leucocephalus*, Savig.) peered down on the water from the top of the highest trees for hours. Flocks of noisy crows (*Corvus ossifragus*, Wils.) sat on drifting logs to feed on small fish and crustaceans. Lonely racoons (*Procyon lotor*, Ill.) visited the banks at the wildest spots on the river to warm themselves in the full heat of the sun. And the fallow deer, driven by thirst, cooled itself in shallow and shaded places.

A few shy jaguars[19] at windbreaks became frightened at the approach of our vessel and quickly fled into the dark primeval forest. However, the alligators became less numerous the nearer we approached the Arkansas River, and it seemed to me that these creatures do not inhabit the Mississippi above the thirty-third degree of latitude.

In the course of the day we passed several islands. Au Beau Soliel and Aux Lapins are the most outstanding. On the morning of the fourteenth we were at the end of a place called La Longue Vue des Ils à Grapin. Here the Mississippi is not only very wide but also flows in a straight direction for a distance of twelve miles, thus affording a very extensive view. About noon we crossed latitude 33° and a few hours later reached a bend in the river. In the middle a large island is located opposite Illichico, a settlement inhabited by a few Indians, Frenchmen, and Anglo-Americans. The poverty-stricken appearance of this place fits well into this extremely wild region.

Immediately upstream from Illichico is the beginning of Spanish Moss Bend (l'Anse à la Barbe), a great bend nearly eight English miles long, the middle of which is almost exactly at 33° 15′ of latitude. Deriving its name from the fact that *Tillandsia usneoides* grows here so abundantly, it imparts to the forest the peculiar character frequently described before. Farther upstream I observed that this parasite decreases more and more and I do not recall having seen it beyond 34° latitude.

---

[19] *Author*: This beautiful variety of cat, quite different from *Felis novahispanica*, Cuv., is somewhat larger than the European wildcat, has elongated black spots on a background shading from bluish gray to reddish yellow. Among the Creoles it is called *chat tigre*. It is fairly numerous in Louisiana and Mississippi.

[Probably the bobcat, *Lynx rufus floridanus* in this range, inasmuch as there have been hitherto no authenticated observations of the jaguar (*Felis onca*) as far north and east as the area between the mouths of the Yazoo and the Arkansas, nor of the ocelot (*Felis pardalis*), either of which, because of its spots, might qualify, though obviously the latter is more logical from "*länglich schwarz gefleckt . . . . Grunde.*"]

When we arrived at the end of the bend night had fallen. We continued traveling, although navigation became more hazardous than it had been during the previous nights because of a great number of small islands.

On the morning of April 15 we were at the northwestern point of Ozark Island, three miles from the mouth of the Arkansas, and we reached this great river soon after daybreak. It was at flood stage, the banks being completely inundated. I could not judge the width of the river bed. I could detect no noticeable difference in temperature between its water and that of the Mississippi. I was not surprised at this since the high water level of the Arkansas was no doubt due to the melting snow on the western prairies, but not that in the highlands of New Spain where the snow does not begin to melt until May.

I add the observation that most of the small rivers which course through the prairies of North America are quite turbid during their high-water period. On finding the Arkansas very muddy, I felt justified in taking that as proof that this river, which receives a great many small streams, must have assumed flood stage because of heavy spring showers falling on the plains bordering the Andes chain.

6

AFTER half an hour the steamboat
left the mouth of the Arkansas. During our stay we had taken on a supply
of wood sufficient for twenty-four hours. The region here is overgrown
with oak trees. With regret I left the river that still hides so much of mystery from the eyes of the investigator, firmly resolving to visit the nearest
Indian villages upstream on my return trip. They constitute some of the
chief depots for the fur trade in western Louisiana. However, this resolve
could not be carried out subsequently, and I had to postpone my proposed
visit to a future and more favorable time.

The White River empties into the Mississippi about sixteen miles above
the Arkansas and is connected by a natural channel with it. A stream of
medium size, it flows into the Mississippi from the northwest. It is navigable for small boats only, and its banks are not developed by aggressive
inhabitants, nor is the ground cultivated to the extent of its larger
neighbors.

In the course of the day we passed several islands and sandbars. This
requires the utmost caution on the part of the pilots, especially in places
where the river is very wide and consequently less deep. I found the
Mississippi unusually wide at Îles au Fer, two islands lying parallel to
each other in the middle of the stream. Overgrown with tall poplars and
many reeds, their gay coloring is in marked contrast to the dark cypresses
of the neighboring banks. Despite all my efforts at questioning I was unable
to ascertain the reason for the name of these islands. I doubt that the
probable iron content of the soil induced the French Creoles to call them
Iron Islands, for above the mouth of the White River another island is
called Lead Island (*Île au Plomb*), and none of this ore is located there.[1]

[1] Le Page du Pratz, reflecting the commercial interest of Antoine Crozat's charter control
of Louisiana (1712–1717) and that of John Law's Company of the West (1717–1723), as

It is often very difficult to determine the origin of place names used by the Creoles. For these people give to islands, rivers, mountains, etc. names of the most insignificant historical events and even of unimportant persons. Thus the regions of Canada and New France owe their names to such unimportant circumstances. The larger rivers retain much shortened or distorted names of the tribes who originally lived near them or in whose doubtful possession they now are. The smaller rivers not serving an original tribe as habitat were and are even today often named for quite an insignificant animal first seen there, or a tree, or the color of the water, or, as is still more customary, the name of the first discoverer. The latter is usually an adventurer who, as a hunter or fur dealer, sought these foreign regions and its wild inhabitants.

During my stay on the Missouri and in the western prairies in company with French Creoles, I had the opportunity to learn for myself at first hand how unknown regions are named. Names thus given may again be changed or entirely forgotten. Instances where mountains or rivers may have several names at the same time are not infrequent, because they are visited by travelers, each claiming to be the first discoverer and each seeking to maintain the right of discovery. In this respect French Creoles and people of English origin rarely agree on names. Even if one accepts the name applied by the other, they usually distort it so that it is next to impossible to recognize the original name.

On the morning of the sixteenth the boat took on the necessary wood supply at a little plantation situated beside a rectangular meadow. Since a natural grass plain in this region of the Mississippi is a very rare phenomenon, I could not refrain from paying it a hurried visit, however insignificant the meadow plot might be. Although growing very short, most of the grasses were in full bloom.

A few pretty flowering plants adorned the beautiful green, and I found a good harvest for my herbarium on this small tract[2] contrasting so markedly to the gigantic shapes of the woods in the nearby virgin forest. For a long time boatmen have observed with interest this little patch of grassland, which in appearance reminded me of a pasture in Germany.

I was not able to find any traces of uprooted trees on its surface, leading

---

well as French interest in developing the Crown Colony thereafter, shows a number of mines in his two maps of Louisiana in *Histoire de la Louisiane* of 1758. Gold, silver, and lead were more often named than real in this period.

[2] *Author*: Among others, *Houstonia coerulea*, Bart., *Draba hispidula*, Mich., *Pogonia verticillata*, Bart., *Anemone thalictroides*, Bart. [These species, respectively, are bluet; *Draba hispidula* = *D. reptans*, Carolina draba; *Pogonia verticillata* = *Isotria verticillata*, whorled isotria; *Anemone thalictroides* = *Anemonella thalictroides*, rue anemone.]

me to the conclusion that it does not owe its origin to an earlier clearing of the ground. Any field well cleared of stumps and roots, if left uncultivated for only two or three years, develops trees several feet high because of the great fertility of the American soil. I was, however, not able to find the slightest vestige of young trees. Only a few ancient oaks proudly raised their magnificent foliage-covered limbs, revealing by their appearance the effect of an open location and the influence of light on vegetation. Everywhere on the edge of this meadow as well as on the banks of the river I found *Cercis canadensis* and *Annona tribola* in full bloom. However, *Itea virginica*,[3] the laurels, and most of the Liliaceae had already shed their wedding attire.

Not far from the just described patch of grass, the St. Francis River flows into the Mississippi. Its course and the volume of water equals that of the White River. Both of these rivers flow almost parallel to one another from the north-northwest into the main stream and higher up follow a course in the same general direction. The St. Francis, or in French, Rivière St. Francis, in Spanish, Rio San Francisco, flows through a swampy plain and is not bordered by high hills as are the Arkansas and the White Rivers.

There are a few lakes near the St. Francis, the most important being Lake Michegama, which is connected with it near its convergence with the Mississippi. The shallowness of the lake and the surrounding stagnant waters may be the reason for the unhealthful climate of this region and its relatively sparse population.

Upstream from the St. Francis the islands in the Mississippi increase more and more, so that one comes near joining the other, and often several such islands, side by side, extend across the bed of the river. The country up to Fort Pickering[4] is almost entirely uninhabited except for wild animals and is so savage, unhealthful, and swampy that its possession will not be contested with them soon. Most of the islands have received their names

---

[3] Respectively, the redbud; the pawpaw; and Virginia willow.

[4] Originally named Fort Adams when Captain Isaac Guion and two companies of the Third Infantry moved south from Fort Washington at Cincinnati in the summer of 1797, the post was renamed Pike, and in 1802 it took its name from Secretary of War Timothy Pickering. The post at Chickasaw Bluffs had been the site of earlier forts built by the French in 1698 and the Spaniards in 1794. It became important as the U.S. took over Louisiana Territory in 1803, but by the end of 1804 it listed a complement of only sixteen soldiers and was closed entirely in 1810.

The government factory at Chickasaw Bluffs adjoining the Fort was opened in 1802 and in the ensuing sixteen years until its closing in 1818 traded heavily with the Chickasaws for furs, tallow, and beeswax.

American State Papers, Military Affairs, I, 176–77; *American State Papers, Indian Affairs,* I, 772, II, 56. Francis Paul Prucha, *The Sword of the Republic: The United States Army on the Frontier, 1783–1846,* 55, 58, 65, 73.

from the French Creoles, the most important of which I shall mention as they are encountered during the trip upstream.

Opposite the mouth of the St. Francis is a rather large island, which, as is customary, bears the name of the nearby river. It is peculiar that at the mouth of almost all rivers flowing into the Mississippi there is an island located so close to the confluence that often there is only a very narrow channel for navigation. As a result of the clay and sand drifting in and deposited there by the action of the counter currents, it becomes dangerous to the rivermen. Islands, connected with one another by sand bars or shallows which at low water protrude above the surface, join one another like an archipelago for a distance of more than forty miles. Since the river has several bends these islands deprive one of views into the distance.[5]

Because of prevailing high water, the great width of the stream, the wildness of nature, and the giant trees, there is not lacking by any means that majestic character with which the Creator impresses His stamp of boundless concern on great and small forms, even in a region not blessed with a large variety of scenic beauty. The group of islands of which I have spoken consists of Îles aux Morvans, à Verdon, au Chenal St. Martin, aux Raisins, and au Conseil (Council Island). The latter is the largest.

After the steamboat had made its way through those shallows we reached President's Island (*Île au President*) as twilight was approaching. It is one of the largest in the Mississippi, being more than twelve miles long and three to four miles wide. Its banks, however, are flat, despite its great size, and the ground, subject to inundation by the river, is swampy and overhung with dense virgin forest.

The night of the seventeenth we passed Fort Pickering. This former military post of the United States is situated on the fourth chain of hills sloping down to the Mississippi and extending from east to west. The area was formerly inhabited by the Chickasaw Indians. With the departure of the warlike aborigines, the fort in later years lost importance and was occupied by only a few soldiers and finally by some half-bloods. A mixture forming a link between the red and white races, they have acquired some of the customs of both.

The development of this part of the state of Tennessee, bordering on the state of Mississippi at the thirty-fifth degree of north latitude, increases gradually, since the soil is very fertile here. The Nanconnah and the Wolf

[5] The correlation of Duke Paul's observations with actual geographical knowledge today for the ascent of the Mississippi and Ohio rivers reveals a high degree of accuracy on his part. Many of his predictions in ensuing pages, moreover, have long since been sustained by economic and commercial developments.

rivers (Rivière du Loup) are two unimportant streams which empty into the Mississippi, and at the mouth of the latter the little settlement of Memphis is located. These small streams have their sources in the Chickasaw Hills and the bordering low plains. Opposite the Wolf there was formerly a small Spanish fort. Now completely demolished, it was abandoned at the time of the surrender of the Arkansas Territory to the United States.

When daylight came I was near another leveling of the Chickasaw Hills known as the Third Chickasaw Bluffs. They descend abruptly from a height of two hundred or three hundred feet to the Mississippi and have no continuation on the opposite bank, which is very flat. An abrupt elevation of such height makes one conclude that this region may have undergone violent convulsion at some time.

At the time of the terrible earthquake which destroyed New Madrid and exerted profound influence on the entire region, from the fortieth degree of latitude down, the effect was especially cataclysmic in these hills, and distinct traces of it are yet visible even to the untrained eye.[6] Although these heights only merit the name of hills, they do not lack the romantic conformation which usually characterizes mountain structures. The abrupt, bare bluffs and the ragged summit of secondary limestone and iron-bearing clay strata, overgrown with the luxuriant vegetation and vigorous foliage so greatly favored by the climate, form a happy contrast to the adjoining virgin forest on low ground marked by the broad, meandering river channel.

Before one reaches the chain of hills, the river makes an abrupt turn from the southwest to the north, whereby the current of the Mississippi is broken with great force upon a sharp pointed, protruding area of land. The American rivermen call this bend, near which is a small island, the Devil's Elbow. At the northern slope of the hills, the river turns to the northeast, forming several islands. Between these and the river banks the channel is so dangerous to navigate, especially at low water, that it has been given the name of *Chenal du bon Dieu* and *Chenal du Diable* (Devil's Raceground), appelations probably owing their origin to the hazardous situation of some boatman during the early days of navigation on the Mississippi.

About noon we were in view of the second ridge of the Chickasaw Hills, which come into view at a considerable distance because the river here makes a bend to the east, runs to the north, and later turns at a very sharp

[6] New Madrid in the county of that name, southeast Missouri, witnessed American settlement as early as 1789 through the encouragement of Spain. It was largely destroyed in 1811 by earthquake, which created Reelfoot Lake nearby in Tennessee, but was rebuilt.

angle to the west-southwest, forming two large islands. The first continuation of the Chickasaw Bluffs extends very close to the second chain and touches the Mississippi between the two bends.

I greatly regretted that I was not able to go on shore and had to content myself with getting only a slight view of this hilly region, which promised material for scientific observation. Its abundant plant life appealed to me from a distance. A beautiful white blossoming bush, probably a variety of plum, enlivened the uniform green of the hillside, whose apparent volcanic character became ever more evident. The outcropping layers of clay produced a varied display of colors, shading from dark yellow through red and brown, indicating the presence of considerable iron content. This ore is not uncommon in the formations along the Mississippi.

A little stream flowing from the hills into the Mississippi indicates by its abrupt and eroded banks that its waters must frequently be swelled by heavy showers. At Point aux Prunes (Plum Point), a promotory on the southwestern bend of the river, are a few sandbars, which, during low water, may actually be passed without danger. In such a wide and swift-flowing river, interrupted by successive bends, sandbars are a common occurrence. They make navigation very difficult even for the most experienced pilot, for the restless masses of sand yield to every influence of current affecting their location. After every high water the greatest precaution is necessary. At low water, even at water of average depth, continuous use of the sounding lead is indispensable. When one is going downstream this is especially difficult and requires the closest attention.

A sandbar and other shallows made their appearance nearby during the earthquake, and a large island disappeared in this region. The Longue Vue des Canadiens (Canadian Reach), formed by the straight course of the river from north to south over a stretch of more than ten miles, affords an extended view. Being full of shallows, this is one of the most dangerous places on the Mississippi, from the mouth of the Ohio to the Gulf of Mexico.

Opposite the little stream Bayou, the river forms a bend to the west. Here the narrow neck of land is cut in two by a channel of some importance. Called New Cutoff, it is, however, too hazardous for larger vessels to use.

It was almost night when we reached the end of the bend to the northeast. The vessel stopped at an open, grass-covered place near a wretched little hut to load wood. I was lucky enough to shoot a beautiful white-headed eagle (*Haliaeetus leucocephalus, Falco leucocephalus,* Wils.). It was an old male, almost nut brown with snow-white head, neck, and tail. The beak, cere, and legs were yellow, and the length of the bird from the tip of its bill to the end of its tail feathers was two feet three inches.

About midnight we passed New Madrid, and it was not until my return trip that I had the opportunity to enter this place in the daytime, a place which has become so well known because of the earthquake on December 16, 1811. The fairly high banks of the Mississippi sank during the earth shock to the level of the average water stand. Great stretches overgrown with heavy timber disappeared entirely and many uprooted trees were moved into the river. Many islands escaped destruction but wide cracks in the ground were opened up and great crevices were created with such violence and velocity that trees standing over them were split wide open from the roots to a considerable height. Many forest creeks changed their course and several new channels and connections with the river were formed. Some new sandbars and islands appeared. The range of the earthquake seems to have followed a regular fault from the northwest to the south and to have been in direct connection with the volcanic center of the North American continent.

Formerly New Madrid was a settlement formed by Spanish colonists, but today the small town is inhabited by Anglo-Americans. The region is indeed very fertile but very unhealthful in the summer, and in recent times it has been frequently subject to inundation. The little Chapousa Creek emptying into the Mississippi close to the town has its origin in a lake twenty-five English miles from New Madrid.

At dawn on April 19 we were in the neighborhood of limestone bluffs, a beautiful white mass rising on the eastern bank to a height of several hundred feet. But farther upriver the bluffs are mixed with iron-bearing clay, whereby the basic color is mixed with reddish layers, presenting to the eye a very pleasant picture. On account of their iron content these bluffs are also called Iron Banks (*Mines au Fer*). The rocks descend quite steeply from a height of two hundred and fifty feet to the Mississippi, and opposite them is a large, well cultivated island, Wolf Island.

In former times (1773) there was a military post on these hills and farther up the stream, not far from the mouth of the Ohio, was located the now abandoned Fort Jefferson on Mayfield Creek.[7]

At nine o'clock I had the long awaited pleasure of seeing the junction of these two great river systems, which may justly be called the pride of creation. I may confess that I was filled with deep emotion and gratitude to

---

[7] The site here described fits more appropriately Fort Massac, on the north bank of the Ohio, ten miles below Paducah, Kentucky, refortified in late May and early June, 1794, from an earlier French fort by Major General Anthony Wayne. Fort Jefferson was north of Fort Washington (Cincinnati) about forty-five miles, established by Major General Arthur St. Clair in October, 1791. Fort Massac continued in operation to 1814, guarding the southwestern Illinois frontier. Prucha, *Sword of the Republic*, 35–36.

the almighty Creator of the universe, who had blessed man with the beautiful gift of receptivity for great and exalted things.

Majestically, and no doubt destined to be witnesses of important epochs in the history of the world, the two amazing and unique water courses of a continent, which a few centuries ago were unknown to Europe, here converge peacefully. The waters of an area of many square miles encompass land stretches and here unite in a single channel. No other continent offers a confluence of two similar rivers. Still in the natural state and almost untouched by human hands, virgin forest regions abounding in wild forms are mirrored in the extensive water surface, whose masses gradually mingle, showing in the mingling the strangest shadings of turbid and clear waters, which characteristically differentiate the water of the Mississippi and the Ohio.

There is a good landing place on a willow-covered point at the junction of the two rivers on the north bank of the Ohio. One also finds here a fairly good tavern, together with the buildings required for the storing of wares, since the steamboats and other vessels exchange their cargoes here. Unfortunately, the banks of both rivers are so low and subject to sudden inundation that no settlements of importance could be established here. Otherwise this would, no doubt, have been done long ago because of the importance of the traffic.

The statement that the highest water during times of inundation at the confluence of these two giant river systems attains a height of fifteen feet above the average water level seems to be readily confirmed by the traces which the floods have left on the adjacent trees.

The increase in trade, a direct result of the ever-growing population of those states situated directly in contact with the great waterways of North America, and the ever-increasing export trade, by way of the southern ports of the United States with New Orleans, the most important loading place, have transformed the banks of the Ohio into well-populated states. Signs increasingly show civilization advancing with giant strides. This region, thirty years ago still a wilderness, might serve many countries of the Old World as a model.

Because of the constant surge of population from the northwestern parts, in a few decades this land, now claimed by roaming bands of Indians, will be occupied. This region by way of the Missouri and the Mississippi is in direct contact with the far north and the endless prairies. It may confidently be expected that in time this fertile part of the United States, so richly endowed by nature and having a climate analogous to that of temperate Europe, will one day become the theater of the New World.

Through moral and inner strength of its unexcelled states, it will ask no odds of the nations of the Old World.

I now ask whether the region about the confluence of these two rivers should not some day become the center of a flowering state and attain importance in the world which will in every way command the respect, attention, and interest of statesmen. Only the effect of unfortunate political conditions could thwart the above-stated premise. I presume, of course, that the valley of the Mississippi will one day be the center of flourishing states. When once awakened to a consciousness of their importance, these regions of the New World will become the object of serious consideration to the thoughtful mind, and even now a steady stream of Europeans is flowing into this region, furnishing ample material for future speculation regarding the history of the human race. Inventiveness and perserverance have prepared man to face the greatest difficulties. He succeeds in transforming the wildest region into an abode satisfying even the most extreme demands. Who would doubt that in America, where civilization has accomplished so much during the last fifty years, there may come an epoch in the history of the human race so exalted as to leave our age-worn Europe far in the background?[8]

According to the observations which we owe to Mr. Ellicott,[9] the mouth of the Ohio is at 37° 22′ 9″ north latitude and 88° 50′ 51″ west longitude from Greenwich. Correct astronomical calculations regarding the confluence of great river systems are always hard to obtain. They rarely agree to the second, for every observer selects a different point for his altitude calculations. The banks of such streams are subject to great changes, influenced by the strong currents and the pressure of counteracting masses of water, especially when, as in the case of the mouth of the Ohio, the banks are not composed of solid rock but of low, soft ground.

The Ohio flows from the southeast into the Mississippi, which here makes a bend to the east. The great volume, the swifter current, and the greater specific weight of the Mississippi check the water of the Ohio, especially during high water, so that great whirlpools develop, making navigation difficult and subjecting lighter craft to much difficulty. The circling

[8] In personal income, many states of the Mississippi Valley would achieve notable rank by 1961: Illinois would rank eighth among the states; Ohio fifteenth; Missouri eighteenth; Indiana twentieth; Iowa twenty-eighth; with Kentucky, Tennessee, and Arkansas occupying positions from forty-fifth to forty-ninth. Edgar Z. Palmer, *The Meaning and Measurement of the National Income*, 325–27.

[9] Andrew Ellicott (1754–1820) conducted the survey extending the Mason and Dixon Line westward in 1785–1786. From 1813 to 1820 he was a teacher of mathematics at the U.S. Military Academy, West Point. *DAB*.

whirls covered with a vast number of bubbles, and the very high, short waves cause one to suspect a great and irregular depth of the river bed at its mouth. The bed, composed of soft masses, changes so frequently that it is necessary to determine the exact depth with the sounding lead.

Statements of different pilots almost never agree, I found by frequent inquiries. The banks of the Ohio near its mouth seem to have changed greatly during the past several hundred years, yet it is improbable that great revolutions, such as the recent earthquake, have produced a disturbing influence on this region.

The well-known Father Marquette and Mr. Joliet, who traveled on the Mississippi in 1673, must be regarded as the first discoverers of the upper regions of the stream. They mentioned the Ohio in their rather adventurous account of the journey under the name of Quabouskigon. At that time its banks were inhabited by the mighty Chuoanous (Shawnees) living in some forty settlements.[10]

The *Maysville* stopped only a few minutes at the tavern to land some passengers. Something happened on this occasion that excited general interest and disturbed the peace in a disagreeable manner. A young merchant whose destination was Louisville complained to the ship's authorities that the sum of several hundred dollars in banknotes had been taken from his pocketbook. He had missed the money only a few hours ago, so the thief must be among the cabin passengers, because the travelers on deck had not been able to enter his sleeping quarters. This complaint greatly embarrassed everybody, particularly the captain. Although the merchant acted very delicately, none of the passengers who were in the large room would leave before the unpleasant case had been resolved and settled. This was most difficult to do, for without police surveillance the thief might find means to escape.

Suspicion centered at once on a passenger unknown to all the others who

---

[10] Jacques Marquette, *Le Premier Voyage qu'a fait le P. Marquette vers le nouveau Mexique et comment s'en est formé le dessein* in *The Jesuit Relations and Allied Documents*, ed. by Reuben Gold Thwaites, LIX, 144.

The Shawnees are linguistically of the Central Algonquian group of Indians, related to the Sac and Fox, the Delawares, and the Nanticokes. In separate bands they occupied the Cumberland Basin of Tennessee and the middle Savannah River area in South Carolina, as of the last third of the seventeenth century. James Mooney in Hodge, *Handbook of American Indians*, II, 531, has them in Ohio past the middle of the eighteenth century, much beyond Marquette and Joliet's observations, though we do not know precisely where the two explorers met them on the Ohio. They were as far north and east in 1756 as the upper waters of the Ohio, however, and throughout the French and Indian War they were the friends of the French and the scourge of the English and Americans, notably along the Kentucky frontier.

had come on board during the course of the journey and had made a studious effort to become intimately acquainted with the young merchant. This unknown man had disappeared at once after our landing, a thing that could not be prevented because he had paid for his passage. Suspicion seemed to be well founded. The captain advised an immediate departure and made arrangements in the tavern for the possible apprehension of the thief. Since the affair had been discussed behind closed doors, the trick worked. The stolen banknotes were found on the evil-doer half an hour after the boat's departure, when the unsuspecting thief could not escape a rigorous search.

I only mention this incident, insignificant as it is in itself, in order that I, a stranger, might not withhold from the Americans the commendation due them for the reasonable procedure they pursued in this matter. During the entire transaction not a rash or hasty word was uttered and no one was personally offended. The merchant, who immediately opposed the decision of all the passengers to institute a search, even seemed to regret having made the announcement of the loss which caused so much disturbance. This calm procedure is to be admired, especially in a country and in a situation where the law has so few means to enter effectually and where, therefore, man is faced with the disagreeable necessity of procuring justice for himself.

Our boat hurried the first few miles up the Ohio with greater speed than I had thought possible in the swift current. This performance can be explained satisfactorily if one considers the pressure exerted by the larger river, causing counter currents at the mouth of the Ohio. This is especially noticeable when the water of the Mississippi is above average level and the Ohio is low. It even happens often that the Ohio is so checked in its course that it overflows its low banks at the confluence of the two rivers, while ten or twelve miles farther up the pilot frequently has to take recourse to the sounding lead to avoid danger because of the low water and the irregular river bed.

Our vessel landed near Cash River on the north bank of the Ohio to take on wood. The ground was too wet to allow me to take a walk into the forest and I had to content myself with a study of the varieties of trees at long range. These did not differ greatly from those of the Mississippi. Nevertheless, I was much interested in the vigorous growth of some climbing plants, especially the grape and sumach (*Vitis palmata*, Vahl., *vulpina*, *Rhus radicans*, Linn. [poison ivy]) whose cycle was evidently soon coming to an end. I must also observe that the nearer I approached the northern latitudes the more I had to admire the luxuriant growth of the parasitic plants.

Though poorer in kinds, the northern clime of the New World seems to show great varieties, which distinguish themselves by the toughness of woody fiber and juicy berries, especially of the grape-bearing *Vitis* appearing in countless numbers. The sassafras, also seen frequently, is favored by the fertility of soil so that it exceeds the bush form and passes over to the tree form. Though this bush of the family Lauraceae prefers a higher location and stonier soil to flat swampland, it nevertheless is frequently seen on the lower banks of the rivers. It has been shown that the roots of this useful plant do not possess the medicinal value which is peculiar to it when collected in dry places. Generally I have found the observation confirmed that, all plants usable in the art of healing which are characterized by peculiar astringent and aromatic qualities, attain their greatest degree of excellence if they do not grow in dark and damp prime forests, lacking light, or in too rich soil, where they grow too rapidly.

Here and there the banks of the Ohio were overgrown with reeds, yet *Miegia macrosperma* (Pers.) attained neither the height nor the density of growth which distinguished this variety of grass in Louisiana, and above latitude 38° it disappears entirely.

The country was enlivened by an extraordinary number of birds, especially by countless parrots and woodpeckers (*Psittacus carolinensis*, Gmel., *Picus pileatus*, Linn., *erythocephalus*, Linn., *villosus*, Linn., *carolinus* (*erythrauchen* Wag.?), Lath., *auratus*, Linn.)[11] competing with one another in an attempt to break the stillness of the forest, or with loud voices interrupting the song of smaller birds. In this the woodpeckers succeeded quite well, and every variety according to kind and relation to size gave to its hammering a peculiar and characteristic emphasis. The restlessness shown by flying from one tree to another, the effort to drive one another from a given locality, the ceaseless cries and chatter from the vast number of these birds was so loud that the parrots and nutcrackers (*Garrulus cristatus*, Cuv.) could outscream them only by occasional outbursts of their sharp voices.[12]

Not far from Cash River is the little settlement of America, and adjoining this is a series of slight elevations composed of limestone where the river has its origin. Opposite the mouth of this river there is an insignificant island, and in its vicinity in the middle of the river are found several cliffs

---

[11] *Psittacus carolinensis*, Gmel. = *Conuropsis carolinensis*, Carolina parakeet; *Picus pileatus*, Linn. = *Dryocopus pileatus*, pileated woodpecker; [*Picus*] *erythrocephalus*, Linn. = *Melanerpes erythrocephalus*, red-headed woodpecker; [*Picus*] *villosus*, Linn. = *Dendrocopos villosus*, hairy woodpecker; [*Picus*] *carolinus* (*Erythrauchen* Wag.?), Lath. = *Centurus carolinus*, red-bellied woodpecker; [*Picus*] *auratus*, Linn. = *Colaptes auratus*, yellow-shafted flicker.

[12] *Garrulus cristatus* = *Cyanocitta cristata*, the blue jay.

against which the water breaks with considerable force. The little town of Wilkinsonville founded by General Wilkinson as a military post in 1801 was later abandoned by the troops. Here are some more boulders in the middle of the river bed, but with careful navigation these shallows are not dangerous.

At noon we reached Fort Massac, occupied by the French in 1757, on the right bank of the river at 37° 12′ north latitude. Its location is really lovely but unhealthful. The Ohio, very wide here and flowing in a mirror-like surface from the east to the northwest, presents a pleasing view. A peculiar formation of heavy iron-containing red earth forms these banks, overgrown with most luxuriant tree and shrub vegetation. The beautiful beech, chestnut, ash, walnut, and oak trees, resplendent in their fresh, dark foliage, appear in sharp contrast to the fainter colored sycamore (*Platanus occidentalis*, Linn.), whose gigantic proportions cause amazement.

The weather had been continuously fair and warm for almost a week, but now suddenly changed as the steamboat reached the mouth of the Tennessee. A strong wind, followed by an icy cold rain, continued into the night and became so severe that the joints of the deck, shrunk during the dry weather, gave way and water came freely into the cabin. My bed was drenched, so that I had to spend the entire night sitting up in a chair, and other passengers shared the same predicament.

Named after the native inhabitants, a most important Indian tribe, the Tennessee or Cherokee flows through rugged regions from the southeast to the northwest and north.[13] Flowing into the Ohio, it is one of the larger navigable rivers for big vessels. Its bed, constricted by highlands, is derived from hard, fossilized matter and packed gravel masses. Collected sometimes in large beds, the latter made navigation uncertain in places, especially since the flow of the water is rapid. Its banks are high, the adjacent land is fertile, and the climate mild. These conditions soon attracted industrious American settlers on their migration westward. Only a few years were necessary to entice the Indians to relinquish the land, either by purchase or by treaty, and the wilderness was soon converted into fields. Cultivation according to European methods insures the well-being of numerous owners.

The Cherokee Indians[14] and their former neighbors, the Chickasaws, by

[13] The Tennessee River, which derives its name, as does the state of Tennessee, from villages of the Cherokee Indians. It is 652 miles from its source north of Knoxville, flowing s.w. to the n.e. corner of Alabama, north across Tennessee into Kentucky, to unite with the Ohio at a point near the southern tip of Illinois.

[14] The Cherokees, a detached tribe of the Iroquoyan linguistic group, at an early period controlled the vast southern Alleghenies from s.w. Virginia, w. North Carolina and South

their wars with the French and their raids into the eastern territories of the United States during the War of Independence, played a role in the history of the world. Through agreements with the government they have given up their former habitat and settled on land assigned to them on the Arkansas.

There they live, tied down in permanent settlements, engaged more in agriculture than the hunt. Having accepted some of the customs and usages of the Europeans, their peculiar inclination to coarseness and cruelty still is noticeable, manifesting itself in unsociability towards their neighbors. The men often leave their homes and fields suddenly, to steal cattle and horses from distant plantations or to make war on the Osages and Pawnees, who roam about the prairies.[15]

The darkness, caused by a torrent of rain that fell in the evening, forced the boat to stop for several hours at Smithville, an unimportant little town. Not until about two o'clock the following morning could the machinery be set in motion again. At daybreak we were opposite the mouth of the Cumberland, which has its source in Kentucky and runs parallel to the Tennessee. Nashville, the capital of Tennessee, situated on this river, boasts a rather lively navigation. Since the geographic location of the Cumberland is the same as that of the Tennessee, and the mountain chain where it has its origin is a continuation of the Alleghenies, the beds of the two rivers resemble each other in many respects.

Carolina, n. Georgia, e. Tennessee, and n.e. Alabama. They warred against the English in the Carolinas during the decade and a half before the War for American Independence, and against the Americans until near the end of the eighteenth century. Under pressure of white settlement, the tribe moved southwestward, ultimately drifting to Arkansas, and by the Treaty of New Echota (Georgia) removed to Indian Territory in 1838–1839, leaving behind, in North Carolina, only a small fragment of their number. The Cherokees were enabled to become literate with Sequoyah's development of his Cherokee syllabary some time after 1820. Cf. Grace Steele Woodward, *The Cherokees*; David H. Corkran, *The Cherokee Frontier*; Althea Bass, *Cherokee Messenger*.

[15] The Osages, a Siouan tribe first noted historically in Marquette's map of 1673, which placed them on the Osage River in southwestern Missouri, were subsequently to range much to the north, sometimes to the west, on various expeditions, one of which saw them allied with the French in defeating the Fox Indians at Detroit in 1714. Pierre François Xavier de Charlevoix, the French Jesuit, met them at Kaskaskia in 1721, and Jean-Bernard Bossu saw them at Cahokia in 1756. After Lewis and Clark had visited with them on Osage River in 1804, the Osages signed a treaty with the U.S. at Fort Clark (shortly to become Fort Osage) in 1808, ceding most of their Missouri and Arkansas lands and agreeing to resettlement in the lands historically remaining to them, i.e., all of present Oklahoma lying north of the Arkansas and Canadian rivers. The latter were further reduced by treaties of 1825, 1839, and 1865, and by Congressional enactment in 1870 to the northeastern part of Oklahoma where they still live. John Joseph Mathews, *The Osages, passim*.

For the Pawnee, consult footnotes 24 and 25 in Chapter 11.

We passed a number of islands called the Cumberland and Sister islands. Despite the continuous rain and a violent northeast wind I observed more and more the striking distinctions between the Ohio region and the lower Mississippi. In regard to location and the more luxuriant and varied vegetation, the Ohio region shows to advantage. The ever increasing cultivation of the soil and the denser population contribute much toward providing a pleasing and inviting aspect to a region already richly blessed by nature, and this picture becomes more and more replete the farther one ascends the river. Appropriately the French called it La Belle Rivière.

In the more settled regions the European traveler sees a rejuvenated fatherland. Frequently addressed in his mother tongue by the many German colonists when he sets foot on land, the German imagines himself transported to the banks of the Elbe or Danube.

Picturesque bluffs of limestone form the northern bank of the river above Horrican Island. Abrupt, tower-like shapes, rising from the bed of the Ohio, present bold, wild groups pleasing to the observer. Among these limestone masses I also saw the much admired cave formations described by many travelers under the name of Cave-in-Rock (La Grande Caverne).[16] Despite my desire, I had to give up the wish to examine more carefully the inner formation and structure of the dropstone[17] and had to content myself with a superficial and fleeting look at this masterpiece of nature.

The cave is formed on a perpendicular cleft, extending to a height of more than one hundred feet, running in parallel layers of limestone. It does not contain as many remains of petrified sea and shell-bearing animals as the limestone formations at the falls of the Ohio, at Cincinnati, or in the mountains of Kentucky. The traces of bones of prehistoric mammals are said to have disappeared from these caves. However, there can be no doubt that more careful investigation and excavation would bring many of them to light.

[16] A historic landmark on the Ohio in southern Illinois below Shawneetown.

[17] *Author*: As a rule the younger common compact limestone, Jurassic limestone, and dropstone have distinct layers and commonly form rounded hills and ridges which occasionally rise in abrupt and grotesque masses. The banks of the Ohio and the Missouri show many such examples which occur even in the flat prairies in the form of great masses. This kind of rock contains a multitude of petrifications of prehistoric shell-bearing mollusks which are known by the names of ammonite, belemnite, fungite, pectinite, terebratulite, astroite, entrochite, echinite, etc. In these limestone formations are caves and grottoes resulting from the revolutions of the earth. In America such caves containing masses of stalactites and stalagmites occur as frequently as in Europe. I found in the grottoes which I had occasion to visit, especially in the stalactite caves near St. Louis, bone fossils imbedded in yellow clay on the floor.

During high water a great part of the cave is flooded by the river. At average low water, however, it is dry and can easily be reached and therefore explored. The cave has frequently been used as a place of refuge on the part of travelers meeting with an accident or seeking to escape inclement weather. The Indians are reported to have made use of it as a hiding place while on war expeditions, sallying forth from it to attack passersby and to molest the colonists. Like all stories dealing with the aborigines, this theme is a favorite subject to the Americans and as unbelievable as other adventurous stories that have been told me about this place.

The summit of the rocky elevation on the north bank of the Ohio near the cave is overgrown with the American [eastern red] cedar (*Juniperus virginianus* [*virginiana*]), its roots penetrating into the clefts and fissures of the limestone and protruding in bunches. This evergreen covering the rocky banks of the upper Mississippi and Missouri, and there attaining a considerable height, prefers to grow on limestone cliffs. Its growth becomes more and more vigorous as one goes north. Forming small clumps of forest, this variety breaks the monotony of the desolate prairies along the river in the northwest.

Passing several dangerous rocks called Battery Rock Bar during the night, we landed early on the morning of April 21 near the Saline at Shawneetown.[18] Here is a very important salt factory supplying the greater part of the United States with this important product.[19]

The little settlement of Shawneetown derives its name from the Shawnee (Chuoanous) nation, which had one of its principal villages here. This Indian tribe had not disappeared entirely, but by frequent intermixture of white blood has departed more from the customs of its ancestors than have the other neighboring tribes. Roaming about restlessly, the Shawnees and the half-bloods who assume this name live on the banks of the Ohio and in the states of Indiana and Illinois, do some agriculture, but mostly hunt and fish. Excepting the Iroquois and Algonquins, whom I only know slightly, they are one of the few tribes living within the inhabited parts of northeastern America inclined to accept the ways of the immigrated European races.[20]

[18] In present southern Illinois, below the confluence of the Wabash with the Ohio.

[19] *Author*: In the United States the common salt or sodium cloride in combination with potassium salt and calcium salt occurs most frequently in the rich springs on the Kenhawa, the Little Sandy River, at Shawneetown, Boone's Lick at Franklin on the Missouri, the saline near Ste. Genevieve—in whose salt beds I found bones of the American mastodon—and in the salt springs of Rivière à la Mine. One should also read on this point Major Long's [Edwin James'] *Account of an Expedition from Pittsburgh to the Rocky Mountains*, Vol. I, page 34.

[20] *Author*: The tribes of the Lenni Lenapes seem to be inclined to accept higher civili-

At the mouth of the Wabash lie three small islands (Brown's Islands) close to one another and leaving only a narrow but deep channel for passage of larger vessels. The mouth of the Wabash into the Ohio at 37° 56' north latitude constitutes the boundary between Indiana and Illinois. Its sources are close to those of the larger Illinois in the neighborhood of the southern point of Lake Michigan and by portages effect a water connection from Canada to the Gulf of Mexico. This connection will in the future be made still easier by canals and is the more probable since the Miami, a river which flows into Lake Erie and is likewise navigable, has its sources near those of the Wabash.

I had no great desire to visit the famous colony of my countrymen, which has the name of Harmony and is situated a few miles up the Wabash. With regret I heard the testimony of every impartial and right-minded American regarding the lot of these settlers, for the most part from Württemberg. Because of a misconceived desire for improvement or a false conception of liberty, they renounced the protection of a parental government which always has regarded the rights of man as something precious and sacred and allowed themselves, by the allurement of speculators, to be placed in a position more humiliating and oppressive.[21]

zation. The efforts of the missionaries among them have evidently not been fruitless. During my journey in the northwestern region among the independent aborigines, I frequently observed with amazement the different stages of civilization among these tribes. How different, for example, are the peaceful Omahas from their coarse neighbors, the warlike Dakotahs (Sioux). Even different tribes of the same nation show contrasts, an example is the harmless Oto tribe (Ouac-toc-ta-ta) and the malicious Iowa (Pa-cho-sché).

[The Leni-lenapes here referred to are the Delawares, and the Delaware Confederacy was the most important in the Algonquian linguistic stock, occupying the Delaware Basin in eastern Pennsylvania and southeastern New York and most of New Jersey and Delaware. After signing their first treaty with William Penn in 1682, they came under the domination of the Iroquois, between 1720 and the French and Indian War. Towards the middle of the eighteenth century they moved westward to the headwaters of the Allegheny, thence to the Muskingum and other streams in eastern Ohio. They warred with the whites to the Treaty of Greenville, 1795, during which period part of them migrated to Indiana, others to Missouri, later to Arkansas, and by 1820 two bands were in Texas. Their later migrations, including to Canada, and to residence in present Oklahoma, form a large history. Hodge, *Handbook*, I, 385–87.]

21 *Author*: In 1831 I saw the colony of Württembergers at Economy near Beaver, which is under the direction of Rapp. The people seemed contented, but could have been happier in their fatherland. Unfortunately many of these countrymen of mine have recently become the prey of adventurers and deceivers.

[Johann Georg Rapp (1757–1847), a Württemberger, founded Harmony near Pittsburgh, Penna., in 1804, removed his communistic group to Indiana in 1815, sold the latter holding to Robert Owen and his followers in 1825, and founded Economy on the Ohio near Pittsburgh in 1824.]

In the afternoon about three o'clock we landed at the small town of Hendersonville,[22] where the Ohio forms a great horseshoe bend more than twenty miles long, while the distance across the neck of the peninsula is scarcely five miles. Hendersonville is a pretty little place which may take pride in having grown to importance in a short time. On the slope of a reddish earth bank, seeming to contain rich iron, this romantic site has a wonderful view of the extensive peninsula which the river makes.

One chain of hills is followed by another and the limestone bluffs appear now in fantastic forms, now in abrupt walls, and then again in jagged points. The farther one gets away from the Wabash, the more beautiful the banks of the Ohio become.

The Ohio seems to have been selected by nature to please the eye of the traveler with a series of uninterrupted and charming scenes, and even though it does not abound in colossal and imposing natural sights, nevertheless so much life and harmony prevail in this picture that even the luxuriant fields of the Tiber and the Arno could not be called more beautiful.

A lovely island, Green Island, is located at the mouth of a creek called Green River. A few miles upstream the Ohio flows for twelve miles in a straight direction. I enjoyed the wonderful view into the distance where an island, on account of a settlement or trade factory of the French, is still called French Island.

Night overtook us in the neighborhood of some sloping banks named for their color, Yellow Banks. These hills approach the left banks of the river near the middle of a bend which the Ohio makes toward the south. Until 1794 there existed an outpost here which by Wayne's Treaty at Greenville was abolished.[23]

Without mishap we traveled the whole night through regions where the river makes many turns. On the early morning of the twenty-second we were at the mouth of the Blue River, flowing from the state of Indiana into

[22] Now Henderson, Ky.

[23] The Treaty of Greenville, 1795, which followed General Anthony Wayne's successful campaign against the Indians of the Old Northwest, contains many cessions by the latter, including a number of tracts surrounding forts or posts, but none relating to the area below the mouth of the Green River, Kentucky, nor yet above Cloverport on the Ohio, also in Kentucky (here conforming to the Duke's specification of the "left banks of the river"). By the Treaty of Greenville the Indians signing it—Wyandots, Delawares, Shawnees, Ottawas, Chippewas, Potawatomis, Miamis, Eel-rivers, Weas, Kickapoos, Piankashaws, and Kaskaskias—gave up two-thirds of Ohio and part of Indiana. Charles J. Kappler, *U.S. Laws, Statutes*, etc., *Indian Affairs: Laws and Treaties*, 3 vols., 57 Cong. 1 sess., *Senate Document No. 452*, II, 30–34.

the Ohio. After being piloted through the shallows, we arrived about ten o'clock at Shippingport, the present destination of the *Maysville*.

I was very glad to leave the vessel. Despite its rapid journey of 1278 English miles, it nevertheless left an unpleasant impression. Because of the excessive number of passengers the steamboat could not offer the comforts and conveniences which under favorable conditions have made American shipping justly famous.

Almost all steamboats from western and southern states destined for Louisville halt at Shippingport, because during average and low water the rapids extending to the anchoring place of the small town make further progress very difficult. During high water the passage is easier, although even then caution is required. In low water it is impossible.[24]

Shippingport is a small place having a few shops and inns, but its location may soon hasten its growth. I secured a fairly good lodging with a family of Swiss origin where German was spoken, and in a short time had transferred all my belongings from the boat to my room looking out on the only important street of the town and on the Ohio. The area around Shippingport is one of the most beautiful and most populous regions of Kentucky.

The nearness of a few important cities, the beautiful banks of the river, the roaring rapids, the hills covered with luxuriant grass and splendid forests, the efficiently utilized and well-cultivated land all around, the neighborhood of two progressive states separated only by the river, the wealth of vegetation, and the countless animals of all kinds enlivening the scene might have awakened in me the wish to tarry for a longer time near Louisville, if the purpose of my journey had not thereby been interrupted.

My earlier plan to continue up the Ohio as far as Pittsburgh had to be given up because no boat could be loaded for this point under eight to twelve days and I should not have been able to return to Louisville before the early part of June. Even if I could have found a vessel to go to St. Louis, it might have been impossible to secure a boat going up the Missouri. All the expeditions of the trading companies are in the habit of

[24] Shippingport (or Shippingsport or Shippinport), Kentucky, of which John Campbell had been proprietor, selling his interest to James Berthoud in 1803, was the lower terminus for heavy steamboats (the *Maysville* was of two hundred tons) in the Mississippi-Ohio river traffic. Lying immediately below the Falls of the Ohio, it afforded a dock and warehouses for the large tonnage undergoing transshipment upstream from the falls, and equally downstream. Thomas Hulme, *Hulme's Journal, 1818–19*, in Reuben Gold Thwaites, ed., Early Western Travels Series, Vol. X, 43; Edwin James, *An Account of an Expedition . . . to the Rocky Mountains*, in Thwaites, *op. cit.*, XIV, 72–73.

departing for this destination in the spring or the autumn. Only exceptionally boats are sent out during the summer months.

On my arrival at Shippingport, the steamboat *Cincinnati*, which ordinarily runs between Louisville and St. Louis, was just about ready to set out for the latter place. After I had secured the certain information that within six weeks I should not have another opportunity to get to the Missouri, I made an agreement with the captain of the *Cincinnati*, and I had no occasion to regret this at any time during the trip. In addition to finding pleasant company, I found the inner arrangement of this boat was very comfortable and clean.

Since the boat was not to depart before the evening of the twenty-fourth, I had a few days' leisure to make excursions in this region and I took full advantage of this. The evening after my arrival I visited the celebrated rapids. These shallows are formed by a drop in the river bed consisting of rocky masses on a hard and stony ground dropping twenty-one to twenty-three feet over a distance of two English miles. Since the water had reached more than the average level, not all of the rocky masses were visible. During the summer season these protrude above the stream's surface. Though the water ran with great speed and broke against the rocks to form funnel-shaped whirlpools, causing a great roar, it did not reach that violence which, at low water and in calm weather, makes the tumult of the stream audible for the distance of a mile.[25]

The rapids of the Ohio by no means resemble a real waterfall, and with some precaution they are not even dangerous to navigation. The government of the state of Kentucky has instituted some very useful precautions to make navigation safe. For example, it has employed several pilots to guide all kinds of vessels through, which is doubly necessary because the different depths often change the course a boat ought to take, and the size and draft of vessels may require the use of different channels. By a bend in the Ohio at the rapids running from east to north to southwest, the pressure of the water against the cliffs is still further increased, and the stronger and more rapid current is therefore on the north bank of the river above Clarksville.

With a few skilled boatmen I entered a small boat and sought to find a way among the rocky banks to that part of the rapids called Indian Chute, through which the greater volume of water forces its way. Not even a steamboat can get up these rapids without cables fastened to the river bank

---

[25] The Falls of the Ohio would become the site of future Louisville. General George Rogers Clark, rafting down the Ohio on his way to the conquest of Illinois in 1778, put in at Corn Island to rest and organize his troops. The city remains in the twentieth century a center for heavy river-borne freight traffic.

and by the aid of the capstan. A very dangerous situation arises if the cable breaks. Some years ago the *Maysville* had a sad experience here and was almost lost, being thrown hard against the cliffs, spring a leak, and reached the bank only with great difficulty.

Since I had a Fischbein hygrometer and a thermometer with me, I attempted to make a few observations of the humidity and temperature of the air close above the water's surface, but the swift passage of the boat made the observations imperfect. The thermometer showed almost no difference in atmospheric warmth compared with that in Shippingport, but the hygrometer changed from 57° to 59°. I had taken precautions against its actually getting wet and exposed it only to the influence of the air. The gravel which covers the bed of the river at the rapids lies on a layer of limestone and sandstone. The latter is of close, scaly structure. This same sandstone occurs most commonly in the bluffs of the Ohio and is cemented by a clay-binding material.

Only after it had grown dark did I return to my lodging in Shippingport. Previously I had landed at the little town of Clarksville, a very unimportant place laid out some thirty years ago directly opposite Shippingport on a slope of an attractive chain of hills.

Early the following morning I was already on my way to Louisville. The road leaves the river somewhat and being on heavy clay soil is almost impassable for wagons, especially during the wet season. The attractive meadowlands, only here and there shaded by scattered tall trees, extend along the river banks up to the nearby rising hills, creating charming grassy areas, adorned in the spring with a multitude of flowers, surprising me most pleasantly.

Open flat areas in the New World enclosed between hills are often covered with numerous grasses and herbaceous plants. Due to the water-rich region, the ground, virginal and left to nature, abounds in vegetation, appearing at times as beautiful, low-growing varieties, then again as bushes of giant size. The wanderer joyfully discovers, among the short-tufted grasses of the *Aira*[26] and the *Paspalum*[27] varieties, lovely orchids scarcely reaching above the ground, and even numerous varieties of the varicolored genus of phlox with heads just stretching above the grasses. Perhaps only a short distance away he finds himself impeded for miles by entangled plants of the extensive family of composites, most of which defy eradication. Tenacious weeds opposing cultivation and growing rapidly, they frustrate the sweating farmer.

Revived by the warmth of the atmosphere and attracted by the blossoms

[26] *Aira*, a genus of some thirty-five grasses.
[27] Another genus of perennial grasses, some of which afford important hay cuttings.

of so many plants, the insect world appears in numbers such as I had never seen in this part of America. They in turn serving as food attracted countless numbers of birds. The vigorous spectacle of an early morning was enlivened by a multitude of creatures, each seeking to derive its food one from the other, and thus distinctly revealing a picture of ever recurring birth and death according to the irrevocable will of Providence, whereby the machinery of our planet, indeed of the universe, is able to function.

I should not have expressed this thought here if it had not been called forth by an accidental observation. With that attention which one at times shows the most insignificant objects, I had been watching the chase a ground beetle made upon a smaller member of its kind, when I was suddenly aroused by a noise. An enormous eagle, in America commonly called the calumet eagle,[28] shot arrow-swift through the air, seized his prey with his mighty talons, and seated himself on a nearby rock to devour it undisturbed.

As the morning hours advanced, more and more wagons and pedestrians appeared on the road to town, carrying produce to market. Here for the first time we were in the vicinity of a U.S. town of size where the area could really be called populated, and where the rural people lived like European farmers, but there was a striking difference between the costumes and manners of the country folk and those of the townspeople. In Louisiana, excepting New Orleans and a few small towns, the planters constitute the majority of the population, investing their wealth in slave-owned colored people. The small remainder are immigrated merchants and a few tradesmen, usually preferring the city to the country.

The reason is partly that the unhealthful climate of the southern states makes living together in large towns undesirable. Further, it is impossible for the working classes in this hot climate to produce their hand-made goods for the same prices that equally good factory-made articles from distant cities are sold. For this reason one finds in Louisiana, as in all southern states, all the various articles needed for human living assembled in every store.

The most fashionable retail stores do not hesitate to sell clothing and leather work of all kinds which are supplied cheaply and excellently by the factories in the northeastern part of the United States. The market in New Orleans is a striking example of this method of doing business. No worker

---

[28] *Author*: Most of the Indians of North America adorn their pipes and other objects of ornament or implements of war with the tail feathers of this eagle, which is identical with *Aquila fulvus* or *melanaetös*. According to Wilson, it is the ring-tailed eagle and is well shown in Part VII, Plate LV, Illustration I. [*Aquila chrysaetus* = *A. chrysaetos*, the golden eagle.]

is able to supply a garment, which the merchant sells for five or six Spanish dollars, for less than twelve or sixteen dollars. Employing a tailor or a shoemaker therefore becomes a luxury, and the inhabitants of the low country prefer to go to the merchants where they can buy more cheaply and, moreover, have the convenience of fitting and selecting their clothes to their own liking without having to depend on the whims of the tradesman.

The situation is entirely different in the northern and eastern states, where cheap living costs support not only the manufacturer but also the tradesman. These two, together with the merchant, who may be regarded as a connecting link between the classes, are able to form close-knit sales organizations in larger towns. In the northern and eastern states, one sees the farmer taking his produce to the market in the cities, as farmers do in Europe, and selling it directly to the tradesmen.

The country folk of Kentucky are more clannish than their neighbors in Indiana, with whom they do not always agree. Many differences in the respective constitutions of the two states may be the cause of this. As the descendants of the old Virginians, Kentuckians are proud, bold, and combative, frequently given to fighting. Unfortunately this casts a shadow on their otherwise good character. Skilled in all manly endeavors, they are characterized by industry and an extraordinary endurance in tedious tasks, especially such as are encountered on journeys. The Kentuckians are known as excellent boatmen on all the rivers of the United States, and as riflemen they have always been the terror of their enemies and of wild animals. The inhabitants of Kentucky still live in such intimate contact with their forests and the wilderness that one need not fear that this vigorous breed of men will lose their bold and attractive manly spirit. Thus I am induced to sing their praise here.

Although slavery has not been abolished in Kentucky, nevertheless Negroes are often helped by Kentuckians in their flight to neighboring states. This is sometimes the cause of unpleasantness arising between them and their neighbors, for Negroes frequently seek Kentucky as a haven of rescue where they are concealed and protected.

The Kentuckians take most of their products, namely smoked and salt meat and maize, to Louisiana, and on these occasions many a Negro slave obtains his freedom. The law, to be sure, forbids hiding runaway slaves and permits the search of homes, boats, and property in which one suspects a hidden Negro. But extensive legal formalities are necessary to do this, so that many fugitives make their lucky escape.

In his clothing, the Kentuckian shows nothing peculiar over other Americans who live in the country. In the summer he wears few woolens or worsteds, and usually his attire consists of a linen shirt, a pair of long trousers, a short jacket of the same material, and a small round felt hat. In the winter he exchanges this light covering for a jacket and a pair of trousers of coarse worsted or wool material. Boots they rarely wear, rather shoes of thick leather or moccasins. The clothing of the women is made of a simple, old English pattern, mostly of linen or calico, with often a quaintly formed straw hat or an even more droll hood. The dwellings of the Kentucky inhabitants, if I may judge by those that I saw and had occasion to visit, are without many conveniences, but were very tidy and sometimes built of brick or stone.

The main wealth of these country people, as of those in almost all the northern states, is great herds of livestock. This is shown by the excellence of their cattle, thriving upon lush pasture-meadows and producing rich milk and great quantities of butter. The breeding of horses has not advanced as far as the condition of the soil and the climate would permit. The introduction of better breeds and greater care are needed. In Kentucky hogs have increased extraordinarily in number, and in the fattening beech, chestnut, and oak forests they prosper abundantly, gaining a high reputation. Salt pork constitutes the main article of export, especially to New Orleans. In America, Kentucky hams have the same reputation that in Europe is given those from Westphalia. Indeed, it makes no difference where this kind of food may have its origin, in America it is everywhere sold as Kentucky ham. All the sheep that I examined had long, coarse wool. Not the slightest attempt at breeding up is shown, and it might require much care and time to improve this branch of agriculture. The pastures are too rich for sheep raising. On the other hand, I am convinced that attempts at sheep raising on the prairies of the northwest would at later times bring good returns.

I entered Louisville at nine o'clock in the morning and was very pleasantly surprised at seeing the clean and well built town, reminding me of a well-to-do provincial town of England. The houses are built of brick several stories high, and especially on the broad main street cutting through the middle of the town, they look good. Everywhere I saw shops and warehouses in which busy artisans showed their wares and offered them for sale.

From every tavern, and there is a large number, I heard voices inviting the passerby to have some refreshment, at least a glass of grog or a gulp of whiskey against the morning air. There prevailed in Louisville such a freeheartedness, reflecting the health and happiness of the inhabitants, that I do not doubt that they are well off and contented. The farmers mingled with the townspeople with a certain sense of cordiality, and I often had to laugh at their mutual wit as they jestingly criticized each other's work or produce. One could indeed distinguish the town dweller from the farm worker by their manner and bearing, but there was not that stiff indifference which in Europe divides the buyer from the farmer.

Louisville is situated on a slight rise at 38° 8′ north latitude in a fairly healthy location, and the first houses were probably built in 1774 by Dunmore, the governor of Virginia, to which Kentucky at that time belonged.[29] Since then, especially in the last twenty years, the town has grown considerably. In 1820 it had 4,012 inhabitants. In the present year, to my knowledge, it has only 250 houses. (As it has grown much since that time, I am convinced that the population has increased by many hundreds.)

Cincinnati and Louisville have kept step about equally with increasing population and prosperity and in the future they, together with Pittsburgh, will probably be the most important places on the Ohio. I had letters of introduction to a few houses in the town, but not intending to stay any length of time, I left Louisville after a few hours in order to investigate the country on the east of Bear Grass Creek, here flowing into the Ohio. From here, Jeffersonville, also a growing young town in Indiana, can be seen, and the Ohio, which above the rapids flows majestically, affords a magnificent distant view over its mirrored surface.

My wandering along the small stream was not without interest for me since I encountered notable objects at every step. Some I found were new to me. Following the course of the water, which flows over a bed of lime-

---

[29] *Author*: Besides Dunmore, the Colonels Logan, Harod, and Boone did much toward developing the region along the Ohio and also the regions farther to the west which thirty or forty years ago were still in the state of nature. Boone died at an advanced age in the neighborhood of Franklin on the Missouri.

[Lord (the Earl of) Dunmore, then Royal Governor of Virginia, established the fort of his name at present Pittsburgh in 1773, but what became Louisville was of later accidental founding, as noted in footnote 25 *supra*. Dunmore's war of 1774 with the Indians of the Ohio Valley and his subsequent highly unpopular position and actions as the Revolutionary War drew on are better remembered. *DAB*.

[Benjamin Logan (1743–1802) accompanied Dunmore as lieutenant in 1774 in his Indian war, joining Richard Henderson a year later in the latter's scheme for the settlement of Transylvania, saw action in 1778 when the Indians invaded Kentucky, and then in 1780 and 1782 led retaliatory expeditions against Indians in Ohio. The most influential Kentuckian during the Revolution, he received appointment by George Washington later to the Board of War in the West, served in the Kentucky constitutional convention of 1792 and in the electoral college which elected its first governor. He failed of election to the governorship in 1796. *DAB*.

[James Harrod (1742–1793) was one of a canoe party descending the Ohio to the Falls in 1773, returning in 1774 to the mouth of the Kentucky, which he ascended with thirty men to survey and build cabins at what became Harrodsburg. He later completed the town development, which was the first settlement in Kentucky. His military service against Indians in 1777, 1779, and 1782 with George Rogers Clark against the Shawnees on the Miami is notable. *DAB*.]

stone, to the heights where Louisville and Shippingport are located, everywhere I found tilled fields and barns and meadows alternating with light forests. Wherever there was a moist spot hundreds of butterflies fluttered about in the air, and I succeeded in catching a few rare specimens. Some of these light-winged creatures of the air must have lately escaped from their chrysalis, for a vast number of the same kind covered adjacent objects, pointing to the fact that the caterpillars must have been hatched in a common mass web.

Even the *Papilio marcellus* and *turnus*, which in North America are very common, I found flying in great colonies. Small varieties often do this in unbelievably huge numbers, so that on the Missouri my boat was so covered a few times by *Papilio nicippe* and *archippus* that we did not know how to rid ourselves of the little tormentors and could not even open our mouths.

Several birds aroused my interest partly because of their song and partly because of their beautiful plumage. For the first time I observed a considerable number of orioles known in America as Baltimore bird (*Psarocolius Baltimorus*, Wagl.).[30] In company with another member of this genus though far less handsome (*Psarocolius castaneus*, Wagl.),[31] which I had already observed in Louisiana. They lived in pairs in tall trees, quite contrary to the habits of the *troupials*, to which the orioles belong.[32]

I have hardly ever seen so many birds of prey in one area as here. Perhaps these harmful creatures were attracted by the great number of other inhabitants of the air. To judge by their flight, most of them belonged to the sparrow hawks (*Daedalon*, Savig.). I shot specimens of two species, the

[30] *Psarocolius baltimorus = Icterus galbula*, Baltimore oriole.

[31] *Psarocolius castaneus = Icterus spurius*, the orchard oriole.

[32] *Author*: Both of these birds formerly belonged to the extensive genus *Oriolus* of Linnaeus, which in recent times has been separated into many divisions. Wagler includes *Oriolus baltimorus, spurius* (*castaneus*), *phoeniceus* and several others in the new genus *Psarocolius*. Cf. *System. Av.*, Auctore Dr. J. Wagler, P. I. Stuttgart et Tübingen, smt. J. G. Cottae, 1827.

By other natural scientists these, and also other birds related to them, have been classified under the species *Icterus, Cassicus, Xanthornus, Agelajus*, etc., most of which live together in hordes and have the same habits as our starlings. *Oriolus mutatus, spurius* and *varius* have been confused with one another. *Oriolus spurius* is Buffon's *Carouge de Cayenne* and Brisson's *Baltimore batard du Canada, Oriolus mutatus* is Wilson's and Wagler's *Psarocolius castaneus*.

On the other hand, *Oriolus varius* seems to me to be a separate species. In their habits these two birds quite resemble our oriole, and their piping song is about the same. The bill of these and a few closely related species which I shot in tropical America is more rounded at the tip and more bent forward than is the case in *Psarocolius phoeniceus* and *Haemorrhous* (*Cassicus ruber, Briss. le cassique rouge*).

[The systematic reasoning here will be obvious to all ornithologists who have followed Robert Ridgway and James Lee Peters, and the more or less final ordering as well.]

Falco pennsilvanicus, Wils., and *Falco velox*, Wils. The latter I had learned to know at New Orleans. The Pennsylvania hawk is a beautiful and skillful bird, larger than our sparrow hawk and resembling the hawk *Falco palumbarius* in his habits.[33]

In Shippingport I was surprised by the sight of a great number of fish and other aquatic creatures of the Ohio which had been caught for me by fishermen whom I had sent out in the morning. Here I saw for the first time the catfish (*Pimelodus catus, Silurus catus*, Catesby), a sheat-fish with a great spinous dorsal fin and very common in the northern rivers of America, and on the upper Missouri it often represented my only food supply. *Pimelodus caudafurcatus*, Lesueur, and another variety of catfish, different from *Pimelodus catus*, likewise is commonly found in the Ohio and is one of the most desired food fish.[34]

Several turtles had also been caught, among them one with a leather-like shell, belonging to genus *Trionix*. Measuring nine inches from the tip of its extended head to the end of its tail, this turtle was an adult female containing a number of fully developed eggs. The leathern covering had a soft feel and yielded to the pressure of the finger. The color of the dorsal side was light gray, interspersed with small, scattered black spots. The animal disseminated no odor of musk and was entirely different from the genus determined by Bartram and from *Trionix ferox*.[35]

Tired from my long walk and the sultriness of the day, I had luckily reached my room when a terrific thunderstorm and a drenching downpour set in, soon flooding the streets of Shippingport and even the interiors of the houses were not spared. Until far into the night the rain continued, the lightning and thunder prevailed without a moment's cessation. By this time I had become so accustomed to the awe-inspiring scene in America that I could only see the magnificent side of it, and though the elements raged ever so severely I did not have that feeling of anxiety over impending danger that I feel in Europe.

[33] *Falco velox*, Wils. = *Accipiter striatus velox*, a race of the sharp-shinned hawk. *Falco pennsilvanicus*, Wils. = *Buteo platypterus*, broad winged hawk. *Falco palumbarius* = *Accipiter gentilis*, goshawk.

[34] Fresh-water fish classifications were as yet unsettled in Duke Paul's time. *Pimelodus* is a genus of primarily South American catfishes. The genus *Ictalurus* embraces the channel catfishes of several species, of which *I. furcatus*, the great blue cat; *I. punctatus*, the channel cat proper; and two other species of the genus are widely distributed. Also of wide distribution (east of the Rockies) is the bullhead, of which *Ameirus nebulosus*, is most representative. Jordan, *A Guide to the Study of Fishes*, II, 179–80.

[35] The Trionychidae formerly applied to both Old World and New World species, but the flapjack turtles constitute for the New World a separate genus, *Amyda*, of the subfamily Trionychoidea.

I have been interested in noting how rarely houses and other buildings are struck by lightning, in spite of the heavy thunderstorms. Often I have asked myself the question whether it is on account of the many forests, the great lakes, or the sparse population. Even in the prairies this is unusual, and single dwellings surrounded for miles by grassland are very rarely hit by lightning. On several occasions I had the opportunity to see lightning strike trees near me but found, upon examination, that no great damage was done to them. Oaks and poplars are most exposed to electric discharges, while some varieties of trees are spared almost entirely. This I observed in several varieties of ash and walnut trees and also in most of the birches of North America.

The electrometer showed before and during the thunderstorm that the air was supercharged with electriicty, and its great excitability and mobility indicated the multiple differences of electric tension in the different air strata, causing mutual discharges to follow in rapid succession. The fact that, during a heavy and continuous rain storm, the electricity of the upper air layers is not soon exhausted might be explained if one assumes that opposite forms of electricity exist in the upper and lower strata of air which, during the rain, are continuously regenerated. What role hydrogen plays in this can be decided only when the assumption of several modern natural scientists, that positive electricity is produced by light, heat, and oxygen, and negative electricity by light, heat, and hydrogen, has been either refuted or proven by further experiments and observations.[36]

Early on the morning of the twenty-fourth I had to take my baggage on board the *Cincinnati*. After being assigned my place, I was informed that all passengers would have to board by noon, since an exact hour could not be set for the departure of the steamboat. This was inconvenient to me, since I had planned to utilize the noon hours to inspect the right bank of the Ohio. There was much talk about a hot sulphur spring on Silver Creek, and on this trip I contemplated examining it.

When I appeared on the *Cincinnati* at the appointed hour, I found my suspicion of non-adherence to a punctual departure confirmed, and learned that the boat would not leave before night. The passengers were given their dinner and permitted to leave the boat if they desired but were told to return without delay upon a given signal, a cannon shot. I found this

---

[36] This passage, one of the most suggestive in the travel account, indicates Duke Paul's familiarity with Robert Boyle's seventeenth-century scientific work, particularly with gases, as well as the findings of his contemporaries, John Dalton in atomic theory, Michael Faraday, Joseph Henry, and Hans Christian Oersted in magnetism, electricity, and the beginnings of electrical field theory, between 1820 and 1835, the latter year coinciding with the Duke's writing of his narrative.

method very considerate, for on other vessels the passengers often are not permitted to leave the boat because of the danger of being left behind. When the steamboats have to lay by, as is often the case, this is unpleasant.

On boarding the *Cincinnati*, I made the acquaintance of Mr. Du Bourg, then bishop of New Orleans and St. Louis (and now bishop of Montauban in France), one of the most revered and best informed men I had the good fortune to know in the New World. The charming and helpful friendship with which the bishop had the goodness to recognize me entitles me to express my most sincere thanks to this priest, who is equally as noble in mind as in heart. Mr. Du Bourg, on his return trip from Washington to St. Louis, was completing his journey on the *Cincinnati*. His intelligence did much to make my stay on the boat and in St. Louis most pleasant. We devoted the afternoon to a walk and talked about Europe, which Mr. Du Bourg had but recently left, and the latest and most interesting news from that part of the world he had absorbed while in the eastern states.[37]

About five o'clock we heard the sound of cannon. Hastening on board, we still had to wait until after seven o'clock, because some repairs on the boiler caused further delay. The *Cincinnati* belongs to the older boats and was somewhat dilapidated, but it looked inviting to me because of its interior furnishings and cleanliness. Also there were but few passengers, whereby more order and more room was assured. I must say that the trip from Louisville to St. Louis was one of the most comfortable I have had in the United States, and on leaving the *Cincinnati* I should not have dreamed that six months later I should see this boat sink under my feet.[38]

The evening was clear and cold, the last rays of the sun colored the hills and houses of the nearby town blood red. Before it had become night we had already progressed several miles. The moon shone with a soft light that illuminated the picturesque landscape, and we should have advanced a considerable distance during the night but for a dense fog after midnight which forced us to stop and wait for the coming of morning. Through the fog and the thunderstorm of the twenty-fifth the air cooled to 39°. The previous day had been very hot and we reacted sensitively. The fog dispersed sufficiently about nine-thirty o'clock to allow us to depart, and at eleven o'clock the boat reached the mouth of the Blue.

On the banks I observed several large birds, which after close examination I took to be turkeys (*Meleagris gallopavo*, Linn.). Although these

[37] For Bishop Duborg's career, see footnote 17, Chapter 7.

[38] The age of the *Cincinnati* was less than met the eye. First on the Mississippi run to St. Louis only seven years before was the *General Pike* in 1816. But as will be seen in Chapter 12, the *Cincinnati*, young as she was, would perish after she was barely under weigh to New Orleans with the Duke aboard in November, 1823.

chicken-like birds have disappeared gradually from the eastern part of the United States, they are still found in large flocks on the Ohio and its tributaries, on the upper Mississippi, and especially on the Missouri. In the domesticated state this bird has been introduced from America into Europe, where its numbers have greatly increased. This lazy and stupid fowl exercises so little precaution that, despite its great increase, it will in time become extinct.[39]

On account of some unimportant damage, the *Cincinnati* had to stop at four o'clock for three hours near a settlement on Anderson Creek. I took advantage of this delay to climb among the nearby limestone bluffs. They contained petrified sea animals, and I gathered a considerable number of them. I also shot a few rare birds, among them *Picus querulus*,[40] which betrays itself by a melodious song. The *Cercis canadensis* and *Prunus virginianus* were in full bloom,[41] and I occasionally observed *Hamamelis virginica*,[42] its oddly perforated leaves appearing in the pale green of their youthful garment.

During the night of the twenty-sixth the boat traversed a great distance. Since the wind blew from the east no fog formed and the temperature that morning sank to 48°. The alternation of hot and cold weather makes the climate of Ohio, even in the spring months, dangerous for persons disposed to suffer from catarrhal and rheumatic troubles. During the latter half of April the thermometer rose to between 83° and 88° almost every noon in the Ohio region and at night, especially toward morning, fell considerably.

At three o'clock in the afternoon we passed the mouth of the Wabash. At Battery Rocks and the Great Cavern the captain had the kindness to stop for a moment so I could cast a fleeting glance into the cave. It was dry despite the fact that the river had risen somewhat, and I observed pools of water only here and there which, however, did not have any peculiar taste. This cave served night owls and bats (*Strix asio* ? *Vespertilio monachus*, Raf., *Vespertilio megalotis*, Raf.) as an abode.[43] These creatures

[39] As A. W. Schorger has shown in *The Wild Turkey: Its History and Domestication*, the genus *Meleagris* contains several subspecies, and its distribution in North America was much wider than earlier supposed, practically from coast to coast. Only a few months earlier than Duke Paul's first encounter with the bird, an observer along a creek in Indiana estimated that some five thousand birds passed before him. Far from extinct, the wild turkey now thrives over large areas of the U.S., partly owing to reintroduction by game-management authorities.

[40] *Picus querulus* = *Dendrocopos borealis*, the red-cockaded woodpecker.

[41] *Cercis canadensis*, redbud; *Prunus virginianus* = *P. virginiana*, choke cherry.

[42] *Hamamelis virginica*, witch hazel.

[43] *Strix asio* = *Otus asio*, the screech owl. *Vespertilio monachus* Rafinesque = *Lasiurus*

were stirred up by the noise of our footsteps and I managed to catch a few of them.

That evening I saw the Cumberland River under finer weather conditions than we had had a few days before. Something broke in the machinery at ten o'clock and we had to stop until morning, and thus the night, which was so favorable a time for travel, had to be passed up. At noon on the twenty-seventh we stopped at Wilkinsonville. It was extremely sultry. Since the region along Cash River and in the vicinity of the mouth of the Ohio was still inundated, there were billions of mosquitoes and flies there, making our stay an inexpressible torture. The whole night we could not sleep and I was exceedingly glad when the boat was again set in motion on the morning of the twenty-eighth and reached the Mississippi. The latter was not so high but presented just as magnificent a sight at the exit from the Ohio as at its entrance a week earlier.

Painfully the *Cincinnati* worked against the strong current, creating heavy waves, which caused the boat to rock, as vessels do on large inland lakes during a high wind. The water in the Ohio was higher than that of the Mississippi, nevertheless the latter presented a strong counter-current, and when the boat turned the point which marks the confluence of the two rivers we soon lost all trace of the clearer water and found ourselves in the domain of the Mississippi. When we had passed the island lying in the middle of the river at the mouth of the Ohio, the violence of the current lessened and the boat advanced more rapidly than I had expected the *Cincinnati* could do.

The banks of the Mississippi again presented the often described monotony of low land covered with virgin forest. In the same measure that the cypresses decreased, I observed that the poplars increased, some of them attaining gigantic trunks. The boat landed at Tyawpatia Creek, an unimportant little stream, to take on wood and provisions, which are cheaper here than on the Ohio. I was able to fulfill my wish to go into the forest, which for the first time I found not to be inundated. As the boat waited for the rising of the moon, I had time enough to make war upon the inhabitants of the forest, which ended successfully for me.[44]

borealis borealis, the red bat; *V. megalotis* Rafinesque = *Corynorhinus rafinesquii* (Lesson), Rafinesque's big-eared bat.

[44] *Author*: I shot here *Tanagra rubra, Muscipeta crinita, Muscicapa melodia, cucullata, Turdus lividus, Psarocolius varius? Trochylus colubris, Picus villosus, pubescens, Coccyzus caroliniensis*, Vieill., *Perdix virginianus, Scolopax paludosa*, and many others.

[The above are: *Tanagra rubra* = *Piranga rubra*, summer tanager; *Muscipeta crinita* = *Myiarchus crinitus*, great crested flycatcher; *Muscicapa melodia* = *Vireo gilvus*, warbling vireo; *Muscicapa cucullata* = *Wilsonia citrina*, hooded warbler; *Turdus lividus* = *Dumetella carolinensis*, catbird; *Psarocolius varius?* = *Icterus spurius*, orchard oriole; *Trochylus*

I was amazed to see a few large trunks of *Gleditschia* (French, *fevier*),[45] almost entirely choked by a climbing begonia. Later I found this begonia in abundance near Kaskaskia, but after that no more.

Around morning of the next day we reached Cape Girardeau, a rocky point of land projecting into the stream. Here are located a small number of houses bearing the name of town, formerly populated by French and Spanish colonists. The river bed is quite unsafe in this part because of a number of rocks lying in the river. Moreover, the Mississippi flows very swiftly and tempestuously over these shallows with a sharp drop. Its course is greatly narrowed from the projecting promontory. Over a distance of twelve miles the rocky right bank of the stream rises abruptly to a considerable height of parallel-stratified limestone. At a height of one hundred and fifty to two hundred feet the hills here are very pretty and present a number grotesque shapes, especially in jagged and sharp-edged forms. They contain many caves and grottoes formed by water and other natural agents and are similar to the caves on the Ohio.

Near an island called Île du Diable the boat had to stop to take on wood, detaining us for two hours. The banks of the Mississippi had again become low, yet the forest seemed less dense, consisting for the most part of cottonwood and ash trees, which prefer a dry soil. Here I shot a large squirrel[46] until then unknown to me. I found the taste of the meat, regarded a delicacy by the inhabitants on the Missouri, quite different from that of other squirrels, which is ordinarily characterized by an unpleasant sweetness.

In the afternoon it began to rain very heavily, which was all the more unpleasant as the region we passed through was becoming more and more attractive. The summits of the hills were frequently covered with cedars

---

colubris = *Archilochus colubris*, ruby-throated hummingbird; *Picus villosus* = *Dendrocopos villosus*, hairy woodpecker; *Picus pubescens* = *Dendrocopos pubescens*, downy woodpecker; *Coccyzus caroliniensis*, Vieill. = *Coccyzus americanus*, yellow-billed cuckoo. *Perdix virginianus* = *Colinus virginianus*, bobwhite; *Scolopax paludosa* = *Capella gallina*, common snipe.]

[45] A genus of thorny trees, e.g., the locusts.

[46] *Author*: The hair on the head and back of this squirrel was black; on the neck and belly, yellowish-red; the tail, bright red mixed with black; the ears were covered with short red hair. The rodent teeth were very long and brownish red, the claws grayish black, the skin on the heels and under toes dark brown. The length of the animal from the tip of the nose to the root of the tail, fourteen inches, the length of the tail eleven and one-half inches. The squirrel is different from *Sciurus hudsonius* Schreb., and *vulpinus*. It prefers to live in hilly regions and is found along the Missouri and Mississippi from the 38th to the 41st degree of latitude. It is less numerous, however, than the gray squirrel, *Sciurus cinereus*, Schreb., which it greatly surpasses in size.

[*Sciurus niger rufiventer*, the fox squirrel.]

mixed with deciduous trees, affording a pleasing change to the eye. The weather became so stormy and it got so dark at the approach of night that the boat had to drop its anchor at the mouth of Apple Creek (Rivière à la Pomme).

Although during the night the rain ceased, an extremely dense fog settled on the river and our boat, so much so that we feared we should not be able to proceed even in the daytime. But at the approach of day the fog lifted and it began to rain again. About ten o'clock in the morning the *Cincinnati* reached a most peculiar rock mass in the shape of a great tower rising over one hundred and fifty feet from the average stand of the water. It is called the Grand Tower (*La Tour du Rocher*),[47] and even in olden times was mentioned by Marquette. This strangely formed sandstone, whose height is not in relation to its base, is almost opposite the mouth of the small Obrazo River at its entry into the Mississippi. Formed of huge rock masses, it stands as mute testimony of important changes of the earth.

Only by great events of this kind could the so-called Tower have been torn away from the bank and found its place in a deep, swift-flowing stream. The water of the Mississippi at this place, especially in the channel between the Tower and the right bank, is so greatly hemmed in that it must force its way through with the greatest violence, thereby forming many whirlpools. The water breaking against the rock produces a mighty roar.

The savages, naturally inclined to be superstitious, consider gigantic cliffs, caves, and dangerous places in the river habitations of their gods, especially the master of life, *Oua-can-da*.[48] Several tribes recognize only this one superior being as identical with the god of fire or of thunder. They approach the Great Tower and the surrounding awe-inspiring region with superstitious dread and fear. At the time when the primitive red people were masters of the land the Tower and the nearby rock, Devil's Oven, served the mystic conjurer priests (*Nica-schinga oua-canda-ge* in the language of the tribes of the Osages or *Oua-sa-sche*) as the seat of their inspiration.

[47] Grand Tower, still so named, is in Illinois, opposite Altenburg, Missouri, on the Mississippi.

[48] *Wakonda*, or *Wah'Kon-Tah*, the Great Mysteries, for the Indian tribes of the Chiwere division of the Siouan family (Oto, Iowa, and Missouri) and the Dhegiha division of the same (Omaha, Ponca, Osage, Kansa, and Quapaw) indicates the ultimate power. The Dakota division of the Siouan group, consisting of seven large subdivisions, also used the word and the concept *Wakonda* but with variations from that of the Chiwere and Dhegiha. Cf. J. Owen Dorsey, *A Study of Siouan Cults, Eleventh Annual Report*, Bureau of American Ethnology (Washington, 1884); John Joseph Mathews, *The Osages: Children of the Middle Waters*; Alice C. Fletcher in F. W. Hodge, ed., *Handbook of American Indians*, II, 897–98.

They fancied they heard the voice of the deity in the roaring of the water, or they believed they heard it at this sacred place in their sleep, artificially induced by the use of poisonous herbs, as Pythia heard the oracles of the gods at Delphi. If it had been possible to collect the legends and traditions of the primitive people more completely, one would no doubt have found positive traces of an earlier and greater civilization by these former rulers of the North American continent.

All traditions of the red people point to long vanished but greater epochs of this race, which, lost in the night of eras, have left only insufficient fragmentary conceptions and mythical allusions among their cruder successors. A great difference exists between the various tribes today in regard to the degrees of civilization which they have attained, and there are points of similarity between certain tribes regarding basic traits of character and religious conceptions. At the time of the discovery and conquest of the New World stronger states existed among the Indians, leaving no doubt that in far remote periods of which we have no historical data there must have existed powerful states with a high degree of civilization. These probably reached back to even farther distant centuries than those we know through factual historical events.[49]

The summits of the hills and rocks are covered with dense timber, especially cedar, and this variety of wood also covers the small surface which constitutes the top of Tower Rock. The boat had to hold to the east bank of the river because the journey near the rock, or in the bay-like channel on the west side, is dangerous because of the swift current and a number of shallows. A few miles upstream are several islands, and the bed of the river is enclosed by high hills. Since the rain had eased and the boat had to take on wood I was permitted to go on shore. I noticed a number of tulip trees (*Liriodendron tulipifera*)[50] covering great areas of hills farther north, where they displaced the evergreens. They were already adorned with new leaves, although I made the observation that spring had not made the progress in this region that it had on the banks of the Ohio.

In the night the Bishop left us in order to visit a French school below Ste. Genevieve. He proposed to make the remainder of the trip by land to St. Louis, which he would have to do on horseback, over most difficult

[49] These conjectures about past Indian civilizations have been abundantly sustained by modern archaeological and historical research, but greatly surpassing the cultures and organization of the plains and woodland groups North of Mexico were those of the Maya and Aztecs of Central America and Mexico, and those of the Incas of South America.

[50]*Liriodendron tulipifera*, important in lumbering, the product being known as "whitewood," "poplar," or "yellowwood."

roads. This hardship, undertaken purely from a sense of duty, Mr. Du Bourg did not shun.

During the greater part of the night we remained stationary, and on the morning of May 1 we saw the mouth of the Occoa River.[51] Six miles upstream is Kaskaskia, the oldest French settlement in Illinois. Landing at noon at the mouth of the small Gabarre River, our boat stayed until evening to put off freight and passengers for Ste. Geneviève, one of the oldest French settlements, with two hundred houses and fourteen hundred inhabitants.[52] Mostly Creoles of French origin, they carry on a lively trade in lead from the very rich mines nearby. On the banks of the Mississippi are only a few scattered houses, for the inhabitants have been obliged to build the main part of the town an English mile inland to avoid the inundations by the river.

An Indian of the tribe of Delawares, wrapped in rags and riding a wretched horse, brought a fallow deer, which he offered to sell. He was accompanied by a still more poorly dressed young half-blood of the same tribe. Both individuals revealed but little of a proud and warlike people which distinguished this mighty nation half a century ago. Crowded out by political conditions, the Delaware tribe, constrained to wander from their eastern home along the seacoast and from the region of that river which still bears their name, have settled in the westerly region of the Mississippi near the Meramec River. Here a pitiable remnant of this once powerful nation, the most dreaded enemy of the immigrated Europeans, barely ekes out a wretched existence near their oppressors, and they will soon be given over to certain ruin. The sight of this deeply sunken ab-

---

[51] Occoa = Okaw River, now the Kaskaskia, which since 1891 has emptied into the Mississippi at the town of that name in Illinois dating from 1700. General Georges H. V. Collot's "Map of the Country of the Illinois," 1796, shows Kaskaskia tucked in a bend of the Kaskaskia River on the east and the Mississippi on the West, with ancient Fort de Chartres, first established in 1720 by the French, east of the Kaskaskia and southeast of Kaskaskia village. The town became the capital of Illinois Territory and briefly of the state in 1818, declining rapidly after 1819 when Vandalia became the capital. The Mississippi, slicing through the Kaskaskia floodplain upstream in 1891, threw the town and what became an Illinois island west of the big river. Neil H. Porterfield, "Ste. Geneviève, Missouri," in John Francis McDermott, *Frenchmen and French Ways in the Mississippi Valley*, 141–43.

[52] Sainte Geneviève, Missouri, on the Mississippi opposite Kaskaskia, was founded by the French circa 1735, although the *Grand Champ* (Big Field) at the site of subsequent Sainte Geneviève had been used by settlers from across the river in the 1720's. The town predates St. Louis by nearly thirty years. It was removed from the river bank late in the eighteenth century to avoid flooding, its principal church following suit in 1794. Lead mining in the St. Francis Valley a short distance away began early in the eighteenth century, and there and in St. François County was swift-developing by 1823.

origine, in whose veins still flowed the blood of his brave ancestors, awoke a feeling of sadness in me, a feeling which no doubt everyone who knows the history of these people will share with me.[53]

During the evening we traveled along a region partly hilly and rocky and partly densely wooded, and I noticed that the western banks were always higher than the eastern. The night of May 1 to May 2 was clear and beautiful, and Venus and Jupiter appeared exceedingly brilliant after sunset, a few celestial degrees removed from one another and shining in the western firmament with georgeous splendor.[54]

Toward morning the moon shone gloomily on an awe-inspiring wooded and rocky region. The faint light, causing these parts to appear still more striking and wild, filled me with amazement. The impression which such a landscape makes on me, far from my fatherland in the midst of a strange part of the world, will be appreciated by everyone who has been in a similar situation and who is receptive to such pictures of a wild and romantic nature.

At sunrise we were at a most peculiar hill formation, the Plateau Large. An enormous rocky mass drops from a height of some three hundred feet perpendicularly to the Mississippi. Its form, resembling that of a bisected cone with lower cross-section along the level of the water, is perhaps one thousand to twelve hundred feet long. Macabre crevices, caves, gorges, and tower-like formations in parallel strata marked this rock wall. Another, no less remarkable, layer of sandstone forms a continuation of the main bluff along the bank. This wall thirty feet high, reckoned from the level of the average water stand, and about one thousand feet long, is eroded by the

---

[53] Delaware Indians would play after 1823–24 a notable role as guides and scouts for many U.S. Army and other expeditions moving into the Far West. Of them Black Beaver (b. Belleville, Ill., 1806; d. Anadarko, Oklahoma, 1880) achieved the most distinction.

[54] *Author*: For the geocentric longitude of Venus and Jupiter I found at 90° west longitude from Paris, on May 1, 1823, at six o'clock in the evening, absolute time, the following results:

Geocentric longitude of Venus 2z 11° 39′ 25″, latitude 1° 12′ 54″ N. Geocentric longitude of Jupiter 2z 10° 2′ 17″, latitude of 0° 27′ 3″ S. From this follows that both planets at this time were rather close together in the heavens, for this spherical distance from one another was only 2° 19′ 43″.

Both planets therefore were at the horns of Taurus. Jupiter formed an isosceles triangle with the stars Alpha (Aldebaran) and Eta of Taurus at a distance of about 6½°. At 90° west longitude from Paris Jupiter was in culmination at 2 P.M., absolute time, Venus at 2:06 P.M. Both planets were in the western vertical circle of the horizon at about 8 P.M. In the determination of the above-given geocentric position, the longitude of the sun and the heliocentric longitude of Venus were computed according to Triesnecker's tables, the heliocentric longitude of Jupiter, however, according to de la Lande's older tables.

various depths of water into parallel strata. I counted five such distinctively different layers, though at lower water several more must be visible. This peculiar river-bank formation may justly be called a natural river measurement and may be regarded as an imperishable record of the various levels to which the water has risen. On the opposite side an island divides the stream and affords a very deep and rapidly flowing channel scarcely a hundred feet wide, through which steamboats can only work themselves up by applying all their steam power. The *Cincinnati* used all its power, and yet I noticed that it could move forward but very slowly.

At nine o'clock we landed at Herculanum,[55] a lead foundry which delivers an excellent quality of metal. The lead mines are farther inland and have a very remunerative output, especially at Potosi, a small place fifty English miles from Herculanum. Several inhabitants of Ste. Genevieve and vicinity have interests here. Mostly mined by black slaves, the ore is brought to Herculanum, cast into pigs, and most of it shipped to New Orleans.

After I had viewed the entire arrangement of the plant, I purchased as much lead as I considered necessary for my distant journey. The shot factory located here furnished these goods skillfully rolled and in all sizes. The shot is also shipped to the southern states and constitutes an important branch of trade. For the state of Missouri the lead mines are of greatest value, since the weight of the metal makes distant transportation very expensive, and the need of it, especially in the trade with the Indians and on the hunting expeditions in the northwestern regions, is absolute.

The location of the little settlement, consisting of scarcely twenty houses, is most romantic, being near a truly imposing group of cliffs of varying shapes, some entirely devoid of all vegetation, while others appear to be luxuriantly overgrown. Framed by hills, the valleys back of the little place are swampy, and I noticed a narrow but deep lake shaded by willows, nut trees, sumac, and a beautifully flowering fragrant apple tree (*Pyrus coronaria*, Ait.?).[56] A multitude of song birds let their voices ring out. Among the green of the newly leafed branches was the beautiful sky-blue and light-yellow plumage of *Sialia sialis* and *chrysoptera*, while hidden in the dense foliage the lonely thrush (*Turdus melodus*, Wils.) let its song be heard.

Upstream the banks of the Mississippi continue to be hilly, but the grotesquely formed bluffs disappear gradually, by and by making room for scattered forests of nut, ash, and sugar maple. Many wild turkeys, es-

---

[55] Herculaneum, Jefferson County, Missouri.
[56] *Pyrus coronaria*, Ait., wild crab apple.

pecially numerous gobblers, were sunning themselves on sandy and stony places and their peace was but rarely disturbed by the clatter of the steamboat.

In the vicinity of an island the *Cincinnati* ran on a shallow. We were able to get away only after half an hour of the most strenuous work. The riverbed from Cape Girardeau to St. Louis is in many places uncertain and full of sandbars which frequently change their location and cause much worry for the pilots, especially when going downstream. The boats touching ground remain stuck. Such accidents occasion days of delay and exertion. Even then efforts are sometimes futile. Unless high water comes soon and sets the boat adrift again, it may be lost entirely, because the sand and mud may settle about it to such extent that no power is sufficient to raise the vessel. The most customary and surest, though very difficult, method is to unload and thus make the boat lighter, or to change the main center of the load itself. Such reloading necessitates a long stay and a great loss of time. This is particularly understandable in the fall, when the water is unusually low and the danger of freezing in is added.

We reached the mouth of the Meramec, or Merrimack, a rather important river, at noon.[57] Its water is clear, and at its confluence with the dark-colored Mississippi it forms the often described cloudy mixture which is so disagreeable to the eye. The hard bed of the Meramec is of limestone and despite its rapid flow the river is navigable for small vessels. Its banks are rich in petrifications, even in fossil bones, of which I obtained several, notably a quite defective tusk of an American prehistoric elephant which was embedded in a clay bank.[58]

Above the Meramec I noticed here and there scattered low bluffs on the west bank which were overgrown with sparse trees or low hazelnut bushes and sumac. From the little town of Carondelet, more frequently called Vide Poche,[59] the hills and bluffs decreased more and more and toward the northwest are leveled off to grass-covered lowlands gradually rising to hills. The last bluff which the Mississippi touches here forms a kind of promontory, then the river turns to the northwest, bringing the region about St. Louis, a town of considerable size, into view. Before one reaches this place he passes a large village, Cahokia,[60] lying somewhat inland on

[57] The Meramec River flows 207 miles from the Ozark Mountains north, northeast, and southeast, entering the Mississippi twenty miles south of St. Louis.

[58] Both the mammoth (*Elephas primigenius*) and the mastodon (*Mammut americanum*) inhabited North America, the latter as recently as five thousand to ten thousand years ago.

[59] Carondelet or Vide Poche on the east bank of the Mississippi near St. Louis.

[60] Cahokia on the east (Illinois) bank of the Mississippi nearly opposite St. Louis takes its name from the Cahokia Indians, one of the Illinois Confederacy, dating from 1699, the

the Illinois bank and called *Le Caho.* Inhabited by French Creoles, it is situated in a flat, somewhat swampy region. Along the river this side of St. Louis are a few very pretty country homes with tastefully arranged gardens, giving this beautiful location a charming and lively appearance.

It had become night when the *Cincinnati* reached St. Louis and tied up at the place for steamboats. The town and the many houses along the river considered to belong to it cover a considerable lot of ground. Our arrival quickly became known, and despite the darkness, the boat was rapidly filled with a crowd of curious people as soon as we landed, keeping up a commotion far into the night.[61]

I remained on board because it was too late to find a lodging place and also because I did not wish to leave my baggage. A few passengers from Ste. Genevieve who had been on the *Cincinnati* very obligingly promised to lodge me on the following morning and to guide me to those persons for whom I had letters of introduction. I was not in the least inconvenienced in regard to a lodging place, for the kind-hearted Americans had at once cared for this, selecting spacious quarters such as I needed for my work and the preparations for my further journey.

My German countryman, Mr. Warendorf, and also the superintendent of the French Northwest Trading Company (now American Fur Company), Mr. Pradd,[62] at once extended the friendliest reception to me. Such a reception is exceedingly pleasing to a stranger in a country where the merchant does not consider his personal interest if he can be of service to a person who has been recommended to him or who places confidence in his

year of the location of a Jesuit mission there. Cf. John Francis McDermott, ed., *Old Cahokia: A Narrative and Documents Illustrating the First Century of Its History.*

[61] St. Louis had been founded fifty-nine years before Duke Paul's first visit by Pierre de Laclède Liguest and René Auguste Chouteau, his fourteen-year-old stepson, as the future site of the trading operations of Maxent, Laclède and Company for the middle Mississippi and Missouri rivers. The town had scarcely begun its life when its transfer to Spain by France, along with the former French claims west of the Mississippi, put it under Spanish administration, where it remained until the U.S. took possession of Louisiana from France (which had regained Louisiana in 1800) on March 9, 1804. At the time of Duke Paul's visit, the city counted something over 5,600 citizens. Cf. John Francis McDermott, ed., *The Early Histories of St. Louis, passim.*

[62] Bernard Pratte, born at Ste. Genevieve in 1771, was known to his contemporaries as "General" Pratte, not from the actuality of the military title but from his performance in the defense of St. Louis and Missouri in the War of 1812. He entered the fur trade as a partner in Pratte, Cabanné, and Company, later Berthold, Chouteau, and Pratte, and still later Bernard Pratte and Company. By 1823 Pratte and his associates had contracted for the exclusive purchase of furs obtained by the Western Department of the American Fur Company, John Jacob Astor's organization. Pratte was a member of the Missouri Constitutional Convention of 1820 and played a prominent role in the business affairs of St. Louis. He retired in 1830 and died in 1836. Louis Houck, *History of Missouri,* III, 253–54.

advice. I consider it my duty to repeat that, without the magnitude of un-selfishness and cordial aid of these friends whom I had the fortune of meeting in America, I should never have been able to carry out the purpose of my journey. Through the kindness of the Bishop, most of the prominent residents of St. Louis were informed concerning my goal, and all strove not only to give me the benefit of their advice and help but also to further the execution of my plans.

General Sir Williams Clarke,[63] whose great endeavor contributed so much to the knowledge of peoples and countries and whose name will be justly preserved in history, received me with that cordial and sincere in-terest for which this illustrious man is universally noted. The General, and also Mr. Pierre Chouteau and his brother Auguste Chouteau, to whom the world is indebted for the first authentic report concerning the upper Mis-souri and its western territory, promising me their warmest interest and every possible assistance, kept these promises most zealously.[64]

On my first visit to Mr. Clarke I made the acquaintance of the famed Major O'Fallon, United States Intendant of Indian Affairs on the Mis-souri.[65] He delighted me with a rare friendship and I shall have occasion to mention him frequently in the process of my journey.

[63] The knighthood attached to General William Clark's list of honors is, of course, with-out basis but the encomium is right. The veteran co-explorer of the Louisiana Purchase with Meriwether Lewis, 1804–1806, was serving as Superintendent of Indian Affairs at St. Louis for the second time when Duke Paul was his guest in 1823. His first superin-tendency dated from his return from the Pacific to 1813, when he became governor of Missouri Territory to 1821, the year of Missouri's statehood (he was thought of to run against Alexander McNair for the state governorship); his second superintendency con-tinued from 1821 until his death in 1838. From his first term as superintendent, he served also as brigadier general of militia. Cf. Donald Jackson, ed., *The Letters of Lewis and Clark and Related Documents* . . . ; John E. Bakeless, *Lewis and Clark: Partners in Dis-covery*; Harlow Lindley, "William Clark—The Indian Agent," Mississippi Valley His-torical Association *Proceedings*, 1908–1909, 63–75. "Clarke" in the Duke's account prob-ably derives from the Nicholas Biddle text (1814) of the Lewis and Clark journals.

[64] René Auguste Chouteau (1749–1829), following his youthful co-founding of St. Louis in 1764, became the much-trusted adviser to the Spanish regime there during Spain's occupancy of the Mississippi Valley, 1764–1800. With his half-brother Jean Pierre Chou-teau (1758–1849) he controlled trade with the Osage Indians in the Missouri and Okla-homa areas and continued to dominate it after the Louisiana Purchase. Pierre, a founder of the Missouri Fur Company, was one of the best known fur traders of the West. His sons, Auguste Pierre (1786–1838) and Pierre Chouteau, Jr. (1789–1865) were associated with him in the fur trade, the latter becoming head of the American Fur Company. McDermott, *The Early Histories of St. Louis*, 5–30 et *passim*; Auguste Chouteau, "Narrative of the Settlement of St. Louis," in McDermott, *op. cit.*, 47–59; "Depositions Before the Recorder of Land Titles, St. Louis, 1825" in McDermott, *op. cit.*, 91–97.

[65] Major Benjamin O'Fallon (1793–1842) was reared in part by his uncle General William Clark at St. Louis. He became Indian agent at Prairie du Chien in 1816, negotiated

Formerly territorial governor of Missouri, General Clarke is, as General Intendant of the affairs of all Indian tribes in the Northwest, one of the most esteemed officials of the United States. This post, so important for the peace of the western regions, could not have been entrusted to a worthier man, for all Indian nations respect and honor the name of this general, recognizing him as a father defending their best interests and their rights with that fervor peculiar to big-hearted individuals. His entire effort aims at reconciling the aborigines with the new immigrants, and by a generous and sane behavior of the latter toward their often very unhappy red brothers, to blot out, as much as possible, that stain so sadly blemishing the history of former centuries and the occupation of America. Recognition is also due to the government of the United States for its philanthrophic tendency toward the aborigines, and this is clearly expressed in many ways. The main purpose of the government is to see to it that its citizens do no harm but leave the natives in the full enjoyment of their rights and freedom.[66]

On the very first day of my stay in St. Louis I could, thanks to the generous aid of the French Fur Company, arrange my plans for the continuation of my journey. The directors of the company, promising to equip as quickly as possible a vessel destined for their factory near Council Bluffs, agreed to arrange on this craft a place for me which should be as comfortable as possible. They also promised to supply me with all necessary provisions and goods requisite to sustain us on so long a journey and also articles indispensable for barter and presents for the Indians.

Relying entirely on this promise, I felt perfectly at ease. No time was lost during my stay in the town, yet everything was so faultlessly ordered that nothing remained to be wished for.

I can advise every foreign traveler contemplating going to the upper Missouri or the western prairies to supply himself in St. Louis with all necessities for the journey. Provisions and wares are only slightly higher here than in other places in the United States, and the purchase of such things serving the trade with the Indians requires a careful selection, be-

treaties with the Otos and Poncas in 1817, and on accepting the position of Indian agent for the Upper Missouri tribes (Pawnees, Otos, Missourias, and Omahas) in 1819 was also given the rank of major. He ascended the Missouri with the Long Expedition in 1819 to Council Bluffs, his new agency headquarters. With a number of Pawnee chiefs (who will be touched upon in the Duke's subsequent narrative) he toured the East in 1821, and in 1825 effectuated treaties with fifteen Upper Missouri tribes and bands. Resigning his agency in 1827, he returned to St. Louis. *DAB*, VII, 629–30.

[66] The extent of the U.S. government's failure to meet this estimate of its Indian policy and its subsequent administration of Indian affairs is realistically and fairly traced in Angie Debo, *A History of the Indians of the United States*.

cause of the peculiar stubbornness of the latter. The Indians disdain more useful articles, preferring poorer ones. The trading establishments in the state of Missouri, being acquainted with the inclinations of the natives, make a happy selection for almost all the different tribes and gladly advise the stranger. Even one who would travel by horseback will procure his mount much better and cheaper in St. Louis and that vicinity than in other places and will also easily find a guide who knows the language of several nations. The class of people who can be used for this purpose are usually honest and upright, for the most part Canadians; they can also be taken into the service of the trading companies as oarsmen and hunters.

It is well, however, to select such men as have already attained rank in this service and who have a reputation for sobriety. A liking for intoxicating drink is about the only serious fault these men have. Often required to do extremely strenuous work, the half-bloods are especially prone to drink.

7

COMMENTS ON THE STATE OF MISSOURI — CONFERENCE OF
GENERAL SIR WILLIAM CLARKE WITH THE POTAWATOMI
INDIANS — ARRIVAL OF A BAND OF OSAGES — DESCRIPTION
OF ST. LOUIS AND THE REGION — JOURNEY BY LAND TO ST.
CHARLES — DEPARTURE FROM ST. CHARLES, UP THE MIS-
SOURI — THE CAVE OF TARDIE — THE GASCONADE RIVER —
ARRIVAL AT THE OSAGE.

SOME forty years ago only Creoles of French descent and a few Spanish immigrants constituted the entire population of the state of Missouri. The surrender of the Louisiana territory to the American Union of States was the repeated signal for a multitude of adventurous immigrant families of the eastern states to share in the advantages afforded by a new country, sparsely settled and serving wild Indians as a habitat. Taking possession, the Congress recognized the importance of having the western regions more fully investigated, especially for political reasons. Several expeditions carried out this purpose with great perseverance, enriching the world with a number of most remarkable discoveries.

That vast territory, superficially known under the general name of Louisiana, extending far to the north and west and inhabited by Indian tribes, was explored in a short time by American engineers. Its political boundaries were established. By the surrender of New France to the United States, the latter not only became possessor of all the Mississippi and Missouri rivers but also extended its domain from the eastern to the western coast of America, thereby obtaining direct influence on three of the most important seas of the New World.[1]

In regard to the western ocean, to be sure, this is not so distinctly felt today, but in more distant times this will change. Insignificant as it may seem at the present time, this advantage is certain to arouse the jealousy of neighboring colonies and their mother countries. By treaties, the aborigines

---

[1] Not in 1823 nor in 1835, when the Duke's *Erste Reise* was published, did U.S. dominion extend to the Pacific, the California coast being occupied by Mexico, and Oregon, i.e., present Oregon and Washington, jointly by Britain and the U.S. The convention for joint occupancy, shaped in 1818, continued in 1826, and dissolved in 1846, finally saw Oregon Territory occupied solely by the U.S. to the 49th Parallel.

withdrew beyond certain boundaries and were not allowed to reside permanently on lands assigned to the white civilized population. It was also prohibited to the whites to settle on land belonging to the Indians.[2]

Generally, laws passed by Congress did much to befriend the Indians, and the punctiliously observed decree preventing the sale of whisky and other intoxicating beverages to the natives is as wise as it is humane and forestalls much trouble.[3] How much the use of spirituous beverages demoralizes the Indians can be clearly seen if one compares those living near whites with those living far away from them. The latter are still much better off and more unspoiled than those who come to the towns and settlements for trade on their hunting expeditions. They cannot be kept away from the use of brandy.

Travelers who have only seen the drunken Indians at the trading stations or in the company of equally degenerate people of European descent give us, for this reason, their partisan and partially incorrect observation of the primitive people of North America. From these totally depraved and profligate Indian groups they sketch the entire aboriginal population of North America. How little, for example, do the superficial observations, which the otherwise truth-loving Volney made of a degenerate tribe of Miami Indians in Vincennes, fit many of the northwestern nations.[4] In their midst I made the acquaintance of men who not only could lay claim to the respect of their Indian tribal associates but whose big-hearted and

[2] The pleasant balance of white and Indian assignments here suggested by the author was not a distinguishing feature of U.S. Indian policy in the nineteenth century, if ever, as even a cursory examination of Kappler, *Indian Affairs, Laws and Treaties* will make clear. Constriction of Indian domains and the extinguishment of tribal titles in land went on from decade to decade, to the full flowering of the reservation system after 1870.

[3] Withholding whisky from the Indians, at settlements or trading posts, or on the wide reaches of the Missouri, was more honored in the breach than in the observance, except at U.S. factories. Cf., for example, the reports of Thomas Biddle and Col. Henry Atkinson in *American State Papers, Indian Affairs*, 16 Cong., 1 sess., *Senate Document 163*, pp. 200–204.

[4] Constantin François de Chasseboeuf, Comte de Volney, resided in the U.S. 1795–1798, publishing his observations in Paris on his return there, *Tableau du climat et du sol des États-Unis* . . . (1803), translated and published in 1804 at Philadelphia as *A View of the Soil and Climate of the United States of America . . . and on the Aboriginal Tribes of America*. His observations on the Miamis are in considerable part those of William Wells, a Kentucky captive adopted by the tribe who had fought in their successful campaigns against Colonels John Hardin and Josiah Harmar and Governor Arthur St. Clair. Anthony Wayne, who had defeated the Miamis, expressed frank respect for the Indians and their great leader, Little Turtle, and for their achievements in agriculture. Cf. Gilbert Chinard, *Volney et l'Amerique, passim*; Bert Anson, *The Miami Indians*; Anthony Wayne, Fort Defiance, to the Secretary of War, August 14, 1794, in *American State Papers*, Class II, *Indian Affairs*, I, 490–91.

noble character earned my full esteem and that of all government agents with whom they came in contact. Unfortunately the tendency toward drink so dominates many Indian tribes that the whisky supplied by avaricious neighbors has not only become a cause of humiliation but their complete ruin. An Indian who considers dignified, serious deportment, coupled with the calm, cool power of reflection, as the symbol of manly strength is, when intoxicated, the exact opposite. Wild passion easily misleads him to any act, and his naturally war-like mind indulgently causes him to wield the weapon against his best friend, whose life he would defend with the last drop of his blood were he sober.

The aborigine, to whom nothing is more sacred than peace among his tribal associates, must atone severely for any disturbance of the peace in the midst of blood kin, and an unavoidable death is the voluntary and certain sacrificial offering of him who, while intoxicated, has killed a friend. This characteristic trait of the Indians proves clearly how much they abhor the consequences of excesses, and only a degenerate Indian will forfeit everything for a glass of brandy.

Unfortunately I saw this too plainly among the nations that live bordering the whites and those that roam in such states as Illinois and Missouri. Only vigilant supervision and continual admonition of the Indian agents can keep them in bounds. Many red nations farther distant continue to maintain their nationality and moral freedom with pride.

Missouri and Illinois are among the states most frequently visited by the Indians. Although they are not actually pushed back by the force of arms, nevertheless, there are many unpleasant clashes between the red aborigines and the earliest immigrating Anglo-Americans. By and by most of the nations became reconciled to the new settlers, especially those who were friendly with the French Creoles, through whose mediation difficulties were greatly reduced.[5]

---

[5] In a very real sense, the Treaty of Greenville (1795), closing General Anthony Wayne's campaign against the tribes of the Old Northwest, was the prelude to the forcible removal of the historic tribes of that area southwestward to Illinois, Missouri, Kansas, and finally Oklahoma in the nineteenth century. These tribes were thus thrown against the tribes historically resident in the latter states. Those occupying southerly areas east of the Mississippi—notably the Cherokees, Choctaws, Chickasaws, Creeks, and Seminoles (the Five Civilized Tribes)—fell under Indian removal legislation in President Andrew Jackson's administration, May 28, 1830, and similarly found themselves strangers in the new lands reserved for them in Indian Territory, present Oklahoma. When Missouri attained statehood in 1821, its Indians were gradually removed to Kansas. The detailed records of these migrations of populations are contained in the writings of such scholars as Grant Foreman, Angie Debo, Muriel H. Wright, and A. M. Gibson, noted in the appended bibliography.

The Potawatomis and the Iowas, two tribes that never enjoyed a good name even among their own people, sporadically still make attacks on and commit excesses against the whites. This apparently will end only with the complete extermination of these tribes.[6] The Osages formerly were greatly feared, but now deport themselves quite peacefully, and from the Kansa there is nothing to fear. The Fox and Sac Indians usually do not push far beyond the boundaries of the European inhabitants, but if they are not afraid they might easily be inclined to mischief. Formerly they often visited as far as the Mississippi, turning westward to hunt or even crossing the Mississippi, impelled by the lust for war. (Their latest wars under Chief Black Hawk confirm the truth of this remark written down ten years ago.)[7]

An extremely long time passed after the important discovery made by Father Marquette in the name of France before steps were taken by that nation to utilize and colonize the upper region of Louisiana. For some time New Orleans enjoyed a comparatively flourishing trade, and France seemed to prefer conserving her forces for the coastal regions along the Mississippi and the St. Lawrence. The exaggerated reports of the fierceness of wild and war-like tribes, and perhaps the overstated tales, fabulously augmented, of earlier adventurers in Illinois, apparently induced

[6] The Potawatomis, pictured dramatically in ensuing pages, are of the Algonquian group, therefore originally one with the Ottawas and Chippewas originating on the shore of Lake Huron, later centering at Green Bay, Wisconsin. With the defeat of the Illinois Confederacy in 1769, they began to occupy parts of Illinois; in the early nineteenth century they extended their control to the area of Lake Michigan, from Milwaukee River, Wisconsin, to Grand River in Michigan, east across Michigan to Lake Erie, and as far south as the Wabash in Indiana. They counted fifty villages. When Duke Paul saw them, they were in the process of selling their lands piecemeal, the culmination of which took place between 1836 and 1841. Most had removed to southern Kansas by 1846 and to Indian Territory in 1868. Hodge, *Handbook*, II, 289–93.

The Iowas, however, were of the Chiwere Siouan group, closely related to the Oto and Missouria tribes. At this time they were on Platte River, Missouri, not far from present St. Joseph, and in 1829 on Platte River, Iowa, in both instances trading their furs to the merchants from St. Louis. Lewis and Clark, *Original Journals*, VI, 91–92.

[7] The Sac or Sauk, originating in the eastern Peninsula of Michigan, were of Algonquian stock. When they joined their linguistic kinsmen the Foxes on Fox River, Wisconsin, in the seventeenth century, the two tribes shared both in the wars and in the migrations which became their common lot, though not without periodic quarrels and divisions, notably over the Sauk Treaty of 1804 at St. Louis relinquishing lands east of the Mississippi, leading to the Black Hawk (Sauk) War of 1832, in which the Sauk leader and his Fox allies tried to recover their holdings in Illinois. General Henry Atkinson's troops defeated this force in August, 1832. After the Sauks had joined the Foxes in Iowa, the two tribes relinquished their lands there and removed to Kansas. The schism of 1857 caused most of the Foxes to return to Iowa. In 1867 the Sauks ceded their lands in Kansas for lands in Indian Territory, present Oklahoma, where remnants still live. Cf. William T. Hagan, *The Sac and Fox Indians, passim.*

the French not to waste their forces and leave their most active colonists to a fate which foreshadowed an unhappy ending.

However, the war so unfortunate for France, in which she lost brave Montcalm and with him Canada, completely changed the influence of this nation in North America. After surrendering her lands to Spain in 1762, France lost all her possessions on the North American continent. Many Canadians dissatisfied with English rule, left the place of their nativity, followed the course of the Great Lakes and of the Illinois, and founded settlements at Ste. Genevieve and New Bourbon.

St. Louis was founded a short time later by a company of traders under the firm name of Pierre Laclède, Maxon [Maxent] and Compagnie. Recognizing fully the extraordinary advantages which the location of this town afforded in the trade with the Indians, they sought to make friends with them as much as possible. In 1766 St. Louis received a considerable increase in French Creoles, who preferred the Spanish to the English government. Or more probably they entertained the hope of living without the supervision of any government. The Spaniards, lukewarm in taking possession of the land relinquished by France, did not take active steps to establish a real government until 1766. Since the treaties between France and Spain were veiled in secrecy and were not published, and as Spanish rule was repugnant to the inhabitants of New Orleans, the Creoles vigorously opposed the Spanish ruler and he had to flee with his troops to Havana.

The colony continued to govern itself in the name of the king of France until 1769, and the small settlements on the upper Mississippi were left entirely to themselves. In August of that year, the Spanish Governor [Alexander] O'Reilly, without opposition, took possession of all the territory ceded by France. Without taking cognizance, however, of the prevailing conditions, he gained at the beginning of his reign a reputation for bloodthirsty cruelty, whereby active hatred against Spain was increased and never abated.

Upper Louisiana, not feeling Spanish pressure until 1770, cleared much land on the upper Mississippi and on the Missouri, at the instigation of the managers of the colony. It appears that this eight-year period may be considered among the happiest for this region. The Canadian colonists, active and peace-loving settlers, made friends with the Indians, and in the shortest time possible would have attained a high degree of affluence had not their passion for hunting and their inclination to lead a roving life caused them to neglect their fields. Thereby the colony sometimes suffered want.[8]

---

[8] The pattern of small individual holdings which prevailed in French Canada was repeated in considerable part in upper Louisiana. But the allusion here to the "roving"

During the American War of Independence, Louisiana remained a valued possession of Spain, but in 1780 an expedition against St. Louis was undertaken by the English. Made up largely of Indians from Michili-mackinak, it was frustrated by the timely action of General Clarke, a relative of General William Clarke. On this occasion the Indians, about fifteen hundred in number, disagreeing with the few English, were able to save themselves only by flight. The U.S. General concluded peace with the Indians, treated them liberally, and let them depart as friends. A few Indian tribes, it is true, attempted to attack the separate colonies, even St. Louis in later times, but were nearly always repulsed with losses.[9]

The act passed by the United States in 1787, whereby slavery of colored people was abolished in the Northwest Territory, caused a great migration to the upper Louisiana country.[10] There, under the protection of the Spaniards, such individuals who brought their slaves with them were gladly received. From this period on, the first settlers of Anglo-American stock came to the western regions of the Mississippi and the Missouri. Consequently the Spanish government seems to have studiously aimed at

habits of the French is an over-simplification. The French in the Mississippi Valley were roving after the continent's largest commercial crop at the time, fine and coarse furs, with eager markets in Europe and the orient.

French Canadian traders and trappers, moreover, were a stratified society consisting of *bourgeois* or proprietors; *voyageurs*, subtraders; *manageurs de lard*, pork-eaters or apprentices; and, from some points of view, the most important of the *engagés* or employees, the *hivernants* or winterers, those who managed posts in the winter months. *Coureurs de bois*, originally those who hunted without license or traded illegally, has been applied incorrectly to the class of *voyageurs*.

Of the small holders who stayed in villages or returned to them periodically or retired there, Louis Joseph Papineau said in 1839, "Our people have no ambitions beyond their present possessions, & never want to go beyond the sound of their own church bells." (Quoted in Mason Wade, *The French Canadians, 1760–1967*, 2 vols., I, 185). John Thomas Scharf's generalized portrait of the *voyageurs* and their ways is not an unjust one (*History of St. Louis City and County*, 271–76, 279–84) Cf. Grace Lee Nute, *The Voyageur*, 177–224.

[9] George Rogers Clark, campaigning against the British and their Indian allies in the Illinois country (British controlled) in 1778 took Kaskaskia and Cahokia in Illinois and Vincennes, Indiana. The latter, retaken by Lieutenant General Henry Hamilton, the British commander, in December, 1778, was again taken by Clark in February, 1779.

The defense of St. Louis fell to other hands, notably its Spanish governor, his limited troops, and citizens of the young city. For Captain Fernando de Lebeya's role in its defense, a well-conceived and courageous one, see John Francis McDermott, "The Myth of the 'Imbicile Governor': Captain Fernando de Lebeya and the defense of St. Louis in 1780," in McDermott, ed., *The Spaniards in the Mississippi Valley, 1763–1804*.

[10] The Ordinance of 1787, establishing the Northwest Territory and providing for the creation of not fewer than three nor more than five states from it, with prohibition of slavery, passed the Continental Congress July 13, 1787.

increasing the population of Louisiana markedly, after evacuating a few fortified places on the east bank of the Mississippi. At least the many liberal concessions, more generous than those granted by other colonial powers in America, indicate this.

Evidently it was Spain's purpose to present a strong force against its ever-expanding neighbor to the east, a force which could serve as a protecting wall for the safety of Mexico. Undoubtedly the cabinet in Madrid knew the immense value which possession of Louisiana would afford the trade and the political position of the United States.

The Spanish government at St. Louis even favored the immigration of two Indian tribes, the Shawnees and the Delawares, from across the Mississippi, conceding to them considerable tracts of land.[11] Similar concessions were made to other people, and the land was granted free of fees on the sole condition that actual settlement should be made on it. Consequent to these measures the population grew appreciably. By the time of the transfer of the territory to the United States, about three-fourths of its inhabitants were immigrants. Even the trade with the Indians up the Missouri and on the western prairies was encouraged. The extant French Fur Company of St. Louis spared no trouble and expense to equal the English Northwest Company of McKenzie,[12] and by the end of the past century several enterprising Creoles, notably the Messrs. Chouteau, had penetrated as far as the Arikara and Mandan Indians.

By these various endeavors a great part of the Northwest Territory and a number of mighty nations, whose names formerly had scarcely been heard, became known. The path was prepared for great explorations of later American travelers, such as the Messrs. Lewis and Clarke.

After the cession to the United States, Upper Louisiana was separated from Lower Louisiana, and Missouri formed a separate territory. The elevation of the latter to statehood encountered great difficulties in Congress, for the surrender of Negro slaves was a disadvantage to the proposed new state. Finally, Washington relented on this point and the terri-

---

[11] The Shawnees, of the central Algonquian group of tribes, of which their kinsmen, the Delawares, were the dominant confederacy of early times, had been so long at war with Americans in the Northwest Territory (from the French and Indian War to the Treaty of Greenville in 1795) that a large number of them welcomed the invitation of the Spanish government to join a portion of the Delawares on a tract near Cape Girardeau, Mo., in 1793. Hodge, *Handbook*, II, 535–36.

[12] The North West Company was organized in 1787 by traders in Montreal, whose enterprising representative, Alexander MacKenzie, ventured to the Pacific in 1789. Cf. Sir Alexander MacKenzie, *Exploring the Northwest Territory: Sir Alexander MacKenzie's Journal of a Voyage by Bark Canoe from Lake Athabasca to the Pacific Ocean in the Summer of 1789*, ed. by T. H. McDonald.

tory was admitted. Despite its vast area, the state of Missouri was one of the most sparsely settled, and in 1822 its fifteen counties contained only 66,586 inhabitants. Whites numbered 55,988, free colored 376, and 10,222 were slaves. The Indian population cannot be included. Because of roving living habits, surmises concerning their number deviate more or less from the truth.

On the second day after my arrival, General Clarke informed me that he expected a visit from the first chief of the Potawatomis, some of his most prominent warriors, and a crowd of Indians with whom several disputed points were to be settled. I then learned that this band of Indians had made their camp adjacent to the town. Hastening there, I found them busily adorning themselves according to their manner and putting on such attire as they deemed becoming such an important occasion.[13]

The Potawatomis belong to the dirtiest tribe that I have ever seen. Because of their filthiness, the natural red-copper skin color, especially of the women, had changed to a dark brown. On this background the vermillion and green paints applied to the face and several other parts of the body seemed very repulsive. The men were almost naked except for a white woolen blanket or an old worn piece of buffalo robe and breech-clout. Among most of the Indian tribes this consists of a piece of red or blue cloth drawn between the thighs and fastened in front and behind to a leather belt.

Few of the warriors wore those special decorations with which the chiefs and braves of other nations are pleased to adorn themselves, indicating their rank. These decorations, usually worked with great care, show good taste. The leggings and moccasins of the men and women of the Potawatomis, made of poorly tanned leather and decorated with little pieces of cloth or ribbon, are without embroidery. The use of dyed hair from various animals for embroidery is a peculiar accomplishment of the Indian women,

[13] The presence of the Potawatomis in St. Louis, as supplicants before Superintendent of Indian Affairs William Clark, can be understood in relation to the severe constriction of their range after the War of 1812, in which they had fought for the British, even laying siege to Fort Wayne, Indiana. By the Treaty of Ghent with Great Britain, the U.S. acceded to Britain's insistence that peace be made forthwith between the U.S. and England's late Indian allies. This was done in 1815 at Portage des Sioux, in 1816 at Fort Wayne, in 1818 at various points. Thus the Indian amnesty under the Treaty of Ghent was fulfilled. But at St. Louis in 1816, Fort Meigs in 1817, and Chicago in 1821, the U.S. had exacted cessions from the Potawatomis, among other Old Northwest tribes, of most of their lands in Michigan, Ohio, Indiana, and Illinois. Thus the happy hunting ground which the Potawatomis had won in Illinois from the Illinois Confederacy during Pontiac's War beginning in 1769 no longer provided them the range or the freedoms they had been accustomed to. *American State Papers*, Class II, *Indian Affairs*, Vol. 2, 12, 95–96, 131–35, 168, 257–58; Grant Foreman, *Last Trek of the Indians*, 12–57, maps at pp. 80, 100, 114.

requiring great skill, especially since the poor tools of the Indians are made of the bones of animals or fish. Nearly all of the men wore their hair long, hanging loose. A few had their hair cropped short and only a very few had their heads shaved clean, leaving only a kind of cockscomb, the usual hairdress of an Indian warrior. This singularly cut tuft extends from the brow to the neck, and is usually decorated with deer hair dyed red or yellow, or with the tail feathers of the golden eagle, sometimes with other decorations. This gives the men a very wild but not an ugly appearance, reminding one in a way of the customs of several Asiatic peoples who also shear their heads except for a tuft of hair.

The facial expression of the Potawatomis was more sinister and wilder than that of other nations. By comparing them with a few Osages whom I saw the following day, this observation was especially evident. There is also traceable an expression of suffering in their countenances which I regard as being due to their lost independence and the wretchedness of their existence. Neither the men nor the women can be called ugly, although the latter, in many ways show to better advantage. Unfortunately their faces, which in many instances were pretty, and their handsome, muscular bodies were abominably disfigured by dirt and put-on paint. The practice of piercing their ears in three places and suspending from them rings or chains of little white and blue sticks of porcelain, I found only among the Potawatomis. Some even had a large ring through their nose, a practice which I rarely found among the natives of North America.

After the Indians had made all necessary preparation, and the women, betraying a great liking for ornaments, had put on everything that in their opinion might increase their charm, they struck camp. Their small tents made of hides, and from long usage rigid with dirt, were piled into heaps and, together with a few half-starved horses belonging to the band, were entrusted to the care of a few women. With the chiefs in the lead, the horde now set out.

A flag with the coat of arms of the United States, presented to the Potawatomis some years before by the government, was carried ahead by an old warrior who was painted entirely black. The Indians, arranging themselves in double file, first the men and then the women, followed the chief in complete silence. With faces bearing an expression of severe earnestness and eyes lowered to the ground, they marched through the streets of the town to the dwelling of the General, entirely oblivious to the many people who were attracted by their strange procession, crowding near and following them.

The General received the Indians in a hall especially arranged for such interviews, decorated with a great number of Indian weapons, ornaments,

191

and garments which Mr. Clarke has collected from a large number of nations on his journeys. This collection is very complete and most of its objects, especially the costumes of tribes of the Far West, deserve to be painted and described. Moreover, it is extremely unfortunate that vermin will have destroyed in a short time the best pieces, particularly the beautifully embroidered animal skins.[14]

Easy chairs had been arranged for the chief and the foremost warriors. The General seated himself opposite the chief, whose name was Junaw-sche Wome, or Stream of the Rock. One of the most esteemed men, the warrior with his face painted black, Muk-ke-te Pakee, or Black Partridge, together with four other warriors, Negge-nesch Keek, Nav-kaw Be-me, Wabe-wy, and Centa-wa, likewise sat down while the rest stood up behind them.

Only the men were in the hall. The women and youths remained outside, and only now and then during the deliberation, which lasted for half an hour, a representative of one or the other timidly stuck a head through the door. During the entire session the Indians maintained the utmost seriousness and the greatest stillness prevailed. No one spoke except the General, Stream of the Rock, and the interpreter. Only on important points touched upon did the most prominent men express their approval or disapproval by a slight motion of the head.

The Chief delivered a long and well composed speech concerning the sad condition of his tribe. Complaining especially bitterly about the decrease of game, their most important food supply, due to existing hunting privileges, he begged the General to take appropriate measures against the complete destruction of game and fish along the tributaries of the Illinois. Although the very life of the wild ones was at stake, I could not, despite the closest scrutiny, observe the least trace of passion in his face. From the beginning

---

[14] This is a little noted description of the ethnological objects retained by Clark after the Expedition of 1804–1806 and others he may have acquired thereafter. Paul Russell Cutright has painstakingly traced the fate of the Lewis and Clark Indian collections from the Far West. Some were shipped to President Thomas Jefferson, part of which he retained for his Indian Hall at Monticello, part going to Charles Willson Peale's Museum in Philadelphia. In the early period of his travels, George Catlin got from Clark certain Indian objects which ultimately went to the Smithsonian Institution, Washington. In 1846, Peale having died in 1827, the Peale Museum was broken up, part of the holdings being sold at auction, part being held for display until 1850. In the latter year, P. T. Barnum bought half of the remaining collection, the remainder being acquired by Moses Kimball of the Boston Museum. Barnum's American Museum in New York was destroyed by fire in 1865. The Peabody Museum, Harvard, acquired the Lewis and Clark ethnological holdings from Kimball around the turn of the century. Cutright, *Lewis and Clark: Pioneering Naturalists*, 350–357.

to the end of his speech, the Chief did not pronounce a single word more emphatically than any other.

During the entire transaction the peace pipe went from mouth to mouth, and after each one with face upturned had sent three puffs of smoke into the air, he gave the pipe to the one seated next to him. The General endeavored to satisfy the Indians as much as possible. After he had given the Chief assurance of the friendliest intentions and had admonished him to keep his tribe at peace with the whites, a few gifts were distributed among them consisting of a kind of blue uniform with a red collar for Junaw-sche Wome, woolen blankets, powder, lead, a few knives, sticks of coral, glass beads, red and green paints, etc. Then the session was ended, apparently to the satisfaction of the Potawatomis.

The Chief, attired in his new garment, which contrasted ridiculously with his other clothing, then stepped to General Clarke, shook hands with him, with Major O'Fallon, and with me. The other warriors, one after the other, followed his example. The hall was then filled with women, who until now had stood impatiently in the street. After they had also received their share of presents the procession went back in the former order.

In the office of the French Missouri Company I had the opportunity of becoming better acquainted with Junaw-sche Wome and the Black Warrior. The Chief entered into a lengthy conversation with me, aided by an interpreter who chanced to be present, during which he told me of several customs of the Potawatomies. But these, however, differ so little from those of other aborigines that they do not deserve to be mentioned here, and at a later time I propose to discuss this point more in detail. Finally, Stream of the Rock repeated to me the complaint which he had brought to the attention of the General, reiterating the unhappy position of his people. Forced by need and wretchedness more and more, they have lost their moral strength and are hastening to their ruin.

The Potawatomis are too weak to migrate to the Northwest, which is held by strong and warlike Indians, and they are also much at enmity with the remaining neighboring tribes. Their existence in Illinois and on the southern shores of the Great Lakes will become more desperate as a result of the reduction of hunting and fishing, for these nomadic tribes are not easily persuaded to take up agriculture.

Quite in contrast to the coolness shown during the official interview, I observed that the unimpassioned indifference in a public transaction is by no means stolidity, but really an art characteristic of these people in controlling completely the strongest emotions of their soul during negotiations, to serve the best interest of their nation. Junaw-sche Wome seemed most deeply moved. Several times I noticed tears in his eyes, especially when his son arrived, a handsome young man who would become successor as principal chief after his father's death.

The Principal Chief partook only moderately of the offered whisky, and Muk-ke-te Pakee, the Black Partridge, who had not spoken a word and had not changed his serious, stern look, refused the drink altogether. Now I also learned why this warrior had disfigured himself so strangely. He was in mourning for a near relative. The time devoted to the memory of the dead is characterized among most of the North American Indians by long and inordinately severe fasting, singing death songs, and painting the face white or black. As long as an Indian's face is painted with this symbol of mourning he does not partake of food. If nature makes its demand too urgently he washes and cleanses himself most carefully, but never neglects to lay on the color as soon as his hunger is appeased. At the same time it is also a law among Indians to let their hair grow during the period of mourning. Shearing is regarded as a mode of adornment, and during the time of mourning all ornamentation is avoided.

I traded from the Chief several small articles which were part of his attire, a kind of cap of martin skin decorated with feathers. This was the head-covering of the Indian. All ornaments and clothes of Junaw-sche Wome, and those of other Potawatomis, were really tasteless and clearly showed the poverty of the band.

A group of Osage Indians of the tribe of the Great Osages (called *Grand Os* by the French Creoles),[15] who usually live near the source of the river which carries their name, arrived in St. Louis at the same time that the Potawatomis were there. In small groups they visited the different parts of the town. Since they had no business to transact with the government officials, only a few of these Indians appeared in dress attire, and there were also no important chiefs and warriors among them. Because the merchants did not wish to offend the Osages, a wealthy tribe living on the prairies, where they hunt bison and so have a considerable trade in hides, furs, and horses, they were treated well. In some places they were given more whisky than was good for them, since they had come to purchase their supplies for the next hunting season. The Potawatomis were not so liberally treated.

I saw but few Osages who were sober and most of them staggered about

[15] *Author*: The French Creoles call most of the Indian nations by the beginning letters of their names, *Chis* for Chickasaws, *Pos* for Potawatomis, *Kans* for Kansa, *Mahas* for Omahas, *Mis* for Miamis, etc.

[The Osage Tribe, fairly late in its development, consisted of three bands: the Pahatsi, or Great Osage; the Utsehta, or Little Osage; and the Santsukhdi, or Arkansas Band. Hodge, *Handbook*, II, 156.]

the streets naked, a very repulsive sight. The Potawatomis no doubt also had a desire for whisky but had to do without it because of their poverty. It seemed that they did not live on intimate terms with the Osages and appeared to be afraid of the latter. Soon no Potawatomis were seen in town. At the approach of night they all crossed the Mississippi to go into Illinois.

The Osages have the reputation of being the tallest and strongest Indians in the western territory. Even though their giant size may be greatly exaggerated, I cannot deny that all the individuals of this nation that I had an opportunity to see were very strong and muscularly built. This characteristic advantage, plus similarity of language shared by most of the tribes, betrays their descent from one common stock. The tribes indicating by similarity of language, analogy of facial and bodily structure, manner of living, likeness of customs and usages that they once constituted a common people with the Osages inhabit that great stretch of prairie land west of the Mississippi and Missouri between the thirty-second and forty-first degree of north latitude, bordered by the Andes chain.

The Osages seem to have been the masters of the land much earlier than the Pawnees. At any rate their rather obscure traditions seem to indicate this. It is indeed possible that the Pawnees migrated from the southwest to the north only a few centuries ago and perhaps owe the undisputed possession of the land they now occupy to their great bravery. Living at about the forty-sixth degree of latitude on the Missouri, the separation of the Arikaras from the Pawnees fell into a still later period, and presents striking proof of the peculiar tendency of Indian tribes to separate amicably from one another and choose a remote region for habitation.[16]

Among the tribes related to the Osages must be counted the Comanches, Arkansas, the Great and Little Osages, Kansas, Omahas, Ponkaras, and probably still a few other small tribes. Concerning them, however, there is a complete lack of information because they live in remote western prairies. As with almost all North American people, they are warlike and cruel. I dislike giving up the belief that this inherited sense of irreconcilability against a defeated enemy is more the result of deep-rooted prejudice than a real moral defect of these natives.

Approaching the tribes of the Osages only in a friendly manner, I found many manifestations of honesty, and while I was among the Omahas and

[16] The Arikaras, in language, differed only dialectically from the Pawnees, their Caddoan kinsmen, both originating in the Southwest. The Comanches, mentioned in the next paragraph, were of Shoshonean stock, an offshoot of the Shoshonis of Wyoming, and as such were unrelated to the Siouan linguistic group, of which the Osages were one. The Ponkaras of the Lewis and Clark *Journals* are the Poncas, one of the Dhegiha group of Siouan peoples, again closely related to the Osages.

Ponkaras I sometimes fancied myself being among a horde of Arabian bedouins. These mounted Indians of the prairie have many good characteristics in common with them, but they are perhaps much better than those children of the desert who live almost exclusively by robbery. The time when these people were still united, or at least lived in much closer association with one another, cannot be as far distant as the first glance at the great area occupied by the various tribes might indicate, and the similarity of language is too great for me to believe that the various tongues of the different tribes are only dialects of the Osage language.

Whether the Great Osages, as is assumed by persons best acquainted with these Indian nations, were the mother or main tribe of the other tribes that speak their language is perhaps difficult to decide, for their history is shrouded in great obscurity. I could get only unsatisfactory answers from the chiefs of the Kansa, Omahas, and Ponkaras to whom I submitted the question.

However, their traditions and legends all agree that a long time ago all these tribes lived peacefully together as one great nation. In spite of the similarity of language and customs, these nations became hostile to one another because of mutual transgressions on the hunting grounds assigned to each tribe. Since they also live in perpetual feuding with neighboring powerful tribes, namely the Pawnees and Dakotahs or Sioux, their numbers have become substantially reduced and it is possible that several small tribes may have died out entirely. I found now and then in old traditional war songs of the Kansa and Ponkaras obscure traces regarding the immigration of the Pawnees from the southwest and confused legends concerning the first battles with this brave nation. These legends agree in many respects with those of the Pawnees and prove that this period belongs to modern times, perhaps only a few hundred years ago. The Pawnees are far better educated than the people of the Osage tribes, and many customs, especially religious ones and human sacrifice, prove an earlier acquaintance with the people of southern Mexico, perhaps even with the Aztecs.

Among the Pawnees there is a tendency to go to the Southwest on all their expeditions of war and robbery, which is quite contrary to the habit of the nations who speak the Osage language. The latter tend to direct their expeditions to the west and the north.

Through the intermediation of the agents of the United States, the above mentioned tribes have become reconciled with one another and have even succeeded in bringing about peace between themselves and the Pawnees. The latter and the Omahas especially have become friendly with one another, which was a good move on the part of both nations, ending definitely the continuous attacks of the wild Sioux. The Omahas and the

Ponkaras live on the hunt of the bison and the catching of beaver and otter. Although near their villages they raise some maize. Requiring almost no care, it is left to nature after it has come up and been hoed a little.

The Arkansas, Osage, and Kansa Indians also hunt bison on the western prairies, but devote themselves more to the hunt in the woodlands which shade the Mississippi and the Missouri. They carry on an extensive trade in bear and deer hides, for which the trading companies often pay as high as a Spanish dollar each in barter. Since firearms are preferred to bow and arrows in the forest hunt, almost all the Osages and Kansa are armed with guns. On the other hand, those tribes living on the prairies manipulate the bow with great skill and strength. I found scarcely any guns among them and they use them but little, if any, in hunting bison.

As is known, these huge mammals are overtaken by the Indians on horseback at top speed and are slain with arrows. This method of hunting is a striking testimony to the great bravery and skill of the Indians. The Pawnees and the Ponkaras are known as the best horsemen and hunters, and I had the opportunity to convince myself of this fact on several occasions.

After the Indians had left St. Louis I directed my attention to the town and its surroundings, which present many things that deserve the attention of the natural scientist and the geographer. Having made the acquaintance of a great number of people immediately after my arrival, almost every day, through the kindness of these citizens of St. Louis and neighboring communities, I was invited on new and interesting excursions. Frequently I had the pleasure of very agreeable company, even that of intelligent and extremely charming ladies. The metropolis of the state of Missouri may be justly proud of counting among its leading citizens some of the most cultured people in the western states, and it seemed as if the French Creoles and the immigrant Anglo-Americans vied with each other at every social gathering as to who should excel. The latter have given up much of their stiff and unbending nature in their association with the carefree Creoles, who adhere to a French lack of constraint. Though the differences of customs and language still distinguish the two nationalities, the two people have come much nearer to each other and will be brought still closer by the bonds of friendship and marriage. A complete fusion does not seem improbable.

Since most of the French Creoles have acquired a certain proficiency in the English language, and because it seems more difficult for the Anglo-Americans to master the French language, it is probable that the English language may gain the upper hand in a shorter time than might be expected. Even the lower class of people feel the necessity of learning this tongue more and more. The majority of the people in this part of the country are immigrants from Indiana, Kentucky, and Tennessee, who for some time past made their settlements on the west banks of the Mississippi and the Missouri. Rarely does one find French people living near the farms of the Anglo-Americans, and those who do live there are obliged to speak English.

In the larger towns where Creoles live, considerable numbers of the male youths work as boatmen on river vessels. These are also in a position where a knowledge of English is an absolute necessity. For these various reasons I found but few individuals of this class of people who could not speak the English language fluently. To these must be added further facts, the transactions in the courts of law are handled in English, the bulk of business is carried on by Anglo-Americans, and finally the recently established schools are conducted only in the English language.

As in Louisiana and other states where black slavery still exists or where the memories of this institution still abound, so also in Missouri there is a sharp separation between the white and the colored. However, this relation applies more to the higher than to the lower classes. It does not reach that ridiculous level, as in the southern regions, where even the most miserable person of unmixed European blood would regard it an absolute degradation to eat at the same table with the richest quadroons.

This prejudice against colored people does not extend to the full-blood Indians, who are treated as free individuals and whose chiefs even demand manifestations of preference and esteem. The free Indian, too proud of his color and freedom to bear any humiliation, would seek to avenge in a bloody manner any disparagement shown him. For this reason, prudence requires that Europeans not confuse the independent and unspoiled tribes with other colored people.

The half-bloods are generally not regarded very highly, but their behavior rather than their color is the reason. Although there are exceptions, of course, it cannot be denied that generally many of these mixed bloods live a dissolute life and are given to immoderate drinking. Neglected education and improper upbringing of these people is largely responsible for this.

Almost all men of whatever color, class, or station living among the Indians or often meeting them keep Indian women, and have children by them. Since the Indian girls are easy to approach and rarely refuse a cultured man an act of kindness, and in their association with hunters and traders have an opportunity to satisfy their liking for ornaments, these women, called squaws, are very common. Many return with their children to their tribes, and there the latter, especially if they are very young, remain among their kinsmen, assume their customs, and can be distinguished from the rest only by a lighter skin color and often by striking European features.

Other half-bloods, on the other hand, are brought up by their fathers and share their mode of living. Many such children receive no education. When they have reached a certain age they are often left to their own fate and must seek to provide their own subsistence in a miserable manner. Such persons usually hire out as boatmen and hunters to the trading companies, or go to their Indian kinsmen. There, with a thin veneer of European culture, they reveal a degree of immorality which is unknown even to the wildest savage. They may be regarded as one of the main causes of the decay of the Indians.

The few half-bloods who have the good fortune to receive a better up-bringing usually learn the language of the different Indian tribes and serve as interpreters of the government officials or the trading companies by whom they are gladly engaged. It must be said of this class of people that they are generally clear-headed fellows who, if they are so minded, can accomplish much. They are usually good hunters, show tremendous endurance at their work, and have a sound body capable of defying the destructive influence of the climate and also the greatest excesses. Being naturally inclined to laziness, indolence, and combativeness, they must be held in strict discipline, and at times become a great burden to the traveler.

The white inhabitants of St. Louis constitute the majority over the colored population of either African or American descent. During my visit there were as many families of immigrants of Anglo-American stock in the town as there were Creoles, and in a short time they will constitute the majority. There are many more free colored people than slaves in St. Louis, and the latter are more and more on the decrease, since many Negroes and mulattoes obtain their freedom.

The climate of St. Louis (at 38° 39' north latitude), similar to the climate of temperate Europe, makes it possible for whites to work, whereby slaves become less and less necessary. Moreover, wages are not as high as in the southern states, and the price of black slaves is much higher than in Louisiana, Georgia, and Florida. The few slaves are treated most gently by their masters, I should say, and much better than many free servants in Europe. Many acquire property and most of them could purchase their freedom, if they did not prefer this scarcely noticeable subjection to a freedom which would leave them dependent upon others anyway, especially since they probably would have to work much harder.

As proof of this, consider that a Negro seldom becomes a run-away. This happens frequently in other states causing many difficulties. The Negroes of St. Louis are honest, good natured, and generally thoroughly devoted to their masters. In most families they are treated as members of the family and are attached to the children of their masters with a boundless love. In general, the Negroes are obedient, gentle, and sober people, and one would be mistaken if one would judge all black Africans by the few Negroes that roam about in Europe.

Only the most unheard of mistreatment could have induced the Negroes of Santo Domingo to rebel against their masters. This is certified by the many clear-thinking Creoles who witnessed the bloody catastrophe, and the noblest manifestations of love and self-sacrifice shown for their masters in the time of terror will find a place in history to the glory of the Negroes and the honor of mankind. A Mr. T. was saved by a young Negro slave at great risk, and put on board a ship that sailed to a port in the United States. When the vessel reached its destination, Mr. T., a very young man, found himself in the distressing situation of being entirely without means, his money spent because he had assisted other refugees who were as destitute as himself. The Negro disappeared suddenly and after a few days the rescued white man received a few hundred dollars and a brief note that the Negro had sold himself into slavery and had sent the money thus obtained to aid his former master. All investigations instituted by Mr. T. remained futile. The noble African had carried out the magnanimous deed so secretly that no trace has ever been found of him to date.

St. Louis, principal town in the state of Missouri, has risen to a very respectable city. Broad streets, some already partly paved, and quite pretty houses, also a new Catholic church built in good style, give the town a pleasing appearance. In addition, the town is enlivened and supplied with many warehouses and stores furnishing all sorts of goods. The houses recently erected and the church are built of brick. The interior of the church is decorated with a few paintings which Mr. Du Bourg brought along from France, and in the bishop's dwelling a library, quite large for St. Louis, has been collected. With praiseworthy generosity this genteel man has not withdrawn these books from public use.[17]

The Bishop's home is very limited, since a part assigned to Mr. Du

[17] Bishop Louis Guillaume Valentin Duborg (1766–1833), born in Santo Domingo and ordained a Sulpician in Paris, came to Baltimore in 1794. He was named first president of Georgetown College in 1796. After sojourns, 1799–1812, in Cuba and Baltimore, he became Administrator Apostolic of New Orleans. After 1816 he settled temporarily in St. Louis, where he built the Catholic church and school for youths. He arranged for the location of the Jesuits (including Father Pierre Jean de Smet) in St. Louis in 1822. St. Louis Academy, established in his time, became St. Louis University in 1832. *DAB*, III, 473–74; John A. Paxton, Preface to *St. Louis Directory and Register* (1821) in John Francis McDermott, ed., *The Early Histories of St. Louis*, 65–66.

Bourg himself has been surrendered by him for open school purposes. In this respect, too, the Bishop has rendered the state of Missouri a great service, for it is due to his untiring zeal that such institutions so necessary to the education of youth have come into being. Besides these schools under the direction of the Catholic clergy in St. Louis, several other educational institutions are headed by Americans and Englishmen. Formerly the Catholic Church held the dominating position among churches of St. Louis and even now has a large number of adherents having every reason to be proud to be under the direction of so clear-thinking a church officer as their Bishop. This is a great advantage for a religious body in a country where the state does not meddle in church affairs and where there are such great differences of religious opinion and so many religious sects as in the United States.

After Catholics, the Methodists and Presbyterians are the largest, and only a few residents belong to the Episcopalian, Lutheran, and Reformed churches. There are few Quakers, and the remaining sects scarcely deserve mention. In praise of these religious sects I must say that all are mutually tolerant with each other, each reserves its opinion to itself, and the differences of faith cause no quarrels. Even the Catholic Creoles combine with the other sects against the Irish if the latter, because of an inherited inclination to quarrel and because of incompatibility, make fanaticism a pretext for unlawful action.

I took advantage of the first free moment to visit those peculiar *tumuli* which owe their origin to a mighty people of long past centuries who disappeared from the scene without leaving behind the least historic trace. Located just north of the town some distance from the Mississippi, these great monuments[18] of ancient American building art, whose purpose has not yet been fully determined, seem to share the age of those extensive

[18] *Author*: There are more than twenty of them which Major Long surveyed carefully in the year 1819. See [Edwin James] *Account of an Expedition from Pittsburgh to the Rocky Mountains, performed in the years 1819 and '20*. Philadelphia, 1823. Vol. I, page 59, footnote.

[Duke Paul is referring to the Cahokia Mounds located four miles northeast of East St. Louis, Illinois. W. K. Moorehead of the University of Illinois, who did the principal archaeological work on them beginning in 1920, placed them in the Middle Mississippi phase, dating from A.D. 1200–1500. Originally there may have been three hundred mounds at this site, of which eighty-five smaller mounds and Cahokia Mound itself survive. The latter covers sixteen acres, measuring 710 feet east to west, 1,080 feet north to south, at the base. Archaeological recoveries include highly developed pottery, copper and mica ornaments, pipes, and projectile points. Cf., Moorehead, *The Cahokia Mounds*, University of Illinois *Bulletin*, XXVI, No. 4 (1929), *passim*. Titian Ramsay Peale, *The Ancient Mounds at St. Louis, Missouri, in 1819*, Smithsonian Institution *Annual Report*, 1861 (Washington, D.C., 1862), *passim*.]

earthen mounds so common in the central part of North America, which claim to have been erected by the Indians for the purpose of defense. I noticed several of these mounds which were more than fifty feet high and had a relatively extensive circumference, and most probably they were originally still higher, unless their summits were intentionally left flat to form a plateau. The mounds form a sort of cone with an oval base. From several angular projections, which in time have been covered with layers of earth, one may conjecture that in former times these conical mounds have had a pyramidal form.

All the mounds are composed of fine clay, which, during long periods of time, must have assumed great hardness. These clay pyramids have gradually been covered with layers of humus earth and are overgrown with scattered trees, shrubs, and herbaceous plants. The trees do not show a very healthy growth, which may be due to the fact that the roots cannot penetrate the hard clay masses composing the center of the mound, and the fertile crust is not thick enough to afford the necessary nourishment. In order to obtain definite information concerning the inner construction of these Indian monuments, it would necessitate cutting them in two and the base would have to be examined at least to the level of the adjacent ground. This would be an expensive undertaking and the result might be nothing more than the discovery of bones and implements. Investigations of this kind would have to be made to settle the question as to whether these mounds are burial grounds of the Indians or if they are memorials dedicated to the name of single chieftains or many warriors who fell in battle.

Even today it is not uncommon among the Indians to cover the dead bodies of persons held in high esteem with a heap of stones or other decay-resisting material, such as bones, horns, antlers, etc. These mounds, which I saw on my second journey in large number near the Rocky Mountains, do not attain a great height nor do they have a great circumference. The custom of roaming Indians to add to such piles by throwing similar material on them is based on religious superstitions, but such practices, however, cannot enlarge those mounds materially. In addition, the Indian burial mounds of recent times in no way resemble the mounds seen near St. Louis, for even the material of which they are formed is different.

Here and there among the North American tribes there prevails the custom, practiced by ancient as well as modern peoples, to honor a great chieftain after his death by bloody human sacrifice. Indeed, even the sacrifice of the wives, as of the Hindoos, shows what great sacrifices the Indians were capable of bringing to the graves of their chiefs and friends. As proof of gratitude for the dead, satisfying the purpose of providing a memorial to their memory, it is even conceivable that earlier nations performed a tedious and difficult piece of hand labor, repellent to the red aborigines of America.

The practice of providing the dead with all the things he needed during his life or stimulated his senses is based on the belief of the Indians that after death they must make use of the things which are buried with them on their journey to a far off country. For this reason, weapons, clothes, and even food are placed in the grave. Often a man's best horse is killed (similar practices, according to Azara, prevail also among the races of South America, especially among the Charruas) and, as mentioned before, the widows are willing to accompany their husbands on the long journey, though this rarely occurs now.

In any event, the great artificial earthen mounds had a religious significance, be it what it may, and if their flat tops are artificial it may easily be possible that they, like the pyramid-shaped monuments of the Aztecs (at Cholula, Papantla, and San Juan de Teotihaucan) in Mexico, may have been the sites of temples and sacrificial rocks. The scholarly companions of Major Long seem also to have been of this opinion.

In company of a few of the best families of St. Louis, I visited the stalactite caves to which I have earlier referred. These caves are located half an hour's walk from town in a flat region densely overgrown with hazelnut bushes and other forms of vegetation, grasses, and herbaceous plants, which seem to constitute the transition to more distant prairies. The entrance to the largest of these caves is very narrow, and we could only crawl in with difficulty, and since the clay floor of the cave was slippery and wet, this was an involved undertaking for the ladies accompanying us.

Near the entrance the cave forms a rather large chamber, and the arched ceiling with many columns of stalactites, some of which reached the floor, afforded a beautiful sight. On close examination, however, I found nothing remarkable in this cave, which has a considerable depth, but its remoter parts could not be reached without the aid of a crowbar. We therefore had to be content with viewing the foremost chamber into which we dug to some extent, revealing neither traces of prehistoric shell-bearing animals in the limestone nor petrified bones in the clay floor. The temperature in the cave was very cold compared with the outside air and the thermometer fell from 75° to 62°.

The floor of the cave was so wet from water dripping from above that at every step we sank in above our ankles. Greatly disappointed by the exaggerated accounts of the size and beauty of the cave, I was compensated in another way, however. For to me, a stranger, everything was new, even though it might be insignificant. The company with whom I visited the cave had taken their slaves along to light our way. These coal black figures bearing burning torches in their hands appeared in sharp contrast to the white people, some of whom were elegantly dressed, and this contrast did not escape even those who were used to such a sight. Among the ladies this feeling manifested itself in hard-to-suppress timidity, while it caused the gentlemen to burst out in loud laughter. The Africans added their grinning smiles, making their faces yet more eerie, and caused the whole group to appear odder still.

On the sixth of May, while I was at the country estate of Mr. P. Chouteau, [Sr.], a violent thunderstorm accompanied by heavy hail set in. Hailstones, many weighing several ounces, covered the ground in some places some inches deep. This thunderstorm was followed by others almost every day during my stay in St. Louis, without, however, reducing the oppressive heat. On my excursions I regularily got drenched, which was harmful to my health, for the usually cold showers were followed by stinging hot sunshine. Despite this I was richly compensated daily by widely varying additions to my collection. The region about St. Louis is well suited to this purpose. Partly hilly and partly flat land, prairie or covered with forest, it feeds a large number of animals and plants preferring these different environments.

On May 10 the vessel equipped by the Missouri Company was loaded and put in shape to undertake the journey to the factory near the Council Bluffs. The necessary crew, for the most part Canadians or Creoles from Cahokia, had assembled around their patrons and were newly clothed and armed by the sponsors.

All my supplies were on board. A portion of the room near the starboard was covered as nearly watertight as possible and furnished for my convenience. I had all my belongings, including my field bed, taken on board that morning. I ordered my servant [J. G. Schlape] to go aboard and ride as far as St. Charles, a small town on the Missouri not far from its confluence with the Mississippi, and to await my arrival there. My plan was to go overland by way of Fleurissant to the plantation of Mr. Auguste Chouteau, in order to make the acquaintance of this venerable old man.

In St. Louis I had taken into my service a Creole named Louis Caillou. Agreeing to accompany me as far as the Kansas, he had promised, if I so desired, to procure for me another companion there. Caillou was well acquainted with the country, an excellent boatman, familiar with all the hazardous places on the Missouri, and at the same time a very good hunter and marksman, qualifications especially important to me. In addition, a rather old but still very useful Canadian, Baptiste de Rouain, was likewise at my disposal. He would accompany me as far as Fort Atkinson.[19]

[19] The mark of François Caillou and the signature of François Derouin appear on the

The gentlemen of the company, showing that they put great confidence in me, requested, in a way, that I have general supervision over the expedition, and for this reason they assigned no clerk to the boat. They were also so kind as to put the entire crew at my disposal if I should have need of them. The company did everything imaginable and with the greatest unselfishness to lend a helping hand to my undertaking.

Not until ten o'clock in the forenoon of May 12 was I able to leave St. Louis. The reason for this was the fact that I wished to travel to St. Charles on horseback. After spending several days in a fruitless effort to procure saddle horses, I had to settle on mounting a two-wheeled cart, the only conveyance with which one might dare travel the extremely bad roads. All the saddle horses offered me were totally unfit for my purpose. They were either too weak or lame or blind, and I would not have dared to undertake a half hour's ride on such creatures, not to speak of making my way through bottomless ground in dense forests or over steep, rocky hills under an oppressive sun. My one-horse, uncovered cart offered no comfort nor did it warrant any hope of reaching my destination unharmed.

At the beginning, after one has passed the last houses of St. Louis, the road to St. Charles leads for two English miles over hills overgrown with bushes of hazelnut, oak, walnut, and sumac. After that one travels through prairie for a distance covering about six or seven miles. This prairie, however, is not only a grass-covered plain but also supports a mass of tall weeds and low wooded plants. The ground seems to be very fertile and could easily be made suitable for agriculture. The road so far proved to be tolerable, but the thunderstorms coming one after another had not left a dry thread in my clothes. However, they soon dried in the burning heat, which beat on us between showers, and this time very light clothing came in good stead. Beyond the prairie there was again a hilly region with underbrush consisting of hazelnut bushes, reminding me of the forests of southern Germany. As is known, the forests are set on fire during the dry season to improve the cattle pasture. Since the fire spreads with tremendous speed,

document dated October 30, 1819, approving Bishop Dubourg's creation of the new St. Louis Church and the adjoining school for youth. Earlier, on May 14, 1797, Lieutenant Governor Zenon Trudeau included in his report to Spanish authorities the testimony of Francisco Derouin, an employee of Clamorgan, Loisel and Company, known as the Spanish Missouri Company, concerning his trip up the Missouri River to the village of the Octatas (Otos) in 1796–1797. Trudeau noted that Derouin was then 24 years of age and that he could not write. If he is the de Rouain of Duke Paul's trip, he would have been 50 years of age at their meeting. There is no certainty, however, that either of the documents here cited establishes the identity of Caillou or de Rouain. Frederic L. Billon, *Annals of St. Louis in Its Territorial Days, 1804 to 1821,* 420–23. A. P. Nasatir, *Before Lewis and Clark,* 109, 516–17.

it does not harm the roots of the bushes, for the ground is not heated very much by the running flames, and in the spring new shoots come out which by fall are several feet high.

In the little town of Fleurissant is a cloister, and the sisters busy themselves with the education of the children. Here the road becomes extremely bad and in the low places, especially in the hollows after the fallen rain, the horses sank above their knees in the black mud, and my driver seemed to be a past master in upsetting the cart. Often, at the worst places, I had to jump from the cart to avoid breaking my neck in the overturning.

Mr. Auguste Chouteau's plantation is a few miles off the road, and in Fleurissant I had to engage a guide, who assured me that he could take me to my destination by the nearest path known to him. Starting on foot with the guide through the dense forest, after traveling several miles up and down the hills, fighting our way through underbrush, we arrived at a lonely cabin. The inhabitants surprised me with the disagreeable news that the Creole had lost his way completely and that we were now farther from Mr. Chouteau's place than we had been when I had left my cart to its fate.

Intrusting myself to a new guide, I arrived four hours later at Mr. Chouteau's at the approach of night. After traveling over a very rough road I was extremely tired. But I soon forgot the miseries of the day because of the cordial and most charming reception of my kind host, a vivacious old man of seventy-three.

On the gray morning of the following day, accompanied by a young mulatto, I went out to hunt in the nearby forest. We penetrated a hilly wilderness and crossed a creek greatly swollen because of the many heavy showers. Since we soon encountered wild turkeys I could not resist the temptation of pursuing them through the dense undergrowth against the urgently repeated warning of my companion. I was fortunate to shoot several but in the pursuit got so far into the wilderness that the mulatto had great difficulty in finding a passable path because of a heavy overcast sky.

Holding on to bushes, we had to let ourselves down several steep slopes, extremely hazardous because of the stony but slippery ground, and not until noon did we reach a ford where my companion considered the water shallow enough to wade through. In this hope we were also disappointed, for even at this place the little stream was deeper than the height of a man and exceedingly swift, so that it would have been impossible to have got across with our guns dry.

After a long search we found a dead nut tree hanging over the water. With great skill the mulatto crawled over it and safely brought our guns. When I had crawled half way across, my companion came to meet me in order to assist me in the difficult treck. This natural bridge, however, was not made to bear the weight of two men and broke in two. We both plunged into the water and I should have drowned had I not been lucky. In the nick of time I seized the roots of a tree projecting into the water and held on to them until the mulatto, a good swimmer, had saved himself and come to my aid. After this bath, a very cold and violent rain accompanied me on the way back, and dripping wet I reached Mr. Chouteau's place in the afternoon, where my host had become very anxious about me.

Despite the accident I had met with, I was so lucky as to have increased my collection abundantly. In addition to a few rare birds I had shot a large marmot. Because of its piping call it is called *sifleur* by the Creoles. It lives in holes in the ground, climbs trees very well, attains a size larger than that of the European hares, and is identical with *Arctomys empetra* of Schreber. This animal, very common along the Missouri, has long hair and its head is extremely flat in front. It has short fore feet with five toes, of which four are supplied with short, curved nails, while the fifth toe is only rudimentary and blunt. The tail is short with long hair, and the color of the creature is gray on the back and rust brown on the sides.[20]

I was very sick and had all the symptoms of a severe rheumatic fever. Despite a heavy sweat I noticed no improvement, had a sleepless and very restless night, and on the following morning, despite every effort, I was unable to get up. My good host and his kind wife did everything imaginable to help me and to cheer me up, and Mr. Chouteau shortened the time by relating many most interesting observations concerning the Indians on the upper Missouri. All bore the stamp of absolute truthfulness, for he had made many trips.

It is a great pity that Mr. Chouteau never felt the urge to publish his many collected experiences among the aborigines, a modesty which I found almost exaggerated in view of his vast information and fine culture. Indeed, I am of the opinion that the accounts of all travelers, even those of unimportant persons, dealing with the northwestern part of the American continent should receive special attention. They would come in good stead some time when serious attempts are made at settling the land between the Missouri and the sea which has been seen by MacKenzie.[21]

[20] *Marmota monax*, the woodchuck.

[21] Auguste Chouteau set down his memories of the founding of St. Louis and the course of the early fur trade on the Missouri and its tributaries in a journal, which, according to his son Gabriel, writing in 1882, was "replete with information." The journal was lent by the younger Chouteau to Joseph Nicolas Nicollet, the French explorer who ascended the Mississippi and mapped the upper stream for the U.S. government (published 1843). The manuscript while in Nicollet's possession was lost in a fire; only a fragment from an earlier draft survived in St. Louis. Auguste Chouteau's depositions before Theodore Hunt, recorder of land titles in St. Louis in 1825, add to the record. Meriwether Lewis had set a series of

The prevailing opinion that the climate of America north of latitude 50° is too severe for human habitation, and that the ever prevailing cold and long winters make this region inaccessible to Europeans, has been successfully refuted by the English, rightfully with good results. There is no doubt that the country on the upper Missouri from northern latitude 47° to the mountains and the high plains occupied by the Blackfeet and Assiniboin Indians[22] is a cold country because of its location.

Those prairie-covered high plains between the northern and western mountain chains running uninterruptedly along the Missouri, the Yellowstone, and the Eau qui Courre (Running Water River)[23] must be several thousand feet above the sea level of the Gulf of Mexico, if one may judge by the rapid current of the Missouri. The lands, however, between the northern mountains and the Sea of MacKenzie belonging to the English Northwest Company are situated much lower and are by no means as infertile and cold as a few geographers, drawing from unreliable sources,

---

questions for the elder Chouteau to answer in 1804, but we have no record of the answers, if any. He did, however, supply extensive notes to the Indian Office in 1816 on the Indians of the upper Missouri and Mississippi rivers. Grant Foreman, "Notes of Auguste Chouteau on the Boundaries of Various Indian Nations," *Glimpses of the Past*, Missouri Historical Society Publications, VII (1940), 119–140. McDermott, *Early Histories of St. Louis*, 47–59, 91–97, 133–63.

In addition to Meriwether Lewis, among his interviewers, Auguste Chouteau talked at length about historical matters with Duke Paul Wilhelm of Württemberg in 1823, the members of the Marquis de Lafayette party in 1825, Duke Bernhard of Saxe-Weimar in 1826, and many others of lesser name, until his death in 1829.

[22] *Author*: The Blackfeet Indians (*Pieds Noirs*) and the Assiniboins, the latter a tribe of the Great Dakotah or Sioux Nation, roam between 47° and 55° of north latitude and between 105° and 125° west longitude, west from London, in which I encountered both tribes in 1830.

[The Blackfeet, of Algonquian linguistic stock, consist of three divisions, the Siksika or Blackfeet, the Kainah or Bloods, and the Piegans, all of the northern Plains, extending from the North Saskatchewan River, Canada, to the streams tributary to the Missouri River in Montana. In Duke Paul's time they may have counted nine thousand people. Cf. John C. Ewers, *The Blackfeet, passim.*

[The Assiniboines, with whom the Blackfeet were almost constantly at war in the eighteenth and first half of the nineteenth centuries, were of the Siouan group, originally part of the Yanktonais. They were located between Lake Superior and Hudson Bay about the middle of the seventeenth century, later drifting to the vicinity of Lake Winnipeg and still farther northwestward to the Saskatchewan and Assiniboin rivers, allying themselves with the Crees. They were at war with their kinsmen the Sioux throughout most of the historic period, especially during their southward forays into the Montana country. Cf. Edwin Thompson Denig, *Five Indian Tribes of the Upper Missouri*; James Larpenteur Long, *The Assiniboines* . . . ed. by Michael Stephen Kennedy.]

[23] Eau qui Courre = Niobrara River.

were pleased to maintain. The view expressed by several such authors that perpetual ice covers the fields of North America from the forty-eighth degree of latitude northward is based on error, deserving correction no more.

According to most careful observations made with great accuracy by Lewis and Clarke, the climate of the western American coast is very temperate and not colder than that of Europe at the same degrees of latitude. There is no doubt, however, that eastern America, from 30° north latitude upward is colder than that of Europe and northern Africa at the same latitude. All lands covered with dense forest enshrouded by a humid atmosphere are cold in winter and hot in summer, and all the observations made with the hygrometer plus the abundant rainfall indicate that eastern America is subject to this condition.

How much the clearing of the forests and the cultivation of the soil contribute to raising the temperature is shown in France and Germany, lands where formerly the animals of the far north lived in comfort. This is also proved by the cold winters of northern Asia situated at the same latitude as Germany. Further, it is known that in earliest times the valleys of Greece were covered with masses of snow, which now barely cover the summits of high mountains. Even the countries that border on our own temperate fatherland, Russia in its unpopulated territories, and also Poland, in part covered with dense forests, are subject to the most severe winters. What a difference there is in the climate between Moscow and Berlin for example!

With all these facts at hand, I was not, however, able to explain the sudden chilling of the air during the winter months in Florida and Louisiana, for in North America it is not only the all-penetrating northwest wind but also the cold east wind that reduces the temperature strikingly. In no analogous northern or southern latitude of our earth do such severe frosts occur as in the southern part of the United States. In New Orleans I saw the thermometer fall to 19° in January, in Pensacola it fell to 22° in the same year, and in St. Augustine in eastern Florida ice is a common occurrence. As is known, the southern hemisphere of our planet is relatively colder than the northern, and yet such conditions are unknown in Buenos Aires and Cape Town which are several degrees farther from the equator. Between New Orleans and Cairo, however, which are situated at about the same latitude, no comparison can be made regarding the lowest thermometer readings in the winter months.

At noon of the fourteenth, Caillou, whom I had engaged in St. Louis as a traveling companion, came with the news that the boat had safely reached St. Charles. Therefore, despite a violent fever, I had made arrangements at once to go there and to leave the home of my generous host. I could not ride a horse, so two horses were hitched to a four-wheeled wooden wagon, and I was made as comfortable as possible.

In company with the younger sons of Mr. Chouteau, I started on the way, traveling on a poor forest road and over the hills to the banks of the Missouri opposite St. Charles.[24] The road led past that creek in which I had come so near drowning. The place where we crossed was not much more than three feet deep and the wagon passed through safely. As a precaution my companions had taken axes and saws along, using them frequently to remove many obstructions in the forest.

The woods consisted of sycamore, walnut, lacquer trees, white and red oaks, poplars, linden, and black beech, a twining begonia the *Annona triloba*, the *Menispermum canadense*, a *Tecoma*, several *Smilax* varieties, together with many other bushes and climbing plants of most luxurious growth. Frequently I saw the tracks of fallow deer, which must be numerous in this region. I also saw many turkeys. Some of them flew into the highest trees and remained sitting motionless there.

After two hours we arrived at the banks of the Missouri. The sky was heavily overcast, the wind blew, and it rained continuously. The first sight of the Missouri afforded me a magnificent and never-to-be-forgotten spectacle, augmented by the opportunity to see it at high water and in stormy weather, making the native wild region appear still more impressive. In the home of an eighty-three-year-old Canadian, Mr. Chauvin, to whom I had been recommended by Mr. Chouteau, I found a friendly reception for the night.[25] I was very much in need for my fever threatened to become more and more severe.

Early, at five o'clock on the fifteenth, we left Chauvin Ferry, where I had spent the night. Here is a ferry to take people and vehicles across to St. Charles. The crossing is not always without danger, since the raging current of the Missouri in the vicinity of its mouth makes crossing on flat vessels very difficult.

Throughout the night the storm and rain continued, but toward morning the wind subsided, changing to a gentle southwest breeze. I had to be carried to the room which had been assigned to me on the boat and there

[24] By this time Augustus Aristide Chouteau, the eldest son of Auguste Chouteau, was 31 (b. October 21, 1792; d. 1833); Gabriel Sylvestre, the second son, 29 (b. December 31, 1794; d. June 18, 1887); and Henry P., 18 (b. February 11, 1805; d. November 1, 1855). Billon, *Annals of St. Louis*, 164–70.

[25] Jacques Chauvin, son of Joseph Chauvin of Kaskaskia, holder of a large land grant achieved in the Spanish period opposite St. Charles. Houck, *History of Missouri*, II, 20 n., speaks of his death in 1826 at 83.

put to bed, feeling so sick that I doubted my own recovery. This condition prevented me from making any observations for several days, although these would have been of great importance to me in this region, especially in regard to the velocity of the current of the Missouri.

The land along the banks of the stream, at some distances from St. Charles, is low and covered with particularly tall cottonwoods and syca- mores. The linden trees, which farther up the stream occur frequently, were somewhat scarcer here. The Missouri had inundated the low forest regions so completely that it was nearly impossible to set foot on land, making our journey most difficult, for now the boat could be propelled but slowly upstream by means of oars. It was impossible to put the crew on land to pull the vessel.

During the night of the sixteenth a frightful thunderstorm raged, ac- companied by an exceedingly heavy downpour, flooding the inner room of the vessel. The joints in the roof of the boat had yielded, permitting the water free entrance. Despite all precautionary measures at our command I was drenched in my bed as if I had spent the night under the open sky.

At daybreak the wind was so strong from the southwest that we had to lay by until evening. As a result of the cold I had contracted my fever be- came so high that I not only suffered from the most intense headache but at times lost consciousness, and between these paroxysms I almost famished from thirst. Consumption of the muddy, clay-charged Missouri river water produced intense convulsions of the stomach and vomiting, aggravating my condition. My companions prepared for me concoctions from the fresh roots of sassafras and sasaparilla, which in these parts seem to render good service in combating rheumatic-gastric fevers.

Finally, toward four o'clock in the afternoon, the wind subsided a little and allowed us to think of the continuation of our journey. The river here is full of shallows, and indeed our boat touched bottom three times, luckily without suffering great damage or causing a long delay. After we had advanced two English miles night overtook us and we halted. The sky had become clear and the air cooler, whereat the insects, which for several days had been quite unbearable, became slightly less troublesome.

As the morning of the seventeenth was clear with no trace of fog, which in the southern part of the state of Missouri is not an infrequent occurrence, even in May, we set out at three o'clock at the red break of day. The bright red light of the sunrise foretold a strong wind. Soon beginning to blow from the southeast, it permitted us to hoist sail on our boat.

The sails used on the boats designed in the United States for river and lake service are much too simple and awkward to permit a rapid journey, for they can be used only when the wind blows directly from the back of the vessel. The boats themselves, very clumsily built, are calculated only for safety to meet the extreme dangers of navigation on hazardous rivers, and for this reason no high sails can be utilized. Despite this imperfect equipment, we advanced a distance of nine English miles by noon, and at this time the wind ceased but later began to blow from the south.

By three o'clock we were at the mouth of a creek, La Femme Osage, also called Petit Osage, about fifteen yards wide and, to judge from the high banks, it may rise to a considerable height after heavy rains. Because of the unfavorable wind setting in, the boat remained near this little stream, and the crew prepared their night's camp on the bank. This was very necessary, to dry the thoroughly soaked baggage. I had myself carried from the stuffy cell into the open air and tried to warm myself by the fire.[26]

During the day I had felt better. My whole body, however, was covered with red, inflamed and painful spots, causing me to guard carefully against taking further cold. Luckily for me, the night remained favorable. I broke out in a great sweat, which was the crisis. Thereafter complete recovery followed.

Immediately upon landing, my hunters had gone out to hunt. Returning late, each claimed to have got a shot at something, but none brought anything. A distinctly visible double-halo around the moon attracted my attention. In the course of half an hour these halos had disappeared, and a few short but strong gusts of wind came, followed by complete calm.

During the entire night the melancholy song of the whipporwill (*Caprimulgus vociferus*, Wils.)[27] could be heard. In America, too, the appearance of this strange nocturnal bird arouses the superstition of ignorant people. For a long time I could not determine the originator of this song. Changing its location constantly, the creature was heard only in damp places in the dense forest. Finally I was so fortunate as to shoot a bird. Closely related to it is the nighthawk (*Caprimulgus carolinensis*, Catesb.),[28] like

[26] Osage Woman's River, in Lewis and Clark, emptying at the northeast bank of the Missouri, 21 miles from the confluence of the Missouri with the Mississippi. Six miles up Femme Osage Creek Daniel Boone had settled in 1798, along with several Kentucky families.

[27] *Caprimulgus vociferus*, for the whip-poor-will, still prevails.

[28] *Caprimulgus carolinensis*, chuck-will's-widow. Duke Paul's scientific name is the correct one but his common name might mislead some readers. The nighthawk, *Chordeiles minor*, another New World caprimulgid, produces a roar when it brakes a steep dive with set wings—a sound responsible for the local name "bull-bat"; but it is the chuck-will's-widow that claps its wings. The nighthawk's roar is to be heard by day and in morning and evening twilight, but not during "dark nights."—George Miksch Sutton to S. L., August 18, 1972. For the searcher after priorities, Duke Paul used the English "Whip-poor-will" for *Caprimulgus vociferus* Wils., and "Night-Hawk" for *Caprimulgus carolinensis* Catesby.

the European goatsucker, betraying its presence during dark nights by clapping its wings.

On the morning of the eighteenth we left our camp very early. Tall timber covered the low banks of the river, which were overgrown with dense growths of wild grapevine. Its blossoms filled the air with aromatic fragrance. Since the sky was overcast it was sultry. The thermometer rose to 73°. In this region the Missouri is divided by an island that is several thousand paces long. The right bank, opposite this island, constitutes a series of timber-covered bluffs composed of parallel strata and their summits assume the most varied formations and shapes. The left bank, on the other hand, is flat and flooded during every high waterstand on the river. Only with great difficulty, by strenuous pushing and pulling, our boat advanced among the many sandbars, shallows, and entangled clusters of tree trunks. Nevertheless we had advanced five miles by noon and were in the vicinity of several houses on the left bank of the river. Inhabited by Creoles since 1804, this village, called St. Jean, was the most remote settlement of Europeans on the Missouri.[29]

Here we made a halt of several hours, allowing the crew to rest. In the middle of the river were some newly formed islands. As yet completely bare but everywhere covered with the white wooly seed of the cottonwood, they will soon be overgrown with this variety of wood, so common here.

Noticing many head of cattle running wild in these parts, and fresh meat being a necessity, I bought a two-year old steer in the settlement for four dollars. On the boat for three days we had eaten nothing besides hard biscuits and salt pork. For me, as a patient, this was not especially pleasurable. The steer was soon shot and dressed and the boat could continue its journey after this short delay.

The limestone cliffs on the right bank beautified the landscape more and more, and their manifold clefts and deep caves made a picturesque sight. The most remarkable of these caves is called Grande Caverne, or Caverne à Tardie, and is perhaps fifty feet deep. In regard to shape and rock formation, I found a striking similarity between this grotto and the previously described cave in Ohio.[30]

In the evening we landed at a false river (*chenal*), or a small branch of

---

[29] At St. Jean or St. John's, just below the mouth of La Charrette Creek, Régis Loisel met Lewis and Clark for the first time, in 1804, as they began their journey up the Missouri. The village then counted seven houses and as many families, apparently all French. Lewis and Clark, *Original Journals*, I, 29.

[30] Both Brackenridge, *Views of Louisiana*, 203, and Lewis and Clark, *Original Journals*, I, 27, accept *Tavern*, but *Caverne à Tardie* in Duke Paul and in fact is more likely. The French name signifies its attractions to *voyageurs* long absent but now loitering at the cavern on the way home.

the river, and had a good supper from our meat. I now felt strong enough to venture on land and saw several deer confidently feeding on the bank, but because of a strong wind I could not approach them and had to return without having accomplished my purpose. This area of the Missouri is enlivened by two tanagers, the *Tanagra rubra* and *coerulea*.[31] However, they appear very seldom and are to be counted among the most beautiful birds of North America.

We left our ship's camp at four o'clock in the morning on May 19, but we had hardly covered two miles when a violent gust of wind from the south compelled us to lay by. The danger was great. Tall timber standing close to the bank was being drawn into the river by the power of the water. A few huge old trunks fell into the water close to the boat. We could have been submerged without being rescued had they fallen on us.

Continuing by means of the tow-line on the left bank, we covered four miles. About twenty-five miles from St. Charles the right bank became flat again, contrary to the individual rock groups rising on the left bank. In the afternoon we had a short but violent thunderstorm, after which I sent my hunter out to hunt. Mr. L. Caillou and I went out together, too, but on account of the thicket and the many windbreaks we could not get a shot. Often six to eight trees, some of them of enormous circumference, lay broken and decayed on top of one another, overgrown with weeds, chiefly common nettles as tall as a man.

It was almost impossible to climb over these obstructions and even the thickest leather of which our clothes were made did not protect us against the burning stickers of the nettles and the thick thorns of the climbing roses and buckthorn. The as yet undetermined roses decorated the tops of the trees with countless pink blossoms, affording a pleasant contrast against the dark foliage of the primeval forest. My hunter came back late, causing me much anxiety. He had wounded a deer and in trailing it had been delayed. Hearing the repeated discharging of our firearms, he had, however, found his way back despite the intense darkness. During the night several heavy thunderstorms followed one another and again drenched our boat.

The morning of the twentieth promised neither favorable nor clear weather, but the wind turned to the east. I entertained the hope that we might continue our journey more speedily than before. In this expectation I found myself disappointed however. Soon after our departure from St. Charles the seed of irregularity and unlawful behavior toward superiors had been planted among the crew, and during the previous night this had

[31] *Tanagra rubra* = *Piranga rubra*, the summer tanager. *T. coerulea* = *Guiraca coerulea*, the blue grosbeak.

matured into serious trouble. With much difficulty I succeeded in getting the men into action at about seven o'clock in the morning.

We had scarcely advanced four miles when the quarrel broke out anew, and despite all my admonitions an open and furious attack against the boat leader, Dutremble, followed. Since he did not have the necessary courage to quell the rebellion, four of the most desperate fellows took their property and the guns which had been issued them by the French Company as part payment for their services. As there was no doubt that the worst kind of quarrel and possibly bloodshed would follow, I applied all my eloquence to calm the better-minded part of the crew. When I had won them over to our cause, in company with my reliable companions we forthwith instituted drastic measures. Thereupon the instigators became frightened, and since we happened to be close to the land, they jumped from the boat and fled into the forest. Considering it ill-advised to have the well-armed fugitives pursued, I had difficulty in restraining the remaining crew from doing so. I never heard anything more of the runaways, who probably had turned to the English settlements.

The boat leader was placed in an embarrassing situation by this most disagreeable incident. In all there remained only thirteen able men on board, and from the very outset there had been too few men to battle the high water. Now we had to lay by for the time being. Dutremble set out on a return to St. Louis by land to announce the deplorable incident to the merchants and to recruit additions to the crew. I considered it advisable to inform the trading company [Berthold, Chouteau, and Pratte, the "French Fur Company"] of everything in a detailed written report and requested them to suggest a safe means of avoiding similar vexation on the journey. I remained with the boat at a promontory on the left bank, with the understanding that we should continue with the aid of the sail, should favorable wind set in. Dutremble with the reinforcements would follow by land. In any event the Gasconade River was agreed on as a place of rendezvous, in case he should miss the boat.

In the afternoon I went into the forest to inspect this region. The promontory at which we had landed consisted of an island formed by a false channel of the river and a little stream. Walking along the edge of the water I saw several deer, some hogs that had become wild, and some turkeys, but only got a shot at the latter. Opposite the boat the neighboring bank rose to a gentle height on which were seen a few poor cabins. On the left bank the nearest habitation was over two English miles away.

During the night it stormed severely and the Missouri suddenly rose several feet, continuing to rise all of the twenty-first. Caillou, whom I had sent to the above-mentioned dwelling, on going away had waded through the narrow arm of the river, but at his return found it so swollen that he had to swim through it. About ten o'clock in the morning the sky cleared and we had a fine, though windy, day, but this was most welcome. We were in need of fresh meat, and all who could handle a gun were sent on the hunt.

However, all our efforts were without avail, due not to lack of game but to the swampy region and the impenetrable underbrush in the forest. Finally, on the following morning, I was fortunate to shoot a deer, and since on the hunt it is usually the case that success follows success, every hunter brought back something on his return at noon. Our supply was bountiful.

On this same day a cloud of insects descended upon us toward evening and we were horribly tormented. In addition to these troublesome guests some very beautiful butterflies flew about us (*Papilio turnus, thoas, marcellus, ephestion, troilus, plexippus, atalanta, phlaes*, and several other undetermined varieties). During the night my men caught several specimens of *Bombyx polypheums* which is common here.[32]

The air was sultry and threatening. When I went hunting very early the next morning I was surprised by quite miserable weather. I was thoroughly drenched, even though I had taken refuge under a densely foliaged cottonwood. During this storm lightning flashed and thunder rolled uninterruptedly, and the lightning struck several times close to me. Since my gun had become useless, I had to return without accomplishment. I decided to take a few of our men with me and visit a dwelling six miles away to purchase some provisions.

The way led across the above-mentioned channel of the river. The water was very high and extremely swift. However, many trees and much driftwood had collected at the mouth. Over this we crawled with much difficulty. Following a forest path, I observed a few extraordinarily fine sycamores which were from three to four meters in circumference and probably fifty yards high. At the first house we found no livestock. It was all in the forest, and not even hogs could be procured. At the second house we found some very uncivil people, especially a ninety-year-old fellow whose whole aim was to overcharge me and to make fun of our distress.

Over four hours on our way, we had come through deep clay mud, and yet our pleading could not induce these hard-hearted people to offer us the

---

[32] *Papilio turnus* = *Papilio glaucus* Linnaeus, the eastern tiger swallowtail butterfly. *P. thoas* = *P. cresphontes*, giant swallowtail butterfly. *P. marcellus*, the zebra swallowtail butterfly. *P. ephestion* = ? *P. troilus*, the green-clouded swallowtail butterfly. *P. plexippus* = *Danaus plexippus*, the monarch butterfly. *P. atalanta* = *Vanessa atalanta*, the red admiral butterfly. *P. phlaes* = *Hylephila phyleus*, the fiery skipper. *Bombyx polypheums* = *B. mori* or possibly *B. mandarina*, in either case a silk-worm species.

least refreshment. Very much disgruntled I went my way, leaving the impolite old man with his swine. On our return I found the opportunity to buy a lean chicken. Divided among six persons, it afforded only a scant meal.

On the evening of the twenty-fourth Dutremble came, bringing five men with him. Among these were three Negroes and one mulatto, all slaves owned by the partners of the French Missouri Company. At the same time I received a very polite letter from the company asking me in the future to look after their interest on board the boat.

During the night we were visited again by several loud thunderstorms and a heavy downpour. Yet in the morning it cleared and we looked forward to a fine day. Going ahead on foot along the river bank to a place which the Creoles call Chaurette, [La Charrette] named after a creek which flows here into the Missouri, I shot two head of game. Left on the edge of the water with a marker, they were happily found by the crew and taken on board. Here both banks of the stream are very flat, overgrown with heavy timber, and the river contains several small islands. Since the wind was favorable I had to go on board shortly.

By noon we had covered eleven miles and landed for a short time on a large island called Ile aux Boeufs,[33] probably so-named because of the large number of bison that once populated it. Opposite the point of the island were several houses. The inhabitants had much livestock, but cultivated the extremely rich soil of their fields very poorly, as, on an average do most Americans.

The ground on the left bank of the Missouri not far from these settlements rises to rather high cliffs of limestone, against which several houses were built. As is customary along the banks of this stream, they are situated not very close to the river. The Ile aux Boeufs is almost six English miles long and two miles wide. A small creek by the same name, flowing from the west to the east into the Missouri, has at its mouth a width of about fifty or sixty feet. Although it extends a considerable distance into the land, it is navigable for small boats only a short way because of its rocky bottom. Along its banks many pioneers, perhaps as many as one hundred families, have settled lately. The bank of the island was so densely overgrown with wild grapevines that it was impossible to put the crew on land to pull the boat by the tow-line.

The wind had ceased entirely so that the sail could not be used, and we moved along very slowly. With great difficulty I made a path for myself

---

[33] Buffaloe Island in Lewis and Clark, *Original Journals*, I, 29. La Charrette, which preceded it in the Duke's itinerary, is associated with Daniel Boone's Missouri career, closed by his death in 1820, according to some authorities at or near La Charrette.

through *Geprötz*, almost impenetrable underbrush, searching for some houses, which I found at the northern end of the island. Here, seemingly well-to-do people lived. Very obliging, they sold me a large amount of provisions and a fat hog at a most reasonable price. As it happened to be Sunday, I found many people at one of the houses. They had come from the opposite bank not far from the island. They all received me in a friendly manner but gaped at me as if I were some wonder-animal, plying me with most peculiar questions. The costumes of the women were so striking that I could scarcely refrain from laughing. Wearing a kind of pointed hat of queer shape they looked ludicrous.[34]

The American in the remote territories have very little or no conception of Europe and regard our continent as a truly fabled land. I believe I may dare make the assertion that, regarding my fatherland, I heard more rational judgments expressed by Indian chiefs than by the white inhabitants of the interior of this land.

In this the total lack of schools among the scattered settlers and the great indifference toward everything that does not concern them immediately are to blame. Above all, my European weapons aroused the disparagement of these good country people. Accustomed to their long, clumsy rifles, shooting a very small bullet, and not understanding how I could get along with my short German rifle, they challenged me to give them a sample of my skill.

Since I am a fairly good shot, at the start I intentionally acted as if I were inexperienced, requesting the Americans to set up a target and shoot first. Satisfied to do so they laid a round piece of wood, near six inches in diameter, on a stump about thirty-five paces away. One of those present, boasting not a little of his skill in shooting, took the first shot and hit a full inch under the target. Hereupon I went back eighty paces and luckily split the piece of wood in two at the center. This aroused general amazement.

During the contest several of my companions had arrived, among them Caillou and old de Rouain, both known as good shots and jealous of their skill. They also came out victors. When I finally retired several hundred paces with my rifle, an extremely good one, and began to shoot from this distance, the Americans, changing their notion in regard to my weapon, could not sufficiently express their admiration.

On the whole the immigrants in the western states shoot fairly well with their rifles, but only at a short distance of thirty or forty paces. They are

---

[34] "Style is as style does," but these women were not wearers of the pointed hats or Normandy blues of France via Canada and the upper Mississippi Valley. Rather they were immigrants from Kentucky and Tennessee of both before and after the War of 1812. Compare Brackenridge, *Views of Louisiana*, 137–38.

far surpassed by the inhabitants of Tennessee and Kentucky. The French Creoles on the Missouri and upper Mississippi also outdo them and are much more daring and untiring as hunters than the westerners.

During this contest, evening had approached and our boat came by very late. Arrangements were made for supper, which I partook of with good appetite, for on this day I had walked ten English miles over very bad roads. When darkness came most of the families who had come to visit on the island left the little colony, rowing back across the Missouri to their habitations. Several young men and a girl got into a canoe made of a hollowed-out tree trunk. Since the lads were in high spirits, the shaky craft, losing its equilibrium, turned over in the water. On the Missouri, however, girls are as good swimmers as boys, and the whole scene passed by without serious consequences amid the uproarious laughter of all.

We left our camp at break of day on the twenty-sixth after a beautiful night and traveled along the densely wooded hills of the right bank of the stream. The overhanging branches of the trees beat ceaselessly against the boat, tearing several objects off the deck. Much time was lost. I observed a great number of lindens and oaks among the forest trees. These prefer rich soil. By this preference they identify places best suited for settlements.

The arm or channel of the Missouri through which we had to pass, separating the island from the river bank, is not over twenty yards wide in many places, and in very dry weather is even said to dry up entirely. Four English miles from this island and the river becomes extremely wide and contains several important islands overgrown with cottonwoods of enormous dimensions.

It is almost impossible to shoot birds and small animals with shot in the tops of such trees. About noon we stopped at the mouth of a creek in a lonely, hilly region populated by many snakes, especially rattlesnakes. I was very much surprised to find such a small number of flowering plants on the banks of the Missouri, which is so rich in various trees and bushes.

Thus I observed during the course of the entire day only one single blossoming umbelliferous plant, *Panax trifolia*, Linn., which the Creoles correctly call *ginseng*. Its properties are well known in the country.[35] Among the pod-bearing plants, the *Amorpha herbacea* and another plant closely related to it (perhaps an *Aeschynomene?*) were very luxuriant on newly cleared land, but their flowers were not yet fully developed.[36] Called wild indigo by the people, its blossoms used as tea are said to be a good remedy for purifying the blood. These plants disseminated a highly unpleasant odor, and I found the leaves attacked by caterpillars.

[35] *Panax trifolia* is here out of its range; probably *Panax quinquefolius*.

[36] *Aeschynomene* is unlikely in this range; possibly a *Cassia* or a *Desmodium*.

The poisonous sumac, *Rhus toxicodendron,* growing here abundantly, because of the narcotic properties of the leaves, causes headaches. It shares this characteristic with the pawpaw variety, *Annona tribola.* Again I made the unpleasant observation that the American nettles burn much more intensely and grow much more luxuriantly than our European varieties. Furthermore, there are more varieties of this weed.

In grasses I found this region poor. On the other hand, a low Syngenesia not yet in bloom, with large umbrella-shaped leaves, covered the ground of the entire forest area.[37] Out of the crevices of the rocks sprouted a few ferns with very delicate leaves, and one small red mushroom appeared as the only specimen of this kind. On waste spots I found some twenty-foot-high dry stalks of an annual helianthus which seemed to agree with a variety, *Helianthus annus,* that I observed in the prairies in various forms.[38]

About three o'clock in the afternoon we reached Shepherd's Creek or Rivière aux Bergées.[39] Equal in width with the Boeuf, it has more than thirty navigable miles for small boats, and its banks are fairly well settled. Only twenty-five years ago it was the hunting ground of the bear hunters and beaver trappers. In recent times these animals have been vastly reduced in numbers, and only the fallow deer has held its own. But it, too, is becoming scarcer because of hunting pressure.

Two miles from Shepherd's Creek our boat got into such an entanglement among tree trunks that we were in imminent danger of stranding and seeing our boat burst wide open. At first no one had the courage to jump into the water and swim among the tree trunks to fasten a line to a tree on the bank in order to pull the boat back. Caillou, the boldest and most skillful of them all, finally plunged into the surging Missouri, and after courageously defying the hazards he reached a tree trunk projecting from the water. Catching hold a drifting log, he swam with its aid through all obstacles, including a whirlpool, threw the line with great skill over an enormous sycamore which had fallen into the stream, swam back with the line again, and thus pulled the boat out of its dangerous position.

On that same afternoon the crew had to endure severe hardship in navigating around a rocky promontory that projected into the river, and they had to push and pull the boat along the bank where undergrowth was densely entangled with grapevines. Opposite Shepherd's Creek, the rocky

[37] The leaves suggest *Podophyllum pelatum* (Berberidaceae), the May-apple.

[38] *Helianthus annus,* one of the sunflowers.

[39] Shepherd's Creek or Rivière aux Bergées empties into the Missouri perhaps a dozen miles above Buffalo Island.

left bank gradually rises to rather high hills, and the river, its bed narrowed by two rows of hills, flows much more rapidly than near its mouth. Despite this increased current and other hindrances, we had made a splendid day's journey of fifteen English miles. Along this entire distance we had seen only here and there traces of former settlements. Continually sinking banks and constant widening of the river had forced the inhabitants to forsake their homes.

Often I heard the bank, undermined by the current, cave in amid loud noise resembling the report of a cannon fired at some distance. At night this noise, together with the roar of the river and its whirlpools and the creaking and grinding of drifting trees, caused a horrendous uproar.

Sneaking about the forest that evening, I succeeded in killing some game but because of the approaching darkness had to leave a part of my booty in the lurch. With the aid of bright moonlight, I returned late to the boat, badly stung by nettles. The night was clear and cool. The thermometer sank from 83° to 59°. Nevertheless, all sorts of mosquitoes and other insects liking the nearness of water tormented me. But we suffered especially from wood ticks of varying size and variety burrowing everywhere into the skins of animals and humans. Usually their head remains in the wound, producing a burning and festering sore.[40]

On the morning of the twenty-seventh we broke camp at three o'clock. I walked ahead of the boat for a distance of four miles along the bank and again encountered several abandoned cabins. Around these several head of cattle and a few horses were grazing, and since these animals were not wild I surmised that the inhabitants might have settled farther inland.

As the morning was clear and cool and a brisk wind was blowing, the boat overtook me at five-thirty. Completely drenched with dew, I boarded it. In this region the river is very broad and slower, the right bank is low, while the left bank is bordered by high bluffs. About noon we reached the island Maline, which is three English miles long, not very wide, uninhabited and overgrown with cottonwoods and willows. Not far from this island is the inhabited Otter Island or Ile de la Loutre. In its middle one sees the now occupied Fort de la Loutre, once an important place in the

---

[40] *Author*: Among the spider-like creatures in the Missouri forest there are two species especially which I should propose to be named *Ixodes humanus* and *Ixodes cruciger*. One of them preferably selects the human body as its host and has several deep red spots on its belly. The other, marked by a distinct yellow cross, is found less commonly on humans than on animals, which are literally seeded with them.

[*Ixodes humanus* did not come into the scientific literature until 1844 when it was named by Koch.

[*Ixodes cruciger* failed of notice by the rest of the scientific world.]

wars with the wild Indians.[41] On the west side of the river the Otter Creek empties at a short distance above the island of the same name.

During the afternoon a heavy thunderstorm with showers reduced the heat and the mosquitoes but also delayed us several hours. Since the twenty-fifth the Missouri had begun to rise markedly. For me this is an unpleasant situation since the journey can be greatly delayed by too high water. Among the articles most necessary for our convenience, and over-looked in equipping our boat, was a usable canoe and a strong rope fit for pulling the vessel. The one which we had on board was so worn that I feared every day it would break in pulling against the strong current, leaving our boat to the mercy of the power of the water, from which it could not have escaped unharmed.

For some days I had observed that the water of the Missouri had be-come much lighter in color, leaving a much smaller amount of clay deposit. I concluded that the increased volume of water might be caused by a flood of the big Osage and the Kansas rivers, which carry clear water, and that they might be very much swollen by heavy rains.

After the storm had subsided somewhat we went on, but the crew had to exert all its strength to move the boat by rowing and pulling. Late in the evening, reaching the mouth of Ash Creek, or Rivière du Frène, we halted. During the night we experienced a heavy rain accompanied by a thunderstorm lasting from eleven o'clock until morning, leaving not a dry spot in our boat. The Missouri rose three feet this night and was covered with thick foam and a lot of driftwood, which growth betrayed the fact that it came from the far north. I was justified in concluding that melting snows must have begun in that part of the mountains where the great tributaries supplying the main stream of the Missouri have their sources.

This rising of the northwestern tributaries of the Missouri causes the second main period of high water, occurring usually near the end of May or the early days of June. At about this time the rivers of the prairies farther to the south are also high, due to almost continuous heavy rain, and for this reason I surmise that the highest water of the river comes about this time. The snow covering the northern prairies from the forty-fourth to the forty-seventh degrees of north latitude melts during April under favorable conditions, keeping the river at a fairly high state. This

---

[41] Fort de la Loutre = Fort Clemson, located on Loutre Island at the junction of the Loutre and Missouri rivers, created in February, 1812, but not by the army. The time was four years after Fort Osage had been erected by the garrison of the First U.S. Infantry commanded by Captain Eli B. Clemson, hence its name. According to Houck, earliest settle-ment on Loutre Island began in 1807 with the arrival of four Anglo-American families. Houck, *History of Missouri*, III, 98, 137, 145. Frazer, *Forts of the West*, 71, 75–76.

hardly exceeds the medium level, depending on the faster or slower melting on the ground.

On that part of the Andes chain lying north of the peak of New Mexico, by the Americans commonly called Rocky Mountains, the snow which has fallen during the winter at altitudes of 3,000 to 4,500 feet melts in May. On the eastern slope of these mountains originate La Platte, the Yellowstone, and all those rivers known as the sources of the Missouri. These are almost all at floodstage at the same time. Added to this is the heavy rainfall, which in this month drenches that part of the country east of the mountains. The snow in the higher regions of the Andes chain begins to melt only during the mid-summer, bringing about the third period of high water on the Missouri. This can be considered the least important period and usually keeps the stream at a fairly high level for several weeks. The lowest water, on the other hand, occurs in the months of September and October. At this time all the sandbars and shallows are visible, and navigation with larger boats downstream requires the greatest caution.

At ten o'clock in the morning we met a large boat coming from the Kansas River belonging to a certain Mr. Curtis, who has established himself as merchant at the mouth of that river.[42] From the crew of that boat we learned that the Missouri was very swift and dangerous and that the water apparently was still rising. The sky was dark on this day and threatening rain. At the same time the air was sultry and filled with billions of insects. The thermometer registered 75°, the de Luc hygrometer 65°.

About noon we were opposite the Chenal de la Pensée along a rocky bank overgrown with a variety of trees. (*Tilia americana, Fraximus juglandifolia, Quercus montana, lyrata, stellata, alba, Acer saccharinum, Juglans nigra, fraxinifolia, compressa, Virburnum lantanoides*, Mich., *Celastrus scandens, Crataegus coccinea*, and others.)[43]

---

[42] Cyrus Curtis, trader upstream at the mouth of the Kansas and farther up the latter stream, doing business principally with the Osage Tribe, was encountered on the Missouri nearly five years earlier, December 24, 1818, by the Missouri Expedition at its winter quarters on Cow Island, 380 miles upstream from St. Louis. Gale, *The Missouri Expedition, 1818–1820*, ed. by Roger L. Nichols, 28, 43–44.

[43] *Seriatim* these species are: *Tillia americana*, the basswood; *Fraxinus juglandifolia* = *F. americana*, the white ash; *Quercus montana* = *Q. prina*, unlikely in Duke Paul's range, more likely *Q. muhlenbergii*, chinquapin or chestnut oak; *Q. lyrata*, the overcup oak, which is out of range, more likely *Q. macrocarpa*, the bur oak; *Q. stellata*, the post oak; *Q. alba*, white oak; *Acer saccharinum*, silver maple; *Juglans nigra*, black walnut; *J. fraxinifolia* Lam. = *Pterocarya fraxinifolia*, an oriental species unlikely here, whereas *J. cinerea*, the butter nut, is likely; *J. compressa* = *Carya ovata*, the shagbark hickory; *Virburnum lantanoides* = *Viburnum alnifolium*, a species of the eastern U.S. and out of range here,

The vessel stayed the whole afternoon along the right bank, although the crew sought to force it ahead as much as possible, but this hard work was beset with many difficulties. When it began to get dark two boats loaded with pelts from the far north shot at arrow speed down this fast-running stream. Here we were not far from the mouth of the Gasconade River, which is very much swollen and more than sixty yards wide.

The Gasconade is one of the more important rivers, and in this respect resembles the Meramec.[44] Both rivers have their sources rather close together. On its banks, where the settlements are, a few water mills make their somewhat rare appearances in the state of Missouri. Some years ago at the mouth of the river an island was built up and is now overgrown with willows and cottonwoods. The left channel now has water only during flood stage, and it was covered with scattered trees uprooted by the force and turbulence of high water.

Toward evening I observed on the rocky banks numerous specimens of *Laurus sassafras*, *Aqilegia canadensis*, and *Dracocephalum variegatum* in full bloom.[45] This evening was again sultry and the sky was covered with solid clouds. On the twenty-ninth we started very early but only covered two English miles. The rising river was terrifying and carried so many logs that we were in constant danger of meeting with an accident.

With tremendous difficulty we reached the bank at a low place and secured the boat as tightly as possible to several trees. The water continued to rise and soon the land was completely flooded. Our situation became still more precarious. However, nothing of importance happened except that the river rose another foot and a half by evening. During the night the sky cleared and a gentle northeast wind began to blow. As this became stronger in the morning and then completely turned to the east, we risked leaving our hiding place with the aid of the sail and oars.

Traveling around an island overgrown with willows, we luckily reached the left bank. However, this too was flooded, but a short distance ahead high rocky bluffs of striking formation constituted the bank. Their summits were covered with trees, and among these the sassafras appeared in bush

---

therefore the reference is to one of the other species of black haw, some of which occur where Duke Paul was then located; *Celastrus scandens*, the bittersweet; *Crataegus coccinea*, *nomen ambiguum* possibly composed of two species, both of the eastern U.S., and impossible to identify from the several species of red haw or hawthorn of the area of the Duke's immediate travels.

[44] The Gasconade River, 250 miles long, rises in the Ozark Plateau and flows north into the Missouri in Gasconade County, Mo.

[45] These species are: *Laurus sassafras* = *Sassafras albidum*, sassafras; *Aquilegia canadensis*, columbine; *Dracocephalum variegatum* = *D. virginianum*, dragon head.

form. On such rocky limestone soil its roots are very aromatic and constitute an excellent purgative and sweat-producing remedy. The flat bank, only a few paces from the abrupt bluff, is overgrown with impenetrable bushes and a few tall cottonwoods, oaks, and beeches (*Fagus ferruginea*, Willd.).[46] As the dwellings of the settlers are usually situated further inland, we had not seen a cultivated spot on the banks of the river for three days.

The high bluffs on the left bank formed a striking contrast to the very low, heavily timbered right bank. These limestone banks, tower-like peaks, cubical and pyramidal structures, and great isolated masses of stone formed an odd group of formations such as I had not seen during the course of my journey. There were many caves in this limestone. Caillou, who had hunted bears in the region, had many interesting things to tell concerning the location of the caves and their depth, which is said to be considerable.

The customary style of pursuing the bear in this dangerous place is to hunt it during its winter sleep, while it is the fattest. But this fashion of hunting may be fraught with difficulties and many dangers. Even the climb to the mouth of a cave, which is usually very narrow, requires a good deal of caution. However, the bear does sleep so soundly that the hunter, if he is provided with a light, could slip up close to its den. The experienced hunter easily recognizes the bear's deep breathing and heartbeat. Rarely do fewer than four or five hunters enter a cave occupied by a bear. And it is seldom that more than one bear occupies such a cave. Though these animals live socially together in the fall, they are always accustomed to separate in the winter. When the hunters have come close to a den, one of them raises the torch high and the others open fire. In the narrow enclosed space the torch naturally goes out. Of course the hunters have to take deadly aim, for a bear that is merely wounded can easily do great harm. Only excellent, skilled hunters or Indians pursue this method of hunting. In rocky regions such as this, bears are plentiful and hunting may be most profitable. Caillou assured me that in one hunting season he had shot more than forty bears.[47]

Near a brook I saw a rickety cabin about two hundred paces from the bank. The fence of the field had been carried away by the water, and the whole presented a picture of great desolation. One finds such wretched huts scattered here and there in Missouri, usually inhabited by poor people,

---

[46] *Fagus ferruginea* = *F. grandifolia*, the American beech, although it is at this geographical point slightly out of its presently known range.

[47] The species here referred to is *Ursus americanus*, the black bear, formerly common to the forested regions of North America, rather than the more feared species *Ursus horribilis*, the grizzly, which, however, was not unknown to the middle reaches of the Missouri River in earlier times, as Hall and Kelson (*Mammals of North America*) have shown. In 1804, the Lewis and Clark party killed a dozen or more black bears between the Mississippi and Kansas rivers.

especially Irish or Indian half-bloods. Their roving, inconsistent style of living is not suited to secure a permanent settlement. Such individuals live outside the law of the social order, establish a cabin now here, now there, and clear a small field for the cultivation of a little corn, and at the first opportunity again leave the settlement. Relying more on their guns than on their hands and patience, these persons constitute a transitional link between civilization and the unrestricted wilderness. In my opinion they are lower than the Indians, for these, by need and by the bonds of blood and friendship, recognize the advantage of social union, hereditary customs and morals, even though fixed laws or compulsory obedience to real authority are unknown to them.

Out of the rocks close to the bank the *Juniperus prostrata*,[48] similar to the European juniper, grew abundantly, its berries beginning to turn blue. The sugar maples also covered these hilly regions, but they did not grow much over twenty to thirty feet high. This beautiful and useful variety of timber, preferring a high location, constitutes solid forests farther upstream. The art of cooking sugar from its juice is, of course, not foreign to the Americans, but the trees in these forests on the Missouri, naturally have not suffered as much as those in the more populous eastern states.

During the whole day I failed to see the *Aquilegia canadensis*, which farther back grew so profusely. On the whole I noted a great lack of flowering plants, while earlier their striking appearance had repeatedly arrested my attention in that fruitful climate. An *Asarum*, with roots the odor of ginger and large round leaves, adorning the banks of a creek, caught my eye. Its roots do not have the nauseating effect of the variety found in Germany which is such a poor substitute for *ipecac*. The plant also seems to be different from the Canadian *ipecacuanha*.[49]

The wind had started again and we traveled fairly rapidly. The thermometer was at only 63° and the de Luc hygrometer at 60°, but soon changed to 57°, for there had been a heavy dew in the morning. By noon we reached a great cliff, called Caverne à Montbrun.[50] Here a small creek,

---

[48] *Juniperus prostrata* = *J. horizontalis*, but Missouri is too far south for this species at this time. Possibly a dwarfed specimen of *Juniperus virginiana*.

[49] *Asarum canadense*, wild ginger.

[50] Caverne à Montbrun, lying between Little Tavern and Tavern creeks in Calloway County, Missouri, was called Monbrun Tavern in Lewis and Clark, *Original Journals*, I, 36, and was named for Stephen Boucher de Mombrun, a relative of Jacques Timothe Boucher de Mombreun of Kaskaskia. Louis Houck, *The Spanish Régime in Missouri*, 2 vols. I, 197–98.

Rivière de la Caverne, flows among the jagged bluffs and empties into the Missouri. The rock mass, about three hundred feet high, hangs at least thirty feet over the edge of the stream. The lowest strata are especially hollowed out deeply forming a very considerable chamber which in crescent form extends about one hundred feet along the little stream and the Missouri. In the chamber thus formed several hundred persons could find shelter from rain and inclement weather. The moss of stone along the level of the water, permeated by several veins of crystaline limestone, was in sharp contrast with the gray and dark yellow, iron-impregnated rock and held my interest for a long time.

This chamber formed by nature has played a role in the history of this land. During one of the wars between the whites and the aborigines it served a long time as a dangerous hiding place for a band of the Indians under the leadership of a French Creole from Canada named Montbrun. Caillou further related to me that, at a time when the Great Osages carried on an expedition against the Sac and Fox Indians, he was in danger of losing his life in this shelter, owing his escape only to good luck.

One night he was in the cave with thirty Osages, and by chance some Fox Indians camped in the ravines and bushes surrounding this rock. The Fox, some one hundred in number, instead of at once attacking their enemies by surprise, first held a council and painted their bodies according to their custom, a practice which seems to be peculiar to all aborigines of North America before an important undertaking. By good fortune one of the young Osages crept out of the cave during the night to look for something and discovered the enemies. Noiselessly he returned to his tribesmen, who, together with the whites accompanying them, still had time to escape in their canoes and flee downriver.

I found many traces of Indian painting on the walls of the cliff. Among them a few representing men in war-like attitude were very well preserved. Since the dyestuff, red ochre, does not resist the weather well, I concluded that the band of Indians must have camped here lately. It seems that it is a common practice among the Indians of America to engrave symbolic figures on the bluffs along the rivers. Such portrayals of men, animals, and idols were, wherever I had the opportunity of observing them, at a very much elevated location on the most precipitous bluffs near the edge of the water, but always high enough that even during the crest of the water they could not be reached by the stream.

I will confess I never found drawings of this kind in places that could not be reached by a person skilled in climbing, and for this reason the images painted or engraved on stone by the aborigines of North America do not deserve the attention that those discovered by Mr. von Humboldt on the rocky banks of the Orinoco do, and which probably belong to a much older period.

The above-mentioned small creek originates in the meadows crowning the plateau of the highland which the banks form. Almost opposite the mouth, a little to the north, is an island bearing the same name as the cave. Two English miles long but relatively narrow, it is covered with tall cottonwoods and uninhabited. The elevation of this island is too high to be inundated by the flood. It is peculiar how the bluffs, which form the Caverne à Montbrun and the bank of the creek, cease so suddenly, as if cut off, allowing the river to increase greatly in width. The two banks then appeared flat and were at that time inundated by the Missouri. Frequent violent thunderstorms must occur here, for everywhere I observed many trees shattered and charred by the lightning.

Where the different kinds of trees have the same height, it seems that the electric discharges most frequently strike the cottonwoods. Nut and ash trees, even oak and linden, are rarely destroyed by lightning, and for this reason they are usually sound to the top. However, the tops of cottonwoods are almost always dead. The many American oaks, on the whole, enjoy an especially luxuriant and strong growth. Only a few of them attain the dimensions of the European stone oak, which by no means belongs to the trees of the Old World distinguishing themselves by great height and wide circumference. But one may reckon the American oak among the healthiest and soundest trees, as is shown by the sturdiness of their growth and the luxuriance of their foliage.

The manifold coloring of the American forest, already mentioned by me and by other travelers, especially as it pertains to the hilly regions, was more splendid on the Missouri than on the Ohio. To the beauty of its banks the Ohio owes its French name of Belle Rivière. The coloring of the hillsides is simply incomparable in the autumn months after the first slight frost.

Despite the swift current, the brisk east wind moved us quickly ahead. One English mile from the Caverne à Montbrun the flat land ceases and low bluffs, not over a height of one hundred feet, reappear. As may be surmised, the limestone bluffs that constitute these banks are continuous, even though they frequently do not extend above the level of the Missouri. Their shape and formation is almost everywhere the same, and in many places they form shelves and projecting cliffs that are hollowed out farther down. From a personal investigation which I undertook at noon, I found the higher layers much harder and less fragile than those at the foot of the cliff near the stream. The parallel strata showed a remarkable difference in regard to their thickness and density. Near the surface of the water they were friable and permeated by veins of gypsum, irregular in shape, fusing with other layers, milk colored, almost transparent, and breakable into flakes. I observed geodes with crystallized surfaces, and as one approaches the higher levels the strata become thicker.

At this bank the current increased in swiftness, and it was miserable and dangerous work to advance the boat, especially since the wind, which had been most favorable in the morning, began to subside. As the vessel had to be kept as near as possible to the bank, the overhanging branches beat against it constantly and the boat repeatedly bumped against the tree trunks protruding from the water. We had to strike our sail and lower the mast lest the former be torn without fail and the latter broken. To control a vessel in deep and rapid current by merely pushing with poles is beset with many difficulties. Despite ceaseless exertion, our crew could scarcely move our boat one hundred paces. After an hour the wind again increased considerably and the sail was hastily raised. We had traveled for a scant half-hour when a sudden gust of wind billowed the sail from the side and threw the vessel with great force against the bank. A thick branch, coming in contact with the rear cover of the deck, tore the rudder loose. I chanced to stand close to the rudder but luckily escaped harm. Immediately thereafter a second overhanging tree struck the boat and seized a young American from Virginia, a Mr. Payne traveling with us as passenger to Fort Atkinson. He was at once hurled into the Missouri. One of the Negro slaves happened to be nearby and jumped after him. After several vain attempts he was able to save the young man, who by the blow and also by the struggle in the water had been rendered almost unconscious.

In repairing the deck and fitting in a new rudder several hours passed by, but the loss of time was made up again, thanks to a very favorable wind and the less rapid current. When we again set out the boat was hardly two miles from the Caverne à Montbrun.

The bluffs suddenly disappeared on both sides at this place, but scarcely one thousand paces farther on they rose again to considerable height. The land lying between was very low and thoroughly flooded. The stream does not extend to the foot of the bluffs but is separated from them by fifty paces of low land, which was also under water. Large masses of dangerous driftwood had settled on the bottom and therefore required greatest caution, especially as we traveled with the sail hoisted.

On the northern end of Taverne Island the Missouri becomes very wide. In the neighborhood of a forsaken and fallen-down cabin a rather wide creek flows into the river. Leaving this creek to our right and favored by the wind, we crossed over to the other bank, which was low and inundated although covered with willows and in the distance cottonwood trees. Here we became entangled in a mass of driftwood thrown together by the wind and current. A few of our crew succeeded in swimming around it and thus piloted the boat out of its dangerous position.

Then we halted, being fourteen miles from the Gasconade River. Therefore he had made a hard day's journey. It was a fine warm evening and the sun set in the most beautiful red. As night approached the wind died down to a perfect calm, but this was by no means desirable because the mosquitoes, becoming very much alive, again increased their miserable activity. The month of May ended with fine weather on the thirty-first.

Starting early on our way, at the outset we had great difficulty rowing past a small willow-grown island. Both banks of the river seemed low and I could see distinctly that the river was falling. Passing the small island, we reached the left bank and at the same time the wind increased to such a degree that we could make use of it. Quickly we passed an island called La Grande Isle au Vase, on which several small islands touch. The name itself indicates that this island has lately been made by the river, for among the Creoles the word *vase* means saturated soft clay originating from the deposits in the water.

Such ground becomes as hard as rock in the dry season of the year and develops many fissures, which make walking over it most difficult. On the other hand, when this clay is wet, one is in danger of sinking into it over his knees at every step. The willows prefer, and thrive on, such land, covering vast stretches of it. This I observed especially the farther we pushed upstream toward the north. There were great waves on the Missouri and the surface carried much driftwood.

From Isle au Vase to the Caverne à Montbrun the boatmen reckon twelve miles.[51] At noon the wind quieted down and the crew was forced to gain the right bank to use the tow-line. Here we saw the first inhabited house we had seen in three days. Its occupants were so obliging as to offer me a fat hog and a vessel full of milk. Since they would take no pay I made them a counter present of a pound of coffee, an article of luxury which the settlers in the remote parts can procure only with difficulty, for the stores are few and often long distances away.

Not far from the house rise rocky hills which mark the course of Bear Creek, or Rivière de l'Ours. This small stream is very unimportant, hardly navigable to canoes, and empties through the west bank of the Missouri a few miles upstream. The whole day remained clear and cool, and the

[51] Isle au Vase (Little Muddy or present Middle River) to Caverne à Montbrun was reckoned at eleven miles by Lewis and Clark (*Original Journals*, I, 36).

insects noticeably decreased in number, as they avoid bright sunlight and fair air.

My whole body was lacerated from the bites of mosquitoes and wood ticks. The bites caused by the latter had become festering welts that were hard to heal, while the stings of the mosquitoes caused burning blisters which often hurt severely for several days. The tormenting inhabitants of the air frequenting the banks of the Missouri were for the most part *tipulariae* of the mosquito family. In the daytime they are joined by multitudes of no less torturing wasps and horseflies, *tabanus*. As is known, the Creoles of America call the bloodsuckers *maringuins* to distinguish them from fly-like *moustigues*. These latter are scarcer in the colder climates and more of a plague in the tropical countries, where the mosquitoes are also numerous. The important influence which the nature of the water itself exerts on the existence of these insects, whose larvae live in the water, is sufficiently well known. The observations made in this regard in other parts of America I found confirmed in regard to the streams that empty into the Missouri, and I noticed especially that the lighter or darker color of the water, and also the smaller or larger amount of earthy deposit carried by the rivers, had an important effect on their presence.

In the afternoon I took a walk to the top of a nearby fairly steep hill and did not return until late in the evening. These hills are covered with a layer of extremely rich humus soil two or three feet thick. The trees growing on these hills are rather far apart, so that many open places appear which, in part, are overgrown with dense brush, consisting of sassafras, sumac, and woodbine, and in part by a luxuriant growth of grass. Most of the tree trunks indicate a strong healthy growth, and especially vigorous were the *Gleditschia*,[52] whose delicate feathery leaves suggest a scene from the tropical zone. The great lack of songbirds in this part of the Missouri struck me as being odd.

For several days I had scarcely heard the song of even a single small bird. Now, seeming even noisier than they were, the piercing cries of flocks of restless parrots and the occasional hammering of a red-headed woodpecker broke the death-like silence of the woods. Infrequently I encountered single gallinaceous birds with their broods, not yet fully fledged, seeking to escape my gaze by hastily running away. In the hilly regions

---

[52] *Author: Gleditschia triacanthos*, by the French Creoles called *Févier piquant*, in contrast to *Févier des bois*, *Gleditschia inermis* and *monosperma*, Walt., which latter also occur frequently in the western part of the United States [*Gleditsia inermis* = *G. triacanthos forma inermis*, a thornless variant of honey locust. *G. monosperma* = *G. aquatica*, water locust found near St. Louis but here too far west.]

turkeys are scarcer during the months of May and July than in other seasons. To provide food for their young, they seek out the nettle-covered low banks of the streams, and only when the young can fly do they go farther inland.

Toward evening the sky became overcast, the wind died down completely, and the awe-inspiring night stillness was interrupted only now and then by the crashing of a falling tree and the noise of an undermined bank caving in. Just before daybreak there was severe lightning and thunder, the former igniting several trees close to us which burned with a slow flame. But not a drop of rain fell. The Creoles, somewhat timid during a thunderstorm, were as terrified by this scene as I was arrested by it as a magnificent spectacle of nature.

Early on June 1 we maneuvered around the old tree trunk that on the previous night had caused us to halt our journey. Very slowly we advanced along the right bank, for at every pull new hindrances barred the channel, which was close to the bank. The high water, swift current, and great amount of driftwood seemed to make it impossible to find a way out. Neither were we favored by the wind or air. It was very sultry and oppressive.

At seven o'clock the boat was opposite the mouth of the rather large Grande Rivière au Vase.[53] It is swift and for seventy miles is navigable to boats, but a little dangerous because of its many rapids and its partly rocky and uneven bed. This stream flows for the most part through meadows, and the adjoining regions are well suited for cultivation; indeed quite a number of settlers have established themselves there already.

On the right bank of the Missouri, about two English miles from our night's camp, two creeks empty into the river, almost too insignificant to deserve mention. Opposite the low east bank, high bluffs descend almost perpendicularly to the water and are washed at all seasons by the water of the river, which is very deep here. These create exceedingly dangerous places, as the pressure of the swift current breaks with great force against the projecting point of the cliff. In addition to this, not far from the bank a number of small islands connecting with one another extend close to the Côte sans Dessein.[54] Standing out but a little above the water, they are in part covered with low willows, in part are bare, forming shallows and

[53] Grande Rivière au Vase = Auxvasse Creek in Calloway County, Mo.

[54] Côte sans Dessein, located near the present town of Tebbetts, north bank of the Missouri, some six hundred yards long and narrow, on which Brackenridge found half a dozen French families in 1811. It was to have Louis Roy's and Joseph Tibeau's block houses, against which the Indians made assaults in the War of 1812. Houck, *History of Missouri*, III, 113, 125–26, 143.

sandbanks. Because of their muddy banks and the driftwood lodged below the water's surface, they are a great hazard to the boats.

At noon we stopped at Bear Creek, or Rivière de l'Ours, whose banks are inhabited. This creek originates in the meadows and later near its mouth runs through that series of rocky hills which, as was already stated, extends to the bank of the Missouri. This region, formerly noted for the great amount of game, was frequently visited by Indian and Creole hunters. Now, however, as everywhere in settled regions, game has been vastly reduced in numbers.

Opposite Bear Creek another small stream, La Petite Rivière au Vase, empties into the Missouri. Our trip led slowly past several insignificant houses, some cleared places, and also a few hills of slight elevation. At a low place a few miles from the mouth of the Osage River we made preparations to spend the night after a short but difficult day's journey.

An unbearable and threatening thunderstorm, with sultry heat and a sky full of countless insects, had enervated everybody. Much as the continuous rain at the beginning of our journey on the Missouri had put my patience to the test, I would gladly have seen a return of that wet period, for the frequent electric discharges connected with it at least reduced the heat and checked the insects, which now, favored by the climate, spread an indescribable unrest and exceeding pain to all living beings. My expectation was disappointed. It did not rain. The stifling atmosphere remained and there was no thought of sleeping.

Held back by many obstacles, we traveled on the following morning through a swift current close along the west bank as far as a few islands marking the mouth of the Osage.[55] As the boat's master, Dutremble, had to go on business to Côte sans Dessein on the other side, the vessel remained idle until his return.

On the bank were found several houses occupied by French people, who showed much pleasure at our arrival. Several of the boatmen were either friends or kinsmen of theirs. These good-hearted people showered me with solicitude and with a multitude of questions which I could not answer, because they gave me no time. Especially active and zealous was a heavy woman of Indian descent who had been stolen from the Pawnees as a child and had been brought up among the Creoles. By her great talkative-

[55] Osage River, 360 miles in length, is formed by the junction of Marias des Cygnes and Little Osage rivers on the border of Bates and Vernon counties, Mo., flowing east and northeast, entering the Missouri east of present Jefferson City at Dodd's Island, Cole County, Mo. It takes its name from the Osage Indians, who were encountered there from the earliest period of French exploration in the seventeenth century to the time of Lewis and Clark.

ness and acquired French customs, quite in contrast with the usages of her nation, she furnished eloquent testimony that it is not race but education that determines the moral development of man.

I found maple sugar of excellent quality at these settlements, and my attention having been called to its superb taste, I made careful inquiry into the process of its preparation. The sap of the sugar maple contains much vegetable sugar, which is obtained by boiling it to the desired consistency. By careful procedure one could easily obtain complete purity of the cooked mass, free from slimy and other foreign particles. The dirty brown color, which makes this useful substitute for the sugar of the West Indies distasteful to many people, could also be remedied. Should the price of ordinary sugar rise in the United States, the preparation of maple sugar would certainly receive greater attention.

Immediately after our arrival I went hunting with the son of the house, a young half-blood. I saw a large brown wolf, perhaps the same species which Prince von Neuwied has made known under the name of *Canis campestris*,[56] which also seems to occur in North America. This beast of prey fled shyly but swiftly over the hills, and it seemed to be larger than the ordinary American prairie wolf (*Canis latrans?*). This latter wolf resembles our European wolf almost completely, but prefers grass covered plains to the wooded, hilly regions.

[56] *Author*: *Canis nubilus?* Without determining this species of wolf more accurately I refer the reader to the remarks of Major Long's *Journal*, Part I, page 168. [*Canis lupus nubilus* Say.]

[Maximilian zu Wied-Neuwied, here referred to, was widely traveled in the Western Hemisphere, and while his *Reise in das Innere Nord-Amerika in den Jahren 1832 bis 1834*, 2 Bände, mit Atlas (Coblenz, 1839–41), has been highly regarded for its views of Indians, particularly of the Far West, and its romantic overtones, it remains that the Prince was a significant natural scientist who named a number of species and for whom species were named. His report on the mammals observed during the expedition appeared in *Archiv für Naturgeschichte*, Band XXVII, 181–88 (1861), and Band XXVIII, 65–90 (1862). This material also appeared in single-volume form as *Verzeichnis der auf seiner Reise in Nord-Amerika beobachteten Saügethiere von Maximilian Prinzen zu Wied, mit vier Tafeln* . . . (Berlin, Nicolaische Verlagsbuchhandlung, 1862). His work on reptiles was printed in *Nova Acta Academia Caeseria Leopoldina-Carolina*, Band XXXII, 1–41, and in volume form as *Verzeichniss der Reptilien, welche auf einer Reise im nördlichen Amerika beobachtet wurden* (Dresden, Druck von E. Blochmann & Sohn, 1865). His papers at Neuwied Castle, immeasureably greater in extent than the contents of the *Reise in das Innere Nord-Amerika*, and complemented by some four hundred paintings, drawings, and sketches by his artist on the tour, Carl Bodmer, were in the process of being transcribed under the direction of the late Stanley Pargellis of the Newberry Library, Chicago, and Savoie Lottinville of the University of Oklahoma, when they were purchased by the Northern Natural Gas Company, Omaha, and may now be seen at the Joslyn Art Museum of that city.]

At a distance of two miles inland from the river bank high and steep hills covered with fertile earth rise out of very flat and wet forested lowland. Luxuriant vegetation of timber and bushes grew on these hills, and the *Tradescantia virginica*[57] and a dainty feathery acacia (*Mimosa illinoensis* ? Mich.)[58] spread out like a lovely carpet. The red mulberry tree, occurring in almost all of temperate North America, was often found in moist places exposed to the light. The trees yielded a great abundance of juicy and refreshing fruit, resembling the sweet cherry in taste, and a vast number of birds were attracted. At the approach of a person, the latter flew twittering and screaming into the interior of the woods. I noticed again a large number of thrushes and cardinals, which had been missing for some time. These were young birds whose plumage did not show the beautiful red of the mature males.

The heat rose to the almost unbelievable height of 93° and not a breeze stirred. Nevertheless, I went further into the country and climbed several high hills. I found traces of saline water on a few steep slopes, where it oozed out rather freely and moistened the soil. Fresh tracks of animals indicated that these places had been visited by wild game, even bears. On the dry, sunny places in these hills I encountered several large rattlesnakes who announced that we disturbed their safety by our approach. They made their presence known by rattling at a distance of more than twenty paces.

Cautiously approaching the dangerous reptiles, from a short distance I could distinctly see how they fixed their gaze steadily on me and vibrated the end of their tail with unbelievable rapidity. On account of their clumsiness, it is a rare occurrence that these admittedly wicked rattlesnakes attack or pursue a person, and they are less dangerous than is usually assumed. The rattling and the rigid stare of their eyes reveal more the feeling of fear than of anger. There is scarcely a case on record in which these snakes have injured a sleeping person, but it is true that their love for warmth often brings these nasty guests into the neighborhood of night camps of travelers, indeed even under their blankets.

I was amazed, when I heard the rattling sound of a snake, to find a large black snake instead of an ordinary rattler, which behaved, in the position and movement of the tail, very much like the latter. Believing that it also belonged to the family of poisonous snakes, I dared a fight with the snake, which it fortunately lost. When I examined it more closely I found that I had erred in respect to its danger, for it was entirely harmless. It belongs to the common adders and differed but little from the common black

---

[57] *Tradescantia virginica* = *Tradescantia virginiana*, the spider-wort, but *T. ohiensis* and *T. subaspera* are more common at this geographical point.

[58] *Mimosa illinoensis* = possibly *Desmanthus illinoensis*, the prairie mimosa.

variety of this region, previously described.[59] The rattling, although much fainter than that of the rattlesnake, was probably caused merely by the violent shaking of the hard shell of the end joints of the tail. Nature seems to have endowed defenseless snakes with the means to terrify an approaching enemy and thereby to save their own lives.

In the later course of my journey no other case of this nature came to my observation and I content myself by calling the attention of naturalists and travelers to this one. In addition to this black snake I also discovered a rattlesnake with three yellow longitudinal stripes on its back and three rattle joints on a very short tail. It seemed to be a new variety and I shall not fail to make known this and several other unknown varieties later on.[60]

The art of charming snakes, especially poisonous snakes, by whistling and the use of superstitious ceremonies, is one of the magic wonders with which [East] Indian jugglers have long worked on the credulity of weak-minded persons. In order to gain superiority over their fellow men, some Creoles have succeeded in mastering the secret and know how to lend this business all the mystical dignity constituting the customary formula of such meaningless actions. The purpose is the deception of the simple.

When I had come back to the river bank an old Frenchman maintained with great and solemn earnestness that he possessed this art and requested me to follow him into the forest after the completion of the meal. Although I was extremely tired I could not resist this invitation, for I, in a way, flattered myself that I should be able to see through the deception. In this I succeeded beyond all expectations.

Conducting me to a decaying tree, the trickster began to whistle, after having conjured the good and evil spirits with all sorts of incantations. As I had foreseen, several perfectly tame rattlesnakes, accustomed to his well-known call, crawled forth and approached the presumed magician. With commanding voice he admonished me to go away from the poisonous reptiles. Not finding it necessary to obey this order, I soon convinced myself, to the great chagrin of my companion, that the poison fangs had been torn out of the mouths of the snakes.

It seems probable to me that one can attract the snakes during the mating season by imitating their peculiar whistling sound. Snakes then approach

[59] The eastern coachwhip, *Masticophis flagellum flagellum*, in the absence of more complete data, would be the choice of Robert G. Webb, the author of, *inter alia*, *Reptiles of Oklahoma*, although he does not rule out as a possibility the black rat snake, *Elaphe obsoleta obsoleta*. Webb to Savoie Lottinville, November 2, 1971.

[60] Only two rattlesnakes occur in the locality in which Duke Paul made his observation: the western massauga, *Sistrurus catenatus tergeminus*, and the timber rattlesnake, *Crotalus horridus horridus*, neither of which, however, is characterized by three yellow longitudinal stripes on the back. The specimen seen was probably aberrant. *Ibid.*

the whistling person but, on looking sharply, they flee hastily. This the snake charmers take advantage of, maintaining that because of sympathy or apathy the snakes can do them no harm. At the same time I am convinced that the odor of many objects, especially smoked leather and the infusions of many leaves and roots, are repulsive to snakes, that they become stupefied by them and unable to strike. Indians and Creoles generally use gunpowder internally and externally as a remedy for rattlesnake bite. I have become convinced of the effectiveness of this simple remedy, and believe myself justified in recommending it, especially since every traveler in the wilderness carries his powder horn with him. The Indians, however, have other antidotes, and never undertake a distant journey without them, maintaining with the utmost assurance that without sympathetic incantations no remedy would be effective.

The night was oppressive, with lightning and thunder in the east. Still, we left our camp at the gray dawn the following morning. Immediately beyond the dwellings where we had spent the night and a part of the previous day, a hilly region formed the river bank. These wild bluffs extend to the mouth of the Osage, where several cabins have been sparsely scattered. On the left bank rises an isolated round-topped hill called the Côte sans Dessein. This bank is inhabited by American settlers. Formerly a few Creole families stayed here hunting and trading. The decrease of game and the advancing population constantly crowding, the Indians subsequently drove away this class of unsteady people, whose temporary settlements depended on both.

Between the Côte sans Dessein and the mouth of the Osage River, which we reached at about eleven o'clock in the forenoon, lie small, narrow islands. I counted six, covered with timber. Traces of destroyed houses indicate that they were once inhabited. The Osage is here some two hundred yards wide,[61] at the average stand of water, and carries clear, drinkable water. Originating in the vast prairies between the Kansas and the Arkansas, it is full of rapids and for the most part flows over a rocky bed. Several streams of some importance empty into it.[62] Of these several are navigable for canoes and even for larger boats.

[61] The author estimated the distance at ninety *Toisen*, an old French measure used also at that time in Württemberg. It was equal to about 2.1315 yards.

[62] *Author*: Among others, Rain Creek, *Rivière de la Pluie*; Little Saline Creek, *La Petite Saline*; the Maniga; False Fork, *La Mauvaise Fourche*; Whitewood Creek, *Rivière au Bois Blanc*; farther on, *Marais de la Douceur*; Potato Creek, *Rivière aux Pommes de Terre*; Grand Creek, *La Grand Rivière*; *La Rivière à Moreau*; Slave Creek, *La Rivière aux Esclaves*; Grand Rapids, *Le Grande Rapide*; the Niangar [Niangua]; a second small Saline; Cave Creek, *La Rivière de la Caverne*; and Rivière Marie.

8

I had occasion in the foregoing chapter to mention those aborigines after whom the first discoverers named the Osage River. Even today they live undisturbed in the possession of the sources of this river and the prairies adjacent to them. The habitat of these Indians has been moved somewhat farther to the west, but on the whole this change could have no important influence on the mode of living and the customs of this nomadic people.

The hunt, constituting the main source of food for this nation, is limited because of the advancing European population and extends to the wooded regions bordering on the Missouri and its tributaries but not to the boundless prairies which support the bison. In former years the Osages could maintain their hunting rights only by incessant wars with other nations that lived farther east. The persistent trapping of beaver on the part of the Creoles has, of course, deprived the Indians more and more of an important source of income. If we consider that the attention of the aborigines was really attracted to this part of the hunt by the value which this kind of pelt commanded in the European trade, we must naturally conclude that the reduced trapping of beaver indeed deprived the Indian of an article of trade, but certainly not of a means of real subsistence.

The Osages perhaps may still be considered among those aborigines who enjoy ownership of the richest hunting grounds. The favorable position which their bravery and warlike disposition secures to them among the neighboring tribes serves the Osages as a strong protective wall against hostile attacks, as well as against the mutually intolerable incursions of still other tribes. And this must be regarded as one of the main causes of the decrease of the latter.

Almost all adjoining wild tribes were repulsed with great losses following their attacks on this powerful and courageous nation. The important defeats which the Kansas, the Fox, and Sac Indians, indeed even the Pawnees, had to suffer at their hands, allayed even in these mighty and vengeful tribes the blood lust which must be considered the evil demon of the Indians, and compelled these nations to negotiate pacts of peace and friendship with the Osages.[1] They won their victories almost always in the open field. Endowed by nature with striking size and bodily strength, the Osages, mounted on their spirited horses, despised every kind of treacherous attack by which, especially in small wars, the cunning savage seeks to gain victory.

The Osages were less cruel than the neighbors, and for this reason human sacrifices are unknown to them. In the area of his lodge an Osage rarely murders a captured enemy, but is satisfied with the scalp of his fallen opponent. He abhors the eating of human flesh. Obeying the authority of his chiefs and the counsels of his old men, he acquires with surprising ease the advantages which accrue to a regulated society, and it would not be easy to find an Indian nation to whom the bonds of social union are as dear and holy as to the Osages. Excepting the Pawnees, no Indian tribe venerates the Highest Being, the Master of Life, as fervently as they, and their priests are therefore held in high esteem. Indeed no Osage undertakes an important transaction without asking the advice of the priests and without preparing himself by fasting, severe penance, and sacrifice.

I return to the continuation of my diary. A mile from the mouth of the Osage a rocky chain of steep bluffs extends along the Missouri. The east bank, on the other hand, appears low and more inhabited. The circumnavigation of a low island, overgrown with thick willows which nearly touch the right bank, gave us much trouble, increased greatly by a strong current and a mass of driftwood. We had to spend the night near a small stream, the Rivière à Moreau, falsely called Morrow Creek by the Anglo-Americans.

Fortunately the night was clear and unusually cool. To our dismay, the river rose a foot, and we feared that the already high water would rise still higher. From noon until evening we had been able to make only three English miles. At daybreak of June 4 we reached an important island

---

[1] The Grand Pawnees were a principal obstacle to Osage pursuit of the bison on the western plains until 1820–21, but thereafter, with the Great and Little Osages claiming most of the old Pawnee lands in northern Oklahoma, the latter tribes were making two buffalo hunts a year, wintering on the Cimarron or the Salt Fork. George E. Hyde, *Pawnee Indians*, 123.

which is called Ile aux Cèdres.[2] This island is about three English miles long and one wide. It owes its name to Cedar Creek emptying opposite its point. On the hills through which the creek winds its way, the well-known tall juniper grows abundantly, constituting the only evergreen on the lower Missouri. The Creoles commonly call it *cedar*. [*Juniperus virginiana*, the eastern red cedar.]

In the afternoon the boat stopped at a so-called town, consisting of three wretched cabins, named Jefferson.[3] Some goods destined for this place were being unloaded, whereby much time was lost, so that the night came on and prevented us from continuing our journey. As the inhabitants of the place did not invite me to visit with them, and since it had got too late for me to explore this inhospitable region, I regretted so much more the loss of precious time.

Our crew, having borne so many dangers and having become wearied by privation and the slow progress of our journey, gladly accepted the opportunity to indulge overly in whisky, which was to be had in excessive amounts. The men, under the pretext of the aforementioned business, obeyed neither the orders of the faint-hearted Dutremble nor the admonitions of my companions and returned to the boat late in the evening dead drunk, some badly beaten up. In their intoxicated state they had been encouraged to fight and had been so thoroughly thrashed that I feared to find them unfit for work on the following day, and even could foresee that I might be forced to prolong my stay in this small but dangerous town.

Before we arrived at Jefferson, I had noticed that some of the crew had put on their better clothes, which caused me to suspect that it was their intention to stay on land for some time. Since the current along the bank where the town is located was very swift, I had suggested to the boat master that we lay by on the opposite bank, where there was a good landing place, unload the small amount of goods there, and let the inhabitants of the place worry about receiving them on that side. Dutremble was unwise enough to yield to the request of the crew and let my advice go unheeded.

When finally, in order to avoid serious trouble, we decided to inaugurate stern measures that evening, he got into a heated argument with the drunken men, the outcome of which would doubtless have been that he

[2] Cedar Island, about three miles in length and covered with heavy cedar growth, was long a landmark for Missouri travelers, Lewis and Clark, the Missouri Expedition of 1818-20, and Stephen H. Long, among others. It lay between Moreau River and present Jefferson City.

[3] This "so-called town" had been chosen as the capital of the newly admitted state of Missouri in 1821 but was not to become such until 1826. St. Charles, which had been the territorial capital, retained the honor of state capital until the latter date.

would have been attacked and mistreated if my men had not protected him and brought him through safely. Almost the entire night was passed amid such noisy scenes that, on the following morning, it was with the greatest difficulty that we got the crew into action. Not until eight o'clock did we get everything ready for our departure. By noon we reached Joncar Creek.[4] Close to the bank an island carries the same name. It is really only a sand-bar, separated during high water from the bank by a channel, and is at the most not more than a mile long.

We took advantage of the high water and rowed in the channel close along the bank. The sky was overcast, the air was very sultry, and the hills were enshrouded in clouds of fog. The thermometer rose to 88°, and clouds of mosquitoes increased the discomfort of the insufferable heat.

At the mouth of Joncar Creek the right bank forms a low point, called Pointe à Ducharme, which extends into the stream and only in the back-ground is it bounded by rocky bluffs. Its existence is subject to those catas-trophes by which the American rivers so easily change their form. This flat point of land incidentally occupies a distance of more than six English miles. The Petite Manitou runs through Pointe à Ducharme and empties into the Missouri a mile above the lower end of the Pointe.[5]

The left bank rises to moderately high hills, which extend as far as the mouth of Petite Bonne Femme, or Little Good Woman Creek,[6] and in front of it forms the Cap à l'Ail. This cape takes its name [ail = garlic] from the edible bulb which grows there in great abundance but which I did not have a chance to see myself. The whole ridge of the hill is sometimes called Côte à l'Ail, which name is probably correctly applicable only to the above-named point, where the river makes a turn to the west. The Indians, who love the taste of onion-like plants, have given this region a name which I could not ascertain despite all my efforts. Some tribes are said to visit these hills even now occasionally on their raids to gather onions, which thereby, of course, become even scarcer. I was sorry not to be able to see this prob-ably useful plant, whose cultivation might be worth-while fostering, but I had to hurry my journey as much as possible.

We traveled along Pointe à Ducharme and spent the night at an isolated dwelling. At the approach of night there came a brief but very powerful

---

[4] Joncar Creek = Jonquière Creek, called Zancare by Lewis and Clark (*Original Journals*, I, 39), empties into the Missouri from the south.

[5] Little Manitou, twenty-two and one-half miles above Cedar Island, located in present Moniteau County, Missouri, the county name being a corruption of "Manitou." It flows from the south into the Missouri.

[6] Petite Bonne Femme Creek is approximately eighteen and one-half miles above present Jefferson City, emptying into the Missouri from the north.

gust of wind, followed by complete calm. The dense dark clouds enshrouded the night in an awe-inspiring darkness, and toward morning the heavy vapors dissolved into just as heavy a rain. This lasted only until eight o'clock and caused a very welcome coolness, which unfortunately terminated shortly, giving way to heat just as oppressive.

The Missouri formed several small islands, which in summer are dry, but in the course of several years may grow into fairly large ones. They lie for the most part close to the bank and are formed by channels of the enormously wild river during periods when high water forces its way not only through the adjoining low lands but also through the apparently impenetrable forest.

Gradually such outbreaks make deep and permanent beds, which, after a distance of several miles, flow back into the main stream. The uprooted trunks of giant trees soon decay in the moist location and are covered with layers of clay by succeeding floods. On such ground cottonwoods and willows soon prosper, their rapid growth being hastened by the fertile soil. Soon the forest, mixed with bushes and herbaceous plants, again assumes its former dense form.

The flat banks, be they large or small, even the islands, which at low water are connected with the bank and are not overgrown with tall timber, were called *battures* by the Canadians and the French of New France, and also by the first white inhabitants of Missouri and the first discoverers.

If, however, the banks are covered with tall timber they are called *côtes basses*. In general I am making use of the terminology used by the Creole hunters for rivers, hills, etc. They either have reference to historical data which mark the first discovery of the land, or are of genuine Indian origin. The newly immigrated Anglo-Americans and Irish, as is well known, are often outcasts from the population of the eastern states who have escaped the restraints of a well organized government. They sneak their way almost without means into the new states. In part too ignorant to understand the names that have been given to places, or too selfish to retain them, they distort them. In this perversion of names they have their equal only in the ancient Romans, and in recent times the French.

The government has bought from the Indians the greater part of the land along the Missouri and the Osage as far west as the Kansas, and from the little Liberty Creek east as far as Prairie du Feu. A large number of such ne'er-do-wells as mentioned above and much more ably described by several writers, especially Cooper, than I ever could, who failed in their former settlements, hoped to find a new Eldorado in the extensive possessions of the United States along the Missouri and Mississippi. In this, these roving loafers found the boon of a convenient region where they could withdraw from the restraints of law and order, with which they so long had been at odds.

From St. Charles to the Kansas, the entire area along the Missouri and all its large and small tributaries has been abused by such people during the last twenty years. Here and there, however, one finds better individuals, who have sold their land holdings in the east and have come west to buy new land. These must be regarded as useful citizens of the state. Such settlers are easily recognizable by their fertile fields, better homes, and considerable livestock. However, their number is small in comparison with those who took up land without asking the government or paying for it. Except for the clothing and the pale white complexion by which the new arrivals are easily distinguished from the old Creole population, the newcomers might be taken by the traveler for a wild tribe, different from the aborigines, whose main characteristics and dark sides of their being were indolence, a decided inclination to dishonesty, drunkenness, and revengefulness. Hospitality, that quality characterizing all humankind and appearing to be sacred to the wildest savages of all lands, seems to be completely foreign to them. I do not recall one instance of having met with a single manifestation of sympathetic feeling, especially among the Irish of the western region.

At noon we stopped at the termination of Pointe à Duchârme. The hills on the opposite bank began to lose themselves in Cap à l'Ail, where they disappear entirely. High hills rise, on the other hand, on the right bank and seem to be separated from the stream by narrow strips of low land or by scattered rocky parts. A large stone mass towers thirty feet above the water close to the bank. It is a blunt cone with a level top, fifty feet in circumference. During high water it constitutes a dangerous hazard to navigation, and by no great margin our boat was nearly split in two on it.

Opposite this rock is the mouth of La Petite Bonne Femme. It is rather wide and navigable to small boats for some forty miles. Originating on the prairie, it waters an important stretch of forest. The left bank hereabout becomes low, and beyond the above-mentioned conical rock the bluffs suddenly cease as if cut off, giving way to level land densely overgrown with virgin forest. At its beginning we halted on the evening of the fifth, after making only six English miles. Since the water had gone down noticeably, it would have been an easy matter to make a much greater day's journey, especially since several intervals of fine wind might have been utilized if the crew had not been so obstinate.

After the last incident of insubordination, the spirit of insolence and disobedience against the boat-master had increased to such an extent that the navigation of the boat depended more on the will of the crew than on that of Dutremble.

Every noon and night, camp was determined by the crew, who stopped any time that it suited them, and if the officer interposed objection he was attacked and intimidated with the vilest and most abusive words. The water in the hold of the boat, which had accumulated through seepage and frequent showers, disseminated a pestilential stench. In vain we applied all our eloquence to induce the crew to dip out the tepid water. Caillou and old de Rouain in the end had to perform this repulsive task themselves, so that it might be possible to sleep in the boat and to protect the goods in the vessel against spoilage.

The hunters had gone out at noon despite the rain. Mine came so near a rattlesnake that he was almost bitten. In damp weather these snakes do not rattle at all or so imperceptibly that one is hardly warned by them. Their mating season comes in May and June, when they are even more dangerous. My hunter had the courage to seize this large rattlesnake. It was a real *Crotalus horridus*, Linn., which has on a gray background a very distinct pattern showing a black zigzag running stripe on its back. The reptile measured five feet three inches in length, six inches in circumference, and had thirteen rattles.

On the morning of June 7 we could not start until nine o'clock. The crew offered as an excuse the fact that during the night it had rained heavily, whereby the bank had been too slippery to permit pulling the boat by the tow-line. Since at the beginning of the journey the crew had performed a like duty under more trying circumstances, I could not understand the real cause for this delay. All morning, and also a good part of the day and night, the crew played cards. Having no money, they played for whisky, which was issued to them daily in certain portions, and the result was that the winners got drunk, while the losers, to whom the beverage by habit had become a necessity, gave vent to their displeasure by the most violent utterances. They then begged for an extra issue of whisky, and the boat-master on several occasions had been so weak as to give in. Had I not interfered with a firm hand there would have been no end to this mischief. I promised the crew an extra amount from my own supply on condition that they should abstain from card playing and work diligently. Otherwise I threatened to turn over those whom I knew to be the instigators of the trouble to the sheriff in Franklin for punishment. Since the men recognized that I was in earnest, the threat worked, at least as long as the boat was in the state of Missouri.

We traveled slowly along a bank but after we had gone scarcely two miles we had to stop, because of heavy rain, at the northern end of a small island called Petite Bonne Femme. After an hour the clouds scattered and our journey was continued. I saw an isolated cabin whose inhabitants were occupied in ferrying people and livestock across the river. I again made the observation that day that the left bank of the Missouri was much more settled than the right. In the afternoon it again rained so hard for an hour that the hold of the boat was immediately filled with water. Thus we were held up once more for several hours. At four o'clock we rowed around the Little Manitou, a rock of more than one hundred feet in height and fifty feet in width whose smooth steep walls were decorated with Indian paintings and pictures of idols.[7]

Close to it an unimportant creek flows into the river. A picturesque little island in the middle of the Missouri increases the romantic touch of this peculiar region, which bears the genuine stamp of a virgin America, until now spared the ax of the settler, still invested with the garb of long past centuries.

A rather long, flat region begins at the mouth of the little stream and extends in the direction of the river bank. As is usual after a heavy downpour, the sky became very clear and bright in the evening, and we were still able to make four miles. In the background rose beautifully shaped hills separated from the river by a not very wide plain covered with truly giant trees. Despite several showers, the river fell several feet during the night.

Earlier than usual on June 8, we started traveling around the bend of the river, called Pointe à Manitou. Having to pass through quantities of driftwood heaped against the bank, and because of a contrary north wind, we had to stop at an island called Ile du Rocher Percé.[8] The wind blew the whole day with great force from a direction opposite to our course. The only advantage which we had from it was that we had no mosquitoes. It was impossible to move ahead in any way; all our efforts were frustrated by the storm, which abated only that evening. I wanted to use the afternoon by going on the hunt with the hunters, but we all soon returned empty-handed.

During the night the storm died down completely, and on the following morning the sun greeted us with unusual splendor. The sight of fine

[7] Both Lewis and Clark (*Original Journals*, I, 40) and Surgeon Gale (*The Missouri Expedition*, 16) wrote of these "uncouth paintings," respectively in 1804 and 1818.

[8] Roche Percée, or Split Rock, names also for the crag nearby, the island, and the creek emptying into the Missouri from the north in Boone County. Duke Paul's rendering, *Rocher Percé*, Split Crag, is etymologically more nearly correct. In the unfortunate way of mapmakers, the stream is now Perche Creek.

weather induced me to use all my persuasive power to urge the crew to make an early start. We succeeded in covering four miles before our customary breakfast time. We were at this hour near a small house at the end of a sandbar which extends to the Little Manitou and derives its name from this rock.

At this place there is a large island located in the middle of the river which is called Ile du Rocher Percé. This island is very low, overgrown with fine trees, nettles as tall as a man, and with *Equisetum* [horse tails]. During the night the river had fallen a foot and a half and it was to be expected that the Missouri would soon recede to its average water level. In the background of the above-mentioned dwelling a rugged and wild chain of rocky hills rises, hardly a mile long, and at last drops abruptly into the river on the right bank.

My men caught a dainty heron[9] scarcely as large as our *Ardea minuta*, and so extremely vicious that we could hardly come near it. This bird stayed alive a long time, took the food we offered him, and finally became quite tame. On that same morning we dug a marmot out of its den. Extraordinarily large, it weighed about fifteen pounds and was a pregnant female whose young were not yet fully matured. The meat of this American marmot is fat and edible. It and that of the squirrel were a desirable food for me.[10]

When we had reached the end of the chain of hills we passed along a low bank overgrown with cottonwoods. The age of the cottonwoods apparently indicated that the land had been but recently reclaimed from the river. In the background rose taller and thicker trees, and among the cottonwoods other varieties of timber intermingled. This bank, formerly inundated, now stood six feet above the water. Here and there I observed separate sandbars and shallows visible above the surface of the water. From the side where I saw the island in question, I take it to be entirely grown over with timber and perhaps uninhabited, because it is subject to periodic inundations.

The left bank of the Missouri is hilly in part, throughout strewn with huge boulders and quite expressive of the generally wild, rough character of this region. Opposite the northern end of the island is the pierced rock,

---

[9] *Author*: Head, upper part of neck, and back were dark cinnamon brown, wings somewhat lighter colored in the middle. The throat and head feathers white and long, a few with a longitudinal stripe of darker color. On the breast a broad, dark brownish ring, the feathers with a light border on the tips. Belly white. Beak and iris of the eye yellow. Feet light green, length sixteen inches. *Ardea exilis*, Wils. [George Miksch Sutton suggests an imperfect description of the least bittern, that is *Ardea exilis* Wilson = *Ixobrychus exilis*, as described from Jamaica by Gmelin.]

[10] *Marmota monax*, the familiar woodchuck of the American areas east of the dry plains.

Rocher Percé, and in my opinion a quite unimportant group of rocks, representing to the explorer no other curiosity than a cave passing through the point of a rock, one of the most unimportant formations of this kind and perhaps a few paces long.

At a distance of three miles from the island the river turns to the west, and the chain of hills, to which Rocher Percé belongs, trends toward the north. Too, the left bank flattens out to a low region, losing its above mentioned romantic character.

Now traveling for a distance of almost three English miles between two completely level banks, I fancied transference to the lower Mississippi country whose primeval forest was but little different from this present one. Soon, however, I saw high bluffs sinking steep and abruptly into the Missouri, at the foot of which enormous masses of water broke with tremendous force. As the crew had made only a short halt at noon, this day's journey made up, in a measure, for the previous day, which had been almost completely lost. The finest weather favored the journey, and a gentle but cool north wind, by reducing the temperature, made the strenuous work easier.

In the afternoon about four o'clock, I was surprised in a pleasing manner. We sighted a vessel in the distance coming down the river and recognized it at once as an Indian pirogue. With the swiftness of an arrow the boat, occupied by naked forms, came straight towards us. At a distance of two hundred paces an Indian sitting at the bow arose and with upraised arms made the sign of peace customary among these people. A moment later the pirogue laid by on the right side of our boat.

There were twenty well-armed Indian warriors of the Iowa Tribe[11] and with them a white interpreter. By signs the Indians made us understand the purpose of their journey. They were on the way to St. Louis to nego-

---

[11] *Author*: This tribe of Indians calls itself in their own language Pa-cho-sché. [Pa-hodje, according to Maximilian zu Wied, *Reise*.] They are now, as will be shown in the course of the story, united with their kinsmen, the Otos, Ouac-toc-ta-ta, in one village on the Platte (Rivière Platte). But a few bands of this tribe, which is accused of treachery, still roam along the Grand (Grande Rivière) and along the Missouri.

[Here and elsewhere Duke Paul has a firm grasp of certain Indian language keys and linguistic relationships. The Iowas are, along with the Missourias, kinsmen of the Otos, with whom they form the Chiwere division of the Siouan family. All three, according to tribal tradition, originated in the Winnebago Tribe. In Duke Paul's time (1822–1824), the Iowas were on the Platte and the Grand Nemaha rivers, later removing (1829) to the Platte River, Iowa, a few miles above the Missouri line. Lewis and Clark (*Original Journals*, VI, 91–92) dealt with them rather thoroughly. Duke Paul's "Ouac-toc-ta-ta" for Otos, like "Pa-cho-sché" for Iowas, may owe something to Edwin James, *Long Expedition*, which has it variously, "Wahtohtata," "Wah-tok-ta-ta." But the Duke's own phonetic renderings are sufficiently unnoted hitherto to spring from his original investigations.]

tiate with the government officials regarding several disputed points. The truth of this declaration and the friendly intention of the Indians was confirmed by the interpreter. The boat's crew, which at first sight of the Indians had hastily seized their arms and had shown no slight fear, began to be calmed. Despite the admonitions of old de Rouain, who himself looked by no means courageous, they began, one after the other, to lay aside their guns and recover from their surprise. This seemed to me a very strange occurrence, since I had believed that the presence of a few armed redskins should be nothing new to a class of men who had spent most of their lives in the American wilderness.

All our warlike precautions seemed to have failed completely to make an impression on the Indian warriors. None of them showed the least mistrust, nor the slightest indication of a feeling that might betray fear. Had I not heard so much of the art, peculiar to these wild tribes, of concealing the strongest emotions and the most intense passions behind an apparently perfectly calm facial expression and a secure outer bearing, I should have been forced to believe that all our precautionary measures had totally escaped their attention, or that they attributed them entirely to different reasons than their own sudden appearance. Nevertheless it did not escape my attention that the looks of the chiefs, despite their pretended indifference, revealed the hearty contempt which must arise in the soul of every fearless person when he sees opponents on whose faces are imprinted the traces of the greatest cowardice.

The Indians, whose purpose it was to obtain some information from us and whose entire position and time of their visit revealed nothing hostile, remained sitting motionless, hands resting on their paddles. Among them were two high chiefs and several warriors distinguished by their bravery.

As I learned later, the chiefs were called Pee-lan, the Crane, and Wa-mo-no-kee, the Thief. The former was the one who had made the sign of peace and he alone carried on the conversation through the interpreter. He addressed himself to me and to Caillou, as he perhaps took us to be the ones of highest rank.

Because they give some concept of the sparing speech of the Indians, I repeat in essense his words, "The warriors of the Pa-cho-sché have left their brothers and have come down the Mother of Rivers to visit and smoke with their father in the great village of the Long Knives. Blood had flowed, but now the tomahawk is buried under the branches of the sycamore. Our father will smoke with his red children, and will not let them return home with empty hands."

Thereupon he extended his hand to us and with every handshake he repeated the brief expression, "How."

Not until then did the other Indians rise slowly and one after the other extended to us his hand. All the warriors were, as mentioned before, completely naked except for a leather belt through which was drawn a strip of blue cloth to cover the private parts. The color of their bodies was the darkest red, and most of them had their hair shorn smooth except for a tuft at the back. The rims of the ears were perforated in four places, from which hung small sticks of porcelain and small glass rods. Among other articles of decoration were tobacco pouches made from the skins of several skunks (*Mephitis*), quite nicely decorated with embroidery of porcupine quills.

The Indians did not have with them any weapons other than bows and arrows, tomahawks, and knives. The bows were quite simple, some made of yellow wood of a yet undetermined variety of tree of the family of Anonaceae, which is no less beautiful than mahogany, and others made of ash and walnut wood with strings of artistically twisted sinews of deer. The quivers were of plain leather tanned brown, containing about one hundred arrows made of ordinary arrow-wood (*Coruns florida*, Linn, commonly called *bois de flèche*), supplied with iron tips and adorned with turkey feathers. The iron tips constituting the weaponry of the arrows were rather skillfully wrought by the Indians from old knife blades and iron tires. The latter, as all iron, has a great value among them and are artistically worked over. Despite the scantiest tools, often consisting merely of stone implements, the Indians are skilled smiths and know how to make many household articles themselves.[12]

The pirogue in which the Iowas traveled downstream was made of hollowed-out logs, very skillfully tied together, so that one could, if he desired, separate them in an instant. The canoes which are used for lighter traffic on the streams of northwestern America are usually hewn from the trunk of the Canadian cottonwood, a piece of work requiring great skill but which nevertheless can be performed in a day by a few fast working men. So the tree, which in the morning still stood in all its leafy splendor, that evening already cuts through the swiftly flowing currents. Canoes are vessels in which only a few persons can find room. A pirogue, however,

---

[12] Until they were closed in 1822, government factories, or trading posts, among the Indians stocked, among other items, scalping knives, rifles and other firearms, gun powder, beads, wampum, cloth, thread, awls, brass bells, blankets, bar and sheet iron, vermillion, and other common items for wilderness life and warfare. The private factories, whose interests largely dictated the closing of the government factory system, traded similarly, and both sets of agencies received furs and peltries, beeswax, tallow, and a few other items in exchange for their trade goods. Thomas L. McKenney to Henry Johnson, Chairman of the Committee on Indian Affairs, January 23, 1822, in *American State Papers, Indian Affairs*, 17 Cong., 1 sess. (Washington, 1834), II, 329–37.

holds many persons, and sometimes it too consists of only one log. But even the primeval forests of the Missouri and Mississippi furnish rarely such giant forest trophies.

From the earliest times, since the Europeans have made the acquaintance of the Iowas and other tribes related to them along the Mississippi and the Illinois rivers, complaints were heard concerning the faithless, cruel, and thieving character of these savages. Ultimately this must lead to the complete extermination of their nation. They usually break every peace shortly after it is made and begin hostilities with unheard of cruelty.

This once numerous nation, which was constantly involved in wars with many enemies, was reduced, even at the time of my stay in America, to about two hundred members; I had the opportunity of seeing the entire remnant of these people, either at the trading posts of the French Missouri Company near Fort Atkinson or in the settlement of the Otos on the Platte.[13]

Through the interpreter who accompanied the chiefs to St. Louis I learned the true reason which induced these Indians to undertake a journey so incompatible with the customs of their tribe. The Iowas, attacking and robbing moving American families near Franklin, had carried away several young women. Threatened with war by the governor, the leading men of the tribe saw themselves compelled to put aside their pride and beg the General Intendant [General William Clark] for clemency, to avert complete annihilation of the tribe.

The Iowas owe their extrication to the humane character of General Clarke and the beneficent inclination which the government of the American Union of States holds in regard to the already weakened Indian nations.

The timidity of old de Rouain changed to fright and at first amused me not a little. This was soon explained by the observation that the old man had discovered among the warriors acquaintances who may have awakened unpleasant recollections in his soul. He poured out a long recital which was everything but complimentary to the Iowas and bore the stamp of exaggeration founded on cowardice. Being acquainted with the language of the Pa-cho-sché and knowing himself in perfect safety, he made the most useless and ridiculous reproaches to the warriors, even committing the indiscretion of threatening several with death should he encounter them in the forest.[14]

---

[13] Lewis and Clark estimated their number in 1804 at eight hundred; in 1829, the Secretary of War placed them at one thousand; the least round figure, that of George Catlin in 1836, is 992.

[14] In his accounting to the U.S. House of Representatives for the years 1820–1822,

This was intended especially for an elderly warrior with sinister and malicious eyes. In earlier times he had been the leader of a strong war party which had mortally wounded de Rouain's brother during a raid. Rouain himself had fallen into the hands of the Indians. Refraining from taking his life, they followed a custom common among most of the tribes of North America, contenting themselves with each giving him a blow across the shoulders with a red painted stick. This procedure is not to be regarded as an act of cruelty but is only a superstitious custom of these nomadic warriors. Renowned warriors are contented to touch their opponent slightly. The playfulness of the young men, inspired perhaps by the odd appearance of de Rouain, was not satisfied with merely letting it be a touch. At last de Rouain was left almost dead in the forest. The threats with which the gray-haired old man gave vent to his feelings, however, completely failed of their purpose, for the one to whom they were addressed listened with incomparable calmness to what Baptiste had to say. After the latter had scolded in unbecoming manner for a good half hour, the warrior replied coldly,

"My father is mistaken. The scalp of his brother is not the medicine pouch of his friend."[15]

Could a feeling of compassion have found room in the soul of the warrior I believe that the frail and pitiable exterior of de Rouain would have touched him. The Indian rarely forgives an insult that is done him and even though he is complete master of the art of enduring in silence, nevertheless, in secret he broods apparently only on vengeance, though he may have to postpone it for a long time. On the other hand the Indian feels an unbounded respect for old age which almost borders on superstition. He respects the gray hair even of an enemy and never will offend an old person with words, even though the white hair of the latter may not protect him from a violent death. Apparently to this, de Rouain, who is nearly ninety, owed the lenient treatment of the warrior.

The Iowas offered me some of their weapons and other things of slight value in exchange for brandy. I did not consider it advisable to make this trade since I foresaw harmful consequences. After I had distributed a few small presents and tobacco among the Indians they departed from us, seemingly satisfied.

former Territorial Governor William Clark, ex officio Superintendent of Indian Affairs for Missouri, listed "Francis Derouin" as a payee "for services as interpreter for two days, $3.00." *Ibid.*, II, 292.

[15] *Author:* The French Creoles call the leather pouch in which the Indians keep the articles necessary for their mystical worship, *sac de médecine*. I make bold to translate this word literally, with the comment that such objects are skins of animals, bones, skulls, scalps, pipes, wampum, etc.

At five o'clock we passed a small saline creek [La Petite Saline] which would not arouse the interest of the traveler except for its large content of salt, which might in time make it quite valuable. From now on the stream was bordered by long, low banks, *battures*, or high, timber covered land, *côtes basses*, alternating with one another. The water in the Missouri had fallen so much that I could notice many places where the bottom of the river bed became visible and even formed sandbars. In many places the water was so shallow that even our flat-bottomed boat could hardly be pushed ahead, and only with the aid of poles. With great difficulty and strenuous work, we succeeded in making two miles beyond the saline creek, and in the night we had to endure a slight rain with a sultriness which attracted an insufferable number of flies and mosquitoes. Despite the utmost weariness we could not sleep.

The morning of the tenth requited us, for the air became cool, and by poling and rowing we had arrived at an island, the Ile du Grand Manitou, whose banks consist of many shelves. It is two miles long but narrow and partially overgrown with cottonwoods. At eleven o'clock we reached the point of this island. I estimated the distance from this point to the saline creek at five English miles. At daybreak the hunters started out and came back with a fallow deer. On the hooks which I had set out a fine fish of the sheat-fish family was caught. I took it to be a *Cataphractus costatus*, one which I had not seen until then. Of the scaly fish, several excellent kinds are found in the waters of the northwest of America.[16] All fish of prey, their scales, often forming an impenetrable armor over the whole body, are so strong that they can resist the effect of firearms.

Our journey continued along the right bank, which remained low from shallow water. The left bank on the other hand rose to high bluffs sloping abruptly into the water. These bluffs contain many caves and clefts. This

[16] *Author*: Among others, there belong to the family of bill-fishes an as yet undescribed scaly bone fish, *Lepisosteus*. The bill is twice as long as the skull, somewhat turned up and very pointed. The upper jawbone is almost flat, the lower one shorter than the upper. The head is scarcely half as long as the body. The scales are rhomboid, indented, in parallel rows, and form sharp points at the caudal fin. The first rays of the ventral fins form a double saw. The shape of the fish resembles the shark and its length is three feet. The color is bluish, shading into milk white. In the Mississippi.

[The sheatfishes, *supra*, are more properly the Old World catfishes. In all likelihood the fish which the author caught was one of the smooth-skinned New World catfishes.

[The bill-fishes the author refers to are of the genus *Lepidosteus*, of which *L. osseus* is the long-nosed variety, *L. platystomus* the short-nosed. Both are garpikes. The alligator gar, *L. tristaechus*, which attains twenty feet or more and is common in the streams feeding into the Gulf of Mexico, is notably the species requiring gunshot to be killed.]

row of hills, called La Côte du Grand Manitou, extends six English miles along the stream to the mouth of a creek.

By evening we were opposite the end of this chain of hills. Here the Missouri makes a sharp curve to the west, and the already low left bank of the river changes suddenly into shallows, so that our boat touched bottom, although it drew only two feet of water. The yellowish gray color of the water of the Missouri, impregnated with clay, made it impossible to recognize such places, and the sounding lead usually leaves the boatman in the lurch in a swiftly flowing current, with the boat moving slowly upstream. After the boat had been set afloat again, it nevertheless seemed impossible to get directly across the stream to the deep water along the rocky bank. With the greatest difficulty we had passed rapids hard by the bank, and now we had to recross it with the current greatly endangering our lives.

The current carried us swift as an arrow toward a pile of driftwood dominated by a giant sycamore trunk lying in the way of our boat. With a loud roar, the river, running in short, high waves, leaped in a huge surf over all objects barring its course. The only outlet the water could find was among the piled up debris, for in the bed the rapids created many whirlpools. As if by a miracle the boat turned through the most dangerous places without striking the driftwood. Finally, far below the rapids, we reached the deep and quieter channel on the opposite bank of high and rocky leaning cliffs. As a precaution I had caused my best and most necessary things to be taken on land, since Caillou, whose expert knowledge had been shown anew on this occasion, had earlier called my attention to the great danger. My concern was therefore centered only on those men whose services required their presence on the vessel, several of whom could not swim.

Without delay we once more rowed upstream, after the crew had succeeded in turning the boat and steering against the current. With much exertion another mile was made, at which point we halted at a suitable place. I scarcely recall having spent a more magnificent evening in the New World than that which followed this painfully lived-through day. The sun set in a most beautiful purple, and a gentle east wind cooled the air so completely that even the mosquitoes had to give up their restless activity.

Very early on the morning of June 11, a strong favoring wind rose, lasting several hours and bringing us soon to the Big Manitou. Here we could see the end of a chain of hills of the same name. A rock decorated with genuine Indian painting throws a weak light on the crude conceptions of the idolatrous worship of the wild aborigines. Here the Indians occasionally bring sacrifices to an evil being whom they fear,[17] and in outline the idol in symbolic form seems to assume the shape of an animal. Judging from the effect which the weather has had on the coloring material, it clearly pointed to a remote time, a time when this mass of stone served the aborigines for the performance of their mystic worship. It even seemed to me as if the painting had been frequently renewed, and the paint on several other better preserved drawings was especially fresh and bright. With considerable skill and proportion, they quite clearly represent battles and hunting expeditions of the aborigines.

Although all drawings of this kind have a peculiar character, it cannot be denied that in the stiff forms, which seem distinctive of all primitive specimens of art, there has been developed a certain talent which from ancient times characterizes most of the primitive peoples. It is expressed in the imitation of objects, especially those of hieroglyphic nature, and gives occasion to important historical study regarding the origin and distribution of the human race.[18]

We again crossed the stream at the nearby island called Ile de la Grande Bonne Femme on the right bank of the river. Here we encountered a plague of a new and most peculiar kind. Entire billions of butterflies belonging to the European *Aegeria* covered the vessel and all objects, hindering almost every activity in that they ceaselessly darkened our eyes and hands, even clinging fast to our nostrils and flying into our mouths while we spoke or breathed.

In the hot belt of the New World this phenomenon seems to occur more frequently. While navigating with difficulty along the south side of the island of Cuba in May, 1494, Christopher Columbus stated that he had met with a like phenomenon. I myself recall having seen huge swarms of migrating butterflies on the swampy coast of Cuba, especially in the region of Battayano. In all probability these insects had but recently escaped from

---

[17] *Author*: This evil spirit is called among the tribes which speak the language of the Osages, *Pi-scherti Ua-kanda*, or *Ua-kanda Pische*, in contrast to the good spirit or master of life, *Ua-kanda*. [See also John Joseph Mathews, *The Osages*, 28ff.]

[18] Cf. Robert H. Lowie, *Primitive Society*; James Mooney, *Calendar History of the Kiowa Indians* (*Nineteenth Annual Report*, Bureau of American Ethnology, Washington, 1898); Karen Daniels Petersen, *Plains Indian Art From Fort Marion*; Peter John Powell, *Sweet Medicine: The Continuing Role of the Sacred Arrows, the Sun Dance, and the Sacred Buffalo Hat in Northern Cheyenne History*.

For the author's reference to "stiff forms" (absence of perspective), cf. Oscar Brousse Jacobson, *Kiowa Indian Art: Watercolor Paintings in Color by the Indians of Oklahoma* (Nice, France, Szwedzicki, 1929); and Jacobson and Jeanne d'Ucel, *Les Peintures Indiens d'Amerique* (Nice, Szwedzicki, 1950).

Paul Wilhelm, Duke of Württemberg
(*Courtesy Stadt Bad Mergentheim*)

Sioux Camp, watercolor, probably by Rosshirt from suggestions by
Duke Paul of Württemberg
(*Courtesy Stadt Bad Mergentheim*)

Mackinaw or cordelle boat on the Missouri
(*Courtesy Missouri Historical Society*)

General William Clark, by Gilbert Stuart
(*Courtesy of Mrs. Daniel R. Russell*)

Metea of the Potawatomis
(From Thomas L. McKenney and James Hall,
History of the Indian Tribes of North America)

Above: Wy-eeyo-gah, Iowa.
Below: Black Hawk, Sauk
(From George Catlin, *Letters and Notes
on the Manners, Customs, and Condition
of the North American Indians*, plates
130 and 283)

Horse Chief, Grand Pawnee
(From George Catlin, *Letters and Notes on the Manners,
Customs, and Condition of the North American Indians,*
plate 138)

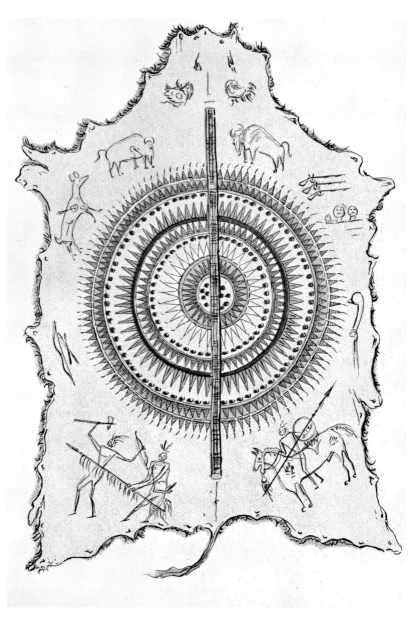

Mandan buffalo robe
(From George Catlin, *Letters and Notes on the Manners, Customs, and Condition of the North American Indians*, plate 312)

their chrysalis, and since they had metamorphosed as a community they had not yet had time to disperse.

About noon we were opposite the mouth of the small La Bonne Femme River, which should not be confused with the Petite Bonne Femme.[19] The right bank of the Missouri changed here to moderately high rows of bluffs perhaps measuring no more than one hundred feet in height. The sun burned intensely, with no breeze, and the thermometer rose to 88° in the shade. However, with that the air was clearer and the heat more tolerable than on sultry days with lower readings on the thermometer.

The left bank is low, and near it, at the mouth of the Grande Bonne Femme (Big Good Women Creek), are several small islands overgrown with willows.

In the afternoon at five o'clock the boat reached Franklin, a small, but not entirely unimportant, town where I noticed only two well-built houses at the time. All the rest were merely wooden shacks.[20] This town on the left bank of the Missouri counted about five hundred inhabitants, mostly Anglo-Americans and Irish. In the midst of wild aborigines and surrounded by forests, its location was in many respects very much exposed to the attacks of the wild hordes, and the carelessness of the inhabitants showed itself only too plainly by the few measures that have been taken for the security of the place.

The locations of newly built towns, removed from the mouths of the

[19] Bonne Femme Creek of today empties into the Missouri at Franklin Island, Howard County, Missouri.

[20] Franklin's antiquity and appearance in its early days have been matters of differing opinion. When Brackenridge visited the area in 1811, he found a "flourishing settlement," on the north bank of the Missouri in Howard County, part of an extensive farming area stretching up and down the river for five or six miles in each direction. Braxton Cooper, a "worthy man," who with his father and brothers presided over the salt works near the mouth of the Mine (now the Lamine) River, flowing into the Missouri some six miles west of a settlement on the south bank to be known as Boonville, was his host during a short stay. The latter settlement had been founded a year before (in 1810) and consisted of seventy-five families, "the greater part living on the bank of the river, in the space of four or five miles" in Cooper County. Franklin was to be lost to floods, New Franklin downstream taking its place.

In what follows in Duke Paul's narrative, it may be kept in mind that the settlers on both banks of the river, at Franklin and at Boonville, were principally of Irish and Anglo-American stock from Kentucky, devotees of a whisky now known round the world. Lewis and Clark, Brackenridge, and Gale all wrote enthusiastically of the land, the soil, and the future of farming in the area. It came to be known as the Boon's Lick Country, more closely associated with the efforts of Daniel Boone's two sons, Nathan and Daniel Morgan Boone, than with the old frontiersman himself. The two sons had worked the salt springs in the neighborhood as early as 1807, at Salt Creek west of Franklin. H. M. Brackenridge, "Journal," in *Views of Louisiana*, 210–11; Gale, *The Missouri Expedition*, 18.

large tributaries of the Missouri, are, in my opinion, poorly chosen, for these towns are usually inhabited by merchants, who sooner or later may leave if the population and trade should increase on the Osage or the Kansas.

On the right bank atop a high cliff opposite Franklin are found a few scattered cabins, whose inhabitants, jealous of Franklin, hold their settlement to be a town and named it Boonville. Hardly an hour had elapsed after our arrival until the effects of the near-by saloons were clearly seen. The entire crew was drunk and created much noise. Under the circumstances it is incomprehensible to me that we had no accident because gunpowder constituted the main portion of our ship's load, and the indiscriminate use of pipes could have caused an explosion at any moment.

I had decided to go on land the following morning, since neither the town nor the inhabitants appeared very inviting. Soon, however, I received visits from all sorts of stupidly bold and curious people addressing me with all manner of indiscreet questions. Their intention seemed to be to make fun of me as a stranger. When they saw that they did not gain their purpose, they committed other incivilities and even tried to gain possession of my papers and things while they decried me as an adventurer and spy.

In order to rid me of these unpleasant guests, my valet in the meantime interested Caillou and a few boat hands, who were not yet entirely drunk, in my behalf, requesting the obtrusive company, with whom I was engaged in a lively discussion, to return to shore. The Franklinites did not seem inclined to do so good naturedly.

Speaking again in my own behalf, I was finally lucky in persuading both parties to leave the boat and settle their affair on land. A terrible fight resulted. During this time a Frenchman, Mr. Benouai from Bordeaux, a well disposed man, came on board to quiet me. Benouai promised the full protection of the law if I would stop at his house. He urged me not to accept an invitation of the young people who, under the pretext of friendship, would try to take me to their tavern in order to start a quarrel there. He also advised me not to leave the boat unarmed. Soon recognizing the sincerity of his intentions, I promised the obliging Frenchman a visit on the following day.

Under the pretext of reconciliation, two persons came to me and, after offering some awkward apologies, requested me to accompany them to the boarding house to celebrate a feast of reconciliation. At first I excused myself in a polite manner, but when they became more and more insistent and laid hands on me, I chased them from the boat amid the uproarious laughter of their comrades. As this decisive manner seemed genuinely popular with the Franklinites, they let the affair stop there.

Since the journey by water went extremely slowly, I resolved to travel by land to the Kansas and await the arrival of the boat there. From Franklin a passable road leads to the mouth of this great river, where all further white population ceases and only a few wild people live. There the traveler can view nature in her virgin state, unchanged. I longed very much for these wildernesses because of the chances of better hunting and the abundance of animals of all kinds.

Even though the habitations of civilized people are few and far apart, all freedom loving animals retreat from them to the completely uninhabited regions, especially in the western part of North America, where such regions are still so numerous. In the populated countries of our civilized Europe, the wild animals find but little real solitude and for this reason they stay in uninhabited and lonely forests. There their survival is even protected and no hindrance is placed in their way, but some die out entirely, as many beasts of prey have done when existence is incompatible with the nearness of man and such creatures as are useful to him.

To prepare for my land journey I went to town early on June 12, accompanied by Caillou, and made my way to the house of Mr. Benouai. Even on the day before, he had endeavored to procure a few horses for me. Saddle horses could not be provided here, as was the case in St. Louis, and only weak, worn-out animals were available. I had to be content to take an extremely wretched and frail one-horse cart (which on the morning of my departure was hastily repaired with nails) to make a journey of over sixty hours along a very poorly kept road, or more correctly stated, to walk this distance.

There was just room enough in the cart for the driver and my very scant baggage. A small boy of fourteen dared to drive this conveyance through an unknown wilderness, where dwellings are often many miles apart. I had left my servant on board the boat to watch my property and my collections, which caused me great worry.

At half past ten we finally started to move out, despite intense heat and a hot southeast wind. The rough trail, dignified with the name of road, was so poorly defined that the traveler often lost it from sight altogether, and it contained so many trees broken off by the wind and so many swampy places that I often spent hours in overcoming these obstacles in our path.

Before one reaches the Kansas River, the Missouri must be crossed twice, the first time at Pierre de la Flèche, and the second in the neighborhood of Tabeau Creek.[21] The road to Pierre de la Flèche by way of the river, a distance of twelve English miles from Franklin, led through a sparsely

[21] Pierre de la Flèche, now Arrow Rock, is in Saline County on the southwest bank of the Missouri, taking its name from the stone used by the Indians for arrow-making. Pierre de

inhabited region. For the first two miles the way was passable. The forests consisted of beautiful trees spaced apart and a dense composite undergrowth of herb-like plants. Magnificent groups of trees were created by the numerous sycamores mixed with luxuriant gleditsia, locust, ashes, and oaks.[22]

A swamp hard by the road bordered the latter for more than an English mile. This stagnant water was covered with aquatic plants of the genus *Typha*, *Potamogeton*, and *Rumex*. A beautiful flowering Nymphaea also delighted my eye.[23] Countless water fowls took wing in fright and a huge flock of *Anas sponsa*[24] passed over my head. From a botanical and ornithological point of view this region seemed engrossing, and I regretted very much that I did not have the opportunity to remain a longer time.

At the end of the swamp the adjoining hills flattened out and a lowland, for the most part inundated by the river, took its place. Our cart broke down for the first time in a deep hole, but after a stay of two hours was

---

la Flèche Creek (which now omits the articles) is some five miles upstream from the rock. Tabeau Creek, possibly named for Pierre-Antoine Tabeau, a notable diarist employed in the upper Missouri trade by Régis Loisel, empties into the Missouri two miles west of Dover in Lafayette County, Mo.

[22] *Author*: Further, I frequently observed: *Gymnocladus canadensis*, *Paphia flava*, *Anona tribola*, *Laurus sassafras*, *Vitis riparia*, *Tilia americana* and *glabra*, more rarely, *Symphoria racemosa*, *Menispermum lyoni* and *canadensi*, *Queria canadensis*, and as yet undetermined *Achillea*, *Cacalia atriplicifolia*, *Zanthoxylon clava herculis*, *Liatris pycnostachia*, *Cucubalus stellatus*, *Rudebeckia purpurea*, *Ostrya virginica*, *Geum album*, *Myosotis virginiania*, an *Amaranthus*, *Urtica pumila* and other nettles which I could not determine, cover all low situated land that is subject to inundations from the river.

[*Gymnocladus canadensis* = *G. dioicus*, Kentucky coffee tree; *Annona tribola* = *Asimina tribola*, pawpaw; *Laurus sassafras* is *Sassafras albidium*; *Vitis riparia*, the riverbank grape; *Tilia americana*, basswood; *Tilia glabra* = *T. americana*; *Symphoria racemosa* = *Symphorcarpos rivularis*, or *Symphoricarpos albus*, both of which are out of range: he probably saw *Symphoricarpos orbiculatus*, buckbrush; *Menispermum lyoni* = *Calycocarpum lyoni*, cupseed; *Menispermum canadense*, moonseed; *Queria canadensis* = *Paronychia canadensis*, forked chickweed; the undetermined *Achillea* is possibly *Achillea lanulosa*, western yarrow; *Cacalia atriplicifolia*, pale Indian plantain; *Zanthoxylon clava herculis* = *Zanthoxylum clava-herculis*, which is out of range, the reference therefore being to *Z. americanum*, prickly ash or toothache tree; *Liatris pycnostachia* = *L. pycnostachya*, blazing star, gay feather, or button snakeroot; *Cucubalus stellatus* = *Silene stellata*, starry campion; *Rudebeckia purpurea*, *Rudbeckia purpurea* = *Echinacea purpurea*, purple cone flower; *Ostrya virginica*, *Ostrya virginiana*, the horn beam; *Geum album* = *Geum canadense*, white avens; *Myosotis virginiana*, *M. virginica*, forget-me-not; an *Amaranthus*, one of several species of the genus; *Urtica pumila* = *Pilea pumila*, clearweed.]

[23] *Typha* is the genus of cat-tails; *Potomogeton* refers to aquatic plants, the pond weeds (Potomogetonaceae or Naiadaceae); *Rumex*, to one of the docks or sorrels; Nymphaea, the family of the water lilies.

[24] *Anas sponsa* = *Aix sponsa*, the wood duck.

temporarily repaired by Caillou, who fortunately had provided himself with an ax. During this time, countless blood-thirsty mosquitoes stung me. They seemed to like the interior of the forest even better than the region close to the river bank.

We made seven more miles through swampy primeval forests, during which time I had ample occasion to make unpleasant observations concerning the lack of skill of our young American driver. About four o'clock in the afternoon we reached an isolated house on the Missouri opposite Pierre de la Flèche.

Here lived the owner of the ferry on which one crosses the river. The inhabitants of the wretched hut were poor but good-hearted people, and we stayed an hour to rest. In Franklin I had provided myself with a few necessary provisions, but in the haste of departure Caillou had forgotten them. This loss was to me very unpleasant, for the package contained several bottles of rum. In this great heat, drinking water unmixed with some kind of spirituous drink is very harmful and may produce fever. In the house we could get nothing at all to eat except some old milk which had almost turned to cheese and some dried-out cornbread. This constituted dinner.[25]

The bank forming the Pierre de la Flèche is high and composed of beautiful rocks. This chain of hills on the right bank of the Missouri is hardly twelve English miles long and it gradually runs over to the lowland which extends as far as Franklin. A small stream, called Rivière à la Mine,[26] empties into the Missouri four English miles from Franklin. There, near its mouth, a large island, two English miles long and overgrown with high cottonwoods, causes a narrow channel between it and the bank.

Nothing remarkable occurred during my crossing of the river on a raft. Requiring almost an entire hour to get across, the raft had to be pulled half an English mile up the stream. The current in the neighborhood of the rocks called Pierre de la Flèche is extremely swift and it was most difficult to make the raft fast on the right bank. We climbed a rather high, steep hill on which nut trees and sassafras grew. On the ridge of these

[25] The Duke's hosts were probably one or both of the Ferrill families, John, the father, or his son Henry, long-time trappers earlier on the Missouri and operators of the ferry at Arrow Rock, according to Louis Houck, *History of Missouri*, III, 115. The temptation to compare their guest's reaction to their rude cabin and fare with that of contemporary and slightly later travelers—such sophisticates as Washington Irving, Henry Leavitt Ellsworth, Charles Joseph Latrobe, and Count Albert-Alexandre de Pourtalès—must be resisted. It would be only a matter of days until the Duke, progressively more agreeable to the wilderness, would relish roasted bear meat on a sandspit in the Kansas River.

[26] The Lamine River is six miles west of Boonville in Cooper County.

hills the timber becomes thinner. Forest and prairie alternate with one another. The vegetation becomes more luxuriant, the dense underbrush gives way to grass-covered spaces, and more and more the region takes on a lighter aspect clearly indicating the transition from the forest region to the prairie.

Half a mile farther to the west, one begins to see larger stretches over-grown with herbaceous plants and scattered clumps of brush such as sumac, walnut, and sassafras (*Rhus glabrum, copallinum, Juglans procina, Quercus ruba, echinata, Populus angulata*, etc.)[27] and also scattered oaks and poplars of most slender shapes bearing the stamp of unhindered growth. Tall plants, among which I observed as yet undetermined *Aquilegia*[28] with very small light blue blossoms, also *Acnida cannabina* and *ruscocarpa*[29] which attained a height of five to six feet forming an edge around the forest, at last gave way to the short prairie grasses whose light green carpet, yet unbleached by the rays of the sun, reached to the blue horizon among hills of soft, wave-like elevations. (This prairie is called Prairie à la Mine, after the river that originates on it and flows through it. It is connected uninterruptedly with the great prairie region of North America and is bounded in the west by the Cordilleras of New Spain.)

This sight I enjoyed for the first time after I had climbed a slight rise, on whose summit was one of the last of the above-described clusters of trees. It appeared picturesquely beautiful when it presented itself to the eye for the first time, but loses much of its interest, for its monotony wearies the senses. Illumined by the golden rays of the nearly setting sun, the charming picture in its simple beauty was still more captivating and reminded me of the sea in still majesty touching the sapphire blue of the darker vault of the wonderful heavens—happy evenings I had spent in the midst of the great ocean under a tropical sky. There the emotions of man are deeply touched, and the soul of man is filled with devout praise of the Creator.

After traveling on for a short distance over the prairie, we stopped at a cabin of a kind-hearted family of settlers. At first sight this dwelling ap-

[27] *Rhus glabrum* and *copallinum* = *R. glabra*, smooth sumac and *R. copallina*, shining sumac; *procina* (*porcina*), probably *Carya glabra*, pig-nut hickory; *Quercus ruba* = *Q. rubra*, northern red oak; *Quercus echinata* = *Q. cerris*, an Old-World species, but he probably saw one of the white-oak species; *Populus angulata* = *P. deltoides*, eastern cottonwood.

[28] This *Aquilegia* is one of some forty species of herbs, columbines of the buttercup family.

[29] *Acnida cannabina* and *ruscocarpa* are synonymous for a species of Amaranth, also known as *Amaranthus cannabinus*, limited to the eastern or Atlantic states; the reference is probably to *Acnida tamaricina*, water hemp.

peared very poor, but presently we observed the inhabitants and saw signs of considerable well-being, which in this blessed region cannot fail to come as a result of diligence and industry. Entirely unacquainted with luxury, these people lacked the most necessary conveniences inside their cabin. They had considerable wealth in livestock and farm implements, yet I could not find a table on which to enter the necessary remarks in my diary. I had to use a turned-up butter churn for this purpose.

The woman of the house busied herself at once, making preparations for supper. In comparison with the meager dinner at the ferryman's house, it was quite ample.

During the night we were threatened by a severe storm from the northeast, whereupon it became so cool for this season that the effect was felt in the interior of the cabin. In the morning the wind subsided and we could start in good time. To the first and nearest dwelling in the prairie, which was to be near the Missouri, the distance was twenty-eight English miles, a stretch which one could cover perhaps in one day during the dry season in the summer.

We followed the tracks of a wagon which must have preceded us for some time, but the tracks were still recognizable to the trained eye of my companion. In this manner we traveled in intense heat until noon, through a grassy plain apparently extending unendingly to the west and the south, interrupted only occasionally by scattered wooded spots. Such brush, with trees rarely attaining a considerable height, when seen from a distance, looks like groups of islands rising from the lap of a calm ocean. The sea-green color of the prairie, the peculiar wave-like movement of the tall grasses as they are stirred in the breezes, that peculiar appearance of the air, the mirage playing on the horizon and resembling a body of moving water (which the Arabs call "the thirst of the Gazelle") misleads men and animals famishing from thirst. This synthesis contributes much to the deception. The searing heat, intensified by a dry and burning southwest wind, had wearied our thirsty horse to the extent that it could go no farther after having made a distance of eighteen miles.

Going ahead and off to a side, I was finally fortunate in finding a spring among a few stunted trees, but the water was warm and muddy. Despite my yearning for a drink I could not make up my mind to taste it. At that time I was still a novice and not sufficiently acquainted with the hardships of a journey through the wilderness. Later I had to accustom myself to drink water much worse than this merely to stay alive. At that time I was also of the opinion that tepid and turbid water was enervating and, because of the repugnance which one felt on drinking it, must be unhealthy. This is, however, by no means the case, for, on the contrary, consuming cold, refreshing spring water is said to be extremely harmful, and even the Indians never drink it as cold as it comes from the spring.

My little driver, afraid to spend the night on the prairie, allowed the exhausted horse scarcely the necessary noon rest and after half an hour drove on. On the prairie the unskilled traveler must make use of the compass in order not to lose his way, since he misses every landmark which is visible only to the keen and experienced eye of the native. I therefore took refuge in the magnetic needle. My companion would pay no heed to it and soon lost the right direction. We found it again only after taking a far, roundabout way.

With the setting of the sun the scorching heat lessened, and at eleven o'clock at night we reached a lonely cabin. However, it was impossible to stay because of the number of insects and the stifling heat. The inhabitants, too, seemed little pleased by our late visit. During the night a heavy dew formed, so that I was thoroughly drenched and in this condition found the coolness of the morning quite unbearable.

The house where we had spent the night was not far from the Missouri, separated from this river only by a swamp and a narrow wooded strip. From the nearness of the stagnant water, I could easily explain the excessive number of mosquitoes that during the night had stung me so horribly. My whole skin was inflamed as if from the sting of nettles.

On the fourteenth we continued our journey at eight in the morning. The day's task was smaller and the region might have more inhabitants. On the prairie we passed through the previous day, it was most desolate. Only a few birds enlivened this lonely region, in addition to a few deer and elk,[30] which at a distance of one thousand paces fled shyly from us.

In herbaceous plants this prairie is also poor and very rarely did I observe blossoming plants. Among these I was interested in one of the Syngenesia with large but not yet fully developed flowers, probably a *Rudbeckia*, whose roots have the unpleasant odor of the rattlesnake during its

---

[30] *Author*: *Cervus major*, Say (*Cervus canadensis*, Cuvier; *Cervus strongyloceros*, Gmelin.). It is the elk of the Americans and considerably larger than the European elk (*Rothirsch*), and is their finest member of the entire deer family.

[The American elk, better called wapiti, its Indian name, thus distinguishing it from the European elk, *Alces alces*, to which it is not related, is *Cervus canadensis canadensis* Erxleben (the species seen by Duke Paul), or one of five subspecies. Historically, elk distribution ranged from the New England states to Vancouver Sound, northward in British Columbia, Alberta, Saskatchewan, and northern Manitoba, southward into Georgia, Louisiana, Texas, New Mexico, Arizona, and parts of Utah, Nevada, and California. Now largely a mountain dweller, the elk in 1822 was also a prairie and plains species. Hall and Kelson, *Mammals*, 1000–1003.]

mating season. Moreover, here and there in moist places grew a *Datura*, which differs from *D. stramonium* only by having larger and more lobed leaves, and a *Sambucus*, growing in clumps as low bushes.[31]

Until three o'clock in the afternoon we continued our journey without interruption. As we neared the Missouri, the country assumed a more wooded character, which finally gained the upper hand entirely. The Rivière à la Mine runs almost parallel to the bed of the stream for a distance taking about twenty hours to cover, and with the many tributary creeks this little stream waters a grass-rich area. Its rich fertility would invite cultivation if it were not so poor in timber. For the raising of horses and cattle there is no better location, but for sheep raising the climate does not seem to be conducive, and the wool is poor.

Even before the approach of night we reached the Tabeau River. Emptying into the Missouri and flowing between high banks, it is swift and deep during the rainy season. Even now its bed had six to eight feet of water, and I found the water strikingly cold. I stopped at a house whose inhabitants were of German origin. They felt an unspeakable pleasure in hearing themselves addressed in their mother tongue. Judging from the hospitable reception I received, I concluded that they were well-to-do. There was nothing lacking to satisfy our hunger. For people who have health and an inclination to work industriously, this fruitful land, properly used, yields all the blessings of a generous nature.

Refreshed by a bath in the cool stream and strengthened by wholesome food and a real bed during the night, I was able to start my journey again the following morning at an early hour. As we had to travel over a poor and stony road on the ridge of a chain of hills sloping to the Missouri, we had the greatest difficulty in making headway with our conveyance. Finally we reached the river, where we proposed crossing near a little, now abandoned, town of Brington.

The right bank, La Côte du Soldat de Duchaine, bounded by low hills, touches upon a swamp, Marais du Sorcier, which has the worst reputation among the aborigines and immigrants, and gives occasion to all sorts of rumors and stories.[32] It is indeed incongruous how the Indians, with their

[31] The Syngenesia constitute a Linnaean class, including the composites. *Rudbeckia* is a genus of some thirty species of North American perennial herbs, mostly cone, yellow-flowering, e.g., black-eyed Susans. *Datura*, a genus of widely distributed herbs, shrubs, and trees of the potato family, includes *D. stromonium*, the Jimson weed; all of the species in this classification are narcotic and poisonous. *Sambucus* is a genus of trees and shrubs, rarely of herbs, making up the elders, which produce berry-like fruits, here the elderberry.

[32] Of l'Isle du Sorcier, Brackenridge in 1811 had much the same set of observations: "The superstitious boatmen believe that a wizard inhabits this island; they declare that a man has been frequently seen on the sand beach, at the point, but that he suddenly disappears,

pronounced bravery and their contempt for all danger, fear the influence of spooks and wicked spirits. These Indians also share with the ignorant lower classes of Europe the superstitious belief of assigning supernatural beings a definite, limited area within which they are said to manifest their influence.

From Brington to Pierre de la Flèche is considered sixty English miles, a distance we made in two and one-half days. Because of the wretched condition of our wagon and hindered by the bad roads, I had made almost the entire distance on foot. This was especially difficult on the fifteenth because of the hilly and stony ground, and was still more taxing because of the almost unbearable heat, which every noon rose to 92° or 95° in the shade.[33]

My companion, the Creole, a man to endure the utmost hardship, called this a pleasant walk and often ran barefoot over the hot stones with a pack of eighty to one hundred pounds suspended from his long rifle. He it was who procured all necessary things for us, loaded and unloaded our baggage, and cared for the horse, because our driver was only a boy, hardly able to stand the long trips in the sun.

The Creole was the last to go to bed and the first at break of day admonishing us to start. With it all he ate only a little and drank only water. His whole wardrobe consisted of a leather jacket, a pair of linen trousers, and a woolen blanket. Only such race of men, accustomed, almost as if in a play, to endure the gravest dangers and privation, could succeed in discovering and populating the endless regions of the New World.

After calling for a long time and waiting in vain for the ferry people who lived on the opposite bank, Caillou was obliged to cross the Missouri on a rickety boat which he fortunately found on the bank. After an hour he brought the ferrymen, rough and unobliging Irishmen. They first entered into long spate of bargaining with me, but nevertheless after crossing they demanded twice as much as the price agreed upon.

On the left bank the road is extremely bad and undefined. I had to travel either through a bottomless morass and great stretches of standing water, or over hard, bumpy, sun-baked clay ground. Much of the region was overgrown with impenetrable brush and thorn, and in part also with nettles as tall as a man. Here our wagon broke down completely and our horse became so lame that the suffering of the animal aroused our pity. The large amount of game, especially the great number of turkeys, the sight of countless birds, notably huge flocks of parrots, and also the splen-

---

on the approach of any one."—"Journal of a Voyage up the Missouri River in 1811," in *Views of Louisiana*, 215.

[33] The Duke's course took him to a crossing between present Lexington and Wellington, Missouri, after which he would bear northwestward to Liberty.

did, luxuriant shapes of trees in full bloom, all would have repaid me amply for the strenuous foot journey if my attention had not been diverted in a painful manner by countless insects.

In the evening, burdened with a considerable load of game, we reached a group of houses called Blufftown.[34] Here I found a pretty good tavern and, dissatisfied, I left the wretched wagon and the little driver to their own fate, paying the lad for the entire contemplated journey.

The owner of the tavern agreed to provide me with a horse to carry my baggage, and over these arrangements for the continuance of my journey, by this new means the whole evening and a great part of the next morning passed by. All types of people from the neighborhood gathered, for the tavern at Blufftown seemed to be the meeting and amusement place of the region. Several women had also come along, and among these there were a few who could lay some claim to beauty, and conscious of this advantage, they showed off before the others.

As a stranger I was especially favored, particularly when the customary diversion of the American, rifle-shooting, was resorted to, and my exceptionally good gun won for me the best prizes. Target shooting is the most passionately pursued form of sport of the inhabitants of the northwestern states. Much money is made and lost. The best shot is preferred here, as he is in the Tyrol and Switzerland, and rarely loses favor with the women. In a country where guns are of as much importance as they are in the wilderness of the New World, this is easily understood.

The people of the upper Missouri travel almost always on horseback, and I believe that I have hardly ever seen anything as bizarre as the pose of the women riding. Too, the entire attire of the women, more comical than their odd carriage, a mixture of the old and the new, was funny. They wear a white linen hood, a cone-shaped pointed cap like a truncated sugar loaf, and twice as high as the head covering of Wendic women in the Lausitz.[35] Earlier I had seen similar costumes among the American women, but never of such an exaggerated form. They wear their hair either in long curls or shorn quite short, and the waist is forced into ill-cut, tight jackets, distorting the whole figure.

Finally the next morning, after much fruitless effort, I was presented

---

[34] Missouri had two Blufftons at the time, the one above the mouth of the Gasconade mentioned by Zebulon Montgomery Pike (*The Expeditions of Zebulon Montgomery Pike*, ed. by Elliott Coues, 3 vols., II, 368–69), and the Bluffton in which Duke Paul found himself in 1823, lying two miles north of the Missouri and serving as the county seat of Ray County. Houck, *A History of Missouri*, III, 185.

[35] A region in East Germany (modern Silesia), originally occupied by a Slavic group, the Wends.

an old horse, almost blind, on which my belongings and, in case of extreme fatigue, myself were to be transported to the little town of Liberty.[36] This place, twenty-four miles from Blufftown, is situated on a small stream which empties into the Missouri almost opposite the mouth of the Kansas.

At eight o'clock we finally started. The heat began early to be quite unbearable. The way led through the woods and a number of creeks and brooks, whose crude bridges had been washed away, or along steep, bumpy hillsides. My packhorse unendingly stumbled and fell, and I even feared whether I would reach Liberty alive.

After covering twelve miles, I saw the bank of the winding Fish Creek, or Rivière aux Poissons, which is navigable in canoes. Fairly deep and muddy, it has bad-tasting, gray water. We crossed on a raft and stopped for an hour at the house of a settler, the first house we had seen since morning. In the forest one could not rest because of mosquitoes, moreover our poor, tired horse swam in his own blood from the countless bites of gadflies and horseflies.

The country teemed with deer and wild turkeys, so tame that they sunned themselves and their broods close to the house and were not in the least disturbed. The next dwelling was another six miles away. In its proximity a hot engagement between Osage Indians and settlers had taken place a few years ago. The former had made several thieving raids and stolen many cattle and horses. Despite this, the Osages were not as much feared as the Iowas, whose raids were usually accompanied by murder and plundering. The region of the newly settled land between the Grand River, or Grande Rivière, and the Kansas was severely harrassed, and isolated settlers could barely maintain themselves in spite of the greatest vigilance.

To the left, not far from the trail on which I was traveling, was an extensive swampy meadow stretching toward the Missouri, about eighteen miles from the last night's camp. At some points the country is vividly beautiful, and a chain of high hills extends from the north to the southwest toward the banks of the river. Not until it had become dark, about nine o'clock, did we reach Liberty Town after a day's journey of almost twenty-six English miles. This time my Creole was so tired that he could not have gone a step farther. The exceptional heat of some 100° in the shade had produced in us a feverish condition which might have had serious consequences, but fortunately passed with mere fatigue.

Liberty consists of a few poor log cabins put up for temporary use. The tavern where I spent the night was crowded with people who did not make

---

[36] It lies thirteen miles north northeast of present Kansas City, Mo. It was only recently settled on a permanent basis, probably not earlier than 1820, when the settlements even this far west began to take form after the War of 1812.

arrangements to retire until about midnight. The resulting noise in the small room of the house and the horrible heat occasioned by the presence of so many people were little suited to accord a weary traveler necessary rest.[37] To give the reader an idea of the innocence and the naturalness of the customs of this land, so far removed from the heart of civilization, I will only remark that the daughters of the house, young girls of fifteen to sixteen years of age, out of the kindness of their hearts and touched by my utter exhaustion, publicly suggested that I share their bed with them since it was the only comfortable sleeping place in the whole house.

As before, I again had a hard time the next day, which was June 17, getting two horses, one to be used by myself and the other for Caillou, who was sick and seemed to be suffering. My intention was to ride to his acquaintance's cabin on the Missouri, three miles from the confluence of the Kansas, in order to rest there a few days, and during the absence of my boat to make several incursions into the interior of the country to the west and along the Kansas River.

This cabin, whose inhabitants were hunters only, was fifteen miles from Liberty on the slope of a chain of flattening hills. Since no road or trail led thither, we rode through the woods in a straight directional line. After we had broken our way for several hours over high hills and through dense brush and deep creeks, we happily touched upon a traveled footpath. The horses which we had got in Liberty were not bad and surmounted the

---

[37] Aside from the normal activity in northwestern Missouri resulting from the thrust of settlement after the War of 1812, the longer-standing fur trade along the Missouri River, and overland trade with the Kansa and other villages to the west, the beginnings of the Santa Fe trade originating at St. Louis and Old Franklin were producing their own electric shock, even where the thinly held frontier was defined by the confluence of the Kansas and Missouri rivers.

William Becknell, himself a veteran of the War of 1812, had moved overland from the Missouri River in September, 1821, reaching Santa Fe on November 16, and returned to Missouri late in February, 1822. His party, however, was not the first to excite Missourians with tales of the Spanish-Mexican trade possibilities to the Southwest. Robert McKnight, Samuel Chambers, and a number of other adventurous souls set out for Santa Fe in 1812, aroused by Pike's account of his experiences half a dozen years earlier, returning to St. Louis in 1821 after a nine-year-incarceration by the Spaniards. Hugh Glenn and Jacob Fowler had also ventured into the hitherto forbidden Spanish-Mexican country, they in advance of Becknell. Glenn reached his destination, Santa Fe, late that year.

The combined accounts of the fortunes to be made in trade between Missouri and New Mexico were enough to stir the imaginations of some scores of their contemporaries, some of whom may indeed have been Duke Paul's tavern companions at this moment in his narrative. Cf. Pike, *The Journals of Zebulon Montgomery Pike, with Letters and Related Documents*, ed. by Donald Jackson, 2 vols.; Jacob Fowler, *The Journal of Jacob Fowler*, ed. by Elliott Coues; Josiah Gregg, *Commerce of the Prairies* [1844], ed. by Max Moorhead.

obstructions of the near impassable territory with more ease than I had supposed. After six hours of riding, I saw the hunter's cabin close at the foot of a hill.

This man, known as Grand Louis throughout the region, had been mentioned to me by many as being hospitable and rather good natured.[38] Among his own kind he is at least the best hunter and trapper, a good shot with the rifle, and a courageous man. By his enormous physical strength and his daring he is the terror of thieving Indians and wild animals in his neighborhood. This true son of the wilderness, reared in the dense forest and in the communion of Indian tribes and company of hunters and boat-men, whose inclination to drink and immorality often exceeded the bounds of all human dignity, had under his leather jacket a heart sensitive to better feelings. He would have been a rare example among his kind if he had not at times darkened the brighter side of his character by an intemperate liking for whisky.

These remarks regarding a man on the whole unimportant are pardonable, because Grand Louis plays a brief role in this story and because it is the duty of the observing traveler to convey pictures with which he comes in contact, of men as well as nature.

When I entered the austere cabin, the master of the house was absent; however, his wife, a good-natured woman and her seventy-year-old mother, a Creole of really remarkable qualities considering her station, were there. I was received with the utmost kindness, and a noon meal, as good as the circumstances afforded, was prepared right away.

Toward evening the host himself came home, but on account of the high water the hunt had not been very successful and there was a noticeable shortage of provisions. The settlers living in remote parts, to be sure, have cattle, hogs, and chickens, but they do not like to kill their domestic animals as long as there is hope of providing for themselves by hunting. In order to be of help, we went on the hunt the next morning on the opposite bank of the river, which there terminates in a low point.

This region lies beyond the boundaries of the United States and is the property of the aborigines. My feet now trod for the first time that endless realm of the northern part of the New World not dominated by people of European origin. All the military arrangements undertaken by the United States are directed to the safety of the settlements and trade.

The heat was again so unbearable that I could scarcely make any move, and the high nettles made the wild, dense forest still more inaccessible.

---

[38] A Louis Louisgrand, originally from Cahokia, had settled near St. Charles in 1799. Hunting and trapping being at best extensive undertakings, it is easily possible that Grand Louis, now operating far to the west, was the same man. Houck, *History of Missouri*, II, 87.

Despite the great amount of game, I was able to bring in only one deer, for it is extremely difficult for the inexperienced to hunt in thicket.

A group of Indians of the Kansa tribe roamed through the forest. I could get sight of only a few men, completely naked except for the breech cloth. In the afternoon several Creole hunters and half-bloods, with a number of Indian women and children, camped on the right bank of the river opposite the cabin of Grand Louis. These hunters soon came to pay my host a visit and they repeated this visit the next day, but on both occasions were drunk, and despite their natural good nature, they were disgusting in this condition.

The Indian women in their company, all concubines and squaws, deported themselves in the manner customary to their people. Scantily dressed in red and blue cloths with decorations consisting of glass beads, coral and porcelain sticks, and faces stained with red, blue, and green paints, they disfigured their pretty faces no little.

During my three-day stay with Grand Louis, several Anglo-Americans of both sexes came to the cabin to see me, probably prompted by curiosity. They were monosyllabic people who always left in anger because we could not satisfactorily answer their curious questions, however much we tried.

The unnatural heat, which during the whole day had prevailed between 95° and 104°, became more and more punishing, causing greater discomfort, for our skin was more sensitive because of countless mosquito bites. During the night of the nineteenth a terrible thunderstorm visited us and a mighty rainstorm deluged us, threatening to wash away everything, but it did not cool the air.

On the morning of the twenty-first it began to rain hard and the wind turned to the northwest, whereupon the sultry heat was somewhat eased. Since the Missouri had flooded the lowlands and little worthwhile could be done, either in the pursuit of natural sciences or in hunting, I decided to go to the Kansas River. I borrowed a large pirogue, which in case of emergency could hold ten persons, and, despite the unfavorable weather, departed in company with Caillou, Louis, and an elderly Canadian named Roudeau.[39]

The river here makes a considerable turn to the southwest, and the right

[39] The already elderly Joseph Robidoux had established a trading post close to present St. Joseph, Missouri, before 1820. He could have been in the vicinity of the mouth of the Kansas at the time Duke Paul encountered one of the Robidoux, or it could have been his son Joseph who moved freely between St. Louis and his posts along the middle Missouri River. Cf. Houck, *History of Missouri*, II, 253, who credits his grandson Joseph with the subsequent founding of St. Joseph.

bank, running out to a low point, is overgrown with tall cottonwoods. In the background this low land touches on squatty hills, which probably constituted the actual river bank a long time ago. While we rowed near the bank the dogs startled a large skunk,[40] which sought protection in the willow bushes along the bank. To drive away its pursuers, who stopped from time to time, it threw its fluid on them trying to chase them away. The whole environment was so vilely polluted that we all had heavy headaches from it and were forced to leave the bank. The skinning of such an animal is the most terrible task one can undertake, and only the beauty of the specimen can compensate one for such an ordeal.

Not far from the mouth of the Kansas a very small creek, the Eau Bleue, flows into the Missouri.[41] At its confluence with the Missouri the Kansas is some eighty to one hundred fathoms wide and very deep. Its water is clear but its current is sluggish. For this reason I found its temperature several degrees warmer than that of the Missouri. It was at about an average water level, and despite the fact that it had been receding for a month, I found the banks at its mouth flooded and the river itself choked, due to the considerable height and pressure of the water of its adversary. At first glance it seemed indeed as if the water of the Kansas were flowing backwards, a phenomenon explained by the slow flow of the Kansas and the swift current of the Missouri. At any rate, the counter pressure of the one against the other is so strong that I could observe the effects of it in the Kansas as many as twelve miles upstream.

The settlement of the fur traders, two large dwellings, were scarcely more than half a mile further up on the right bank of the Missouri, and I went there in order to visit the owners, the Messrs. Curtis and Woods. No one was at home except the wife of the latter, a Creole and daughter of old Mr. Chauvin with whom I had spent the night near St. Charles. The entire population of this little settlement consisted of only a few persons, Creoles and half-bloods, whose occupation is trade with the Kansa Indians, some hunting, and agriculture.[42]

[40] *Author*: With a narrow white stripe on the forehead and two very wide stripes on its back terminating in the tail. Twice as large as *Mephitis putorius* and also different from that of Dupraz. Probably a new variety.

[The subspecies seen was within the range of *Mephitis mephitis avia*, but in any case it was one of the striped skunks, of which there are several subspecies.]

[41] This is the point where, twenty-four years earlier, Daniel Morgan Boone, the son of Daniel, had trapped. Near the point where the Kansas flows into the Missouri, the Lewis and Clark party had camped for three days. Lewis and Clark, *Original Journals*, I, 59.

[42] The settlement in which Duke Paul found Cyrus Curtis and Andrew Woods was upstream from the confluence of the Kansas, on the Kansas side. It thus lay within present Kansas City, Kansas. Cyrus Curtis was an independent fur trader whom the Missouri

Here I also found a youth of sixteen, whose mother, a member of the tribe of Sho-sho-nes, or Snake Indians, had accompanied the Messrs. Lewis and Clarke, as an interpreter, to the Pacific Ocean in 1804 to 1806. This Indian woman married the French interpreter of the expedition, Toussaint Charbonneau, who later served me in the capacity of interpreter. Baptiste, his son, whom I mentioned above, joined me on my return, followed me to Europe, and has since then been with me.[43]

I remained for dinner with Mrs. Woods and after the meal rode again to the Kansas. Its banks are at first quite low, but a mile further up on the left side several sandstone bluffs rise in steep, sheer walls, but after a short

---

Expedition had met on the river as it progressed upstream in 1818 and going downstream on the return to St. Louis in 1820. Andrew Woods had become a partner in Manuel Lisa's re-organized Missouri Fur Company in 1819. By 1823 both men were in the Chouteau fur enterprises, of which the present settlement was an outpost, first taken up by François Chouteau, son of Pierre Sr., in 1819, and as such they were in the orbit also of the American Fur Company, John Jacob Astor's creation. Gale, *Missouri Expedition*, 43, 52, 84; Richard E. Oglesby, *Manuel Lisa and the Opening of the Missouri Fur Trade*, 172.

[43] Soon after the Lewis and Clark Expedition reached the Mandan-Hidatsa villages near the mouth of the Knife River, near present Stanton, North Dakota, October 26, 1804, they hired Toussaint Charbonneau, who had formerly been employed by the North West Company and knew the Hidatsa language, as an interpreter, along with René Jesseaume, another French Canadian who had also lived among the Indians on the Knife.

Charbonneau had two Indian wives, one of whom, a Shoshoni, bore the name of Tsa-ka-ka-wias or Sacagawea, a former captive of the Hidatsas whom Charbonneau had purchased at about fourteen years of age. Her subsequent services to the expedition are matters of both fact and romantic legend.

At Fort Mandan, which the explorers had built on the east bank of the Missouri some seven miles below the mouth of the knife, Jean Baptiste, the son of Sacagawea and Toussaint Charbonneau, was born February 11, 1805, partly with the aid of rattlesnake rings administered, according to Meriwether Lewis, to the mother in labor (Lewis and Clark, *Original Journals*, I, 257–58). Thereafter the young Baptiste was known to the members of the expedition as "Pomp," short for Pompey. The youngster and his mother remained with the expedition until it had gone to and returned from the Pacific to the Mandan-Hidatsa villages in August, 1806.

The Charbonneaux, however, did not accompany the expedition on its return to St. Louis, even though William Clark had "offered to take his little son a butifull and promising child who is 19 months old to which they both himself & wife were willing provided the child had been weaned. they observed that in one year the boy would be sufficiently old to leave his mother . . ." (Clark in *Original Journals*, V, 344–45). Accordingly Pomp was later taken into the Clark household in St. Louis and sent to school. When the nineteen-year-old youth went with Duke Paul to Germany in 1824, he was to have another five years of education in Europe. His subsequent life would be devoted principally to services to various travelers and explorers in the West as guide and interpreter. Cf. Harold P. Howard, *Sacajawea* (Norman, University of Oklahoma Press, 1971), *passim*; Grace Raymond Hebard, *Sacajawea, a Guide and Interpreter of the Lewis and Clark Expedition* . . . (Glendale, The Arthur H. Clark Co., 1933), *passim*.

distance these bluffs run out to give way to a level plain with high trees. A long and very low sandbar touches upon the bank and extends over almost the entire bed of the river, which is forced into a narrow but very deep channel. We worked our way eight English miles upstream. The right bank rose to lovely wooded hills. Following the bend of the Kansas to the southwest, they are bounded by a long but very narrrow plain.

We spent the night without food on the sandbar, and since it had become cool, we were not molested by many mosquitoes. The whole next day was scheduled for the hunt. By daybreak of June 22, however, the wind turned to the south, and the warm air brought such countless numbers of insects that I cannot recall having ever, earlier or later, seen so many of them. At the edge of the water I had only a foretaste of the tormenting guests that descended on us in the woods.

Barely penetrating a hundred paces into the thicket, we were swarmed upon and covered by mosquitoes to such an extent that we could scarcely see and recognize each other at a distance of twenty paces. This was also the probable reason why we did not see any deer. However, my companion, Louis, was attacked by a huge black bear when he, imitating the call of a fawn, tried to attract a deer to himself. This call is the customary unsportsmanlike means which the American hunters use during this season to get a deer into shooting range, and is the principal cause of the reduction of this fine game, usually shot only for its hide.

When bears are in the vicinity, they frequently come running to the place from which the bleating voice emerges, because fawn meat is a delicacy for these animals of prey. During the mating season, from the beginning of July to the middle of August, the male bears are extremely vicious, even to the point of attacking a man. My companion would therefore have had a hard time if his rifle had failed, since I was fifty paces away from him in the dense woods. However, he shot the bear through the head so that it died instantly. I saw two other bears, which, however, were not as bold as the first and at our approach hastily left their lair. It is amazing to observe in what great numbers these animals inhabit the region on the Kansas and some neighboring streams.

On the sandbars in the river we often found holes filled with turtle eggs the size of partridge eggs. These are hatched by the warmth of the sun. Turtle eggs and the shot bear afforded us a delicious noon meal, all the more desired since we had not eaten anything for twenty-four hours.

Because of the huge number of mosquitoes I had to give up my plan of going farther up the Kansas, and so we prepared for the return. The sun was still high in the heavens as we rode down the Kansas and the Missouri and reached Louis' dwelling.

By the twenty-fourth the large boat had not yet arrived and I began to fear an accident. This, and also the lack of my mosquito netting, which Caillou had forgotten in Franklin and without which I could not sleep, induced me to start downstream to meet my crew. I had two small canoes tied together and seats put across these. In this manner one is safe from upsetting in the current and has a comfortable craft with enough room for persons and goods. However, such a boat cannot be used in going upstream.

A more accurate description of the banks of the Missouri I shall reserve for the account of my return journey on the boat, which, because of its slow course, provided more leisure to observe the region, limiting myself here to mention only briefly that we reached Fort Osage, a military establishment recently abandoned, on the evening of the twenty-fourth. Its location on a hill surrounded by forests and prairies is really picturesque.[44] Four miles farther downstream we made our night camp on a level bank.

At dusk many deer and wild turkeys came out of the forest to the river and sandbars to cool off, a splendid sight. During the sultry day we had frequently encountered deer sunning themselves at the edge of the water, and having had a successful hunt, we left these wild creatures in peace. But we ourselves during the night were attacked by our strongest and mightiest foes, the mosquitoes.

On the morning of the twenty-fifth a dense and impenetrable fog suddenly formed, veiling all objects and obscuring them from sight. Thus we were obliged at our leaving to seek the middle of the stream to avoid accidents. This, however, was incompatible with the purpose of my journey, for in this manner I might easily pass the big boat without being aware of it. Luckily I saw it about ten o'clock in the forenoon, not far from the

[44] Fort Osage, on the south bank of the Missouri above present Sibley, was at a site singled out by Lewis and Clark in 1804 for its strategic value (*Original Journals*, I, 56), and to it General Clark returned in the autumn of 1808 for its establishment by the First U.S. Infantry under Captain Eli B. Clemson. Its location, description, and an account of the rich flora up and down the Missouri for five miles in each direction, together with its elevation seventy feet above the Missouri on a commanding bluff, are subjects dealt with by George C. Sibley, who was the government factor (quoted in Houck, *History of Missouri*, III, 149), Brackenridge (*Views of Louisiana*, 216–18), Gale (*Missouri Expedition*, 23), and many others.

At the site, General Clark had held the treaty council with the Osage Indians in the summer of 1808, to induce the tribe to cede its traditional lands east of a line from Fire Prairie south to the Arkansas line, and to resettle in the neighborhood of the fort, whose factory would also serve the Iowas and the Kansa Indians. The fort was closed during the War of 1812, regarrisoned in 1815, and closed permanently in 1827 on the establishment of Fort Leavenworth on the west bank of the Missouri twenty-three miles above the mouth of the Kansas. Duke Paul had evidently missed the fort as he moved overland from Franklin.

houses where on June 15 I had been taken across the Missouri. Lying near a bend in the river close to an island on the right bank called Ile du Chenal Tigre,[45] or Ile du Marais Apaqua, it was detained by the fog.

Soon after my arrival the boat set in motion, and the tedious journey upstream began anew. The right bank here is hilly, the left however very low, and the Missouri winds to the northwest. A deep and navigable arm of the stream, called Chenal de la Prairie des Sacs, cuts off this bend.

We wanted to take advantage of this shorter way but had to return unsuccessfully since we found the entire channel blocked by drifted logs. Here I shot my first American golden eagle, a splendid large specimen, the tail feathers of which are highly valued by the Indian, for they constitute the greatest warrior ornament. This rare eagle has been accurately described and pictured by Wilson.[46]

Whether the *Aquila imperialis* (described in Temminck's *Manuel d'Ornithologie*, Part I, page 36) and which Temminck and Bechstein regard as a separate species, is also found in America, I cannot say[47] The Creoles call the golden eagle *oiseau à calumet*, because the Indian warriors decorate their pipes with its feathers. The one I shot, a mature male, with outspread wings measured eight feet, two inches.

In the night a violent storm with heavy rain and vehement thunder claps attacked us. On the twenty-sixth the journey was most dangerous and the channel on the edge of the island was entirely covered with driftwood and trees felled by the wind. Moreover, the swift current made the passage through such obstacles extremely hazardous. Luckily we soon left the dangerous places behind us but unavoidably reached a new arm of the river, which passage also caused us no little trouble.

Gaining the end of the channel, we found the water too shallow to let the fully loaded boat go through. The whole crew therefore had to get into the water to lighten the boat, and with the greatest effort it was pulled with the tow line over the sandbar.

Thereafter we encountered a place in the river strewn with uprooted trees, seemingly an impassable obstacle to most boatmen. The American boatmen, however, accustomed to exert almost superhuman energy if the occasion demands it, succeeded in performing this feat after ceaselessly working for more than five hours. We naturally made only a short day's

---

[45] Panther's Island between Hicklin Lake and Lexington, in Ray County. There has been much geographical confusion at this point, for which see Coues, *The History of the Lewis and Clark Expedition*, I, 27n.

[46] *Aquila chrysaetus* = *A. chrysaëtos*.

[47] *Aquila imperialis* = *A. heliaca*, which is Eurasian.

journey, remaining for the night on a sandbar in Chenal à Hubert. The channel forming a horseshoe-shaped island, takes up a small creek.[48]

During the night two boatmen, the most irresponsible of our crew, seized my canoe, escaping down the stream after stealing articles from their comrades. I have never heard anything more of these men.

In the morning I found a four-foot catfish, *Pimelodus catus*, on my set hook. At noon we reached a small island in the middle of the river. The neighboring bank is of low but attractively shaped bluffs. Two and one-half miles from our night camp the Missouri makes a great bend to the northwest. When we reached the point on the left bank, a strong gusty wind arose. Setting sail at once, we sailed around the promontory. Attempting to avoid some old logs, we ventured more than a hundred steps from the bank into swift current. The wind suddenly ceased. The swift current carried the boat quickly with it in its grip, throwing it against the rocks on the right bank.

The entire crew stood with poles on the left side of the boat, and by the exertion of the many men the vessel was saved. Now the boat had to be worked around a dangerous rock by means of the tow-line fastened to a tree. In the afternoon the wind arose from the northeast, aiding us to pass quickly over a perilous shallow, Batture du Chenal du Sorcier,[49] about four miles long. About five o'clock, noticing that the low banks were broken by a chain of low hills, I soon recognized the region of Blufftown where I had spent a night.

For some days Caillou had been suffering from a very painful and inflamed wound on his right hand. I watched hourly, fearful that gangrene would set in. Since he could not do any work, I had hired a Canadian half-blood of the Slave Indian nation to assist, a useless fellow, however, and a decided drunkard.[50]

Toward sundown a boatman from the upper Missouri came on board. Having participated in the unfortunate expedition of Mr. Ashley against the Arikaras, he brought the first news of this tragic affair, to be followed

[48] Chenal à Hubert, or Hubert's Slough, and Hubert's Island, together with two creeks entering the Missouri in Lafayette County, Missouri, all together constitute one of the largest etymological puzzles in the long history of Missouri River exploration. The creeks evolved into the Great and Little Snibar or Sniabar. The unraveling is Coues' in *The History of the Lewis and Clark Expedition*, I, 27n.

[49] Likely in the vicinity of Little Blue River of today, in Jackson County.

[50] Slave Indians = Etchareottine ("People Dwelling in the Shelter"), Athapascans formerly occupying areas west of Great Slave Lake, Canada, possibly brought this far south by French Canadians operating along the Middle and Upper Missouri. Hodge, *Handbook*, I, 439.

by others just as distressing.[51] I induced Caillou to take the opportunity to return with this boat master to St. Louis, because I was very much concerned about him. With tears in his eyes he left me.

With the water still very high, we traveled slowly on the twenty-eighth. The air was sultry and soon there came a heavy downpour. The right bank is low. A gust of wind from the south finally drove us forward rather quickly, appreciably helping our exhausted crew over several dangerous places. Toward evening we entered an arm of the river, the Chenal de la Prairie du Flux. This channel is deep but not wide, separating a meadow from the tall timber of the flat bank. Here we spent the night.

The next morning a brisk northeast-by-north wind arose and we could hoist sail early. At six o'clock we reached the mouth of the passage, staying on the right bank lined by bluffs. Fort Osage ends one of the highest points of this chain of hills covered by prairie. The fort commands a good military position, but at present consists of only one wooden house occupied by a single family. This forms the boundary line against the Indians on the right bank of the Missouri. On the left bank, however, as far as Liberty Creek, the land belongs to the state of Missouri. Close to the fort I met Mr. Curtis in a boat from the Kansas and delivered to him the letters from his trading company. Below the fort, in the neighborhood of the bluff, the current was so strong and the journey so difficult on account of a whirlpool

---

[51] The disaster suffered by the William Henry Ashley-Andrew Henry fur-trading expedition on the Missouri near the mouth of the Grand River, when it was attacked by the Arikaras, with whom the party was trading in the first days of June, 1823, will be dealt with in detail at footnote 44, Chapter 9.

The Arikaras or (popularly) Rees, of a Caddoan sedentary culture, are closely related to the Pawnees, whose language, except for dialectical differences, they share. Both groups originated in the Southwest, moved, according to tradition, to the Missouri Valley, where they parted, the Skidi Pawnees settling in the area of the Loup River, Nebraska, the Arikaras continuing northward on the Missouri but ranging as far south as present Omaha. In such location, the Arikaras were inevitably thrown against Siouan groups in their own westward migrations.

When Lewis and Clark met with the Arikaras in 1804, they had three villages near the mouth of the Grand River in present north-central South Dakota. Here the explorers learned much about the tribe from Pierre-Antoine Tabeau (*Tabeau's Narrative of Loisel's Expedition to the Upper Missouri*, ed. by Annie Heloise Abel), and one of their party, Sergeant Patrick Gass, set down many detailed observations of their ways and culture. (*A Journal of the Voyages and Travels of a Corps of Discovery, under the Command of Capt. Lewis and Capt. Clarke of the Army of the United States*, ed. by David McKeehan).

After their troubles with the whites in 1823, the Arikaras rejoined their Skidi Pawnee kinsmen on the Loup in Nebraska, but two years later returned to the Missouri. By the Treaty of Fort Laramie, 1851, they were confirmed in their lands west of the Missouri, and late in the century were located in the vicinity of Fort Berthold, North Dakota, along with their early allies, the Mandans and Hidatsas. Hodge, *Handbook*, I, 83–86.

that we could not have gotten farther without the aid of the wind. However, the wind became so strong that the boat, tilted on its side by the pressure of its sail, began to dip water. Had the wind not ceased presently our vessel would have been lost without fail, for near an unavoidable whirlpool an enormous log extended across the channel. We would certainly have struck it, for the sail, being fastened too tightly to the mast, could not be taken in. After advancing four English miles more, we made camp on the left bank opposite a small island.

On the following day the air was so oppressive and sultry, a result of the heavy rain, that the mosquitoes again had free play. Since no wind arose we had to work with the towline. Despite this our journey progressed rather well. Both banks are low, and the left was very sparsely settled. On the low land under tall trees the ground was covered with nettles as tall as a man. Hardly ever have I seen so many parrots in one place. When I shot one of these from a tree, where hundreds of these birds were sitting, the others did not fly away but were merely satisfied to make a frightful outcry. The same is true if they sight a bird of prey. The meat of these parrots is tough and black. However, fish like it and so it is used for bait by anglers.[52]

About fourteen English miles from Fort Osage low bluffs rise, and behind these is a low plain, three miles long, overgrown with willows and impenetrable bushes. In this region we spent the night. Here I found in full bloom *Asclepias syriaca* and *amoena* together with *Solanum carolinianum*.[53]

On July 1 we again started out at four in the morning. Not far from our night's camp the little Pichiky Creek flows into the Missouri. Its banks are said to contain much lead ore. A group of islands, Iles de Vincent, farther up the stream, forms several passages. By evening we reached the end of a very low bank seven miles long, La Batture à Bénit.[54]

In a hilly region I saw a rich coal bed, long known by the Creoles to exist, but they do not make use of it on account of the abundance of wood. La Batture à Bénit is cut in two by a channel of the river which shortens the way by four miles. The water in it is very deep, the bed muddy, and the current swift. It therefore required much exertion to wind ourselves

[52] The Carolina parakeet (*Conuropsis carolinensis*) was the immensely plentiful species Duke Paul saw here as well as elsewhere on his American tour.

[53] *Asclepias syriaca* and *A. amoena* (probably *A. purpurascens*) are two species of the milkweed family. *Solanum carolinianum* = *S. carolinense*, the horse nettle, a species all too familiar to the traveler but here referred to again because of its flowering.

[54] At Bénite (now Mill) Creek in Jackson County. Coues, *Lewis and Clark Expedition*, I, 32, traces the original name to an *hivernant* in the employ of the Missouri Fur Company in 1811. The coal seam nearby had been noted by Lewis and Clark as a "bank of stone coal on the north, which appeared to be very abundant."

through it. The dense undergrowth of willows intertwined with grape-vines made it impossible to walk along the bank to pull the boat by the tow-line. Poling the boat upstream over a muddy bed is very difficult work. A few men fell into the water on this occasion, letting their poles stick in the mud, and the swimmers had great difficulty in regaining them.

Numerous tracks of deer, racoons, and turkeys betrayed a region rich in game. Several large white cranes, *Grus americana*, flew over my head. An exceedingly pretty bird, larger than the European crane, it is found rather numerously in the northern prairies of the New World.[55] I also secured a *Buprestis* with fine metallic sheen, which in respect to beauty of color is almost as fine as the Brazilian *Curculio imperialis*.[56]

The mouth of the passage, entirely blocked with tree trunks, we had reached very early in the morning. It caused us much work, and almost the whole day passed in gaining a distance of thirty paces. To clear and open it for passage, men who could swim armed themselves with axes to cut logs and branches. In the meantime evening had come. Opposite this mouth was a large island along which we traveled for another two miles. A frightful and yet majestic thunderstorm arose in the east. Never have I seen more beautiful cloud formations, nor more light changes of striking colors from reflections of the rays of the setting sun. Uninterrupted light-ning and thunder augmented the impression offered by the awe-inspiring spectacle. In the coolness of the evening we all took a bath. One of the men got into deep water and a whirlpool. Without the utmost daring of the swimmers, he would not have been saved. The thunderstorm con-tinued into the night, and there was such consistent lightning that I could read the whole time, thunder making sleep impossible.

On the third our day's journey consisted only of crossing the river to the opposite bank. Following the thunderstorm, a violent southwest-by-west wind set in which did not allow us to advance a step. I spent the day botanizing but was not very lucky. I did find a large number of insects living on the decaying wood on the bank. During the night the wind from the southwest-by-west increased to tornadic proportions, with repeated electric discharges. When the lightning several times struck close to the boat, the crew, fearing that one of these bolts might strike our gunpowder-loaded boat and most certainly blow it up, went a considerable distance away for their place of rest.

Luckily, the danger passed and the storm cooled the air perceptibly.

[55] *Grus americana*, the American whooping crane, which, with perhaps fewer than sixty-five survivors, is now (1972) anxiously guarded against extinction.

[56] *Buprestis* is the type genus of the Buprestidae, the beetles. *Curculio imperialis* is one of the snout beetles.

(In the evening at six o'clock it was 94° and the following morning, the Fourth of July, it was 73°.) The morning of the Fourth of July was clear and beautiful. Traveling around the point constituting the left bank, we made three miles before breakfast. The right bank is hilly and running thus to the southwest extends as far as the Kansas.

Old Baptiste de Rouain and my servant undertook to find by land the cabin of Louis. At this time I dismissed the Canadian half-blood, a lazy, useless person, because he was afflicted with an ugly contagious disease. At noon the wind became very strong again. We had reached a promontory, an hour's walk from the bluffs on the western slope where Louis' cabin is located.

As the boat apparently could get no farther, I also went ahead on foot to find his cabin. At the beginning, the way led along the bank through almost impenetrable bushes, among which a thorny *Crataegus*[57] tore all of of my clothes badly. Fighting my way through with my knife in hand, I reached the mouth of a creek which was very deep and muddy. I followed the course of the creek upstream for more than three miles until I found a suitable place to wade through.

By an indistinct footpath I arrived at an abandoned cabin. From here I found a well-marked way to the river. On its bank I walked along the hills for another mile to the hunter's cabin and found no one at home. Across the river on the right bank at the place where the hunters had their encampment during my former visit, I noticed many Indian tents and a lot of Kansa Indians camped.

[57] *Crataegus*, one of the thorny shrubs, the hawthorns, any of the species of red haws.

9

WA-KAN-ZE-RE, a chief of the Kansa
Indians, called Le chef americain by the Creoles, is highly esteemed by his
tribe, which, like those of most of the aborigines, is divided into several
bands joining each other but rarely, while going on the hunt or gathering
in their great village. By these terms one must think of a stable habitat,
where subordination under a single head comes only when the greatest
danger requires it.[1]

Among the whites Wa-kan-ze-re is markedly esteemed because he was
one of the first of his tribe to induce the Kansa, formerly hostile aborigines
and cruel towards the settlers and fur traders, to adopt a friendly attitude
and enter into trade with the Europeans. Since the beginning of this
century this influence of that chief and some other respected Indians has
been very noticeable. A man of more than forty, with a large, somewhat

---

[1] The Kansa Tribe, one of five comprising the Dhegiha group of the southwestern Sioux,
is closely related to the Osages, somewhat less so to the Quapaws, linguistically. In the
historic separation of the five elements of this Dhegiha group, the Osages remained on the
Osage River, Missouri, while the Kansa went up the Missouri and briefly settled on the
south side at the mouth of the Kansas River. They then removed farther up the Missouri
to the northern boundary of Kansas, where Cheyenne attacks forced them back to the mouth
of Kansas River. They were on the Blue River in the early part of the eighteenth century.
By 1815 they were on Kansas River at the mouth of the Saline. They had earned the oppro-
brium of Lewis and Clark in 1804: "At present they are a dissolute, lawless banditti; frequently plunder their traders, and commit depredations on persons ascending and descending the Missouri River."—*Original Journals*, VI, 85. They were much at war with their
neighbors, so that by 1822, a year before Duke Paul's visit with them, they counted, according to Major Benjamin O'Fallon, the Indian agent, some 1,850 people, a figure much
reduced from earlier times. The tribe relinquished its lands in northern Kansas and southeastern Nebraska in 1825, thereafter removing to Council Grove, Morris County, Kansas.
In 1873 they removed to Indian Territory adjoining the Osages. Hodge, *Handbook*, I, 653–
66; William E. Unrau, *The Kansa Indians: A History of the Wind People* (Norman,
University of Oklahoma Press, 1971), *passim*.

corpulent figure and a serious, commanding expression on his face, he conveys the poise and the calmness of bearing which show so advantageously in the character of the American aborigines.

Like most of the chiefs who have visited the eastern states to negotiate with the officials at the seat of the Congress, he shows in his behavior that he fully recognizes the advantages of European customs. Nevertheless, he is aware that the laws of the Europeans are unsuited to the nations close to the state of nature and that sudden acceptance of such laws would bring harm to them.

I learned immediately after my arrival that the Indians had heard about me and were curious to make my acquaintance, and for this reason had postponed their departure several days. Taking a canoe, I had myself paddled across the river.

The camp was pitched near the river bank, and little children were bathing. The women were scraping hides nearby which they tan, color white, or smoke brown, so that they become soft and do not shrink if wet. As the men had seen me coming, they all gathered together at the tent of their chief and seated themselves in a circle near him.

He sat on a steer hide while his followers lay about on the bare ground. At my approach the Indians sat up. Wa-kan-ze-re stepped up to me and extended his right hand with the brief expression, "How!" their customary sign of friendship. He led me to his seat, on which I had to sit, while he, like the others, threw himself on the ground, a sign of especial respect.

An Indian warrior, with a face adventurously painted with red stripes and a head shorn smooth, then made a speech in a loud, drawling voice. The meaning was translated by the interpreter about as follows:

The tribe of Kansa, he said, regarded me as a close brother of the great chiefs beyond the great sea in the east. These were mightier than all chiefs (*ka-hi-ge*) of the red people, and as mighty as the great father of the long knives. Further, eternal peace with the whites had been made, and that their meeting with me had long been their wish.

After the speech was finished the chief handed me a roll of paper containing a treaty with the government, whereupon all the men got up, and one after the other shook hands with me.

I read the treaty aloud and the Indians continuously expressed their satisfaction, although they naturally did not understand a word of the content. To this scene the women and children were admitted and stood behind the men, but did not sit down.[2]

[2] Treaty of October 28, 1815, of peace and friendship between the Kansa and the U.S. Charles J. Kappler, ed., *Indian Affairs: Laws and Treaties*, 4 vols., II, 86.

I admired the calm bearing of the assembly. No one but Chief Wa-kan-ze-re, the interpreter, and myself spoke. The Chief had a large peace pipe brought, smoked, or rather took a few puffs, then gave it to me, whereupon I did the same. During this, the men raised themselves slightly from their reclining posture, directly reclined again, and finally each one after the other drew three puffs.

The Chief had brought to him a fine bow of yellow wood, a dozen used arrows, and his red head ornament. And with his special esteem he then presented them to me.[3]

On this occasion he told me that, through the mediation of the American agents, he was on friendly terms with most of his neighboring tribes, especially the Sioux (Dakotah), Pawnees, Sakis,[4] Otos, Osages, etc. He stated that this was not the case with the Iowas, however, and that the irreconcilable and malicious character of the latter tribe was to blame for this.

The men were mostly naked, except for an apron on the breech-cloth. This covering usually consists of a piece of blue or red cloth drawn between the legs and fastened to a leather belt in front and behind. On only a few of the men did I see leggings and moccasins. Their bodies were scarred and scratched by thorns. Each had a knife in his belt. The sheath for this knife was a double piece of leather with a broad edge, in which a triangular cut was made and through which the belt was drawn, holding the sheath in place. Their knives were the ordinary kind common in the inland trade.

The Kansa rarely have modern rifles, and in their ignorance still prefer the poor rifles of English manufacture, although the fur traders, hoping to increase the returns from the Indians' hunt, have exerted every effort to persuade them to the contrary. Their bows, ordinarily of walnut, short and stiff, are very simply worked and are used with iron-tipped arrows carved from the wood of *Cornus* or *Cephalanthus*.[5]

They use these weapons less and less frequently and only in hunting the bison, which is disappearing more and more from their hunting grounds. Like other mounted Indians, they overtake these mighty inhabitants of the prairie on horseback, piercing them at close range with their arrows. In war, the bow and arrow of the Indian is more dangerous than the firearm,

---

[3] In all probability the wood of this particular bow was *bois d'arc* or Osage orange, *Maclura pomifera*, which was first collected by Meriwether Lewis in the spring of 1804 and first described by Constantine Samuel Rafinesque in 1817. Lewis's specimen went to President Thomas Jefferson. Lewis and Clark, *Original Journals*, VII, 295–97.

[4] Sakis = Sauk Indians.

[5] *Cornus*, a genus of hardwood shrubs and small trees, the dogwoods and cornels, having extremely fine-grained, hard woods. *Cephalanthus* is a small genus of American shrubs of the madder family, buttonbush is *Cephalanthus occidentalis*.

which the western tribes do not know how to use well. Carrying very far, the bow and arrow never fail and do not easily betray the marksman in the bushes.[6]

Sometimes the tips of the arrows are only hardened in fire, and yet their effect is deadly. The armament of arrows is made to serve one of two purposes, for war or for hunt. For the first, the tip is cut in acute angles and is provided with a barb to remain lodged in the wound. The other has obtuse angles and can be drawn out. The quiver is made of deer skin and the bow is carried in a separate case attached to the quiver. Like all Indians, the Kansa are passionate smokers. In neatly decorated pouches made of the skins of small animals they carry tobacco and a substitute for it consisting of the leaves of *Rhus typhinum*[7] and the bark of a *Cornus*, which is called kinnikinnick. Usually these small animals are carefully skinned so that head and toes stay on the skin, the inner tail is decorated with colored quills of the porcupine, and the feet are hung with metal disks and tassels. Even larger animals, such as the fish otter, are worked up for pouches with utmost skill.

The women wear aprons of cloth around their hips, and many of them have very neatly worked and richly decorated leggings. I saw a few pretty faces among them, and both sexes are characterized by handsome figures and dark-colored skin. The warriors usually have their heads shorn, except on the back of the head they have a kind of cockscomb and two long braids.

On the other hand, the women and children boast of their handsome, smooth, glossy hair. The men occasionally leave a few hairs on their chins, but otherwise painstakingly pluck out all the other hair from their entire body. The ears of both sexes are perforated four times lengthwise, and in every incision hangs a bundle of blue and white porcelain sticks, which are valued highly by these Indians. The richer among them wear strings of such porcelain sticks around their necks and flat armbands of thin plated silver above the joints of their arms. Children of both sexes are entirely naked to their twelfth or fourteenth year.

Since the weather became stormy, I had to embark in my unstable canoe sooner than I had desired, so as to achieve the opposite bank. The skill of my boatman luckily overcame the high waves on the river, which toyed with our hollowed-out log canoe. Since it is mandatory to maintain the

---

[6] The late Walter Prescott Webb's analysis of fire-power (in *The Great Plains* and *The Texas Rangers*) accords an additional virtue to the bow and arrow, in comparison with the single-shot rifle or pistol in this era: rapidity of fire in the bow was not to be matched until the introduction of repeating rifles and side-arms, at least at short range.

[7] *Rhus typhinum* is *R. typhina*, the staghorn sumac. More likely *Rhus glabra*, smooth sumac.

equilibrium in such a canoe, persons whom one does not trust in this capacity are made to lie down flat in the bottom of the canoe, as in a coffin, and are not allowed to stir. Even so, Indian canoes upset frequently. Since the Indians can all swim like fish, this does not bother them much, and usually they are able to save their few belongings. Only rarely does an Indian or a Missouri hunter let a companion drown, but they always take the precaution to let the victim swallow enough water to make him incapable of hindering the rescuer by untimely movements.

In the evening I was visited by a prominent Kansa called Sa-ba-no-tsché, that is, Standing Black Man. His mission was to announce a visit of his chief on the following day. This warrior was a handsome man, at least six feet tall, of athletic figure, and very vain, for he asked at once to be given a mirror that he might arrange his head ornament, consisting of an embroidered band and the rare mark of honor of a red-dyed deer tail. He seemed to be a good man. He spoke very sensibly with us and especially admired my weapons.

My double-barreled rifle appeared to him to be very practical, and he quite naïvely advised me to take it along if I should roam through the woods alone, since one could not be too much on his guard against men and animals in this region. I had some brandy set before him. However, he only sipped of it. Such moderation is rare in this country. At last we parted after we had presented gifts to one another, and with repeated assurances of friendship, the very satisfied Indian went away.

It was late evening when the large boat arrived, after I had anxiously awaited it, because the weather had become stormier. The wind howled frightfully, and fierce lightning flashed through the cracks in the hunter's poorly built cabin. The next morning, however, the sun shone brightly in all its glory and a cool breeze blew towards me. From July on, thunderstorms and rain became more and more frequent, but the oppressive heat increased day by day. Thus the traveler welcomes such storms, since they relieve him, at least for a few hours, from the scourge of stinging insects.

The Indians arrived early, the men seating themselves in a semi-circle with the chief in the center. The speaker of yesterday began to talk and with great emphasis shouted several complimentary remarks aimed at me. Hereto the entire company nodded approval. I had some brandy and tobacco distributed and gave the chief some presents. Whereupon he took the peace pipe and handed it to me as a token of deepest friendship, at the same time delivering an address with much decorum. Naturally I could not understand its content, since the interpreter was not there. This unfortunate circumstance soon brought the meeting to a close. All the Indians arose and one after the other gave me his hand. I must say in honor of the

Indians that I did not see one of them drunk, although the opportunity was not lacking, for the half-bloods and Creoles set them a bad example. All had indulged immoderately with whisky.

Despite my precaution of sending the vessel forward early the next morning, it progressed only for half an hour upstream, halting at a low place on the left bank. Part of the crew, absenting themselves secretly, lay drunk on the bank. The heat rose to 108° and brought a severe thunderstorm after it.

To protect myself against the rain, I was obliged to go to Louis' house, where I had to endure the repulsive sight of the drunken men. The deplorable lot of the poor housewife, with a sick child in her arms, grieved me greatly. With danger to my life, I was compelled several times to tear knives and rifles out of the hands of these quarrelsome fellows. Outside the rain fell in torrents, but the stupefying effect of brandy subdued the raging-mad band in time.

By daybreak the missing members of the crew were rounded up and put on board, and since the wind had risen, the boat departed. To overtake it, I had to walk five English miles through woods and over swampy land overgrown with nettles as tall as a man. The vessel was a mile above the mouth of the Kansas, where it chanced to stop. I could not have followed farther, for on the way I had lost a shoe in the mud and my foot had been badly torn by thorns. To replace my loss I took a canoe to the fur traders', but let the boat continue its journey. My companion again became so drunk that I had to leave the canoe in the lurch. A young half-blood showed me the way back, and after I had waded through a muddy arm of the river four feet deep, I overtook the boat (on July 7).

Above the mouth of the Kansas the right bank is low. Then it rises to hills overgrown with luxuriant timber. A flat bank follows the drop from these bluffs, and six miles farther the river makes a bend to the north and later to the northwest. Opposite a small stream called La Petite Rivière Platte, we stopped for dinner. This river winds through the hilly, heavily timbered area to the left.[8]

It originates in the prairies between the Missouri and the Rivière des Moines, whose waters flow into the Mississippi. The rock formation which forms the bed of the Petite Platte is remarkable. This rapid-flowing stream rushes over a mass of obliquely fissured limestone, separating the latter into rectangular blocks and giving the bed the appearance of a checkerboard.

The thermometer again rose to 105°, and the crew almost succumbed

[8] The Platte River of Iowa-Missouri, three hundred miles in length from its point of origin in Union County, southern Iowa, to its confluence with the Missouri in Platte County, northwest Missouri, approximately fifteen miles northwest of Kansas City.

at their work. For this reason we made only three English miles. Near an island, the river bank makes a great bend from east to west and thereby forms a broad basin. Here stagnant bodies of water are connected with the river, their surface covered with many swampy plants, especially a beautiful water rose (*Nymphaea sagittata*).[9]

Between two islands the right bank rises to picturesque bluffs, and passing rocky cliffs alternating with lowlands we reached a large island at five o'clock, in the language of the Kansas called Wa-sa-bae-wa-kanda-ge. (The Creoles call it Ours de Médecine.) It is separated from the mainland by a deep channel and forms a flat-shaped arc from the east to the southwest, following the direction of the main current. Opposite the island is a place on the hilly right bank where formerly an Indian village was located, which the fur traders call Le Village de Douze, the Village of the Twelve, as it is twelve hours from the mouth of the Kansas. When in recent times Fort Atkinson on Council Bluffs was abandoned, General Leavenworth established a new military post here, about which more will be told in my account of the second journey.[10]

Despite the swift current which the Missouri creates in the passage that separates the island from the mainland, we reached the end of it. And aided by the wind we made twenty-five English miles on this day. On the eighth the wind was intermittently favorable. The great prairies extending to the crests of the hills that border the stream glitter in their pale green between the scattered groups of trees. The dense growth of the hilly,

---

[9] *Nymphaea sagittata* = *Nuphar sagittaefolium*, which is out of range.

[10] The landmarks mentioned in this paragraph, in the vicinity of present Leavenworth, Kansas, were notable to other travelers, Perrin du Lac, Stephen H. Long, Lewis and Clark, and Joseph Nicolas Nicollet, though the latter's Park Island has been transmuted to Spar Island. Lewis and Clark had more trouble than Duke Paul did with *Wahkan'da wakhdhi*, the Place Where Wah'Kon-Tah Was Killed. But his rendering does well enough, and the name Bear Medicine Island conforms to earlier French and American renderings. Whether to agree with Lewis and Clark that the Indian village mentioned was an old Kansa Indian site, or with Coues (*History of the Lewis and Clark Expedition*, I, 36–37), who seems to accept Nicollet, that it was Kickapoo, is a question. The nearby island is today Kickapoo Island, located just above Fort Leavenworth.

Fort Leavenworth, named for Colonel Henry Leavenworth (1783–1834), by whom it was founded in 1827, would become a principal defensive position for the protection of the Santa Fe trade. In 1881, at the direction of General William Tecumseh Sherman, it became the center for the Command and General Staff School of the U.S. Army, which it continues to the present. It is located twenty-two miles northwest of Kansas City on the west bank of the Missouri.

Fort Atkinson, established by General Henry Atkinson (1782–1842) in 1819, was located at Council Bluffs, on the west bank of the Missouri, nine miles north of present Omaha. It was the largest western fort between 1819 and 1827, when it was abandoned.

primeval forest gradually disappears, until the timber hardly reaches the end of the hills close to the stream.

Later on the forested area again increases somewhat. A scant sixty hours farther up the Missouri, the prairie gradually gains more in extent and finally covers even the elevated river banks, forcing the trees into those low regions which are subjected to the annual inundations of the mighty stream. In these low lands, called *pointes basses* by the Creoles, the fertility of the soil produces very resplendent trees. From the sources of the Missouri and its great companion stream, the Yellowstone, one sees the bleak wilderness on the banks of both streams broken by miles of continued cottonwood groves, appearing like islands in a seat of prairie grass.[11]

At eight o'clock in the morning a large island, Ile à la Vache, lay before me. A fort with a garrison was formerly located on this island, but it was moved because of its unfavorable location.[12] On this day I frequently saw deer and turkeys on the river bank. Often I observed that the class of poplars, which on the lower Missouri and Mississippi is so common, and called by the Anglo-Americans cottonwood, more and more gave way to the Canadian poplar.

Moreover, the *Assimine*, that *Annona* (*Orchidocarpus* [*porcelia*] *tribola*, Mich. [*Annona tribola*, Willd.]), noted for its excellent fruit, becomes scarcer the closer one approaches latitude 40°.[13] Although the varieties of trees still grow luxuriantly, one cannot help noticing the gradual disappearance of certain kinds of trees, and it seems as if the mentioned degree of latitude has a remarkable effect in the geographic distribution of plants, especially in northern America. The forests are indeed so densely overgrown with native shrubbery and so impenetrable that even wild animals can hardly wind their way through them. However, a lack of pretty, blossoming herbaceous plants presents the botanist no wide field to make extensive investigations. This section is also poor in birds. Excepting cries of turkeys, parrots, and crows, one hears but rarely the voice of a song-bird.

[11] For the importance of the broad-leaved cottonwood (*Populus deltoides*) to explorers and trappers, see Cutright, *Lewis and Clark: Pioneering Naturalists*, 86–87. The Canadian poplar mentioned *infra* by the author is more likely *Populus sargentii*, the plains species.

[12] Ile à la Vache = Isle des Vaches or Isle de Vache in Lewis and Clark, later and now Cow Island. Stephen H. Long met with the Kansa Indians here, August 24, 1819, and it was here that the Missouri Expedition of 1818–1820 wintered during its first year out. Gale, *Missouri Expedition*, 28 ff.

[13] *Assimine* fr. Indian *assimin*, French *asiminier*, yielding generic *Asimina*; *Orchidocarpus* = *Orchidocarpum* = *Asimina*; *porcelaria* = *Porcelia*, a genus of five species of Central and S. American plants (Annonaceae); *Annona tribola* = *Asimina tribola*, pawpaw.

Strong wind drove the vessel to the edge of a chain of hills called Côte du Sahône, where we spent the night on a small island. This region takes its name from the gravestone of a chief of the Sioux nation who recently was buried here, having died on his way to St. Louis.[14]

We had advanced fourteen leagues. During the night a heavy downpour drenched the boat. For three days rain had fallen in torrents. The total rainfall in America is so enormously heavy, despite long periods of drought, that relatively more water falls than at the same latitudes in Europe.

The storm had not cooled the air, and when we started at four o'clock on the ninth, the thermometer already registered 85°. Since the boat could be pulled forward only very slowly on account of a complete calm and the swift current, I climbed the hill on which the grave of Sahône was, but found nothing noteworthy. The ground was covered with impenetrable bushes of sumac and elder. Separately *Acacia illinioensis* [*Desmanthus illinoensis*, prairie mimosa], Michaux, and a *Sesbania* with purple blossoms grew amid dense grasses [*Amorpha canescens*, lead plant?].

Not far from this place, the prairie touches the edge of the stream and loses itself in an invisible distance among the hills. At this place there was formerly an Indian village of the Kansa Nation, called by the Creoles Village de Vingt Quatre, probably because of the distance of twenty-four hours from the Kansas River.[15]

The aborigines had left it not long ago to establish a new village. Numerous sites of camp fires and recently abandoned huts constructed of tree branches made me conclude that Indians had camped there only a few days before. However, these shelters were not those of the Kansa but rather those of the Iowas or Otos.

The prairie disappears again into a series of rocky hills stretching directly north, separated from the Missouri by an extensive, low wooded point, extending from the south to the east. The river bank here is very low. Opposite the prairie runs a long willow-covered grass bank which does not bear one's weight.

Toward evening I went ashore, hoping to find some game. After I had

[14] Sahone as the name of a Teton subdivision of the Sioux appears in Meriwether Lewis's *A Statistical View of the Indian Nations Inhabiting the Territory of Louisiana* [1805], in *American State Papers, Indian Affairs*, 9 Cong., 1 sess., 1806, 714–15. The chiefs of the three subdivisions or bands of the Sahone mentioned by Lewis were Ar-kee-che-tur of the Sahone proper, War-min-de-o-pe-in of the Tak-chan-de-su-char, and Sharlo-ka-hâs-câr of the Saho-ne-hont-a-par-par. Which had died we do not know. Lewis classed the Sahone among other Tetons as "the vilest miscreants of the savage race."

[15] Brackenridge (*Journal*, in Thwaites, *Early Western Travels*, VI, 164–65) places the first Kansa village site twenty-eight miles above the mouth of the Kansas.

struggled for an hour through man-high nettles, a turkey gobbler led me to the edge of a plot bare of trees, but overgrown with tall stalks of *Rudbeckia* and *Sylphium*, entwined with *Dolichos* (*Dolichos lignosus?*)[16] and wild grape vines so densely that it required an hour to advance a distance of two hundred paces.

At first the low point of land did not look as extensive as it really was, and I sought to reach the eastern bank in the hope of encountering the boat. The sun had set when my attention was arrested by a peculiar odor, and I also noticed several places in the dense bushes where the branches and nettles had been bent down. Suddenly I heard a noise and in the twilight I recognized a large bear coming straight at me. Upon my firing the animal collapsed. Because of the darkness, however, I had shot too low in the head. He arose again and attacked me anew. I had no time to reload my rifle but fortunately saw a thick uprooted sycamore and took safety behind this windbreak. The bear followed to this place, but was too weak to climb over it, so that it was easy for me to finish him.[17]

I reached the bank of the river, and despite the darkness of night, by the dim light of the moon I realized how far my distance from the boat must be. On firing several shots I received no answer, and so I had the questionable pleasure of walking along the bank. The thicket was impenetrable and I could not get back to my former path. It was very dangerous to walk along the bank, which was very high and hollowed out by the current. The moon set in the meantime. After two hours holding on to trees and roots, groping my way along in the darkness, suddenly the ground gave way under me and I plunged into the water. Clinging to branches of grape vines and becoming so entangled in the vines in the fall, I nevertheless succeeded in getting a firm footing. Then, by shooting away my entire supply of powder, I was able to attract the attention of my crew. About midnight my servant and four men came, having cut a path through the bushes to liberate me from my dangerous position and to lead me back to the boat.

The night was cool. In the morning of the eleventh the first rays of the sun had already promised a hot day. We started early. At eight o'clock, four miles from where we had spent the night, we reached the place where I had come to the Missouri the previous evening. At nine o'clock we met a

[16] *Sylphium* may have been one of four species of rosinweed or compass plant. *Dolichos lignosus*, hyacinth bean, Asiatic, which is unlikely; possibly *Amphicarpa bracteata*, hog peanut.

[17] This adventure with a male bear suggests an atypical experience with the black species or a typical one with the grizzly. In the latter case, the incident has significance for zoologists concerned with the historic eastern limits of *Ursus horribilis*.

large boat belonging to the [American Fur] Company coming from Council Bluffs. On board was a certain Rodger, commonly called Bell, in the service of the Company, who had been sent out to meet the vessel in order to encourage the master to a speedier journey. In the Fort of the Otos, near the factory of the Bluffs, they were avidly awaiting the cargo which had been so long delayed by the high water. The Indians did not have enough powder and lead left for their main hunt. If this turned out badly it would mean a great loss to the trading company.

Both banks of the river are flat in this region. The Missouri, falling for a few days, now began to rise again. During the afternoon we caught a horse, which pleased me greatly. The hunters had apparently lost him in the previous autumn. I resolved to accompany Rodger on a trip over the prairie to Council Bluffs, and towards that end I planned to load the horse with the most necessary baggage and food supplies. According to the judgment of all, current travel on the right bank of the river was most difficult, since one had not only to work his way through almost impassable regions but also to anticipate a lack of water during the hot season.

The night of the twelfth was beautiful, but towards sunrise the sky became overcast. Beginning to thunder, the storm discharged itself somewhat northerly and gave expression only by several violent claps and pouring rain for nearly half an hour. The sky thereupon became clear again and the thermometer registered 79° in the shade at six o'clock.

The horse captured the day before was saddled and loaded, and we started on the way. It would have been impossible to ride through the dense thicket on the banks of the river. The wild grape entwined the dense bushes, especially dogwood, to such an extent that a pedestrian had to make use of his knife to cut through. With great difficulty the horse was gotten through. Such an impenetrable thicket usually forms a wall along the stream and is rarely wider than two to three hundred paces.

Indeed we soon entered into lighter timber, with underbrush of high nettles and cattails (*Equisetum riparium*, M. [a horsetail or scouring rush, here named by the author but undescribed]). This formed the inner parts of the forest lands dividing the Missouri between hills and meadows here. The horse protested against going through these burning, prickly plants and began to rub itself against every tree, so that my baggage was considerably damaged.

Still, I did not give up hope of driving the horse farther on, but the farther we penetrated the higher and denser the nettles became. Swarms of gadflies, flies, and mosquitoes swarmed around us, tormenting the horse so much that it continually rolled on the ground, disarranging all of my things. At last the animal became so obstinate that it could not be budged by any means. There was nothing to do but finish unloading it, for a part of the load had already fallen off and was lost in the woods. With the horse's load on our backs, my companion and I hurried for the river bank several miles away, where we spied the boat at too great a distance ahead of us to overtake it with our burdens. Rodger left me, therefore, to bring men from the boat, and in the course of several hours my baggage was once again on board, after we had hacked a way through to it with the aid of axes and knives.

I had found the boat at the mouth of a channel which forms an island on the left side of the river and is called Ile à Rivet.[18] As the wind had changed to the east, we could make the passage with the aid of sail, but after we had the island at our back the wind subsided. This was very unpleasant for now we had to cross to the right bank and travel through heavy current along a shallow containing but little water and much driftwood. Despite every exertion with poles and oars, the crew was unable to overcome the force of the current. There was nothing else to do but to pull the boat by the tow-line. To do this, the men had to get into the water, and there being too little water near the bank to float the boat, they then had to wade in the stream, with water above their hips, for more than half an hour.

The Missouri here makes a curve to the northwest. The left bank presents to the eye hills overgrown with grass. They are separated from the stream by low timber and bushes. This bend is seventeen English miles from Village du Vingt Quatre. The low bank itself is three miles long. After traveling on for two more miles, we came to an island, Ile de Grand Détour, as the sun was going down.[19]

The boat master decided to ascertain that evening whether the channel was navigable, and his stay far into the night caused me no little concern. Finally he came with the information that the channel was impassable, as its entrance was blocked by driftwood.

The night was very beautiful and clear. Indeed the clear nights in July already were refreshing. However, on the morning of the thirteenth, the temperature betrayed what was in store for the coming day, as the thermometer rose to 85° by eight o'clock, not a breeze stirring. At daybreak we set out, holding to the left bank of the island. The boat was propelled with oars and poles.

[18] Rivet Island near the east bank of the Missouri, nearly opposite present Bean Lake, Missouri, named for a soldier in Étienne Veniard, Sieur de Bourgmont's command ascending the Missouri in 1724.

[19] The Missouri opposite present Atchison, Kansas, bends northeastward, and about two miles beyond the turn Grand Détour Island was thus near modern Rushville, Mo.

On the bank, all sorts of driftwood had been washed up, and the water shot through the middle of the stream with tremendous force. Both banks of the Missouri are low here and overgrown with tall timber. At the mouth of the channel Grand Détour, great masses of driftwood had been piled up, extending far into the stream and embracing part of the island. Travel along this pile of timber was most difficult and dangerous. Since there was neither a long cable nor a skiff on board, the swimmers again had to prove their skill by swimming against the swift current for a distance of over one hundred paces while holding on to the line, which they then had to make fast. From the deck of the boat it was then wound to its tied end. Had the line broken, the boat would certainly have been lost. Never in my life have I seen such imperfect equipment with which to navigate a river. One should imagine our danger on the swiftest river in America far removed from all human assistance.[20]

The entire bank above described constitutes a shallow covered with driftwood, which already protruded out of the water, extending to the middle of the river, as the waters had receded. Beyond Grand Détour the Missouri makes several bends. In its background grass-covered hills glisten, indicating a vegetation of social grasses occasionally mixed with clumps of bushes, replacing the wooded banks more and more. The region as far as Prairie du Serpent Noir, seven miles from Détour, is very monotonous. Willows and poplars covering low banks intertwine with impenetrable shrubbery.

On the whole the vegetation is scant. Where the water had receded from the banks of the Missouri, I found on grassy spots *Cassia chamaecrista*, a few *Dolichos*, and a *Desmodium* and *Cyperus*. In dry places, an *Impatiens*, closely related to *Noli me tangere*, two *Acnida*, a tall *Sonchus*, and *Rudbeckia laciniata*, and *Epilobium*, and a tall, new herbaceous plant belonging to the Onagraceae. Besides these there were several Umbelliferae and composites which had not yet developed their blossoms.[21]

[20] John James Audubon would develop similar feelings about the Missouri when he saw its powers first-hand in 1843. Audubon, *Audubon in the West*, ed. by John Francis McDermott, 87.

[21] The plants here are roughly identifiable as follows: *Cassia chamaecrista* = *C. fasciculata*, partridge pea; the *Dolichos* are wild vines of the Fabaceae family; *Desmodium* is one of the tick trefoils; *Cyperus* are wild vines of the Fabaceae family; *Desmodium* is one of the tick trefoils; *Cyperus* is a genus of several species of umbrella sedges of the Cyperaceae; the *Impatiens* mentioned as being closely related to *noli me tangere* indicates a species in appearance like a forget-me-not; the two *Acnida* specimens were of the amaranth family; the tall *Sonchus* refers to an Old World sow thistle noted by Pursh for the eastern U.S. as early as 1814; *Rudbeckia laciniata* is the golden glow; *Epilobium* is a genus of willow herbs; and the tall herbaceous plant of the Onagraceae refers to a family of which *Epilobium* is one genus. *Umbelliferae* = Ammiaceae, the carrot family.

In places where the water washed the bluffs there appeared a very pretty *Euphorbia*, several inches high with blood red spots on the leaves,[22] several *Asclepias*,[23] and *Aguilegia canadensis*.[24] The edge of the prairies is marked by bushes of *Rhus typhinum*.[25] Beyond these are dense clusters of composites, especially *Helianthus*[26] and *Silphium*,[27] whose genera in the New World are so rich in species.

This region is also poor in bird life. Still, I found several rare birds of prey, as for example *Falco borealis* and *hyemalis*, both belonging to the Asturinae,[28] *Icteria sibillatrix*,[29] the *Coccycus erythrophtalmus*,[30] and great flocks of parrots. I found no Saurians at all, only one of the Batrachia[31] (and this is a rare specimen), three or four Chelonia,[32] on the other hand I found rather many Ophidia,[33] especially rattlesnakes.

The Missouri is poor also in fish, limited almost to the genera *Pymelodus*, *Cyprinus*, and *Perca*.[34] Freshwater snails are also not common, however, in the stagnant water left by the river I found a few large and beautiful bivalves.

Toward noon a gentle southeast wind arose but did not do us much good. The heat again reached the extraordinary height of 102° in the shade; similar atmospheric heat I have never observed in tropical countries. In the evening a cloud of mosquitoes tormented us, but during the clear night they were driven away by a rising wind. The wind continued until morning, so we could utilize it for our journey.

About seven o'clock we reached Prairie du Serpent Noir extending along the east and bordering on the bank of the Missouri. It is a continuation of the great prairies between the Missouri and Mississippi and watered by the

[22] The *Euphorbia* here could be *E. maculata*, nodding spurge; *E. supina*, milk purslane or *E. heterophyla*, painted leaf.

[23] *Asclepias* is a genus consisting of the milkweeds.

[24] *Aguilegia canadensis* is a species of columbine, the only one in the area.

[25] *Rhus typhinum* is the staghorn sumac, better *R. typhina*, out of range; possibly *R. copallina*, winged sumac, or *R. glabra*, smooth sumac.

[26] *Helianthus* is the genus of sunflowers.

[27] *Silphium* is a large genus of tall North American perennial herbs, mostly yellow-flowered, the rosinweeds and the compass plant.

[28] Accipitridae embraces the goshawks, but the genus *Falco* now belongs in the Falconidae. Here *Falco borealis* = *Buteo jamaicensis borealis*, the red-tailed hawk, and *F. hyemalis* = *Buteo lineatus*, the red-shouldered hawk.

[29] *Icteria sibillatrix* probably = *I. virens*, the yellow-breasted chat.

[30] *Coccycus erythrophthalmus* is the black-billed cuckoo.

[31] Batrachia = Amphibia.

[32] Chelonia, the turtles.

[33] Ophidia, the snakes or serpents.

[34] *Pymelodus* = *Pimelodus*, a genus of primarily South American catfishes.

small Black Snake Creek. A little north of this creek is a factory manned by government agents and built for the Saki, Otogami (Fox Indians) and Iowas. This trading post, concealed by trees and bushes, is on the slope of a low chain of hills running from north to south between the Missouri and the Grande Rivière.[35]

The prairie here presents one of those picturesque views in which this great river is not very rich. In the background rise limestone hills in strange regular cones and pyramids, resplendent in the freshest sea-green. From a distance they resemble those Indian burial mounds which I had observed near St. Louis and in other places on the Mississippi. Scattered trees and bushes separate the grassy parts from the fringe of woods, the trees becoming fewer and fewer and soon disappearing altogether, leaving to the eye only prairie and sky.

The low right bank is just as dreary and desolate as the left is smiling and attractive. A flat bank, covered with low willows and exposed to floods at every inundation, only serves stinging insects as a habitat. The Missouri here makes a turn to the northwest, with hills continuing along this bank to form abrupt slopes that resemble great walls. The slopes must have been formed in recent times, for I distinctly noticed how great masses of earth had been violently torn off. The ground is undermined by the strong current. By and by the hills will be entirely engulfed by the stream and their place will be occupied by an immense water basin. Here at the slope of the hills the great Serpent Noir empties.[36] Doubtless of Indian origin it probably was named for a chief of the Sac Indians.

We followed the left bank in a straight direction toward the west to a point where the river again turns to the north. The wind was strong from the south, unfavorable for the boat and our journey. Finally, at noon, we reached the end of the bend and could hoist the sail to reach a small island by nightfall. The banks are covered with poplars and willows. I noticed much game and turkeys, drawn to the edge of the water by the heat. Throughout the night there was thunder and lightning but no rain. About midnight the wind calmed and it became very cool.

On the fifteenth both banks of the river were piled with driftwood in

[35] The prairie, the stream, and the hills here referred to are all of the Black Snake Hills area, where Joseph Robidoux, Jr., not the government, was operating a trading post, and where John James Audubon also visited in 1843, shortly before the establishment of St. Joseph, Missouri.

[36] Great Serpent Noir, as a designation, makes more sense than at first appears, as Coues found equally for the Lewis and Clark acceptance of Nadawa, Pike's Nodawa, and Long's Nodaway, which is today's name for the river forming the border between Holt and Andrew counties, Mo., as it flows into the Missouri. These cognates all mean snake, and the river was long called the Snake. Coues, *History of the Lewis and Clark Expedition*, I, 41 n.

many places, so that the journey went ahead with utmost difficulty. I found some hunters who had been here for some time because of the abundance of game. They had salvaged a barrel of brandy from the wreckage of a boat and with it plied some of our crew. The latter came back intoxicated and started all sorts of controversies on the boat. With difficulty they were subdued.

About noon a large pirogue came downstream to us. In it was a Mr. Pratt, the son of one of the managers of the Company.[37] He brought three men with him to assist us and also informed us that the Blackfeet Indians on the Yellowstone River had killed a large company of hunters and fur traders. For me this was disquieting news, especially since I had planned to travel in that region.[38] Mr. Pratt presented me with a large skin of a grizzly bear, the only one that had been killed by the hunters this year.[39] This bear, though still young, had torn apart two Indians and had been killed only after a hard struggle.

In the evening we reached a large island separated from the left bank

[37] The "Mr. Pratt" who was a son of a manager of the company refers either to Sylvestre Pratte or to Bernard Pratte, Jr., just which we are unable to determine from this distance. Bernard, Sr., became significant in the Missouri fur trade as a partner in Pratte, Cabanné and Company in 1816. The company was reorganized in 1820 as Berthold, Pratte, and Chouteau (the so-called French Fur Company) which latterly (in 1823) became Bernard Pratte and Company. With John Jacob Astor's establishment of the Western Department of the American Fur Company at St. Louis in 1822, Pratte saw an opportunity and acquired from Astor in 1823 exclusive rights to purchase furs from the Western Department, an arrangement continued to 1834, when Pratte, Chouteau and Company (as it was renamed on Bernard Pratte's retirement) acquired the Western Department outright.

At the time of Duke Paul's meeting with Pratte, the latter and his brother were moving back and forth between St. Louis and Fort Kiowa on the upper Missouri, a quarter of a mile above the mouth of the Yellowstone and twelve miles above Andrew Henry's Fort Recovery, constructed in 1822 for the William H. Ashley fur enterprises.

Another distinguished German, Maximilian zu Wied, would go up the Missouri ten years later, under the American Fur Company banner, first on the *Yellowstone*, then on the *Assiniboine* from Fort Union. Bernard Pratte, Jr., "Reminiscences of General Bernard Pratte, Jr., *Missouri Historical Society Bulletin*, VI, 59–71; Oglesby, *Manuel Lisa and the Opening of the Missouri Fur Trade*, 167ff.

[38] "The large company of hunters and fur traders" killed by the Blackfeet consisted of Robert Jones and Michael Immel and five of their men of the large party representing Joshua Pilcher's Missouri Fur Company, near Pryor's Fork of the Yellowstone in Montana, May 31, 1823.

[39] *Author*: On my second journey in 1830 I had an opportunity to see many of these giant beasts of prey. I postpone a detailed and accurate account of these monsters for my account of the second journey. [As indicated in the Editor's Introduction prefacing the present volume, the Duke's plan for a volume on the second trip was not to be fulfilled in published form, and there is reason to believe that he did not get around to preparing it in manuscript form.]

by a channel into which the Nandawa River empties.[40] The channel dividing the island is over five miles long and contains almost clear water, because the upper inlet is very small and the Nandawa pours all its water into it. The island is relatively much longer than it is wide and is overgrown with scattered trees and ferns. The left bank of the channel, on the other hand, is inaccessible because of dense bushes and intertwining grape vines. The grapes, beginning to turn purple, hung in countless clusters from the vines. In this area the *Annona tribola* is also seen rather frequently, but becomes rarer farther toward the north and disappears entirely at latitude 40°. The same is true of *platanus*, the root bearing *sumac*, and *tecoma*. On the other hand, many kinds of stately oaks are on the slopes of the hills.

Never did I see so many tracks of wild animals as I saw here, whole packs of wolves, among them those of the black wolf, which I had seen even in Mexico, and it seems closely related to the wolf of the pampas, of Prince Neuwied (*Canis campestris*). This wolf must absolutely be put in a class by itself. It differs completely in manner of living and in form from the two wolves described by Say (*Canis latrans* and *Canis nubilus*), of which one is a genuine jackal and the other has the characteristics of the wolf of the Ardennes. This wolf is more cinnamon brown than brown, darker in the winter, lighter colored in the summer, larger than the Siberian lycaon which has a superior pelt, but in form and habits approaches the Mexican coyote, the coastal wolf of the hot zone with a much lighter colored pelt.

In general America has many wolves and foxes, and in regard to these animals the zoologists are yet very much in disagreement. This condition will not be solved soon, for there are many differences and varieties, differences in age and size in the same genera.[41]

The presence of hunters and Indian camps draws packs of wolves. These animals find excellent protection in the tall prairie grass and in the dense forests and are hunted but little or none at all. And since they rarely attack horses or people, nothing is done to hinder their increase, which is greatly favored by nature. Seemingly these beasts of prey know this full well for they do not shun the presence of man, but follow like dogs the camps of Indians.

[40] Nandawa = Nodaway River, which empties into the Missouri immediately below the town of Nodaway, Mo. Its source in Iowa is far to the south of the Des Moines source.

[41] Individual variations in *Canis lupus*, the gray or timber wolf, from nearly white through gray, rufous, and dusky to pure black, have led historically to false classifications and not a little misunderstanding. *Canis latrans*, the coyote, is represented by three subspecies possible in this area: *Canis latrans latrans* Say of the Long Expedition, *C. latrans thamnos* and *C. latrans frustror*.

After some time I saw again large cottonwoods and sycamores, several yards in circumference in the forest. Most of the trees on the edge of the stream are of frail and stunted growth, because they are subjected to severe storms and all the effects of weather. They cannot reach a great age for after thirty or forty years they are usually undermined by the stream and torn away.

Despite every exertion, we did not reach the mouth of the channel and had to spend the night in a place overgrown with willows. Such willow thickets are the favorite habitat of insects, and are therefore avoided by travelers. Toward morning of the following day, a pouring rain set in lasting until noon. Afterwards the sky cleared.

The Nandawa is at its mouth thirty fathoms wide, its course is sluggish, and its bed muddy and in places deep. The stream, originating in the prairie not far from the sources of the Rivière des Moines, is navigable in canoes for sixty miles. Much driftwood covered with foam lay at its mouth, and a very swift current indicated the nearness of the Missouri, whose high water had decreased hardly at all.

We had to wind our way with much danger and toil along the bank. The strong current had piled the driftwood, leaving but little room for a passage. Advancing scarcely two miles, we were compelled by approaching night to lay by. In the night a thunderstorm came and it rained until morning. Swarms of mosquitoes filled the air, permitting neither rest nor sleep. Especially notable for the first time, a fly, an inch long and having a painful sting, made its appearance. Many insects, particularly a large sand flea, were able, despite all the precautions we employed, to penetrate the fly net. Thus this last means of protection was made useless.

On the seventeenth the air remained sultry and the sky overcast. Due to stagnant water, the stench in the hold of the boat became unbearable in the hot, moist atmosphere. Several of our crew became sick, and I feared the outbreak of a nervous fever, especially since none of the men could be prevailed upon to unload and clean the boat.

About three miles from the mouth of the Nandawa, very high, meadow-covered hills rise on the right bank, called Les Côtes du Loup. These hills extending for a distance of six miles along the stream count as some of the highest in the Missouri region, reaching a height of five or six hundred feet.

Also on this day we dragged along slowly as we almost succumbed to the sultry, oppressive heat. Next morning the wind rose from the north and the thermometer dropped back to 79°. At the same time a slight rain fell, although the de Luc hygrometer only registered 65°, which even in clearer weather is the ordinary condition on the Missouri during the month of July. Often, however, the hygrometer rose to 70° and 80°.

About eight o'clock we reached the mouth of the Wolf River.[42] Opposite is an island and the banks themselves adjoin the prairie. In the immediate vicinity of the stream there are dense bushes with tall weed-like composites. A low ridge forming the right bank is overgrown with lindens, sycamores, and ash-leaved trees. The *Cercia canadensis* and a low growing plum bush bearing round edible fruit grew from the cracks in the rocks.[43]

Near these heights the stream turns to the west. The left bank is low and wooded with tall timber, and the right bank is a lowland overgrown with willows. Here our crew, unfortunately, found a full barrel of whisky which had been washed there by the stream. In the middle of the stream is a rather large island called Ile à Salomon which, according to my calculation, is located exactly at latitude 40°. At the point of this island we stayed for the night. It was fine weather and a cool wind blew from the northeast. Unmindful of this, clouds of insects of every dimension covered us.

The whole day long canoes with men of Mr. Ashley's company had come down the river, mostly wounded men who had taken part in the fight with the Arikaras. They, too, had fished up brandy and were for the most part drunk.[44]

[42] On earlier maps, Rivière du Loup, hence the author's earlier usage of Côtes du Loup. It is more properly Wolf Creek, emptying into the Missouri in Doniphan County, Kansas.

[43] *Cercia canadensis* = *Cercis canadensis*, the redbud. The author's low-growing plum bush is possibly *Prunus pumila*, the sand cherry noted by Sergeant Charles Floyd during the early stages of the Lewis and Clark expedition.

[44] William Henry Ashley, lieutenant governor of Missouri and general of militia, had mounted, with Andrew Henry, his partner, the second of two private fur-trading ventures into the upper Missouri country in the spring of 1823. Henry, leading a trapping brigade to the confluence of the Missouri and Yellowstone rivers a year earlier, had made the first thrust by the recent partnership formed by these St. Louis residents. He and his men had gone into winter quarters to await Ashley's second party, which left St. Louis on March 10, 1823, in two keelboats, the *Rocky Mountains* and the *Yellow Stone Packet*, propelled by sail and hand-operated side-wheels supplemented by tow-lines or cordelles.

The expedition was undertaken in spite of warnings of Indian troubles on the upper Missouri, notably Major Benjamin O'Fallon's report as Indian agent to the Secretary of War (U.S. Senate, 18 Cong., 1 sess., *Senate Document No. 1*, 55, 61). Four hundred miles above Council Bluffs near the mouth of the Grand in northern South Dakota, Ashley came upon two Arikara villages, where trading began June 1. Next day it became known that one of Ashley's men had been killed by the Indians, and shortly thereafter the Arikara assault began. Among Ashley's men were such redoubtable figures as Jedediah S. Smith, William Lewis Sublette, and James Clyman. They and thirty-seven companions on the Missouri River beach withstood the Arikara fire for a time, but finally made for the boats, many swimming. Thirteen of their number were killed and eleven wounded, two of the latter dying shortly.

Moving downstream from the Arikara villages, the two boats rested; Ashley then dispatched the *Yellow Stone Packet* to solicit aid from Major O'Fallon and Colonel Henry Leavenworth, commandant at Fort Atkinson opposite Council Bluffs. Leavenworth and

On the morning of July 19, the wind still blew as it had during the night, and the sail could be used to advantage in several places. For some hours we traveled along a lowland with sparse trees which grew there leaning over onto the bank. Then we reached a chain of hills whose sheer walls formed the banks of the river. This bluff is a shaley clay formation whose summit is covered with sand a few feet deep. In the background appeared the prairie, losing itself on the horizon. A large island, the name of which is unknown to me, lies near the left bank, separated from it by a channel probably cut by the stream, for the timber on the bank of the island shows the same age, and the varieties of trees are the same.

At the above-mentioned shale formation, the river turns to the northwest, its right bank an abrupt slope. From there on we got to a rather high chain of hills and at the western extension of these hills the Namaha, or Nimaha, River flows into the Missouri. This river, about forty fathoms wide at the mouth, flows from the southwest to the northwest through the prairies.[45] Its right bank, just before flowing into the main stream, touches upon the heights from which it takes its name. Its left bank is flat, however, and overgrown with low willows. The right bank of the Missouri, also overgrown with willows and formerly a shallow of three miles length, is bordered by tall timber.

During the day I observed large swarms of *Crysomela* covering the willows along the bank. Although these social beetles always appear in huge swarms, I was at a loss to explain how millions of these creatures, as if by magic, could occupy a defined section of land on both sides of the river,

six companies of the Sixth Regiment boarded boats for the Arikara villages on June 22, to be joined June 27 by Joshua Pilcher and sixty men of the Missouri Fur Company, Ashley and his men on the *Yellow Stone Packet*, a number of Sioux at the mouth of the White River, and Henry's men from the Yellowstone River, the combined forces assembling at the mouth of the Teton July 30.

The ensuing attack on the Arikaras was abortive, but the Indians sued for peace at the sign of a second attack, Leavenworth accepting. From these details it becomes clear why some of Ashley's men, with many wounded, had come down the Missouri from Council Bluffs in canoes: the *Yellow Stone Packet* and the *Rocky Mountains* were occupied with the first major military campaign against the Indians of the upper Missouri.

There is no accounting for the barrels of whisky which enlivened Ashley's men and threatened Duke Paul's crew, unless, as is probable, they had floated free from a boat upstream, victim of one of the Missouri's many snags.

John E. Sunder, *Bill Sublette: Mountain Man*, 33–53; Dale L. Morgan, *The West of William H. Ashley, 1822–1838*, 24–56; Russell Reid and Clell G. Cannon, eds., "Journal of the Atkinson-O'Fallon Expedition," *North Dakota Historical Quarterly*, IV (1929), 5–56.

[45] Both the Big Nemaha, which flows from Lancaster County, Nebraska, to the Missouri near present Rulo, and the Little Nemaha, lying north of the Big Nemaha and joining the Missouri in southeast Nemaha County, Nebraska, flow in a southeasterly direction. Here Duke Paul evidently refers to the Big Nemaha.

and then disappear without a trace. After careful examination I observed two kinds of these Chrysomeloe, one a most beautiful green with a golden sheen, the other with five black stripes on the yellow outer wings.[46]

The lovely *Papilio thoas* distributed over all of North America appears here also, and the *Papilio marcellus*, *ephestion* and *plexippus* are very common.[47] The latter goes far to the north and seems to be distributed over all of America, apparently not only the whole continent but also the islands, and under the most varying conditions.

On the twentieth I touched again the prairie along the river, which extends beyond hills entirely divested of trees, the soil composed of limestone and washed-up sand deposits. This alluvial formation deserves a closer examination. Especially so because this region for miles contains thick layers of easily slacking coal, wherein the forms of the original wood can still be distinctly traced.

This region bears the name Tapon-glé-sé.[48] Highly remarkable are the thick veins of coal imbedded in parallel layers of limestone and clay along the banks of the Missouri and its tributaries. These coal beds become even more enormous as one approaches the sources of the great river. Near the mouth of the Yellowstone and in several regions of the upper Missouri one can see great layers piled on top of another and reaching the crests of mountain masses more than one hundred feet high. Wholly submerged forests appear with fully developed trees of gigantic growth still standing. These layers, piled five and six, one above the other, are separated by strata of soft limestone and beds of clay, making a strange display of color which is visible at a great distance.[49]

The journey along the rocky cliffs of the Tapon-glé-sé was very dangerous on account of the many projecting rocks and the swift current. Six miles from the mouth of the Nimaha, the Missouri turns to the north and often times a low point of land separates the river from the hills containing

[46] Chrysomelidae, a family of small leaf-eating beetles. The two mentioned here are *Captocycla bicolor*, the golden tortoise beetle; and *Leptinatarsa decemlineata*, the species with black stripes on yellow, the Colorado potato beetle, so-called, which, before the introduction of potato culture, lived on sandbur foliage.

[47] The Linnean family Papilionidae, formerly applying to all the butterflies, now is confined to the swallowtails, of which *Papilio thoas*, Thoas' swallowtail, and *P. marcellus*, the zebra swallowtail of the group of kite swallowtails, are two. *P. ephistion* may here be confused with, possibly, *P. ornythion* Boisduval, a common Mexican and southwestern black.

[48] Tapon-glé-sé (possibly from the old form *tapon* and *glissé* in French). These exposed plugs or strata of coal are not mentioned at this point in Lewis and Clark.

[49] *Author*: On my second journey in 1830 I visited these coal beds on the Yellowstone and the upper Missouri. In due time I shall report my observations.

the coal beds. The left or northern bank is low and overgrown with tall trees.

A beast of prey had killed a deer and covered it so skillfully that I was inclined to believe that it had been done by human hands. Although the animal had already begun to decay because of the intense heat, the boatmen could not be restrained from eating of this unappetizing thing, for all of our food supplies had been spoiled by the excessive heat. The bacon had become rancid and the pickled meat was alive with large maggots. Our flour supply was almost exhausted and our hardtack, mouldy and spoiled. A wound on my foot prevented me from going on the hunt, and my hunter too suffered most acute pain in his limbs.

We rode along two bends which the river makes to a row of hills on the right bank, and despite nasty places and violent current, covered fifteen English miles. A fairly strong southeast wind allowed us to use the sail. The night was clear and cool. On the following day we rode round a bend in a northwesterly direction. The southern bank had little timber, but more tall weeds and low bushes, impenetrable so that a man can hardly make a hundred steps in an hour. The ground is also bad, sandy, and mixed with iron ore, and is considered wasteland. A man in a boat came toward us from the Fort of the Otos with a letter urging our boat master to greatest speed.[50]

An island in the middle of the stream was divided from the right bank by a rather wide channel, through which we passed. A small stream, Ta-kio, or Tar-ku-yu, empties into the Missouri near here from the east.[51] It winds among a series of prairie covered hills which present a surprising sight. Its bed is deep and muddy. Another creek bearing the same name also flows into the river farther down.

After the Missouri makes several unimportant bends in a distance of four miles, there is seen a long narrow island covered with willows. A narrow, rather shallow channel separates it from the right bank. Opposite the northern point of this island the Nish-na-ba-tona flows into the Mis-

[50] Of the Fort of the Otos, we will hear more in the present chapter, but private factories or trading posts catering to this tribe, the Kansa, and the Iowas, were early formed along the Missouri and the Platte. The Mr. Bennet mentioned by William Clark (*Original Journals*, July 14, 1804) as trader with the Otos and Pawnees in 1804 below the Little Nemaha was François Marie Benoît, one of Manuel Lisa's fur traders. Between this point and the mouth of the Platte, and for thirty miles up the latter river, the Otos lived until 1841, meeting at many points with fur company representatives. Oglesby, *Manuel Lisa*, 23 ff.

[51] The three forks of the Tarkio River rise in Montgomery County, Iowa, and flow south, uniting at Tarkio, Mo., thereafter flowing into Missouri River.

souri.[52] Below this stream the bank of the river is a prairie running back into the hills, where scattered trees grow.

The meadows through which the Nish-na-ba-tona flows are made unsafe by bands of roaming Iowas and Sacs lying in wait, ready to rob lone traveling hunters and fur traders. The right bank of the Missouri from the Platte to the Nimaha serves as the hunting ground for the friendly Otos.

The Iowas live in perpetual warfare with the western Indians between the Missouri and the Rio Bravo del Norte. Among these one reckons, as being of the same original stock, the great and little Osages (Osa-gua), the Arkansas (Apaches), the Kansas and other Indians called *Indianos l'laneros bravos* by the Spaniards of New Mexico.[53]

The Iowas belong to the O-tschan-gra, Winnebago nation, as do also the Fox, Oto, Sac, and other Indians who roam more peacefully between the Mississippi and Missouri.[54] To the Nadowess Dakotahs, or the Sioux nation, belong all the tribes which the French call in general the Sioux. These are the most populous tribes.

The Pawnees and Arikaras seem to be tribes which have been driven from the western regions to the border of New Spain, and perhaps they once inhabited the mountains of Sierra de las Grullas, for the Indians living there are said to have many points in common with them. The Arikaras (Rees), although surrounded by tribes of other hostile aborigines,

[52] The East Nishnabotna, rising in Carroll County, Iowa, and the West Nishnabotna rising nearby in the same county, join at Riverton, Iowa, the Nishnabotna continuing its southward flow to join the Missouri above present Corning in Atchison County, Mo.

[53] Rio Bravo del Norte = Rio Grande. The Iowas were fairly early thrown against their distant kinsmen, the Dakota Sioux, in the vicinity of the Blue Earth River in south central Minnesota. Their subsequent movement southwestward brought them into contact with a much more serious threat, especially as they reached the Missouri-Nebraska-Kansas frontier, in the Apaches, first, later the Comanches.

Étienne Venyard, Sieur de Bourgmont, in France's interest in commercial thrusts to the upper Missouri and westward to the Rocky Mountains, attempted with some success to bring the Iowas, Missourias, Kansa, Osages, and other lower Missouri tribes into peaceful relationship with the Comanches in 1724, the year following his establishment of Fort Orleans at the mouth of the Grand in present Carroll County, Mo. Pierre Margry, *Découvertes et Établissements des Français dans l'Ouest et dans le Sud de l'Amerique Septentrionale (1614–1754)*, 6 vols., VI, 388–448. George E. Hyde, *Pawnee Indians*, 23–48.

[54] O-tschan-gra = Otchagras (Thomas Jeffreys, *The Natural and Civil History of the French Dominions in North and South America*, 2 vols., I, 47). The Winnebagoes are of the Siouan linguistic family, and their language is shared by the Oto, Iowa, and Missouria tribes. The Sauks, or Sacs, and Foxes, on the other hand, were of the Algonquian linguistic group. For the influence of the Central Algonquians on the Winnebagoes, see Hodge, *Handbook*, II, 958–61.

seem not to be related to the northern Indians, but speak a dialect more related to that of the Pawnees.[55]

The twenty-second was a beautiful but hot day. The Missouri here forms a large elongated island, and like most of the islands in these parts it has no definite name. Here the eye enjoys many surprising vistas over picturesque meadows, beautiful sea-green grass standing out in striking contrast to the yellow coloring of the cliffs, with high, sloping walls rising in huge masses and dotted sparsely with tree clumps, especially poplars. Their silvery leaves glisten in the sun. Altogether, a striking change of colors. Masses of grayish yellow waters of this very wide stream roll amid this scene, now rushing, now smooth as a mirror. And it seems to be increasing rather than decreasing toward its sources, for in its upper regions it often appears wider than the Mississippi at its mouth.

A row of bluffs, thinly covered with timber, extends from east to west and then suddenly ends at the mouth of the little Nimaha. This unimportant stream, bordered by the prairie, joins its right bank on the above named hills, and at its mouth forms a small island covered meagerly with willows. Its channel on the north side probably dries up in the hot summer. For two miles from the little Namaha the bank of the Missouri borders on the prairie. The left bank, however, is low and wooded, and in the background an arresting chain of hills is covered with a rich carpet of luxuriant green grass, extending from the southeast to the northwest, and at last again reaches the river, which it had left at the mouth of the Nisch-na-ba-tona. Our boat traveled along the right bank to a willow-covered point, where the river turns from the north to the northeast.

The observation of the calculated eclipse of the moon this evening was of much importance to me. It could not have come under more favorable circumstances. The sun set in splendor and the moon appeared half eclipsed when I saw it rising above the forest-fringed plain. A small cloud floated past it at the total eclipse occurring between 9:30 and 9:40 o'clock. It hung perfectly free in the sky, colored dark red, the left surface appearing lighter than the right. I could not recognize the *mare crisium*, but could see the lower dark spots on the opposite side.

The point where we were was, according to my calculation, at 40° 38′ north latitude and 98° 44′ west longitude from Greenwich, and that means that it is at the same latitude as the capitals of the warmest countries of Europe: Naples, Constantinople, and Madrid. But how noticeable is the difference of the temperature here and that at the same latitude of Europe.

[55] The Pawnees and the Arikaras are of the Caddoan group, the former having moved northward to Nebraska in historic times, the latter to the upper Missouri in South Dakota.

While the summers in the middle regions of the Missouri resemble the climate of Egypt (mean temperature of both 90° to 92°), the winters approximate the climate of Moscow.

The Missouri is at times covered with a slab of ice six feet thick and with four to six feet of snow. These variations of climate in the northern half of the North American continent are under the natural graduation of climates in similar conditions common to all of the regions east of the Cordilleras as far south as latitude 28°.

On the other hand, those parts lying to the west of the mountains have a much more equable climate. As an illustration I shall only mention the following: The mouth of the Columbia River (46° north latitude), the village of the Arikaras and Quebec are almost at the same degree of latitude; while the winter on the Columbia resembles that of southern Germany, the last two regions are rigidly cold such as is scarcely felt in Königsberg or Moscow. The Presidio de San Francisco, St. Louis, and Washington are all between latitude 38° and 39°; while in the first named place oranges and figs thrive, thick ice masses cover the Mississippi and Potomac during January and February. At San Ildefonso in the province of Sonora in Mexico tropical plants grow on the east coast of the Sea de Cortes; on the other hand, between latitude 29° and 30°, at New Orleans and St. Augustine in eastern Florida the thermometer in my presence fell to 19°, and thick icicles hung from the rigging of our ship.

From latitude 28° on, along the Gulf of Mexico, the striking phenomena of winter cease. In the colony of New Smyrna (28° 45′ north latitude) even frost is quite rare. And the coast of Matamoros from the Rio Bravo del Norte on and also the whole peninsula of Florida from the 26th degree on do not suffer the chilling northwest wind as severely as the above-named regions are subjected to, nor do they have frost. For this reason tropical plants do so well there.

Early on the twenty-fifth we traveled along the right bank of willow-covered lowlands and scattered patches of tall timber. Several islands have been formed in the river six miles from the Namaha, some in the middle of the Missouri, others close to the bank, separated by narrow channels. We had to turn around in one of them, as the mouth was blocked. Our crew found a barrel of whisky in the mass of driftwood and the greater part of the men got drunk and so were useless for that day.

At noon a canoe arrived with three men who had been sent out to meet our boat. The journey was thereby not speeded up. Such additions of men were always of little use, since they invariably caused a disturbance and were grudgingly or not at all willing to lend a helping hand.

Several islands of varying size lie linked together in the river, chain-like,

separated from the bank by channels of differing width. They seem formerly to have been part of the mainland. The banks bordering on the prairies
are overgrown with stunted timber. Miles of prairie touch upon the river
bank, and near the edge of the water grow hemp-like weeds and low sumac
bushes, forming an impenetrable mass.

For the first time I saw several *Oenothera*[56] and a very handsome
Assclepias,[57] a genus rich in manifold varieties in America. We reached a
large island, called Île à Beau Soliel, perhaps the largest in the Missouri.
A broad deep channel separates it from the right bank. The night was very
clear and cool, and in the morning there was a dense fog and heavy dew.

During the morning we traveled along the right bank, staying the whole
day along this side of the stream. The water seemed to be rising slightly,
and once we had to row along a chain of hills whose high limestone cliffs
formed the steep bank. The remaining stretch is a wilderness, which, as
usual, consists of impenetrable weeds and dense masses of willows. The
prairie either is in the near background or comes to the edge of the water.
The river makes only one bend to the north.

We had a most beautiful and cool night. On the twenty-fifth the boat
reached a bend in the river to the northwest, a dangerous place. The current
runs over a shallows with many tree trunks and creates a violent whirlpool,
where many vessels have met their ruin. In the middle of these rapids the
current grabbed and turned our boat with such fury that we were obliged
to seek the left bank, a meadow with man-high grass. The force carried us
back a mile and at eight o'clock that morning, after working for four hours,
we still were two miles downstream from the place where we had spent the
night.

A tall, dense-growing, reed-like variety of grass (*Saccharum*) was in
bloom and covered the prairie for a great distance from the bank.[58] I
noticed huge swarms of butterflies belonging to the Danaidae,[59] related to
Papedusa. They were hard to catch, as are most of the butterflies of this
region.

A rather strong wind had risen from the north. Although unfavorable
to our journey, it was nevertheless welcome because it reduced the heat and
drove away the mosquitoes.

[56] *Oenothera*, evening primroses.

[57] *Assclepias* = *Asclepias*, a genus of the milkweed family.

[58] *Saccharum*, a genus of Old World tropical grasses, of which *S. officinarum*, the sugar
cane, is one. *Andropogon* sp., the big bluestem, the "leek green grass" noted by William
Clark, is one of the greatest of western grasses and may be the one here noted by Duke
Paul, or it could have been Indian grass, *Sorghastrum nutans*.

[59] Danaidae, the family of monarch butterflies, the swarms referred to being, in all probability, *Danaus plexippus* Linnaeus, the monarch.

The previously mentioned chain of hills, running from the east to the northwest, parallels the Missouri and at no place is distant from it. Limestone cliffs and attractive shelves alternate with one another to form great bare areas, and then are again resplendent with luxuriant grass. Along these low hills the Nisch-na-ba-tona winds from the southeast to the northwest, almost parallel to the Missouri. Its source is not far from the Missouri and there is a place where the two streams are only a few English miles apart. This region is called, by the Creoles, La Traite du Nisch-na-ba-tona.[60]

Despite the indescribable heat and the very few rain showers to alleviate the sun's glow, the green of the meadows and the foliage of the trees was still as fresh as in the spring. In other hemispheres at the same latitude, where the heat of the summer is less intense but the winters more mild (as for example in the warmer parts of Asia), the vegetation begins to die even at the end of July, and in August the green of the grassy regions has completely changed to a dead yellow. The prairies of North America, however, even in the regions that border on the hotter belt, seem to enjoy a much longer life. This may be due to the milder and more regular winds. Moreover, I believe this phenomenon may be caused by the greater atmospheric humidity. While I made three hygrometric observations each day in the western part of America on the banks of the Missouri, the de Luc hygrometer rarely registered below $55°$, even on the hottest days. The average was between $62°$ and $64°$. Compared with this, the humidity of southern Europe and especially the middle of Asia will differ approximately by $15°$. Mornings after sunrise a heavy dew had usually formed, reducing the temperature of the air slightly.

The river now makes a great bend enclosed by meadows, with a green chain of hills in the background. I never saw the Missouri as wide as here, more than two English miles wide. Even now that the water is falling this is very noticeable. The right bank is low and willow-covered, and a channel forms an island. Within a week the river has fallen seven feet. But it rose slightly during the night after the rain on the twenty-fifth, but hardly enough to earn mention.

A short distance above the great bend, a low bank projects far into the stream, bordered by many shallows. The Missouri is forced into a very narrow but deep bed with a swift current, making the opposite bank, together with a mass of driftwood, most dangerous.[61]

[60] Nishnabota Trace or Trail.

[61] Great Bend, one of several of the same name mentioned by the author, clearly seemed, here as elsewhere, to merit its designation. Of one of these, John James Audubon said in 1843 that it was twenty-six miles around by boat but only three miles across on foot. The present one seems to be located southwest of Langdon in Atchison, County, Mo.

A mile farther up north the vegetation in the area is changed. The right bank, some fifteen feet high, has tall timber. The left bank constitutes a continuation of the long low point at the great bend, the beginning of prairie. A fifty-foot wide channel separates a willow-covered island from the bank. We tried a passage through this channel but had to give it up, as the water was too shallow.

My men caught a catfish (*Pymelodus*) of extraordinary size. This fish, belonging to the *Siluria*, seemed to me distinctly different from those I found in the Ohio.[62]

The heat had been extremely intense the whole day, and the northeast wind cooled it but little, for from ten to five the rays of the sun beat down every movement of air. Such calm becomes unbearable since all means of relief are lacking on the Missouri. Springs of cold water are most scarce, and the fresh water from the river must usually be left standing for two or three hours before it can be drunk, because the earthy particles settle very slowly. Even though it is kept in the coolest place that can be found, it takes on the temperature of the air. The water of the Missouri has a temperature of 85° to 88°, making it almost undrinkable unless some alcohol is mixed with it. For three weeks I had nothing to drink but this muddy water, without becoming sick, proof that river water, especially when mixed with earthy matter, is less harmful than the water of cooler springs. This experience is common on the Missouri and the Mississippi. The night was cool, but unmindful billions of mosquitoes swarmed in the air.

With the earliest light on the twenty-sixth we tediously started to pull the boat along the right bank, a slowed-up journey made dangerous by the driftwood washed up along the bank in huge piles. The willow-covered lowland ceased, sparse timber appeared, and here the land changed into prairie. In several places scattered trees, bare and leafless, covered considerable areas. These places resemble clearings which the settlers are in the habit of making with the aid of fire and then abandoning them to nature. The cause is indeed the same, for in the autumn the Indians set the dry prairie on fire and so lay whole forests in ashes, the wind driving the fire on until it reaches the river. Of course the scattered trees in the prairie are not consumed by the flames, but the bark is dried up near the roots, and life is ended. In the forest the fire seizes the lower branches of the trees and also the bushes and climbing plants. Like a sea of fire, the flames, driven by the wind, surge high in the air to consume the finest forest for miles around.

The prairie near the bank touches upon a chain of hills which two miles

---

[62] *Pymelodus = Pimelodus*, a primarily South American genus. The species seen could have been either *Ictalurus furcatus*, the great blue catfish, which reaches 150 pounds, or the much smaller *Ictalurus punctatus*, the white channel catfish. *Siluria = Siluridae.*

farther up comes close to the stream. Scattered bushes resembling plantings in a park grow on this prairie. The left bank is a lowland, bordered by an island separated by a broad channel. At the mouth of this channel a boat had recently been wrecked.

Not until noon did our boat reach the hills mentioned above, which for a distance of two miles skirt the right bank and consist of limestone and sandstone. These friable and loosely joined masses slip into the river during falling water, especially noticeable at one of the hills projecting far into the river. For this reason the Creoles call this hill Grand Debouli, a name also applied to an island farther down the river (Ile du Grand Debouli).[63] In the course of time this row of hills will disappear entirely.

The prairie, uniting completely with the hills, is dotted with stunted trees with top branches dead. For the most part they are walnut and oak trees (*Juglans nigra, fraxinifolia* [better *Carya*, hickory or pecan], and *Quercus phellos, obtusifolia* [*imbricaria*] etc.).

The Missouri, making a great bend here, is very dangerous because of rapids flowing over shallow places, especially during falling water. Beyond this place at a higher bank several cottonwood trees undermined by the river tumbled into the stream directly before and behind our boat. In such manner the Missouri gains in width in these higher areas, and the soil is then deposited in others, where it narrows them.

In a swampy place I observed a *Typhaceae* in bloom (but it was not *Typhaeceae angustifolia*) similar to that found in European lakes and ponds, but differing from it by having a thicker flowering club and narrow leaves. The American aspen[64] of Michaux appeared here and there among the willows and other woods. It is very difficult to distinguish it from *Populus angulata*, Willd. In general, all the aspens mentioned by Michaux and most of those brought to Europe differ but little from the ordinary Mississippi poplar or cottonwood. These again resemble the Canadian poplar yet have points of difference. North America is really very rich in poplars or aspens, whose manifold varieties extend to the tropical regions. Mexico grows excellent trees of this kind on the slopes of the Cordilleras, in the hottest part of that region, and also on the central plateau in the environs of the capital city.

The night of the twenty-sixth to the twenty-seventh was cool, but the morning became sultry and rainy. Immediately after our departure we had to pass a dangerous place, and here our rudder was wrenched out by a tree

[63] Irregular, from French *débouler*, to fall precipitately.

[64] *Populus tremuloides*, quaking aspen, is out of range; possibly *P. sargentii*, plains cottonwood.

stump projecting from the water. Carried away by the current, it was overtaken and brought back by our swimmers.

The wind rose out of the south by southeast with considerable force aiding us in our journey. I reached the row of hills on the right bank, called Côtes de la Table, a grass-covered area with occasional patches of timber, presenting a pleasing appearance. At a point where the river makes a turn to the west at the foot of the neighboring heights the little Rivière de la Table flows into the Missouri. The right bank of the Missouri is low land, separated from a large island by a channel that dries up in the summer, but which may really be considered as a part of the mainland. The channel still contained enough water to float our boat and we passed through it in half an hour, shortening our journey by at least three miles.

Now the river again turns to the west. The right bank, piled with driftwood, is a high, flat point. We crossed over to the left side and here the bank is low and overgrown with willows. The journey was dangerous because of the swift current, also the wind struck us from the side. The river makes a great bend to the north and forms many sandbars. A row of grass-covered hills (named after a nearby creek, Côtes de l'Eau qui Pleure) extends for a considerable distance.[65] Here the Missouri is very wide in several places and is made unsafe by shoals and sandbars. The left bank is the continuation of a great point bordered by hills and prairie.

Both of the streams mentioned above are only small creeks with names taken from the Indian language. In the late summer they dry up entirely. Their beds contain deposits of fatty clay which formerly served the bison and deer as licks during the autumn season. These animals have not been seen here for years, having been frightened away by the military establishment at the Council Bluffs.

Since the traffic between the whites and the nations who dwell in considerable numbers between the Platte and the Eau qui Courre had greatly increased and the Indians are supplied with firearms, the bison, falsely called buffalo by the Americans, have withdrawn a hundred hours' distance. In a few decades these animals will probably cross the Rocky Mountains and penetrate into the western regions of the New World, which do not seem to have been made suitable by nature for their habitat.[66]

[65] l'Eau Qui Pleure or Weeping Water Creek, which empties into the Missouri from the west at the point where Otoe and Cass counties, Nebraska join, got its name in Perrin du Lac, more than thirty years earlier. Noted by William Clark (Coues, *History of the Lewis and Clark Expedition*, I, 50).

[66] The American bison (*Bison bison*) was well established east as well as west of the Mississippi when the earliest Europeans arrived in the New World. East of that river, its habitat extended to most of the states and regions except the Great Lakes, Florida, New Jersey, and New England. In the West the plains bison ranged from northern Mexico to

The prairies about the creek Qui Pleure were covered with half decayed skulls and large bones of these giant oxen. My companion assured me that only five or six years ago he still hunted the bison here. On my arrival at the Otos' trading post I was consoled in that I would encounter them after a few day's journey along the Elkhorn River. However, I had to travel farther north, over one hundred English miles, before I sighted these creatures for the first time.[67]

The wind blew uninterruptedly the whole day with equal velocity. At noon we reached two large islands (Les Iles à Trudot). The first and larger one of these is separated from the land by a narrow and deep channel. The other, a mile farther up, is nearly in the middle of the river. The stream turns to the northwest by west and an hour farther on forms a large island, called Ile aux Barils.[68] This island lies nearer the left bank, and the main current flows along the right bank. Here begins a long chain of hills bordering the right bank of the Missouri, forming a continuation of the prairie, where only scattered trees of average height grow, resembling our orchards on a meadow plain.

The deer grazing in large herds are like our herds of cattle, and the many crows and ravens (*Corvus major, Corvus americanus, mihi*, the American crow; [respectively, *C. sinuatus* Wagler, 1829, and *C. corone* Wilson, 1811]) about the same as ours in color and size, reminding one of their European relatives.

Many sandbars in the stream, appearing now in the middle and then again near the bank and in part covered with water, made the journey more difficult.

---

the Rocky Mountains; in the mountains the wood bison (some scientists say it differed so little from the plains subspecies as to be unworthy of separate classification) ranged from Colorado northward to subarctic Canada.

White hunting pressures on eastern herds developed largely from extending patterns of settlement; progressive extinction of these herds is relatively easily traced, e.g., for such states as Kentucky and Pennsylvania. The pattern in the West was of a different character: as the robe and hide trade developed between whites and Indians, the old food-fiber-clothing dependence of the latter upon the plains herds gave way increasingly to barter uses. This in turn was largely replaced by commercial hunting after the Civil War, so that by 1876 the massive western herds were exterminated.

Frank Gilbert Roe, *The North American Buffalo, passim*; Carl Coke Rister, "The significance of the Destruction of the Buffalo in the Southwest," *Southwestern Historical Quarterly*, XXXIII, No. 1 (July, 1929), 43–50; Wayne Gard, *The Great Buffalo Hunt, passim.*

[67] *Author*: On my journey up the Missouri in the year 1830 I encountered the first bison near the settlement of the Arikara Indians, about at latitude 45° 50' north.

[68] Nicollet called the four islands noted by Lewis and Clark Trudeau's, but others called them Five Barrel Islands.

I saw many wild geese (*Anser canadensis* and *hyperborea*) and shot an old gander drifting past our boat and unable to save himself by flying away. The Canadian goose, the most widely distributed variety in North America, is incorrectly named and might be called much more appropriately *Anser nigricollis*.[69] The German variety, called *Anser leucopsis* by Wolf and Meyer, has the same white cheeks as *Anser canadensis*. For this reason the name *leucopsis* is likewise not suitable and might lead to confusion if geographic distribution did not separate the two varieties. The black neck of the Canadian goose is rather distinctive.

We stayed overnight at a promontory of the above-mentioned hills at a place called Pierre à Calumet.[70] During the night a heavy thunderstorm accompanied by north wind overtook us. The morning of the twenty-eighth was clear and beautiful. The boat moved along the right bank around a wooded point on which a strip of prairie enclosed by hills extends to the Missouri. Crescent-shaped it terminated at a grass-covered cliff which projects far into the river. The cliff, called Oeil de Fer, or the Iron Eye, derives its name from an Indian of the tribe of Otos who is buried here.[71]

Among all primitive people of America a burial mound, especially that of a chief, is a sanctuary. These are usually peculiar places or on conspicuously shaped hill formations. However barbarous against their enemies, the Indian peoples never touch a grave to desecrate it, not even that of their worst enemy. This is not done because of magnanimity but because of superstitious fear, a feeling singular to untutored races. Near this cliff a small creek flows into the Missouri.

Beyond the heights the river turns to the west. A large island is separated by a deep and rather wide channel from the right bank. The distance from the end of this island to the mouth of the Platte River is reckoned to be six miles. A row of rocky hills touches upon the river to form a very stony bank.

These heights, called Côtes de la Rivière Platte, reach to this river. The first height is overgrown with timber. The main wood varieties are *Mespilus americana*, *Quercus phellos*, *nigra*, a *Prunus*, the *Tilia americana* and *Fraxinus nigra*.[72] All these trees lack the fine growth and the luxuriant

[69] Avoiding color description, the Canada goose is now *Branta canadensis*.

[70] Calumet Point, not noted by Lewis and Clark, on the Nebraska side.

[71] Perrin du Lac's name for the hill; to him the Indian history is also traceable.

[72] *Mespilus americana*, unknown; possibly *Amelanchier arborea*, service berry, or *Pyrus ioensis*, western crab apple. *Quercus phellos*, willow oak, is out of range, suggesting rather *Q. imbricaria*, shingle oak. *Q. nigra* suggests *Q. marilandica*, black-jack oak, or *Q. velutina*, black oak. *Prunus* could have been *P. americana*, American plum; or *P. serotina*, black cherry; or *P. virginiana*, choke cherry. *Tilia americana*, basswood. *Fraxinus nigra* is here out of range, but *F. pennsylvanica*, red ash, and *F. lanceolata*, green ash, were both common near the mouth of the Platte.

foliage of their kind on the fertile heights of the lower Missouri. Farther back the hills run out gradually into the common form of the region, the grassy plain stretching into uninterrupted prairie.

We spent the night at a little creek where two slopes join. The high banks are covered with grass. The night seemed rather cool at 73° and we were chilled, no doubt because our bodies had become accustomed to the heat. No mosquitoes were heard, and even the bats of the genus *Molossus* ceased flying about us. There was also a heavy dew especially toward morning.

By seven o'clock in the morning on July 29 we had reached the great Platte River. Here the hills dipped suddenly to form a level point covered with cottonwoods. Several islands of varying size lie at the mouth of the river, and for this reason it flows into the Missouri at its fullest width.

The Platte, called Rio de la Plata by the Spaniards of New Mexico, is rightfully entitled to its name. It is very shallow and because of many rapids and sandbars is not navigable. Undoubtedly it is the largest tributary of the Missouri and is one of the main rivers of North America. Its source, though not quite definitely determined, is found in the enormous ice masses in the northern Cordilleras of Mexico in the region of perpetual snow, north of the great James Peak between northern latitude 40° and 41°.[73]

The sources of four great rivers, the Rio Bravo del Norte, the Rio dos Arcos (Arkansas), the Rio Colorado de Natchitoches, and the Rio de la Plata are all found in the Sierra de Grullas, or Crane Mountains, and are not far from one another. Excepting the Rio Bravo del Norte, all flow into the territory of the United States to empty into the Missouri or Mississippi.[74]

After a regular course from the west to the east of almost two hundred

[73] *Author*: Concerning the Platte River and its geographic position, the journal of Major Long is the only reliable source. I therefore refer to the work of this traveler, to whom science owes such a debt. [The Platte is formed by the North Platte, 618 miles long, rising in Jackson County, northern Colorado, flowing north into central Wyoming, and turning south, southeast across the Nebraska border through west central Nebraska, and the South Platte, which it joins in Lincoln County, Nebraska, to flow 310 miles to its confluence with the Missouri below present Omaha. The South Platte is 424 miles long, rising in Park County, Colorado. "The northern Cordilleras of Mexico" is therefore a misnomer for the period in which the Duke is writing: the Platte drainage lies well north of the Arkansas, which, in present Colorado, defined in part Mexican territory lying southward, to the north-south line to the west adopted in the Adams-Onis Treaty of 1819 between Spain and the U.S.]

[74] Rio Bravo del Norte = Rio Grande. Rio Colorado de Natchitoches = Red River. Crane Mountains appears in Alexander von Humboldt's *Carte Générale du Royaume del la Nouvelle Espagne* (1811) as Sierra de las Grullas, now designated the Sawatch Range in central Colorado.

German miles through an uninterrupted prairie region, but rarely broken by scattered trees and bushes along its banks, the Platte empties into the Missouri (at 41° 2' north latitude and 99° 4' west longitude from P.).

Among the most important tributaries to the Platte must be mentioned the Elkhorn (Corne de Cerf). Near its mouth is located the village of the Otos, and many Indian tribes roam its banks and the adjoining prairie. Several of these living along the border of New Spain are distinguished by their lust for robbing.

In the territory of the United States the Pawnees are the most numerous of the tribes. Peacefully inclined toward the Americans and Frenchmen, they are the irreconcilable enemies of the Spaniards. The Weta-pahatos, the Kiaou (Kiawa), the Cheyennes, the Arapahos (Arapahoras of the Mexicans), and the Apaches are less numerous, and the Spaniards know them by the name of *Indianos l'Laneros bravos*.

A great sandbank joining an island and covered with much driftwood closes the mouth of the outlet of the Platte. Where the banks were somewhat elevated, countless bank swallows (*Hirundo riparia* and *viridis*) had nested. The handsome *Sterna* with black head and white band on the forepart of its head streaked about. The belly is grayish white, the back and quill feathers darker, wing feathers grayish-black, and the feet yellow.[75]

As far as the shallow little Butterfly Creek (Rivière au Papillon), the banks are covered with timber, later no more with trees but only meadow growth.[76] On the sandbanks close to the water were low willows, whose seed easily takes root. The left [west] bank continues to be low and overgrown with cottonwoods. Then a stretch of prairie comes close to the bank, extending as far as a row of hills called Côtes à Kennel, on the slope of which the American Company at that time had a factory.[77]

[75] *Hirundo riparia* = *Riparia riparia*, the bank swallow or sand martin; [*Hirundo*] *viridis* = *Iridoprocne bicolor*, the tree or white-bellied swallow, a species that does not nest in banks. A bank-nesting swallow that Duke Paul might have seen is the rough-winged swallow, *Stelgidopteryx ruficollis*. The *Sterna* was probably *S. albifrons*, the least tern, the only tern of interior North America having a white forehead when in breeding plumage, according to George Miksch Sutton.

[76] The French name has stuck and Papillion is the county seat of Sarpy County, Nebraska, the latter named for Jean Baptiste Sarpy, the St. Louis businessman and fur trader.

[77] The Council Bluffs area was so situated that it could hardly avoid a post by any of the major interests in the Missouri Fur Trade: Fort San Carlos of the Missouri Commercial Company, 1795; Régis Loisel's post of 1802; Manuel Lisa's Fort Hunt after the War of 1812, later Fort Manuel, 1819; Cabanné's Post, representing Bernard Pratte and Company; and, earlier, Pratte and Vasquez above Council Bluffs. The American Fur Company operation here was the fruit of Ramsay Crooks' zealous competitiveness for the Company as head of its Western Department. Nearest the mouth of the Platte was the Missouri Fur Company post Bellevue, replacing in 1823 Fort Manuel farther up the Missouri. Houck, *History of*

We reached this settlement by sundown after traveling along a meadow overgrown with tall nettles and flax-like weeds. The little Mosquito Creek flows into the stream from the left between willows. I set out from the boat in order to deliver my letters to the overseers of the American Company and stayed there overnight. Here I noticed traces of some Indian tents in the yard having belonged to Iowas who had gone to the Fort of the Otos.

After breakfast I found a Spanish mule, bridled and saddled before the house, to carry me to the fort, twenty-two miles from the Côtes à Kennel. It seems to me impossible to make such a long trip in the intense heat with such a wretched creature. I was assured by the guide, however, an old half-blood employed by the trading post as interpreter, that such a mule could cover forty English miles in a day with a load of three hundred pounds on his back. Though this seemed unbelievable to me, I mounted the mule and trotted up the hill on a narrow footpath.

This bad trail, in part blocked by fallen trees and windbreaks, ran for more than four English miles over rather steep heights overgrown with heavy brush and tall weeds. My mule, however, went on with nimble steps and did not stumble once.

Beyond this miserable trail the prairie begins, bordered by the hills, and is lost in unending distance to the western horizon. The plant growth of these plains seemed different in many respects from that of the prairie farther south, the grass is shorter and not as luxuriantly green as that which I had seen earlier. Many plants, mostly annuals, were in bloom, and many of them were known varieties such as *Helianthus, Silphium, Rudbeckia, Tagetes,*[78] and other composites. They either stood singly in the prairie, as for example the sunflower, or they formed dense clusters in moist places and on the edge of small creeks. Many smaller plants, covering the grassy land carpet-like, had ceased blooming or were just unfolding their rather insignificant flowers. To these belong several legumes of the genus *Delea, Astragalus, Kennedia,* etc. The *Opuntia* of northern America was also seen here and there, but only sparingly compared with the regions farther north.[79]

My companion seemed to be in a hurry and let his horse go in a stretch-

---

Missouri, I, 252–53; Sunder, *Joshua Pilcher,* 55–56; Phillips and Smurr, *The Fur Trade,* I, 412.

[78] The other genera having previously been identified, only *Tagetes,* the genus embracing the marigolds, needs this identification; he probably saw *Dyssodia papposa* or the genus *Ratibda.*

[79] *Delea* is *Dalea; Astragalus,* a large genus of herbs of the pea family: the milk vetches. *Kennedia* = *Kennedya,* a genus of Australian woody vines of the pea family. *Opuntia,* a large genus of cacti, including *Opuntia polycantha,* prickly pear.

ing gallop. The mule did not lag and performed just as well. In an even gait with the best of wind, he covered at least four German miles in that burning heat. The mules of New Spain, although small and unimposing, far surpass the European mules. Laden with the heaviest loads, they are driven by the *ariero* (the Spanish mule driver) over thirty miles in a day through hilly country and on bad roads. In running they often surpass the horses, and the hunters of New Mexico frequently use good mules to overtake the bison.

The Missouri, making a great bend to the north, and also the Platte, can be seen in many places from rises. The beds of both seem equally wide. The prairies gradually slope from the heights to reach the Missouri in a low point covered with scattered trees. A chain of bluffs touches the river at the end of the bend, forming enormous walls of stratified limestone.

When I reached the hills near our stream, the foot trail became very bad again, passing through weeds fifteen to twenty feet high, so entangled that I had the greatest difficulty in working my way through.

The trading post of the Otos is situated among the hills on the slope close to the river.[80] In order to reach it, however, I had to ride around the entire ridge of the hill. I found the trail almost impassable, for very few people travel this way, and the richness of the soil produces rank vegetation overgrowing the path which but recently had been cleared with much toil.

The building of the French Company, to which they apply the name fort, is set near a small creek whose steep banks enclose it almost like a wall. The house is rather firmly put together and has chimneys of brick. The agent of the company, Mr. Robidoux, having been informed of my coming, received me with much politeness and had a room prepared for me.[81]

[80] *Author*: In the year 1823 the company still existed under the name of Campagnie Française, to distinguish it from the American Fur Company, and engaged in the fur trade in the Northwest. It was organized by Creoles [Berthold, Chouteau, and Pratte]. When the American Company ceased to be a closed trading union, the French Company united almost all fur trading interests under the name American Fur Company, under the presidency of Mr. Astor of New York, and this company carried on the business with little competition within the territory of the United States. Among the oldest founders of the fur trade belonged the Chouteau family of St. Louis. They are still greatly interested in the trade, and Mr. Pierre Chouteau [Sr.] is now the director of the company in St. Louis, the place where all important undertakings start. [The Oto Post, to be named Cabanné's Post in the autumn of 1823, when J. P. Cabanné succeeded Joseph Robidoux, Jr., as factor, dated from 1822.]

[81] Joseph Robidoux, Jr., born in 1783 at St. Louis, was in the midst of an active and long career which had early taken the directions pursued by his father, a native of Kaskaskia, in frontier commerce and fur-trading. He had established a post at Blacksnake Hills in the

Near the creek in front of the house a large number of Iowa Indians was camping, having come here because of fear of the Sioux or Dakotahs (of the tribe of Yanktons) with whom they live in irreconcilable enmity. They were under a new leader, who at that time seemed to be their priest. Most were in deep mourning because of a recent defeat in which the Yanktons had killed one of the best leaders of the Iowas, Oua-i-a-ka, Le Coeur Dur (the Hard Heart) and in addition some of their warriors. Their women and children had been abducted by the savages, and a few of the former had been killed. I was shown a woman who had saved herself by fleeing, and she had traveled barefoot a distance of over one hundred German miles in two weeks. She had had no food other than roots and onions that grow on the prairie. To strengthen their friendship with the Iowas, the agents of the government had ransomed a small boy, bringing him back to his parents.

Since I had the opportunity of acquiring some information about the Iowa Indians during my stay, I shall record the following observations, hoping that they may not become tiresome, in a sketch dealing with the mode of living and the customs of an American primitive people who have become almost extinct.

A few character traits markedly distinguish the Iowas from neighboring tribes. They place a high esteem on matrimonial fidelity, and the mothers guard the chastity of their daughters. For this reason one finds fewer prostitutes among them than among the Pawnees, Sioux, Kansa, and other tribes. Further, the love of parents for their children and relations among each other deserve mention. Friends never forsake one another in danger, and bravery is a quality desired by all these natives. With these qualities progressive education could accomplish much with them, even though they may appear ever so crude.

Recently a great chief of the Dakotahs was killed, and a man sixty years old, called Nan-ki-pa-hi, voluntarily hurled himself to his death. When he heard of the death of his friend, Nan-ki-pa-hi called out to his even older wife, "Old one, my chief is dead. I am accustomed to live with him. We must die with him."

---

environs of present St. Joseph, as earlier indicated, and at Council Bluffs, Robidoux and Papin were in partnership with Berthold, Chouteau, and Pratte, the latter a fur-forwarding system for the American (Astor) Fur Company, Western Division. Laforce Papin would continue in the fur trade to 1842, the year of his death, and Robidoux in various interests to 1868 at St. Joseph. Maximilian zu Wied, *Travels in the Interior of North America, 1832–1834*, 4 vols., ed. by Reuben Gold Thwaites, Early Western Travel Series (Nos. 21–24), I, 257n.; IV, 111, 112, 121; Edwin James, *Account of an Expedition from Pittsburgh to the Rocky Mountains*, 4 vols., ed. by Reuben Gold Thwaites, Early Western Travels Series (Nos. 14–17), II, 143n.

The old woman followed and Nan-ki-pa-hi on his horse charged at full speed into the enemy. He called with a loud voice, "Where the scalp of my friend hangs there may mine be also."

Pierced by a hundred arrows, he fell, and with him his wife. Ancient and modern history relates few instances of such true friendship, and how can it be possible that one should despise a people that count such men in its ranks?

The dwellings of the Iowas are similar to those of other American nomadic peoples. Usually they consist of skins spread over willow poles, bent bow-fashion. Others resemble conical tents and are covered with bison hides. One family lives in a tent lounging on blankets. A fire burns on the ground in front of the hut. Food consists mainly of maize and meat, boiled in kettles without salt. The food is eaten with knives and spoons made of the horns of the bison.

The Iowas eat the meat of all sorts of animals, roots, and the bark of trees. Dogs are regarded a delicacy. They do not readily take up agriculture, although their kinsmen, the Missourias and Otos, live in fixed villages and cultivate large fields of maize and pumpkins. The American government has not succeeded in confining the Iowas to a fixed habitat. Even the Otos and Missourias will remain in their villages only during the time of seeding and harvesting their crops. The remaining time they devote to hunting the American bison and the deer.

It seems probable that through the efforts of Major O'Fallon the Iowas may be united with the Otos and the Missourias. The latter live together in the same villages, and in reality they share little of their culture, but act as one tribe standing by each other in war and in peace.

The efforts of a benevolent government, through highly estimable men who represent it, have averted many a bloody encounter among the Indians. Every possible effort is being made to consolidate friendship between the nations, and only the greed of trade can disadvantageously affect the efforts of the government and its agents.[82]

The Iowas call themselves Pa-cho-sché in their own language which may be translated into Gray Snow from *Pa*, snow, and *cho-sché*, gray. They seem to have descended from the Nyo-ta-sche, or the Missourias, and to be related to the Quac-to-ta-tas, or Otos, and perhaps some other wild tribes whose customs and language are strikingly similar to theirs. At the end of the seventeenth century these nations became known to the first French

---

[82] *Author*: Unfortunately the recent war with Black Hawk, a chief of the Sauk Indians, with whom the Iowas were associated, has changed much to the disadvantage of both parties. This bloody war developed shortly after my second visit. I myself was a witness to the beginnings of this most serious event.

navigators. It is possible that the Iowas descended from the Winnebagos, the Qui-ne-pe-gong, or O-tschan-gra (Big Fish), who in former centuries constituted a powerful nation.

The religious cults, the customs, and also the dialects of the nations named above are in their totality in greatest agreement, and lend weight to the opinion that these people had a common origin. These traits furnish much more conclusive evidence regarding their origin than do their legends which are exaggerated praise of the bravery of their forefathers. It seems that the various nations dwelling between the Great Lakes and the Mississippi formerly lived in Canada, were driven out of these parts, and followed the direction of the lakes. They speak somewhat confusedly of a colder region than they now inhabit, and they also seem to have an indistinct notion of a sea lying to the east, which they call the Great Salt Lake.

Concerning their external aspect, most of them have a pointed nose, high temples, a very arched forehead, lower cheekbones, fuller lips, and deeper groove above the chin than the members of other nations. A slighter body and less athletic build distinguish them from the Osages, the Omahas, and the Kansas, from whom they also differ in facial structure. The features of the Iowas are manlier and wilder than those of the last named people.

It is worth mentioning that one rarely encounters ugly women. The outline of their faces is regular and pretty, and they do have some similarity to the facial forms of the Asiatic people and also to the people living in Wallachia, Servia, and Poland. Moreover, they resemble all the American nations that I have had an opportunity to see. The copper color which is seen in the skin of brown people is not found among them. Their very long hair is always carefully arranged. Usually their clothing consists of a bright colored skirt of calico or cloth, leggings of blue or scarlet cloth set with beads or coral, and moccasins decorated with hog bristles or porcupine quills. The men have a very light beard, the hair being pulled out as soon as it is noticed. Most of them cut off the hair of their head except a tuft on the back of the cranium to which they fasten the red-dyed tail of a deer. This war-like decoration may be worn only by those who have carried out a bold stroke or have robbed an enemy of his scalp. Most of them wear a belt about their loins and leather shoes (*aka-tsche*). Leggings (*aku-tu*) are luxury articles and instead of the bison robes, which are rarely found among them, they wear woolen blankets of red, white, or green color.

Both sexes have small feet, muscular and well proportioned limbs, shining pitch black hair, coarse, however, as horsehair. With both sexes, it is usual to have each ear pierced in four places. In these holes they fasten porcelain ear pendants. They often pay high prices for these luxuries and for their bracelets of porcelain rings.

The language of the Iowas has many gutteral and nasal sounds, but it does not lack expressiveness. The voices of the women are screechy. The religious beliefs of these people are mixed with traits of mythology, and in this respect they have something in common with religions of the ancients. They present their god, called Wa-kon-dah, with the aid of symbols, and it does not seem that they venerate these images or manitous as God himself, but only as figures of him. They know that the Master of Life is invisible, but by showing him commanding lightning and thunder it reveals that their belief is analogous to that of primitive peoples and similar to that of the inhabitants of northern Europe, who likewise armed their first gods Jupiter and Wodan with lightning.

Their cult divides itself into several parts. According to their religious tradition, there originally lived eight persons who busied themselves solely during their short lives with the happiness of their people. After their deaths the souls entered the bodies of eight different animals, each of which is venerated by a different sect, and each sect preserves its image as a symbol. This is exhibited only on solemn occasions, chiefly before their war parties start on the march.

The first sect worships Tu-num-pe with the figure of a bear. Tu-num-pe was the first who ate raw meat. The other sects worship Aro-tschon and Tsche-hi-ta, the eagle, Cu-tsche, the turtle dove, and Pa-he, the beaver, who, according to their tradition, discovered the art of making fire by rubbing two pieces of wood together.

Among the savages no two persons of the same sect may marry. This determination secures internal unification among them. When a young Indian makes a choice among the daughters of another sect he goes on the hunt, takes the game he procures, presenting it as it is to his father or nearest kin, who ties it on his horse and takes it without delay to the designated place, leaving it without saying a word. After some time the wooer himself appears. He must learn for himself that the game his father brought is being prepared, and if he is invited to the feast in preparation, he recognizes this as proof that his proposal has been accepted. Immediately his father or nearest relative selects the horses and other objects intended for the wedding present, and these the engaged person takes to the dwelling of his sweetheart. According to the customs obtaining among the Iowas, he at the same time becomes the possessor of all his wife's younger sisters. The practice of polygamy allows him to use them, but he is permitted to dispose of one or more of them to his friends without giving offense to his relatives. Uncles and aunts are honored quite as are father and mother, and cousins like brothers and sisters.

At the death of a near relative the whole family either pulls out or cuts off their hair. The signs of deep mourning in this case are very strict abstinence, the wearing of garments of mourning, and the blackening of the face. It is amazing to what degree the savages carry this complete and voluntary abstinence from all food, even in the face of the most urgent promptings of nature. A chief or a brave warrior is buried with much pomp. His best weapons are placed in the grave with him and his finest horses are presented as a sacrifice. His corpse, frequently fully armed and fully clothed, is laid in a narrow, deep grave, and covered with earth and stones to protect it against the depredation of wolves. Small mounds are raised over the grave and decorated with the tails of horses and other tributes befitting a warrior. These burial places are respected even by their enemies, and sites where they are located are sacred.

I must add, however, that the nations of the northwest of America expose the bodies of their dead on high scaffolds or in trees, surrounding them with the most costly effects. The Mandans and the Gros Ventres so place them around their villages and on the prairie. The sight of these corpses and the remains of the belongings of the dead surrounding the homes of the savages awaken in the mind of the traveler the thought that death can snatch one's friend from him but can not blot out the memory of the departed.

Their dances and their burial ceremonies are accompanied by loud howling and terrible grimaces. If one of their number meets death at the hands of an enemy, they gather to curse the murderer, threatening him at his return with the most appalling treatment.

I was present at the burial of a chief who, with four warriors and a woman, had been killed at the same time. The howling and wailing of the widows hidden among the bushes on the adjoining hills heightened the effect. The ceremonies were held as preparation of the warriors starting on the warpath to avenge the suffered insult. The dances and songs indulged in on this occasion were ridiculous and at the same time abominable. From one side the men approached, from the other the women, dancing by twos. After meeting they formed a group of dancers, exactly as one sees in the drawings and descriptions of celebrated travelers who have visited the islands of the Indian archipelago in the South Sea. The dancers really took no steps, but hopped stiffly without bending the knees, their legs held close together, accompanied by the beat of a drum, the rattling of long gourds half filled with seeds, and the sad complaining song of those present.

I observed three kinds of dances among them, the dance of amusement, the funeral dance, and the dance preliminary to a military expedition. Only to the first two are women admitted, and the last is performed by men only, those warriors appearing ready to go into battle, disfigured by barbarous painting, carrying tomahawks and battle axes. One of their most famous warriors exemplifies by true-to-life pantomine his heroic deeds and by an expressive address tries to inspire and inflame the minds of his surrounding companions in arms, emphasizing the distinction which his brilliant achievements have brought him.

The costume of the women when they participate in joyful festivities is often bizarre and ridiculous. I saw the daughter of a chief wearing over her skirt the old livery of an English servant. Another Indian woman who had scarcely more than a girdle on wore a straw hat all decorated with feathers, and an old matron wore a dragoon's uniform and a round hat. The chiefs and warriors do not participate in the dances of the young people, but are merely spectators, standing around passing the peace pipe from mouth to mouth.

The Iowas have the same manner of conducting war as do other nations of North America. For a general war the entire nation is aroused. If, however, only a few warriors take up arms against a hostile tribe, then it is only party strife. The latter combats are the more common and are usually inspired by a wish to avenge an insult to one's own family, or against an entire tribe.

If the war is a general war, the nomadic hordes assemble at a chosen place for a war council, which at times may last for weeks. On such occasions the foremost chiefs display their wisdom and eloquence, while the young warriors dispute among themselves as to which of the elders deserves most honor. It is known that primitive people have the gift of eloquence, and that they like to embellish their language with flowery phrases. In the council, however, they try to convince by logic based on truth. They never indulge in personality disputes while in council. Once a war plan has been agreed on, it is kept with an inviolable seal of secrecy in the heart and comes to life only at the moment of its execution.

If an offended Indian desires satisfaction for some wrong, he besmears his face, avoids every association with his tribe, takes himself to an out-of-the-way place, and from there lets his death song resound. Braves and young warriors who are inclined to take his part silently lay an arrow at his feet, and if he considers his group strong enough, he washes and dresses himself with care, gathering his adherents for council.

It is most dangerous to meet such a war party. Marking their trail by plunder and murder, they are cruel and unforgiving toward their enemies, and all their neighbors, especially the whites, are their enemies.

Seemingly between the Iowas and the Sioux no means of reconciliation exists. So intense is their hate for one another that they issue challenges, even at the trading posts, should they chance to meet there. I myself was the witness to such an incident at the Fort of the Otos.

The Iowas are not cannibals any more, though they do scalp their foes, that is, they cut off the skin with the tuft of hair (*nan-to-tscha*). The fights become especially fierce if they surround one of their warriors to protect him from the disgrace of being scalped.

They rarely take prisoners, but because of their barbarity kill their enemies, even women and children.

10

THE FORT ATKINSON ON THE COUNCIL BLUFFS — THE VIL-
LAGE OF THE O-MAHAS — MEETING WITH THE O-MAHA
INDIANS — THE RIVER EAU QUI COURRE — THE PONCARA
— THE WHITE RIVER — VOLCANIC REGION — SIOUX
INDIANS — THE FACTORY OF JOSHUA PILCHER.

A few days after my arrival at the
fur trading company's factory[1] I decided to visit the military post at the
Council Bluffs located two geographic miles upstream, and in the absence
of the commanding officer, who was on an expedition against the Arikaras,
to visit my earlier acquaintance, the Indian agent, Mr. O'Fallon. At that
time Fort Atkinson was still in its best condition and could be called the
foremost military post bordering the independent Indians. Since then it
has been destroyed, for it seemed advisable to bring the armed forces closer
to the white population.[2]

The way from the post to the fort led in part through graceful forests of
oak and sumac with a dense undergrowth of brush, in part through prairie
with tall grass and broad-leaved plants of the composites, and over a ridge
of hills gently sloping toward the river and toward the prairie to the west.

[1] The site remains as at the end of Chapter 9, the Oto Fort of Berthold, Chouteau, and
Pratte, soon to be named Cabanné's Post, for details of which see Dale L. Morgan, *The
West of William H. Ashley*, 243n.

[2] Fort Atkinson was a product of the so-called Yellowstone Expedition of the army in
1819–1820, which got as far as present Fort Calhoun, Nebraska, near Council Bluffs. The
temporary site, Engineer Cantonment, was a mile north of Lisa's trading post. Colonel
Henry Atkinson, commanding officer of the expedition, chose the more permanent site, three
miles above Council Bluffs on the Nebraska side in a cottonwood grove "on an extensive
river bottom," the buildings of which were begun October 4, 1819, and completed October
17. Flooding the following spring forced relocation on higher ground, the new fort being
called Cantonment Missouri, subsequently renamed in Atkinson's honor on order of Secretary of War John C. Calhoun. Ironically, it was to be abandoned when Atkinson was made
responsible for locating and founding of the infantry school at Jefferson Barracks near St.
Louis in March, 1826. John Gale, *The Missouri Expedition, 1818–1820: The Journal of
Surgeon John Gale, with Related Documents*, ed. by Roger P. Nichols, *passim*; Nichols,
General Henry Atkinson: A Military Career, 47–116.

Despite the intense heat, the vegetation was exuberantly luxuriant, with lovely green meadows. A narrow, difficult trail led me at first for an hour's ride through dense growing bushes and then into the open prairie. Now I saw the Council Bluffs, one of the most picturesque points along the often all too monotonous banks of the great river. From almost every direction the tasteful, whitewashed buildings of the fort could be seen at a considerable distance, and for me it was a genuine pleasure to see the dwellings of civilized men, yes, a small town again after months of separation in the wilderness.

The garrison indeed merited this name, for there were several hundred troops stationed, and many of them had their homes here. In addition to these there were many families whom circumstances had drawn hither. Except for St. Charles and Franklin, Fort Atkinson was perhaps the most populous place on the Missouri, and in the matter of agriculture the environment was most favorable. Its military arrangement and its location were gratifying and solid. It did not deserve to be abandoned so soon.

The real reason why the government of the United States gave it up is not clear to me, unless the transportation of certain necessities to the place was too difficult, or that the place proved to be too unhealthful.[3] Since it is extremely difficult to send troops up the stream, and since strife with the aborigines will not cease as long as there are any independent Indians, peace of the western region is by no means any nearer just because an important garrison has been established below St. Louis, and in that location there is as much chance of sickness as higher up the river. Of course, in case of necessity, troops could be taken up the Mississippi and the Missouri by steamboat, but only to such a point where either stream becomes too hazardous for this kind of vessel.

During the last wars between the whites and the aborigines, the great nations living along the Platte and the Missouri were not hostile toward the Americans, which should be counted a most fortunate situation. I should not advise the government of the United States, however, to rely too much upon the assurances of friendship on the part of any of the Indian tribes, since unforeseen and unimportant circumstances may react so violently upon the irritable nature of the Indians that the paternal attitude and purpose of the American government might be frustrated all too easily.

---

[3] Colonel Atkinson, on orders from Secretary of War Calhoun, had begun raising food-stuffs as early as the spring of 1820, so that by October he was able to report harvesting 250 tons of hay, 13,000 bushels of a superior Indian corn, 4,000 bushels of potatoes, and between 4,000 and 5,000 bushels of turnips. The farming operations were in large part a response to a devastating outbreak of scurvy among the troops the previous winter. Nichols, *General Henry Atkinson*, 74–75.

I venture to say that under the exemplary military colonization system which the United States has begun, whereby a garrison can provide itself with the means of subsistence for years, even at a vast distance from the border, the political position of the Union might necessitate extending such military posts as far as the Rocky Mountains, indeed even to the western coast, and in this way the connection between the two oceans would be established. The realization of such a thing still has to be left to the distant future, but surely it is included in the plans of the government, which has already done so much to open lines of communication for the public traffic and for world trade.

As I stated above, the garrison has been removed and in 1830 I saw instead of a flourishing colony only a heap of ruins and the smoke of Indian camps where a few years before civilization and military discipline reigned. Nevertheless, I permit myself to give a rather detailed description of the place, for such an account will furnish an accurate idea of the American military colonies in general, and this post might again become one of some importance in the further extension of American settlements.

As is known, Captains Lewis and Clarke were sent out in 1804 by the government of the United States on an exploratory expedition with the purposes to ascend the Missouri to its sources, to find a pass through the Rocky Mountains, and then advance down the Columbia River to the shores of the western ocean.

These officers, whose three-year undertaking was crowned with the most favorable results, arrived about the end of July, 1804, in this region where the military post was located, calling the place the Council Bluffs, because here they had a meeting with the Otos.[4] The location on the Missouri, where several of the larger nations of the aborigines lived together in a relatively narrow space, and the proximity of the Platte River, at the mouth of which more or less dangerous war parties of the upper and lower Missouri were accustomed to roam, of necessity demanded the establishment of a military post for the protection of trade with the aborigines and for the safety of the colonists beginning to settle as far as the Kansas River.

The above-named officers submitted their reports and suggestions as urgently as possible to the president and through him to Congress. The government first decided to establish Fort Osage with General Clarke undertaking this expedition. However, the reasons invoked by Lewis and Clarke were so urgent and trade so hampered by roving Indians that the

[4] Cf. Document 326, "The Nicholas Biddle Notes," in *Letters of the Lewis and Clark Expedition, with Related Documents, 1783–1854*, ed. by Donald Jackson, 512. Meriwether Lewis's address to the Otos, August 4, 1804, is Document No. 129 in the same work, 203–208.

government finally induced Congress to send seven hundred men under Colonel Atkinson to the mentioned region.[5]

This expedition consisting of riflemen and the Sixth Regiment of regulars was equipped with everything necessary for the construction of the fort, the cultivation of the surrounding country, and the maintainance of the men who arrived at the Bluffs on October 12, 1819.

The first location selected was a low point about three miles farther up stream than the Bluffs, not far from a swamp. In the summer of 1820 a serious epidemic broke out, manifesting itself by successive swellings of limbs. Called scurvy by the local physicians, it does not seem to have been diagnosed accurately, for three hundred of the men perished from the effects of this disease. An earlier flood, the proximity of the swamp, and the consumption of rancid salt pork may have been the cause of the sickness.[6]

The romantically situated hills sloping abruptly toward the river were chosen as a suitable location for a military post, and in 1820 was called Fort Atkinson. The location of the establishment was very well selected at 41° 27′ north latitude in a region freely swept by the breezes and commanding completely the surrounding country and the Missouri River, which is not very wide here for a distance of 1,000 paces.

The fort itself was a square structure, its sides each two hundred American yards long.[7] There were eight log houses, two on each side. The fort had three gates, and on the river side there was only a passage under the inside houses. Each house—25 feet wide and 250 feet long—consisted of ten rooms, with a roof sloping toward the inside. On the outside wall each room had a shooting loophole ten feet long. The interior court was a large grass-covered square. In the center stood the powder house built of stone. Around the fort, at a distance of fifty paces, ran a fence with three gates. Outside the fort on the northwest side was situated a council house about fifty feet long, consisting of a hall and a smaller room where the government agents negotiated with deputations of the Indian nations and chiefs.

In addition, on the northwest side of the fort were several small houses intended for the supplies of the artillery, and the gunsmith had his smithy

[5] For Fort Osage, see footnote 44 in Chapter 8 of the present book.

[6] The high incidence and devastating effects of scurvy at the post are fully detailed in Surgeon John Gale's letters of January 23, and February 5, 16, 23, and 25, and March 19 and 20, 1820, in Gale, *The Missouri Expedition*, 118–26.

[7] Colonel Atkinson, reporting to Secretary of War John C. Calhoun, October 19, 1819, described the first large installation as barracks forming a square "each curtain presenting a front of 520 feet." The second establishment, begun in the summer of 1820, was more than a mile from the original site, on higher ground but lacks specifications, except as here given by Duke Paul. Sixteenth Congress, 2 sess., *House Executive Document No. 110*, 169–71.

here also. The remaining buildings outside were located on the banks of the Missouri below the fort. In these buildings were housed the store for the personal needs of the establishment, moreover, the bakery, the smithy, and the shop for the cabinet makers and the carpenters.

On the south side was the gristmill and a sawmill driven by oxen and, for this region, said to be completely equipped. A storehouse of three stories, the lower floor for spirituous beverages, the second for salt pork, and the third for dried cereals. Another storehouse two stories high contained all the materials and hardware required in the agricultural undertakings at the fort.

The agricultural endeavor near the fort was excellent. A considerable stretch of land along the Missouri south of the fort, and separated from the prairie by a row of hills, had been converted into wonderful garden land. Here the finest European vegetables were grown. I found our common white cabbage, our kind of beans, onions, and melons of excellent quality.

The watermelons in this region are of unusually fine quality and size. On the border of the garden the soldiers grew Italian millet, the tufts of which are used for making brooms in Southern Europe. Large cornfields and wheatfields surrounded the settlement, and on some farms in the neighborhood much livestock was raised. The fine prairie, with its excellent grass, encourages horse raising, and the hay for winter feeding is of the best kind.

The opinion of the government regarding military posts is very sensible. It not only pays, feeds, and clothes its soldiers well, but also requires of them strict industry. The American military establishments must be looked upon as great industrial centers to provide the post with all its requirements even beyond its needs, naturally excepting the raw material, as for example, cloth, linen, and leather. Some of their artisans are very clever and produce the finest work. In 1823 it was still necessary for the government to supply the post with salt meat and brandy. In the following year the garrison hardly needed it anymore. The extended cattle raising sufficed and replaced the unwholesome salt meat, and a recently established distillery prepared the necessary brandy.

The military discipline in the United States is good, with service strict but moderate. The rations in the cantonments are the same for the officers and soldiers, namely, ¾ pound of beef, ¾ pound of salt pork, also one gallon of whisky per month, and vegetables, in season more than abundant and obtained from their gardens. The soldiers working in the shops always obtain double rations of brandy.

The spirit of the corps of officers here was equally good and all members spoke with the greatest respect of the organization of European armies.

The companies were cadres of forty men. At Fort Atkinson there were generally ten companies stationed.

On my arrival I found Mr. O'Fallon engaged in a conference with some chiefs of the Otos, and also a peculiar case. By a strange adventure, a party of hunters from Montreal in Canada, mostly Iroquois and half-bloods, had, after a hunting expedition to the western regions, come to the Council Bluffs to seek the aid and protection of the American government. These hunters, reckoned among the most fearless people on the American continent, had left their home on the St. Lawrence some years ago in a party of about thirty with their families, and in the manner of Indian hunters and beaver trappers they had undertaken an expedition to the west for the sources of the Saskatchewan River and into the Rocky Mountains, where beaver trapping is still productive.

As long as they hunted on British territory everything went well, but when they crossed the demarcation line of the United States they were attacked by Crow and Cheyenne Indians, and in addition to several killed, they had to leave some of their women and girls behind. In order to have these returned to them the Iroquois had undertaken the extremely dangerous march to the Bluffs, succeeding after many bloody encounters with the Indians. The intendant looked after these brave people as best he could, promising them every possible aid. In the course of my account of my second journey I shall have occasion to touch upon this incident once more.[8]

Late in the evening I left the fort, having made previous arrangements for my further journey. As I contemplated going by land, Mr. O'Fallon had the kindness to look after the preliminary preparations. The extreme heat of the day was considerably reduced in the evening by the shadows of a dark thunderstorm, and I was obliged to lead my poor horse over the

[8] Iroquois Indians, with French Canadian trappers, some of them of part Indian blood, were frequently employed by both the North West Company and the Hudson's Bay Company in the Northwest after 1813, as revealed in Alexander Ross's first-hand narrative of these years, *The Fur Hunters of the Far West*, ed. by Kenneth Spaulding, supplemented by another first-hand account, Ross Cox, *The Columbia River*, ed. by Edgar I. and Jane R. Stewart. The group here mentioned had deserted from the Snake Country brigade sent out by the Hudson's Bay Company in 1822, ending up at Fort Atkinson "after incredible wandering," as Dale L. Morgan has characterized their experience in *Jedediah Smith*, 120–22, 144–46, 396. As Henry Atkinson, now a brigadier general, and Major Benjamin O'Fallon, U.S. agent, Indian Affairs, were to report to Secretary of War James Barbour, following their treaty-making journey among the northwestern tribes in 1825, the Blackfeet, rather than the Crows and Cheyennes, were the bitter antagonists of "foreign traders" northwest of the three Forks of the Missouri. American State Papers, *Documents, Legislative and Executive, of the United States*, Class II, Indian Affairs, Vol. II, 14 Cong. 1 sess. to 19 Cong., 2 sess., inclusive, 607.

narrow trail, overgrown with almost impenetrable brush. At midnight we finally reached the factory very tired and nearly eaten up by insects.

My arrival caused a great stir among the Indians, who were encamped on the lowlands. Having been awakened by the baying of the dogs they had seized their weapons. These Indians live in perpetual fear of an attack on the part of their deadly foes, a band of Yankton Sioux, who roamed about these regions. Their fear was not unfounded, for on the following day some of the young men of the Yanktons tried to slip into their camp. To this end they had swum across the river and had hidden in a low place close to the river bank. They were accidentally discovered and were driven away by a few shots.

With great difficulty Mr. Robidoux procured a couple of usable horses for me. These and a couple of mules seemed sufficient for a journey of several hundred miles across the prairie. The horses and pack animals were in good condition. Such creatures stand a journey very well and often become fatter while on the march than near the settlement, for the horses cannot be driven far out because of the danger of being stolen by the Indians, and consequently the grass near the post is largely grazed off.

Mr. Robidoux engaged two men to accompany me. One was a man named Rodger and called Bell, who was mentioned in a previous chapter, and the other a half-blood named Monbrun, also called La Malice, an experienced hunter, a sinister fellow of genuine Indian nature. Courageous and faithful, he had no fear of other Indians, which is rare among these people. Moreover, he was highly respected among the neighboring tribes.

On August 9, about noon, we left the Fort of the Otos. This time I chose a wider and more comfortable way, fearing the frisky pack animals might ruin my baggage. After such mules and horses have free run on the meadows for some time, they are extremely fractious, and the traveler has a lot of trouble with them. This is the constant complaint of natural scientists, who often lose their best instruments and collections on their expeditions. The pack animals and also their keeper were a constant source of vexation to me. They always found occasion to impede the progress of the journey, to which I will repeatedly refer later in my story.

In the hope of finding a better trail I was disappointed, for in many places the way led through tall bushes entwined with grape vines and other climbers. Every moment I had to stop because one or the other animal had shaken off its pack.

The ridges separating the river from the grassy prairies are often over four hundred feet high and very steep. The trail led to a place on the slope where formerly a settlement had been but now had again become entirely wild. Only a tumbled-down fence and some maize growing wild betrayed former cultivation. Everywhere the grass was luxuriant and many beautiful plants were in bloom. A little creek, almost dry, delayed me, for the horses sank in the mud to their knees. Threatening thunderclouds darkened the sky and only with difficulty I reached the Bluffs.

A violent storm broke, and for several hours one of those terrific electric displays discharged flash upon flash. The thunder never ceased rolling. One can scarcely form a conception of this in Europe. At the same time rain fell in torrents for many hours, threatening to flood the low places. Horses as well as cattle in the meadows suspect the danger that accompanies such forces of nature, and one sees them in droves at the approach of a thunderstorm seeking high and protected areas. Later on my journey I observed that the American bison practices similar precautions.

The horse that had been assigned to my servant proved so miserable that I had to send it back. Through the kindness of the officers I was able to replace it with a better one.

Horses are twice as expensive at the Council Bluffs as at St. Louis, and at the factories on the upper Missouri can hardly be procured at all, excepting poor Indian ponies that usually do not stand the hardship. The better Indian ponies can be bought from the Indians only at exorbitant prices, and for this reason travelers ought to procure their horses at St. Louis.

Later I regretted very much that I had not followed the advice of my friends, to make the trip from St. Louis by land. In that way I could have extended my excursion to the Rocky Mountains and would have been spared the monotonous trip on the Missouri. When, seven years later, I left St. Louis in the middle of the winter, some of my horses stood the entire trip despite the severe season.

I left the Bluffs at noon on August 10. The way led through the tall grasses of the prairie, but the region abounds in hills with gentle slopes. About four English miles from the Council Bluffs I came upon one of the sources of the Little Butterfly Creek. It contained only shallow water, and the horses sank to their bellies in the muddy bed.

Another source of the same creek, two miles farther on, was entirely dried up. From the top of a ridge I soon thereafter saw the Elkhorn River. Following a high plateau, I reached this river, called Corne de Cerf by the Creoles. In a picturesque place, its left bank is bounded by limestone bluffs, the summits of which seem to be covered with trees and bushes. The left bank broadens into a prairie and continues thus to the Platte River.

Several elk (*Cervus major*, Say) sought safety in flight. I had the horses and baggage taken across the river. The water was clear and despite recent rains was not very swollen. As it was late evening, I halted and made camp on the bank of the river. Despite the cool night the mosquitoes tormented me unmercifully, and they did not desist even in the morning, when the dew was heavy.

A small variety of wolf, called *Canis latrans* by Mr. Say, repeatedly came close to our camp during the night, disturbing us with its repulsive and complaining howl. This beast of prey is a genuine jackal, having the same habits and mode of living as his kin in the old world. Although this American jackal does not run in such large packs as the jackal of the Orient, it is distributed over a larger area and is so much bolder than the larger species of American wolf. These *Canis latrans* with the greatest cleverness steal any object they can get hold of. They follow the caravans of the Americans and also those of the Indians camps, showing but little fear of man. They are always in the wake of a great herd of wild bison. Since their pelts are worthless they are rarely hunted, and they are often seen in parts where there is no game or the food supply is scarce, which mainly consists of the remains of such animals which were slain by hunters and Indians. Having drawn an accurate picture of this formerly unknown wolf I contemplate publishing it later, together with the rest of my natural historical subjects.[9]

On the following morning we broke camp at daybreak. We followed the river, riding through very tall grass. Several small lakes and swamps touch the river. The stagnant water contained reeds, a specie of *Typha*, and countless waterfowl inhabited these parts. Of these I will mention only *Anas americana*, *Anas boschas*, *Anas sponsa*, and *Mergus cucullatus*.[10] I also saw the calumet eagle, *Aquila fulvus*, Temm.,[11] whose beautiful tail feathers, as is known, are used as decorations by the Indians, and the *Falco ulliginosus*, Edw. This marsh harrier seems to be widely distributed in America. I found it in the swampy regions of tropical America just as frequently as in the north, even in different seasons, indeed in the middle of winter in high latitudes.[12] The surface of the water was covered with the leaves of a *Nymphaea*, a *Potamogeton*, and a broad-leaved *Sagittaria*.[13]

[9] The translator and editor have no record of this and other drawings, which may have been lost during World War II. But Duke Paul's *icones ineditae* at Schloss Rosenstein, Stuttgart, contain two dozen finished paintings of mammals and 86 of birds, of which four of each are reproduced in the present volume.

[10] *Anas americana* = *Mareca americana*, the baldpate; *Anas boschas* = *A. platyrhynchos*, the mallard; *Anas sponsa* = *Aix sponsa*, the wood duck; *Mergus cucullatus* = *Lophodytes cucullatus* (Linn.), the hooded merganser.

[11] *Aquila fulvus* Temm. = *A. chrysaëtos canadensis*, the golden eagle.

[12] *Falco ulliginosus* Edw. = *Circus hudsonius* (Linnaeus), the marsh hawk.

[13] Nymphaea, a family of aquatic plants to which the water lilies belong; *Potamogeton*, one of the aquatic herbs, the pondweeds; *Sagittaria*, a genus of aquatic plants of the water plantain family, including *S. latifolia* and *S. cuneata*, two species of arrowhead, offering edible tubers.

We rode about fifteen English miles along the Elkhorn, and after that reached an elevation on which the short curly grass attained a height of scarcely three to four inches. From the top of the rise I could see the village of the Otos, situated on the Platte River, close to a sheer bluff of white chalk-like limestone.

At noon we camped for a few hours in the shade of some trees, near an almost dry little creek, called La Petite Prune, named after the wild plums growing on its banks. A wide high plateau stretched before my eyes to the west and north.

Toward evening we encountered our first antelopes. The French Creoles call it *cabril*, also *cabris*. Of the beautiful species of the numerous antelope family Ord has correctly defined the genus *Antilocapra*.[14] Of all the goat-like animals, as far as I know, this American prairie antelope is the only one that has forked horns. The females have no horns, but those of the bucks are strongly beaded at the core. When the animal is two years old prongs appear, pointing several inches from the head to the front. Finally, these become several inches long and the remaining prongs curve to the inside, as with the least antelopes. The horns are a dark black-gray, often attaining a length of a foot and several inches. In the summer the skin of the prairie antelope is dark brownish yellow on the back, with the under side of the belly shining white, and a yellowish rump patch. Over the top and front of the head a dark stripe passes along the eyes and over the nose. The hoofs resemble those of our goats and are blunter than those of other antelopes. The teeth show no difference in general and are like the teeth of other antelopes. In size they are between the fallow deer and the doe, but vary greatly according to age and sex. Smith calls this antelope *Dicranoceros furcifera*, and Cuvier places it between *Aegonoceros*, Sm., and *Tetraceros*, Leach.

I consider the designation *Antilocapra americana* as more fitting since the head and the hoofs would classify them among the goats, their mode of living, however, among the antelopes.

Few animals show so many peculiar qualities in their mode of living as does the *cabril*. No animal in the world is as curious, exposing itself recklessly to danger. In regions where they are not exposed to continuous harassment, they boldly approach every object that looks peculiar to them. At the sight of horses and men they do not run away, but come right up to

[14] *Antilocapra americana* is a subfamily of the hollow-horned ruminants. It is not an antelope but is so called in North America. Ten years after Duke Paul saw his first antelope, Carl Bodmer was to see it too and to capture it in a painting entitled "Missouri: Jagd des Cabril, 1833" when he accompanied Maximilian zu Wied into much the same area.

them, and even if they are driven away, they return again and again, bleating almost like a doe.

No animal has afforded me greater entertainment than these harmless antelopes, and the Indians hunt them only in case of dire need, because their skin is of little value and the meat is hardly equal to that of the goat. Even in places where the *cabril* is disturbed by hunters and fur traders it is an easy matter to take them. The hunters hide themselves at the place where the antelope frequents, previously setting up a red stick or some other striking object at some distance from them. If the hunters have chosen the wind right, the antelope will come running to the object that attracts its attention and will return even if the hunter misses his shot.

A small creek, called La Mauvaise Rivière, or Bad Creek, caused us much and repeated trouble in getting the horses and mules across. I myself sank up to my shoulders in the mud, as I carelessly risked going in a treacherous place, but was pulled out with considerable difficulty. At the ford, which the Indians consider the only possible one, were found the skeletons of horses and mules that had become mired. The Eau qui Courre, or Running Water, one of the larger tributaries of the Missouri, is the only stream that I have found to be more treacherous than the Mauvaise Rivière. A very insignificant creek, it flows into the Elkhorn a few miles farther on.

We camped here for the night because there was no drinking water at another place. We were horribly bitten by mosquitoes, which prefer the muddy water. To escape this torture, I ordered a very early start on August 12, and, moreover, it was necessary, for the heat became unbearable, and a very long day's journey across extremely dry prairie had to be made to reach the large village of the Omahas on the Elkhorn.

The way led through a most desolate region, which only prairie land can present, and on account of the prevailing drought we saw no living creature except a few *Calidris* (*Tringa*) *bartramia* and *rufa*, Wilson,[15] which are common here as in all prairies of western America. Flocks of *Fringilla pecoris*[16] flew about the horses, and were so affable that they sat down on the pack mules near me to eat the insects covering the animals. There were also others, entirely ash gray, which at first I took to be young birds of the same species in their plumage. But since they were even more sociable and also had a different flight, I was inclined to consider them a different species.

Fringilla pecoris, which naturalists count among the weaver birds, a

---

[15] *Calidris* (*Tringa*) *bartramia* = *Bartramia longicauda*, the upland plover; [*Calidris* (*Tringa*)] *rufa* = *Calidris canutus rufa*, a new world race of the knot.

[16] *Fringilla pecoris* = *Molothrus ater*, the brown-headed cowbird.

migratory bird which trades the high north in the winter for the southern part of the United States, in its flight resembles the swallows and in its mode of living the starling. The mature males are of the most beautiful blackish brown color with steel luster and the females are light brown. The Americans call them cowbirds, and Wilson furnishes us an excellent illustration and a long description of this bird, which is a member of the large family of American gregarious birds.

The heat rose during the day to 102° and became unbearable for man and beast. About five o'clock in the evening, completely exhausted, we reached some sand hills which supported only meager bushes. On the eastern slope of these hills were two deep holes filled with clear water, the edges of the holes overgrown with swampy plants. From the summit of these elevations I saw the Elkhorn in an expansive plain, dotted with many skulls and skeletons of the bison, which at that time still frequented these regions during the winter. Since then these giant creatures of the prairie have withdrawn farther and farther and it is possible that the Ponca or even the White River is now the geographic boundary of these animals along the Missouri. This boundary is constantly being pushed farther to the north and west, because the demand for the valuable hides of these animals, together with the wantom destruction at the hands of hunters roaming over these regions, is bound to reduce their number greatly.

My servant [J. G. Schlape], since our departure from the Council Bluffs, had not been feeling well. Struck with complete exhaustion from over-exertion and heat, he became seriously ill, and all the symptoms of a nervous and gastric fever appeared.

A little stream that comes from the south to the west and flows into the Elkhorn was entirely dried up, frustrating our hope of finding water for our famished animals. We were able to reach the banks of the Elkhorn only by the greatest effort. Despite the lack of water and an intolerable heat, we had this day gone a distance of about thirty English miles.

During the night a heavy thunderstorm passed over us. Previously a hurricane-like storm had blown from the southwest for several hours. Suddenly the wind ceased and the downpour came, weighing down and crushing the shelter my men had put up. We were drenched. My tent was blown down by the storm and was now being washed away with all other objects that were not too heavy to be carried along. I felt especially sorry for my German servant, who in the intense paroxysms of fever was not able to get up and received but scant help in the general bedlam of the storm and during the total darkness that enveloped everything.

The breaking day illuminated the destruction which the storm had wrought. Giant cottonwoods, along the Elkhorn and stretching near the village of the Omahas, lay on the ground, either uprooted by the storm or shattered by lightning. The river was changed into a torrent, and the earth huts of the Indian village, abandoned during the summer, were under water. Since the Indians are accustomed to planting corn, pumpkins, and watermelons in the spring and harvesting them in the fall on their return from the hunt, it seemed likely that the terrible storm might have wrought tremendous devastation here. This was, however, not the case, for the Indians are so clever in the choice of their various fields and so accustomed to such storms that the crops will rarely be harmed. It is remarkable that even hostile parties roaming in the summer through the settlements of Indians regard the plantings of their enemies sacred and leave them un-molested, a vital policy upon which the rapidly decreasing tribes must of necessity depend.

With much effort my men collected our scattered belongings and dried them as much as possible. During the night the horses and mules had strayed away and had to be brought back with difficulty. At nine o'clock my men found it possible to cross the Elkhorn, which is shallow near the village of the Omahas. If the rain had continued a little while longer it would have been impossible to cross on this day, and I realized keenly the mistake of not having followed the advice of Monbrun, who had wanted to cross on the previous evening despite the long march.

I utilized the following morning to inspect the Indian huts. In some were articles which the natives had left behind. The huts of various sizes, most of them large enough to accommodate comfortably several families, were round in structure, forming a dome above the ground, made of long bent poles, bound together by a wickerwork of willows, and covered with a thick layer of earth. The floor of the huts had been excavated two or three feet deep and covered with a layer of very hard clay. Around the inner walls were elevated sleeping places of wickerwork covered with fairly well worked mats, resembling bunks in the cabins on ships. In the center of the earth roof of the dirt huts was an opening through which the smoke can escape, and under this opening is an arrangement to hang the cooking kettle. The door, which in all the huts is to the south, is nothing more than a round hole through which one must crawl to enter. On their hunting expeditions the Indians make use of leather tents of tanned bison hides in the shape of a sugar cone. Affording the necessary scanty shelter for eight to twenty persons, they are supported by three interlocking poles, often twenty feet long, which the Indians must carry with them because of the lack of timber. This is inconvenient on their nomadic journeys. In the huts I found a few worthless objects of no intrinsic value. Assuming them to have been forgotten I desired to take them along. Monbrun, who accompanied me, would not allow me to do so, saying that all objects thus left behind were *ua-kan*, which puts upon them the stamp of inviolability.

So also the fields, the graves, and many symbolic signs are *ua-kan*, or bewitched, to the very superstitious and predestination-believing Indians. This is caused by the priests or tricksters, who know very well how to take advantage of the prejudices and superstitions of the people. Under a veil of mystery, which they throw over every natural thing, and by some slight knowledge of the art of healing, or by prophesying of every probable event, they know how to beguile the mind of the Indians in such a manner that they do not dare to undertake anything without the advice of these men. These medicine men constitute a unique caste whose manner of living differs completely from that of the rest of the Indians. They lead a care-free, lazy life, do not take part in the hunt or in war, have themselves supplied with the best food, and the whole day long smoke their kinik-kinik, or Indian tobacco, said to be the principal ingredient by which they work their sorcery and conjuration against the evil spirits.

Since the customs of the different nations present many points of simi-larity, nevertheless, I observed that the *ua-kan* is interpreted in a very broad sense, especially among the tribes of the northwest, where it is very similar to the taboo of the inhabitants of the Sandwich and Washington islands. The peculiar customs which I observed at the burial of their dead among the Mandans, Gros Ventre, and Assiniboins remind me of the prac-tices of the Moaris, the inhabitants of the Pacific, to which I shall return in the course of the account of my second journey.

When the weather cleared, the region around the village was enlivened with many birds. A tree-covered spot in the middle of the prairie came to resemble an island in the center of the ocean. The bare prairie affords nourishment for only a few inhabitants of the air, unless it be for such as live on grasshoppers and other insects. Moreover, they have no protection against birds of prey and no water. In addition to buntings and flycatchers, I saw great flocks of *Cassicus phoeniceus*,[17] which prey on the cornfields, also *Fringilla caudacuta* (*Emberiza cryzivora*),[18] *Tyrannus rapax, Tyran-nus ferox*, which Wilson classifies under the name *Muscicapa crinita*,[19] moreover *Vireo gilvus*[20] and others. These birds are preyed upon by several

---

[17] *Cassicus phoeniceus = Agelaius phoeniceus*, the red-winged blackbird.

[18] *Fringilla caudacuta* (*Emberiza oryzivora*) = *Dolichonyx oryzivorus*, the bobolink, a sharp-tailed icterid that Duke Paul considered finchlike because of its short, heavy bill.

[19] *Tyrannus rapax = Contopus virens*, the eastern wood pewee, a small flycatcher; *Tyrannus ferox = Myiarchus crinitus*, the great crested flycatcher, described by Linnaeus in 1758 and placed in the genus *Muscicapa* by Wilson.

[20] *Vireo gilvus*, the warbling vireo, described by Vieillot in 1807 and thought to be new by Wilson, who gave it the name *Muscicapa melodia* in 1812.

kinds of hawks, among which I observed *Falco columbarius*, *Falco hyemalis*, and *Falco sparverius*.[21]

We had scarcely left the village when four completely naked Indians armed with bows and arrows came towards us. My companions, taking them to be Sioux, jumped from their horses. This caused the Indians to halt and make friendly signs, by which we recognized them as Omahas. They came happily toward us, shook hands with me, declaring that a large number of Omahas were returning from the hunt to camp at a point nine miles away, that a second group was approaching the village, and that a third under their principal chief Te-re-ki-ta-nau, also called On-pan-tanga, the Big Elk, had gone to the Pawnees. Thereupon the young men left us but soon returned, bringing ripe watermelons and ears of corn just in the milk stage, to make a very good meal.

A high ridge extends for a distance of two miles along the left bank of the Elkhorn and is separated from the latter by a meadow overgrown with tall grass.

Soon after, while roaming through the region, I saw over the heights and along the river a large number of Indian warriors, forerunners of the main body, all armed with bows and arrows. These were for the most part young men selected for this purpose; among such Indian outposts one rarely finds warriors of high rank. Usually these ride together in the center of the main body, in order that, should an attack be made upon their people, they may hasten to the point where the danger is the greatest, or cover the main body consisting of women and children, the old men, and the baggage.

Indians are experts in skirmishing. Every nation has a number of enemies, with war parties following every move of their Indian camps, therefore marches are conducted with the utmost precaution. Patrols are thrown far out, and constant communication is maintained between the outposts and rear guard and the main column.

The Omahas, Poncas, Kansa, and Osages, as I have stated above, formerly belonged to one great nation. They are still united with one another by similarity of language and are constantly on hostile terms with all of the tribes of the Sioux or Dakotah.

The Sioux are extremely cruel enemies and even wreak their vengeance on defenseless women and children, while other nations are satisfied merely to make them prisoners. They are also barbaric, often torturing captive warriors with studied cruelty. They make the lot of captive women and children less hard, usually adopting and incorporating them into

---

[21] *Falco columbarius*, the pigeon hawk or merlin; *Falco hyemalis* = *Buteo lineatus*, the red-shouldered hawk; *Falco sparverius*, the American sparrow hawk or American kestrel.

the victor nation. The inhuman practices of the Sioux are shared by the Arikaras and Blackfeet Indians, both of whom may be reckoned among the wildest and most blood-thirsty nations on the American continent. It is evident that the Omahas and Poncas are at a disadvantage when compared with the Sioux, in that they have fewer firearms than the latter, for it is much more difficult for them to procure rifles, inasmuch as the returns of the hunt are much smaller than those of the Sioux. Clearly, the wealth of the Indians depends upon the returns of the hunt.

I counted between four and five hundred young men during a ride of two hours, ranging in age from twelve to eighteen years, who were returning to their village at this time, because their corn, one of their favorite foods, was half-ripe. After awhile came scattered groups with their pack horses. The men rarely carried anything except their weapons and for the most part were horseback, while the women and girls carried great loads held fast by straps drawn around the forehead. The pack horses, very lean and excessively loaded, carried the entire spoils of the hunt, which included large bundles of dried bison meat for the autumn provision. The earlier mentioned tent poles, called *loges* by the Creoles, three or four in number, depending on the size of the tent, hung from the side of the pack with one end trailing far behind on the ground. Small children were lying in the oddest positions on top of the loads without being tied thereto and without falling off.

The second chief of the Omahas, called Hui-ru-gnan, or Man of Courage (l'Homme de Valeur), had established camp on the left bank of the Elkhorn, and I observed that the greater number of tents were erected around his. I have already stated that only a part of the Omahas were returning to their village. Of these a part remained for the night with their chief, while the other part sought to reach the village. When they caught sight of us one mounted Indian came galloping up. He was an old warrior, Ua-bac-tié, who was sent by the chief to invite us courteously to come to the camp. On learning from the interpreter who I was, he deported himself most respectfully toward me.

I now rode into the camp and pitched my tent close to the bank of the river. More than one hundred tipis were already set up, each of them housing two to four families. By evening there were four times that number standing. Hui-ru-gnan, surrounded by his own bravest warriors, received me in his tent, a peace pipe in his hand. He asked me many questions, revealing a good mind and manifesting a dignified behavior such as I should not have expected from an Indian. Offering every aid in his power for the continuance of my journey, he showed such a lively interest that I could not doubt his friendship. Here I again remark that a certain degree of politeness is peculiar to the Indian, and that these people have advanced much farther in social life than one usually assumes.

Hui-ru-gnan is a very tall, stout man with an expressive face, of calm bearing and unrestrained deportment. Since he noticed that I was tired, he induced me to go to my tent and gave strict orders that the roving women and children should not disturb me in my rest. He was very desirous to provide hospitality for me and my men and promised to spend the evening with me.

An Indian named Oa-schin-ga-sa-bae, or Black Bird (l'Oiseau Noir), stationing himself before my tent and the camping place of my men, declared everything to be *ua-kan*, at times employing very drastic measures when young men and women inclined toward theft approached. This young warrior was the son of the greatest chief of the Omahas, who until his death exerted a considerable influence over his own and also the neighboring friendly tribes. In the further course of this report I shall speak more concerning old Oa-schin-ga-sa-bae, who at the time of the Lewis and Clark expedition was the mightiest chief of this region. His burial is on a hill on the right bank of the Missouri, called by the Creoles La Butte de l'Oiseau Noir.[22] His son went to Washington after the death of his father and was among the first Indians of the upper Missouri introduced to Congress. A loyal friend of the whites, he has now become the foremost chief of the Omahas.

After a few hours Hui-ru-gnan and four old men who formed his retinue arrived. Presenting him with some tobacco, I hosted them with coffee, of which the Indians are very fond. Since my interpreter had come I began to barter with the Indians for some small articles, especially weapons. The bows and arrows of the Omahas are exceedingly good and an Omaha will pierce the biggest bison bull with his arrow as he chases it on horseback.

The nation of the Omahas must be very populous, for although I had counted several thousand Indians, there were always new groups coming

---

[22] The site is described in Lewis and Clark, *Original Journals*, I, 106, entry of August 11, 1804. Lewis has Black Bird's death occurring "4 years ago," or in 1800, from smallpox, although the epidemic among the Omahas occurred in 1802. The Chief had arrested James Mackay's ascent of the Missouri in 1795, out of which came, incidentally, the map used by Lewis and Clark. Brackenridge, in *Views of Louisiana*, 229–30, says that the Chief controlled his tribe and many surrounding Indian groups by threats to use arsenic, which he had procured from a trader. Both Brackenridge and Irving (*Astoria*, 161–65) describe his burial on horseback, upright. At the time of Lewis and Clark, the burial mound was surmounted by a pole on which they affixed a "white flage bound with red Blue & white." George Catlin sketched the grave site in the 1830's (Plate 117, Vol. II of three vols., *Letters and Notes on the Manners, Customs, and Condition of the North American Indians*).

by.[23] The division under Hui-ru-gnan by no means constituted the majority of the people, for in addition to the division that had moved to the Pawnees, there was yet another that was at the Eau qui Courre (as the Creoles call the Running Water), where they were encamped with the Poncaras. Friendly nations often visit each other and hunt together.

Toward sundown the young people without discrimination of sex bathed in the river in the presence of all the people. They saw no impropriety in appearing nude before us to laugh at our European dress. The whole night through the Indians intoned their songs, joyful paens as well as death songs. Both constituted a horrible howling in which the dogs and the wolves of the wilderness joined.

Nothing in the world is more frightful than these all-night-long barbaric concerts accompanied by crude instruments. Among the nations of the upper Missouri and the Rocky Mountains which I visited several years later the war chants and death songs were in conjunction, moreover, with terrible tortures and disfigurations, to which the Indians submit to appease the evil spirits.

The dogs of the American aborigines have pointed ears and a drooping tail, constituting a unique species, as does the dingo of the South Sea Islands. Of course, one also finds many cross-breeds and bastards of European dogs. The original breed of these dogs seems to derive from the coyote.[24] Howling, but not barking, they growl and bristle up their hair. They approach one quietly and bite without warning, especially Europeans. The Indians must have domesticated these dogs long before the (white Spanish) discovery, and old Indians assured me that they had heard their forebears relate how they had tamed the wolves. The wolves will follow bitches in heat and breed bastard dogs. I had occasion to observe this myself.

On August 14 I made preparation to continue my journey early, and most of the Indians had already started before daybreak. Of the three or four hundred tents only five were still standing. The chief and several other Indians of high rank came into my tent to take leave of me and accompanied me out of camp.

[23] Other Siouan groups may have been visiting the Omahas during Duke Paul's visit, for Meriwether Lewis's "Statistical View of the Indian Nations Inhabiting the Territory of Louisiana" in Lewis to the President of the United States, April 7, 1805, gave small figures for the principal village at Eau qui Courre and the head of Wolf River: 60 lodges, 150 warriors, and a total of 600 souls. He estimated the warriors ten years earlier (1795) at 700, adding that the smallpox in the autumn of 1802 had reduced their number to fewer than 300 men. By 1829 the tribe was estimated at 1,900. *American State Papers, Indian Affairs*, 9 Cong. 1 sess., No. 113, February 19, 1806, 705–707, 709.

[24] This is a possible ancestor, but the more likely one is *Canis lupus*, the wolf.

A small stream, Rivière des Frénes [Ash River], empties into the Elkhorn near the camp ground. My travel companions advised me to follow the course of this stream upwards. At noon a heavy thunderstorm lasting for two hours forced our caravan to halt. In the afternoon the air cooled and a strong southeast wind rose. A Ponca Indian accompanying me discovered a body of Indians near evening whom he recognized as belonging to his nation. He rode to meet the group, and in the course of half an hour came galloping back accompanied by three men. Among them was a chief of the Poncas, named Ua-bac-tié. He rode a most beautiful horse and invited me to visit his camp. I accepted the invitation.[25]

I interrupt the thread of my story to say a few words concerning the horses of the Indians. All Indians west of the Missouri and Mississippi belong to mounted tribes. The horses brought to Mexico and Florida by the Spaniards became wild in the course of time straying about the prairie and wilderness. Also a large number of horses were stolen each year from the Spaniards by the Indians on their raids, and French colonists of New France and Louisiana experienced similar losses. Since, however, the French settled New France much later than the Spaniards settled Mexico and had fewer horses, the Indian horses from the Spaniards crossed but little with the blood of French horses brought from Normandy and Picardy. The nature of the Indian horses has been changed and even their physical appearance, due to the long period they have existed in a foreign part of the world. Now they resemble the parent stock very little.[26]

At a cursory glance one might mistake them for horses from the steppes of Eastern Europe. Long hanging manes, long necks, strong short fetlocks and a straight back make them appear similar to the horses of Poland. Probably the lack of up-breeding by good stallions of prime Spanish stock may be the chief cause why the horses of the prairie have degenerated so much. In Mexico horse-breeding was undertaken with great zeal and often the finest stallions were imported from Europe to maintain a good breed of horses, and, indeed, the Mexicans had better horses than were found in trade in Spain, where horse breeding is on the decline.

One finds among the Indian ponies now and then noble animals of beautiful form; however, these are so rare and valued so highly that it is

[25] Lewis and Clark, who, in the Biddle text, estimated the Poncas at fifty men at the time of their meeting with them at the mouth of Ponca Creek in Knox County, northern Nebraska, September 5, 1804, placed their number at some four hundred some years earlier. *Original Journals*, I, 140.

[26] For the dispersion of the horse in North America, see Frank Gilbert Roe, *The Indian and the Horse*, map at p. 78. Alfred Jacob Miller's first-hand observations of the relations of the Indians to their horses are given in Miller, *The West of Alfred Jacob Miller* (1837) ed. by Marvin C. Ross, *passim*.

almost impossible to trade for them. On the whole the horses of the Indians are most enduring, content with the often meager feed that they can find on the prairie. In the winter they must seek scant feed under deep snow, enduring the greatest hardship. Even when the intense cold forces the Indians to abandon the prairie, compelling them to seek the protection of the wooded regions along the rivers, the horses must be satisfied with twigs of the aspen and willows or feed on the rushes of the horsetail (*Equise-tum*). In the winter the horses are therefore uncommonly lean, but they recover quickly in the spring. It is unbelievable how much the Indians can accomplish with their horses, what burdens the latter are able to carry, and what long distances can be covered with them in a short time.

The Indians are extremely bold and daring riders, shown especially in their hunting of the bison. In this dangerous work it is often difficult to whom to ascribe greater skill, the rider or the horse. Since the Indian who manipulates the bow and arrow cannot use the reins, he must leave the horse entirely to its own discretion. The animal must be carefully trained to approach the bison within a few paces, staying close to the powerful and often angry bull, ready at all times with the utmost swiftness to evade all charges of these terrible opponents.

Ua-bac-tié had just returned from the hunt and on that very morning had seen bison. This made me most impatient to see these colossal inhabitants of the prairie, a desire of long-standing. I now hoped to meet the bison in a few days, since several herds had crossed the Eau qui Courre Rivière, even coming into the vicinity of the Omaha village and to the Elkhorn.

The Indian chief seemed a sincere and good man, and on the whole the Omahas and the Poncas may be regarded as the best Indians on the Missouri. These two nations and the Mandans had never killed or robbed a white man up to the time of my first visit. Unfortunately the character of the Omahas and the Poncas has become worse since then and mistakes may be to blame for that. These are difficult to avoid when dealing in trade with the Indians and bartering for furs. Also the decrease of the hunt is likely to bring about complications.

I presented Ua-bac-tié with a few small gifts, knives, tobacco, etc., and received in exchange a beautiful bow of yellow-wood. This beautiful variety of wood is highly prized by the Indians and would, indeed, be suitable for the finest furniture if it could be brought into the market. The tree from which the yellow-wood, actually reddish wood, is taken is called *bois jaune* by the Creoles and belongs to the family of Urticaceae (*Maclura aurantiaca?*).[27] It grows on the eastern slopes of the Cordilleras between the 33° and the 40° north latitude.

[27] The range suggested for *Maclura aurantiaca* (*M. pomifera*), the Osage orange or

I left the small camp of the Ponca chief and rode on for some hours, crossed the Rivière des Frénes, and spent the night on its banks under a grove of maple trees. This maple was the *Acer negundo* from whose sap one can also make good sugar. This variety also grows far in the north, while the sugar maple prefers a more moderate climate. I observed it even in the vicinity of the Rocky Mountains, where the forested regions become more numerous, and here and there even crowd out the prairie.[28] During the night the thermometer fell to 41° and a heavy dew soaked us thoroughly.

On the fifteenth of August the way led through an interminable wilderness in a northwesterly direction. I found no water, not even in the bottom of a creek bed which I reached as night approached. After dark, Monbrun succeeded in discovering some water in a creek, its banks surrounded by high and almost barren hills. Here I ordered a halt to be made.

The horses had covered a distance of thirty English miles and therefore were extremely tired and thirsty. The heat had risen to 95°, and a hot, oppressive wind from the southwest (which in the North American prairies takes the place of the *sirocco*) made it almost intolerable. My servant had been transported to this place with the help of my men and the Indians, for as long as he was conscious, he could not decide to stay behind with the Omahas. But now his condition had become so serious that I expected his death momentarily. I was therefore placed in a great predicament, for it was impossible to make a longer stay here because of the lack of provisions. Many antelopes appeared on the ridge of the neighboring hills or came to the stream to drink, but because they were extremely shy we made a fruitless hunt for them.

On the morning of August 16, after a most difficult ride of six hours over high hills and through deep ravines, we reached the Eau qui Courre not far from its junction with the Missouri.[29] This river is bordered by steep hills, but these run out a short distance from the mouth of this stream, where stretches of low lands border both sides of it. The southern bank

bois d'arc, by the phrase "eastern slopes of the Cordilleras" is misleading, inasmuch as Lewis and Clark had sent a specimen to Thomas Jefferson, together with a letter description (the first known to science) from their staging station at the mouth of Wood River, above St. Louis, in 1804. Lewis and Clark, *Letters*, 170–71.

[28] In the springtime of 1805, Meriwether Lewis noted *Acer negundo*, the box elder of the maple family, on the Missouri downriver from the mouth of the Yellowstone, but Duke Paul's is a much more inclusive and descriptive statement. *Original Journals*, I, 323.

[29] Eau qui Courre = the Niobrara River. Major Stephen H. Long had called it the Running Water during his trip to the Rocky Mountains in 1819–1820. Fifteen years earlier Lewis and Clark identified it as River "Que Courre" (*Original Journals*, I, 138). The original Ponca-Omaha designation, Niobrara, however, has prevailed.

near the mouth expands into a beautiful meadow region with tall grass. The northern bank is covered with tall timber and a wooded plain joining upon a row of hills, where it connects with the Missouri to form a triangular wooded point. The mouth is about 42° 37′ north latitude and 98° 8′ west longitude from Greenwich.[30]

When we reached the river I saw two Indians on horseback galloping from a rise on the opposite bank. These good people had seen my group approaching and had come to show us a good place to ford the river. Its bed in places contained much quicksand and the water flowed swiftly.

The Eau qui Courre had been discovered in early times by French fur traders, and, if I am not mistaken, the brothers Chouteau were the first white men to tread its banks. It was more accurately determined by the Lewis and Clarke expedition, which reached it on September 4, 1804, and called it Rapid Water River. The engineers of that expedition found it to be seventy-six [152] yards wide at its mouth. This was, however, a survey made at the lowest stand of the water. When I crossed the same river seven years later,[31] in the middle of winter, it was unusually rapid, broad and deep, and caused us a great deal of delay and difficulty because of the large amount of drifting ice. This time it was not deep but so swift that in places three or four feet deep the horses had the utmost difficulty in wading through. At the same time the bed of the stream is very uneven, full of sandbars and muddy places caused by deposits of clay, which are extremely slippery. These banks and also those of the nearby Missouri are formed of yellow ochre, an observation which did not escape Lewis and Clarke.

On the whole, the region north of 42° 30′ north latitude takes on a character strikingly different from that of the lower Missouri. Great masses of volcanic rocks take the place of the sandstone and limestone formations which prevail farther down the river. The pleasing green meadows are replaced by bare, lava-covered rocks from now dead volcanoes, and the existing vegetation is cactus and yucca covering wide stretches of land, reminding the traveler of a desert clime.

Strikingly peculiar and manifestly unique is the geographic distribution of plants, which shows the greatest analogy to the temperate volcanic plateaus of Mexico and Peru and seems to have been transferred, as if by

[30] *Author*: Unfortunately I could not make accurate measurements, since all my instruments had either been lost or had become completely useless. On my second journey the sky was covered because of a bad snowstorm. [Duke Paul's location of the junction of the Niobrara with the Missouri lacks several minutes of being accurate for latitude, and the junction is slightly west of 98° west longitude.]

[31] I.e. in 1830, on the Duke's journey of 1830.

magic, from the regions of the Andes into the midst of the central plains of the North American prairie regions.

The splendid *Bartonia*, also belying the climate to which it belongs, is confined to a very limited space and covers the inhospitable banks of the rivers with its beautiful flowers. This plant belongs to the cacti and has been superbly illustrated by Barton.[32]

The yucca, which I mentioned earlier, seems also to be new. It sends out a flowering stalk with large white blossoms resembling *Yucca aloefolia*. The plant itself becomes scarcely more than two or three feet high. The seeds germinated perfectly in my garden and tolerated the climate of southern Germany. Of the cacti is the *Opuntia missouriensis*; the other, not yet definitely determined, is a small *Mamillaria* with splendid red blossoms which I should like to call *septentrionalis*. (This *Mamillaria* has been erroneously confused with *Mamillaria simplex*.)[33]

When I entered the bed of the river large flights of ducks and geese took wing, and several wolves (*Canis nubilus*, S.) fled from their hiding places into willow thickets. Here I saw for the first time the northern hare, probably different from *Lepus variabilis*. In the winter this hare is snow-white down to the toes and lower part of the paws, which are yellowish. The tips of the ears are dark black shading into a light brown color. This hare is very large and in the summer it is light brown except the belly which is entirely white.[34]

The two Indians reported that the chief of the Poncas, Chu-ge-ga-chae, the Great Smoke, or La Boucanne, was present in this region. Since I could not help the condition of my German servant, I resolved to surrender the unfortunate man to the mercy of the Indian chief. Deciding to have this ruler of the wilderness, whose good character was generally recognized, called, and contrary to the advice of my companions, I caused a halt to be made. The small camp was therefore set up on a rise near the river bank. I asked the Indians to explain to their chief the deplorable condition of the sick man and to appeal to his sympathy. The Indians galloped away and soon disappeared beyond the hills.

[32] *Author*: *Bartonia ornata*, Nutt. (*Flora of North America*, by W. P. C. [B. S.] Barton, Table 81). The *Bartonia nuda* appears likewise, but more rarely than *B. ornata*. [*Bartonia ornata* = *Mentzelia decapetala*; *B. nuda* = *Mentzelia nuda*.]

[33] *Mamillaria septentrionalis* = *Coryphantha missouriensis*, former not in Curt Backeberg, *Die Cactaceae* (6 Bände; Jena, Gustav Fischer Verlag, 1962). For the complications in *Mammillaria simplex* Haworth, see Backeberg, 3377–78. *Opuntia missouriensis* is now *O. polycantha*, prickly pear.

[34] *Lepus variabilis* is a Greenland species. The more likely identification of the species seen by Duke Paul is *Lepus townsendii campanius*.

I utilized the remainder of the day to examine the surrounding country and added a few good plants to my herbarium. Strikingly pretty legumes entwined the short grasses, and the *Cassia chaemachrista*[35] with its beautiful yellow flowers and its mimosa-like feathery leaves covered the low places on the bank of the river. A *Gelega*[36] and a *Desmodium*[37] (*Hedysarum slutinosum*, Wild.?) were found. The sticky hulls of the latter had become ripe and clung so tightly to our clothing that they could not be loosened even with the aid of a knife. However, this *Desmodium* is a very pretty flowering perennial with rose red blossoms that stay in bloom for several months. The higher prairie supports an abundance of *Dalea*[38] and *Astragalus*[39] and also a very luxuriant *Melilotus*,[40] which must furnish an excellent fodder.

Of trees I saw the American cedar (*Juniperus oxycedrus* [*J. virgiana*]) extend a considerable distance up the Missouri, as far as 45° of latitude reaching an important height. It furnishes a very solid and useful timber. *Tetrao phasianellus*[41] was found here and there, and its habits are the same as those of *Tetrao cupido*. A large pretty grosbeak, brown with yellow underbelly with white spottings, lives either singly or in small flocks in these parts, and seems to frequent the wild cherry trees of the prairie. These cherries producing dark red fruit in grape-like clusters have a pleasing, cooling taste.[42] A variety of plum with fairly large red fruit is seen frequently in the prairie, but does not form such large clumps as farther north, where the cherries, too, cover large tracts of land and constitute a main source of food for the Indians in the summer.[43]

By daybreak Chu-ge-ga-chae arrived with a group of Indians and his son, Ka-hi-ge-schin-ga, which in the language of the Indians means Little Chief. They had ridden the whole night and had very tired horses. Chu-ge-ga-chae was a man of fifty, tall, and very stout, and had an extremely large nose disfiguring his face. Unfortunately, this Indian chief, known for his bravery and goodness of heart, died a few years ago and lies buried near the place where we had our meeting. A large cairn marks the place where

[35] *Cassia chaemachrista* = *C. fasciculata*, partridge pea.

[36] *Gelega*, one of the large family Gelegeae, in all likelihood of *Astragalus*, of Leguminosae.

[37] *Desmodium*, one of the tick trefoils.

[38] *Dalea* = *Parasela*, a large genus of the Fabaceae or pea family.

[39] *Astragalus*, one of the milk vetches.

[40] *Melilotus*, one of the sweet clovers.

[41] *Tetrao phasianellus* = *Pedioecetes phasianellus campestris*, prairie sharp-tailed grouse.

[42] *Prunus virginiana*, the choke cherry; or wild black cherry, *Prunus serotina*.

[43] *Prunus americana*, wild plum.

the remains of an Indian rest, a man of excellent character who deserved a better fate than that of being a chief in the prairie. His generous deeds refute the adventurous and absurd descriptions applied by some travelers to defame a people whose customs and practices they are in no position to judge, because they have no understanding.

At his arrival he manifested his sincere distress over the sad condition of my servant and promised me most solemnly to give him all the aid that was in his power to give. Among the Poncas with him was a Creole who had lived among the Sioux as an interpreter, looking even wilder than the Indians themselves. He seemed, however, to be a good man, praised Chu-ge-ga-chae highly and assured me without reservation that I might be without concern regarding the care the sick man would receive, the chief entertained every hope for his recovery, and that the patient, once having arrived at the Indian camp, would receive the best of care. All these promises were indeed fulfilled punctually and unselfishly. The sick man's health was completely restored and a few months later he was brought back to Fort Atkinson.

After I had spoken with Chu-ge-ga-chae for a short while concerning his affairs and his relations with the Sioux, I gave the signal to break camp. The son of the Chief, together with some of the warriors, accompanied us over the adjoining hills to a rise from which one could see the procession of the Poncas, or Poncaras, as they call themselves in their own language.

The whole tribe had followed their chief during the night and were apparently still several miles away. These Indians advanced in the same order as had the Omahas, but they maintained a strong and well-armed rear guard as protection against a possible attack on the part of the Dakotahs or Sioux.

Ka-hi-ge-schin-ga advised me to follow the trail the Poncaras had made up the Ponca River in order to avoid a scarcity of water.[44] From the source of this river I was to hasten in a northerly direction and cross the rocky wilderness which separates the Ponca from the White River. At the same time he admonished me to supply my caravan with sufficient water, since we would not find any water over a distance of fifty English miles.

About ten o'clock in the morning we reached the Ponca at a place where one could look down on the Missouri. Tall cottonwoods shaded this little stream, whose charming banks broke the monotony of that region most agreeably. Not far from this place is a most remarkable fortification of nations long extinct belonging to the past ages of America. On a conical elevation are breastworks in the form of a circle, more than a hundred

[44] Ponca Creek, rising in Tripp County, southern South Dakota, flows southeastward, nearly paralleling the Missouri, which it joins near the 98th Meridian.

paces in diameter, and in its entire circuit it had stood up well for many centuries. This fortress was a part of warfare entirely different from that practiced by the Indians of today, and the selection of the site itself proves that the fortification was designed for a considerable stay.[45]

It is surprising how little the Indians of the lower Missouri region know of the art of protecting themselves against a sudden attack by means of well-executed devices of defense. The Indians of the country farther north, on the other hand, are much more skillful in this, knowing how to secure themselves on their expeditions against a sudden attack by constructing barricades of tree trunks, and also attempting to protect their villages by strong palisades. Near the Rocky Mountains I found four-sided fortifications made of tree trunks placed together. These originated with the Blackfeet and Assiniboins, and sometimes such fortifications were found to number six or eight in a series at some distance from one another.

While crossing the Ponca I shot a deer of that variety called by the Creoles *chevreuil à queue noire*, and which Mr. Say has quite correctly classified as *Cervus macrotys*. This species belongs to *Cervus dama* without palmated antlers and attains the size of the European deer, appearing to constitute a transition to the elk. The antlers of this deer are forked, and usually grow longer than those of *Cervus virginianus*. Striking are the extraordinarily large ears of this deer, as is also the black spot on the short tail. Farther towards the northwest this deer becomes more numerous, while the Virginia deer becomes rarer. The color of the adult blacktail deer is red shading into yellow, somewhat lighter than the Virginia deer. In their mode of living they are alike.[46]

The Ponca flows almost in a straight direction to the northwest, parallel to the Eau qui Courre, here and there shaded by fine oaks and cottonwoods. High hills often force it into a narrow channel, or, spread out, its banks touch on extensive meadow lands. The summits of the hills are covered with short curly grasses among which the Missouri cactus grows. The bed of the river is sandy, the banks, steep and high.

In the afternoon a cold northwest wind rose, reducing the temperature of the air from 73° to 50° and forcing me to get out my warmer clothing, since I had become quite unaccustomed to such changes in temperature. I

[45] Compare William Clark (Lewis and Clark, *Original Journals*, I, 135–37), who drew the accompanying map of the so-called fortifications. Thwaites, in a footnote, was of the opinion that these formations were of wind-blown origin.

[46] Although Constantine Samuel Rafinesque is credited with the first description of the mule deer (1817), it was William Clark who on September 17, 1804, gave the description of Private John Colter's kill, *Dama hemionus hemionus*. Its ears, like those of the mule, evoked from Meriwether Lewis in 1805 the name which has stuck.

spent that night among some willow bushes and cottonwoods on the bank. The cold during the night might have pained the wolves, for they howled so pitiably that I could not sleep. At midnight the sky became clear and the thermometer registered 36°. On the morning of August 18 a thick hoar-frost covered the region and the entire vegetation mourned because of the sudden change in weather conditions, with the thermometer registering a few lines above freezing. The Ponca is scarcely 1800 Rhenish feet above sea level, so that here is added proof as to how strongly the northwest wind acts upon the thermometer even at the middle latitude in North America.

High hills compelled us to leave the Ponca a few miles to one side, to reach the plateau lying between the Ponca and the Eau qui Courre. Here I saw a peculiarly formed rock formation in the plains, called Pan-haesch-na-bae by the natives and Buttes de Médecine by the Creoles.[47] This re-markable hill rises out of the middle of the plain, appearing as a four sided rock, four to five hundred feet high, with abrupt sides, and on the flat summit boulders lie scattered. This striking rock and also an isolated high hill, almost two degrees to the north in the vicinity of Grande Detour, called Man-haesch-na-bae, or La Grande Butte de Médecine, are most noteworthy points for the geographer. Their longitude and latitude ought to be accurately determined. Since my way took me close to this formation, I regretted exceedingly the loss of my instruments, which made observa-tions of this kind impossible.

Every traveler making long and strenuous journeys by land will have reached the regrettable conclusion that it is next to impossible to keep the barometer in usable condition. The same is true of astronomical instru-ments, which are either made useless by moisture or are broken by trans-portation on the backs of pack animals. Moreover, it is absolutely impera-tive to carry two or three barometers for the purpose of checking. On the great flat prairies one can often make use of the ship's sextant and can thus obtain fairly accurate latitudes. As this was the only instrument for eleva-tions which was in tolerable condition, I employed it several times. It was discovered, however, upon my return to Europe, that this expensive in-strument by Campbell fell short of the requirements which I had set for it.

Longitude can be determined more accurately by the declination of the moon and other astronomical observations than by the longitude watch. This delicate instrument may not safely be intrusted to the back of a mule, for usually the jerking movement of this animal causes the instrument to deviate from the accuracy of its gauge. Mr. von Humboldt had the re-markably good fortune to carry out this extremely difficult work more successfully than any other explorer, because of the painstaking care he

[47] At present Butte, Nebraska.

devoted to his instruments, and it has been incomprehensible to me how this great scholar, amid the enormous privations on his extensive excursions, managed to make such an abundant collection of astronomical and physical observations.

Easterly toward the Missouri great clouds of smoke arose. It was a prairie fire, beginning even in this season to consume the prairie grass. These fires gradually extend over the entire boundless prairie region and devour the grass in late autumn in a sea of flame.

At noon I reached the Ponca River fifty miles upstream from its mouth. A new spectacle surprised me here, for all the hills on the opposite side [west bank] were covered with huge herds of bison. These were the first animals of this kind which I had seen in the wild state. Crossing the river, we made preparations at once for the hunt.

We tried to hide behind a ridge to the leeward of the animals, which approached us. Horses and mules were fettered and bound together as much as possible with strong thongs of bison leather such as the Indians use. In our haste, however, we forgot to take the load, including my overcoat and the water container, from the back of the mule, an oversight which I later was to regret very much.

The half-blood Monbrun picked out the fittest of our horses, saddled and bridled it in Indian fashion, and then galloped away, round about, behind hills, and through ravines. He was in the midst of the herd before the animals were aware of it. Carefully he had considered the wind, allowing him to ride his horse at a fast pace into the center of the herd.

Suddenly one could see countless bison running about in extraordinary confusion, and the whole prairie, far and wide, as if it were alive, was one great turbulence of excited animals. Not knowing which way to go, they ran to and fro. At first it seemed as if the herd would turn to the northwest, but suddenly changing their course they rushed with violent speed between the Ponca and the hill where our pack animals were. The region where Monbrun had come upon the herd was now pretty well cleared of the creatures, and there I saw him resting on his horse after he had killed three of the bison.

I found protection from the approaching herd behind a boulder and observed how the vanguard of the animals, frightened at the sight of our horses and mules, rushed in a straight line toward the river. Now the enormous beasts passed close by me, and for more than an hour I had the opportunity to see the animals at closest range, an unaccustomed sight which filled me with amazement.

Only after considerable time does one become accustomed to the sight

Urus americanus ♂ , *Bos Bison*, Lin. [*Bison bison.*]
(From *Icones ineditae*, Paul Wilhelm of Württemberg, "Atlas: Säugthiere,"
Schloss Rosenstein, Stuttgart)

Cervus macrotis, Say. [*Dama hemionus*, mule deer.]
(From *Icones ineditae*, Paul Wilhelm of Württemberg, "Atlas: Säugthiere,"
Schloss Rosenstein, Stuttgart)

Sciurus carolinensis, Gmel. [Gray squirrel.]
(From *Icones ineditae*, Paul Wilhelm of Württemberg, "Atlas: Säugthiere,"
Schloss Rosenstein, Stuttgart)

Mephitis Chinga, Liehbenss. *M. Americana seu hudsonica*, Bich. *Viverra Mephitis*, Lin. [*Mephitis mephitis avia* Bangs, striped skunk.]
(From *Icones ineditae*, Paul Wilhelm of Württemberg, "Atlas: Säugthiere,"
Schloss Rosenstein, Stuttgart)

Otus asio ♂. [Screech owl, male, red phase.]
(From *Icones ineditae*, Paul Wilhelm of Württemberg, "Atlas Vögel,"
Schloss Rosenstein, Stuttgart)

Mareca americana ♀ [♂ .] [Baldpate or American widgeon.]
(From *Icones ineditae*, Paul Wilhelm of Württemberg, "Atlas Vögel,"
Schloss Rosenstein, Stuttgart)

Coccyzus ludovicianus P. v Württ. Florida, Louisiana.
[*C. minor* (Gmel.), mangrove cuckoo.]
(From *Icones ineditae*, Paul Wilhelm of Württemberg, "Atlas Vögel,"
Schloss Rosenstein, Stuttgart)

Podilymbus maculirostris P. v Württ. *Colymbus seu Podiceps carolinensis?*
[*Podilymbus podiceps* (Lin.), pied-billed grebe.]
(From *Icones ineditae*, Paul Wilhelm of Württemberg, "Atlas Vögel,"
Schloss Rosenstein, Stuttgart)

of such huge animals; then they become a familiar and indifferent spectacle to the traveler, and unconcernedly the hunters pass among them to kill only those animals that are needed for food. It is hard to think that from sheer wantonness countless numbers of these harmless creatures are uselessly sacrificed. It is extremely easy to hunt the bison with firearms after one has once learned the necessary advantages of this method of hunting.

A most disagreeable accident caused me the greatest inconvenience. Despite the precaution and care with which my men had fettered and tied the pack animals, misfortune willed it that a rush of bison should run just in the direction of the area where the animals had been left behind. They became so frightened that they broke away, freed themselves of their fetters and fled with the utmost speed. A mule carrying my coat and the water container also escaped. The whole evening was spent in hunting for the lost animals, but they were not found until the following morning, all except the mule, which could not be located again. Probably frightened by the pack which had perhaps become loosened, he must have followed the herd of bison. This loss was most distressing, especially since it involved the loss of the water container, and this was particularly regrettable, as I was about to traverse the already-mentioned desert region and necessity demanded that we should be supplied with drinkable water. My men helped to make good this loss the next day by drying the bladders of the bisons, blowing them up and filling them with water. This water, however, took on such a repulsive taste that it was almost impossible to make use of it.

During the night a heavy storm with thunder and lightning passed over the plain, ending in a heavy downpour. The ceaseless rolling of thunder, the sharp electric discharges, and the bellowing of the large herds of bison in heat, badly frightened by the weather, rushing headlong to the Ponca, gave this night a special character, the true stamp of the wilderness.

I felt the loss of my overcoat very much, since I had nothing to protect myself against the cold rain. About midnight the storm passed and the moon lighted the gloomy landscape. Great herds of bison passed close to our camp and a few bulls approached fearlessly to within a few feet. Since a scant fire had to be maintained, but with great difficulty, it seemed to me that these animals were blinded by the light and yet attracted by it. It has been my experience that wild animals like to come near a fire, often so close that one can kill them.

Rodger brought back early the next morning the run-away horses. Still hoping to find the mule, I decided to roam until noon over the plain that separates the Ponca from the Eau qui Courre, and to use the time to observe the bison at as close range as possible, and to shoot some of them. Of the bulls only the tongue was edible during the breeding season. They disseminate a pungent odor of musk, which is even more repugnant than that of the stag during the breeding season.

That morning I was surprised in a peculiar manner. While I was behind a steep hill, I saw several heads protruding over the ridge, and I recognized them at once for Indians. I made several signs of friendship, and soon an Indian warrior climbed to the summit of the hill and waved a blanket. Since I recognized this as a sign of friendship intended for me, I waved my handkerchief. The Indians withdrew, disappearing toward the west, all except the one who had given the sign. He approached me unarmed and gave me his hand.

He was a tall, handsome man of about thirty years whose face and body, however, were made quite ugly by a layer of white chalky earth. Directing my attention to the bison I had killed, he then pointed in the direction of the Eau qui Courre, repeating the word Poncara. He also pointed to the north and several times called Wa-schi, which means white people. I now understood the Indian was saying that he belonged to a war party that had gone out after the Poncaras, and that many Americans and Creoles were coming from the north. By this he meant that the expedition of Colonel Leavenworth against the Arikaras, for a large body of Sioux had gone with the United States officer as auxiliary troops. The Indian warrior now began to dress the bison which I had killed, and we parted as friends.

I must remark that the Indians, even if they are in a region abounding in game, avoid as much as possible killing an animal when they are on a war expedition, in order that they may not be betrayed to their enemies by the remains. Therefore, especially if they spend a long time in a hiding place, they sometimes suffer the direst hunger.

Later I learned that I had not been mistaken in regard to the Indians. They were Sioux of the Teton tribe. These Indians are called *Si-schan-ko*, or Burnt Posteriors, that is, *cu brulé*, not *bois brulé*, or Burnt Wood, as they are often called incorrectly.[48] The group I saw comprised only twenty

[48] Their own name, as recorded by Ferdinand V. Hayden for the Brulé Sioux, is slightly more accurate linguistically but varies little from Duke Paul's rendering here. Burnt Thighs is the French translation of the Brulé tribal name. The Brulés in Duke Paul's time were occupying almost precisely the area recorded for them by Lewis and Clark in 1804–1806. The latter called them Bois Brulés, or Burnt Woods. They were a division of the Teton Sioux, warring on the Arikara and ranging for wild horses to the Platte and the Arkansas valleys in the first half of the nineteenth century. Somewhat past the middle of the century they began to range with the Southern Cheyennes, and in the great raids in 1865–1866 by the latter they were very active as allies over an area stretching from northwestern Kansas, Nebraska, Colorado, and the Dakotas. George Bent, *Life of George Bent Written from His Letters by George E. Hyde*, ed. by Savoie Lottinville, *passim*. Hodge, *Handbook*, I, 167–68.

men; the whole party numbered perhaps over a hundred. During my stay among the Pawnees this war party disturbed the latter near the Platte River, and the invaders lost their chief in an engagement with the Wolf [Skidi] Pawnees.

My men joined me at noon. They, too, observed that the Indians were much concerned, because the latter had recognized them as Sioux and did not trust them absolutely. The Sioux are dangerous only as enemies and as such they are cruel and bloodthirsty; as friends they are correspondingly loyal and extremely grateful. In the course of my journey I had, by chance, the good fortune to render a favor to a Sioux of high rank. On my second journey, in the midst of winter, under the terrible climatic conditions of this area, the warrior's son, at great personal sacrifice, rescued me and my companions from a most critical situation.

Though very tired from walking through the tall grass and fatigued by the terrible heat, I continued my journey. Near evening we crossed the Ponca and stopped there several hours to rest our exhausted horses. We had ridden through countless herds of bison. Since the wind was favorable, they allowed our retinue to come close to them. The old bulls even remained lying in the river without taking flight and eyed us calmly. These huge, formidable colossi, relying on their enormous strength, seem to defy almost any enemy. The cows, on the other hand, are very shy and it requires caution on the part of the hunter to slip up on them. The great herds maintain a peculiar order on their march and thus make broad trails, sometimes several feet wide tramped out deeply, and frequently several such trails run one beside the other to form regular roads.

The Creoles and the Canadians call them *chemins de boeufs*. Since we were obliged to ride in such trails freshly made by the herds, we had to exercise the utmost caution in the selection of camp sites: if the wind doesn't apprise the bison of the proximity of the camp, they will walk right through it, stampeding the horses and often endangering the men and the baggage. These animals, especially old bulls and old cows, follow the trail stubbornly and if the vanguard has once passed over an object, the others do not allow themselves to be deterred by any circumstances.

The evening was very beautiful; toward ten o'clock, however, a strong wind arose followed by a thunderstorm with pouring rain, yielding nothing to the one yesterday. Lightning hit the ground uninterruptedly, striking some nearby trees. Frightened herds of bison fled in utter confusion, seeking the ravines of the hills or the wooded banks of the river. Amid the flashes of lightning we saw them often close to our camp.

Howls of the wolves, bellows of the bulls, and the din of the elements made the loneliness of the dark night even more tangible than that of the previous one. Toward morning the sky cleared again. The rising sun dispelled the clouds, and the wind rose in the southeast, so that from August 20 to September 3 we had no more rainfall. While the heat of the day was broiling, the nights began to be very cool. In this region of the Ponca the ground rises more and more and takes on a volcanic character. The bare heights, their summits covered with iron-bearing lava, testify to the activity of only recently extinguished subterranean fire. Some craters do not seem to be fully cooled off yet. Here I found sulphur and iron-bearing rocks covering the craters of the more distant volcanoes. On average, these lava flows contain iron.

The Ponca is forced into a narrow bed between the sides of mostly wall-like, abrupt cliffs. Only here and there are the banks shaded by low trees, cut by deep bison trails. At intervals of two to three hundred paces the stream had to be crossed, for the narrow canyon afforded no other way out. A large number of bison grazed in this gorge and at our approach fled over the hills. On this day we killed many of these animals. The cows were extremely fat and their meat excellent. It excels the best beef. The cows are a third smaller than the full-grown bulls. The calves, born in March and already fairly large, were reluctant to leave their dead mothers, even attacking the hunters courageously when they attempted to approach the bodies. The wounded animals ran away and offered fight only when severely pressed.

Loaded with meat, we moved to a convenient place to break for dinner. While my companions prepared the meal, I made use of the time to study the country. From an elevation I could distinctly see the Eau qui Courre and the Ponca. These two rivers run almost always parallel to each other. The region is hilly, overgrown with short grass, and furrowed by deep hollows which one has to climb in and out of with much effort. The Eau qui Courre seemed broad and swollen, a result of the heavy rainfall of the previous nights.

Many antelope in small groups of three or four dotted the prairie, and as far as the eye could reach I saw herds of bison. My men thought I was lost and were just ready to start a search for me. Despite the great heat, I had them break camp and we continued the march, which was especially difficult for the bed of the Ponca was so muddy that the pack animals sank to their bellies. We had to cross the river five times. The bison had trampled the banks of the stream, and in some places had made deep wallows in the bed itself, causing some of our mules to plunge so deep into the water that our baggage was soaked. In some places, particularly higher upstream where the Ponca divides into two branches, the water was shallow and the banks were overgrown with dense willows and American dogwood.

We spent the night on an island formed by the stream. The hungry wolves of this region, scenting fresh meat, ventured so close to camp that during the night we had to kill several of them to rid ourselves of the bold tormentors. The specimen we killed did not differ from *Canis nubilus* and *Canis latrans* which I have often mentioned earlier in my work.[49] They appeared in several shades of color and in several varieties. I do not propose to classify them as different species, although this family of predatory animals does not appear more numerous anywhere than on the extensive continent of the New World. The lack of hair gives many of these wolves a revolting appearance, and their bodies contain many patches that are entirely bare. There are many malformations among these animals, and I believe that I am safe in stating that *Canis gibbosus* of Mr. von Humboldt, the *izcuintli puzzoli* of the Mexicans, and other members of the wolf family may only be abnormalities of a widely distributed variety.

The *Canis lycaon*,[50] which if I am not mistaken, is considered by Harlan among the American wolves, is at any rate different from the Siberian, and is probably a separate species. In the far north there appears also a large, powerful wolf with a short tail of dense hair, which in size and in its mode of living approximates the wolves of northern Europe and furnishes a good pelt. I think that this animal also represents a different species, perhaps *Canis gigas*, T., of which I have made a most careful and true drawing.[51]

During the night of August 24 the thermometer sank to 50° and the mosquitoes began to diminish. My men had spent the night on guard, because all sort of signs had caused them to fear the nearness of a party of mischievous Indians.

Rodger suffered intense pain from a peculiar injury to his hand, which occurred when he attempted to capture a porcupine. The quills of these animals (*Hystrix dorsata* [*Erethizon dorsata*, Fr. Cuvier]) produce ugly

---

[49] The author's handling of these two species, here more fully than elsewhere, indicates his familiarity with Thomas Say's work as zoologist with the Long Expedition of 1819–1820 in the same area, although he probably did not see it in finished form until after his return to Germany in 1824. Edwin James, *Account of an Expedition from Pittsburgh to the Rocky Mountains*, I ,169 (*Canis nubilus* Say); I, 168 (*Canis latrans latrans* Say). Hall and Kelson, *Mammals of North America* give twenty-four subspecies of *Canis lupus* and nineteen of *Canis latrans*.

[50] *Canis lycaon* = *Canis lupus lycaon* Schreber (1775: type locality Quebec), formerly ranging from the southern end of Hudson Bay to the St. Lawrence, southward to northern Florida, northwestward and north to s.e. Missouri and the Mississippi.

[51] *Canis gigas* T. = *Canis lupus gigas* Townsend? The latter is distributed from northern Nevada to a point two hundred miles north of Vancouver Island, but its date of description is 1850, hardly possible of inclusion in Duke Paul's publication date of 1835. We have no trace of his drawing of the species mentioned.

wounds which heal poorly if the quill breaks off in the wound. Instead of coming out by festering, it penetrates deeper into the flesh and may even result in the loss of a limb.[52]

In the morning a strong wind blew from the east, reducing the heat. At noon the thermometer registered 62°. I had to ride frequently across the swampy and ever more swampy Ponca. The herds of bison did not decrease in number and by noon the entire plain was covered with these animals. In the afternoon it began to rain and the wind turned to the northeast. Toward evening the sky cleared and the air became painfully cold. The source of the Ponca, which we followed after it divided into two branches, contained less and less water and eventually became completely dry.

I computed the length of the river from the junction of its two branches to its confluence with the Missouri at about one hundred and forty English miles, counting all the bends, of course. Without the latter the distance may amount to only a little more than one hundred English miles. The latitude of our night's camp of the twentieth to the twenty-first I calculated at 42° 40′ north latitude.[53]

The region southwest of the sources is a rather level prairie, extending thus as far as the Eau qui Courre. To the north and east, however, an exceedingly wild region sets in with chains of hills of volcanic origin from north to east. The summits of the hills are for the most part extinct craters but still bearing the stamp of recent eruptions. Jagged limestone cliffs with crusts weathered black, surrounded by enormous layers of encrusted lava, porphyry, and iron-bearing boulders, have liassic formations at their base,[54] where I found many good petrifications with many surfaces shining in beautiful colors.

The meager iron-bearing soil supported only stunted prairie grass, lichens, and mosses of the lowest order. The weathered lava, however, produced the cactus, yucca, and *Bartonia*[55] mixed with sparse bulbous plants. In the spring and summer the blossoms of these plants cheer this extremely desolate region somewhat. Except for this slight decoration, nature has given these parts the stamp of a dry and waste region. Only in isolated places where water accumulates in the spring a few taller plants

---

[52] *Erethizon dorsata = Erethizon dorsatum bruneri* or *E. dorsatum dorsatum.*

[53] At the northernmost forks of the Ponca he was in present south central Tripp County, South Dakota, nearly a full degree north of his stated latitude.

[54] Lias, from Teutonic, stone; in geology, Liassic is the oldest division of the European Jurassic Age of the Mesozoic Era, usually a limestone.

[55] *Bartonia*, now *Mentzelia*, a genus of small herbs of the gentian family, usually yellow-flowered.

grew, such as the earlier mentioned beautiful *Helianthus*[56] and a very pretty *Polygonum* with red flowers resembling buckwheat.[57]

The journey was now continued in a direction straight to the north in an attempt to cross a chain of rocky hills. These hills towered to a considerable height above the plains and thus cannot be unimportant. After a march of three hours we reached the first row of these hills. They form truncated cones or cylinders with bare summits strewn with cubical boulders or columns. I rode past two hills of dazzling whiteness, of which one, marked by broad black bands, resembled a large tower, reminding me of the tower-like rock formations in the Pirna region of Saxony.

From here a twenty-mile plain extends, interrupted only by small rises, and the spaces intervening represent the beds of dried up creeks. This wasteland is desolate and uninhabited. Here and there we saw a lone bison, hunting its sparse and miserable feed on adjoining heights. Antelope fled a short distance ahead of the horses, stopping frequently to observe us more closely, and then take flight again. Great packs of hungry wolves followed our group at a slight distance, uttering their terrifying howls from time to time.

These waste regions were swept by a cold northeast wind which was extremely penetrating and against which I could hardly protect myself. We made forty English miles on this day, finding not a drop of water anywhere, so that on that night man and beast had to go thirsty. The cold increased so quickly that the short, curly grass was covered with hoarfrost, and the thermometer fell to 26°.

At the very earliest next morning we broke camp, although I was quite stiff from the cold. We cut in a northerly direction through the wasteland until noon, when we reached the hills bordering the plain to the northeast. A small river with sparsely wooded banks snakes along the base of these hills. On the older charts this stream is called Shannon's River. My expectation met great disappointment. The river bed was dry. Thus we were doomed to endure torturing thirst for a still longer time. The wind had subsided toward morning, and at once the heat rose to a degree that was alarming to men already famished by thirst. I had the horses unsaddled and we camped in the shade of a few lindens and oaks [basswoods and bur oaks].

I was very much surprised to find doves and other song birds here, and concluded from this that some pools were nearby. However, despite every effort, no water could be found. After an hour's rest, we broke camp again in order to leave this desolate region as soon as possible, a region which

[56] *Helianthus*, the sunflower.

[57] *Polygonum*, a genus of herbs, the knotweeds. Here possibly *P. pennsylvanicum*.

357

may justly have some similarity with one's conception of Hades. High, conical, sharp-pointed, black-burned, rocky hills are separated from one another by deep, steep-walled ravines strewn with huge boulders or broken by deep holes. Wide-mouthed caves open into the sides of the walls and contain lava and cinders. Craters of extinct volcanoes, now filled and covered with ashes and other volcanic matter, testify by their funnel shaped depressions to their former extent and location.

After a dangerous ride of two hours we had passed over this ridge, the picture of which will remain deeply impressed on my mind, leaving the natural scientist a wide field of investigation. Manifestly these regions deserve more accurate and diligent study, which unfortunately seems impossible during the hot season because of the lack of water. In the spring, on the other hand, these difficulties do not obtain, and more excursions of longer duration can then be undertaken without hazard.

It is remarkable that such wide stretches of volcanic formation are so frequent in the New World. Rising right out of the high plateau, they themselves support only a scant vegetation but are often surrounded by the most luxuriant plant life. It seemed to me as if the high plateau of this part of the Missouri country rose in strata one upon the other, and though the single, almost sudden, elevations may amount only to a few hundred feet, the conclusion is unavoidable that the central plateau rises several thousand feet above the sea level.

Soon we entered another similar high plain, which was bounded on the north by high hills, extending perfectly level for seven miles. Here, too, nature seemed to have died out. Neither birds nor mammals were to be seen. My companions were of the opinion that the White River was beyond the ridge. According to my calculations, however, this stream was yet twenty English miles away. The most tormenting thirst compelled us to ride as rapidly as possible and since the ridge opened to the northeast, we rode through deep ravines and found, as I had surmised, a wilderness surrounded by high hills instead of the White River and drinking water. For fear of famishing we continued our way into the night.

The moon illuminated the desolate region with a bright glow, and the hope of finding water made us forget our weariness. However, the rough ground, being full of holes and containing many prickly cacti, presented too many obstacles to allow us to go farther by night. Without food and tormented by the most acute thirst, we had to stop for the night. After midnight dense clouds rose along the horizon, but it did not rain, and the cold again became most painful.

Early on the twenty-third my men and horses, exhausted by thirst, had to start again. I estimated the distance to the White River at fifteen English miles. The country continued to present the same aspect, always desolate, full of boulders, bearing the imprint of subterranean fires that produce wasteland. Beyond a height two Indians were making signals with a small mirror on which they caught the rays of the sun, signs which can be seen at a vast distance. The sight of human beings filled me with joy and my men with terror, because they always dreamed of enemies. Surmising that the Indians might be Cheyennes or Sahones,[58] the terror of travelers, my men refused to move on. I insisted on my purpose of advancing without delay. It would be better to face a fight with the Indians than to die of thirst; moreover, the lay of the land was such that we could reach the White River without getting into an ambush. I was also of the opinion that the Cheyennes might be encamped near the Rocky Mountains, and that there might be no danger from the Sahones, since they likely were engaged with their arch enemies, the Arikaras.

Finally, about ten o'clock we saw the White River in a narrow tree-covered valley surrounded by high hills. The Creoles call this river, Rivière Blanche. We reached it after descending a steep hill overgrown with *Opuntia* and almost impassable, being strewn with boulders and broken lava. A few tall cottonwoods surrounded by a growth of thick grass stood in the dismal valley.

The White River flows over a bed of white clay, its water so impregnated with the latter that it resembles a thin gray paste at low water. The river is not deep but contains great stretches of quicksand and beds of clay which dry up quickly after the recession of the water to its regular bed. The deeper layers remain soft and slimy, so that one sinks into it deeper and deeper at every step. The horses sank so deep into the soft ground that finally we had to wade through on foot. Though I was extremely thirsty I could scarcely make myself drink of the water in the river, the slimy stuff was so repulsive. My companions, however, drank it with greedy excess and at once felt severe colic-like pains. We tried in vain to cook something, but the water remained thick and no sediment would settle, which, by contrast, the water of the Missouri does almost immediately.

We stopped for an hour, time which the men spent in worry and fear. We had hardly resumed our march when three Indians came toward us. My men jumped from their horses, standing ready to shoot. I called it to their attention that there were two men and a woman approaching, and that three persons coming in broad daylight could have no evil intentions.

[58] Sahones, Sahowns in Lewis and Clark, more properly Sagonas, were a band of the Hunkpatina division of the Yanktonai Sioux.

They were an elderly man, a youth, and a young woman carrying a basket. They belonged to the tribe of the Yanktons, a member of the Sioux or Dakotah Nation, who live in peace with the Americans. The man told much about the expedition which the Americans had made against the Arikaras but how it had failed its purpose, and he described most accurately the way to the nearest American factory, perhaps twenty miles away. The woman gave me a basket of wild plums, which in this region are of excellent quality and are of a variety not yet described.[59]

I sought to compensate them for the gift by some tobacco, powder, and flint stone, for the man had a gun, but the youth had only a short lance. The Indian also reported that the people whom we had seen on the hill were likewise Sioux of his tribe accompanying some hunters of the Missouri Fur Company, whose business it was to supply the post with game.

The way we now took was a most difficult one. We had to wade through the shallow river nine times, since its flow watered the narrow valley closed in between high hills. Plum trees and *Hypophaea canadensis*, called *graine de boeuf*,[60] somewhat sour berries, grew on the banks of the river and also grow in large numbers on the upper Missouri. Soon I saw several young Indians busy hunting, and I asked one of them to guide us to the factory, which was ten miles away.

Leaving the White River, we had to climb hills that rose one thousand feet above the bed of the Missouri to a high plateau. From its northeastern slope the Missouri and the factory building could be seen. About two miles from the Missouri, the hills descend abruptly. The slopes, composed of weathered lava, are sparsely covered with cacti and grass.

The wind blew violently from the northeast and the thermometer rose to 88° in north shade, an unbearable heat. Across the Missouri I saw *Ma-na-ka he-si-tah*, a volcano which in 1823 still sent out smoke and which I shall mention again in the following chapter.

Extremely tired, even exhausted, we reached the foot of the hills and rode across the level prairie separating the Missouri from the hills. Here I saw one of the colonies or towns of barking marmots, *Arctomys ludoviciana*, called *chiene de prairie* by the Creoles. In countless numbers they undermine vast stretches of land, socially inhabiting extensive dens and tunnels. This small dainty animal, about the size of the European squirrel, has a tail a few inches long, is yellow, and usually sits so that the upper part of its body protrudes from the opening of its burrow. The barking voice of this remarkable rodent resembles that of a small dog, and at the approach

[59] Possibly the American plum, *Prunus americana*, native to the Great Plains.

[60] *Hypophaea canadensis* = *Shepherdia argentea* Nuttall, the silvery buffalo-berry, French bullberry, or beef suet tree.

of danger these animals continue barking until they slip into their holes, disappearing so quickly that one can hardly kill them by a shot.[61]

About eight hundred paces from the Missouri tall cottonwoods and oaks rise and a small creek enters the river near the point where at that time the factory stood. Since then it has become completely dilapidated. Mr. Joshua Pilcher, then superintendent of the Missouri Fur Company, received me at the factory in the most cordial manner, and I soon felt compensated for the many endured privations.[62]

[61] *Arctomys ludoviciana* = *Cynomys ludovicianus ludovicianus*, the black-tailed prairie dog (from George Ord, who gave it the name in 1815 here repeated by Duke Paul). Lewis and Clark encountered it in Boyd County, Nebraska, in 1804 and thus introduced it to science, although the French and Spanish explorers and, of course, the Indians, had long known it.

[62] Joshua Pilcher, whose career is fully detailed in John E. Sunder, *Joshua Pilcher: Fur Trader and Indian Agent* (Norman, University of Oklahoma Press, 1968), was at this time a partner in the Missouri Fur Company's fur-trading ventures in the region, and as such a competitor of the newly arrived William H. Ashley expedition, which was thwarted, as we have seen, by the Arikaras. In letters and newspaper articles he was bitterly criticizing Colonel Henry Leavenworth's conduct of the punitive military campaign against the Rees, as he called them, which began August 9, 1823, only two weeks before Duke Paul's arrival at his trading post, Fort Recovery, on a small island in the Missouri just north of the mouth of the White River.

11

SIOUX INDIANS — FACTORY ON THE GRAND DÉTOUR —
RETURN BY WATER TO THE COUNCIL BLUFFS — THE STAY
THERE — JOURNEY TO THE OTOS AND PAWNEES.

THERE was great activity at the factory. Mr. Pilcher and a large number of his men had been part of the expedition against the Arikaras and had returned only a few days before. Several bands of Sioux Indians had joined him and were now camped around the trading post. Some of them were in want of food supplies. Since the march of so many Indians and whites along the banks of the river, the bison had withdrawn, and the hunt was very sparse for the needs of the people. Despite the prevailing shortage I was nevertheless treated most hospitably and was invited by Mr. Pilcher to spend a longer time in that region.

Dejectedly I learned that it would be impossible to continue my journey farther upstream, perhaps as far as the Mandans, for there were no posts occupied by white men, and the bands of friendly Sioux had all gone west to the Rocky Mountains because of the lack of game. The Arikaras, no doubt, roamed in small bands over the country and would cut down every traveler without mercy. Without considerable escort it would also have been impossible to go upstream by boat and, in addition to the immense danger, the journey could not be carried out before the arrival of cold weather. Much against my will I was therefore compelled to postpone my plans until a future time and to content myself with studying the immediate environment.[1]

[1] After the Ree Campaign, Joshua Pilcher of the Missouri Fur Company had returned to Fort Recovery, where he would compete in the more limited theater with Berthold, Chouteau, and Pratte, who kept open Fort Lookout twenty miles upstream. He had closed Fort Vanderburgh, constructed in 1822 and named for his close friend, William Henry Vanderburgh, twelve miles above the mouth of the Knife in present North Dakota. The Arikaras had forced that.

It was a strange turn of events, only a dozen years after Manuel Lisa, Pilcher's predecessor in the Missouri Fur Company, had shown Henry M. Brackenridge the friendly

Since three different tribes of the Sioux nation, namely the Tetons, the Yanktons, and the Sissetons, were camping in this area, I at least had the opportunity at that time of seeing these people in their native environment.[2] This somewhat compensated me. I had heard so many exaggerated reports regarding the Sioux. In St. Louis they were described as the wildest savages, the treacherous enemies of all whites and of all neighboring Indian tribes, the terror and the plague of the upper Missouri. Therefore it was a great surprise to me when I was clearly convinced of the opposite. It is true that this warlike nation, the separate tribes of which are closely bound together, has offered a longer and more stubborn resistance than many other American aborigines and has been depicted in the blackest colors by neighboring tribes, who generally hate and fear the Dakotah tribes and who do not want them to make common cause with the descendants of the Europeans.

True it is that the Sioux are cruel and treacherous in war and as an enemy, that they occasionally ate the bodies of their slain enemies,[3] that their great poverty and the lack of the most necessary means of subsistence have often misled them to commit robberies and other illegal treaty acts against fur traders and other hunters. Since the American government had succeeded in checking the hostile influence of the Sioux and the American agents have been able to win their confidence, the many tribes of the Dakotahs belong to the more loyal of the aborigines under the care of the American government. These conclusions I also confirmed on my second journey, during which I met most of the tribes of the Sioux and had the opportunity of living with them for some time.

The chief of the Yanktons, or *I-hank-tome* as they are called in their

sights of the Arikara villages. Wilson Price Hunt, going upstream at the same time for John Jacob Astor's Pacific Fur Company, had brought to the Arikara country two other scientist-travellers, Thomas Nuttall and John Bradbury, the former more occupied with gathering roots than studying Indians, according to the French boatmen, while the latter accompanied Brackenridge, who later wrote a superb description of the Arikaras. Brackenridge, *Views of Louisiana*, 240–302.

[2] Of the eight large subdivisions of the Siouan family, the Tetons, Yanktons, and Sissetons fall in the Dakota-Assiniboine group. The Tetons ranged west of the Missouri, although they had first been met by Hennepin in 1680 in Minnesota; the Yanktons, also encountered by Hennepin at Leech Lake, were described by Long as ranging east of the Missouri; the Sissetons had earlier ranged northeastward from the Mississippi but in Lewis and Clark's time and after were at the headwaters of the Minnesota. Hodge, *Handbook*, II, 736–37, 989–90, 580–82.

[3] Such evidence as exists suggests cannibalism among the northern Indian groups was war- or religious-ceremonial. Cf. Franz Boas, "On Certain Songs and Dances of the Kwakiutl of British Columbia," *Journal of American Folk-lore*, Vol. I, No. 1 (April–June, 1888), 49–64; Hodge, *Handbook*, I, 200–201.

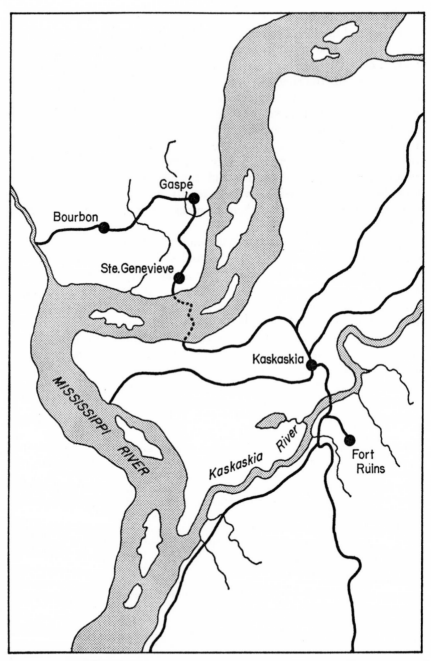

Ste. Genevieve and Kaskaskia (After Georges H. V. Collot's Map of
the Country of the Illinois in *A Journey in North America*)

own language, named Scha-pon-ka, Le Maringuain, or The Gnat, was at the factory and seemed to be a special friend of Mr. Pilcher's. With him were encamped between fifty and sixty warriors, together with some women and children. The majority of the band, said to number four hundred warriors, had scattered over the prairie. Besides the Yanktons, there were also some Tetons at the fort. Their leaders were said to be near by, farther upstream at Grand Détour at the factory of the French Missouri Company. These Sioux were very much excited at the result of the expedition against the Arikaras, and it seemed to me that the members of the Fur Trading Company also were not pleased with the results of this war.

After more careful examination of the circumstances, however, I cannot disapprove of the action of Mr. Leavenworth, the commander of the expedition. Undoubtedly this officer could have caused a mighty blood bath among the Arikaras, and many women and children would have lost their lives or would have been prey to the cruelty of the auxiliary Indian tribes.

General Leavenworth[4] and his expedition surprised the village of the Arikaras before the Indians had time to evacuate it. The settlement of the Arikaras on the Missouri consisted of two villages on the west bank of the river, separated only by a creek. The earthen huts of the Indians are of such construction that only the effect of heavy artillery could molest the inhabitants. The Arikaras, numbering over one thousand warriors, had supplies for more than a month and probably possessed a considerable amount of powder and lead.

The fur traders and Indians urged Mr. Leavenworth to risk a charge and this opinion was also shared by several regular officers of the American troops. Later I convinced myself on the spot that Mr. Leavenworth was entirely correct in declining this demand. His regular troops were much too weak to carry out a successful charge against well-fortified earthen huts, which would be defended with the greatest stubbornness, and, moreover, the commanding officer could not at all rely upon the allied Indians and the hirelings of the Fur Company, however great the courage of the leaders.

The proposed charge would undoubtedly have been repulsed, whereon the wounded would have been given up to the unrestrained cruelty of their opponents. Since the regular troops could not sufficiently encircle the settlement of the Arikaras, and since the Sioux, displeased with the slow progress of the siege, relaxed in their vigilance, the besieged, with the cleverness peculiar to the Indians, succeeded in departing their village

---

[4] Henry Leavenworth would not achieve general officer rank until the following year, 1824. Francis B. Heitman, *Historical Register and Directory of the U.S. Army*, 2 vols. (Government Printing Office, Washington, D.C., 1903).

during a dark, stormy night. With few exceptions they succeeded in reaching the open prairie. The regular troops suffered but few losses on this expedition. The Sioux, however, on several occasions having had sharp encounters with the Arikaras, counted a good many dead and wounded.

At first the few pieces of artillery brought up on boats by the American troops had inflicted some damage on the Arikaras. The latter soon learned, however, to dig themselves in inside their huts, securing themselves against even the cannon shot. If one now considers the small body of usable American regular troops, the costly nature of transportation into remote regions, and also the considerable loss by illness, one must conclude that it would have been an act of madness on the part of the commandment to have risked the lives of soldiers against a band of Indians living so far from every settlement in so disadvantageous a terrain. This is so much more valid since the expedition had the misfortune to lose a large boat, loaded mostly with ammunition, on the way up the Missouri, the bed of which is notoriously hazardous to navigation.

I must beg my readers to pardon me if I have wearied them by a detailed recital of an apparently unimportant military operation on the other side of the ocean. Since, however, this work will probably be read in the United States also, I consider it my duty to defend the cause of an officer who has been adversely criticized in the public press of his fatherland because of this expedition. In my estimation he has rendered his fatherland important services by the moderate, yet firm, stand toward the Indian nation during the time he was in command of the upper Missouri.

The Sioux differ from the nations farther south by letting their hair hang down long, never shearing their heads. In common with other nations of the Northwest, they have the habit of smearing their braids with a resin, a loathsome practice indulged in by both sexes. In general they are much dirtier than their neighbors, the Omahas and the Poncaras. The art of tanning leather and embroidering pretty, colored designs with porcupine quills has been advanced to a high degree of perfection. Both sexes frequently wear a leather skirt, which the warriors decorate with the scalps of slain enemies and the tufts of hair of stolen horses. The Sioux use firearms more than the other western nations, and their bows and arrows I found less efficient than those of the more northern nations. They had only few good horses and these had been stolen from the Pawnees and Omahas.[5]

During my stay the warriors performed victory and death dances while the scalps of slain Arikaras were borne around on poles. Such dances are also performed in honor of a stranger, and on such occasions it is customary

[5] Roe's previously cited map indicates that horse dispersion had not begun to benefit the Dakota Sioux much before 1770.

to present gifts to the Indians, which practice in the end became burdensome to me, but also afforded me the advantage of trading for all sorts of ornaments and weapons of these Indians. Their distress was so great that at last they even sold the conquered scalps and holy relics, specimens which I was subsequently unable to obtain from other nations despite all my efforts.

The lack of food is at times so great among the Indians that they consume all sorts of things that would seem most unwholesome to other human beings. They often eat tanned or dried skins, grasshoppers, tree bark, and all sorts of roots. Among the latter are the bulbs of an *Allium* and the root of a *Psoralea*, called *assinniboi*, which is rather scarce, but contains much nutriment and furnishes a starch which the fur traders farther north also use for a food.[6] The Sioux, moreover, prepare much pemmican—meat dried in the air, preserved in leather sacks, and beaten into a powder. In the far north it is also made of fish. Mixed with the fat of the bison, pemmican constitutes the commonest food of the Indians and the fur traders.

On the twenty-fifth of August I crossed the Missouri to visit the smoking hill I mentioned in the preceding chapter. It is called by the Indians *Ma-na-ka he-si-tah*. I do not know definitely what that word means, for it seems to me that the same word is also applied to the White River. At times entirely different objects seem to have the same name among the Indians. It is impossible, despite all pains a traveler may take, even with the aid of an interpreter, to make himself entirely understood by the Indians. The lack of linguistic knowledge of the interpreter is chiefly at fault.

On the ridge of the hill I found several tumuli, or artificial mounds, composed of piles of stone containing the remains of celebrated chiefs of the Sioux nation. Having arrived at the summit, I found few if any traces of a recent eruption and was convinced that this volcano had been extinct for some time. It showed the same formation as the hills on the opposite bank. Nevertheless, every morning I could discern distinct traces of haze which, according to trustworthy persons, disappear entirely at times and then reappear in the form of dense smoke. On my second journey this phenomenon was not observed either in the summer or in the winter, and I cannot attempt to offer an explanation.

Toward the Missouri the slope is very steep and broken by many ravines. I found a path by which it was possible to descend. The steep slope, composed of calcareous earth, extends to the foot of the hill, where outcrop-

---

[6] *Allium*, one of three wild onions. *Psoralea esculenta* was first described by Frederick Pursh in 1814 from the dried specimen brought back by Lewis and Clark (and still preserved in Philadelphia).

pings of clay and slate beds are observed. Here I found some petrified ammonite, ostrea, and serpent stone, the upper surface with a metallic luster resembling mother of pearl. The banks of the Missouri in this region abound in the remains of similar shell-bearing animals, most of which show the above characteristic.

On my return to the trading post I found a certain Toussaint Charbonneau present. He lived as an interpreter among the Gros Ventres and had accompanied Messrs. Lewis and Clarke to the west coast in this capacity. This Charbonneau had been sent out by the clerk at the factory at Grand Détour to invite me to visit there. I was very glad to do this, since that trading post was only twenty English miles away, and I hoped to see some Sioux Indians there.[7]

The next morning early I started on the way leading through a barren, desolate region, about which there is not much to say. On the summit of a rather steep hill sloping to the Missouri many cacti were growing. A wide plain extended toward the west. To the north a high, solitary rocky hill rose in the prairie, called La Grande Butte de Médecine by the Creoles. Visible at a vast distance, it is held in mystic awe by the Indians and their medicine men.

During the entire ride I saw no living creature, except a few prairie birds, nor even any antelope, which ordinarily inhabit the most barren and waterless regions.

We did not reach the factory until evening. Consisting of a few buildings, it is surrounded by a high palisade. Even from a distance I could see the leather tents of the Sioux like pointed sugar hats, their size varying according to the number of families that inhabited them. Some of these can shelter eighteen to twenty persons. Sometimes requiring twenty and even more bison hides, these leather tents are sewed waterproof and drawn over several poles tied together at the top, where an opening lets the smoke out. This opening is covered with a leather flap which can be turned to suit the direction of the wind. In the center of these tents, which the Creoles call *loges*, is a hole in which the fire is built. From one of the poles the cooking kettle hangs perpendicularly over the fire.

The tent is fastened to the ground by means of wooden pins and resists the most inclement weather and the severest storms, and even in the winter requires only a meager fire to hold the warmth. These leather tipis are much more useful than canvas tents and completely protect against moisture. The chiefs and celebrated warriors set up poles before their tents on which they hang their weapons, medicine bags, the tails of horses, etc.

[7] The site is Fort Kiowa or Lookout, held minimally open by Berthold, Chouteau, and Pratte. This was the Duke's farthest penetration of the Indian country in 1823.

The camps of the Sioux, who are a really nomad nation, have therefore a striking oriental appearance and no people resemble the Bedouins more than they.

The clerk at the factory, a born Frenchman, met me and apologized for having so few means at his disposal to provide some comfort for me. The post was indeed without provisions, and the Indians suffered extreme hunger. There were two Teton chiefs there. One of them was called Inga-mo-na-kute, Celui qui Tire le Tigre, or He Who shoots the Tiger, and the other was Schinga-ka, l'Enfant or the Child.

The Tetons appeared to me wilder and less civilized than the Yanktons, and as they had lost more men in the war against the Arikaras then the other tribes, they were sunk in deep mourning, ceaselessly howling their songs of lamentation. There were several in the camp who had been severely wounded and were being nursed with utmost care by their relatives. Here I had the opportunity of observing how skillful the Indians are in healing even most severe injuries, and with what patience and resignation the wounded Indians bear the most intense pain.

The region about this post presented so little that was worth seeing, and the vegetation was so poor and so little different from the parts I had already seen that it was not necessary to prolong my stay, and it was in such dire need of provisions that every visitor must have been a highly troublesome burden.

For this reason I returned to Mr. Pilcher early on the following morning. He was so kind to equip a small boat for my return journey to the Council Bluffs, large enough for ten persons and my baggage, and Mr. Leclerc, his clerk,[8] accompanied me down stream. In addition to this clerk there were on board two Americans, an Irishman, two half-bloods, and a Negro.

On the twenty-ninth I left my friendly host. At first the journey progressed slowly, for a strong southwest wind hampered the efforts of the oarsmen. High bluffs rose on the banks of the river near the mouth of the White River. This opening scarcely could be seen by the travelers because of an intervening island.

After a storm a beautiful night followed. We camped on the east bank of the river under tall cottonwoods. Early the next morning I saw some high bluffs rising above the Missouri, called Côtes à Bijou, named thus by a certain Bisoton, who formerly lived here as a trader.[9] These steep

[8] Narcisse Leclerc, whose hot temper would later lead to troubles at Cabanné's Post, in 1832. Sunder, *Joshua Pilcher*, 101–102.

[9] Louis Bijou, who had early ascended the Missouri to the Three Forks for Manuel Lisa's Missouri Fur Company, gave his name to Côtes à Bijou. The company post also

limestone bluffs rise more than 1,000 feet above the bed of the river to present a wild and magnificent sight. The right bank is level and covered with dense curly grass, but at a distance of several miles a chain of hills rises. Some distance from this place a grass fire had wrapped the prairie into a black shroud. The hunters killed a deer, a *Cervus macrotys*, which had grazed near the banks among the high bluffs.[10] I also succeeded in shooting a *Falco mississippiensis* (Wilson III, 35, 1, Mississippi kite), a splendid specimen which Wilson has pictured masterfully.

On this day the heat rose to 88°, with a gentle breeze from the southwest, but it did not prevent us from traveling fairly rapidly. On an island in the Missouri I saw several bison bulls, but we left them unhunted since we had no time to lose and did not need any provisions. Shortly thereafter our vessel reached a group of islands, called Les Trois Isles, and not far from there I noticed high bluffs of striking limestone formation constituting the projection of high hills. These cliffs form sheer towers, and there were huge boulders composed of white chalk-like limestone wrenched loose by some gigantic force.

The boat had to pass close to these cliffs because of the deeper channel, and here an incident occurred that filled my companions with the greatest fear. Suddenly, as the boat passed close along the rock we saw a tall Indian warrior on a projection of the cliff, who motioned to us to stop our boat. My companions at once took up their weapons, terrified by this sudden encounter. Only Mr. McNair, a brave and resolute American who was on board, and Mr. Leclerc did not lose their heads, but had the boat go to shore at an inaccessible place under a high bluff. Even if we had tried to reach the middle of the stream we could not have escaped the bullets of the Indians, who doubtless were hidden behind the rocks. Thus it was at least possible to protect ourselves fairly well against sudden attack.

The Indian now threw his weapon aside and came within a few feet of us. He was a tall, handsome man of commanding figure and seemed to be a chief whom Mr. Leclerc, who knew the Sioux tribes, recognized as an Indian from the upper Mississippi or from the St. Pierre River. At any event, caution was extremely necessary, for he belonged to the tribe of Sissetons or Sissatons, who had hitherto lived in enmity among the Americans. The Indian declared in a loud voice that he had not come with the intention to be hostile, although it had been entirely in his power, for the

---

named for him in Brulé County, South Dakota, figures in John C. Luttig's *Journal of a Fur Trading Expedition to the Upper Missouri*, ed. by Stella M. Drumm, kept during Luttig's clerkship on Lisa's expedition of 1812–13: pp. 35, 88–89, 104, 106.

[10] *Cervus macrotys* (*Cervus macrotis* Say) = *Dama hemionus hemionus* (Rafinesque), the mule deer.

previous night he had been near our camp. He had swum across the river to speak to us at this place, which vessels could not circumvent at this season of the year. The Sioux further declared that he had heard from several Tetons of my arrival at Grand Détour and had wished to see me. The open face and the bold manner of the Indian warrior standing unarmed before us took from my companions all distrust and they laid down their guns.

Immediately the Indian made a motion and I saw between thirty and forty men rise. They had hidden so cleverly that it had been impossible to notice any one of them, although they were so near that a single suspicious movement on our part would without fail have cost all of us our lives. They were for the most part handsome young Indians accompanying their chief on a war expedition. I remained uninformed concerning its purpose.

The chief, of whom I can say that but few Indians left so lasting a memory with me as he did, declared with the utmost frankness that he had formerly been a dangerous enemy of the Americans, but that he had made peace by an agreement in Fort St. Pierre and would undertake no further hostilities.[11] After this interview we pushed off again, and on this day proceeded yet four miles farther downstream.

In the vicinity of our night's camp I saw fresh tracks of Sioux Indians, who probably had crossed the river with an entire camp. I recognized clearly how they had prepared rafts to transfer their baggage. Such rafts are simply constructed and usually consist of four willow poles tied together in a square and then covered with branches. Onto these tottering vessels the baggage is tied, and the Indians push the raft ahead of them while swimming. Horses are usually driven into the water and an Indian leads the horse that is the best swimmer out into the stream, whereupon the remaining horses are accustomed to follow.

Early on the morning of the thirty-first a heavy fog surprised us, forcing us to lay by at a large island. This island was entirely overgrown with cedars and called reasonably Île aux Cèdres.[12] A strong wind dispelled the

---

[11] Both chronological and geographical confusion may result from the Chief's statements here: Commissioners William Clark, Ninian Edwards, and Auguste Chouteau had shaped the U.S. treaty of peace and friendship with the Indians of St. Pierre, Minnesota, River, July 19, 1815, at Portage des Sioux. These were the Sissetons. There would not be another formal treaty until July 15, 1830, at Prairie du Chien, not Fort St. Pierre, a stopping place but not a fort of Bernard Pratte and Company until 1831, named for Pierre Chouteau, Jr. The latter was a quarter of a mile west of the Missouri River, three miles above the mouth of the Teton River, thus some three miles n.w. of the present city of Pierre, South Dakota.

[12] Probably Little Cedar Island of today, in Charles County, S.D., notable also for "the backbone of a fish 45 feet long," seen nearby by Lewis and Clark, now identifiable as the

fog but forced us to seek shelter in a bay on the west bank of the river. Since there was nothing left to do for the remainder of the day, I went on the hunt in company with the two Americans and the Irishman. We soon discovered a herd of bison, approached these animals within firing range, and killed four of them. A wounded bull fled into a ravine, and it required five or six shots to dispatch him. My companions shot him several times in the head, but the bullets did not make the slightest impression on the thick skull with its dense mat of hair.

A bad prairie fire, driven quickly by a strong wind, spread like a giant sea of fire over the prairie toward the west and approached the Missouri with giant strides, covering the entire horizon with smoke and flames. This magnificent sight lasted deep into the night until the river set a barrier against the fire.

On September 1 the storm subsided and fine weather with a gentle northeast wind set in, which favored our travels. Early we reached an island where the remains of an abandoned factory were to be seen, formerly called Fort van der Bourg.[13] Nearby I saw a peculiarly shaped double hill with conical summits, called Le Tour. The banks of the Missouri were inhabited in many places by countless swallows (*Hirundo viridis*, Wils.), which live socially together in the manner of our cliff swallows [*Riparia riparia*, bank swallows]. In the night it began to rain heavily, which was the more disagreeable as we had to endure it without shelter.

On the following day I found the region less hilly and the banks of the river, especially at the Ponca and the Eau qui Courre, very beautiful. At the Ile à Bon Homme we stopped for dinner and I succeeded in killing a big deer (*Cervus major*) with large antlers.[14] Since I had not shot a finer specimen of this variety of deer, I had it prepared and this, because of the prevailing heat and the size of the animal, caused us much difficulty. However, I succeeded in bringing this specimen to Europe in fairly good condi-

---

remains of a reptile of the Cretaceous period. Coues, *History of the Lewis and Clark Expedition*, I, 113, 113n.

[13] The site is so close to Pawnee House, where Jean Baptiste Truteau or Trudeau spent the winter of 1796–97, in one of the early penetrations of the upper Missouri country by the Spanish Commercial Company of St. Louis and himself, among others, that it is easy to suspect Duke Paul of mistaking it for the later (1822) Fort Vanderburgh twelve miles above the mouth of the Knife in present North Dakota, about which he had doubtless heard. Tabeau, *Tabeau's Narrative, passim ad Truteau*; Sunder, *Joshua Pilcher*, 38–39.

[14] Bonhomme Island lies below, rather than above, the mouth of the Niobrara in the county of that name in present South Dakota, as indicated by the author. It was confused in Tabeau, *op. cit.*, but not in Trudeau, "Trudeau's Description of the Upper Missouri," ed. and trans. by Annie Heloise Abel, *Mississippi Valley Historical Review*, VIII, 165.

tion where it is now displayed in Stuttgart. In the evening we landed at Ile aux Boeufs, where I saw the last bison.

The next day we passed the mouth of the Rivière à Jacques. High limestone bluffs rise here on the east bank of the river. The journey was again delayed by a violent storm followed by rain lasting throughout the whole night.

On the following day the rain ceased about noon. High hills touch upon the west bank of the river not far from the mouth of the Vermillion River. Here I saw countless flocks of swans and pelicans flying in wide circles overhead or hunting their food on the sandbanks of the river. In the afternoon the weather was fine and the boat succeeded in reaching the mouth of the little Iowa River.

On the morning of the sixth I saw the Sioux River, whose bed is muddy and deep. The river flowing from the east into the Missouri is one of the most important tributaries of the great stream. In the vicinity of its mouth high hills of limestone formation rise.[15] Not far from the Sioux River on the opposite bank of the Missouri a level plain stretches out, which in the south is bordered by a wooded chain of hills. Here one sees the remains of Indian settlements originating from the Omahas, who frequently settled this region, exchanging their dwelling place on the Elkhorn for that in the vicinity of the Missouri.

The hilly right bank of the Missouri shows beautiful formations of outcropping rocks, the slopes toward the river are abrupt. The forests are luxuriant and begin to show different varieties of timber, and the climatic influence of the nearness of the fortieth degree of latitude is clearly expressed in the plant and animal world. *Meleagris gallopavo* and *Psittacus carolinus* seem rarely to cross this boundary, but appeared in huge flights farther down stream.[16]

From the Missouri on the highest summit of the hilly ridge one can see the burying place of Oa-schin-ga-sa-bae, or Black Bird, the great chief of the Omahas. He played an important role among these Indians, and his friendship was enjoyed by the fur traders and the Americans. This chief acquired such a great respect among the other Indians by his courage and resoluteness that he exercised a truly despotic power over the lives of these people. The great awe which the Indians held for Black Bird, whose reputation as warrior and medicine man was equally great, is attested by the pompous burial accorded him. His best horses and his weapons were buried with him. Some even assert that his wives were buried with him, but this I doubt.

[15] Big Sioux River of the present flows into the Missouri at Sioux City, Iowa.

[16] Respectively, the wild turkey and the Carolina parakeet.

The Indians, even the hostile tribes, when they roam this region, do not fail to carry stones to his burial mound, and on my second journey when I revisited this grave, I found new stones added and the whole mound considerably enlarged.

In a previous chapter, at the occasion of my visit to the camps of the Omahas, I mentioned the son of this chief, who, after the death of his father, accompanied the American agent to Washington.

The following day we were delayed the whole day near Côtes à Woods because of adverse winds and the strong current. However, early on the eighth we reached the Petite Rivière des Sioux and camped that night at the mouth of the Rivière aux Soldats, or Soldiers Creek, both of which flow into the Missouri from the east. Opposite our night's camp the west bank rises to moderate hills, which extend to the Council Bluffs and are used as pasture for the cattle of the garrison. A row of narrow swamps overgrown with tall weeds touch the right bank of the river.

Early on the morning of the ninth I reached the Council Bluffs. I had the boat lay by that I might pay my respects to the commandant. In the person of Colonel Leavenworth I found a very well-educated officer. He received me with extreme courtesy and very obligingly promised me aid for the continuance of my journey. The Colonel suggested that I ought to visit the Otos and Pawnees. Both nations were at their settlements on the Platte River at that time. He promised to give me an escort of an officer and sufficient number of men, and it was decided that I should begin the journey in a few days.

Since Mr. Leclerc wished very much to reach his post at Côtes à Kennel, where his presence was urgently needed, I had to consent to leave the Council Bluffs on that same day and prepare myself for the impending land journey at the Fort of the Otos.

An exceedingly unpleasant incident occurred that evening. One of our companions had become drunk at the Council Bluffs and in this condition started quarrels on the boat. The risky condition of the intoxicated man made it necessary for us to stop in order to avoid any possible accident. Shortly before the boat reached the bank, the inebriate succeeded in securing a knife with which he meant to stab Mr. McNair, who had patiently tried to calm him. This intention was frustrated, but during the struggle the drunk had wounded one of the half-bloods in his abdomen so severely that we despaired of the man's life. The boat having landed, the evildoer fled and escaped further pursuit. Later I learned that this man had previously committed several crimes while in a drunken condition.

Early the following day we reached the trading post of the Otos, where I took leave of my companions, who continued their journey down the stream. I did not find Mr. Robidoux there but did meet Mr. Cabanné, one of the members of the French Company, who is now a leading member of the American Fur Company. I had previously made the acquaintance of Mr. Cabanné, a native Frenchman, in St. Louis.[17] Since nothing of importance happened during the stay at the Fort of the Otos, I shall proceed with the account of my journey to the Pawnees.

On September 17 I went to Fort Atkinson and betook myself at once to Colonel Leavenworth, who had been so kind as to have a dwelling prepared for me and my men. My servant, whom I had been obliged to leave as a sick man with the Poncas and of whom I had heard nothing since, had been restored to health through the care of these Indians and had arrived at the fort the day before. Colonel Leavenworth, wishing to do everything to make this new and difficult land journey as comfortable as possible, ordered Captain Riley of the Sixth Infantry Regiment, a First Sergeant, and the interpreter of the fort, a half-blood of the Iowa nation, plus a few soldiers to accompany me. Before we started I was warned by several persons regarding the half-blood, and Captain Riley would also have been glad to leave him behind had he not been so indispensable. The company of the captain became even more pleasing to me, since he was a very resolute man of the highest character and on this as well as on my second journey gave abundant proof of his friendship. Since then he has been duly advanced in rank.[18]

I have previously mentioned that the autumn makes itself distinctly felt at the beginning of September, the nights especially are cold, and the wind extremely strong. At the fort, due to its high and exposed location, the nearness of the winter made itself keenly felt. I think that I can safely say that the September nights in northern Prussia and even in Russia could not be colder. The hot days in contrast to the low level of the thermometer at night had caused the most stubborn fever at the garrison, and a large number of soldiers had fallen victim to it. Even then men were dying there every day despite the rigid sanitary arrangements made with minute detail in every respect by the commandant. Proof of the great stubbornness of typhoid fever! Often death follows within several hours of the first symptoms of the disease and does not spare even the men who appear healthiest.

The cause of the evil, which is of a purely miasmatic nature, could not be determined by the physicians, for in the matter of diet the greatest pre-

---

[17] J. P. Cabanné, a native of Pau, capital of the Department of Basses-Pyrénées, southern France.

[18] Captain Bennet Riley, commanding officer of a company in the First Battalion of the Sixth Infantry, would distinguish himself in the Mexican War, for which he was decorated. Fort Riley, Kansas, established shortly after Riley's death in 1853, is still operative.

caution had been exercised. The soldiers had been sent to camp on an airy elevation several miles from the Missouri, where they are supplied with only fresh food. At first it was thought that the trouble was due to fish or drinking water, both probably without cause. The proximity of evaporating swamps could exert no bad influence, since the surfaces they encompassed were relatively small. I believe that the true cause is to be sought in the isothermic condition of the air and also to the constant succession of extraordinarily hot days and very cold nights. A condition when extremely hot winds follow sudden cold air masses could not fail to produce illness. I cannot deny that I was very much concerned that one or another of my company might suddenly become sick, whereby the continuation of my journey would have met interference. The Canadian Iroquois whom I had seen on my first arrival at the Council Bluffs had for the most part become victims of the climate, and of the few men who were left several died later on.[19]

On the morning of September 19 we rode away at the appointed hour. Our small caravan was joined by a few traders, who, driven by speculation, desired to go to the Pawnees to trade mules. These they hoped to dispose of farther south. Such men have an inherent fear and thus like to join more courageous men in order that under their protection they can carry on their trade in safety.

Neither Captain Riley nor I cared for the company of the interpreter and the traders, therefore I suggested that we should let the mule buyers go their own way. Captain Riley, however, restrained me, for he believed that the interpreter meant to profit from the purchases of these mule traders, and that he might be inclined to play us a bad turn with the Indians if he was thwarted in his expectation.

A strong wind blew from the east, striking us with such force when we reached the elevation between the fort and Butterfly Creek that we had difficulty in guiding our horses. The vegetation of the prairie had dried up. However, the low prairie roses were splendid with their four or five dark red seed pods, only a few inches high, in dense clumps at the top of the stalks. The pretty *Helianthus* had also ceased blooming and had scattered

[19] Before medical research and treatment had established the causes and cures for several often fatal diseases (typhoid fever and malaria were two), it was common to attribute them to bad air or low-lying, often swampy, living or camping sites. *Salmonella typhosa*, the bacterial source of typhoid, is usually water- or food-borne, occasionally (perhaps not more than 3 per cent of the cases) from "carriers," i.e., persons who transmit the disease long after they have themselves survived it. Careful sewage disposal and sanitary handling of foods are best defenses.

its seeds, and this was also true of most of the other *Syngensia*. Only a single bush-like aster with small blue blossoms was still very luxuriant.

Butterfly Creek, which we reached about three o'clock in the afternoon, at the place where we had to cross exhibited banks which were lined with dense plum bushes and a kind of sumac. The water was so low that the horses sank into the mud to their bellies. Three low chains of hills separated this creek from the Elkhorn River. On the east side the Elkhorn is bordered by rather abrupt rises, and the other bank joins a low plain. The crossing of this river was made without any trouble, since it is not deep and has a hard bed. We crossed it nine English miles from its confluence with the Platte. The nearest village of the Otos lay in a westerly direction before us. An Indian trail in the prairie led through extremely dense grass almost as tall as a man.

However luxuriant the grass is, the prairie is poor in herbaceous plants, except for a few *Asclepias* and *Dalea*. I observed great numbers of *Xanthornus phoeniceus* and *Fringilla pecoris* flying about in huge flocks like our starlings, for the birds were already assembling to begin their migrations to the south. *Tetrao cupido* often flew out of the tall grass. The Creoles confuse this beautiful variety of chicken with the pheasants inhabiting the prairies in the summer and winter, moving to the vicinity of the corn fields, where they gather in large numbers.[20]

The *cupido* belong to the few known species living gregariously like pigeons, and at the approach of danger, or in order to rest, settle together in tall trees which bend under their weight. The males have distentible membranes on each side of the neck, which they can inflate with air like two bladders. Under the ears several long feathers protrude, which the birds erect at will. In size, the *cupido*, commonly called the prairie hen by the Americans, is about that of the grouse and in their flight and color both sexes resemble the European grouse. The meat is rather tough and of dark color, and in this *Tetrao cupido* is entirely different from *Tetrao umbellus*, another North American variety of chicken, which may be considered the closest relative to our hazel grouse.[21]

As it grew dark we reached the Platte River, very broad and shallow, its

---

[20] *Tetrao cupido* = *Tympanuchus cupido* (Linn.), the greater prairie chicken or pinnated grouse, the eastern (nominate) race of which, known as the heath hen, ranged formerly along the Atlantic seaboard from New England southward to the Potomac River. The bird Duke Paul saw was *T. c. pinnatus*, the more northern of the two western subspecies.

[21] *Tetrao umbellus* = *Bonasa umbellus*, the ruffed grouse of forested parts of northern North America. The hazel grouse, *Tetrastes bonasia*, ranges widely in Eurasia.

bed consisting of soft sand. At low water stand a great number of sandbars appear and at such times the river is divided into many channels, permeated more or less with quicksand, which makes crossing hazardous for the uninitiated. None of us was able to find a ford, for the opposite bank was very steep.

The village of the Otos was still half an hour's ride farther up the river. On the side where we were the bank was overgrown with dense bushes, affording no good place for a night's camp. For this reason Captain Riley advised that we should try fording the stream yet that same evening. To me this seemed impossible to execute. However, I did not wish to oppose the captain and so we rode onto the sand. The horses sank in to their knees. For half an hour we rode upstream keeping ourselves between two channels of the river.

In the meantime it had become dark and very cold. The Captain, approaching the opposite bank, tried to guide his horse into the main channel but got into deep water and quicksand from which only the aptness of his horse rescued him. At this moment we saw some fires on the crest of the hills on the right bank and heard the voices of several Indians. Unfortunately the interpreter had stayed behind. I feared that the Indians might not heed to calls, but in this I was mistaken, for in a short time two young men came swimming across the stream.

As the interpreter had then arrived, we learned that the river was so treacherous and dangerous to ford that it would be impossible to undertake it at night. Moreover, the Indians declared that under no circumstances could they serve as our guides in the dark, for they seemed to place but little confidence in our ability to swim.

Consequent to this unpleasant news we had to consent to ride back and occupy the spot which in the evening had appeared too bad for a camp. Captain Riley had the tent pitched in the middle of the densest underbrush in order to protect us as much as possible from the biting north wind. The sky was heavily overcast and all indications of bad weather seemed infallable. Nevertheless, there was only a strong wind and no snow fell. The thermometer, however, dropped to 23° during the night. The north wind blew hard until the morning of the 20th, and being entirely unaccustomed to the cold, I nearly froze to death.

At seven o'clock we broke camp. The Indians had spent the night with us and sat outside our tent stark naked, smoking their pipes. We forded the main channel of the river in low water where the Indians crossed regularly, opposite the Indian village on a hill. Even so, most of the horses had to swim, but mine, being the tallest, had the water come half way up to its breast. As the water was extremely cold, we felt the chill so much more acutely, especially since most of the men had to swim while holding the manes of their horses.

On the bank I was awaited by the chief of the village, Isch-nan-uanky. This man seemed to be sincere and friendly to the whites, and in 1821 had been to Washington with Mr. O'Fallon. There, with Anpan-tanga, the chief of the Omahas, he had distinguished himself before all other Indian warriors.

The road from the river to the village led through a plain, in part over-grown with grass and in part planted to corn, and joining this was a low but steep-walled chain of hills of disintegrated limestone. Here the village was built. We climbed the hill to the dwelling of the Indian. This village con-sisted of about forty earthen huts, occupied in common by the Otos and their kinsmen, the Missourias. As the Otos were at that time on friendly terms with the Iowas, I also noticed several families of this nation among them.

The chief led us to his hut, which he shared with six other families. Al-lowing our men to pitch their tents on the side of the village, we resolved to rest for a day, because the cold and stormy weather would make the continuation of the journey vexingly difficult.

If one has seen one Indian earthen hut, one can have a clear idea of all others. Almost all nations with fixed dwellings make use of about the same style of construction and inner arrangement, with only slight differences, those farther north excepted. The latter have huts which are much larger, because in the intense cold they are obliged also to winter their horses in them.

The construction of the huts is about as follows:

A circle of forty to eighty feet in circumference is measured out on the ground, and tall poles, fifteen to twenty feet long, are set in the ground in a circle of thirty to forty feet wide at an angle of sixty degrees, making them then twelve to fourteen feet above the ground. These poles are fastened together at the top. On these, other poles are laid to form a conical roof. The door is a rectangular hole, four feet high, and the en-trance is protected on the outside by a covered passage at least twelve feet long and four feet high. The entire hut is then, to the point of the roof, which remains open as a chimney, closely woven with willow branches, and the entire structure is covered with a layer of earth or clay two to three feet thick. In the center of the hut, which has a floor tamped hard like a threshing floor, there is a round hole to serve as the hearth. Over it almost continuously hangs a large kettle of copper or of sheet iron, traded from the dealers at a high price. Formerly the Indians utilized stone vessels, a custom which still prevails among some nations in the northwest. This kettle serves all the inhabitants of the hut as a common cooking vessel, and is proof that great unanimity exists among these people.

At times along the interior wall of the hut there are twelve to sixteen partitions woven of willow reeds. These are again divided in the middle and contain beds three or four feet wide, supplied with mats to serve as sleeping quarters. Mats are also spread on the floor for seats, but these are generally intended for the chiefs and other distinguished men. Youths, also the women and children, must sit on the bare floor. At the peak of the hut there is usually a pole and, tied to it, a medicine pouch containing symbolic objects to serve the Indians in their mystical practices.

Much has been written concerning the superstitious religious beliefs of these uncivilized people and their inclination to fetishes. It is exceedingly difficult to determine the truth, since their priests act very mysteriously regarding their idolatrous service and usually supply the curious person with untruths. This much is certain, most of the Indians are pure theists and their symbolic forms are simply intended to ban the evil spirits which they recognize. Their insensate fear of the influence of such ghosts has unfortunately led them to a kind of worship which befogs the reason of a child-like people. Ignorant travelers have confused this with a real worship of God.

Observation has unfortunately shown that, even in the most civilized states of Europe, certain sickly apparitions are being used to confuse the susceptible public mind with cacodemonic trickery, and we, therefore, need not be surprised that such evil seed also produces its sad fruit among a naïve and ignorant people.

No intelligent person nowadays will but maintain that this suggested kind of sickly apparition merits, and indeed requires, the serious attention of the physician, the philosopher, and the humanitarian. No expert will deny that the ordinary diagnosis and therapeutics are insufficient to judge correctly these abnormalities of soul-life in order to prescribe an adequate treatment. With deference and admiration we pay our respect to those of our far-seeing investigators who examine more closely the mysterious associations of the physical and psychic in our nature and who, so to speak, have illumined even the darkness. But if the outer as well as the inner world has its dark sides, one ought not devote his entire attention to the darkness or the dawn, or even that beloved twilight, ignoring the broad light of day.

The Indian in his natural state gives the psychologist a hard problem to solve, in the determination of his mental faculties. In many important moments of life, he appears thoughtful, resolute, firm, taciturn, and endowed with much moral strength, while he recoils weak and irresolute from things which seem unexplainable to him, and in which he fancies the influence of evil spirits and of magic. Taking advantage of this weakness, their medicine men, who are at the same time their priests, cleverly make use of sickness and other occurrences to serve their own selfish ends. A long time will elapse before the night in which their souls are shrouded will become illumined, and indeed this period may never come for them. Their tribes will probably disappear without a trace before they can reach a higher degree of civilization. How difficult it is for a people to renounce superstitious beliefs. Such beliefs prevail even among civilized people in multiple guises, sneaking in the darkness to enter and bar the way to cultural progress in our century.

In the dwelling of Isch-nan-uanky it was cleaner than it ordinarily is in Indian huts. The chief brought leather cushions to sit on, said to be a distinction, and gave me some presents as a counter compliment for those that I had given him. These presents consisted of all sorts of ornaments which the Indians, especially the warriors, value most highly. His own head ornament was particularly elegant, consisting of colored hair, feathers of the calumet eagle set with porcupine quills, and a comb artistically carved from bison bone. He requested the Otos present to offer me their possessions for barter, and in a few moments I had a large heap of things lying before me. The selection was hard to make, for I did not wish to deplete my supply of wares in return for accepting too many articles.

I saw an old man called Hu-nan-schuch, over eighty years old, but still very vigorous. Presenting this man some tobacco I tried to learn from him something concerning the earlier history of the Otos. He was indeed inclined to tell me everything he knew about. Thus I was informed of many barbarous practices, the cessation of which must be regarded as a step forward in the moral development of the nation, and this advance must be attributed to their acquaintance with the whites. This old man distinctly remembered the first time his people saw the first white Creole.

After a stay of several hours I requested permission to go to my camp. I found, however, that my men had gone away. Instead of pitching the tent close to the Indian village, they had encamped a distance of three miles away in a spot among some trees on the Platte River. Although I had to walk this distance on very bad and slippery ground, I could not criticize the caution of my companions. They wished to avoid the intrusion of the young people and the women, who are inclined to stealing.

The sky had become clear and fine weather prevailed. Despite the distance to the Indian village, the young Indians molested me the remainder of the day by their visits and their begging. This annoyance was increased by a few older men, who found pleasure in the taste of whisky, which the mule buyers had unfortunately secretly brought along.

In the evening a cousin of the chief, named Uaschi-mica, arrived. A handsome man, he brought me a small present. After he had gotten a small glass of whisky he demanded more, and this being refused he became angry and abusive, so that Captain Riley had to chase him away. The Indian submitted quietly to this and went on his way. During the night the people left us unmolested. Only the chief came begging our pardon for the intrusion of his cousin and giving us the assurance that none of his people would allow anyone to bother us in the least from now on.

The night was clear but so cold that the thermometer registered 19°, and the water had a crust of ice, a finger thick. Such early frosts at 40° of latitude are rare occurrences, even in northern Europe, and in America are so much the more surprising at this latitude, for often, even into the month of November, warm and beautiful weather holds.

On the following morning we broke camp early in order to reach the thirty miles distant second, and larger, village of the Otos that same day. Since the trail led through the village, we had to make a wide detour around it.

Indians had buried one of their number the day before on a hill which we had to pass. Among several aborigines of western America, the custom prevails of distributing the effects of the deceased among the friends and relatives. At the same time prizes are earned by athletic events. These games consist of foot races, throwing, jumping, etc., and in these contests the women also take part. In this we find a similarity with the peoples of great antiquity, proof that in the progressing history of mankind and in the kinds of peoples similar customs may prevail, but this does not prove that the various nations are kin to one another.

Among the more civilized peoples of America, especially on the central plateau of the Andes, the customs and practices prevailing at the time of the first invasion of the Spaniards go back to the historical traditions of several nations of antiquity.

In the areas of Mexico which the Aztecs and Toltecs inhabited, I was amazed when I looked upon the great ancient remains, which time and decay have not blotted out but have left the record of these ancient nations. These remains, as well as these hieroglyphics and architectural art, have a striking oriental character, in some respects resembling the Egyptian. Nevertheless, it is hard for me to agree with the opinion of several very astute scholars who hold that the primitive culture of these people had come from Asia. More accurate and detailed investigation reveals something genuinely and distinctively American.

It is a peculiar fact that, even in the oldest and most imperfect drawings of the primitive people of America, the facial form of the human figures always bears the type of a pure, primitive American race, whose physiognomy is strikingly different from the Asiatic. Even if a migration of people from Asia had taken place, it seems improbable to me that the traces of culture which we find among the Peruvians, Mexicans, and the people of Natchez had been carried over from Asia.

It seems to me that the germ for higher development of these people is rather to be sought in their more advanced community life, where savage customs have endured, and the perfection and refinement in those customs find expression in secular and religious laws. All this is the consequence of an increased population, where people must feel the necessity of preservation to a much higher degree than do small groups of men who are able to provide their means of living in an easier manner.

The distribution of the previously mentioned prizes of honor of the deceased was just taking place, and I had an opportunity of seeing several of the athletic events myself. The young Indians proved as agile and skillful as the women and girls betrayed clumsiness and awkwardness, provoking much laughter, which terribly embarrassed them. It is striking that the females of these rather crude people, though endowed with well-formed bodies, possess so little skill in physical exercise, swimming perhaps excepted, and are so very inferior to men. The cause is to be found in the demanding work they must do and the heavy burdens they must carry from youth on, while the education of the men consists in the highest development of physical functions.

For a distance of three or four miles our way from the Platte to the larger village of the Otos led continuously through the prairie. From the first village to the second one finds neither a creek nor any other watering place. This makes travel over this trail extremely difficult for men and horses in the hot summer. We did not suffer from this need, but were, however, miserable from the effect of a very cold northwest wind, which blew violently.

On all sides the Indians had set the prairie afire, such fires running over vast stretches with unbelievable speed, causing dense smoke to darken the sky. Especially pretty were the valleys of tall grass on the Platte, where surging flames advanced amid extraordinary crackling.

Since the prairie fire surged all around the great village of the Otos, we were obliged to ride through the fire in the manner of the Indians. This cannot be called a dangerous undertaking, for the burning region is usually not very wide, and one rides against the wind to cross the flames. Mine, a gentle horse accustomed to this kind of thing, galloped through the fire without suffering the least damage. My companions, however, could not all boast of the same good luck. One of the soldiers, a poor rider and mounted on a mule, was thrown into the burning grass, but escaped with only his hair and clothes singed.

The Indians know how to fire the prairie with great skill and how to take advantage of a favorable wind. Despite the fact that all around the village the grass was burned, the cornfields nearby were unharmed. I saw women and children busy gathering corn.

At the approach of our party a large number of Indians gathered and surrounded our group. The foremost chiefs, who had been informed of our coming, had met us half a mile out. The leader of these, Schon-ka-pè, wore a red uniform and a three-cornered hat with feathers, looking very odd with an otherwise bare body. The second chief, Schoch-mo-no-koch-fi, a fine looking tall man, wore only a loin cloth, which was most becoming to his dark-red Indian skin. Surrounded by a large crowd of people of all ages, the Chief accompanied Captain Riley and me to the village lying high on an elevation beside a creek which flows into the Platte.

We had, as usual, to accompany the first chief into his hut, where the ceremonies prescribed by the Indian concept of courtesy took place. This hut was also clean and in this regard differed from the rest. I could not stay in it for long, however, because the thick smoke of the fire was driven back by the strong wind. To this was added the preparation of a most nauseating meal in my honor. It consisted of freshly killed dog and jerked, dried bison meat. This choice meal was boiled with corn in a kettle which for a considerable time had needed a good scouring. A most unappetizing horn spoon was used for skimming. Only the direst hunger and the utmost self-control could have induced a European to have partaken of the food.

In the eyes of the Indian connoisseur, dog meat is a very choice delicacy, and no feast of any importance is celebrated at which this favorite food is lacking. If one can overcome his inherited revulsion for dog meat, one may find it edible enough, and I have seen many Europeans, who, while among the Indians, liked it. The Indians prefer it to any other meat.

I left the hut for a few moments, but Captain Riley called me back, remarking that the Indians would be very much offended should I disdain their meal. He said that I should control myself, and at least pretend to partake of it. I therefore returned, but was again overcome with repugnance when some dirty old woman picked the meat out of the kettle with her filthy hands and greedily sipped the meat broth out of hollowed hands. Exerting all my will power to suppress the terrible nausea I felt, I could not force myself to swallow an entire spoonful of the food which Schon-ka-pè handed me. But when I sipped of it the Indian was satisfied, since that was sufficient to appease Indian etiquette. He even was so polite as to excuse himself that he could not serve me with anything better, knowing that Europeans found no pleasure in the Indian culinary art. He declared further that the butchering and eating of a dog as well as the smoking of the peace pipe were manifestations of good will in his tribe, and that they were followed by a sincere bond of friendship. This chief, and also the other Oto Indians, subsequently gave me on my second journey the greatest and most unmistakable proof of the truth of this promise.

Taken all in all, I can assert that most of the aborigines deport themselves with more poise and decency in their social life than the descendants of many white Europeans who live near them and whose crudeness often exceeds the bounds of decency. Yet, in their self-satisfaction and conceit these whites apply the name of barbarian to their more sensible and unspoiled Indian neighbors. Many whites satisfy a low egotism by calling the Indians faithless, false, and cruel, and compare them with cannibals.

I have often taken occasion in this report to mention the errors and the virtues of the Indian and I leave it to the judgment of my readers to draw for themselves a picture of the Indians after the various sketches that I have presented. I add that many nations, especially those living in the Northwest, are very hostile toward whites, particularly the fur traders from the United States. In war, like all Indians, they commit terrible and barbarous deeds upon their prisoners and slain enemies, causing men since the discovery of America to fear the Indian people.

This is by no means true of all the tribes. Some have befriended the European settlers and have not tortured to death living captives, nor enjoyed tormenting them, nor eating their flesh to satisfy their hunger and revenge. To eat human flesh, especially the heart and other viscera, is a terrible practice, which even the Blackfeet and the remotest tribes of the Sioux seem to have given up. These and a few tribes of the northwestern country and of the interior of New Spain must no doubt be numbered among the wildest and most savage nations on earth, and can only be compared on the basis of customs with some of the savages of South America and New Holland.

A good example and strict supervision over the morals of men employed by the fur traders, with the strict observance of the laws forbidding the introduction of whisky into the regions occupied by the Indians, are the safest means of preserving peace with the latter. To the credit of the

United States, it has exerted itself vigorously in these matters, especially keeping a watchful eye on the actions of such speculators who cheat the Indians in trade and try to deprive these poor sons of the wilderness of the returns from the ever-decreasing bounty of their hunts.

It is a great advantage that the various companies trading with the Indians have united to form the American Fur Company, and that the means at their disposal are sufficient to meet all competition. Their own interest makes it requisite on the part of the company to see to it that the continued income of their trade is sustained, and to this end they must let the Indian kill only just as much game and fur-bearing animals as the demand for this commodity requires. They must not allow them to destroy the hunt, which is the sole means of subsistence of the Indians. The members of the American Fur Company are respected and honest men and the directors at St. Louis under the younger Mr. P. Chouteau could not be better chosen.

It seems appropriate that I should once more mention a class of people, who by the position they occupy, can become highly dangerous to the agents of the government and also to the fur trader. These are the half-bloods who are used as interpreters. These persons, born of Indian squaws (squaws are Indian women who associate with white men as their concubines), have inherited the vices of the Europeans and the characteristics of the Indians.[22] Reared by their father, they have also learned his language, and growing up without education, they know no other occupation than to use the skillfulness of the two tongues to their advantage. Since from their mother's side they are equipped to stand the hardships which life in the wilderness demands, most of them are good hunters and good horsemen, and they render excellent service if they can be kept from the ex-

---

[22] As A. F. Chamberlain indicates in Hodge, *Handbook*, II, 629–30, the word squaw is defined as an Indian woman: "From Narraganset *squaw*, probably an abbreviation of *eskwaw*, cognate with the Delaware *ochqueu*, the Chippewa *ikwé*, the Cree *iskwew*, etc. As a term for woman *squaw* has been carried over the length and breadth of the United States and Canada, and is even in use by Indians on the reservations of the West, who have taken it from the whites."

Marriage among American Indians, seemingly a simple affair to white observers or those who became intermarried, was in fact surrounded by social codes and primitive legal restrictions of the type analyzed by Karl N. Llewellyn and E. Adamson Hoebel in *The Cheyenne Way: Conflict and Case Law in Primitive Jurisprudence*, among others. Wife-lending, a form of courtesy, was not uncommon among Indians of the West. The extent of intermarriage between white trappers and traders with Indian women was considerable in the first two-thirds of the nineteenth century, even if, as with Manuel Lisa and Mitain, the stately daughter of the Omahas, the white man had an Indian wife for the wilderness and a white one for civilization (Edwin James, *Account of an Expedition from Pittsburgh to the Rocky Mountains*, I, 244–49, I, 183).

cessive consumption of alcohol. There are some who are very useful and can be relied upon. And I have seen some among them who are outstanding for their faithfulness and sobriety and are ashamed of the wild excesses practiced by the low class of Creoles.

My companions had conveyed my baggage across the above-mentioned river and had there pitched camp. The Indians had not obeyed the orders of their superiors, so I was surrounded at every step by a large crowd of people, whose curiosity and boldness exceeded all bounds. With much trouble my baggage was arranged and, despite the utmost precaution, the children and women stole all sorts of articles they could get their hands on. I noted the great difference between the inhabitants of the larger and those of the smaller village. Here also the Indians brought all sorts of nonsensical trifles for sale and became more and more obtrusive the more I tried to get rid of them. The women and girls allowed themselves wide license, which could hardly be reconciled with the idea of propriety, and a few of the men with loud insistence demanded whisky. Captain Riley, who knew the better side of the Otos, could not account for this rudeness.

It seemed to me that the cause lay in our interpreter, the half-blood who, taking advantage of our ignorance of the language, had incited the Indians against us and called their attention to the whisky which the mule buyers had. When toward evening the disturbance appeared to have reached a point of danger, several prominent warriors, among them Isch-nan-non-ge-he, La Crinière, or The Curry Comb, a splendid chief, proceeded to take stern measures, all much the more necessary as Captain Riley began to lose his patience. Hereupon a circle was drawn around the camp and the Indians were forbidden to cross this line. Even the girls were not allowed to cross this boundary after dark, and this seemed to insult the Indian beauties very much.

My suspicion toward the half-blood was not unfounded. Late in the evening, Schon-ka-pè came and by means of sign language expressed his suspicion also, declaring that he had seen Ua-schi-mika talking to the interpreter. Also he called attention to the fact that the former had not come into camp with us. Captain Riley, now suspecting trouble, ordered a watchful eye kept on the half-blood and that Ua-schi-mika should not be admitted to the camp. Despite this, the half-blood brought this Indian to Captain Riley. At first he acted very friendly, but could not hide his meanness long. He became more and more suspect, and the Indians finally took him away, keeping a watchful eye on him to avoid further trouble.

On the following morning I had further proof of the wickedness of the interpreter, which, through the wise precautions of the Chief, averted trouble. The mule buyers also began to see how the half-blood had harmed them by his avaricious purposes, and they were unable to make a trade. Now we all desired to get away in the hope of finding another interpreter among the Pawnees. The chiefs sent a reliable Indian ahead to the nearest village of the Pawnees to announce our coming.

At ten o'clock on the morning of the twenty-third we were again on the move, accompanied for several miles by the chiefs and a number of Indians. That evening we reached the Platte River not far from the mouth of the Wolf, which the Americans call Loup Fork, or Wolf Fork. Near the mouth of this stream the water of the Platte is forced into a narrow channel, hence the river here is deep and swift. Having to cross it, we went a few miles farther upstream to the vicinity of a large island overgrown with tall timber, and there found a ford which, because the accompanying Otos were familiar with it, allowed us cleverly to cross the Platte that same evening.

The next morning we broke camp early. The way led over a prairie mostly burned over. We reached the first village of the Pawnees, surrounded by cornfields and situated in the fertile plain of Wolf Fork. This settlement is inhabited by the Great Pawnees, who are divided into two divisions, and another division of these people is settled a few miles farther to the west. (One of these bands is called Republican Pawnees by the Americans.)

The Wolf Pawnees have separated from the Great Pawnees and they live twenty miles farther up Wolf Fork. Despite the earlier disagreement which occasioned a separation, the two tribes are on friendly terms, and these three tribes of Pawnees constitute the most populous nation among the independent Indians. Among themselves all Pawnee tribes are friendly, even those living farther to the south and west, though they are perpetually involved in wars with the Spaniards and Americans.[23]

---

[23] The Pawnees, a large confederacy of the Caddoan Indian group in historic times, called themselves *Chahiksichahiks* or Men of Men, but were said, perhaps mistakenly, to be known from the term *par'iki*, horn, from the hairdress which made the scalplock stand in an erect curve. Their principal bands, really tribes, consisted of the Chaui or Grand Pawnee, the Skidi or upper Pawnee, the Pitahauerat or lower Pawnee, and the Kitkehahki, an up-stream group, all of which centered in the eighteenth and early nineteenth centuries in the Platte Valley. They were raiding into New Mexico against the Spaniards as early as the fore part of the seventeenth century for horses, were probably heavily involved in the disaster to the Villasur Expedition of 1720 in Nebraska, but were not unfriendly to the French, notably Bourgmont, 1724–26. They were almost never at odds with the U.S. but were enemies of the Sioux, southern Cheyennes and Arapahos, and Comanches. They were closely related to the Arikaras. The best existing portraits of this large group (perhaps 12,500 people in Duke Paul's time) appear in Charles Augustus Murray, *Travels in North America*, 2 vols., I, 235–473; John Treat Irving, *Indian Sketches: Taken During an Expedition to the Pawnee Tribes* [1833]; and George E. Hyde, *Pawnee Indians*, 88ff.

Hardly had our party been noticed from the village when large divisions of Indians came to meet us. Many of them were mounted and the area teemed with horses and mules constituting the wealth of these inhabitants of the prairie. Two chiefs, Ta-rari kaúa ó, Long Hair, and Laopeku-leschar, approached us first, welcoming us with much cordiality. A large number of people from both villages had come together to gape at us with open curiosity, for many among them had scarcely ever seen so many whites together, as the women and children do not follow the men on their expeditions.

The high respect with which the chiefs of the Pawnees are regarded was shown at once by the excellent order that prevailed everywhere and by the decorous behavior of the young people, a markedly great contrast to the behavior of the Otos. The chiefs informed us at once that it would be necessary for us to make our night's camp inside the village, since a party of Sioux, the same as I had met on the Ponca, was stirring up the country and had indeed already committed several murders. That Sioux chief carried on his hostile trade with great caution, and despite all their bravery the Pawnees had not yet succeeded in locating this Dakotah with his few warriors.

Schakè-ru-leschar, the first chief of the second village, had arrived in the meantime and invited me to visit him on the following day. I assured this Indian how gladly I would accept his invitation and spend the day with him, but also made him understand how I would be pleased to see very many Pawnees, as I had heard that this nation was still very numerous. The chief promised me to bring together as many of his people as possible explaining at the same time that the Pawnee nation numbered as many heads as the stars in the sky and that they could not be counted.

Of their huge number of people the Pawnees are extremely proud and should they become hostile they would be exceedingly dangerous. Those on the Wolf River were never ill disposed toward the French Creoles and the Americans, while their hate toward the Spaniards and the Mexicans knew no limits. Against the population in the eastern Provincias Internas, along the Rio Bravo [Rio Grande] and in Texas they wage a relentless war of extermination. It seems as if these people and also the Comanches, Arapahos, and other Indianos L'laneros Bravos originally came from the region now occupied by the New Spaniards and that the sword of the conquerors had displaced them from their former habitations. However, a few Indian tribes related to them which occupy the inaccessible mountains and wooded regions of the Cordilleras, such as the Bolson de Mapini, the Sierra de las Grullas, etc., owe their independence solely to the wildness of the land inhabited by them, and from hiding places they become the scourge of the ranchos (that is, settlements devoted to the raising of cattle and horses) by uninterrupted raids.

The Pawnees are proud of the great damage which they in their time have inflicted upon the descendants of the Spaniards, and that even in the earliest times of the conquest they fought hard battles against the *Conquistadores*. Of the latter they still possess many trophies.

A Creole named Alexander Coté arrived with the chief of the Grand Pawnees. Fully conversant with the language of the Pawnees, he rendered me good service, whereby the malicious projects of the half-blood were stopped.

On the morning of the twenty-fourth, arriving at the second village, I was amazed at the mass of people whom I found there. This settlement is located at 41° 21′ north latitude and 97° 51′ west longitude. Schakè-ru-leschar had escorted me there and was joined by Leki-tauè-leschar, the second chief.[24] Here too, we had to make our camp within the village which, because of the splendid discipline that obtained among the Pawnees, caused us no inconvenience.

According to my wishes the chiefs had assembled a great number of Indians on a wide plain adjoining the village, all lined up in the best order. A compact circle was formed by the old men and warriors, and the women and younger people were behind them. The chief delivered a long address in which he stressed the advantages of friendship with the Americans and painted in vivid colors the fine traits of his nation.

In their clothing and in the manner of painting their skin the Pawnees differ but little from the neighboring nations. The warriors usually wear their hair long, sometimes the braids are even pasted together. They are not inclined to shear their heads as the Otos and the Omahas. Sticks of porcelain, such as are sold by the traders, are considered of great value,

[24] *Author*: I must remark here that Indians often change their names and for this reason some of the names do not agree with those mentioned in Major Long's expedition, although most are the same individuals. I am following my diary strictly in the account.

[The intimate contacts of the Long Expedition with the Pawnees at Engineer Cantonment, below Council Bluffs, in early October, 1819, including the recovery of zoologist Thomas Say's possessions earlier taken by the Indians, as well as Indian Agent Benjamin O'Fallon's council with the Pawnees on October 10, appear in Edwin James, *Account of an Expedition* . . . in Thwaites, *Early Western Travels* (Vols. XIV–XVII), XIV, 229–50; and subsequent events in XV, 149–64, 203–220.

[The struggle between Long Hair and Sharitarish, presumably the first of that name, or White Wolf, also called Angry Chief, for control of the Grand Pawnees continued for many years after 1806. By 1811, Sharitarish had control of the Chaui or Grand Pawnee, the Kitkehahkis, and the Pitahauerats, displacing Long Hair among the Grand Pawnee, who had gone to the Skidis. Not until Long Hair's death in 1822 was victory fully his, however.]

and they wear them in their ears, around their necks, and around their wrists.

The religious concept of the Pawnees seems to be more complex than those of the neighboring tribes. Besides the Master of Life, they worship the sun, moon, and stars. Until relatively recently the Pawnees had the barbarous custom of burning captured enemies alive, sacrificing them to the sun or the morning star. This gruesome worship will, perhaps, soon cease entirely. A few years before my arrival, a war party had stolen a young Spaniard. A certain Mr. Woods, informed of this and with the aid of the chiefs, happily rescued the unfortunate boy. Generally, the Pawnees are less cruel than the other neighboring nations.[25]

In the night the Sioux had dared an attack upon several Pawnees, but while pursuing them fell into a set ambush and were in turn attacked with great courage by the Pawnees and most were killed. The leader of the Sioux fell in this engagement and his head and the scalps of the remaining Sioux were brought into the village, where the Indians sang the death song around them. The whole day the young men practiced games of arms, in which they showed great skill, especially in throwing spears and large heavy disks.[26]

During the night several girls, whose main purpose seemed to be to steal, sneaked into the camp of our men. Indeed they succeeded in carrying away all sorts of things. Two young men and a woman imposed themselves on me with the intention of selling me a leather shield. The woman placed herself very gently against me trying to direct my attention to herself in order to obtain some small gifts. After I had bought the shield from the young people I let them go unhindered. However, it was quickly discovered that a fine blanket belonging to Captain Riley had been stolen.

In the darkness of the night it had been impossible to distinguish the faces of the visitors. Also the theft had been carried out with greatest dexterity, for I had not let the intruders out of my sight. The captain had the chief come at once and demanded satisfaction. Next morning the Pawnees

[25] It was the Skidi branch of the Pawnees which practiced the rite of Morning Star, centering in human sacrifice, at this period. In 1817 an Ietan (Ute) girl captive was saved from the rite partly by the opposition of Lachelesharo, or Knife Chief, partly by the direct intervention of Pitalesharo, his son. Both of the later intervened in 1818 to save a young Spanish boy from a similar fate. Hyde, *Pawnee Indians*, 102–111.

[26] This otherwise unrecorded attack by Sioux suggests continued incursions in 1823 by the Brulés, who in the early years of the century coveted and often got Spanish horses from the Pawnees, frequent raiders on and south of Red River, with whom they fought in 1807–1808, according to the Pawnee winter counts, and again in 1813 when they broke up the Indian fair on the North Platte. Hyde, *Pawnee Indians*, 107.

brought the blanket back, for the thief had been betrayed by his own companions.

In company with many Indians we started on the twenty-sixth to reach the Wolf Pawnees.[27] The way led in part through a hilly region covered with short grass, in part through lowlands dense with weeds, and I also saw several large swamps overgrown with reeds on which numerous flocks of *Xanthornus phoeniceus* bestirred themselves, making a noisy clamor.

We were received with particularly great solemnity by the Wolf Pawnees and at once conducted to the dwelling of the chief. A number of Pawnees were just returning from the hunt and their pack horses were laden with meat. The bison had this year come close to the village and were still to be found at a two or three days' journey. These Pawnees had met Arapahos and a distant band of their own nation, the Schkiri-Uruk or tatooed Pawnees (Panis Piqués of the Creoles), and of the latter a few families had come along on a visit with the Wolf Pawnees.[28]

The tatooed Pawnees belong to the more evil tribes. I was therefore most curious to see these people and some of them were brought to me at once. These were two men and a young woman of most handsome appearance and tatooed from head to foot with black dots, representing all sorts of clever designs. They wore leggings and blankets of very fine, well-tanned antelope leather, otherwise they were completely bare. The light color of their skin was in marked contrast to the dark copper red of the other Pawnees whereby this tribe is distinctive.

The Arapahos are similarly supposed to be handsome people, wearing their hair in long braids stuck together with resin, too, perhaps of *Liquid-ambar storaciflua* [*L. styraciflua*]. (I surmise that the Arapahos are a branch of the Blackfeet, Pieds noirs).[29]

---

[27] Wolf Pawnees here = Skidi Pawnees, whose historic winter home was on the forks of Loup River in east central Nebraska.

[28] Schkiri-Uruk here = Panis Piqués, or Tattooed Pawnees, which refers to members of the Wichita Confederacy, perhaps identifiable with the people of Quivira met by Coronado in 1541 at the Great Bend of the Arkansas in central Kansas. They were on the South Canadian when Barnard de la Harpe met them in 1719. It appears that the Panimahas or Skidis, to whom they were related, as they were to all Pawnees, maintained close relations with them and frequently lived with them between 1750 and 1850. It is worth noting that *Schkiri-Uruk* does not appear in synonymies. The Tawehash as a designation for a principal division of the Wichitas appears in early Spanish accounts, but the most frequent designation by the Spaniards of New Mexico was the Jumanos. All were Caddoans, doubtless springing from the Hasinai of the Trinity and Angelina river valleys of Texas.

[29] Both the Blackfeet, that is, Siksika or Blackfeet proper, the Kainah, and the Piegan, on the one hand, and the Arapahos, on the other, are of the Algonquian group of the Plains. The Atsina broke off from the Arapahos, perhaps within historic times, associating them-

I received a scalp of a Padauka. The long luxurious hair growth had the same characteristics making it a much desired addition to my collection.

These Indians wear all sorts of feather ornaments and have beautiful bows of yellow wood (*Maclura aurantiaca*, Nuttall). I traded for a few and also arrows that were armed with flint arrowheads.

A young Indian who could speak broken Spanish was pointed out to me. This Indian had been captured near the mission of San Antonio and dragged by the Spaniards to the interior of New Spain. There he had been baptized. Later finding the opportunity to escape, he returned to his people. Here we have another proof of the keenness and cleverness of the Indians.

In the evening Lale-lure-schik and Ta-rare-kak-schà, The Ax, leaders of the tribe, together with Alexander Coté and one of the subordinate priests, came to bring me the news that the oldest men and the medicine men had counseled with one another agreeing to introduce me to the mysteries of their temple, as I had previously expressed this wish. I gladly accepted the invitation and followed my guide, however without the company of Captain Riley. We passed through nearly the entire village in silence, gaped at by an enormous accompanying crowd of Indians, chiefly boys and girls who could not comprehend at all why the priests should grant a white man admittance to their sanctuary.

On the outside the temple differed from other round huts of the village only by its larger size and the fact that on top of it there was a pole to which were fastened some bundles of corn, probably a sacrifice to a deity.

At the entrance a priest, painted entirely black, awaited us. After mumbling a few words he let me, the interpreter, and the chiefs crawl through the low opening. The latter put aside their bison robes before entering and followed silently behind us into the interior of the hut.

The whole interior, with walls lined with reeds, seemed large enough to contain over one hundred persons. In the center was a large fireplace where a few chips of sumac and sassafras glowed. This scant light only sparingly illumined the wide space of the hut. In the background opposite the entrance was placed a kind of altar. On it I noticed the skull of a bison and also a human skull. Over it was fastened a pair of antlers painted red and decorated with cloth strips. Beside the altar stood two bundles of corn with filled ears.

All this was hardly discernible in the darkness of the hut. After I had spent a few minutes in the interior in silent anticipation, from beneath the altar suddenly a very old man rose and walked slowly and significantly

selves with the Siksika. The division of the Arapahos proper into their existing northern and southern groups occurred after 1820.

toward me. With piercing glance he scanned me from head to foot, and for several minutes he observed my every move sharply. He was of medium stature and heavy build, with a wrinkled brow revealing a stern and mysterious being. His hair, which among the Indians becomes gray only in extreme old age, was cut short. Between the small, sparkling, dark-brown eyes rose a very curved, pointed nose. The color of his body had been changed from its natural copper red to black by extensive rubbing with grease and resin. Instead of clothes, he wore over his naked body a bison robe with the hair to the outside.

Before he broke the silence he threw a handful of stinking weeds into the fire. Gravely he addressed me with a strong voice. The translation by the interpreter sounded about as follows:

"It is known to us that you have come over the great salt lake from the east to visit our red brothers who live toward the west. The Long Knives in their village by the great stream (Council Bluffs) have indicated to the nation of the Pawnees that you are a man of high station, from a country toward the rising of the day star, and that you are disposed to smoke the pipe, to celebrate the feast of peace with us, and partake of our food, as one brother with another.

"You have not come into our country to trade with us nor to throw down all sorts of useless trash or poisoned drink, as so many do, for our best property, nor to enrich yourself by our poverty. You wish to tell us something new about your country, for it is true you know much in your land that we do not know, and we know something that you do not know.

"I regard you and the other white people as a father, for you desire our good, and are wiser than we!

"My father, the Long Knives to the east have done us good and love us, but the bearded people toward the west near the mountains hate the red people, and since the time of our fathers have driven us out and killed us. Therefore we drink their blood and hate them, for our country was toward the evening.

"We love the Master of Life (*Oua-kan-da*). He created the earth and air, rain and clouds. He is the Master of Lightning and Thunder. Behold this head of the bison. He created it for us, and when we sacrifice to him, He gives us luck in the hunt. When we sacrifice the ears of corn, our harvests succeed. Behold the skull of the enemy. We sacrificed him. He was a mighty warrior of the Osages (*Oua-sa-schè*). Since then our enemies have been slain, and the name of Pawnee is a terror to them."

When the address was ended, he threw some more weeds on the fire, showed me the peace pipe, and at last gave me a gift of very valuable wampum. Put together of the seeds of a variety of palm and the seeds of a leguminous plant (*Glycine?*) from tropical regions, it was purported by the priest that it had been bequeathed from father to son. This was evidently of southern origin and was valuable to me as proof of the migration of these people. Moreover, the priest showed me old Spanish weapons of the sixteenth century, which, according to his declaration, had been captured a long time ago in a war which the Pawnees had fought with the Spaniards in the mountains to the west. He spoke of several Indians of his nation who on their raids had gotten as far as the mouth of the Bravo River. Later I had the opportunity of seeing a few and to convince myself of the truth of this assertion.

When the old man had finished showing me the curiosities of the temple, I asked him about many customs which are part of the Pawnees' religious service. The priest maintained that human sacrifice had taken place among them, as among the other neighboring nations, with the difference that they selected only one of their captured enemies and treated the rest as prisoners. The one chosen for sacrifice was kept in the priest's house for a long time and was well nourished. On the day when the morning star, which holds an important place in their religious observances, shone the longest, he was tied to a post, killed with arrows, and then burned with the customary ceremonies. In the ashes the priest would read the future, for the Pawnees believe in pyromancy.

According to the declaration of the priest, the Pawnees abhor the consumption of human flesh and in this they are not like other American aborigine nations. I asked the old priest whether the Pawnees worshipped the sun, moon, and stars as God, but he answered evasively,

"The Master of Life causes the sun to shine in the day as a reminder of Him, and in the evening the moon to glisten. All fire comes from heaven, and the Master of Thunder can be served only with fire."

It is certain that the Pawnees worship the stars, and their course has an influence on their actions. I asked him if he knew that the morning and evening stars were one and the same heavenly body. He was content to reply that at the time when the evening star shone the morning star could not be seen, and vice versa.

In regard to the little Spaniard whom the Pawnees had captured at Taos and intended to sacrifice, the priest said that it was true that the Long Knives had heard about that matter, and he praised very highly the brave and humane deportment of Mr. Woods of the Fur Company. I finally inquired whether he really believed that the ceremonies which the priests and old men made use of to protect their fields against the attack and destruction by hostile parties and wanton boys had any effect.

395

"Great father," the priest replied, "if the enemies and the boys did not believe in that, the old men would starve and the priests perish."

I now hastened my return to the Council Bluffs to prepare for my return journey to St. Louis. My supply of presents was entirely exhausted, so I decided to begin my return trip on the following day, being completely satisfied with my reception and my stay with the Pawnees. Two young Indians were to act as my guides, and Captain Riley considered it expedient to return to the garrison by the nearest way, without going again to the Indian settlement.

On the twenty-seventh we reached the small Beaver Creek toward noon and spent the night on Shell River, where we saw a herd of elk.

On the following day we met a party of Omahas who were going to the Pawnees. These Indians had run into some fleeing Sioux and had engaged them in combat. Two Omahas were killed. Among the other Indians the Omahas are reputed to be cowardly, and their young people sometimes are great cowards. That night we camped on the Elkhorn, and at noon on the twenty-ninth we reached Fort Atkinson.

I close this chapter with a short list of names of some Iowa and Oto Indians which I have gathered. These may give some conception of the sound of the language of these people. Major Long has compiled in his valuable reports of his journeys an extensive vocabulary of these people. This is, however, in English, which should be transcribed into German so that it might be pronounced correctly. I have also added the names of the Indian chiefs in the French dialect of the Creoles and from it translated into German.

Iowas or Pa-cho-sché

CREOLE LANGUAGE	INDIAN	ENGLISH
La petit étoile	*Misch-nè-ké*	The Little Star
Le temps clair	*Ké-ra-ma-ni*	The Clear Weather
La pluie qui marche	*Ni-you-ma-ni*	The Passing Rain
La grande aile	*Aou-srè-schè*	The Great Wing
La nuée blanche	*Ma-hosch-ka*	The White Cloud
La bois brulé	*Nan-ta-schô*	The Burnt Wood
Le petit ours blanc	*Man-to-nié*	The Little White Bear
Le petit plat	*Ouas-ke-y-niè*	The Little Dish

Otos or Ouac-toc-ta-ta

Le calumet qui branle dans le manche	*Oua-sa-ni*	The Peace Pipe which Turns on the Stem
Le voleur	*Miè-scha-schan-sè*	The Thief

Qui frappe l'Osage	*Oua-sa-schè-sa-kè*	He Who slays the Osage
L'ours debont	*Manto-na-niè*	The Standing Bear
Le petit homme sans pareil	*Mok-schi-ke-sé-nan-niè*	The Little Man without an equal
La mauvaise humeur	*Oua-i-pischko-né*	The Bad Humor
Le soldat	*Ouâ-scha-ki-tâ* (also *Man-sa-ki-tâ*)	The Soldier
Le tailleur de robe	*Oua-ro-ni-sâ*	The Blanket Maker
Le vermillon	*Man-schu-schè*	The Vermillion
Le Boeuf	*Schè-tô-ka*	The Bison
Celui qui marche vite	*Ouasch-ka-ma-ni*	He Who Walks Fast
Celui qui a ce qui lui apartient	*Oua-ni-mi-man*	He Who Has What Belongs to Him
Le nez blanc	*Oua-pan-schas-ka*	The White Nose
———	*Oua-gre-na-nie*	(I was unable to get a translation.)
Celui qui arrache	*Oua-nan-schè*	He Who Runs Away
Le midi	*Pi-ru-tan*	The Noon
La petite tortue	*Kè-ouâ-nie*	The Little Turtle

397

12

CONTINUATION OF THE JOURNEY TO ST. LOUIS — DEPAR-
TURE BY THE STEAMBOAT *Cincinnati* — THE STEAMBOAT
HAS AN ACCIDENT AT STE. GENEVIEVE — THE STAY THERE
— JOURNEY TO NEW ORLEANS — RETURN TO EUROPE.

MY preparation for the return jour-
ney was soon made. I had reason to be in a hurry, for the autumnal storms,
fog, the smoke spread by the burning prairie, and the low water level made
the journey down the river not only tedious but dangerous as well.
Through the friendship of the commandant, a vessel which had supplied
the fort lay ready to take me on and to begin the trip to St. Louis at once.

On October 2 I left the Bluffs. Between the fort and the factory of the
Otos is a place called Engineer Cantonment. Here the expedition of Major
Long made its preparation for the western journey. It is noteworthy because Mr. Graham, an officer of the United States, made very correct
astronomical observations and found for this place a north latitude of
41° 25′ 39″ and a longitude of 95° 43′ 53″ west of Greenwich, or 18° 43′
53″ west of Washington. Therefore the Bluffs are 2′ farther north, at
about 41° 27′.

For the first six days no hindrance stood in the way of our journey, and
since the wind was favorable, about noon the fog, a daily occurrence
morning and evening, disappeared. The ship's master, a certain Mr.
Francis, knew the river intimately. In the vicinity of the Nandawa, however, the burning prairie flashed to the right bank, setting the forest on
fire. From then on a mighty and almost impenetrable smoke filled the air,
while the fire, extending with giant strides and consuming the timber with
a terrible crackling, sprayed sparks for miles around. The Indians living to
the east also set the dry ground on fire, and since the delta between the
Missouri and the Mississippi produced tall grasses, weeds, and vast
stretches of forest, both banks of the Missouri soon witnessed this mighty
struggle of the elements, which man had loosed for the destruction of
organic matter.

Drifting in the middle of the river and watching the giant Missouri bordered by a mass of fire for miles, we saw a truly horrifying but magnificent sight. Particularly at night, the spectacle defied description and the boldest imagination would seek in vain to depict it in true and vivid colors. The burning of the prairie and forests is practiced more and more by the aborigines and by the settlers. Through the prairie fires, the grass becomes more luxuriant in the spring, but the forests are in part devastated and in many places in the western states one now sees only miserable bushes and the charred stumps of former forest trophies, once mighty and virgin forest.

Frequently we ran onto Indians, but we did not think it advisable to comply with their repeated invitations to come on land. We guessed their purposes only too clearly, namely to beg for whisky from the ship's master, who is strictly prohibited by the American agents from distributing whisky among the natives.

On the ninth the boat reached the Kansas. I remained several hours and picked up the son of Toussaint Charbonneau, who would accompany me to Europe. Here my men caught an unusual snake which is called hog-nose snake and which the Creoles consider poisonous. The *Heterodon simus*[1] (*la camuse*) is peculiar because of the oddly upturned tip of its nose consisting of one piece. This, together with the flat, viper-like head, gives the snake a very curious appearance. But it is quite harmless and has no poison fangs.

A band of Kansas was also encamped here and were in the act of selling the spoils of the hunt and drinking up the proceeds in whisky. The Indians had just killed a large, extraordinarily fat bear, which I bought of them. The meat of the black, red nosed bear, *Ursus americanus*, is excellent and resembles that of the best wild boar, and has nothing distasteful about it, for the bear lives almost exclusively on vegetable matter.[2]

For several days we had been gathering many ripe persimmons. The fruit of this *Annona* is undoubtedly one of the most delicious products of the North American forests.[3] The fruit is not only most nutritious, pleasing, and full of aroma, but also wholesome. Many Anglo-Americans do not like it and are prejudiced against it, but it is a favorite food of the Creoles, and the Indians gather it with great care. It is peculiar that it is harmful to hogs and is avoided by these animals. The geographic distribution of this useful tree, which by careful attention would also prosper in

[1] *Heterodon simus* = *H. contortrix*.

[2] Hall's terse characterization is "Bears are omnivorous," and this includes *Ursus americanus*, the black bear.

[3] Persimmon, *Diospyros virginiana*, of the Ebenaceae, not Annonaceae.

southern Germany and bear fruit, extends only a few minutes north of the fortieth degree of north latitude.

To avoid scenes such as we had on the Kansas on our trip up the river, we broke camp as soon as possible. It was indeed high time, for several of the boatmen had found acquaintances. Moreover, Grand Louis, from the other side of the river, having heard of my arrival, had come across and started a quarrel with some men of our crew. But the master of the boat was resolute enough to put an end to this nuisance, and since the boat was equipped by the military authorities it was easier to maintain discipline. At three o'clock we cast off and made a considerable distance on our way.

Up to now the crew had been compelled to subsist on very meager rations, for at the time of our departure from the Bluffs the provisions, especially flour and hardtack, had become scarce. The results from hunting had also been most unrewarding as far as the Kansas, for we had only a short time to go on land, and the forest fires made it impossible. Thus it was decided to stop at the first prosperous looking settlement and barter for the most needed supplies. Below Blufftown the boat laid by.

In the houses where I called I found several inhabitants of the neighborhood who had returned from a meeting of the Methodist Church. This sect is one of the most widely distributed in the United States of America, and with the Anglican and Presbyterian churches constitutes the majority of the Protestant population.

Concerning the practices of this congregation, especially their camp meetings, much has already been written and almost every traveler in the United States has drawn a picture of these night scenes and represented them more or less romantically. This much is certain, that this peculiar manner of worshipping God, a mixture of piety, superstition, and raving bordering on fanaticism, furnishes enough material to emphasize definite characteristics. It is perhaps one of the most unfortunate developments of recent times that out of the lap of the pure Christian church such abnormalities could have grown.

Since I have touched upon this subject, I permit myself to add a few remarks on church conditions in the United States, which I have obtained from reliable sources.

In a union of states, as is the United States, in which the government declines to exercise any supervisory rights over the various religious congregations, it is but natural that there should develop an ever-increasing difference of opinion in religious matters, and therefore it is easily explained that North America has become the place of refuge and the home of all the various religious practices.

The Roman Catholic Church indisputably occupies in the United States a high place, commanding a respect which its members owe unquestionably to the strict observance of the prescribed church commandments and to the recognition of one universal head of the church. For this reason the venerable structure has not been split by sectional beliefs. A stranger who travels in the United States, no matter to which Christian church he belongs, must admire the high sense and tolerance and harmony which prevail among the Catholics, especially among the Creoles of French extraction. Even the extraordinary prejudice separating the colors in the slave states disappears before the altar of the Lord, and here no separation takes place, however much it may exist outside the temple. In some Protestant churches this unfortunately is not the case, for here prejudice extends even to the threshold of the house of God. Though unfortunately a necessary policy may separate the whites from the colored people in public life, it is certainly contrary to the high teaching of Christianity to carry this separation to the throne of God.

Christian churches, or rather the followers of certain religious beliefs, unfortunately hate each other in the United States just as vehemently and relentlessly as they do in other countries, as shown by the attacks of the Presbyterian theologians against the Catholic clergy. This abuse for a time filled a large number of American newspapers, but remained ineffective. Although they were learned to a high degree, they were at the same time in the least degree tolerant.

To give accurately the number of Catholics in the United States or to establish a correct census of the population of this country regarding religious organizations is an almost impossible task, due to the fact that one cannot rely upon the available data and because the figures are constantly changing. They operate under nine bishops and one archbishop. During recent years the bishopric of Ohio alone had an increase of between four and five thousand immigrants, most from Alsace and Switzerland, attracted by the flourishing condition of the church here. This should be attributed to the zeal of the recently deceased Bishop Fenwick, a most reverent man.

The Presbyterians are the oldest Protestants in the United States, as they count the so-called Pilgrims of New England among their forebears, whom the persecution of the then prevailing church at the time of Cromwell had driven out of England. The puritanic spirit continued to prevail among them even in the New World and gave birth to the notorious Blue Laws, a number of cruel and petty church statutes. The formerly persecuted later became the persecutors.

More genial, though not less strictly adhering to the precepts of Calvin, are the followers of the Church of Scotland, who allow those of other faiths to share the Lord's Supper with them. While the followers of Cameron, the Covenanters, in North America calling themselves Reformed Presbyterians, bar their church to every one who does not belong to their society. Not so intolerant is the Church Organization of Independents, or Congregationalists, also adherents of Calvin, for the most part in the New England states, and calling themselves independent because they allow every congregation to settle its affairs by a majority vote. Brownians and Sandemannians are only variations of those of the Scottish Presbyterians and do not have many peculiarities.

Since the law allows everyone to adhere or turn to any religious party he may desire, even without the consent of his parents, it sometimes happens that each member of a family belongs to a different church congregation without disturbing the organization and peace of the household substantially. But surely this is not conducive to a deeper and more sincere spirituality of the members of the family. This mixture may in fact be partially the reason that in most families one may observe a certain estrangement and coldness in the daily association of the members, which appears unpleasant to the stranger. At the same time this complex condition of the family does surpress the spirit of persecution which might otherwise manifest itself harmfully, and it makes easier the union of great religious organizations, which because of the differences in their teaching, but mainly through the marked contrast in their worship services, would seem utterly irreconcilable.

At the present time, for example, the Presbyterians and the Methodists understand each other very well. Formerly the Presbyterians most severely criticized the camp meetings, but now they themselves and also many of the Lutherans hold meetings in the open. The Protestant Episcopal and also the Dutch Reformed congregations likewise show here and there a tendency to follow this example, and their clergymen will have to adjust themselves to these views and merely try to bring into harmony as much as possible the demands of time with the rules of morality.

These churches have indeed already begun, in at least a few states, to accept the so-called new measures, such as protracted meetings that sometimes last for weeks, during which services are held in the forenoon, afternoon, and even in the evening. Then communal sermons, exhortations, prayer meetings, and personal witnessing of experiences alternate with singing of hymns and trips to the anxious-seat placed about the altar, where reassurance-seekers and those who confess their sins are seated.

For the performance of benevolent purposes the above-named organizations have united with the Baptists, whereby missionary and bible-society work have gained uncommonly much, especially in the remote regions, and every unprejudiced person will rejoice over this. It cannot be denied that these basically good institutions have not always been handled with an equal sense of impartiality and unselfishness. (Dr. Meyen, for example, complains, probably justly, about the missionary work of the North Americans in the Sandwich Islands.)

The Lutheran or Reformed German, especially if he resides in the country, with faithful heart clings to the church of his fathers and is happy and contented. The natural sense of justice of these confessional relatives makes them tolerant to the approaches of others and allows quarrels with other faiths seldom to arise. Their clergymen have one great merit, that of great modesty. They preach the gospel in the manner of the illustrious founder of their church, and among the Reformed the gentle spirit of Zwingli always manifests itself.

The English Protestant Episcopal Church did not become fully organized in the United States until the years 1785 and 1789. The general synod of this church organization is divided into two houses, the house of bishops and that of the clergy and lay deputies. The presiding Bishop White of Pennsylvania,[4] the late Bishop Hobart of New York,[5] and Ravenscroft of South Carolina,[6] have won great merit for their church. With no less extraordinary zeal, Bishop Chase of Ohio has worked for the establishment of a college, now flourishing under the name of Kenyon College in Knox County of that state.

The Moravian Brothers have indeed created much good in the United States. The educational institutions at Bethlehem and Nazareth in Pennsylvania and at Salem in North Carolina are used by many American families of high station, especially for the education of their daughters. One needs only to be acquainted with the spirit of the presiding officer of this church in Pennsylvania, the Patriarch Andrus, who has dedicated the remainder of his life to the service of his church and at an advanced age has said goodby to Europe, perhaps forever, to take upon himself the duties of a bishop. On my second journey I had the honor of making the acquaintance of this man and being filled with esteem for this church body. In America the heads of churches are also respected as art patrons, and until now no one but they have performed such oratorios as Haydn's *Creation* with an orchestra of more than one hundred musicians, a distinction in

---

[4] William White (1748–1836), first Protestant Episcopal Bishop of Pennsylvania (1786), author of a number of substantial theological-historical works.

[5] John Henry Hobart (1775–1830), rector of Trinity Church, New York City, assistant bishop at 26, later bishop.

[6] John Stark Ravenscroft (1772–1830), first Episcopal bishop of North Carolina (1823).

which New York and Philadelphia cannot yet compete with little Bethlehem.

The Methodist Church, whose two main branches, the American founded by the Wesley brothers,[7] and the Calvinist whose founder, as is known, was Whitefield,[8] have united in America as the Methodist Episcopal Church, and its many clergymen preach in circuits, trying to forget the old separation and to make the union complete. Still, there are many adherents to this organization who can hardly be considered as Methodists, as the Methodist Baptists.

There are the Lutheran Methodists who have introduced into the Lutheran Church new measures mentioned above. The Unitarian Methodists (New Lights), who by screams and other extremes give vent to their religious feelings, in some places fully equal the real Jumpers. And the United Brethren in Christ, who have their own bishops and count among their members many Germans. There are the Bible Christians. The African Methodists consisting of Negroes and mulattoes who accompany their services in the churches or in the fields with horrible shrieks, bodily contortions, jumps, and convulsions, in which the last sub-branch and followers of Albrecht, a German sect, almost equal them.

The Methodist Episcopal Church is trying to eliminate the frenzied excitement which was once so common at their camp meetings, and the excessive screaming and raving of the audience at such gatherings caused by the highly inflaming sermons. Nowadays one can attend meetings at which there is no trace of any excess, and one is indeed often surprised by the fervor, indeed without exaggeration, the richness and even classic eloquence, of their preachers.

The Society of Baptists is also divided into several branches. Among the English Baptists are listed the Calvinistic Baptists; the Free Will Baptists, who are found mainly in New England; the Free Communion Baptists in New York state and hated by others because of their liberality; the Baptists of the Ten Principles in Rhode Island and New York; the sabbath-celebrating Baptists; the followers of Alexander Campbell,[9] who

---

[7] John Wesley (1703–1791) formed the doctrines and the religious revival with his brother Charles at Oxford, England, in the years 1728–1735, in the latter year departing for Georgia. Methodism proper began with his return to England in 1738, and by 1739 was assuming a vigorous role.

[8] George Whitefield (1714–1770), a powerful speaker, was attracted to Wesleyan doctrine in 1735 and went to Georgia from England in 1838. After 1840 he was the leader of Calvinist Methodism.

[9] Alexander Campbell (1788–1866) founded the Disciples of Christ or "Campbellites," also Bethany College.

by his disputations and writings has made himself famous and has won many adherents to Chiliasm, especially in Kentucky and the Mississippi Valley; the Fullerians; and finally the Universal Baptists.

Among the German Baptists, the Anabaptists are very numerous and called Dunkers and Bearded Men, because they usually wear long beards. The people who are now so friendly and orderly, who are such outstanding farmers, and who provide for the education of their children, are the descendants of the old dissatisfied German Anabaptists, who under Carlstadt, Münzer, and Bockholt did so much harm. But they were brought to better disposition by Menno Simons, after whom they are called Mennonites. Different from these are the Amish, who do not insist upon rebaptism but allow either immersion or sprinkling as a form of baptism. Their tolerance also extends to their domestic relations. Both of the above societies observe love feasts, to which they welcome all other Christians. The Amish are often inclined to the teachings of the reappearance of all things (*Wiederherstellung*), and are disinclined toward Calvinism.

The Universalists have a different teaching, in that the future life will not bring punishment for sins committed in this life. They are increasing tremendously, largely due to the fact that their authors Baillou and Skinner, the publishers of the *Trumpet*, and others are, in their way, clever Bible interpreters. It is understandable that the other orthodox churches view this only with alarm, and the unification of various great church organizations can be attributed mainly to the desire to work thus with greater success against the Universalists. Their number cannot be determined, but it is very large.

Among the Friends, or Quakers, actual strife has broken out. The spirit of discord must have become great on earth if its influence could sever this honorable society, noted for its gentleness and tolerance. The group which developed in the lap of this community is purely deistic, rejecting as mystical fanaticism the idea of inner and outer light so dear to genuine old Quakers. The Quakers have nothing in common with the Shakers, though the latter are sometimes called Shaking Quakers. The view held by the latter, that they can worship God by dancing and clapping of hands, is a horror to the Quakers.

From the neo-Quakers to the Unitarians the transition is a very natural one. These Socinianists have among them gifted writers and excellent pulpit speakers. They have achieved large numbers only in the Atlantic states, chiefly in Massachusetts, but in the West and South of the Union they are looked upon with disgust, as are the Universalists.

Concerning the Separatists of Württemberg, I have already mentioned them earlier. It is a pity that the good will of these people, the spirit of orderliness, unity, and obedience which they manifest constantly and in deed by great tests of sacrifice, had not been treated more humanely and rewarded more nobly by their principal officers. As affairs now stand, they have become the victims of the selfishness of Rapp or the deceptions of Proli.

The Mormons are equally the victims of some fanatics, who dream of a golden book which an angel is said to have brought from heaven. They gathered first in Geauga County in Ohio, then went down the Ohio into the state of Missouri, where they were persecuted in Jackson County, and thus were induced to move on.[10]

On a higher plane than the just mentioned fanatics are the followers of Swedenborg,[11] who have strong congregations in the Atlantic parts of the United States, and it cannot be denied that they number among their followers persons of the finest and most enlightened way of thinking.

Of the smaller sects I have either learned nothing or have not wished to say anything in order not to draw this out too far. I now return to the conclusion of the report of my journey.

On October 19 I stopped at the town of Franklin again, but this time was received much more courteously than at the time of my other visit, for the good citizens of Franklin may have become convinced that they had been mistaken in me.

From this day to the twenty-third, when I reached St. Charles, the fog ceased, but on the other hand a cold northeast wind hindered the travels of the boat very much, and at night the air was sharply cold. Regularly before sunrise the thermometer fell to 23° or 25°. The vegetation changed its form very rapidly, the colder weather caused the trees to put on their autumnal garb, but the premature beginning of winter caused the leaves and the weeds to die completely. Exceedingly picturesque were the various colors with which nature adorns the different kinds of trees in America during the autumn. The vast variety of the different deciduous trees presents shades that vary from dark red to light yellow, for almost every variety of tree has colors peculiar to itself after having been touched by the first frost. In the warmer latitudes, however, a number of trees and bushes with evergreen leaves lend still different shades of color. The great cottonwoods are particularly pretty with their sturdy trunks entwined to

---

[10] The Mormons, members of the Church of Jesus Christ of Latter-day Saints, had their founding under Joseph Smith in upstate New York in 1830, reassembled at Kirkland, Ohio, in 1831, moved thence to Independence and Far West, Missouri, after which they went to Nauvoo, Illinois, where violence forced them to migrate to the west bank of the Missouri at present Omaha in 1846, and in the spring of 1847 under Brigham Young they made their final trek to Utah.

[11] Emanuel Swedenborg (1688–1772) was the Swedish mystic.

the very top by climbing sumac (*Rhus radicans*, [poison ivy]) whose luxuriant leaves change to a blood red, while the tops of the cottonwoods are a mixture of their dying leaves in yellow and light green.

The bare islands, now protruding from the river because of low water, were the gathering places for huge flocks of geese and pelicans, so that the islands, when seen from a distance, appeared as if covered with snow. The beautiful, white-feathered American snow goose (*Anser hyperborea*)[12] gathered among its kin on its way to the tropical zone. (In February 1831, I shot this goose in the lagoons at Tampico on the Mexican coast.)

On my arrival in St. Charles the wind began to blow very hard, and it seemed that the arrival of the boat in St. Louis might be delayed for several days. Therefore I decided to cross the river and spend the night at Chauvin's Ferry, and from there I intended to start early the next morning for St. Louis by land.

Despite the painful cold, I started early on the morning of the twenty-fourth, a wagon having been lent by my kind host, and I reached St. Louis in a few hours, for the road was much better than it had been in the spring. Since there was no suitable opportunity to continue my journey to New Orleans, I utilized the time to visit the Messrs. Chouteau at their country homes and there I was showered during my stay with manifestations of hospitality.[13]

On November 3 I boarded the steamboat *Cincinnati* on which I had made the trip from Louisville and had enjoyed such fine treatment. The boat carried a heavy cargo of lead, which was still increased at Herculanum,[14] so that the journey was made increasingly difficult and dangerous thereby, because of the low water. The boat ran on shallows several times during the first two days, but luckily was set free again and thus we reached Ste. Genevieve very early on the sixth. Since this little place is half an hour's walk from the river and several passengers and some freight had to be taken on board, the boat lay by for several hours.

It had become penetratingly cold. A strong northwest wind and snowstorm drove all the passengers to shelter. The boat had advanced but for a quarter of an hour when a terrific impact scared everyone from his rest, and the cry, "The boat is sinking!" created panic, terror, and great confusion.

---

[12] *Anser hyperborea* = *Chen hyperborea*.

[13] Again at Florissant, north of the city on Cold Water Creek, where the author had visited Auguste Chouteau at the beginning of his Missouri River adventures earlier in the year.

[14] On the Mississippi in Jefferson County, Mo., and the center of the lead trade at the time, with two shot-towers, among other manufacturing facilities for that metal.

The *Cincinnati* had run with tremendous force on a snag, one of those dangerous tree trunks that lay in the bed of the river. The lower hold of the boat had been pierced through and through. With remarkable presence of mind and the utmost intrepidity, the captain of the steamboat and the machine engineer tried to restore order in the midst of the confusedly milling masses and make the necessary arrangements for the rescue of the passengers and their belongings. All this in the short time left before the boat was expected to sink completely.

Regarding this unfortunate accident, I cannot give enough praise to the captain, who, though part-owner of the boat and its cargo, yet directed all his efforts toward the prevention of probable accidents among the passengers.

Fortunately the accident occurred close to the riverbank, and the pilot cleverly succeeded in reaching a place which was not too deep before the boat sank entirely. By order of the captain, the whole crew was engaged to their utmost in rescuing the passengers and their baggage. They succeeded in putting all ashore, which was extremely fortunate, for in the prevailing cold and the stormy weather only a few could have saved themselves by swimming. I lost but few of my belongings, though everything was thoroughly drenched.[15]

With abundant good will and hospitality, all the passengers were received by the good citizens of Ste. Genevieve, and during my stay there I was the recipient of much kindness and goodness on their part. A real, honest people of true Creole stock live there, people who dislike to leave their villages, reminding me of the early times of colonization. In customs and in architecture, they remain faithful to their nationality and would rather bear the consequences of the adverse location of Ste. Genevieve than abandon the place, which is sacred to their patron saint.

One finds only a few Anglo-Americans settled here, for the distance from the river and the low elevation of the place is not very favorable to trade. Many inhabitants are owners of lead mines in the interior of the country and send their black slaves to work there. The production of this ore and the trade in it are a rich source of the economic well being in the southern part of the state of Missouri.

I found very good accommodations with the Janis family for my stay, which lasted for several weeks. I was treated in the friendliest and most obliging manner in their house.[16] By the middle of November, winter had

[15] *Author*: It may be considered among the oddest whims of fate that seven years later, almost on the same spot, the steamboat *New Jersey*, a new and most handsome vessel on which I was traveling, sank under the same circumstances.

[16] Jean B. Janis, the son of Nicolas Janis, whom Houck describes as a member of "one

set in in earnest and the region was often covered with deep snow. But this did not prevent me from making frequent excursions, especially to the east bank of the river. There I found several separate homes of very honest Creoles, who aided me in my hunting and accompanied me into the forests.

Even in the midst of winter the naturalist finds here plenty of harvest, especially waterfowl, which abound in the cold season of the year in extraordinarily large numbers, such as *Anas boschas, sponsa, Valisineria albeola, marila,*[17] *Mergus cullatus,* and many others. Also the land birds of the north had arrived: *Fringilla hudsonia, Emberiza leucophris, Parus bicolor, Tetrao cupido,* and they increased my collection from day to day.

The primeval forest is rich in various kinds of timber. The mightiest trunks of the sycamore rising above their forest companions stand majestically among locust trees and *Gymnocladus canadensis* [= *G. dioicus,* Kentucky coffee tree]. The *Diospyros* is yet in part laden with fruit, and the traveler is often surprised in the midst of winter to find such good fruit amid deep snow.

In these woods are still found many wild turkeys, who in the fall gather in great flocks. They are here hunted with dogs to chase them out of the thickets. Then the birds flying to the highest tops of the trees allow themselves to be stalked rather easily. I saw several sea eagles of exceptionally large size and shot one of them. Wilson had pictured this eagle in the seventh volume, plate 55, number 2, under the name *Falco* (*Haliaeetus*) *ossifragus.* I take this to be a young bird belonging to *Haliaeetus leucocephalus.* It is entirely brown without a white head and tail.[18]

As I had to go back to St. Louis once more, I chose to go by way of Cahokia, and for the purpose hired a conveyance from a Canadian who had settled on the other side of the river. The way led over a bad road through the hills to a small Creole settlement, Prairie du Rocher.[19] Here I found

of the most ancient families of that ancient settlement," Kaskaskia, was himself born in Kaskaskia in 1759 and distinguished himself as a young ensign under George Rogers Clark in the recapture of Vincennes in February, 1779, from the British. He had been a resident of Ste. Genevieve since 1776 and died there in 1836. Houck, *History of Missouri,* I, 353–54.

[17] *Valisneria* [sic] *albeola* = *Bucephala albeola,* the bufflehead; [*Valisineria*] *marila* = *Aythya marila,* the greater scaup; *Fringilla hudsonia* = *Junco hyemalis,* the slate-colored junco; *Emberiza leucophris* = *Zonotrichia leucophrys,* the white-crowned sparrow; *Parus bicolor,* the tufted titmouse, actually a non-migratory species; *Tetrao cupido* = *Tympanuchus cupido,* the greater prairie chicken.

[18] I. e., a juvenal individual of the bald eagle. Duke Paul's identification of Wilson's drawing is correct, for the tarsometatarsus of the bird shown is featherless.

[19] Prairie du Rocher, like Kaskaskia and Ste. Genevieve, dated from the French era, in the first quarter of the eighteenth century. Above it on the Mississippi was the site of Fort de Chartres, constructed 1753–57 on the designs and engineering of François Saucier, ceded by France after the French and Indian War and occupied by the British in 1765. Encroach-

many lakes and much swamp land covered with tall reeds and cane, inhabited by countless numbers of wild ducks flying about in unbelievably large flocks. Hunting for these ducks yields a rich harvest at the market in St. Louis. The taste of the American duck is much preferable to that of ours, perhaps because the American duck finds more abundant food.

Cahokia, or Le Caho, one of the oldest settlements in Illinois, was formerly inhabited by a tribe of aborigines, of which the French, when they took possession of these parts, found a great many different tribes. The French Captain Bossu has left us some interesting information regarding them and also regarding the first settlement.[20] Cahokia is a very insignificant place, inhabited for the most part by Creoles, and its location is a low, unhealthful region. The male youths of this place usually hire out as boatmen on vessels going up the Mississippi and the Missouri and spend the winters with the fur traders among the Indians.

Because the river carried much drifting ice, the crossing in the horse boat was rather tedious, and I had to limit my stay in St. Louis to a few hours, for otherwise I might have found my crossing delayed for several days.

A steamboat, the *Mandan*, which had been out of service for some time, was put in readiness by the first of December to take the passengers of the *Cincinnati* and some freight to New Orleans. The obliging owners had equipped this boat as well as possible, and I boarded it on December 5. Although the journey proceeded rather slowly because of the shallow places in the river, and because the dark nights demanded great caution, we nevertheless arrived without mishap in the capital city of Louisiana.

It would tax the patience of my readers if I were again to describe the regions which I mentioned in the account of my journey up the river, and a characteristic picture of the Mississippi banks wrapped in their winter garment is too monotonous to reproduce. The giant trees are completely divested of their leafy ornaments, relieved by the only green things, a few climbing plants and Mississippi reeds.

---

ment of the Mississippi spurred the latter to abandon it in 1772. Two earlier Forts de Chartres adjoining Kaskaskia, a few miles down the Mississippi, the first in 1720–1722, destroyed by the Indians in 1727, and the second a few years later, preceded it. "François Saucier, Engineer of Fort de Chartres, Illinois," by Walter J. Saucier and Kathrine Wagner Seineke, in John Francis McDermott, ed., *Frenchmen and French Ways in the Mississippi Valley*, 199–227.

[20] Jean-Bernard Bossu, *Nouveaux Voyages aux Indes occidentales* . . . 2 vols. (1751–1757; 1757–1762), I, 144–59. Cahokia probably dated from 1699, remaining a French frontier center until after English occupation, 1763–1765, of the Illinois country, after which it lost much of its French population to Spanish Louisiana along and west of the Mississippi.

Below the 36th Parallel the evergreen trees become more numerous; laurel and magnolia, more frequent at the 35th Parallel; and the *Olea americana*[21] and *Liquidambar storaciflua*[22] occur rather abundantly. The latter is a splendid tree growing in the regions from the east coast of North America to the heights of the Cordilleras, and thus takes in a vast geographic area.

At New Madrid the boat stopped for several hours, however not long enough to permit me to view at close range the area made notable by the great earthquake. I therefore reserve a more detailed account for a report of my second journey, when I stopped there for a longer time.

Most remarkable is the difference which the vegetation assumes below the 34th Parallel. It seems as if this region had been selected by nature to be the dividing line between the warm and the temperate zones. The Mississippi reeds suddenly attain tremendous height and great thickness of stem. The cypresses, *Schubertia disticha*,[23] cover themselves with Spanish moss, *Tillandsia usneoides*. The green of the non-deciduous trees stands out prominently, and among these are the great laurel oak[24] and the luxuriant *Magnolia grandiflora*. Spring-like air dispelled the ice of the raw winter and only now and then the effects of the northwest wind reminded one of the colder regions. Dwarf palm and yucca reassure one of the nearness of tropical influences. The bare cotton fields give way near New Orleans to large sugar-cane plantations, where the harvesting and preparation of the raw sugar occupies the plantation Negroes completely.

On December 19 I reached the chief city of Louisiana, where I found some things changed. One year is quite sufficient to bring about a great alteration in such an industrious city, and when I entered New Orleans again several years later, I could hardly recognize the town, such a great number of new structures had been erected, some on the site of older houses, others in places which at my first visit had been far remote from the suburbs of the city.

Since no frost had occurred yet in Lower Louisiana, the country enjoyed its green attire and was the gathering place of a multitude of inhabitants of the air, which in the winter exchange the northern for the southerly regions.

[21] *Olea americana* = *Osmanthus americanus*, the devilwood.

[22] *Liquidambar storaciflua* = *L. styraciflua*, the North American sweetgum. Its range is vast, from the southern border of Pennsylvania to central Florida, west and southwest to eastern Texas and the southeastern corner of Oklahoma, but it does not extend farther westward.

[23] *Schubertia disticha* = *Taxodium distichum*, bald cypress.

[24] *Quercus laurifolia*. "Laurel oak" is sometimes also applied to *Quercus imbricaria*, the shingle oak.

My business in New Orleans was soon attended to, since a large part of my collection had already been shipped to Europe. A good ship to France was ready to go to sea. I left New Orleans on December 24 on board the brig *Smyrna*. Many friends accompanied me on board, taking cordial leave. Among these was a Württemberger, Mr. Frauenknecht, who after Mr. Teetzmann's death became a partner in the business. Since then he has shown me many a proof of his friendship.

Before the brig *Smyrna* reached the Balize and could be piloted into the sea, my patience was put to a severe test. Until January 7, 1824, we drifted on the waters of the Mississippi or had to lie at anchor for days, and the prevailing south winds brought to life countless mosquitoes, which attacked me relentlessly with their bites.

The alligators, too, had been activated by the warmth to leave their muddy river bed and stick their heads above the surface of the water. Several of these creatures were shot, one of which, wounded in the head, was brought on deck alive. Despite the intense cold which we encountered on the journey while crossing the ocean, this alligator made the trip to France in a spare cask and was brought on the land alive.

The contrary wind and my yearning to continue my journey put me out of sorts, and on January 6 I found myself in the pilot house in the Balize when the news came that the wind had begun to be favorable and the *Smyrna* would probably be brought out to sea that same evening. At that time steamboats, neither upstream or downstream competed with one another in towing boats at a reasonable cost into position to begin their journeys.

The hope of reaching the sea that night was frustrated, but I found myself early the following morning in the channel where the salt water and the river water mix and where the counter-currents form huge heaps of mud and earth so dangerous to navigation. The enormous pressure which the volume of river water exerts upon the sea is noticeable for a long distance, making itself felt several miles from the mouth by a gradual decrease of the current, which varies, naturally, depending upon the higher or lower water level in the river. For this reason the difference in the coloration of the water is not always as clearly defined as it was at the time of my first trip up the river.

In the meantime the *Smyrna* quickly left the land behind and the coast vanished gradually from sight. I fixed my eyes on it until the last sign of it had vanished without a trace in the waves of the sea. An emotion-filled moment overcame me as the last bit of land was lost from sight. I had received so many manifestations of friendship in the United States, and everywhere my journey had awakened the interest of the inhabitants. The people had been most obliging. Even the plain countryman had furthered my undertaking, through his inherent kindness, without conceiving its purpose.

I was filled with respect for many excellent institutions of states which are approaching a higher development and destiny with giant strides. My wishes for their country certainly combine with those of my American friends that the wise laws of the Union of States, founded on reason, may remain unchanged by innovations, a memorial to the venerable founders, and that the great philanthropic work may go on unhindered. Domestic peace, strict administration of the laws and respect for the same, general freedom of trade, and a peaceful and honest policy toward foreign countries, these were the aims before the eyes of Franklin and Hamilton, and their achievement was advanced by the wise administrations of Washington, Madison, and the two Adamses.

The purpose of my journey was to get to know the nature and the people of a distant part of the world. I have endeavored to describe them faithfully and impartially. Even though I have not engaged in mere criticism of the errors and frailties of this hospitable land, as so many others who have written about America have done, I do not believe that I have been less faithful to the truth.

On the morning of the tenth we were in sight of the coast of Cuba, east of Pan de Matanzas, and on the following day, therefore, close to the Cuban coast at 23° 40′ north latitude and 81° 57′ west longitude from Greenwich. The weather continued to be favorable. On the fourteenth and fifteenth we sailed through the channel of Santaren, turned around the coast of Florida, and on the fifteenth at eight o'clock in the morning we were at Cat Keys, where we had to tack on account of the northeast wind which had set in.

Until the twenty-second at 33° 58′ north latitude and 69° 28′ west longitude, therefore near the Bermudas, the weather remained clear and favorable. Gloriously the sun rose and set, illuminating the horizon with the most wonderful red. The waves appeared as clear as a mirror, and numerous dorados and bonitas engaged in rivalry with flying fishes and dolphins. Also large cetaceans appeared frequently in the warmer regions. A number of sea birds, especially gannets (*Dysporus sula*) and sea gulls, flew about the ship and a beautiful frigate bird (*Tachypetes fregata*) was shot by me.

The thermometer continued to register between 65° and 73°. I had become quite unaccustomed to the hard west wind which blew from the twenty-third to the twenty-sixth. The wind strength changed to a storm, and on the twenty-ninth, at 40° 36′ north latitude and 54° 21′ west longitude, we felt the effects of the Bank of Newfoundland, which every navigator who crosses this rough region of the sea in the winter months must experience.

From now on the sea fought us with huge waves, and the ship was tossed about so violently that the rolling action became unbearable. The waves struck with such force over board that part of the railing was shattered. Water barrels and other gear were washed into the sea and it was almost impossible to remain on deck. Fortunately, we sailed before the wind, since it came from the northwest, rarely blowing from the northwest by north.

The cold had risen to a most painful stage. The thermometer sank to between 5° and zero, hail and snow skiffs filled the air, and in between there was occasional lightning and thunder. The creaking of the masts, the whistling in the storm-torn rigging, the heavy pounding of the waves, the eternal rocking of the boat, and the vast quantities of water that penetrated through the door of the cabin made the situation exceedingly unpleasant.

On the thirty-first, at 42° 20′ north latitude we sighted a sailboat at sea, reaching it in the course of an hour. It was a schooner-brig from Mobile bound for an English harbor. This vessel was in great distress, but on account of the high sea and the strong wind we could not send out a boat to get more accurate information regarding her condition.

On the days from the sixth to the seventh the storm subsided a little, but on the eighth it broke out with redoubled fury, pursuing us to the height of Cape Finisterre at latitude 48° 46′. Now came dense fogs, becoming so much more dangerous the nearer we approached the English channel. On the twelfth we sailed into that passage and luckily had clear weather. On the fourteenth at two o'clock in the morning we sailed past the lighthouse of Kaskets to the southeast by east at a distance of ten miles.

The coast of France now unfolded its high rock walls. We approached Cape Harfleur, took on a pilot, and reached Havre-de-Grace by two o'clock. Simultaneously, another vessel under an American flag was signaled. Strangely it was the brig *Ido*, which had left New Orleans at the same time as the *Smyrna*, and despite the stormy weather had accomplished the ocean crossing in exactly the same time as we had.

Sources Consulted

Abrams, Le Roy. *An Illustrated Flora of the Pacific States.* 4 vols. Stanford, Stanford University Press, 1923–60.

Adams, James Truslow, and Coleman, R. V. *Atlas of American History.* New York, Charles Scribner's Sons, 1943.

American Ornithologists' Union. *Check-list of North American Birds.* Sixth Edition. Lancaster, Penna., 1957.

Anson, Bert. *The Miami Indians.* Norman, University of Oklahoma Press, 1970.

Austin, Oliver L., Jr. *Birds of the World.* New York, Golden Press, 1961.

Bakeless, John E. *Lewis and Clark: Partners in Discovery.* New York, William Morrow, 1947.

Barbour, Thomas. *The Birds of Cuba.* Memoirs of the Nuttall Ornithological Club. No. 6. Cambridge, Nuttall Ornithological Club, 1923.

Bass, Althea. *Cherokee Messenger.* University of Oklahoma Press, 1936.

Bent, George. *Life of George Bent Written from His Letters by George E. Hyde.* Ed. by Savoie Lottinville. Norman, University of Oklahoma Press, 1968.

Billon, Frederic Louis. *Annals of St. Louis in Its Territorial Days, from 1804 to 1821.* St. Louis, n.p., 1888.

Boas, Franz. "On Certain Songs and Dances of the Kwakiutl of British Columbia," *Journal of American Folk-lore,* I, No. 1 (April–June, 1888), 49–64.

Bogner, Harold F. "Sir Walter Scott in New Orleans," *Louisiana Historical Quarterly,* XXI, No. 2 (April, 1938) 423–42.

Bond, James. *Birds of the West Indies.* Boston, Houghton Mifflin Company, 1961.

Bossu, Jean-Bernard. *Bossu's Travels in the Interior of North America, 1751–1762.* Tr. and ed. by Seymour Feiler. Norman, University of Oklahoma Press, 1962.

————. *Nouveau Voyages aux Indes occidentales* .... Paris, 1768.

Brackenridge, Henry Marie. *Views of Louisiana; together with a Journal of a Voyage up the Missouri River, in 1811*. Pittsburgh, Cramer, Spear, & Eichbaum, 1814.

Bradbury, John. *Travels in the Interior of America* in Reuben Gold Thwaites, ed., *Early Western Travels*, V. Cleveland, The Arthur H. Clark Company, 1904–1906.

British Museum (Natural History), Department of Zoology. *Catalogue of the Birds in the British Museum*. 27 volumes. London, 1874–98.

Brown, Joseph Epes. *The Sacred Pipe: Black Elk's Account of the Seven Rites of the Oglala Sioux*. Norman, University of Oklahoma Press, 1953.

Butel-Dumont, Georges-Marie. *Mémoires historiques sur la Louisiane* .... 2 vols. Paris, 1755.

Carey and Lea (publishers). *A Complete Historical, Chronological, and Geographical American Atlas, Being a Guide to the History of North and South America, and the West Indies ... to the Year 1822*. Philadelphia, Carey and Lea, 1823.

Catlin, George. *Letters and Notes on the Manners, Customs, and Condition of the North American Indians* .... 3 vols. London, Published by the Author, 1841.

Chasseboeuf, Constantin François de, Comte de Volney. *Tableau du climat et du sol des États-Unis* .... Paris, 1803.

————. *A View of the Soil and Climate of the United States of America: with Supplementary Remarks upon Florida; on the French Colonies on the Mississippi and Ohio, and in Canada; and on the Aboriginal Tribes of America*. Philadelphia, 1804.

Chinard, Gilbert. *Volney et l'Amerique*. Baltimore, Johns Hopkins University Press, 1923.

Clark, William. *The Field Notes of Captain William Clark, 1803–1805*. Ed. by Ernest Staples Osgood. New Haven, Yale University Press, 1964.

Corkran, David H. *The Cherokee Frontier: Conflict and Survival, 1740–1762*. Norman, University of Oklahoma Press, 1962.

————. *The Creek Frontier, 1540–1783*. Norman, University of Oklahoma Press, 1967.

Cotterill, R. S. *The Southern Indians: The Story of the Civilized Tribes Before Removal*. Norman, University of Oklahoma Press, 1954.

Cox, Ross. *The Columbia River*. Ed. by Edgar I. and Jane R. Stewart. Norman, University of Oklahoma Press, 1957.

Curtis, Nathaniel Cortlandt. *New Orleans: Its Houses, Shops, and Public Buildings*. Philadelphia, J. B. Lippincott Company, 1933.

Cutright, Paul Russell. *Lewis and Clark: Pioneering Naturalists*. Urbana, University of Illinois Press, 1969.

Dale, Harrison C. *The Ashley-Smith Explorations and the Discovery of a Central Route to the Pacific, 1822–29*. Glendale, Arthur H. Clark Company, 1941.

Debo, Angie. *And Still the Waters Run*. Princeton, Princeton University Press, 1940.

———. *A History of the Indians of the United States*. Norman, University of Oklahoma Press, 1970.

———. *The Rise and Fall of the Choctaw Republic*. Norman, University of Oklahoma Press, 1934.

———. *The Road to Disappearance: A History of the Creek Indians*. Norman, University of Oklahoma Press, 1947.

Denig, Edwin Thompson. *Five Indian Tribes of the Upper Missouri: Sioux, Arickaras, Assiniboines, Crees, Crows*. Ed. by John C. Ewers. Norman, University of Oklahoma Press, 1961.

De Terra, Helmut. *The Life and Times of Alexander von Humboldt*. New York, Alfred A. Knopf, 1955.

Dorsey, J. Owen. *A Study of Siouan Cults*. Eleventh Annual Report, Bureau of American Ethnology. Washington, 1894.

Engelmann, George. *The Botanical Works of the Late George Engelmann, Collected for Henry Shaw, Esq*. Ed. by William Trelease and Asa Gray. Cambridge, Mass., J. Wilson and Son, 1887.

Ewers, John C. *The Blackfeet: Raiders on the Northwestern Plains*. Norman, University of Oklahoma Press, 1958.

———, ed. "Of the Arickaras," by Edwin T. Denig, *Bulletin of the Missouri Historical Society*, VI, No. 2 (January, 1950).

Firmin Didot Frères (publishers). *Nouvelle Biographie Generale*. 46 vols. Paris, Firmin Didot Frères, Fis, et Cie., 1875–1912.

Foreman, Grant. *The Five Civilized Tribes*. Norman, University of Oklahoma Press, 1934.

———. *Indians and Pioneers: The Story of the American Southwest Before 1830*. Norman, University of Oklahoma Press, 1936.

———. *Last Trek of the Indians*. Chicago, University of Chicago Press, 1946.

———. "Notes of Auguste Chouteau on the Boundaries of Various Indian Nations," *Glimpses of the Past*, Missouri Historical Society Publications, VII (1940).

Fowler, Jacob. *The Journal of Jacob Fowler Narrating an Adventure from Arkansas through the Indian Territory, ...* Ed. by Elliott Coues. New York, Francis P. Harper, 1898.

Frazer, Robert W. *Forts of the West: Military Forts and Presidios and Posts Commonly Called Forts West of the Mississippi River to 1898.* Norman, University of Oklahoma Press, 1965.

Gale, John. *The Missouri Expedition, 1818–1820: The Journal of Surgeon John Gale With Related Documents.* Ed. by Roger L. Nichols. Norman, University of Oklahoma Press, 1969.

Gard, Wayne. *The Great Buffalo Hunt.* New York, 1959.

Gass, Patrick. *A Journal of the Voyages and Travels of a Corps of Discovery, under the Command of Capt. Lewis and Capt. Clarke of the Army of the United States.* Ed. by David McKeehan. Minneapolis, Ross and Haines, 1958.

Geiser, Samuel Wood. *Naturalists of the Frontier.* Dallas, Southern Methodist University Press, 1948.

Gibson, A. M. *The Chickasaws.* Norman, University of Oklahoma Press, 1971.

———. *The Kickapoos: Lords of the Middle Border.* Norman, University of Oklahoma Press, 1963.

Goetzmann, William H. *Army Exploration in the American West, 1803–1863.* New Haven, Yale University Press, 1959.

Greenberg, Joseph H. *The Languages of Africa.* Publication 25, *International Journal of American Linguistics,* Supplement Vol. 29, No. 1, Pt. 2, Bloomington, Indiana University Research Center in Anthropology, Folklore and Linguistics, 1963.

Gregg, Elinor D. *The Indians and the Nurse.* Norman, University of Oklahoma Press, 1965.

Gregg, Josiah. *Commerce of the Prairies* [1844]. Ed. by Max L. Moorhead. Norman, University of Oklahoma Press, 1954.

———. *Diary and Letters of Josiah Gregg.* Ed. by Maurice Garland Fulton and Paul Horgan. 2 vols. Norman, University of Oklahoma Press, 1941, 1944.

Hagan, William T. *The Sac and Fox Indians.* Norman, University of Oklahoma Press, 1958.

Hall, E. Raymond, and Keith R. Kelson. *The Mammals of North America.* 2 vols. New York, Ronald Press, 1959.

Hall, E. Raymond. *Names of Species of North American Mammals North of Mexico.* Lawrence, Museum of Natural History, University of Kansas, 1965.

Hassrick, Royal B. *The Sioux: Life and Customs of a Warrior Society.* Norman, University of Oklahoma Press, 1964.

Haynes, Bessie Doak, and Edgar Haynes. *The Grizzly Bear: Portraits from Life.* Norman, University of Oklahoma Press, 1966.

Hebard, Grace R. *Sacajawea, a Guide and Interpreter of the Lewis and Clark Expedition* . . . Glendale, Arthur H. Clark Company, 1933.

Heitman, Francis B. *Historical Register and Directory of the U.S. Army.* 2 vols. Washington, D.C., Government Printing Office, 1903.

Herskovits, Melville J. *The Human Factor in Changing Africa.* New York, Alfred A. Knopf, 1962.

Historische Commission bei der Königlichen Akademie der Wissenschaften. *Allgemeine deutsche Biographie.* 56 vols. Leipzig, Duncker & Humblot, 1875–1912.

Hodge, Frederick Webb. *Handbook of American Indians North of Mexico.* Bulletin 30, Smithsonian Institution, Bureau of American Ethnology. 2 vols. Washington, 1910.

Houck, Louis. *History of Missouri.* 3 vols. Chicago, R. R. Donnelley and Sons Company, 1908.

———. *The Spanish Régime in Missouri.* 2 vols. Chicago, R. R. Donnelley and Sons Company, 1909.

Howard, Harold P. *Sacajawea.* Norman, University of Oklahoma Press, 1971.

Hulme, Thomas. *Hulme's Journal, 1818–19.* In Reuben Gold Thwaites, ed. *Early Western Travels,* Vol. X. Cleveland, Arthur H. Clark Company, 1904.

Humboldt, Friedrich Heinrich Alexander Freiherr von, and Aimé Bonpland. *Voyage de Humboldt et Bonpland.* 30 vols. Paris, 1805–34.

———, and C. S. Kunth. *Nova Genera et species.* 7 vols. Paris, 1815–25.

———, and Hermann Hauff. *Reise in die Aequinoctial-Gegenden des neuen Continents. In deutscher Bearbeitung von Hermann Hauff. Nach der Anordnung and unter Mitwirkung des Verfassers.* Stuttgart, Cotta'sche Verlag, 1859–60.

Hyde, George E. *The Pawnee Indians.* Denver, University of Denver Press, 1951.

———. *Red Cloud's Folk: A History of the Oglala Sioux Indians.* Norman, University of Oklahoma Press, 1937.

———. *Spotted Tail's Folk: A History of the Brulé Sioux.* Norman, University of Oklahoma Press, 1961.

Irving, John Treat, Jr. *Indian Sketches: Taken During an Expedition to the Pawnee Tribes [1833].* Ed. by John Francis McDermott. Norman, University of Oklahoma Press, 1955.

Irving, Washington. *The Adventures of Captain Bonneville, U.S.A., in the Rocky Mountains and the Far West.* Ed. by Edgeley W. Todd. Norman, University of Oklahoma Press, 1961.

———. *Astoria; or Anecdotes of an Enterprise Beyond the Rocky Mountains.* Ed. by Edgeley W. Todd. Norman, University of Oklahoma Press, 1964.

———. *A Tour on the Prairies.* Ed. by John Francis McDermott. Norman, University of Oklahoma Press, 1956.

419

————. *The Western Journals of Washington Irving.* Ed. by John Francis McDermott. Norman, University of Oklahoma Press, 1944.

Jacobson, Oscar Brousse. *Kiowa Indian Art: Watercolor Paintings in Color by the Indians of Oklahoma.* Nice, France, Szwedzicki, 1929.

————, and Jeanne d'Ucel. *Les Peintures Indiens d'Amerique.* Nice, France, Szwedzicki, 1950.

Jahreshefte des Verein für vaterländische Naturkunde in Württemberg. Nekrolog von Oberstudienrat Dr. von Kurr. 18. Jahrgang, 1862. Seite 20–24.

James, Edwin, comp. *Account of an Expedition from Pittsburgh to the Rocky Mountains, Performed in the Years 1819 and '20: Under Command of Major Stephen H. Long. From the Notes of Major Long, Mr. T. Say, and Other Gentlemen of the Exploring Party.* 2 vols. Philadelphia, H. C. Carey and I. Lea, 1822–23.

————. *Account of an Expedition from Pittsburgh to the Rocky Mountains* ... in Reuben Gold Thwaites, *Early Western Travels*, Vols. XIV–XVII. Cleveland, Arthur H. Clark Company, 1904.

Jeffreys, Thomas. *The Natural and Civil History of the French Dominions in North and South America.* 2 vols. London, 1761.

Johnson, Allen, et al., eds. *Dictionary of American Biography.* 11 vols. New York, Charles Scribner's Sons, 1946–58.

Jordan, David Starr. *A Guide to the Study of Fishes.* 2 vols. New York, Henry Holt and Company, 1905.

Kappler, Charles J. U.S. Laws, Statutes, etc.: *Indian Affairs: Laws and Treaties.* 3 vols. 57 Cong., 1 sess., *Senate Document No. 452.*

Keating, William Hypolitus. *Narrative of an Expedition to the Sources of St. Peter's River, Lake Winnepeek, Lake of the Woods, &c., Performed in the Year 1823, by Order of the Hon. J. C. Calhoun, Secretary of War, Under Command of Stephen H. Long, U.S.T.E. Compiled from the Notes of Major Long, Messrs. Say, Keating, & Colhoun, by William H. Keating. . . .* 2 vols. London, G. B. Whittaker, 1825.

King, Grace. *New Orleans: The Place and Its People.* New York, Macmillan, 1896.

Le Page du Pratz, Antoine Simon. *Histoire de la Louisiane.* 3 vols. Paris, 1758.

Lewis, Meriwether. *A Statistical View of the Indian Nations Inhabiting the Territory of Louisiana* [1805]. In *American State Papers, Indian Affairs*, I, 9 Cong., 1 sess., 1806, 714–15.

Lewis, Meriwether, and William Clark. *History of the Expedition under the Command of Lewis and Clark.* Ed. by Elliott Coues. 4 vols. New York, Francis P. Harper, 1893.

————. *Letters of the Lewis and Clark Expedition With Related Documents,*

1783–1854. Ed. by Donald Jackson. Urbana, University of Illinois Press, 1962.

————. *Original Journals of the Lewis and Clark Expedition.* Ed. by Reuben Gold Thwaites. 8 vols. New York, Dodd, Mead, and Company, 1904–1905.

Llewellyn, Karl W., and E. Adamson Hoebel. *The Cheyenne Way: Conflict and Case Law in Primitive Jurisprudence.* Norman, University of Oklahoma Press, 1941.

Long, James Larpenteur, as told to Michael Stephen Kennedy. *The Assiniboines: From the Accounts of the Old Ones Told to First Boy.* Norman, University of Oklahoma Press, 1961.

Lowie, Robert H. *Primitive Society.* New York, Boni and Liveright, 1920.

Luttig, John C. *Journal of a Fur Trading Expedition to the Upper Missouri, 1812–1813.* Ed. by Stella M. Drumm. St. Louis, Missouri Historical Society, 1920.

McDermott, John Francis, ed. and comp. *The Early Histories of St. Louis.* St. Louis, St. Louis Historical Documents Foundation, 1952.

————, ed. *The French in the Mississippi Valley.* Urbana, University of Illinois Press, 1971.

————. *George Caleb Bingham, River Portraitist.* Norman, University of Oklahoma Press, 1959.

————, ed. and comp. *Old Cahokia: A Narrative and Documents Illustrating the First Century of Its History.* St. Louis, St. Louis Historical Documents Foundation, 1949.

————. *Private Libraries in Creole St. Louis.* Baltimore, Johns Hopkins University Press, 1938.

————, ed. *Audubon in the West.* Norman, University of Oklahoma Press, 1965.

————, ed. *The Spaniards in the Mississippi Valley, 1763–1804.* Urbana, University of Illinois Press, 1972.

McKenney, Thomas L., and James Hall. *History of the Indian Tribes of North America, with Biographical Sketches and Anecdotes of the Principal Chiefs* .... Philadelphia, E. C. Biddle, 1837–44.

MacKenzie, Alexander. *Exploring the Northwest Territory: Sir Alexander MacKenzie's Journal of a Voyage by Bark Canoe from Lake Athabasca to the Pacific Ocean in the Summer of 1789.* Ed. by T. H. McDonald. Norman, University of Oklahoma Press, 1966.

McReynolds, Edwin C. *Missouri: A History of the Crossroads State.* Norman, University of Oklahoma Press, 1962.

McVaugh, Rogers. *Edward Palmer: Plant Explorer of the American West.* Norman, University of Oklahoma Press, 1956.

Madariaga, Salvador de. *Christopher Columbus*. New York, Macmillan, 1940.

Margry, Pierre. *Découvertes et Établissements des Français dan l'Ouest et dans le Sud de l'Amerique Septentrionale (1614–1754)*. 6 vols. Paris, D. Jouaust, 1875–1886, VI, 388–448.

Marquette, Jacques. *Le Premier Voyage qu'a fait le P. Marquette vers le Nouveau Mexique et comment s'en est formé le dessein*, in *The Jesuit Relations and Allied Documents*. Ed. by Reuben Gold Thwaites. Cleveland, Burrows Brothers, 1900.

Mathews, John Joseph. *The Osages: Children of the Middle Waters*. Norman, University of Oklahoma Press, 1961.

———. *Wah'Kon-Tah: The Osage and the White Man's Road*. Norman, University of Oklahoma Press, 1932.

Mayer, Alfred Goldsborough. *Medusae of the World*. 3 vols. Washington, Carnegie Institution of Washington, 1910.

Mézières, Athanase de. *Athanase de Mézières and the Louisiana-Texas Frontier, 1768–1780* . . . . 2 vols. Ed. by Herbert Eugene Bolton. Cleveland, Arthur H. Clark Company, 1914.

Miller, Alfred Jacob. *The West of Alfred Jacob Miller (1837)*. Ed. by Marvin C. Ross. Norman, University of Oklahoma Press, 1951.

Mitchell, Harry A. "The Development of New Orleans as a Wholesale Trading Center," *Louisiana Historical Quarterly*, Vol. XXVII, No. 4 (October, 1944), 933–63.

Mooney, James. *Calendar History of the Kiowa Indians. Nineteenth Annual Report*. Washington, D.C., Bureau of American Ethnology, 1898.

Moorehead, W. K. *The Cahokia Mounds*. University of Illinois *Bulletin*, Vol. XXVI, No. 4 (1929).

Morgan, Dale L. *Jedediah Smith and the Opening of the West*. Indianapolis, Bobbs-Merrill, 1953.

———. *The West of William H. Ashley, 1822–1838*. Denver, Old West Publishing Company, 1964.

Morison, Samuel Eliot. *Admiral of the Ocean Sea: A Life of Christopher Columbus*. 2 vols. Boston, Little, Brown and Co., 1942.

Morse, Jedediah. *A Report to the Secretary of War of the United States, on Indian Affairs*. New Haven, S. Converse, 1822.

Murray, Charles Augustus. *Travels in North America During the Years 1834, 1835, and 1836*. 2 vols. London, R. Bentley, 1839.

Nasatir, A. P. *Before Lewis and Clark*. 2 vols. St. Louis, St. Louis Historical Documents Foundation, 1952.

Nichols, Roger L. *General Henry Atkinson: A Western Military Career*. Norman, University of Oklahoma Press, 1965.

Nicollet, Joseph Nicolas. *The Journals of Joseph N. Nicollet: A Scientist on the*

Mississippi Headwaters. Tr. by André Fertey, ed. by Martha Coleman Bray. St. Paul, Minnesota Historical Society, 1970.

————. *Report Intended to Illustrate a Map of the Hydrographical Basin of the Upper Mississippi River* . . . . 26 Cong., 2 sess., *Senate Document 237.* Washington, D.C., Blair and Ives, 1843.

Nolte, Vincent. *Fifty Years in Both Hemispheres; or, Reminiscences of the Life of a Former Merchant.* New York, Redfield, 1854.

Nute, Grace Lee. *The Voyageur.* New York, D. Appleton & Company, 1931.

Oglesby, Richard E. *Manuel Lisa and the Opening of the Missouri Fur Trade.* Norman, University of Oklahoma Press, 1963.

Palmer, Edgar Z. *The Meaning and Measurement of National Income.* Lincoln, University of Nebraska Press, 1966.

Peake, Ora Brooks. *A History of the United States Indian Factory System, 1795–1822.* Denver, Sage Books, 1954.

Peale, Titian Ramsay. *The Ancient Mounds at St. Louis, Missouri, in 1819.* Smithsonian Institution *Annual Report,* 1861. Washington, D.C., 1862.

Peters, James Lee. *Check-list of Birds of the World.* 7 vols. Cambridge, Harvard University Press, 1931–51.

Petersen, Karen Daniels. *Plains Indian Art from Fort Marion.* Norman, University of Oklahoma Press, 1971.

Phillips, Paul Chrisler, and Smurr, J. W. *The Fur Trade.* 2 vols. Norman, University of Oklahoma Press, 1961.

Pike, Zebulon Montgomery. *Journals, with Letters and Related Documents.* Edited by Donald Jackson. 2 vols. Norman, University of Oklahoma Press, 1966.

————. *The Expeditions of Zebulon Montgomery Pike.* Ed. by Elliott Coues. 3 vols. New York, Francis P. Harper, 1895.

Pourtalès, Count Albert Alexandre de. *On the Western Tour with Washington Irving: The Journal and Letters of Count de Pourtalès.* Trans. by Seymour Feiler, ed. by George F. Spaulding. Norman, University of Oklahoma Press, 1968.

Powell, Peter John. *Sweet Medicine: The Continuing Role of the Sacred Arrows, the Sun Dance, and the Sacred Buffalo Hat in Northern Cheyenne History.* 2 vols. Norman, University of Oklahoma Press, 1969.

Pratte, Bernard, Jr. "Reminiscences of General Bernard Pratte, Jr.," *Missouri Historical Society Bulletin,* VI (59–71).

Prucha, Francis Paul. *The Sword of the Republic: The United States Army on the Frontier, 1783–1846.* New York, Macmillan, 1969.

Reid, Russell, and Cannon, Clell G., eds. "Journal of the Atkinson-O'Fallon Expedition," *North Dakota Historical Quarterly,* IV (1929), 5–56.

Ridgway, Robert. *The Birds of North and Middle America. Bulletin 50,*

United States National Museum. 10 vols. Washington, D.C., Smithsonian Institution, 1901–46.

Rister, Carl Coke. "The Significance of the Destruction of the Buffalo in the Southwest," *Southwestern Historical Quarterly*, Vol. XXXIII, No. 1 (July, 1929), 43–50.

Roe, Frank Gilbert. *The Indian and the Horse*. Norman, University of Oklahoma Press, 1955.

———. *The North American Buffalo: A Critical Study of the Species in Its Wild State*. Toronto, University of Toronto Press, 1951.

Ross, Alexander. *The Fur Hunters of the Far West*. Ed. by Kenneth Spaulding. Norman, University of Oklahoma Press, 1956.

Scharf, John Thomas. *History of St. Louis City and County, from the Earliest Periods to the Present Day*. Philadelphia, L. H. Everts & Company, 1883.

Schoolcraft, Henry Rowe. *History of the Indian Tribes of the United States* .... 6 vols. Philadelphia, J. B. Lippincott Company, 1857.

Schorger, A. W. *The Passenger Pigeon: Its Natural History and Extinction*. Madison, University of Wisconsin Press, 1955.

———. *The Wild Turkey: Its History and Domestication*. Norman, University of Oklahoma Press, 1965.

Schwäbische Kronik, Stuttgart, Januar 24, 1861 (S. 21); Januar 27 (S. 24).

Seligman, Charles Gabriel. *Races of Africa*. 3rd edition. New York and London, Oxford University Press, 1957.

Seton, Ernest Thompson. *The Life Histories of Northern Animals*. 2 vols. New York, Charles Scribner's Sons, 1909.

———. *Lives of Game Animals*. .... 4 vols. Garden City, Doubleday and Company, 1925–28.

Sinclair, Harold. *The Port of New Orleans*. Garden City, Doubleday & Co., 1942.

Small, John Kunkel. *Manual of the Southeastern Flora* .... New York, John Kunkel Small, 1933.

Smither, Nelle. "A History of the English Theater at New Orleans, 1806–1842," *Louisiana Historical Quarterly*, Vol. XXVIII, No. 1 (January, 1945).

Sunder, John E. *Bill Sublette, Mountain Man*. Norman, University of Oklahoma Press, 1959.

———. *The Fur Trade on the Upper Missouri, 1840–1845*. Norman, University of Oklahoma Press, 1965.

———. *Joshua Pilcher: Fur Trader and Indian Agent*. Norman, University of Oklahoma Press, 1968.

———, ed. *Matt Field on the Santa Fe Trail*. Coll. by Clyde and Mae Reed Porter. Norman, University of Oklahoma Press, 1960.

Tabeau, Pierre-Antoine. *Tabeau's Narrative of Loisel's Expedition to the Upper Missouri*. Ed. by Annie Heloise Abel, tr. by Rose Abel Wright. Norman, University of Oklahoma Press, 1939.

Tauber Zeitung, Mergentheim, September 21–November 4, 1850 (S. 306, 310, 314, 318, 322, 326, 330, 342, 362); Januar, 1855 (S. 26); Juli 24, 1937.

Thomson, A. Landsborough. *A Dictionary of Birds*. New York, McGraw-Hill Book Company, 1964.

Tixier, Victor. *Tixier's Travels on the Osage Prairies*. Tr. by Albert J. Salvan, ed. by John Francis McDermott. Norman, University of Oklahoma Press, 1940.

Trenholm, Virginia Cole, and Maurine Carley. *The Shoshonis: Sentinels of the Rockies*. Norman, University of Oklahoma Press, 1964.

Trudeau, J. B. "Trudeau's Description of the Upper Missouri," ed. and tr. by Annie Heloise Abel, *Mississippi Valley Historical Review*, Vol. VIII, 165.

U.S. Government. *American State Papers: Documents Legislative and Executive*. Ed. by Walter Lowrie et al. 38 vols. Washington, Gales and Seaton, 1833–61.

Unrau, William E. *The Kansa Indians: A History of the Wind People*. Norman, University of Oklahoma Press, 1971.

Vogel, Virgil J. *American Indian Medicine*. Norman, University of Oklahoma Press, 1970.

Wade, Mason. *The French Canadians, 1760–1967*. 2 vols. New York, St. Martin's Press, 1968.

Wagner, Henry R., and Charles L. Camp. *The Plains and the Rockies: A Bibliography of Original Narratives of Travel and Adventure, 1800–1865*. San Francisco, Grabhorn Press, 1937.

Wallace, Ernest, and E. Adamson Hoebel. *The Comanches: Lords of the South Plains*. Norman, University of Oklahoma Press, 1952.

Webb, Robert G. *Reptiles of Oklahoma*. Norman, University of Oklahoma Press, 1970.

Webb, Walter Prescott. *The Great Plains*. Boston, Ginn and Company, 1931.
———. *The Texas Rangers: A Century of Frontier Defense*. Boston, Houghton Mifflin, 1935.

Weiss, Harry Birschoff, and Grace M. Ziegler. *Thomas Say, Early American Naturalist*. Springfield, Ill., Baltimore, C. C. Thomas, 1931.

Wheat, Carl I. *Mapping the Transmississippi West, 1540–1861*. 5 vols. in 6. San Francisco, Institute of Cartography, 1957–63.

Wied-Neuwied, Maximilian Alexander Philipp, Prinz von. *Beitrage zur Naturgeschichte von Brasilien*. 4 B. Weimar, 1825–33.

————. *Reise in das innere Nord-Amerika in den Jahren 1832 bis 1834*. 2 B., mit Bild Atlas. Coblenz, J. Haelscher, 1839–41.

————. *Travels in the Interior North America* . . . . Tr. by Hannibal Evans Lloyd, ed. by Reuben Gold Thwaites. 4 vols. in Early Western Travel Series, Vols. XXI–XXIV. Cleveland, Arthur H. Clark Company, 1906.

Wilson, Alexander, and Prince Charles Lucien Bonaparte. *American Ornithology, or, The Natural History of the Birds of the United States*. 3 vols. London, Paris, New York; Cassell, Petter, and Gilpin, n.d.

Woodward, Grace Steele. *The Cherokees*. Norman, University of Oklahoma Press, 1963.

Wright, Muriel H. *A Guide to the Indian Tribes of Oklahoma*. Norman, University of Oklahoma Press, 1951.

Württemberg, Paul Wilhelm, Duke of. *Erste Reise nach dem nördlichen Amerika in den Jahren 1822 bis 1824*. Stuttgart und Tübingen, Verlag der J. G. Cotta'schen Buchhandlung, 1835.

————. *First Journey to North America in the Years 1822 to 1824*. Tr. by William G. Bek. South Dakota Historical Collections, Vol. XIX (1938).

Zimmer, John Todd. *Catalogue of the Edward E. Ayer Ornithological Library*. Ed. by Wilfred H. Osgood. 2 vols. Chicago, Field Museum of Natural History, 1926.

Index

443